# YEARS OF PERSECUTION, YEARS OF EXTERMINATION

# Years of Persecution, Years of Extermination

*Saul Friedländer and the Future of Holocaust Studies*

Edited by Christian Wiese and Paul Betts

continuum

Continuum UK, The Tower Building, 11 York Road, London SE1 7NX
Continuum US, 80 Maiden Lane, Suite 704, New York, NY 10038

*www.continuumbooks.com*

Published with the financial support of the Centre for German-Jewish Studies, University of Sussex, and the Fritz Bauer Institute, Frankfurt am Main.

First published 2010

British Library Cataloguing-in-Publication Data
A catalogue record for this book is available from the British Library.

ISBN Hardback 9781441189370
ISBN Paperback 9781441129871

Typeset by Pindar NZ, Auckland, New Zealand
Printed and bound by the MPG Books Group

# Contents

# List of Contributors

DORIS L. BERGEN (Ph.D., 1991, University of North Carolina, Chapel Hill) is the Chancellor Rose and Ray Wolfe Professor of Holocaust Studies at the University of Toronto. Her research focuses on issues of religion, gender, and ethnicity in the Holocaust and World War II and comparatively in other cases of extreme violence. Her publications include *Twisted Cross: The German Christian Movement in the Third Reich* (1996); *War and Genocide: A Concise History of the Holocaust* (2003); *The Sword of the Lord: Military Chaplains from the First to the Twenty-First Centuries* (edited, 2004); and *Lessons and Legacies VIII: From Generation to Generation* (edited, 2008). She has held grants and fellowships from the United States Holocaust Memorial Museum, the German Marshall Fund of the United States, the DAAD, and the Alexander von Humboldt Foundation, and she has taught at the Universities of Warsaw, Pristina, Tuzla, Notre Dame, and Vermont. She is a member of the Academic Advisory Committee of the Center for Advanced Holocaust Studies at the US Holocaust Memorial Museum in Washington, DC.

RICHARD BESSEL (D.Phil., 1980, University of Oxford) is Professor of Twentieth-Century History at the University of York in the United Kingdom. He taught previously at the Open University and at the University of Southampton, and has held visiting professorships at the University of Bielefeld and the University of Freiburg. His books include *Germany after the First World War* (1993); *Die Grenzen der Diktatur: Staat und Gesellschaft in der DDR* (co-edited with Ralph Jessen, 1996); *Fascist Italy and Nazi Germany: Comparisons and Contrasts* (edited, 1996); *Patterns of Provocation: Police and Public Disorder* (co-edited with Clive Emsley, 2000); *Life after Death: Approaches to a Cultural and Social History of Europe during the 1940s and 1950s* (co-edited with Dirk Schumann, 2003); *Nazism and War* (2004); *Germany 1945: From War to Peace* (2009), and *Removing Peoples: Forced Removal in the Modern World* (co-edited with Claudia Haake, 2009). He is currently working on a history of violence.

PAUL BETTS (Ph.D., 1995, University of Chicago) is Reader in Modern German History at the University of Sussex, United Kingdom, and Co-director of the Centre for Modern European Cultural History there. Previously he taught at the University of North Carolina at Charlotte. He is the author of *The Authority of Everyday Objects: A Cultural History of West German Industrial Design* (2004) and has co-edited *Between Mass Death and Individual Loss: The Place of the Dead in Twentieth-Century Germany* (with Alon Confino and Dirk Schumann, 2008); *Socialist Modern: East German Everyday Culture and Politics* (with Katherine Pence, 2008); and *Pain and Prosperity: Reconsidering Twentieth-Century German History* (with Greg Eghigian, 2003). His research interests include modern Europe, nineteenth- and twentieth-Century Germany and European material culture. He has been joint editor of the journal *German History*, 2004–2009, and his book, *Within Walls: Private Life in the German Democratic Republic*, will be published in 2010.

ALON CONFINO (Ph.D., 1992, University of California, Berkeley) is Professor of Modern German and European History at the University of Virginia. He has written extensively on memory, nationhood, and historical method. He is the author of *The Nation As a Local Metaphor: Württemberg, Imperial Germany, and National Memory, 1871–1918* (1997), winner of the Smith Book Prize of the Southern Historical Association, and *Germany as a Culture of Remembrance: Promises and Limits of Writing History* (2006), as well as the co-editor of *The Work of Memory: New Directions in the Study of German Society and Culture* (with Peter Fritzsche, 2002) and *Between Mass Death and Individual Loss: The Place of the Dead in Twentieth-Century Germany* (with Paul Betts and Dirk Schumann, 2008). He is now completing a book entitled *A World Without Jews: Germans, Jews, and Memory in the Third Reich*.

DAN DINER (Ph.D., 1973, University of Frankfurt am Main) is Professor of Modern History at the Hebrew University, Jerusalem, and Director of the Simon Dubnow Institute for Jewish History and Culture at the University of Leipzig. He is the author of numerous publications on twentieth-century history, Jewish history, Middle Eastern history and German history, particularly in the period of National Socialism and the Holocaust. His most recent publications include: *Das Jahrhundert verstehen: Eine universalhistorische Deutung* (1999); *Beyond the Conceivable: Studies on Germany, Nazism, and the Holocaust* (2000); *Feindbild Amerika: Über die Beständigkeit eines Ressentiments* (2002); *Gedächtniszeiten: Über jüdische und andere Geschichten* (2003); *Versiegelte Zeit: Über den Stillstand in der islamischen Welt* (2005); *Dark Times, Dire Decisions: Jews and Communism* (co-edited with Jonathan Frankel, 2005); *Gegenläufige Gedächtnisse: Über Geltung und Wirkung des Holocaust* (2007); *Restitution and Memory* (co-edited with Gotthart Wunberg, 2007); *Aufklärungen: Über Varianten von Moderne* (2008). His most important books have been translated into English, Italian, Polish and Hebrew. In 2006 he was awarded the Ernst Bloch Prize, and in 2007 the Italian Premio Capalbio.

SAUL FRIEDLÄNDER (Ph.D., 1963, University of Geneva, Switzerland) is Professor of History – 1939 Club Chair of Holocaust Studies – at UCLA. He is also Professor Emeritus at Tel Aviv University and at the Graduate Institute of

International Studies in Geneva. Among Friedländer's numerous publications on Nazism and the Holocaust, the two most recent are *Nazi Germany and the Jews: The Years of Persecution, 1933–1939* (1997) and *The Years of Extermination: Nazi Germany and the Jews, 1939–1945* (2007). For these works he received the Geschwister Scholl Prize, a MacArthur Fellowship, the Peace Prize of the German Book Trade Association, and the Pulitzer Prize. Earlier important works include *Pius XII and the Third Reich: A Documentation* (1966); *Kurt Gerstein: The Ambiguity of Good* (1969); *History and Psychoanalysis: An Enquiry into the Possibilities and Limits of Psychohistory* (1978); *When Memory Comes* (1979); *Reflections of Nazism: An Essay on Kitsch and Death* (1984); *Probing the Limits of Representation: Nazism and the "Final Solution"* (edited, 1992); and *Memory, History, and the Extermination of the Jews of Europe* (1993).

JAN T. GROSS (Ph.D., 1975, Yale University) is Professor of History at Princeton University. He joined the Princeton History Department in 2003 after teaching at New York University, Emory, Yale, and universities in Paris, Vienna, and Cracow. His works include *Polish Society under German Occupation* (1979); *Revolution from Abroad: The Soviet Conquest of Poland's Western Ukraine and Western Belorussia* (1988); *Neighbours: The Destruction of the Jewish Community in Jedwabne, Poland* (2001) and *Fear: Anti-Semitism in Poland After Auschwitz* (2006). Gross is also the author of several books in Polish, the co-editor of *The Politics of Retribution in Europe: World War II and Its Aftermath* (2000), and the co-editor of *War Through Children's Eyes* (with Irena Grudzinska-Gross, 1981). His research focuses on comparative politics, totalitarian and authoritarian regimes, Soviet and East European politics, and the Holocaust. He has recently finished a book on antisemitism in Poland after World War II and co-authored a study with Stephen Kotkin entitled *Uncivil Society: Communist Implosion in 1989* (2009). He is now writing a book on the plunder of Jews by the local population in Nazi-occupied Europe.

RAPHAEL GROSS (Ph.D., 1997, University of Essen) is Director of the Jewish Museum and the Fritz Bauer Institute in Frankfurt am Main as well as Director of the Leo Baeck Institute London. He is Honorary Professor in History at Frankfurt University and a Reader in History at Queen Mary College, London University. Since 2001 he has been co-editor of the Year Book of the Leo Baeck Institute. He has finished a book on Nazi Morality: *Anständig geblieben – Nationalsozialistische Moral* (2010). His most recent publications include *Carl Schmitt and the Jews, the "Jewish Question," the Holocaust, and German Legal Theory* (2006); *Novemberpogrom 1938: Die Augenzeugenberichte der Wiener Library, London* (co-edited with Ben Barkow and Michael Lenarz, 2008); *Die Frankfurter Schule und Frankfurt: Eine Rückkehr nach Deutschland* (co-edited with Monika Boll, 2009).

WOLF GRUNER (Ph.D., 1994, Technical University Berlin) holds the Shapell-Guerin Chair in Jewish Studies and is Professor of History at the University of

Southern California, Los Angeles. He has taught at the Technical University Berlin and as a visiting Professor at Webster University St. Louis and its campus in Vienna. He worked as a researcher at the Zentrum für Antisemitismusforschung (Technical University Berlin) and the Institut für Zeitgeschichte Munich-Berlin. He was a postdoctoral fellow at Harvard University, Yad Vashem, the US Holocaust Memorial Museum and the Women's Christian University, Tokyo. He is the author of seven books on the Holocaust, most recently: *Jewish Forced Labor under the Nazis: Economic Needs and Nazi Racial Aims* (2006); *Widerstand in der Rosenstrasse: Die Fabrikaktion und die Verfolgung der "Mischehen" 1943* (2005) and *Die Verfolgung und Ermordung der europäischen Juden* vol. 1: *Deutsches Reich 1933–1937* (edited, 2008). He is also the co-editor of *Das Großdeutsche Reich und die Juden: Nationalsozialistische Verfolgungspolitik in den angegliederten Gebieten* (forthcoming 2010). His research interests include mass violence, genocide and state discrimination against indigenous populations, especially in Latin America.

ALAN KRAMER (Ph.D., 1987, Hamburg University) is Professor of European History at Trinity College, Dublin. In the 1990s he published several monographs and articles on West Germany 1945–55, and then turned to the study of the First World War. With John Horne he published the prize-winning book *German Atrocities 1914: A History of Denial* (2001). Further publications include *The West German Economy 1945–1955* (1991); and *Dynamic of Destruction: Culture and Mass Killing in the First World War* (2007). He is currently working on the international history of concentration camps.

TONY KUSHNER (Ph.D., 1986, University of Sheffield) is Marcus Sieff Professor of Jewish/non-Jewish relations in the Parkes Institute and History Department, University of Southampton. He is the author of seven monographs and ten edited collections and is co-editor of *Patterns of Prejudice* and the Parkes-Wiener Jewish History and Culture monograph series with Vallentine Mitchell. His most recent publications include *We Europeans? Mass-Observation, "Race" and National Identity in Britain* (2004); *The Holocaust: Critical Historical Approaches* (co-edited with Donald Bloxham, 2006); *Remembering Refugees: Then and Now* (2006); and *Anglo-Jewry since 1066: Place, Locality and Memory* (2009). His research interests include British Jewish history, refugee and immigration studies; history and heritage; the history of antisemitism and racism; and Holocaust representation.

A. DIRK MOSES (Ph.D., 2000, University of California, Berkeley) joined the Department of History at the University of Sydney in 2000 after studying in Australia, Scotland, the United States and Germany. Before coming to Sydney, he was a research fellow in history at the University of Freiburg, where he worked on postwar German debates about the recent past, a project that appeared as *German Intellectuals and the Nazi Past* (2007). His current interests are in world history, genocide, the United Nations, colonialism/imperialism and terror, about which he has published a number of anthologies, including *Genocide and Settler Society: Frontier Violence and Stolen Indigenous Children in Australian History* (2004) and *Empire, Colony, Genocide: Conquest, Occupation and Subaltern Resistance in World History* (2008), and *The Oxford Handbook of Genocide Studies* (co-edited with Donald Bloxham, 2010).

PETER PULZER (Ph.D., 1960, Cambridge) is Professor Emeritus of Government at Oxford University. From 1984 to 1996 he was Gladstone Professor of Government and Fellow of All Souls College. He held visiting appointments at the School of Advanced International Studies, Washington, DC, the University of California, Los Angeles, the Geschwister-Scholl-Institute at the University of Munich, the Technical University of Dresden, the Humboldt University, Berlin and the University of Leipzig. His works include *Political Representation and Elections in Britain* (1967); *The Rise of Political Antisemitism in Germany and Austria* (1988); *Jews and the German State: The Political History of a Minority, 1848–1933* (1992); and *German Politics, 1945–1995* (1995).

MARK ROSEMAN (Ph.D., 1987, Warwick University) is Professor of History at Indiana University. His research focuses on a wide range of topics in German, European and Jewish history, including life-reform and protest in 1920s and 1930s Germany; Holocaust survival and memory; Nazi policy and perpetrators; the social impact of total war; post-1945 German and European reconstruction; generation conflict and youth rebellion; and Jewish and other minorities in modern German history. His publications include *Recasting the Ruhr 1945–1957: Manpower, Economic Recovery and Labour Relations* (1992); *Generations in Conflict: Youth Rebellion and Generation Formation in Modern Germany 1770–1968* (edited, 1995); *The Past in Hiding* (2000, winner of the Geschwister Scholl Prize); and *The Villa, the Lake, the Meeting: The Wannsee Conference and the "Final Solution"* (2002); *Three Postwar Eras in Comparison: Western Europe 1918–1945–1989* (co-edited with Carl Levy, 2002); *German History from the Margins* (co-edited with Neil Gregor and Nils Roemer, 2006), and *Conflict, Catastrophe and Continuity: Essays on Modern German History* (co-edited with Frank Biess and Hanna Schissler, 2007). He is currently writing a critical synthesis of recent work on Nazi perpetrators.

NICK STARGARDT (Ph.D., 1989, Cambridge) teaches Modern European History at Magdalen College, Oxford. He is the author of *The German Idea of Militarism: Radical and Socialist Critics* (1994), an intellectual and political history of anti-militarist movements in Germany before the First World War, and of *Witnesses of War: Children's Lives under the Nazis* (2005), which offered the first social history of the Second World War through the eyes of children. He is currently writing a new social history of Germany in the Second World War, focusing on military and civilian morale.

# LIST OF CONTRIBUTORS

DAN STONE (D.Phil., 1997, University of Oxford) is Professor of Modern History at Royal Holloway, University of London, where he has taught since 1999. He is a historian of ideas whose research interests include historiographical and philosophical interpretations of the Holocaust, comparative genocide, history of anthropology, and the cultural history of the British Right. He is the author or editor of ten books, including: *Breeding Superman: Nietzsche, Race and Eugenics in Edwardian and Interwar Britain* (2002); *Constructing the Holocaust: A Study in Historiography* (2003); *Responses to Nazism in Britain 1933–1939: Before War and Holocaust* (2003); *The Historiography of the Holocaust* (ed. 2004); *History, Memory and Mass Atrocity: Essays on the Holocaust and Genocide* (2006); *Hannah Arendt and the Uses of History: Imperialism, Nation, Race and Genocide* (co-edited with Richard H. King 2007); *The Historiography of Genocide* (edited 2008) and *Histories of the Holocaust* (2010). He is on the editorial boards of the *Journal of Genocide Research* and *Patterns of Prejudice*, and is currently editing two books: *The Oxford Handbook of Postwar European History* and *The Holocaust and Historical Methodology*.

ZOË V. WAXMAN (D.Phil., 2001, Oxford) is Fellow in Holocaust Studies at Royal Holloway, University of London. Previously she taught at Oxford University. She is interested in witness testimony written both during and after the Holocaust. Her first book, *Writing the Holocaust: Identity, Testimony, Representation* (2006), charts the history of Holocaust testimony from the first chroniclers, confined to the Nazi enforced ghettos, to today's survivors writing as part of collective memory. The book she is currently completing, *Gendering the Holocaust*, focuses on the Holocaust testimonies of women. She is also working on the impact of the Holocaust on Britain and the subsequent treatment of the Jewish survivors of the Holocaust.

CHRISTIAN WIESE (Ph.D., 1997, University of Frankfurt am Main) is Director of the Centre for German-Jewish Studies, Co-Director of the Centre for Modern European Cultural History and Professor of Jewish History at the History Department at the University of Sussex. Previously he taught at Erfurt University and has held visiting professorships at McGill University, Dartmouth College, and Trinity College, Dublin. His publications include *Weiterwohnlichkeit der Welt: Zur Aktualität von Hans Jonas* (co-edited with Eric Jacobson, 2003); *Challenging Colonial Discourse: Jewish Studies and Protestant Theology in Wilhelmine Germany* (2005); *Janusfiguren: "Jüdische Heimstätte,", Exil und Nation im deutschen Zionismus* (co-edited with Andrea Schatz, 2006); *The Life and Thought of Hans Jonas: Jewish Dimensions* (2007); *Redefining Judaism in an Age of Emancipation: Comparative Perspectives on Samuel Holdheim (1806–1860)* (edited, 2007), *Modern Judaism and Historical Consciousness: Identities – Encounters – Perspectives* (co-edited with Andreas Gotzmann, 2007); *Judaism and the Phenomenon of Life: The Legacy of Hans Jonas: Historical and Philosophical Studies* (co-edited with Hava Tirosh-Samuelson, 2008); and

*Jüdische Bildung und Kultur in Sachsen-Anhalt von der Aufklärung bis zum Nationalsozialismus* (co-edited with Giuseppe Veltri, 2009). He is also the editor of Hans Jonas's *Memoirs* (2003). He is currently writing an intellectual biography of Robert Weltsch.

MICHAEL WILDT (Ph.D., 1991, University of Hamburg) is Professor of History at the Humboldt University, Berlin. Previously he taught at the University of Hamburg and did research at the Institut für Sozialforschung in Hamburg. His publications include *Die Judenpolitik des SD 1935–1938: Eine Dokumentation* (1995); *Generation des Unbedingten: Das Führungskorps des Reichssicherheitshauptamtes* (2002); *Volksgemeinschaft als Selbstermächtigung: Gewalt gegen Juden in der deutschen Provinz 1919–1939* (2007); and *Geschichte des Nationalsozialismus* (2008). His research focuses on twentieth-century history, particularly on antisemitism and National Socialism.

# Acknowledgments

The editors would like to express their gratitude to the University of Sussex's Centre for German-Jewish Studies and the Centre for Modern European Cultural History for support in organizing and funding the conference on Saul Friedländer's book *Nazi Germany and the Jews* in June 2008. Saul Friedländer's presence at the conference provided the unique opportunity to discuss a wealth of aspects of his interpretation of the Nazi genocide against the European Jews as well as the future of Holocaust historiography in general and inspired the thoughts presented in this volume. We would like to thank all our colleagues for their valuable contributions and we hope that this book will generate further discussions among historians in the field.

Special thanks go to Diana Franklin and Romy Langeheine for their great help in the conference organization. Generous financial assistance was provided by the German History Society UK and the University of Sussex's School of Humanities, and we are particularly indebted to Dean Steve Burman's interest and support. Translation costs for several essays in this volume were made possible by the Centre for German-Jewish Studies at Sussex and the Fritz Bauer Institute for Holocaust Studies in Frankfurt am Main, Germany. Finally, we would like to thank Continuum Press and especially Michael Greenwood for the smooth and reliable cooperation.

# Introduction

## Paul Betts and Christian Wiese

At one point in his well-known 1986 book, *The Drowned and the Saved*, Primo Levi recounts being asked to explain his experiences at Auschwitz to a classroom of Italian fifth-graders. For him this story perfectly captured the problems of Holocaust historiography. In response to what had become the "obligatory question": "But how come you didn't escape?," Levi replied that there was no possible escape route under the circumstances. Unconvinced, one of the school children on hand summoned Levi to draw a sketch of the camp on the blackboard, which he duly did, "watched by thirty pairs of intent eyes." After a few moments, the ten-year-old offered Levi a sure-fire escape plan: slashing the throat of the sentinel, donning his clothes, racing over to the power station and then deactivating the high tension electric fence, assuring that he could "leave without any trouble." The schoolboy solemnly concluded with the following advice for the Holocaust survivor: "If it should happen to you again, do as I told you. You'll see that you'll be able to do it." For Levi, this innocent primary school encounter inadvertently raised profound issues for him as a survivor as well as for those committed to teaching, writing and remembering the Shoah. As he put it:

> Within its limits, it seems to me that this episode illustrates quite well the gap that exists and grows wider every year between things as they were 'down there' and things as they are represented by the current imagination fed by approximative books, films, and myths. It slides fatally towards simplification and stereotype, a trend against which I would like here to erect a dike [. . .] It is the task of the historian to bridge this gap, which widens as we get farther away from the events under examination.[1]

Levi's elegiac vignette on the desire and limitations of communicating the past is a fitting departure point for a volume on Holocaust history. After all, the necessity to remember is the historian's very stock in trade, and nowhere has this professional mission been invoked more passionately than in the need to record and recall the Holocaust as an organized genocide to destroy European Jewry once and for all. In this regard, the legendary injunction from historian Simon Dubnow – "People, do not forget; speak of this, people; record it all" – supposedly uttered just before the decimation of practically all 30,000 Jews living in the Riga Ghetto in early December 1941, has served as an ethical imperative to honour the dead by preserving their tales and tribulations. This exhortation has been a hallmark of much Holocaust historiography ever since, animating Holocaust survivor Ruth Klüger's claim that "whoever writes, lives,"[2] as well as Alexandra Garbarini's more recent remark that "annihilation is incomplete when memory is preserved."[3] This is why some assert that Holocaust testimonies – whether written at the time or later – are themselves acts of resistance in the face of the systematic destruction of a whole people, tradition and culture.[4] In this way, Holocaust histories are sometimes seen as efforts to provide the desecrated dead some semblance of a proper funeral, and in so doing perhaps help reconcile the living with the dead.

The Holocaust's historians have long been confronted with the conceptual and moral difficulties inherent in trying to narrate the magnitude and man-made monstrosity of the Shoah. It is an extreme case in which the process of remembering itself not only resists fixed perspective and steady scrutiny, but its larger meaning eludes our grasp. The questions that bedevil all historical undertakings about capturing the past take on particular urgency in the face of the Holocaust: How can past events be properly explained, or even satisfactorily communicated? What is to be learned in the end, if anything? And perhaps most profoundly, what is it exactly that we wish to know, and how best to try to narrate it? Such questions have only become more troublesome with the passage of time. Holocaust historiography is not only burdened with the fate of the mil-lions of dead, it also must contend with the passing of the survivor generation. To say that the Holocaust is moving from the realm of experience and witness to memory and representation has become a truism, however, and overlooks the fact that the recollection of the Holocaust has been connected to the problem of representation from the very beginning.

No one has grappled with this question of bridging the gap between experi-ence and memory more profoundly than the distinguished and internationally acclaimed historian, Saul Friedländer. He has published a number of important books on Nazi Germany and the Holocaust, ranging from his early books *Hitler et les Etats-Unis* (1963) and *Pius XII and the Third Reich: A Documentation* (1966) to the two-volume *Nazi Germany and the Jews*, which is the subject of this volume. At times Friedländer has ventured further afield, having written on international politics and Israel, as well as Arab-Israeli relations.[5] What distinguishes his work from many other Holocaust historians, though, is his abiding interest in questions of memory and representation. His 1984 *Reflections of Nazism: An Essay on Kitsch and Death*, and his 1992 edited collection, *Probing the Limits of Representation*, pioneered discussions about the strange afterlife of Nazism and the Holocaust in the media, historiography and public culture, themes that would exercise historians for the next generation. What also makes his work distinctive is that he is both witness and historian, and it is precisely this double existence that has fuelled his life-long preoccupation with the history of the Third Reich.

Nowhere is this sensibility more manifest than in Friedländer's 1979 memoir, *When Memory Comes*. Here he recounts, in fragmentary form, his personal jour-ney from his early Czech Jewish childhood in Prague to survival in Vichy France, and then emigration to Israel. His is a restrained tale of ruptured identities amid a world turned violently upside down, perhaps best captured in the dizzying series of symbolically laden name-changes as emblems of radically shifting identity. As one commentator neatly put it, "For the young Friedländer the public, open spaces and thick texture of a bourgeois Jewish life in Prague are followed by the hidden spaces and shadow life of a young child who changes his name at least five times, from Pavel in Prague to Paul in France to Paul-Henri Ferland in the world of his Catholic refuge to Shaul in Israel and Saul in the international scholarly community."[6] It is Friedländer's evocative acknowledgment of the stubborn irreducibility of the past – to say nothing of its uncanny resistance to being reconciled with the present – that has shaped his existential and professional perspective over the decades. As he confesses in *When Memory Comes*:

> Perhaps I am the one who now preserves, in the very depths of myself, certain disparate, incompatible fragments of existence, cut off from all reality, with no continuity whatsoever, like those shards of steel that survivors of great battles carry about inside their bodies.[7]

Assuming the moral office and professional duties of the historian became one way for him to make sense of his own past, as well as the one that he shared with millions of other Jews across Nazi Europe. As he wrote: "Isn't the way out for me to attach myself to the necessary order, the inescapable simplification forced upon one by the passage of time and one's vision of history, to adopt the gaze of the historian?"[8] What perhaps has characterized his work above all – powerfully on display in his two-volume *Nazi Germany and the Jews* – is his refusal to surrender to any such "inescapable simplification." In it there is no recourse to simple master narratives, such as the "failure of liberalism," "crisis of modernity," "the collapse of civilization," "banality of evil," or more recently, "eliminationist antisemitism." On the contrary, rejecting such general interpretative frameworks is, for Friedländer, precisely what is at stake with the "gaze of the historian." The jarring quality of his autobiography, slicing back and forth as it does in a filmic jump-cut style between his endangered childhood in Europe and his adult life in Israel, attests to his great sensitivity to narrating crisis; one that acknowledges the interpenetration of past and present, confusion and understanding, pain and reason, knowledge and inexplicability. It is this biographical element born of harrowing circumstances that lends his work its rich and unforgettable quality. As Steven Aschheim has remarked, Friedländer's is a uniquely "authoritative custodial voice," whose "eloquent assertion and defense of the historical and moral centrality, as well as the ultimate inexplicability, of the Holocaust" serves as the creative tension underlying all of his work.[9]

How does Friedländer's work fit in with Holocaust historiography? Such a question cannot be fully addressed here, not least because Holocaust literature is a vast and rich record of half a century of scholarship. Nevertheless, Friedländer's work has reflected – and inspired – several dramatic shifts within it.[10] No doubt Holocaust historiography has changed a great deal since its modest beginning. As

Friedländer himself remarked, "[a]t the end of the war, Nazism was the damned part of Western civilization, the symbol of evil. Everything the Nazis had done was condemned, whatever they touched defiled; a seemingly indelible stain darkened the German past, whilst preceding centuries were scrutinized for the origins of this monstrous development."[11] Perhaps for this reason, scholarly analyses of the Holocaust until the 1970s tended to maintain a discernible distance from the events, preferring to view it as somehow linked to wider European developments. In particular the early postwar literature (notably dominated by philosophers and political scientists, not historians) was shaped by two impulses: the first was the so-called totalitarian school, associated with the likes of Hannah Arendt and Carl Friedrich, who claimed an elective affinity between Nazism and Communism; the second grew out of interwar Marxist thinking, wherein fascism was summarily condemned as the political expression of "late capitalism," a view that marginalized the racist dimension of Nazism and the Holocaust altogether. Commentators tended to view the genocide of the Jews, as Omer Bartov has noted, through the "lens of a general interpretation of the crisis of European society and politics," and were "much less concerned with explaining the Holocaust as such." What attention was given to Judeocide was usually written by those interested in the history of antisemitism itself.[12] Whilst the 1980s witnessed renewed empirical attention towards the decision-making process and social structure of the regime, often characterized by the so-called "intentionalist" versus "functionalist" debate, these new histories still interpreted the Holocaust through the eyes of the perpetrators. As a consequence, Holocaust historiography was still "seeing like a state," and a "racial state" at that, whilst the victims did not figure all that much.[13] Mainstream historiography on the Nazi period, moreover, was still slow to integrate the Holocaust into broader histories of the Third Reich. Strange as it may seem today, some of the landmark histories of Nazi Germany written from the late 1960s through the early 1980s barely touched on the Holocaust: the first comprehensive scholarly account of the Nazi regime, Karl Dietrich Bracher's 1969 *The German Dictatorship*, dedicated just 12 of 580 pages to the Holocaust; Martin Broszat's 1981 book *The Hitler State* featured one paragraph directly dealing with the Holocaust; and Gordon Craig's celebrated 1987 book *Germany, 1866–1945* did not mention the Holocaust at all.

But this is not to say that Holocaust historiography was a minor concern. If we recall the early pioneering work of Eugen Kogon, Josef Wulf, Leon Poliakov, Gerald Reitlinger, and Raul Hilberg, for example, it is clear that this literature was already quite substantial by the mid-1960s.[14] Even earlier, Philip Friedman's 1949 review essay of new scholarship on the "Recent Jewish Catastrophe" chronicles the surprising amount of research on the subject less than five years after the liberation of the camps in 1945.[15] However, much of this Jewish, Israeli and Polish historiography found little resonance among mainstream historians in the West. Those who endeavoured to revise the writing of the history of Germany, Germans and the Second World War, such as Hilberg, Poliakov and Wulf, found it difficult to make much headway, as Holocaust scholarship and victim-based testimonies remained outside the broader academic canon and community. Even so, Yad Vashem in Jerusalem and the Jewish Historical Institute in Warsaw continued to do their work, as did a number of other scholars around the world.[16] One of the merits of Friedländer's book is to have effectively incorporated this marginalized literature into his larger historical synthesis, serving as a key, if often overlooked, dimension of his "integrated history" of the destruction of the Jews in Hitler's Empire.

The end of the Cold War marked a sea change in historical consciousness regarding the Holocaust, as it increasingly moved to the centre not just of twentieth-century German history, but to assessments of the twentieth century itself. A variety of newly developed perspectives were introduced to reassess the Holocaust, the most fruitful being the themes of memory and testimony. Whilst such themes were first explored in the 1980s, most famously in Claude Lanzmann's 1985 film *Shoah*, this new approach took off in the 1990s, and gained more and more prominence among historians and Holocaust chroniclers alike. So much so that incorporating the perspectives of the victims became one of the salient features of 1990s Holocaust historiography. In part this was due to the opening up of a range of new archives, especially in Poland and the former USSR, which gave scholars access to hitherto unseen documents about the making and witnessing of the Shoah. It was also related to the expanded work at important centers devoted to preserving Holocaust witness testimonies, such as the Jewish Historical Institute in Warsaw and Yad Vashem in Jerusalem, as well as new institutions like the Holocaust Museum in Washington, DC and the Fortunoff Video Archive at Yale University. What is more, in recent years many witnesses have stepped forward to record their stories before their approaching demise, and the growing public awareness of the Holocaust has doubtlessly encouraged others to tell their stories. Whilst many memoirs and testimonies had been published before, they were rarely folded into more general accounts of the period. In large measure this is due to the fact that much Holocaust historiography, understandably so, has remained strongly preoccupied with the motivation of the killers, and as a result still mostly views the victims as "merely the targets of genocide and not as historical protagonists whose own thoughts, actions and memories have a bearing on the event."[17] In this regard, it is as if Holocaust chroniclers have taken their cue from the Nuremberg Trials themselves, where victim testimony was expressly excluded from the proceedings in favour of official documentation (and defendant testimony), lest the trials be construed as crass "victors' justice" and thus politically and legally illegitimate.[18] To be sure, subsequent Holocaust trials, such as the Adolf Eichmann trial in Jerusalem (1961) and the Frankfurt Auschwitz trials (1963–1965), relied heavily on witness testimonies; in fact, it was at the Eichmann trial where witness testimonies dominated the judicial proceedings.[19] Nevertheless, the early classics of Holocaust historiography – such as Raul Hilberg's three-volume 1961 *The Destruction of the European Jews* or Josef Wulf's 1961 *Das Dritte Reich und seine Vollstrecker* – tended, as Ulrich Herbert has observed, to depict "the murder itself only in distanced terms – out of respect for the victims of course, but also to avoid the charges of sensationalism."[20]

The problem of integrating victim testimony into the history of Nazism and the Holocaust has emerged as one of the new developments in recent Holocaust historiography, and Friedländer's work has been at the center of discussion. This issue was perhaps most openly addressed in his famous 1987 correspondence with the prominent West German historian of Nazi Germany, Martin Broszat. Two years earlier Broszat had published an essay in the West German journal *Merkur*, calling for a new "historicization" of the Third Reich, one that sought to explore the patterns of social "normality" below the barbarism and horror of the regime. The role of Nazi ideology was thus "relativized" in the context of the "normality" of everyday life. Friedländer, in a 1987 essay published in *Tel Aviver Jahrbuch für deutsche Geschichte*, took issue with what he saw as the underestimation of ideology and the dangerous separation of criminality from normalcy in Broszat's "historicization" plea.[21] The two historians then engaged in a series of informal correspondences in 1987. This exchange is sometimes described as one of the key instances of "post-Shoah German-Jewish dialogue," and has stimulated a good deal of scholarly attention.[22] The thrust of the correspondence pivoted around the tricky question of to what extent Germans and Jews, given their radically divergent experiences and perspectives after 1933, could, should and/or must approach the Nazi past differently. For Broszat, the Nazi experience not only has made "German" and "Jewish" history-writing fundamentally incongruous; the Jews' victim status, so he continued, has meant that "Jewish" historiography remains too beholden to emotional memories of the past. As Broszat wrote, "the period still remains bound up with many and diverse monuments of mournful and accusatory memory, imbued with the painful sentiments of many individuals, in particular the Jews, who remain adamant in their insistence on a mythical form of this remembrance." For this reason, he surmised, Jewish memory and historiography did not qualify as "scholarly-scientific investigation." For Broszat, it was precisely the (West) Germans' break with the Nazi past in the 1950s and 1960s that has afforded them the necessary distance and detachment to write more objective and scholarly histories of the period. As he put it, the early postwar "demonological interpretation of the National Socialism" was "concerned more with bringing about a distancing exorcism of the demons than arriving at a historical explanation;" and now that "the field of history and historical studies" is "no longer represented by a generation whose members were contemporaries of National Socialism and became adults before 1945," there is "no longer sufficient reason for the imposition of a general quarantine."[23] By contrast, Jews, so Broszat adds, have not cut their identification or intimacy with this past, and thus their victim perspective remains trapped in "mythic" history-writing and remembrance of the period.[24] Whilst Friedländer's specific epistemological and moral objections to Broszat's views are well known,[25] it was the broader issue of how historians can and should write the history of the period that mattered most to him. Here and elsewhere Friedländer made quite clear that he was neither convinced that (West) Germany's proclaimed full break from the Nazi past had actually occurred in the way that Broszat described, nor that victim perspectives could not be used to write "scientific-scholarly" accounts of the Holocaust.

For years Friedländer has devoted a good deal of his career to pointing out how the "mythic" remaking and remembrance of the Nazi period – hardly the preserve of the victims – emerged as a vigorous cottage industry of cultural life across Europe, the United States and Israel during the 1970s and 1980s. Such views were first articulated in his 1984 book *Reflections of Nazism: An Essay on Kitsch and Death*, in which he took issue with what he called the disturbing 1970s "re-elaboration" of the Nazi past across popular culture, particularly notable in film and popular histories. From the 1970s the imagery of the Nazi past has been undergoing radical change, wherein attention "has gradually shifted from the revocation of Nazism as such, from the horror and the pain [. . .] to voluptuous anguish and ravishing images, images one would like to see going on forever." According to Friedländer, this new dispensation towards an aesthetics of atrocity was characterized by a troubling fusion of kitsch and death, not unlike that found in the 1930s, in which the violent extremism of the regime was being "neutralized" in a kind of sentimental, stylized aesthetic of "accumulation, repetition and redundancy."[26] Several years later he edited a book that explored the problem of representing the Nazi past, *Probing the Limits of Representation: Nazism and the "Final Solution"* (1992); these conceptual concerns found their way into his most recent Holocaust histories.

What characterises Friedländer's "integrated history" of the Holocaust are two conceptual strategies. The first is the idea of expanding the scope of Holocaust history far beyond Germany. Whereas the scope of action in the first volume (1933–1939) naturally covers events in Germany, in the second volume Friedländer masterfully weaves together the story of the annihilation of the Jews across wartime Europe. Here he integrates the story of all of the targeted Jewish cultures in Europe in a vortex of destruction, wherein the continent-wide diversity and distance of Jewish communities is radically negated as the Third Reich catapults its way eastward in 1941 and 1942, bringing millions more Jews (and POWs) under its control. It is a full, Europeanized history of the Holocaust, and as such Friedländer builds on Hilberg's classic work, even if Hilberg himself never ventured beyond German sources. For Friedländer the driving force that incites Nazi action and risk is the power and predominance of racist ideology, what he calls a toxic "redemptive antisemitism." What makes his discussion of ideology so fruitful is how he ventures into the territory of hopes, fears and the imagination, making good on his oft-cited 1984 claim that "Nazism's attraction lay less in any explicit ideology than in the power of emotions, images and phantasms."[27] No less decisive in his Holocaust history is the shocking collapse of European civil society across all national frontiers, including the Churches. One passage from Friedländer's preface may stand as the most damning indictment of all about the collapse of human solidarity across Europe after 1933:

Not one social group, not one religious community, not one scholarly institution or professional association in Germany and throughout Europe declared its solidarity with the Jews [. . .]; to the contrary, many social constituencies, many power groups were directly involved in the expropriation of the Jews and eager, be it out of greed, for their wholesale disappearance. Thus Nazi and related anti-Jewish policies could unfold to their most extreme levels without the interference of any major countervailing interests.[28]

This phenomenon has been noted by other observers. As Jürgen Habermas put it some years ago:

"There [in Auschwitz] something happened, that up to now nobody considered as even possible. There one touched on something which represents the deep layer of solidarity among all that wears a human face; notwithstanding all the usual acts of beastliness of human history, the integrity of this common layer has been taken for granted. Auschwitz has changed the basis for the continuity of the conditions of life within history.[29]

But it is Friedländer who has most effectively shown how this happened step by step, across all national communities.

The second pivotal dimension of this "integrated history" is his endeavour to include the voices of the victims. Friedländer justifies this approach thus:

The 'history of the Holocaust' cannot be limited only to a recounting of German policies, decisions, and measures that led to this most systematic and sustained of genocides; it must include the reactions (and at times the initiatives) of the surrounding world and the attitudes of the victims, for the fundamental reason that the events we call the Holocaust represents a totality defined by this very convergence of distinct elements.[30]

For him, working at the level of microhistory is the most effective way of revealing both the humanity and inhumanity of the events:

It is at the microlevel that the most basic and ongoing Jewish interaction with the forces acting in the implementation of the 'Final Solution' took place; it is at this microlevel that it mostly needs to be studied. And it is at the microlevel that documents abound.[31]

What these sources reveal is the interaction between policy and everyday behaviour, showing how Nazism's "racial morality" drew more and more Germans into active complicity with broader Nazi projects based on increasing disregard and violence towards others.[32]

Friedländer's notion of "integrated history" was certainly present in the first volume of *Nazi Germany and the Jews*. In its introduction, for example, he asserted that his study "will attempt to convey an account in which Nazi policies are indeed the central element, but in which the surrounding world and victims' attitudes, reactions, and fate are no less an integral part of this unfolding history." But it is the centrality of the victims' perspectives as historical witnesses that is the most innovative aspect of the second volume. As he writes: "For it is their voices that reveal what was known and what *could* be known; theirs were the only voices that conveyed both the clarity of insight and total blindness of human beings confronted with an entirely new and utterly horrifying reality."[33] The close-up quality of the diaries provides a fresh perspective in capturing the shocking strangeness and rough quality of the gathering "Final Solution," and in so doing makes disbelief and confusion – blindness and insight – fundamental to the story itself.

This is not to say that diaries have never been used as historical sources before. For decades historians have been using diaries as unique – if not representative – insights into the past.[34] Martin Gilbert's 1986 *The Holocaust: A Jewish Tragedy* was pioneering in building a narrative based almost exclusively on witness testimony. However, the more general interest in using diaries to explore the Third Reich was inspired by the 1995 publication of Victor Klemperer's two-volume eyewitness account of the fateful transformation of Germany, Germans and Jews after 1933, *I Will Bear Witness*, and this book features prominently in Friedländer's work as well. With it came a new commitment to using diaries and memoirs as key historical documents in their own right, though German historians have been much slower to follow this lead from North America, Britain and Israel.[35] Friedländer's work has inspired others to reread the war experience from this perspective. What many historians found most inspiring in Friedländer's first volume was the way in which he used witnesses to give a human scale to the enormous events happening around them, as subjective experience (eyes, ears, pens) became a seismograph of radical social transformation. For example, Nicholas Stargardt, in his 2005 *Witnesses of War: Children's Lives under the Nazis*, uses a range of children's diaries, drawings and eyewitness accounts to show how the war and the Holocaust were understood – or at least witnessed – through the eyes of the young.[36] Peter Fritzsche, in his 2007 *Life and Death in the Third Reich*, draws heavily on diaries, arguing that "they capture something of the conversations that Germans had with one another. They expose the fears, desires and reservations of contemporaries, and they show how they fitted National Socialist words and concepts into everyday life."[37] Others too have used Holocaust diaries and witness accounts to great effect.[38] Notable too is the extent to which scholars have grown more sensitive to issues of gender and generation in Holocaust remembrance,[39] and the same goes for some excellent recent work on visual memories of the Holocaust.[40]

As all the contributors note, there are many issues in Friedländer's book that deserve further thought and attention. Some see it as the end of an era, others as a new departure. Yet everyone seems to agree that the book represents a sea change in historical consciousness. In part this has to do with the problem of distance – yet this is not simply a question of fading memories and altered understandings. More fundamentally, the issue pivots on what and how we want to tell about a past that, for better or worse, has truly gone global.[41] The second issue is one of change. Friedländer puts a great deal of store in the notion of "redemptive antisemitism" as the ideological glue that held the Nazi state and its people together to the very end. But whilst this may have been the emotional impetus behind the mass killings of Jews initiated by the regime, how did it change over time? How did it blend with other apocalyptic fantasies in the latter stages of the war? Another related issue concerns testimony, and in particular, how to integrate the disruptive views of witnesses. In Friedländer's book, for example, why are only eyewitness accounts included, and not post-1945 memories? Why does an "integrated" history of the Holocaust preclude the voices and memories of the survivors after 1945? Is this an effort to protect a more conventional narrative structure from turning into a more open, free form *When Memory Comes* writ large? Or put slightly differently, how does such an "integrated history" of the Holocaust relate to the subject matter's most fundamental characteristic, namely moral, social and physical disintegration? Relevant here is Friedländer's evocation of Walter Benjamin's notion of messianic time in his "Theses on the Philosophy of History," cited by Friedländer at the opening of his 1992 essay, "'The Final Solution:' On the Unease in Historical Interpretation." In it Friedländer begins by quoting Benjamin: "The past carries with it a temporal index by which it is referred to redemption [. . .] There is a secret agreement between past generations and the present one [. . .]. Like every generation that preceded us, we have been endowed with a weak messianic power, a power to which the past has a claim. That claim cannot be settled cheaply [. . .]" Friedländer then concludes his essay – which among other things discusses the notion of *Rausch* as an undervalued historical force of action – by returning to Benjamin's notion of unredeemed history, arguing that the "apparent historical exceptionality" of the Holocaust may be "inaccessible" to both "representation and interpretation," rendering it ultimately "irrelevant for the history of humanity and the understanding of the 'human condition.'" "We," as the Holocaust historian states in his last sentence, "may possibly be facing an unredeemable past."[42] But to say that historians face a Holocaust past that can neither be redeemed nor even fully known is only the beginning. For it begs the question: in what way does this "post-redemptive moment" differ from writing any other history? What is at stake for a new generation of Holocaust historians when notions of "historical exceptionality," "inaccessibility" and/or "understanding of the 'human condition'" have much less conceptual hold? All of these questions register deep shifts in historical and generational consciousness, and how they shape the enterprise of Holocaust history-writing itself occupies a chief concern of this book.

Friedländer's work has addressed these questions in rich and provocative ways. As he makes clear in all of his books, Friedländer sees the main task of the historian as being to: fight against the dull "domestication" of history, to preserve the jarring dissonances of human experience. His Holocaust histories willfully unsettle the mission and meaning of interpretation, revealing how historical agents – witnesses in this case – possess a "disruptive function" and in so doing "shake our prior and well-protected representation of extreme historical events."[43] This is not simply a call for greater historical precision, but rather a plea for trying to better understand man-made worlds of dim perception, fleeting impressions and limited comprehension. However, this problem of fully capturing the past is not particular to the Holocaust. As Alon Confino has written:

> For, in fact, in its inability to be fully captured, the Holocaust is not unusual. It is not that the Holocaust is unique because the historical discipline cannot capture it, but that the extreme case of the Holocaust lays bare the basic fact that the historical discipline can never fully interpret, explain and capture a past, that all interpretations are incomplete, and that all historical understanding is a work in progress.[44]

The Holocaust may have revealed the fragility of humanity and the thin crust of civilization, but it also, as Friedländer and the contributors in this volume show, has exposed the problem of what it is to know.[45]

***

This volume of essays is based on a conference (13–15 June 2008) co-organized by the Centre for German-Jewish Studies and the Centre for Modern European Cultural History at the University of Sussex. It was expressly dedicated to an in-depth discussion of Saul Friedländer's recently published second volume of his landmark history of the Holocaust, *Nazi Germany and the Jews: The Years of Extermination, 1939–1945*. This book, the sequel to his prize-winning first volume on the prewar Nazi years, *Nazi Germany and the Jews, 1933–1939: The Years of Persecution* (1997), has received wide international coverage and scholarly acclaim, and was awarded the prestigious *Friedenspreis* in Frankfurt, Germany in 2007, as well as the Pulitzer Prize for History (US) in 2008. The conference brought together a range of leading historians from the UK, US, Canada, Australia, Ireland and Germany to address the manifold conceptual and historiographical issues raised in Friedländer's new book.

The two-day conference was devoted to investigating aspects of Friedländer's book from a variety of perspectives and to engaging in a critical discussion of several crucial aspects, including his concept of a "redemptive antisemitism" emerging in Germany at the end of the nineteenth century, which perceived the Jews as a demonic threat to German society, as well as his interpretation of the Holocaust as a singular and unprecedented historical event. The conference panels were clustered mainly around four distinct themes: The Holocaust as Narrative Problem; Interpretations of antisemitism in German Society; Mass Killing; and Future Perspectives. The aim of the conference, however, was not simply to evaluate Friedländer's book on its own merits, but rather to use his text as a means of exploring the contours (and future) of Holocaust historiography. Of central concern was to situate his work within the broader terrain of Holocaust studies and European history, as well as to explore the ways in which his book opens up new directions in the knowledge, study and understanding of the Shoah in particular and twentieth-century genocide in general. The tasks identified for future research on the basis of Friedländer's work were, among others, a cultural history of the Holocaust, a more critical analysis of Jewish and non-Jewish testimonies, and a clearer interpretation of the part gender roles played in the Holocaust.

In his keynote address, "An Integrated History of the Holocaust: Some Historiographical Issues," Saul Friedländer outlined the main methodological and moral aspects of his interpretation of the Nazi genocide and discussed the difficulties of providing a "thorough historical study of the extermination of the Jews of Europe, without eliminating or domesticating the initial sense of disbelief" caused by the sheer enormity of this crime. Of central concern to him was how to incorporate individual voices, whose "eloquence or its clumsiness, by the immediacy of the cry of terror, or by the naivety of unfounded hope, tear through the fabric of the 'detached' and 'objective' historical rendition." The historians present at the conference all addressed two main elements in Friedländer's approach: the attempt to restore the voices of Jewish survivors and witnesses instead of emphasizing narratives dominated by perpetrators, and the keen awareness of the ultimate limits of the representation of the Holocaust.

## PART I: *THE HOLOCAUST AS A NARRATIVE PROBLEM*

Alon Confino opens the volume with his wide-ranging essay, "Narrative Form and Historical Sensation in *The Years of Extermination*." In it he devotes particular attention to the problem of historical writing, in this case how to write a historical narrative of the Holocaust that offers explanations of the unfolding events and also suggests that the most powerful sensations about those events, at the time and since, are ultimately beyond words. Confino explores Friedländer's crafting of such a narrative by considering, first, the role of Friedländer's attempt in *The Years of Extermination* to explain the Holocaust and, second, the narrative form of the book. The book is best seen, Confino argues, not primarily as a work of explanation but as a vast narrative that places an explanation of the Holocaust within a specific form of describing that goes beyond the boundaries of the historical discipline as it is usually practiced.

Dan Diner continues in this vein in his contribution, "Kaleidoscopic Writing: On Saul Friedländer's Narrative of the Holocaust." Diner too argues that Friedländer's mode of representation is truly unusual, even bold by the standards of this genre. The short "takes" with which he moulds the text are like those of a filmmaker, and their impact grows cumulatively. The rational diction of commentary takes a back seat; it is restrained, as if the subject matter cannot tolerate anything more than the whispered word. The author remains in the background, yet is made all the more forcefully present through terseness, layering and irony. For Diner, Friedländer's book's style takes its inspiration from that of the chronicle – but it is a chronicle which, unlike the usual ones, does not stand at the beginning of a consideration of historical material, but rather at its end. In its seeming simplicity, the chronicle mode of narrative here proves, according to Diner, to be an effective stylistic form, in the sense that it returns to the source of historical awareness about the possibility and limitations of historical writing.

Tony Kushner then turns to the problem of testimony. As he notes, it has taken many decades after 1945 for the testimony of Holocaust victims to be taken seriously. In so doing Kushner's article on "Saul Friedländer, Holocaust Historiography and the Use of Testimony" charts the shift from the marginalization of survivors and the lack of interest in their accounts immediately after the war to more recent developments, whereby they have gained belated recognition and huge efforts have been made to record their experiences. Kushner analyzes Saul Friedländer's use of testimonies in his integrated history of the Holocaust and discusses the opportunities and dilemmas of using their "disruptive function" in Holocaust history-writing.

Mark Roseman builds on Kushner's essay by testing the limits of the victim-centred approach, asking what the victims can tell us about the perpetrators themselves. In his contribution "Holocaust Perpetrators in Victims' Eyes," Roseman thus addresses a rarely addressed dimension of Holocaust history-writing. Using diaries and memoirs, Roseman explores the issue of how Jewish witnesses reflected upon the perpetrators and their victimhood. As such Roseman adds a crucial element to the social history of the Holocaust by capturing both the proximity and distance, blindness and insight of the victims' view of their masters. Whilst Friedländer's narrative succeeds in restoring agency to the victims, drawing attention to their perceptions of the perpetrators sheds new light on the victims' predicament and self-understanding.

Michael Wildt broadens the discussion by comparing the distinctive approaches of Holocaust historians Raul Hilberg and Saul Friedländer. Whilst Hilberg was particularly interested in the Nazi bureaucratic system and machinery of destruction, looking at the Holocaust mainly from the perspective of the perpetrators, Friedländer treats the Jewish perception and response to the Nazi policies as a constitutive part of the history of the Holocaust. However much the two approaches seem absolutely contradictory, they both meet in trying to tackle an issue that most other Holocaust historians tend to skirt: the problem of finding a language, an idiom to write about the Holocaust. Hilberg wanted to keep close to the original German terms, whereas Friedländer make the voices of the persecuted Jews heard. Yet both had the sense that words can communicate only a fragmentary dimension of what has happened, raising deep questions of narrative and history-writing itself.

## PART II: *GERMAN SOCIETY AND REDEMPTIVE ANTISEMITISM*

In the first contribution of this section, under the title "National Socialism, Antisemitism and the 'Final Solution,'" Peter Pulzer analyzes Saul Friedländer's interpretation of the role "redemptive antisemitism" played in Nazi ideology and the politics of Nazi Germany in general. His argument, slightly different from

Friedländer's, is that whilst antisemitism and racism in general were crucial to determining the policies of the regime and to the conduct of its subordinate organizations, it was less important in securing the acceptance, or at least the toleration, of these policies among the wider population. In so doing Pulzer discusses various interpretations of antisemitism in Holocaust historiography and presents his own view of the virulence of antisemitism within the German population.

Nicholas Stargardt shifts attention to the increasingly extreme fear and vulnerability of the German population during the final stages of the war, and describes how the Nazis' success in portraying the Jews as the driving force behind the war influenced German complicity, silence, or indifference regarding the fate of European Jewry. Moreover, in his article "Speaking about the Murder of the Jews: What did the Holocaust Mean to the Germans?," he explores how Germans perceived the murder of the Jews during the years 1941–45, and discusses whether they were animated by "redemptive antisemitism." His findings are that whereas for Jews the Holocaust framed their understanding of the war, for Germans it was the war that provided their frame of meaning to the Holocaust. Such asymmetry does not make an "integrated history" of Jewish and German responses impossible, but it does complicate it, requiring a wider set of reference points, in the ways in which Germans formulated their hopes and fears about the war.

Christian Wiese, in his article, follows by taking up Saul Friedländer's discussion of the role the history of Christian prejudice played in the emergence of the Nazi's "redemptive antisemitism" and his analysis of the Churches' responses to Nazism. Since his challenging book on Pope Pius XII Friedländer has made it clear that many clerics, particularly senior church leaders who feared that open criticism of the genocide would bring down the wrath of the Nazis on them, remained silent and inactive, except where Jewish converts to Christianity were concerned. In some areas – particularly Croatia – nationalist clergymen egged on the murder squads with their own brand of religiously inspired antisemitism. Pope Pius XII does not come out well, but what strikes the reader yet again is the exemplary evenhandedness with which Friedländer weighs the arguments on both sides in an area that has become more controversial than most in recent years. Wiese's contribution analyzes Friedländer's – slightly changing – representation of the responses of the Churches to Nazism in his different works and put his views into the context of current historiographical debates on the topic.

The relationship between Christianity and the Shoah is also taken up by Raphael Gross in his piece "Konrad Morgen – another Kurt Gerstein? On Morality and the Holocaust." As he argues, Saul Friedländer's early research on the Holocaust started with his work on the SS officer Kurt Gerstein, who witnessed mass murders in the Nazi extermination camps Belzec and Treblinka and contacted members of the Roman Catholic Church with connections to Pope Pius XII in order to inform the international public about the Holocaust. Raphael Gross compares this case to that of Konrad Morgen, an SS judge who conducted investigations against the leaders of several concentration camps, and reflects upon the difficult question of morality under the circumstances of genocidal politics and the ambivalence of figures who, although belonging to the perpetrators or being witnesses of crimes, attempted to influence the events and disturb the smooth implementation of the Nazi "Final Solution."

## PART III:  *MASS KILLINGS AND GENOCIDE*

In his wide-ranging essay, Alan Kramer asks the question of whether the Holocaust can be compared to other mass killings during Europe's "Thirty Years War" between 1914 and 1945. Kramer analyzes the Nazi genocide against the Jews in the context of the transformation of European warfare from the 1890s and tries to differentiate between different ideological motivations for mass violence. With regard to antisemitic violence, one decisive discontinuity to World War I and the period of the Weimar Republic is, according to his view, that genocide was not part of the concept of antisemitism. With this Kramer uses a wider historical lens to test the heuristic value of "redemptive antisemitism" for interpreting the Holocaust.

Dirk Moses opens up the terrain considerably in his contribution. In a critical dialogue with Saul Friedländer's concept of "redemptive antisemitism," Moses works to contextualize Nazi ideology within Hitler's broader imperial visions of genocidal conquest, namely the Lebensraum policy in Eastern Europe. Moreover, he shows "how an imperialist political imaginary functioned in sections of the German political class between the 1890s and 1930s," and in so doing seeks to relate National Socialism and the Holocaust to world history "without subsuming antisemitism and the Holocaust beneath a generic concept."

Richard Bessel broadens the discussion by addressing the violent endgame of the Nazi regime. The massive eruption of deadly violence around the world during the 1940s left as many as 100 million people dead and many more wounded and scarred for life. This was probably the greatest eruption of violence the world has yet seen, and left in its wake a difficult and far-reaching legacy – of loss, of mourning, of disorientation, of bitterness and of hatred. Bessel's article focuses on the murderous policies of the Nazis against the Jews and tries to answer the question why the last months of the war were the deadliest for European Jewry and why the Nazis devoted their energies and resources to implementing the "Final Solution" amidst the threatening defeat of the German army. Racism, from his point of view, is not enough an explanation for this; rather, the obsession with killing as many Jews as possible in death marches was a symptom of the more general violence that accompanied the disintegration of the Nazi regime.

Next, Jan T. Gross addresses the related theme of the relationship between Jews and their Christian neighbours. Gross's approach to Holocaust historiography, particularly regarding Eastern Europe, has been to encourage the reader to view the period through the eyes of the Jews who were in Poland during the Second World War. His contribution points to a phenomenon that is rarely discussed:

the slayings of Jews by their Polish Christian neighbours at a time when Poland's German occupiers were rapidly annihilating its 3.5 million Jews. In this case, Gross analyzes court depositions in the countryside of Kielce Voivodeship where cases of killings of Jews were tried after the war. As such Gross explores the social context and the motivations of such killings, and raises questions of history-writing in relating local violence to organized genocide.

## PART IV: *PERSPECTIVES*

Doris Bergen's contribution identifies key issues in Saul Friedländer's representation of the Nazi Holocaust (the use of chronology, agency, solidarity, and religion) and shows in which way his attempt to provide an integrated history of the Holocaust poses ongoing challenges to any historian engaged in Holocaust historiography. She concludes with some comments about his biography, and the role of biography in his work. Based on the perspectives opened by Friedländer, she outlines the scope and task of future Holocaust Studies.

Zoë Waxman in turn emphasizes in which way Saul Friedländer's work raises the question regarding the role and place of gender during the Holocaust, and why the concept of an integrated history of the Holocaust has to take gender (femininity and masculinity) more seriously. In it she argues that both the history of the perpetrators as well as that of the victims has to be differentiated in terms of the specific circumstances related to gender roles. This applies to the strong link between sexism and antisemitism, to the different treatment of women as well as to the fate of female victims: The idea or hope that women and children would be spared by the Nazis, for instance, contributed to the fact that Jewish women did not – to the same degree as men – try to escape to the East and join partisan groups. On the basis of new sources, she claims, Friedländer's approach could and should be broadened, and the history of the Holocaust rewritten in terms of more gender-specific issues.

Alternatively, Wolf Gruner pleads for a more biographical approach to the Holocaust to better understand how "Nazism transformed Germans into mass murderers." In his eyes, more attention to "biographical accounts" of mid-level technocrats, especially those in the occupied territories, will help shed new light on the under-researched topic of individual socialization, aims and experiences so as "to unearth motives and interests that informed the decisions and actions of the perpetrators." For Gruner, Holocaust historiography is still in need of more work on the networks of decision-makers and responsibility across the Reich, with a particular view towards studying these dynamics in a more local and interregional setting.

Finally, Dan Stone analyzes the process in which Friedländer, over the course of his career, gradually modified his original skepticism towards the historicization of the Holocaust (triggered by his earlier debates with German historians during the "Historikerstreit" in the 1980s) and developed a kind of historicization that preserved the central significance of the Holocaust at the same time. Stone praises Friedländer's *Nazi Germany and the Jews* as a remarkable synthesis that reached a certain telos of Holocaust historiography. On the basis of this achievement, however, Stone claims, recent new developments within Holocaust historiography should be integrated, among them a stronger focus on cultural history, gender studies or anthropological studies.

\*\*\*

Several years ago, a leading German historian, Ulrich Herbert, characterized the promise and peril of historical inquiry into the Holocaust in this way:

> Historical research into National Socialist mass extermination policy has brought to light a process that was so complex, so multi-layered in terms of the perpetrators, so characterized by competition, ambitions, private interests, banality, lust for murder, and petit bourgeois hypocrisy, as well as by political utopianism and ostensibly scientific systems for interpreting the world, that this extraordinarily multifaceted image is ill-suited as a metaphor for political education and, in a sense, cannot even be identified with. And yet the didactic challenge of the history of the Holocaust lies precisely in the fact that it does not lend itself to explanations involving pithy formulations and simple, readily digested concepts or theories. And because the Holocaust possesses no theory or redemptive formula, our need to understand can only be satisfied by continuing to wrestle with the subject.[46]

Friedländer's work has done this more profoundly than any other. His two-volume *Nazi Germany and the Jews*, as many contributors note, has meticulously resisted and challenged the simplification of the Holocaust in the name of historical precision and moral compassion. Friedländer has fought long and hard against any interpretation of the Nazi past, as he explained in his *Reflections of Nazism*, that "easily turns into a rationalization that normalizes, smoothes, and neutralizes our vision of the past."[47] In the preface to his *Probing the Limits of Representation*, Friedländer remarks that "we are dealing with an event of a kind which demands a global approach and a general reflection on the difficulties that are raised by its representation." Friedländer's books are monuments both to a more globalized approach to the Shoah as well as a call to more sensitive historical writing about a subject that "should never have come to be,"[48] and one that stubbornly defies certain meaning or simple lessons.

*Notes*

1   We would like to thank Alon Confino, Mark Roseman, Nick Stargardt and Dan Stone for constructive criticism on an early draft of this introduction. Primo Levi, *The Drowned and the Saved*, trans. Raymond Rosenthal (New York: Vintage International, 1988 [Italian original, 1986]), 157–8.

2  Ruth Klüger, *Weiter Leben – Eine Jugend* (Göttingen: Wallstein, 1992), translated as *Still Alive: A Holocaust Girlhood Remembered* (New York: Feminist Press, 2001).
3  Alexandra Garbarini, *Numbered Days: Diaries and the Holocaust* (New Haven: Yale University Press, 2006), 65, as well as Marion Kaplan, *Between Dignity and Despair: Jewish Life in Nazi Germany* (New York: Oxford University Press, 1998).
4  Zoë Vania Waxman, *Writing the Holocaust: Identity, Testimony, Representation* (Oxford: Oxford University Press, 2006).
5  See for example his *Reflexions sur L'Avenir d'Israël* (Paris: Seuil, 1969) and, with Mahmud Hussein, *Arabs and Israelis: A Dialogue* (New York: Holmes and Meier, 1975).
6  Sidra DeKoven Ezrahi, "See Under: Memory: Reflections on *When Memory Comes*," *History & Memory* 9 (1997): 364–75, here 371.
7  Saul Friedländer, *When Memory Comes* (New York: Farrar, Strauss, Giroux, 1979), 110.
8  Ibid., 144.
9  Steven E. Aschheim, "On Saul Friedländer," *History & Memory* 9 (1997): 11–46, here 11.
10  See the numerous essays dedicated to Friedländer's legacy in the special double issue on "Passing into History: Nazism and the Holocaust beyond Memory: In Honor of Saul Friedländer on His 65th Birthday," *History & Memory* 9 (Fall 1997).
11  Saul Friedländer, *Reflections of Nazism: An Essay on Kitsch and Death*, trans. Thomas Weyr (Bloomington: Indiana University Press, 1984), 11–2.
12  Omer Bartov, "Introduction," in his edited *The Holocaust: Origins, Implementation, Aftermath* (London: Routledge, 2000), 1.
13  James Scott, *Seeing Like a State: How Certain Schemes to Improve the Human Condition Have Failed* (New Haven: Yale University Press, 1998) and Michael Burleigh and Wolfgang Wippermann, *The Racial State, Germany 1933–1945* (Cambridge: Cambridge University Press, 1991).
14  Eugen Kogon, *The Theory and Practice of Hell: The German Concentration Camps and the System Behind Them* (London: Secker & Warburg, 1950); Josef Wulf and Leon Poliakov, *Das Dritte Reich und die Juden: Dokumente und Aufsätze* (Berlin: Arani, 1955); Gerald Reitlinger, *Die Endlösung: Hitlers Versuch der Ausrottung der Juden Europas 1939–1945* (Berlin: Colloquium, 1956); and Raul Hilberg, *The Destruction of the European Jews* (Chicago: Ivan R. Dee, 1961).
15  Philip Friedman, "The European Jewish Research on the Recent Jewish Catastrophe," *Proceedings of the American Academy for Jewish Research* XVIII (1949): 179–211. I thank Mark Roseman for this reference.
16  Michael Marrus, *The Holocaust in History* (London: Penguin, 1993).
17  Omer Bartov, "Eastern Europe as the Site of Genocide," *Journal of Modern History* 80 (2008): 557–93, here 584–5.
18  Donald Bloxham, *Genocide On Trial: War Crimes Trials and the Formation of Holocaust History and Memory* (Oxford: Oxford University Press, 2003).
19  Hanna Yablonka, *The State of Israel vs. Adolf Eichmann*, trans. Ora Cummings (New York: Schocken, 2004) and Devin O. Pendas, *The Frankfurt Auschwitz Trials, 1963–1965: Genocide, History and the Limits of the Law* (Cambridge: Cambridge University Press, 2006).
20  Ulrich Herbert, "Extermination Policy: New Answers and Questions about the History of the 'Holocaust' in German Historiography," in Ulrich Herbert and Götz Aly (eds), *National Socialist Extermination Policies: Contemporary German Perspectives and Controversies* (London: Berghahn Books, 2000), 1–8, here 2.
21  Martin Broszat, "Plädoyer für eine Historisierung des Nationalsozialismus," *Merkur* 39 (1985): 373–85 and Saul Friedländer, "Some Reflections on the Historicization of National Socialism," *Tel Aviver Jahrbuch für deutsche Geschichte* 16 (1987): 310–24. For background, see Ian Kershaw, "'Normality' and Genocide: The Problem of 'Historicization,'" in his essay collection, *Hitler, the Germans and the Final Solution* (New Haven: Yale University Press, 2008), 282–302.
22  Steven E. Aschheim, *Culture and Catastrophe: German and Jewish Confrontations with National Socialism and Other Crises* (New York: New York University Press, 1996), esp. chapters 5 and 6.
23  The correspondence is translated and reprinted in English as "A Controversy about the Historicization of National Socialism," *New German Critique* 44 (1988): 85–126, here 90, 89. The exchange originally appeared in *Vierteljahreshefte für Zeitgeschichte* 36 (1988): 339–72.
24  Nicolas Berg, *Der Holocaust und die westdeutschen Historiker: Erforschung und Erinnerung* (Göttingen: Wallstein, 2003), 447–63.

25   In one of the letters, he notes with irony that "[w]hat created the distancing, what eliminated the
     normal historical empathy is not only the criminal dimension of the regime, but also the abhorrent
     vision of nationalist exaltation, of frenetic self-glorification which so rapidly penetrated practically
     all domains of public life and so much of private life, too." Friedländer, "A Controversy," 105.
26   Ibid., 21, 27, 50. For discussion, see Gavriel D. Rosenfeld, "The Normalization of Memory: Saul
     Friedländer's *Reflections of Nazism* Twenty Years Later," in Dagmar Herzog (ed.), *Lessons and
     Legacies VII: The Holocaust in International Perspective* (Evanston: Northwestern University
     Press, 2006), 400–12.
27   Friedländer, *Reflections of Nazism*, 14.
28   Saul Friedländer, *The Years of Extermination: Nazi Germany and the Jews, 1939–1945* (London:
     HarperCollins, 2007), xxi.
29   Jürgen Habermas, *Eine Art Schadensabwicklung* (Frankfurt: Suhrkamp, 1987), 163. See too
     Michael Geyer, "Resistance as Ongoing Project: Visions of Order, Obligations to Strangers,
     and Struggles for Civil Society, 1933–1990," in Michael Geyer and John Boyer (eds), *Resistance
     Against the Third Reich, 1933–1990* (Chicago: University of Chicago Press, 1994), 325–50.
30   Friedländer, *The Years of Extermination*, xv.
31   Ibid., xxiv.
32   On this theme, see Claudia Koonz, *The Nazi Conscience* (Cambridge, MA: Harvard University
     Press, 1997) and Michael Wildt, *Generation des Unbedingten: Das Führungskorps des
     Reichssicherheitshauptamtes* (Hamburg: Hamburger Edition, 2002).
33   Saul Friedländer, *Nazi Germany & the Jews: The Years of Persecution, 1933–1939* (London:
     HarperCollins, 1997), 2.
34   Lothar Bluhm, *Das Tagebuch zum Dritten Reich: Zeugnisse der Inneren Emigration* (Bonn:
     Bouvier, 1991) and Gustav René Hocke, *Das europäische Tagebuch* (Wiesbaden: Limes, 1963).
     See too Geoffrey H. Hartman, *Holocaust Remembrance: The Shapes of Memory* (London:
     Blackwell Publishers, 1994).
35   See for example the observations by Herbert, "Extermination Policy," 17.
36   Nicholas Stargardt, *Witnesses of War: Children's Lives under the Nazis* (London: Cape, 2007).
37   Peter Fritzsche, *Life and Death in the Third Reich* (Cambridge, MA: Harvard University Press,
     2008), 9.
38   Some of the most important include Lawrence Langer, *Holocaust Testimonies: The Ruins of
     Memory* (New Haven: Yale University Press, 1991); Shoshana Felman and Dori Laub, *Testimony:
     Crises of Witnessing in Literature, Psychoanalysis and History* (New York: Routledge, 1992);
     Henry Greenspan, *On Listening to Holocaust Survivors: Recounting and Life History* (Westport,
     CT: Greenwood Press, 1998); Donald Niewyk (ed.), *Fresh Wounds: Early Narratives of Holocaust
     Survival* (Chapel Hill: University of North Carolina Press, 1998); and Sandra Ziegler, *Gedächtnis
     und Identität der KZ-Erfahrung: Niederländische und deutsche Augenzeugenberichte des
     Holocaust* (Würzburg: Königshausen und Neumann, 2006).
39   Carole Rittner and John K. Roth (eds), *Different Voices: Women and the Holocaust* (New York:
     Paragon House Publishers, 1993); Dalia Ofer and Lenore J. Weitzmann (eds), *Women in the
     Holocaust* (New Haven, Yale University Press, 1998).
40   Barbara Zelizer. *Remembering to Forget: Holocaust Memory through the Camera's Eye* (Chicago:
     University of Chicago Press, 1998) and Lawrence Douglas, *The Memory of Judgment: Making
     Law and History in the Trials of the Holocaust* (New Haven: Yale University Press, 2001).
41   Daniel Levy and Natan Sznaider, *The Holocaust and Memory in the Global Age* (Philadelphia:
     Temple University Press, 2006). Duncan Bell (ed.), *Memory, Trauma and World Politics* (London:
     Palgrave, 2006).
42   Saul Friedländer, "The 'Final Solution': On the Unease in Historical Interpretation," in Peter
     Hayes (ed.), *Lessons and Legacies: The Meaning of the Holocaust in a Changing World* (Evanston:
     Northwestern University Press, 1991), 23–35, here 23, 35.
43   Friedländer, *Years of Extermination*, xxvi.
44   Alon Confino, *Germany as a Culture of Remembrance: Promises and Limits of Writing History*
     (Chapel Hill: University of North Carolina Press, 2006), 8. See too Dan Stone, *Constructing the
     Holocaust: A Study in Historiography* (London: Mitchell Valentine, 2003), esp. 16–30.
45   Peter Fritzsche, "The Holocaust and the Knowledge of Murder," *Journal of Modern History* 80
     (2008): 594–613.

46   Herbert, "Extermination Policy," 44.
47   Friedländer, *Reflections of Nazism*, 102.
48   Aschheim, "On Saul Friedländer," 38.

# 1

# An Integrated History of the Holocaust: Possibilities and Challenges

## Saul Friedländer

"In history," wrote Michel de Certeau, "you begin by putting aside, gathering, thus transforming into 'documents' certain objects that have been distributed differently. This new cultural distribution is the first task. In reality, it consists in *producing* such documents by copying, transcribing or photographing these objects and, in so doing, changing their place and their status."[1] In gathering 'documents' for the history of the Holocaust, several very different archives have been constituted and several quasi-autonomous histories written. This essay will deal with reshuffling or, in other words, reorganizing such previously separate entities in order to produce an integrated history of the extermination of the Jews of Europe.

I shall first define the concept of such an integrated history, then address a few related narrative and interpretive choices and, finally, evoke some issues that were previously downplayed or ignored.

## 1 THE CONCEPT OF AN INTEGRATED HISTORY OF THE HOLOCAUST

The need for an integrated history of the Holocaust had been on my mind for several decades;[2] it became a priority during the debates of the mid-and late 1980s as a result of my confrontation with Martin Broszat, at the time director of the Institute of Contemporary History in Munich, regarding his 1985 article, entitled "Plea for a Historicization of National Socialism." One of Broszat's arguments was directed against what he deemed to be the traditional simplistic, black-and-white representation of the Third Reich; in his view, it had to give way to various shades of gray. In our exchange of letters at the end of 1987, Broszat contended that the Jewish survivors' perception of this past, as well as that of "their descendants," albeit "worthy of respect," nonetheless represented a "mythical memory" that set a "coarsening obstacle" on the path of a rational German historiography.[3]

Such a plea could be interpreted as some sort of intellectual segregation of the work of Jewish historians about the Third Reich. Thus, *Nazi Germany and the Jews*, was meant to show that no distinction was warranted between historians of various backgrounds in their professional approach to this subject, that *all* historians dealing with this theme had to be aware of their unavoidable subjectivity and that all could muster enough self-critical insight to restrain it.[4] What mattered most to me in my own project was the inclusion of the Jewish dimension, along all others, within an integrated historical narrative.

Such a narrative could be identified as follows: First, the history of these events cannot be limited to German decisions and measures only; it has to include the initiatives and reactions of authorities, institutions, and of the most diverse social groups throughout the occupied and satellite countries of German-controlled Europe. Second, at each stage, Jewish perceptions and reactions, collective or individual, cannot and should not be considered as a secluded domain within the general rendition, as they impacted, in various degrees, upon all other elements of this history. Finally, a simultaneous representation of the events – at all levels and in all different places – enhances the perception of their magnitude, their complexity, and their interrelatedness. Let me very briefly address each of these points.

We do not need to belabor the fact that the history of the extermination of the Jews of Europe cannot stop at the borders of the Reich, nor be limited to German decisions and measures only. However, one aspect of the German and European scene, marginalized at times, demands to be stressed: the awareness among European elites and populations of what these anti-Jewish measures and policies were leading to. Nowadays we know that a considerable amount of information about the extermination was available throughout Europe from a rather early stage on. The Polish underground was openly referring to the mass murder as soon as it started;[5] the Swiss federal authorities explicitly mentioned the consequences of the hermetic closing of borders for Jews, in midsummer 1942.[6] In Germany itself, the fate of the Jews was quite openly alluded to at various levels of the population.

"In Bereza-Kartuska where I stopped for lunch," *Wehrmacht* Private H. K. wrote home on June 18, 1942, "1,300 Jews had just been shot on the previous day. [. . .] Men, women, children had to undress completely and were then liquidated with a shot in the back of their neck. The clothes were disinfected and used again. I am convinced that if the war goes on much longer, the Jews will be turned into sausage and served to Russian war prisoners and to Jewish specialized workers."[7] A few months later, Private S. M., on his way to the front, wrote from the town of Auschwitz: "The Jews arrive here, that is to Auschwitz, at a weekly rate of 7 to 8,000; shortly thereafter, they die a hero's death." He added: "It is really good to see the world."[8] In Minden (Westphalia), the inhabitants had been discussing the fate of deportees from their own town as early as December 1941 and publicly mentioned that Jews who were unable to work were shot.[9]

German elites showed precise information. As early as February 1942, Bishop Berning of Osnabrück noted that "admittedly there is a plan to exterminate all the Jews." In recent studies, Peter Longerich, Frank Bajor and Dieter Pohl, Bernward Doerner and, previously, Jörg Echternkamp confirmed an awareness strenuously denied for decades. Echternkamp, in his massive volume on German wartime society, although still minimizing the extent of open allusions to the extermination, nonetheless offered an eloquent summary of that awareness: "The lie of Auschwitz became the lie of German society, whereby secret knowledge of secret evil was passed off as ignorance [. . .] Living a lie was normality in German war society [. . .] Only a few beacons of truth [. . .] rose above the sea of liars."[10]

Let us now turn to the Jewish dimension of this history. Works dealing with German and related policies generally pay little attention to the properly Jewish dimension of the events: The Jews, it is usually assumed, were passive victims, an amorphous mass, whose history could be reduced to mere statistical data: a given percentage of the Jewish population exterminated in such and such a country, a different number in another one, and so on throughout occupied Europe. Yet, important work by Jewish historians, mainly focusing on the Jewish dimension of the events, had been developing since the early 1950s, so to speak behind closed doors. It included the gathering of vast collections of documents, the publication of diaries and the writing of monographs devoted to the everyday lives of the Jews and to their path to death, by country, city, community, ghetto, and camp.[11]

This internal history of the Jewish people during the years of persecution and extermination has most often remained a domain apart, whose traces in the general history of these times were mainly limited to Jewish armed resistance or to the issue of Jewish leadership. In fact, the contribution of this history to our grasp of the Shoah (and thus the need for its integration into the overall narration of the events) applies to a fundamental point. Testimonies left by Jews from all over occupied Europe indicate that, in contradistinction to vast segments of surrounding society, the victims did not understand what was ultimately in store for them. In Germany and in the west, the information available to the Jews had somehow not been pieced together; in the east, the Jewish populations in their immense majority refused to believe that what they heard about other places would also apply to them.[12] This lack of comprehension decisively contributed to the smoothness of the extermination process and to the so-called passivity of the victims. In terms of reactions and initiatives, expecting terrible hardship and even widespread death is one thing, expecting immediate murder, quite another.

The history of the destruction of European Jewry at the level of individuals can be reconstructed from the perspective of the victims on the basis of postwar depositions, interviews and memoirs, but mainly owing to the unusually large number of diaries (and letters) written during the events and recovered over the following decades. These diaries and letters were written by Jews of all countries, all walks of life, all age groups, either living under direct German domination or within the wider sphere of persecution. Of course, the diaries have to be used with the same critical attention as any other document. Yet, as a source for the history of Jewish life during the years of persecution and extermination, they remain crucial and irreplaceable.[13]

I have given priority to the individual voice for yet another reason beyond its testimonial value. The victim's voice, suddenly arising in the course of the narration of these events, can, by its eloquence or its clumsiness, by the immediacy of the cry of terror, or by the naivety of unfounded hope, tear through the fabric of the "detached" and "objective" historical rendition.

Such a disruptive function would hardly be necessary in a history of the price of wheat on the eve of the French Revolution, but it is essential to the representation of extreme historical events such as the Holocaust, which ordinary historiography necessarily domesticates. The individual cries and whispers of the victims draw from the most scholarly historical narrative a primary, sudden and essential emotional response.

It has often been stated that witnessing the Shoah is impossible in essence as, in Primo Levi's words, "those who touched bottom, those who saw the Gorgon have not returned to tell about it or have returned mute."[14] In the abstract this is undeniable. However, no less evident remains the fact that the victims' notations inscribed in the descent towards extermination come ever closer to what the diaries of members of the *Sonderkommandos* almost touched: The moment of murder.

Let us finally consider the third aspect of an integrated history of the Holocaust: simultaneous representation. Only the succession of phases, each presenting the synchronicity of events both throughout occupied Europe and within each country can indicate, as mentioned, the interrelatedness and the very dimension of this history. An example of usually separately described yet related events taking place in the Reich at the end of 1941 may help to clarify this point.

In late December 1941, the decision to exterminate all the Jews of Europe had been taken. At the same time, the main representative institution of the German Evangelical Church, the Church Chancellery, responding to the violently antisemitic stance voiced by a number of local churches adhering to the German-Christian line, issued a statement of its own denying any solidarity with converted Jews. This was made brutally clear in a circular letter published on December 23 by the Chancellery's deputy director, Günther Fürle:

> The breakthrough of racial consciousness in our people, intensified by the experience of the war and the corresponding measures taken by the political leadership, has brought about the elimination of the Jews from the community of us Germans. This is an incontestable fact which the German Evangelical Churches [. . .] cannot heedlessly ignore. Therefore, in agreement with the Spiritual Council of the German Evangelical Church, we request the highest authorities to take suitable measures so that baptized non-Aryans remain separate from the ecclesiastical life of the German congregations. The baptized non-Aryans will have to find the ways and means to create their own facilities to serve their particular worship and pastoral needs.[15]

The Confessing Church protested, but its protest was that of a minority and did not call for any countermeasures.

A few weeks earlier, several Catholic bishops, led by Bishop Preysing of Berlin, circulated a text meant to express support for converted German Jews sent to the "East." The majority of the Bishops' Conference rejected any such motion, even in its most timid phrasing.[16] Of course, neither Protestants nor Catholics addressed the fate of the immense majority of the deportees, the non-converted Jews. In other words, as the deportations from the Reich and the Protectorate were sending tens of thousands of Jews to the East, as the huge massacre of Jews in occupied Soviet territory became common knowledge, and as Chelmno, the first extermination site, had just been activated, Hitler and his acolytes could rely on the passivity of the Christian Churches, the only counter-force that had once challenged the regime about its criminal policies, namely the killing of the mentally ill.

The simultaneity of the decision to murder all the Jews of Europe and the declared non-intervention of the Christian Churches even regarding converted Jews sets the early phase of the "Final Solution" in its wider German context. The same context takes on an additional tragically ironic meaning as, at the very same time, in the last days of 1941, in the Reich and all over occupied Europe, Jews were celebrating their oncoming liberation in view of the Soviet successes on the Moscow front.[17] Only in Vilna and somewhat later in Warsaw did a tiny group become aware that the overall extermination was just starting.[18]

## 2 NARRATION AND INTERPRETATION

A discussion of the narrative form adapted to an integrated history of the Holocaust is primarily meant here at a quasi-technical level. We are dealing with events occurring in Germany, in every single country of occupied and satellite Europe, and well beyond. We are dealing with institutions and individual voices, with ideologies, religious traditions, etc. No general history of the Holocaust can do justice to the significance of this diversity of elements by presenting them as independently juxtaposed. Thus, analytic categories applicable to a study of the perpetrators and to the system of extermination have to be replaced by a succession of temporal frameworks, the only ones which can encompass perpetrators, victims and surrounding society. For this reason and, furthermore, in order to follow the fate of individual Jews, mainly that of the diarists, a chronological representation of the entire process becomes unavoidable. In other words, an integrated history, as presented here, imposes a return to a chronicle-like narration. But, as historian Dan Diner pointed out, not to a form of chronicle that predated conceptualization; in this case, chronicle remains the only recourse after major interpretive concepts have been tried and found lacking.[19]

Such a form of chronicling does not exclude partial interpretations nor does it exclude assumptions about the general historical context of the Holocaust, the collapse of liberalism in continental Europe and the related surge of extreme antisemitism, for example, nor, more specifically, does it exclude assumptions about the historical place of the extermination of the Jews within the vast array of Nazi goals and policies. This last issue brings us back to a point that was implicitly present in Broszat's argument: his objection to setting the criminal policies of the regime at the centre of a general history of the Third Reich.

The promoters of the historicization agenda stressed quite correctly that Nazi crimes had been, out of necessity, set at centre stage for the needs of the postwar trials. Later, according to the same argument, the centrality of the criminal dimension and the black-and-white representation that ensued became imperative, at least for a German historiography aimed at educating the nation (*eine volkspädagogische Geschichtsschreibung*). Thus, according to the same view, the time had come (in 1985) to perceive the policies of the regime within a much wider and differentiated context.

This 'historicization' of the Holocaust resurfaced in a spate of recent studies in which the extermination of the Jews of Europe, although presented as the secondary result of criminal policies, becomes the result of entirely different goals. These goals included, for example, the creation of a new economic and demographic equilibrium in occupied Europe by way of murdering surplus populations; ethnic reshuffling and decimation of Eastern populations to facilitate German colonization or, in the immediate, to ensure sufficient food supply for the *Wehrmacht*; systematic plunder of the Jews of Europe in order to allow the waging of a total war without putting too heavy a material burden on German society or, more precisely, in order to protect the economic and social foundations of Hitler's *Volksstaat*.[20]

These interpretations are often based on new documentary material, but they tend to project the limited or local significance of this material onto an overall explanation of the Holocaust as such. As a result, all such interpretations imply the primacy of instrumental rationality to explain the policies of expropriation, slave labor and extermination. Instrumental rationality means modernity and, implicitly, in most of these studies, the pitilessness of modern capitalism. This brings us back, on a more sophisticated level, to some of the early Marxist attempts to explain Nazism. To analyze these approaches here would be impossible. Suffice it to mention some marginal but telling events that become significant 'anomalies' and put in question the validity of such a paradigm.

What, for example, would be the rationale behind the Reichsführer SS' personal demand, in the summer of 1942, of Finland's prime minister to have his country deliver its 30 to 40 foreign Jews into Germans hands? Why would the Germans take the trouble to deport the small and impoverished Sephardic communities from the Aegean islands in July 1944 while the Reich was crumbling? Or, why would they round up and deport hundreds of Jewish children from France to Auschwitz, a few days before the liberation of Paris?

The only approach that seems plausible in writing an integrated history of the Holocaust – and I am aware that this goes against often used universalizing perceptions of this history – is to consider the Jewish issue as one of the central tenets of the regime's worldview and thus of its policies. "All in all," Goebbels noted after a long conversation with Hitler at the end of April 1944, "a long-term policy in this war is only possible if one considers it from the standpoint of the Jewish Question."[21] This crazed obsession was enthusiastically supported and implemented by Hitler's closest acolytes, by party and state agencies, by officials and technocrats at all levels of the system, and accepted – often supported – by important segments of the population.

The "logic" behind this anti-Jewish passion was constantly spewed by the regime's propaganda. In fact, as Jeffrey Herf has shown, propaganda molded an increasingly ominous image of 'the Jew" as the lethal and relentlessly active enemy of the Reich, intent on its destruction.[22] Thus, within the same hallucinatory logic, once the Reich had to fight on both fronts, East and West, without any hope of rapid victory and with some early intimations of defeat, Hitler opted for immediate extermination of the Jewish enemy. Otherwise, as he saw it, the Jews, like in 1917–18, would stab Germany in the back and destroy the Reich and the new Europe from within. And, after the military situation became ominous, the extermination was accelerated to its utter limits.

## 3  IN CONCLUSION: QUESTIONS, ANSWERABLE AND UNANSWERABLE

An integrated history leads in and of itself to comparative queries and, more generally, to connections that are otherwise but dimly perceived. Let me present one telling example: The glaring lack of an overall Jewish solidarity in the face of catastrophe.

The German Jewish leadership attempted to bar endangered Polish Jews from emigrating from the Reich to Palestine, in late 1939 and early 1940, in order to keep all emigration openings for German Jews only; native French Jewish leadership (the *Consistoire*) ceaselessly demanded from the Vichy government a clear-cut distinction between the status and treatment of native Jews and that of foreign ones. The Councils in Poland – particularly in Warsaw – were allowing a whole array of privileges to members of the local middle class who could afford to pay bribes, while the poor, the refugees from the provinces and the mass of those devoid of any influence were increasingly pushed into slave labor, or driven to starvation and death. Once the deportations started, Polish Jews in Łódź, for example, turned against the deportees from the West. In Westerbork, German Jews, the elite of the camp, closely working with the German commandants, protected their own and put Dutch Jews on the departure lists, while, previously, the Dutch Jewish elite had felt secure and was convinced that only refugees (mainly German Jews) would be sent to the local camps, then deported. The hatred of Christian Jews by their Jewish brethren, and vice versa, particularly in the Warsaw ghetto, is notorious.

Yet, a strengthening of bonds appeared within small groups sharing a specific political or religious background. Such was typically the case in political youth groups in the ghettos, among Jewish scouts in France, and, of course, among this or that group of orthodox Jews. In looking at the big picture, we may reach the conclusion that in the majority of cases, specific ethnic-cultural, political or religious bonds shared by any number of sub-groups took precedence over any feeling of shared 'Jewishness.'

***

On June 27, 1945, the world-renowned Jewish-Austrian chemist, Lise Meitner, who in 1939 had emigrated from Germany to Sweden, wrote to her former colleague and friend, Otto Hahn, who had continued to work in the Reich. After mentioning that he and the scientific community in Germany knew much about the worsening persecution of the Jews, Meitner went on: "All of you have worked for Nazi Germany and never tried even passive resistance. Certainly, to assuage your conscience, here and there you helped some person in need of assistance but you allowed the murder of millions of innocent people, and no protest was ever heard."[23] Meitner's *cri de coeur* addressed through Hahn to Germany's most prominent scientists, none of them active party members, none of them involved in criminal activities, could have applied as well to the entire intellectual and spiritual elite of the Reich (with some exceptions, of course) and to wide segments of the elites in occupied or satellite Europe.

An even more unsettling aspect of the same question arises in regard to the attitude of the Christian churches. In Germany – again with the exception of a few individuals, none of whom belonged to the higher reaches of the Evangelical or Catholic Church – no Protestant bishop or Catholic prelate protested publicly against the extermination of the Jews. When men of good will, such as Bishop Preysing of Berlin or the voice of the Confessing Church, the Württemberg Bishop Theophil Wurm, were ordered to stop their attempts at confidential protests, they submitted.

That an important number of personalities belonging to Germany's intellectual or spiritual elites did not take a public stand against the murder of the Jews is easily understood. That not even a few prominent voices were publicly heard is puzzling; that not a single personality of major stature was ready to speak out remains, as do some other aspects of this history, a continuous source of disbelief.

*Notes*

1    Quoted in Georges Didi-Huberman, *Images in Spite of All* (Chicago: University of Chicago Press, 2008), 97–8.
2    I had already presented this idea in the mid-1970s in a lecture later published as "The Holocaust: An Approach to an Historical Synthesis," in Yehuda Bauer and Nathan Rotenstreich (eds), *The Holocaust As Historical Experience* (New York: Holmes and Meier, 1981), 1–21.
3    Martin Broszat and Saul Friedländer, "A Controversy about the Historicization of National Socialism," in Peter Baldwin (ed.), *Reworking the Past. Hitler, the Holocaust and the Historians' Debate* (Boston: Beacon Press, 1990), 102–28, here 106.
4    Saul Friedländer, *Nazi Germany and the Jews: The Years of Persecution, 1933–1939* (New York: HarperCollins, 1997); Saul Friedländer, *The Years of Extermination: Nazi Germany and the Jews, 1939–1945* (New York: HarperCollins, 2007).
5    Yisrael Gutman, *The Jews of Warsaw, 1939–1943* (Bloomington: Indiana University Press, 1982), 253ff.
6    Independent Commission of Experts, Switzerland – Second World War, *Switzerland, National Socialism and the Second World War* (Zurich: Pendo, 2002), 134.
7    Walter Manoschek, *Es gibt nur eines für die Juden –Vernichtung. Das Judenbild in deutschen Soldatenbriefen, 1939–1944* (Hamburg: Hamburger Edition, 1997), 58.
8    Ibid., 63.

9    See Otto Dov Kulka and Eberhard Jäckel (eds), *Die Juden in den geheimen NS-Stimmungsberichten, 1933–1945* (Düsseldorf: Droste, 2004), 477.

10   Excerpted in Max Hastings' review of Echternkamp's volume, "Germans Confront the Nazi Past," *The New York Review of Books*, February 26, 2009, 17. Regarding the other studies, see mainly Hans Mommsen, "Der Holocaust und die Deutschen. Aktuelle Beiträge zu einer umstrittenen Frage," *Zeitschrift für Geschichtswissenschaft* 10 (2008): 844–53.

11   For these early years, let us mention the names of Philip Friedman, Isaiah Trunk, Joseph Kermish and Mark Dworzecki, among others. For the politics of historiography during this early period, see Orna Kenan, *Between Memory and History: The Evolution of Israeli Historiography of the Holocaust, 1945–1961* (New York: Lang, 2003).

12   For this lack of comprehension throughout most of occupied Europe, see Friedländer, *The Years of Extermination*, 438ff.

13   On the diaries, see in particular Alexandra Garbarini, *Numbered Days: Diaries and the Holocaust* (New Haven: Yale University Press, 2006).

14   Primo Levi, *The Drowned and the Saved* (New York: Summit Books, 1988), 83–4.

15   Quoted in Wolfgang Gerlach, *And the Witnesses were Silent: The Confessing Church and the Persecution of the Jews* (Lincoln: University of Nebraska Press, 2000), 194.

16   Klaus Scholder, *A Requiem for Hitler and Other New Perspectives on the German Church Struggle* (London: SCM Press, 1989), 163.

17   Friedländer, *The Years of Extermination*, 327.

18   Ibid., 328.

19   Dan Diner, "Chor der Opfer. Wucht und Dramatik des Holocaust: Saul Friedländer schildert die Jahre der Vernichtung," *Die Welt*, 30 September 2006, 7.

20   See in particular Götz Aly and Susanne Heim, *Architects of Annihilation: Auschwitz and the Logic of Destruction* Princeton: Princeton University Press, 2002); Christian Gerlach, *Kalkulierte Morde: Die Deutsche Wirtschafts-und Vernichtungpolitik in Weissrussland, 1941 bis 1944* (Hamburg: Hamburger Edition, 1999); Götz Aly, *Hitlers Volksstaat: Raub Rassenkrieg und nationaler Sozialismus* (Frankfurt am Main: Fischer, 2005).

21   Joseph Goebbels, *Die Tagebücher von Joseph Goebbels*, ed. Elke Fröhlich, part 2, vol.12 (Munich: K.G. Saur, 1995), 202.

22   Jeffrey Herf, *The Jewish Enemy: Nazi Propaganda during World War II and the Holocaust* (Cambridge, MA: Belknap Press, 2006).

23   Quoted in Ute Deichmann, *Biologen unter Hitler: Porträt einer Wissenschaft im NS-Staat* (Frankfurt am Main: Fischer, 1995), 372.

PART I

*The Holocaust as a Narrative Problem*

# 2

# Narrative Form and Historical Sensation: On Saul Friedländer's The Years of Extermination[1]

## Alon Confino

> Now all [historical] ideas have a subjective element, they involve imagina-
> tion, historical insight, historical sense – words that speak of a more than
> simply logical activity. [. . .] The historian – at every stage of his activity,
> in the formation of his concepts, and the interpretation of the data – has
> constantly to rely on something in himself that is much deeper and more
> impenetrable than the purely logical association of ideas [. . .] it is pure delu-
> sion to suppose that the non-rational element of historical understanding
> can be banished from that discipline and confined to the category of art [. . .]
> yet if historical feeling has its own hold on truth, that is certainly not to the
> exclusion of aesthetic pleasure. They cannot be separated.
>
> – JOHAN HUIZINGA[2]

In *The Years of Extermination*, Saul Friedländer recounts the history of the Holocaust as an integrated story of the policies of the perpetrators, the behavior of the surrounding European societies, and the world of the victims.[3] It has been received worldwide as an exemplary work of history, for in addressing the most difficult historical topic of all in the post-1945 period it has found the right balance of tone, narrative, and interpretation.[4] And yet it was written by a historian who in the last two decades has strenuously asserted the limits of Holocaust representation. The topic, as we all know, has been at the center of a much larger discussion in the last generation over the meaning of history. Friedländer's words, half *cri de coeur* and half theoretical observation, are well known: "Does an event such as the 'Final Solution' allow for *any kind* of narrative, or does it foreclose certain narrative modalities? Does it perhaps escape the grasp of a plausible narrative altogether?"[5] Consequently, Friedländer's historical reconstruction of the Holocaust in the book exists in tension with his view that the Holocaust resists a plausible narrative. How, then, does Friedländer join in one account the story of the Holocaust and our doubts about the possibility of telling this very story? How does the doubter of a plausible Holocaust narrative narrate the Holocaust?

Friedländer himself articulates this as the main challenge of the book in the last words of the Introduction: "The goal of historical knowledge is to domesticate disbelief, to explain it away. In this book I wish to offer a thorough historical study of the extermination of the Jews of Europe, without eliminating or domesticating that initial sense of disbelief."[6] At the center of my reflections on Friedländer's book is a problem of historical writing: how to write a historical narrative of the Holocaust that *both* offers explanations of the unfolding events and also suggests that the most powerful sensation about those events, at the time and since, is that they are beyond words? By "historical narrative" I understand a story that commingles explanation and description. (This rough definition will suffice at this stage; I will discuss it further as we go along.) I will explore Friedländer's crafting of such a narrative by considering, first, the role of Friedländer's attempt in *The Years of Extermination* to explain the Holocaust and, second, the narrative form of the book. Explanation and narrative form are, of course, connected. But I would like to discuss the two separately, for this helps to articulate certain features of the historical representation of the Holocaust that may otherwise remain obscure. What emerges in *The Years of Extermination* is a narrative that goes beyond the boundaries of the historical discipline as it is usually practiced; this makes it a most appropriate book for thinking, beyond its boundaries, about the nature of historical understanding more generally.

So often one finishes reading a good book about the Holocaust with a sense that, while it explores convincingly issues of context, motivation, and ideology, something is still missing in the narration of the events, a sensation that is not quite definable but is strongly felt. The reader turns the last page of *The Years of Extermination* feeling that Friedländer has captured a sense of the past that, in a sudden flash or slowly along the book's 700 pages, provides a certain illumination about the Holocaust that had not been present before. What exactly is this historical sensation of the past in the book? And what does it have to do with historical writing and understanding?

I

Let us begin by placing the book's challenge in a wider historiographical context. Friedländer's aim – namely, to offer a historical study while keeping the sense of disbelief – is unusual even while it fits within some contemporary trends in historical theory and practice. On one level, Friedländer's book accords with discussions of historical writing and method in the last thirty years, where it has become a staple of historical work to own a historical past precisely by showing the limits of historical knowledge and the constructedness of historical representation.[7] Edward Ayers described this shift eloquently in a meditation on the different narrative forms that appeared in his book, *The Promise of the New South*, published in 1992, and in C. Vann Woodward's *Origins of the New South*, published in 1951. Ayers, a student of Vann Woodward, views *Origins* as the finest Southern history. However, during the forty-one years that separated the publication of the two books historical writing changed markedly, becoming dominated by "a sense of contingency and possibility even within powerful structures [. . .] when the authors let the reader in on the way the argument is being constructed [. . .] when the appearance of coherence and a commanding argument may ultimately be less useful than a reckoning with the limits of our knowledge or understanding."[8] In this respect, Friedländer's aim seems a radical version of a shared concern among historians, namely, that reconstructing the past entails awareness of and openness about the doubts and limits of this reconstruction.

Yet Friedländer's aim is unusual because the historian customarily reconstructs the past, within the limits of the historical method, with the aim of owning a historical reality, not with the aim of owning and disowning this past in the same narrative. The difference comes into sharp focus when we think of significant books that are sensitive to questions of method. Ayers's intention in *The Promise of the New South* (and note also Lyndal Roper's in *Witch Craze*) is precisely to lead the reader into a strange world in order to suspend disbelief; their success is measured by their ability to unlock as much as possible the strangeness of racist and witch-crazed pasts.[9] Friedländer's aim, in contrast, is, at one and the same time, to reconstruct the past and simultaneously to express disbelief about this past. The conventional assumption concerning history books is that the historian engages in a process of familiarization – which consists of reading documents, using evidence, and employing methods – that results in a narrative whose intention is to overcome the past's strangeness. But Friedländer proposes both to engage in the act of familiarization and at the same time to keep a sense of strangeness. For him, the "sense of disbelief" is not simply a problem of historical reconstruction, and is not an obstacle the historian has to overcome in order to portray the period better. Instead, it is a defining characteristic of the period and an element the historian has to integrate into his or her narrative.

What is the role of explanation in this book that aims to provide a systematic historical study of the extermination of the Jews of Europe, without domesticating the sense of disbelief about it? I begin with explanation because nowadays it is considered the main task of historical work.[10] By "explanation" I mean the attempt to provide an answer to the question, "What caused it?" Friedländer knows that on some level we cannot fathom what caused the Holocaust, but he does present a clear interpretation. The Holocaust, he argues, was determined by "the centrality of ideological-cultural factors as the prime movers of Nazi policies in regard to the Jewish issue."[11] The driving force behind the events was a form of antisemitism that saw its mission as that of redeeming the world by eliminating the Jews. Nazi ideology viewed "the Jew [as] a lethal and active threat to all nations, to the Aryan race and to the German *Volk*." One contribution of the book is that it puts to rest any attempt to interpret the extermination of the Jews as a secondary or derivative result of German economic, bureaucratic, and resettlement policies aimed at entirely other goals. It demolishes any explanation of the Holocaust that does not give central place to the Jews, and that views the extermination as a by-product of German intentions and plans that had little to do with them. Ultimately, all those who attempt to understand the Holocaust as caused by institutional and policy-making processes inherent in the Nazi system of government, by the inner logic of National Socialist policies geared toward resettlement and expansion, or by the need to solve immediate, local, pragmatic problems (such as food problems) – that is, all attempts that fundamentally underplay the beliefs and values embedded in the acts of the perpetrators – are bound to end in an interpretive cul-de-sac.

Friedländer also presents an overall interpretive framework. "The events we call the Holocaust represent a totality defined by [the] convergence of distinct elements."[12] The first element is the Germans and their collaborators as the prime agents of policies of extermination, from Hitler, via civil and military agencies, down to ordinary Germans; the second is the reactions and initiatives of the surrounding world – be they occupied countries, the Catholic Church, or belligerent states – with special attention paid to the passivity or support of the population toward the Germans' murderous plans; and the third is the experience of the victims. The history of Nazi ideology and policies thus combines with the history of the Jews, which has largely remained in historiography a world unto itself separate from the history of the perpetrators. In this respect, the book stands out in its attempt to provide "both an integrative and an integrated history" of the Holocaust.[13] The scope is a sort of total history (in a historiographical age that repudiates it) that "penetrates all the nooks and crannies of European space."[14] The narrative is held together by two elements: the centrality of ideology as its driving force and unifying theme; and diaries written by Jews all over Europe that provide their subjective, everyday experience.

The explanation of the Holocaust as driven primarily by redemptive antisemitism is significant for Holocaust historiography, but in itself, I would like to argue, it cannot be determinant to the making of a narrative that commingles familiarization and strangeness. There is a built-in tension between the success of this interpretation in convincing the reader and Friedländer's wish to maintain a sense of disbelief. The more convincing is the answer to the question "What caused it," the greater the domestication of disbelief.

The same is true for the interpretive framework of the Holocaust as an integrated history. The result is convincing. But, again, a compelling rendition of this interpretive framework would work toward domesticating disbelief, regardless of the author's intentions declared in the Introduction. We can understand this by thinking of a book that a generation ago attempted a sort of integrated history of the Holocaust. Leni Yahil's *The Holocaust* was published in English in 1987 with the explicit aim to "interweave [. . .] the intentions and actions of the Nazis [. . .] the behavior of the Jewish communities [. . .] the relations between the Jews and the peoples among whom they lived [. . .] [and] the attitude of the world's nations."[15] The two books are divided by a whole generation of scholarship, which necessarily influenced their method as well as the information at their disposal. But the idea of the Holocaust as an integrated history is shared by both scholars. It is no coincidence that both are Jews: they rejected a history of the Holocaust with the Jews left out or as minor actors.[16]

What kind of a narrative did Yahil produce? Although she states in the introduction that "this history cannot be presented as usual historiography, that is, surveying a series of events, actions, and developments in society," this is precisely the narrative she presents.[17] There is nothing in the narrative form that would correspond to Yahil's idea of the uniqueness of the Holocaust. In this respect, she represents a whole generation of historians who asserted the uniqueness of the Holocaust at the outset of their books, and yet who went on to produce a conventional historical narrative of it. We shall return to this topic below. The interpretive framework of integrated and integrative history, however important, cannot therefore produce by itself a narrative that commingles historical study and disbelief.

The same is true for the attempt to capture via diaries the subjective experience of contemporaries, especially the victims. To understand my argument we need to consider briefly the foundation of this experiential approach. Students of culture have postulated in the last generation that collective representations cannot be reduced to social and political origins. This approach moved away from explanation in terms of functionalist and structuralist models toward, as the editors of the *Annales* put it in a 1989 historiographical statement, "analysis in terms of strategies, which allow memory, learning, uncertainty, and negotiation to be reintroduced to the heart of social interaction."[18] Exploring "the world as representation," to use the title of Roger Chartier's 1989 essay, was ultimately a way to "cast a fresh eye on the social itself."[19] The point of this move to see the cultural as a historical factor in itself has been to capture an additional aspect of the historical reality of the past, not to maintain a sense of disbelief. Even radical cultural studies approaches, which question historical knowledge and whether it exists at all, sought to capture the experience of oppressed people in the past. Scholars have used gender, racial, transnational, and postcolonial categories to undermine hegemonic narratives and historiographical practices precisely in order to bring to life voices, subjective identities, and hidden histories of silenced groups in the past. This was the whole point. And however radical some of the critique of historical knowledge was, scholars of cultural studies let the subaltern speak because in the end they believed, whether they acknowledged it or not, that this voice has a historical materiality that we can still call reality. The cultural approach that seeks to uncover the subjective experience of people in the past cannot, therefore, be used in itself to craft a narrative that keeps its own sense of disbelief.

In a series of publications and talks, Friedländer presented the idea of an integrated history of the Holocaust as the book's major contribution.[20] This idea speaks to the historian in him, and to the wish to set the historical record straight about the Holocaust. But I do not think that *The Years of Extermination* is best seen as an important book because of its explanation and interpretive framework; they are new, but not that new.[21] They are important in this specific historiographical moment, but interpretations come and go. More importantly, they cannot be the main elements of the book because they undermine the quest for a narrative that is both historical and maintains disbelief about the past. Explanation and interpretation are normally used by historians as means of making the past familiar, not of keeping its sense of strangeness. The point is not that Friedländer could have used them better, but that in themselves they present an obstacle to crafting such a narrative. With respect to the Holocaust, then, the challenge is to use explanation and interpretation in such a way that the sense of shock and disbelief is still maintained. It means finding a different way of representing the evidence and telling the story. Consequently, *The Years of Extermination* is best seen not primarily as a work of explanation but, to my mind, as a vast narrative that places an explanation of the Holocaust *within a specific form of describing*.


## II

We can appreciate the claim that I am advancing here by considering the problems of writing the history of the Holocaust. A major historical task since 1945 has been simply to describe aspects of the historical reality of the persecution and extermination of the Jews from 1933 to 1945. The basic task of all history writing – to tell what the case was – was immensely difficult.

After 1945 the Holocaust was generally not considered in public and scholarly circles as a foundational past of European history; the term itself became synonymous with the extermination of the Jews only around 1960. Primo Levi's *Se questo è un uomo* was rejected in 1946–7 by Einaudi and by five other Italian publishers for lack of interest before it was taken by a small publishing house in Turin.[22] Very few major historical works were devoted to the Holocaust until the 1970s. Raul Hilberg's monumental *The Destruction of the European Jews* was published in 1961 after many difficulties. It was rejected by Columbia University Press, Yad Vashem, Princeton University Press, and the University of Oklahoma Press before it was published by a new, small, independent publishing house in Chicago, Quadrangle Books. The 1959 rejection letter from Princeton University Press noted that the manuscript did not "constitute a sufficiently important contribution" and that "readily available" books on the subject existed "in sufficient detail."[23]

Ever since historians finally began, in the 1970s and then with growing persistence and meticulousness from the 1980s onward, to tell the story of the Holocaust, there existed two seemingly contradictory trends in the way people thought about it. On the one hand, there have been doubts in scholarly and public discourse about the possibility of producing a historical representation of the Holocaust at all. Friedländer's view – that "[One] wonders, possibly, whether any historical approach could suffice to redeem, that is convincingly to interpret that past" – is but one expression of it.[24] This state of mind was part of the epistemic crisis in Western culture created by the Holocaust.[25] On this issue, historians reflected, more than they shaped, popular perceptions about the special character of the Nazi past. For a long while, it became *de rigueur* among scholars to state that "Arguably, indeed, an *adequate* explanation of Nazism is an intellectual impossibility."[26] This kind of historical evaluation worked as an emotional, moral, and professional bulwark against telling the story.

At the same time, Holocaust scholarship developed in a diametrically opposed direction. The Third Reich became the single most written about topic in history; a standard bibliography of National Socialism listed 25,000 titles in 1995 and a whopping 37,000 in 2000.[27] What emerged is just how complex the Holocaust actually was. It was not simply a German event, but a European and a North African one (Libyan and Tunisian Jews were sent to Auschwitz). In fact, it was not an event at all, but a series of events. It did not involve just Hitler and several of his cronies, but German society, its economy, and culture as a whole. And it did not involve only the Jews, but was tied to a series of Nazi resettlement plans and murderous policies to redraw the map of Europe, which involved Poles, Russians, Roma and Sinti, the handicapped, homosexuals and lesbians, and others. One lasting contribution of this body of work has been to tell in detail aspects of the military, institutional, ideological, and political history of the Holocaust. One problem this remarkably specialized massive historiography has presented for the historian who wanted to narrate the Holocaust was not that it could not be represented, but conversely that, studied in such detail, it was at times difficult to see the forest for the trees.

Another fundamental aspect of this body of work has been its almost positivist attachment to facts. It answered the difficulty of narrating the story of the Holocaust by turning to the massive accumulation of facts – to the way things were –in order to suspend disbelief, domesticate the past, and undo the strangeness of a racist and murderous world. This body of work has been characterized by the use of substantial sources to tell the story very close to the documents. We can think of the major work by Christopher Browning (with Jürgen Matthäus), *The Origins of the Final Solution*, or of the grand studies of the Third Reich by Ian Kershaw and Richard Evans, who write in the British tradition of empirical, erudite histories. Kershaw's aim in his biography *Hitler. 1936-1945: Nemesis* is to tell "how it came about," while that of Richard Evans in his trilogy on the Third Reich is to "show how one thing led to another."[28] Evans's "central aim" – "to remind readers that [...] 'the past is a foreign country: they do things differently there'"—has an educational motive based precisely on the idea that the gap between the reader and the past must and can be bridged by the historian.[29]

Friedländer's narrative form, to which we shall turn shortly, emerges from the relations between the seemingly contradictory trends in Holocaust historiography discussed above: on the one hand the view that the Holocaust faces inherent problems of interpretation, and, on the other hand, the enormous body of work characterized by detailed empirical evidence. The fact that Holocaust historiography attempted to describe the event as accurately as possible is complementary, not contradictory, to the notion of the limits of Holocaust historical representation. Precisely because of these limits (some real, some perceived), scholars felt – and "feeling" seems to me the accurate word here – that "hard facts" and evidence are the only basis for legitimate historical work.[30] Holocaust historical scholarship is still in many respects cautious, and it comfortably relies on close reading of documents.[31]

Significantly, the two trends often run parallel to each other. Historical studies of the Holocaust have often been separated from the theoretical discussion of the limits of representation. Important scholars who theorized about the Holocaust (Dan Diner, Dominick LaCapra, Dan Stone) were often different from those who wrote its history (Raul Hilberg, Christopher Browning).[32] Friedländer is among the few who did both well. Of course, this distinction is not clear-cut, but it helps to identify an important trend in Holocaust historical writing: in contradistinction to literature, poetry, and other arts, history did not quite find a new form of narrative to express the problems of Holocaust representation and the fact that a sense of disbelief (by Germans, Jews, and others) was a characteristic perception of the event since its inception.

In their conventional – that is, typical – historical writing of the Holocaust, historians implied the opposite of what many had stated about its representational challenge. To be sure, there is something in the common use of historical method that works against a new form of narrative: the need to present the evidence in a logical, orderly, clear way, to keep (some sort) of chronology, to respect relations of cause and effect, to demonstrate with pertinent sources who did what to whom and why. Historians, therefore, acted here as they should: they told stories based on evidence and rules of verification, and by doing this they contributed tremendously to our knowledge and understanding of the Holocaust. The discussion about the uniqueness and representability of the Holocaust was a metahistorical discussion that historians qua historians could not resolve.[33] By producing studies whose aim was to dispel disbelief in the past, they instinctively resisted the cultural notion, often sustained by the same historians, that the Holocaust somehow stands outside of history.

But the gap persisted between the aim of Holocaust historians to overcome the strangeness of the past, on the one hand, and the sense of disbelief that this past has always engendered. It is in this gap that *The Years of Extermination* fits. Friedländer's first achievement is to tell an integrated history of the Holocaust that is a sort of *summa* of Holocaust research of the last generation. This integrated history fulfills his aim to provide a "thorough historical study," but it could not, as we have seen, fulfill his other aim to offer a sense of disbelief. *The Years of Extermination* recounts the familiar political, military, administrative, and ideological history of the Holocaust, and in this way it aims to overcome the strangeness of the past. But the book also has another story to tell, one that gives this familiar history of the Holocaust a new meaning.

This other story is able, first, to capture the elusive historical sensation of disbelief because disbelief, too, was part of the way things were. The historiographical body of work largely banished the strangenesses of the period from the story of the Holocaust instead of integrating them into the narration of how things were. By "strangenesses of the past" I mean those elements that can be captured through an analysis of culture, mentalities, and sensibilities. My point is not that the Holocaust is strange in a particular historical way; for the historian, all pasts are strange. Rather, my point is that the task of the historian ought to be to elucidate the strangeness of the past, not to attempt to overcome it. This is exactly what Friedländer does.

By telling this other story, *The Years of Extermination* is able, second, to bring the problems of Holocaust representation into the historical narrative. The idea that the Holocaust is difficult to represent has been shared and reiterated by historians, literary theorists, and philosophers, but the various tellings about the event did not result in a new or different narrative form of historical writing. The common practice has been instead to begin one's study of the Holocaust by asserting its representational difficulties, while proceeding to narrate it as if these difficulties do not exist.[34] In contrast, the narrative form of *The Years of Extermination* aims at accounting for what happened, but also at accounting for the persisting problems of perceiving and believing what happened.

This sort of historical narrative requires going beyond the usual boundaries of historical writing. This is the reason, I believe, that this book is best seen not for its interpretation of the Holocaust, but for the way its interpretation is embedded within a specific form of describing. Friedländer's book cries out to be perceived and understood formally, as a historical narrative that combines evidence and a poetic act.

## III

The narrative of the *Years of Extermination* is characterized at first sight by unity, order, and coherence. It is strictly chronological, aims at providing the "totality" of the Holocaust, and has a clear organizing and explanatory principle in the notion of redemptive antisemitism. But in fact this narrative is fractured at its core and does not follow the usual mode of historical writing.

Friedländer's narrative is distinguished by the use of Jewish individual testimonies interspersed with the chronological history of the extermination. Commonly, argues Friedländer, the victims' voice was perceived as "a trace left by the Jews that bear witness . . . and illustrates their fate." He uses the voice of the diarists differently: "by its very nature, by dint of its humanness and freedom, an individual voice suddenly arising in the course of an ordinary historical narrative of events such as those presented here can tear through seamless interpretation and pierce the (mostly involuntary) smugness of scholarly detachment and 'objectivity.'"[35]

The result is a narrative marked by violent dislocations and interruptions. On one level, there exists the chronological, political, military, administrative, and ideological story of the extermination; it follows the regular modes of typical historical accounts. But on a different level, this narrative is pierced through by diarists' voices that are not used to bolster empirical evidence or to strengthen arguments about historical causality, but to insert a human dimension that "facts" alone cannot quite capture. They create images in short stories and vignettes that are not so much connected to what comes before and after, as they are startling in their visualness. Different diarists follow one another, they appear, disappear, only to reappear again hundreds of pages later in a loosely joined narrative. The typical historical account acts like the necessary context, the outward reality, to the deep, genuine, existential meaning of the story.

Thus, following an ordinary historical discussion of the events in Holland under the occupation (the policy of the military administration, the reaction of the public, and so on), Friedländer turns to the diary of young Etty Hillesum. Her experience is not narrated as a means to explain, exemplify, or provide proof for the previous discussion. Friedländer does not begin the short page on Hillesum with a common historical phrase such as "The travail of occupation is exemplified in the story of Etty Hillesum." Instead, he starts with "Etty (Esther) Hillesum was still a young woman student in Slavic languages in Amsterdam University during these spring months of 1941."[36] Her story is not offered to provide evidence for a given argument; its meaning lies in its speaking at all, in its existing. For the Nazis, the crime of the Jews, George Steiner once observed, was the crime of being; the meaning of Hillesum's voice is that of being. Her story does not require the historian's justification ("this source illustrates well my argument that . . ."). She is part of the narrative in much the same way protagonists in a novel are (and that is why we accept without question her next appearance 200 pages later and again for less than a page). As readers we do not expect, say, Orhan Pamuk to explain to us how the actions of Shekure move the plot forward in *My Name is Red*; he lets Shekure speak, and we figure the story out.

The historical narrative of *The Years of Extermination* has qualities of a literary narrative. While the literary and poetic aspects are widely accepted as constitutive parts of historical narrative, these kinds of ruptures and breaks are devices associated with works of fiction, and historians do not usually use them.[37] They are anomalous in historical studies. It should be noted that not only the relations between the historical narrative and the diarists' poetic narrative are marked by dislocation, this is a characteristic of the book as a whole. The reader is alerted to the narrative of dislocation, characterized by moving from one scene to another, by the ubiquitous double space that separates the scenes. This is not a tight monograph. Consider the studies by Browning, Evans, Hilberg, Kershaw, Longerich, or any other monograph on the period. (At the same time, Friedländer's narrative is possible in part only because there now exists a massive literature that depicts in detail aspects of what happened.) *The Years of Extermination* is a loosely jointed narrative bounded by strict chronology and the overarching plot of Nazi policies and the ideology of extermination, but one interrupted by voices other than that of the historian.

Some diarists' stories have the air of literary episodes. The diarists speak, and only rarely does Friedländer interject with the authorial voice of the knowledgeable historian, who by virtue of hindsight knows more than the people in the past.[38] He recounts the reactions of David Sierakowiak, a Jewish youngster, scarcely fifteen, to the persecution of the Jews shortly after the Nazi invasion of Poland. "And at that point," writes Friedländer, "the young diarist added a puzzling question: 'is this evidence that the end for the Germans will probably come soon?"[39] Friedländer leaves the question hanging in the air and moves on to the next topic. What is the meaning of it, I noted in the margins when I first read it. But the literary pattern emerges as I went on reading. Friedländer suspends the episode in its particular historical time, holding back from the usual practice of historians, which would be to add a comment that places it in a larger context. The aim is to represent a truth expressed by Sierakowiak without the interference of the "smugness of objectivity" and of historical time that is measured in years and decades.

The attempt to capture Sierakowiak's subjectivity in this specific instant, while History swirls around him, reminds me of Ida Fink's notion of time in her story "A Scrap of Time": "I want to talk about a certain time not measured in months and years. [. . .] This time was measured not in months but in a word – we no longer said 'in the beautiful month of May,' but 'after the first "action," or the second, or right before the third.' We had different measures of time [. . .] during this time measured not in months nor by the rising and setting of the sun, but by a word [. . .]."[40]

*The Years of Extermination* is a total history of the Holocaust that is aware of itself as partial; this awareness forms the formal essence of the text. Friedländer posits the historical totality of the Holocaust as an integrated and integrative story, while at the same time he uses a narrative form that intimates that this history cannot quite be captured. It is a historical narrative against itself. The power of this work is the fundamental ambivalence at its heart, a book built on its own contradiction: describing the past as history and setting at the same time the limits to that describing.

"Style is the bridge to substance," observed Peter Gay in an essay about Jacob Burckhardt.[41] *The Years of Extermination* has a distinct, composed tone, without moralizing and pontificating. The reader discovers the style as he or she goes along; Friedländer does not alert the reader to it. Only once, in a footnote, does he make clear his rhetorical choice: he discusses Janusz Korczak, who walked at the head of the row of children of his orphanage as they all marched together to their death in the Warsaw Ghetto on 5 August 1942: "there have been many descriptions of this march, and quite a few 'literary' embellishments were added to the bare facts, which certainly do not need any added pathos."[42] This style contrasts with writings that see fit to remind us explicitly about the morality embedded in the Holocaust, writings that are always a word removed from moralizing. Among the important historians of the period, I can think, for example, of Omer Bartov and Michael Burleigh.[43] Friedländer's moral presence emerges from his minor tone, which reminds me of the style of Primo Levi and Ida Fink, and of Inga Clendinnen, a historian of the Aztecs who wrote remarkably about the Holocaust.[44]

And yet it should be noted that Friedländer tells a story in black and white, of the entire continent on one side, and the victims on the other. His is a story without "gray zones," to use Primo Levi's famous expression.[45] The story focuses on the complexity of the extermination project and of the Jewish experience, but it does not explore the construction of a genocidal culture and the psychology of the perpetrators and therefore largely avoids the dilemmas faced by Germans and bystanders. The book's focus on ideology as the main motivation for the Holocaust is partial and at times even too simple an explanation. At issue is to offer a description, and not at all an explanation, let alone to justify the explanation via evidence and argument, while leaving the moral consequences of the tale to the moral imagination of the readers. *The Years of Extermination* is concerned with bequeathing to the historical account the moral essence of the event (in contradistinction to historical narratives characterized by the smugness of "objectivity").

The descriptive element of the book is expressed significantly in the issue of causality. The book's overall explanation is that redemptive antisemitism, serving as "*the* mobilizing myth of the regime," was at the core of the Holocaust.[46] Friedländer qualifies this proposition by adding, "depending of course on circumstances, institutional dynamics, and essentially, for the period dealt with here, on the evolution of the war."[47] But if the unfolding of Nazi antisemitic ideology is well described in the book, its origins, reception, and reason for success are taken for granted. If by "causal relationship" historians seek to give an answer to the question of what caused this or that historical case, then *The Years of Extermination* is not particularly revealing. Neither the behavior of Germans and perpetrators nor their genocidal mindset is investigated. Antisemitism is described and assumed, but not explored. Friedländer mentions the "crisis of liberalism and the reaction against communism" as background for the spread of antisemitism, but these factors remain a background, not a cause. At the end, he argues, "there remains but one plausible interpretation": Nazism was a form of "sacralized modernism," of religious elements in modern society.[48] But this well-known interpretation is not explored in the book in order to explain the origins of the ideology, why it was successful, and what were its symbols, especially its religious symbols. Redemptive antisemitism functions in the book as an organizing principle that is effectively evoked and described. But it has an overall presence that orders and answers everything, and ultimately is presented as a given, not as a belief constructed in the crucible of German culture. The notion of ideology employed in this way reflects current historiography, where ideology has depreciated by surplus use and has acquired at times metaphysical explanatory value.[49]

Moreover, the three different levels of the integrated history (Germany, surrounding world, and victims) are not so much causally connected as they are linked by association and by the context created by the historian. The story holds together not because of established causal relationships (among, say, Nazi ideology, occupation authorities, the Vichy regime, and the French public), but because of the description that weaves things together.

Friedländer describes Hitler's suicide on 30 April shortly after 3 p.m., noting that on 1 May, on Doenitz's orders, German radio broadcast an announcement of Hitler's death "at his command post in the Reich Chancellery." The next scene, separated by a double space, tells about Cardinal Bertram's request to his Breslau parish "to hold a solemn requiem mass in memory of the Führer."[50] The meaning of this story is clear from the context, namely that Germans admired Hitler until the bitter end, and mourned his death. But the story is not strictly connected to what comes before or after, and Friedländer does not articulate its meaning (by writing, for example, "a demonstration of the love of Germans to Hitler until the very end is provided by Cardinal . . ."). He leaves the reader to fill in the blank and to draw the meaning of the vignette. This narrative form weakens causal relations in favor of descriptive power.

As a result, Friedländer's book is more of an inclusive history of the Holocaust that discusses three topics that have usually been separated in the historiography (Germans, the surrounding world, and Jews), than it is an integrated history, as Friedländer claims, that interweaves three topics via cause and effect relations into a tight historical narrative. But then again it cannot be such an integrated history precisely because of the "individual voice [that] suddenly aris[es] in the course of an ordinary historical narrative of events [and] tear[s] through seamless interpretation [. . .]."[51] What is gained by using the narrative form that it does – the capturing of a historical sensation of the period – is far greater than attempting to establish a causal relation.

In this respect, the issue of causality along three levels of history in *The Years of Extermination* reminds me of Fernand Braudel's *The Mediterranean and the Mediterranean World in the Age of Philip II*.[52] Braudel perceived the past in this seminal work of the *Annales* school along three waves of different historical lengths of time and space. The first is the *longue durée* of imperceptible changes, of realities that time transforms only with great difficulty, such as the movement of people out of the mountains to settle in the plains. This is a history of the constraints that geography, landscape, and also technology impose on human history. The second is the *moyenne durée*, comprised of cycles of ten, twenty, or at the most fifty years, of economic and social processes such as price curves, demographic changes, and movement of wages. The third is the *courte durée* of those most readily observed, everyday, political events, the *histoire événementielle*. But the three major *durées*, which make up the three sections of *The Mediterranean*, never quite come together. Braudel never fully succeeds in showing how long-range developments influence the events of the period of Philip II. Based on an interpretation of the past comprised of three levels, *The Mediterranean* aspires to be an *histoire totale*; to capture the whole of human activity in the age of Philip II, while *The Years of Extermination* aspires to present the "totality" of the Holocaust as an integrated and integrative story.[53] Both fall short of the authors' intention with respect to linking causally the three levels, while their achievement is to provide a massive and powerful portrait of the period.[54]

We can now go back to the notion of narrative and the relationship between explanation and description. A prevalent opinion among historians favors analysis over description. But this is surely a mistake. "Historical description" is far more complex and fascinating than a theoretically unaware perspective recognizes. It is certainly not separated from explanation. *The Years of Extermination* fits well with Allan Megill's elegant words that "upon descriptions, explanations arise. Descriptions and explanations presuppose an interpretive perspective, and in the best histories they modify and enrich such a perspective."[55] Friedländer turns the event we call the Holocaust into a vast collection of settings, happenings, actions, characters, and experiences. He provides explanations for precise problems (the role of Hitler, the timing of the decision of the "Final Solution," the responsibility of the Catholic Church, and others). But the overall explanation that arises from the description is that the historical method can grandly tell about the Holocaust, while it also requires an additional component to get to a deep human element embedded in it. This imparts to the book a certain feel – of the period, of contemporaries, of the victims, of suffering, of what we call the past – that is remarkable.

## IV

A persistent tension runs through the book: is the book's narrative form specific to the Holocaust or is it applicable to the craft of history as a whole? The tensions and ambiguities between these two positions make this an important book about historical writing, while they also define its limitations. Indeed, the argument about historical understanding embedded in the book should be set free from the bounded context of present-day Holocaust historical representation.

Let us begin this discussion by tracing the intellectual origins of *The Years of Extermination*. They are to be found in *Probing the Limits of Representation*, a book edited by Friedländer and published in 1992, that explored the representation of the Holocaust against the challenge of post-modernism that rejected the possibility of a firm reality beyond the self-referentiality of linguistic constructs.[56] Twice in the introduction to *Probing the Limits* Friedlander cites a sentence by Pierre Vidal-Naquet quoted from Carlo Ginzburg's essay "Just One Witness":

> I was convinced that [. . .] everything should necessarily go through a discourse [. . .] but beyond this, or before this, there was something irreducible which, for better or worse, I would still call reality. Without this reality, how could we make a difference between fiction and history?[57]

*The Years of Extermination* provides a total history of the Holocaust as an irreducible reality by using not just one, but many witnesses.[58] At the same time, Friedländer also intimates in the introduction that "a precise description of the unfolding of events [. . .] [and the] impact of empirical evidence" cannot by itself "carry its own interpretation, its own truth."[59] And he ends by saying: "But the truth aimed at by history's, as opposed here to fiction's, specific form of discourse needs the maintaining of other convergent paths as well [. . .] it does not kill the possibility of art – on the contrary, it requires it for its transmission."[60] The book's narrative commingles two aspects, only seemingly contradictory: its language is tied to reality through a detailed history of the event and the voice of its witnesses, while its form alternates with violent dislocation that is uncommon in historical studies.

A mix of personal and professional considerations explains Friedländer's underlying approach to the Holocaust. We begin with the historian, described by Johan Huizinga at the outset of this essay as having "constantly to rely on something in himself that is much deeper and more impenetrable than the purely logical association of ideas." Friedländer's view of Holocaust history emanates not only from methodological or historiographical considerations, but from his relationship to his work, from the meeting point of personal experience and historical subject matter. Historians prefer to ignore the issue of the relationship of the historian to his or her subject matter, to pretend it does not exist, or just to keep silent about it; it is considered a personal matter, and therefore outside of scholarly detachment and objectivity.[61] But this is a mistake. By leaving out Friedländer's relationship to his work we leave out whole areas of how narrative and interpretive decisions are made. "To miss the emotional intensity of the historical operation is to miss a major part of its meaning," Linda Orr observed perceptively.[62] Part of Friedländer's historical insight comes from intuition, without which no historical work can be written. It is also linked to his experience, as he attempted to translate it into the language of the historian. Friedlander the historian couched his arguments in the language of chronology, context, and evidence, but his personal experience silently intimated that these are not quite enough to make sense of the horror of it all.

This is reflected in Friedländer's view, which placed the Holocaust squarely *"within the relevant historical framework,"* even as he questioned whether it allows "for *any kind* of narrative" and "whether any historical approach could suffice to redeem, that is convincingly to interpret" it.[63] He gave voice to general, public perceptions about the difficulty in understanding the Holocaust, and was able to see the development of Holocaust studies and memory several steps before most. His insights make sense within these contexts; they should be taken seriously as a reflection of historical representation of the Holocaust at a specific period. But as historical insights qua historical they are either wrong or not unique to the Holocaust. History is not supposed to redeem the past and it cannot be asked to interpret it convincingly in all respects. The "Final Solution" does allow for any kind of narrative, historical or otherwise; it is a question of cultural and moral sensibilities in their specific context, and of the author's intention (the comedy of Roberto Benigni's *La vita é bella*, the comics of Art Spiegelman, and the tragedy of Louis Malle's *Au revoir les enfants* are all possible, but would have been shocking in 1950). Historical narratives come in limited varieties, as we have seen with narratives of the Holocaust crafted by historians, and there is no reason to think that any human event forecloses narrative modalities or escapes the grasp of a plausible narrative. I suspect that Friedländer the historian knew all this, but he felt, together with a whole generation, that the usual historical narratives left out an essential element, a historical sensation, about the event.

Friedländer does not argue that the Holocaust stands apart, and yet this is the underlying tone of the book. The individual voices that pierce the historical narrative "would hardly be necessary in a history of the price of wheat on the eve of the French Revolution, but it is essential to the historical representation of mass extermination."[64] Note, too, that Friedländer presents the sensation of disbelief as separate and opposed to "thorough historical study." The narrative form of the book thus seems to fit the particular case of the Holocaust (and potentially other mass exterminations). But the example of the price of wheat is not a good one; no one would deny that this topic demands a different sensibility. The question is whether it would demand a *fundamentally different* mode of historical procedure; the answer to this question is surely "no." The Holocaust is a special event; we feel it, and we feel correctly. But it demands a different sensibility not because it is an event that goes off the charts of regular historical analysis, but because the stakes of interpreting it are higher for human morality and history than the price of wheat. (It would be a different story in a case in which a deliberate human action changed the price of wheat in order to cause massive hunger and death). It seems to me that Friedländer (the historian) would agree with this argument against historical uniqueness, while Friedländer (the person defined by his experience and memories) would wish to preserve some kind of undefined specialness to the Holocaust. He attempted to capture this duality in *The Years of Extermination* by writing a historical text whose formal essence broadens the boundaries of history.

My interpretation of this narrative strategy is that it reveals a certain element of the past that is not quite knowable through ordinary historical narrative, though it clearly existed and is indeed essential to understanding the period. The problem with Friedländer's view about commingling irreducible reality and the possibility of art is not that it is not historical enough, but on the contrary, that it is too limited: this is a sensibility, to my mind, that belongs to *all* historical understanding. His argument, bounded by personal experience, by public and scholarly perceptions of the Holocaust, and by (some) conventions of the historical craft, needs to be set free so that it can become clear that it applies to all historical understanding.

I would like to view the narrative of *The Years of Extermination* from the following perspective. I begin with the assumption that for the historian the Holocaust does not present exceptional problems of representation, but conversely it plainly reveals problems of historical representation overall.[65] Historical sensation is part of all historical reconstruction, which requires going beyond the logical association of events into human elements of the period. Historical sensation is not separate from historical investigation, but they together comprise historical understanding. Johan Huizinga described well this historical sensation:

> There is in all historical awareness a most momentous component, that is most suitably characterized by the term historical sensation. One could also speak of historical contact. Historical imagination already says too much, and much the same is true of historical

vision [. . .] this contact with the past, that is accompanied by the absolute conviction of complete authenticity and truth, can be provoked by a line from a chronicle, by an engraving, a few sounds of an old song. [. . .] Historical sensation does not present itself to us as a re-living, but as an understanding that is closely akin to the understanding of music, or, rather, of the world *by* music.[66]

I interpret this notion of historical sensation to mean two things. It is, first, a necessary awareness on the part of the historian in order to perform his or her task, namely, to reconstruct and to understand the past. It is not only an awareness of the specific context of the past, but also of the total strangeness of the past – we may call it the mystery of the past – that cannot quite be captured by the historical method alone. It demands a certain intuition. Friedländer is a master of the craft because of his historical sensation.

Second, historical sensation also means an essential element in the mental world of people in the past that must be captured by the historian. It is not mystical or irrational: it is based on sources that are painstakingly explored. But it demands a certain intuition to link elements that seem unconnected, to see new ideas beyond convention and tradition. *The Years of Extermination* captures the historical sensation of disbelief through a close reading of diaries, chosen and used according to strict historical method, that endow the book with (what we feel is) a presence of the past. This historical sensation is based on the materiality of the written page, the pen, and the act of writing in the direst circumstances. In this context, familiar sources and events receive new meaning, as when Friedländer recounts the last diary line of Chaim Kaplan, the chronicler of the Warsaw Ghetto, on 4 August 1942: "If my life ends – what will become of my diary?"[67] Huizinga was inspired to write *The Autumn of the Middle Ages* after looking at a painting of Van Eyck. He claimed that in some cases objects of the past can preserve "an aura of the past *itself*," that the past maintains a certain presence in artifacts (such as paintings, furniture, everyday objects, or a book).[68] The diaries transmit a sense of the past itself as if it had survived.

Far from being based on a special method for a special historical case, *The Years of Extermination* is to my mind a model for how to apprehend and to present historical sensation. I associate *The Years of Extermination*, with its rich description of the period, with great historical works such as Jacob Burckhardt's *The Civilization of the Renaissance in Italy* and Johan Huizinga's *The Autumn of the Middle Ages*, which are a source of inspiration for the way they captured a sense of the past.[69] It is in this sense that my argument – that the fundamental importance of the book goes beyond its explanation and interpretive framework – is clarified. The interpretations of Burckhardt and Huizinga are of course important, though many of their arguments have been understandably revised over the decades. But what has endured is the vast description of impressions, sensibilities, and beliefs – in their narratives that are also fractured – that has made it possible for readers to conceive of and imagine the Renaissance and the Late Middle Ages through their chronological and psychological distance.

Historical sensation is part of all historical reconstruction. And here we see the tremendous accomplishment as well as the limits of *The Years of Extermination*. Historical sensation permeates the book, both in terms of Friedländer's approach and in terms of his articulation of a sensation that was essential to the period. But in terms of method he presents sensation as separate and opposed to "thorough historical study," whereas in fact they are united, together comprising historical understanding. And in this respect, *The Years of Extermination* only lays bare more clearly in the case of the Holocaust what is an essential element in all historical understanding.

## Notes

1   This essay was first published in *History and Theory*, 48 (October 2009). I am grateful to the journal and to Wiley-Blackwell for the permission to reprint it. I am indebted to insightful conversations with Amos Goldberg, Allan Megill, Dirk Moses, and Dan Stone, who read earlier drafts of this text. Paul Betts, Herbert Tico Braun, Neeti Nair, and Ilana Pardes shared their ideas with me. The paper was presented at the Lockmiller History Seminar at Emory University, the German Studies Seminar at the University of Tennessee, the research group "Globalization of the Holocaust" at Van Leer Jerusalem Institute, the research group "Ethnography and Experience: Theory, History and Interdisciplinary Practice" at the Institute of Advanced Studies at the Hebrew University, and the conference "Nazi Germany and the Jews: Years of Persecution, Years of Extermination" at the University of Sussex. I am grateful to the participants for the useful comments and discussions.

2   Johan Huizinga, "The Aesthetic Element in Historical Thought," in *Dutch Civilization in the Seventeenth Century and Other Essays* (New York: Frederick Ungar Publishing, 1968), 229, 236.

3   Saul Friedländer, *The Years of Extermination: Nazi Germany and the Jews, 1939–1945* (New York: HarperCollins, 2007).

4   Jeffrey Herf, "The Whole Horror," *The New Republic* (October 9, 2007); Peter Pulzer, "How the Holocaust Happened," *Times Literary Supplement* (January 2, 2008); Richard Evans, "Whose Orders?" *New York Times* (June 24, 2007); Dan Diner, "Jahre der Vernichtung," *Die Welt* (September 30, 2006); Norbert Frei, "Gesichter des Schreckens," *Neue Züricher Zeitung* (October 2, 2006); Ulrich Herbert, "Die Stimmen der Opfer, "*Süddeutsche Zeitung* (September 29, 2006); Volker Ullrich, "Gesichter des Schreckens," *Die Zeit* (September 28, 2006); Ada Pagis, "These Dead That Do Not Stop Living," *Haaretz* (Book Review Supplement) (December 12, 2007), in Hebrew.

5   Saul Friedländer, "The 'Final Solution': On the Unease in Historical Interpretation," in Peter Hayes (ed.), *Lesson and Legacies: The Meaning of the Holocaust in a Changing World* (Evanston, IL: Northwestern University Press, 1991), 23–35, here 32. Emphasis in the original.

6   Friedländer, *The Years of Extermination*, xxvi.

7   We can think of works such as Carlo Ginzburg, *The Cheese and the Worms* (Baltimore: Johns Hopkins University Press, 1980) and Natalie Zemon Davis, *The Return of Martin Guerre* (Cambridge, MA: Harvard University Press, 1983).

8   Edward Ayers, "Narrative Form in *Origins of the New South*," in John Roper (ed.), *C. Vann Woodward: A Southern Historian and His Critics* (Athens: University of Georgia Press, 1997), 40–1.

9   Edward Ayers, *The Promise of the New South: Life after Reconstruction* (Oxford: Oxford University Press, 1992); Lyndal Roper, *Witch Craze: Terror and Fantasy in Baroque Germany* (New Haven: Yale University Press, 2004).

10   Allan Megill, "Narrative and the Four Tasks of History Writing," in *Historical Knowledge, Historical Error: A Contemporary Guide to Practice* (Chicago: University of Chicago Press, 2007), 79.

11   Friedländer, *The Years of Extermination*, xvii.

12  Ibid., xv.

13  Ibid.

14  Ibid., xix.

15  Leni Yahil, *The Holocaust: The Fate of European Jewry, 1932–1945* (New York: Oxford University Press, 1990), 10. Yahil finished writing the first volume in 1975 and the second volume in 1981; the study was published in Hebrew in 1987.

16  Yahil writes from an explicit Zionist perspective that links the tragedy of the Holocaust to redemption in the state of Israel. She focuses, among others issues, on ideological and historiographical issues that were important to Israeli society: why Jews in Europe did not resist the Nazis (in implicit contrast to the behavior of Jews in Palestine) and why Zionist and world Jews did not help more.

17  Yahil, *The Holocaust*, 9.

18  The editors of *Annales*, "Let's Try the Experiment," in Jacques Revel and Lynn Hunt (eds), *Histories: French Constructions of the Past* (New York: New Press, 1995), 484–91, here 487.

19  Roger Chartier, "The World as Representation," in Revel and Hunt (eds), *Histories*, 544–58, here 552.

20  Saul Friedländer, *Den Holocaust beschreiben: Auf dem Weg zu einer integrierten Geschichte* (Weimar: Wallstein Verlag, 2007); Saul Friedländer, "Eine integrierte Geschichte des Holocaust," *Aus Politik und Zeitgeschichte* 14–15 (2007): 7–14.

21  For a discussion of the strengths and weaknesses of current Holocaust historiography, including Friedländer's interpretation, see my essay "A World without Jews: Interpreting the Holocaust," *German History* 27 (2009): 531–559.

22  Ian Thomson, *Primo Levi: A Life* (New York: Metropolitan Books, 2002), 227–35.

23  Raul Hilberg, *The Politics of Memory: The Journey of a Holocaust Historian* (Chicago: University of Chicago Press, 1996), 105–19, 156. The reader who wrote this was Hannah Arendt.

24  Friedländer, "The 'Final Solution,'" 23.

25  The Holocaust is seen now by some scholars, such as Gabrielle Spiegel, as the intellectual and cultural force behind post-structuralism and post-modernism that doubted grand narratives and questioned the meaning of historical knowledge. Spiegel, "Revising the Past / Revisiting the Present: How Change Happens in Historiography," *History and Theory*, Theme Issue 46 (December 2007): 1–19.

26  Ian Kershaw, *The Nazi Dictatorship: Problems and Perspectives of Interpretation*, 3rd ed. (London: Edward Arnold, 1993), 3. Emphasis in the original. The largely historically pointless debate about the uniqueness of the Third Reich and the Holocaust shows what happens when historians get into metaphysical debates. For precisely this argument – that an adequate explanation is impossible – which was made by scholars as a proof of the uniqueness of the Third Reich and the Holocaust, is part of what makes these topics objects of historical investigation in the first place: all interpretations of all events are always partial and incomplete. That is what makes them issues of historical investigation as opposed to topics of religious or ideological certainty, whereby the topic is presented as dogma, catechism, airtight, and beyond doubt.

27  Michael Ruck, *Bibliographie zum Nationalsozialismus* [1995] (Darmstadt: Wissenschaftliche Buchgesellschaft, 2000).

28  Christopher R. Browning, *The Origins of the Final Solution* (Lincoln: University of Nebraska Press, 2004); Ian Kershaw, *Hitler. 1936–1945: Nemesis* (New York: W. W. Norton & Company, 2000), xviii; Richard Evans, *The Coming of the Third Reich* (New York: The Penguin Press, 2003), xix. See also the important study by Peter Longerich, *Politik der Vernichtung: Eine Gesamtdarstellung der nationalsozialistischen Judenverfolgung* (Munich: Piper Verlag, 1998).

29  Evans, *The Coming of the Third Reich*, xx.

30  This can also explain why scholars of the Holocaust showed a certain disregard for, even uneasiness with, current historical trends such as cultural history. Studies of the culture of the Third Reich (in films and literature, for example) or the memory and representation of the Holocaust after 1945 do exist. But using culture and memory to understand the Holocaust as it unfolded is rare. See Confino, "A World Without Jews" and the forum following Dan Stone's "Holocaust Historiography and Cultural History" in *Dapim, Studies on the Shoah* 23 (2009): 52–93.

31  Omer Bartov, "As it *Really* Was," *Yad Vashem Studies* 34 (2006): 339–53.

32    Omer Bartov produced archival work in the first half of his career and theoretical work in the second half.

33    Steven Aschheim, *In Times of Crisis: Essays on European Culture, Germans, and Jews* (Madison: University of Wisconsin Press, 2001), chaps 4 and 10.

34    "The paradox is that, although it has become *de rigueur* for historians to begin their studies by observing that the Holocaust denies notions of progress and civilization, they then often write using a philosophy of history that implies the opposite." Dan Stone, *Constructing the Holocaust: A Study in Historiography* (London: Vallentine Mitchell & Co. Ltd., 2003), 16.

35    Friedländer, *The Years of Extermination*, xxv–xxvi.

36    Ibid., 182.

37    The key text in the last generation is Hayden White, *Metahistory: The Historical Imagination in Nineteenth-Century Europe* (Baltimore: Johns Hopkins University Press, 1973).

38    The point of view of contemporaries that is often unfettered by the hindsight preserved for historians adds to the literary feel of the story. The discussion of the global situation after December 1941, when America entered the war but the Axis powers enjoyed victories, ends with the following question: "Would the strategic balance tip to Hitler's side?" (331), as if we do not know how things unfolded. The author rarely preempts the future with a remark about what will happen. A rare exception is on page 578 when information about Austrian SS captain Tony Burger, who was appointed in 1943 first commandant of Theresienstadt, is added in parenthesis: "(whose main claim to fame – the deportation of the Jews of Athens – was still a year away)." Friedländer also hardly ever uses the term "we" that creates a bond between reader and author, as well as between these two and (some) people of the past.

39    Friedländer, *The Years of Extermination*, 29.

40    Ida Fink, *A Scrap of Time and Other Stories* (New York: Schocken Books, 1987), 3.

41    Peter Gay, *Style in History* (New York: Basic Books, 1974), 156.

42    Friedländer, *The Years of Extermination*, 757, note 133.

43    Michael Burleigh, *The Third Reich: A New History* (New York: Hill and Wang, 2001). Bartov can write about Himmler's logic expressed in his speech to SS leaders in October 1943: "This concept's long-term polluting effects on humanity as a whole cannot be overestimated. No amount of erasing the traces by exhuming and cremating the murdered, bulldozing the death camps, and planting forests over mass graves would purge our moral universe of this redefinition of ethics and decency." Omer Bartov, *Mirrors of Destruction: War, Genocide, and Modern Identity* (Oxford: Oxford University Press, 2000), 29.

44    Inga Clendinnen, *Reading the Holocaust* (Cambridge, UK: Cambridge University Press, 1999).

45    Primo Levi, "The Gray Zone," in *The Drowned and the Saved* (New York: Summit Books, 1989). Even in the concentration camps, wrote Levi, there existed gray zones: "The network of human relationships inside the Lagers was not simple: it could not be reduced to the two blocs of victims and persecutors [. . .] [we cannot] separate evil from good [. . .] It remains true that in the Lager, and outside, there exist gray, ambiguous persons, ready to compromise [. . .] within the gray band, that zone of ambiguity which radiates out from regimes based on terror and obsequiousness" (37, 49, 58).

46    Friedländer, *The Years of Extermination*, 473, italics in the original. See also 478–9.

47    Ibid., xvii.

48    Ibid., 657.

49    See Confino, "A World without Jews" and "Fantasies about the Jews: Cultural Reflections on the Holocaust," *History and Memory* 17 (2005): 296–322, here 301–9.

50    Friedländer, *The Years of Extermination*, 661.

51    Ibid., xxvi.

52    Fernand Braudel, *The Mediterranean and the Mediterranean World in the Age of Philip II*, 2 vols. (New York: Harper & Row, 1972–1973).

53    One difference between the two books is that Braudel posits his three-tier perception of the past as a model for historical understanding overall, while Friedländer's three levels are specific to the Holocaust.

54    J. H. Hexter's article remains a classic. "Fernand Braudel and the *Monde Braudellien . . .*," *Journal of Modern History* 44 (December 1972): 480–539. See also Hans Kellner, "Disorderly Conduct: Braudel's Mediterranean Satire," *History and Theory* 18 (1979): 197–222, here 217.

55   Megill, "Narrative and the Four Tasks of History Writing," 103. Megill, following Hexter, views *The Mediterranean*, which had epitomized for the *Annalistes* the explanatory form of writing known as *histoire problème*, as a form of descriptive history that is no less explanatory and revealing for that (see 94).

56   Saul Friedländer (ed.), *Probing the Limits of Representation: Nazism and the "Final Solution,"* (Cambridge, MA: Harvard University Press, 1992). Hayden White expressed in the volume a compromise position that attempted to escape the extreme consequences of his relativism.

57   Friedländer, "Introduction," ibid., 20. See also 8.

58   Carlo Ginzburg tells in "Just One Witness" the story of two Jewish witnesses who survived the extermination of their communities in fourteenth-century France. Ginzburg brings forth the most radical argument against White's relativism: the voice of one single witness is enough to reach a certain historical reality and therefore some historical truth. Friedlander summarizes in the Introduction Ginzburg's contribution. In the following paragraph, which is very short and separated by a double space, he points out without commentary that at Belzec extermination camp, where 600,000 Jews were massacred, two witnesses survived to tell the tale. Here we can see the origins of the narrative form of *The Years of Extermination*.

59   Friedländer (ed.), *Probing the Limits of Representation*, 7. Friedländer implies that for most historians a description of facts does carry its own truth, setting himself apart from this group. He makes this point in relation to Christopher Browning's essay in the volume.

60   Ibid., 20. He cites Shoshana Felman.

61   See Alon Confino, "The Historian's Representations," in *idem, Germany as a Culture of Remembrance: Promises and Limits of Writing History* (Chapel Hill: University of North Carolina Press, 2006), 1–22.

62   Linda Orr, "Intimate Images," in Frank Ankersmit and Hans Kellner (eds), *A New Philosophy of History* (Chicago: University of Chicago Press, 1995), 89–107, here 90.

63   Friedländer, "The 'Final Solution,'" 23, 32. Emphasis in the original.

64   Friedländer, *The Years of Extermination*, xxvi.

65   Dan Stone writes eloquently on this point in *Constructing the Holocaust*, 30.

66   Frank Ankersmit, *Sublime Historical Experience* (Stanford: Stanford University Press, 2005), 120–1. I use Ankersmit's translation. I found Ankersmit's notion of historical experience insightful for thinking about historical sensation.

67   Friedländer, *The Years of Extermination*, 430.

68   Ankersmit, *Sublime Historical Experience*, 115.

69   Jacob Burckhardt, *The Civilization of the Renaissance in Italy*, 2 vols. (New York: Modern Library, 1975); Johan Huizinga, *The Autumn of the Middle Ages* (Chicago: University of Chicago Press, 1996).

# 3

# Kaleidoscopic Writing: *On Saul Friedländer's* The Years of Extermination: Nazi Germany and the Jews, 1939–1945[1]

## Dan Diner

*On September 29, 1941, the Germans shot 33,700 Kiev Jews in the Babi Yar ravine near the city. As the rumors about the massacre spread, some Ukrainians initially expressed doubts. 'I only know one thing,' Iryna Khoroshunova inscribed in her diary that same day, 'there is something terrible, horrible going on, something inconceivable, which cannot be understood, grasped or explained.' A few days later, her uncertainty had disappeared: 'A Russian girl accompanied her girlfriend to the cemetery [at the entrance of the ravine], but crawled through the fence from the other side. She saw how naked people were taken towards Babi Yar and heard shots from a machine gun. There are more and more such rumors and accounts. They're too monstrous to believe. But we are forced to believe them, because the shooting of the Jews is a fact. A fact which is starting to drive us insane. It's impossible to live with this knowledge. The women around us are crying. And we? We also cried on September 29, when we thought they were taken to a concentration camp. But now? Can we really cry? I am writing, but my hair is standing on end.' In the meantime, the war in the East was entering its fourth month.[2]*

This is how the second part of Saul Friedländer's tripartite monumental work on the Holocaust, *The Years of Extermination: Nazi Germany and the Jews, 1939–1945*, begins. This main section, which deals with the period summer 1941 to summer 1942, is entitled "Mass Murder." Part I, "Terror," covers the period fall 1939 to summer 1941. Part III bears the emblematic title "Shoah," and treats the period summer 1942 to spring 1945.

At first glance, Friedländer's tripartite division of the history of events in the Holocaust appears to be conventional. It moves on through the chain of events in their classical periodization, from the conquest of Poland in 1939 the attack on the Soviet Union in 1941. From the massive murder actions of the *Einsatzgruppen* in the summer of 1941 in the ethnic borderlands of eastern Europe between the Baltic and Black Seas, down to the preparations hatched in early autumn and the first steps to implement a systematic annihilation, the so-called "Operation Reinhard." And from the accelerating measures of an industrial mass murder on to the death marches in the closing phase of the war.

This conventionally received structure provides the historiographic project with its external armature. It constrains the author to preserve the basic patterns of the unfolding of historical events, strictly observing the power of central events. It obliges him to adhere to the canon of what is familiar, disciplining him to pay at all times careful attention to the comprehensive context of the totality of events: the constantly changing circumstances of the conduct of warfare, the basically constant conditions shaped by the great politics of the time, and the enigmatic chess moves and fluctuations of diplomacy. Yet these rather standard norms of classic historiography centered on the history of events prove to be anything but conventional when viewed against the backdrop of the findings of research over the past two decades. This is especially true if one considers that inquiry on the Holocaust increasingly is tending to become more and more devoid of context. By that I mean it is becoming a history of the mass murder which ever more tends to isolate the event of the Holocaust, largely by truncating it from the circumstances of World War II. Such a tendency is marked basically by an approach that pays less and less attention to (a) the causal nexus and significance of events in succession, (b) the weight of decisions correspondingly made and (c) the actions proceeding from these decisions and from persons responsible for them. In their stead, interpretations proliferate which veer off, spinning away from the actual historical events that really occurred. Actions, circumstances and causalities for which responsibility must be borne, and accountability established, are pushed into the background in favor of modes of interpretation that increasingly distance themselves from what actually took place. These tend to break loose from the political-historical girdle of interpretation closely tied to the actual sequence of concrete events in order to shift anthropological generalizations in the shape of phenomena of mass murder as such into the spotlight of analytical attention, beholden to a seemingly supra-historical and comparative perspective. Viewed in this way, the only ostensibly conventional structure of Friedländer's presentation, adhering closely to the sequence of actual events, secures for itself the basic presuppositions of what we actually mean by history. Given his strict periodization of the object of investigation, his approach entails something like a narrative retrieval of the prerequisites of what makes historical judgment as such actually possible.

Another accounting runs right through the three main parts of the book. It has a sequential structure laid out in 10 chapters. These chapters, in contrast with the static girdle of the larger overarching periodization, move within a rhythm of extremely short temporal intervals. One for example is the time-frame June to September 1941 with chapter four, here specially highlighted, whose first scene is based on the diary entry by Iryna Khoroshunova. Here the horrible events of Babi Yar are described from the perspective of a non-participating observer, capturing the gravity and dramatic quality of the incipient genocide. The diary entry rips the curtain from the terrible events, rendering its further course something able to be grasped. This is followed by additional testimonials, blow after blow. The staccato of literalness is oppressive in its authenticity. A variety of contrary perspectives intermesh. The contours of events crystallize in sharp relief through the layered impressions of victims, perpetrators and bystanders. The entire work is permeated by the stylistic device of layering testimonies of individuals which capture events in a powerful, even oppressive immediacy. In this way, the author succeeds in evoking the elements of a direct and immediate visualization and momentary rendering of the past as vividly present.

This aspect of immediate visualization makes use of the structure of the internal sequence of chapters termed "small periodization." This mode of periodization serves, by utilizing various local events, to conjugate both the dynamism and the monstrous enormity of the events unfolding from the summer of 1941 on. The rhythm of this small periodization follows the meshing of two tendencies: events in the course of the war and the ideological thrust which impregnated German action and policy. The Holocaust is thus the product of circumstances that arose in the turmoil of events and were also created by the Nazis themselves, as well as events shaped and constricted by ideological parameters guiding concrete action.

The rapid succession of sequences, one following on the next, is Friedländer's significant stylistic means in his broad canvas of the period of the mass murder. This generates an effect of dramatic acceleration. It leaves the reader with an impression of compelling tension, a kind of crystalline concentration of all that is happening in the *Gestalt* of micrological images, one following rapidly upon the next. Ultimately, the events that cascade from the summer of 1941 on constitute a category of eventfulness that is realized in a totally different tempo of movement from the years of persecution, the period 1933–9, described by the author down to their most ramified details in the first volume of his oeuvre.[3] It was possible to describe that period in keeping with a rhythm which, despite all the drama inherent in that era, corresponded to the beat and tempo of sequences of events, together with their inherent temporal patterning, which are generally appropriate for political-administrative events under the conditions of peace. The certainties of the bourgeois everyday world, which after all still dominate events, even if they are constantly losing their safeguards, may in description help to spotlight those occurrences that are deviating more and more from the expectations of normality. They serve as a means of contrast, as it were, to point up and recognize the ever more frequent deviations from the everyday as they occur, extending to the point of reversing the perimeters of the predictable and what can be calculated: that is, systematic discrimination, exclusion and expropriation by means of special regulations, and on all the way to forced emigration, tantamount to the practice of expulsion. However, the event of annihilation, its speed and massivity in the days of war, can no longer be pictured and represented against a background that is somehow familiar and thus also imaginable, one inscribed with the dimensions of life-world continuity and normality. The annihilation as a turning point that suddenly bursts apart all social relations, in the shape of an accelerating and ever more comprehensive destruction, needs to make use of other stylistic means. One of these is the laconic distance which the author paradoxically prescribes for himself in his description in the face of horror, yoked together with a restrained objectivity that seems almost choking. It permits a kind of decelerating look at the excesses of violence, pausing at times to focus, as these excesses intensify at frightening speed into the full fury of the annihilation.

And as a matter of fact, Friedländer's description is highly unusual, and in terms of the genre of writing, downright daring. The dramaturgy of events proceeds in quick cuts that are almost erratic. The approach resembles that of a filmmaker. The texts are strung one after the next in a way similar to how the perspectives articulated are layered one on top of the next. The ordering as a series suggests a temporal sequence, while layering in strata projects the depth of the horror experienced. Through such a compilation, what unfolds is nightmarish in its power of impression. Commentary and reasoned discourse recede into the background, or are in any case subdued; modulated to a point of such low volume as if the subject could tolerate only a whisper. The author steps back totally into the wings yet is all the more present by the carefully situated aspects of irony and parenthetical remark. This tone resonates with the reserve of the chronicler.

The mode of presentation is indeed analogous to the mode and feel of a chronicle. And here a chronicle that does not, as is otherwise customary, appear right at the beginning of the treatment of a historical subject. Rather, contrary to all expectation, that chronicle is placed at its end. A chronicle-like narrative form proves itself, after the decades of often excessive investigation of the events, to be a brilliant stylistic means in its seeming simplicity: brilliant in that it returns to the unfalsified origins of historical representation, in a sense undermining all interpretations that have accumulated over a long period. Perhaps, after all the years of belabored occupation with the Holocaust, this is the sole still remaining form through which to appropriately describe the object. Something genuinely crystalline beyond all counterfeit has been preserved in this chronicle-like mode of telling.

In its simplicity, however, this view is only seemingly ingenuous. On the contrary: under closer scrutiny, it proves rather to be quite sophisticated. Ultimately, after all, it has passed through the multivocal discourses of complex and complexifying interpretations – only to show that it has had its fill of them. The stagings of the historians, burdened down with theory, are exorcized in a way by the vitalizing touch of direct immediate description. Only in that way does the author succeed in redeeming history from the past. This is done by infusing the strange monstrosity of events with life and vibrancy.

It is likely that Friedländer, after wrestling for decades with the "Final Solution," decided on this path for its description, due in significant part to his own experience with the endless historiographical discourses and public disavowals that ultimately miss the target of the chosen topic. Ultimately, Friedländer himself, whose work from the beginning of his academic career and of his own biographical introspection was under the impress of National Socialism and the Holocaust, went through all phases and layers of scientific investigation and public confrontation with the subject. That trajectory started with his book on Pius XII, his study on the entry of the United States into the war, the vignette on

Kurt Gerstein, his intervention on Kitsch and Death, his prominent participation in the Stuttgart conference in 1984 on the state of research on the "Final Solution," and went on with his own uncanny meeting with Ernst Nolte in 1986 that sparked the early churnings of the historians' debate, and then on to the correspondence with Martin Broszat in 1987 which coagulated into the actual methodological question of historiography and representation.

The steps taken by Friedländer, over decades, through the history of research on National Socialism and the Holocaust, ultimately lead in their *summa* to the impressive mode of sober narrative – though a sober narration which is similar to an epistemic purification pressed through the dislocating funnel of the history of research. And this process can be seen in his work on the annihilation. Sequences constantly become visible that allude to the theoretical controversies, though not specifically mentioning them with a single word. Instead one senses a laconic voice, a profound sense of reserve. And it is that laconic voice and accompanying reserved irony which testifies as a stylistic means that guides to a knowledge that has in the meantime been jettisoned. Instead, events and sequences of events are woven into a meaningful narrative structure in which the modes of narrative themselves acquire an effect analogous to the ordering power of theory. It would certainly be not unacceptably arrogant to express the suspicion that with this work, Saul Friedländer wished to refute Broszat's collective allegation that the Jews, as principle victims of the Nazis, were not only unable to write a sober objective history of those events, but rather were in addition fundamentally biased due to their own mythological understanding of history. As Friedländer again and again intermixes the three possible perspectives in the perception of the Event – victim, perpetrator and bystander – he succeeds in achieving the only appropriate view of events, one that reconstructs history: namely the vantage on events that takes all facets into account on the basis of an ethically grounded empathy with the victims.

The fourth chapter, highlighted here as an example, reflects in an unmistakable way the approach chosen by Saul Friedländer. Along with thick description by witnesses and the frozen, miscroscopically and plastically accurate focus on the acts of murder, the great international contexts are likewise given a broad canvas in the background. And the step-by-step decisions and the actions of the Nazis based on them, eventuating in the deed, are sketched in careful detail. The scales of micro and macro interlock here as if organically. Slice after slice, the relevant events and perspectives for the specific time-frame are prepared. This includes the entry of the United States into the war as that loomed on the horizon as well as the genocidal operations of the *Einsatzgruppen* in the Soviet territories conquered by the *Wehrmacht*. It encompasses the participation of the agitated local populations in the massacres of their Jewish neighbors, and the reactions, a meld of fear, horror and bewilderment, of the Jews, murdered, burned, buried alive, throughout the entire area of the zone of death under the Nazis and their henchmen, stretching from the Baltic to the Black Sea.

To the extent necessary for understanding the historical context, Friedländer goes back into more distant pasts, and does so without falling prey to the dangers of presenting a false breadth of scope. Precisely as a result of the rapid, even abrupt change in action in different spaces simultaneously, made possible by the sharp breaks in description – shifting from Poland to France, the Netherlands to Hungary, Bulgaria to Denmark, Serbia to Lithuania – one can still perceive in the unending multiplicity of circumstances and conditioning factors behind events some sort of unity in what decades later will flow into the emblematic concept of the Holocaust.

For the historian, it is almost an impossible task to describe in a suitable manner these events unfolding within an extremely compressed time. And Friedländer endeavors to avoid any false teleology, such as a focus on the events in the centers of decision-making solely in Nazi Germany. In the face of a project for total annihilation extending across Europe and becoming ever more radical, a final view of things would be inadequate. Such a perspective would overshoot its mark, failing to see the complexity of events and their multifarious ingredients.

How complex and confusing the circumstances are, that ultimately crystallize in a synthesizing description, is evident for example in the seemingly paradoxical fact of spatial thrust: the movement of German military expansion ran spatially from west to east, while the Holocaust advanced in the opposite direction, from east to west. And this was true even when its earlier stages in the form of discrimination, exclusion and expulsion initiated in the territory of the Reich, intensifying after the attack on Poland into a ghettoization of the Jews in the newly established German realm of the *Generalgouvernement*. And then, with the invasion of the Soviet Union in June 1941, leading on to mass murders of an increasingly blanket systematic character. This quantum leap in events, extending to actions of annihilation, fell together with the fury of the notorious *Einsatzgruppen* behind the lines of the advancing *Wehrmacht*. Not until "Operation Reinhard" in 1942 were the Jews in forced ghettoes in the *Generalgouvernement* far to the west of the battlefront seized. And only later were the Jews of western Europe, as well as those in countries more on the periphery, such as Greece, drawn into the vortex of the machinery of destruction. The place of universal implementation, the interlacing of all spaces and times of the Event, is Auschwitz.

In presenting a picture of the total canvas of events, the seeming paradox of a West-East direction of movement in German military expansion and an East-West movement of the Holocaust must be taken into proper account. Due to the interwoven character of events, or more precisely: the fusing of all events into a single happening, this cannot be simply handled by description country by country. The historian has to comply to the complex knotting of all the circumstances moving and driving the machinery of murder. Nonetheless, we cannot avoid taking cognizance of the respective concrete circumstances on the spot. And those circumstances are due to the respective special local situations, while also being bound up with the earlier (pre-) histories of events, especially those of the interwar period that reach on down into the time of the Holocaust.

The complex topography of the Holocaust suggests the need for differentiation. And this complex of differentiation is largely less the product of the respective degree of antisemitism operative and more the outcome of a variety of political constellations encountered in various places. It is striking, for example that Jews in countries allied with Nazi Germany were better able to avoid for a time being seized by the Germans than those, in Poland for example, that were under direct Nazi occupation. This distinction, shaped by diverse events, is already visible in the different way Jews were treated in the Reich and in annexed Austria in 1938. In the Reich down to November 1938, despite all the measures of discrimination, with the Nuremberg Laws as their core, Jews were still somewhat protected due to the presence of a conservative bureaucracy and a level of *Gleichschaltung* that was still incomplete. In Austria, however, which was after March 1938 besides rejoicing the *Anschluss* by the majority of the population also to a certain extent an occupied country, the Jews were directly subordinated to the Nazi authorities. In Hungary, an ally of Hitler's Germany, despite all the discrimination and the regime's measures of persecution, the Jews were not seized and sent to their annihilation until the Germans occupied the country in March 1944. Denmark was occupied in 1940, but the occupation was not the result of mere military conquest. The Danish administration remained largely intact, and the king had not fled. This constellation allowed the Danes to provide a relative degree of protection for the small Jewish community, down to their evacuation to Sweden as a move of resistance. In the Netherlands, the deportation and destruction of the Jews of the country was almost total. By contrast, in Belgium a large number of Jews managed to elude seizure by the Germans. Though the reasons were multiple, one main factor was probably that the Dutch royal house and government had fled into British exile, while in Belgium the king remained on the throne under the German occupation. In the Netherlands, Nazi German rule was direct; in Belgium, it was more indirect, mediated by Belgian authorities. And recall the constellation under an axis power such as Italy or the Vichy regime in France. In regard to the "Jewish question," both had a similar spatially and politically divided position, even though the situations there differed substantially. Thus, there was the spatial division in France between the occupied north and the unoccupied south under the Vichy regime down to 1942 and the Allied landing in North Africa. In Italy, from July 1943 on, with the overthrow of Mussolini and the country's withdrawal from the axis, there was the northern part, now occupied by the Germans, and the generally liberated south. The special situations in Bulgaria and Romania (and they were each quite different from the other – precisely through their very distinctive intermediate situations in the context of a Second World War that consisted of many individual wars, alongside the prime antagonism between Hitler's Germany and the Allies) allow us to see the complexity of a process like the Holocaust. In its implementation it appears to unfold in a straight line, so to speak, giving rise to teleological conclusions, while in reality being composed of a swirling myriad of different components. The most extreme example of an eccentric component in the total picture was probably Finland, where during the siege of Leningrad as part of a continuing Finnish-Soviet war, Jewish soldiers in the Finnish army were in combat against the Russians. There were other peripheral perspectives in this mix, such as that in Spain, where Franco, after victory over the Republicans, allowed Jewish refugees to enter Spain, facilitating their transit on to Portugal. Portbou in Spain's far northeastern corner at the French border is a paradoxical site in view of the comprehensive history of the Holocaust. Walter Benjamin committed suicide on the French side of the border because he feared he would not be able to cross over to the (Fascist) Spanish side.

A basic insight here should be clear: the more *direct* the access of the Germans to the Jews in the respective country, the more disastrous was their fate. Where the Nazis had to discuss and consult with the states and governments close to or allied with them regarding the fate of their Jews, the more difficult was their deportation. If the German occupation had come to pass militarily under conditions of warfare, such as in the case of Poland, with its substantial Jewish population, or if the battles were difficult or even involved an ideological enemy, as in the case of the Soviet Union, threatened from the start with a war of anni-hilation, then the murderous access to the Jews there was direct, lethal and total. The behavior of the local non-Jewish population in all those diverse constella-tions was a substantial factor, but in view of the respective special circumstances not of such decisive importance as some historians contend. Whether the local population traditionally was or was not considered antisemitic probably did not have such a decisive impact on behavior towards them. Far more important were the political circumstances on the ground – the distinction between occupation by means of warfare and non-combative occupation, direct and indirect access to the Jews, etc.

Given the multitude of "situations" involved, the historiography of the Holocaust faces huge challenges of composition. If the events are narrated from the fact of the Holocaust as fait accompli, it is hard to avoid leaving the respec-tive special circumstances aside, or giving them low priority. Ultimately, those circumstances did not significantly contribute to decelerating or even preventing the Holocaust. If one allows the multitude of circumstances into the picture, even if they did not contribute much to hindering the project of the mass murder, and even if they are foregrounded, then the danger is of missing the big picture, and thus also the actual subject as such. Consequently, the suitable fine line of narrative that has to be walked needs to swing between the Scylla of a necessarily ordering teleology and the Charybdis of an unordered multiplicity of realities. The historian, weighing factors, intervenes in that complex, via an ethical empa-thy of nearness that is purified by temporal distance. That is the path along this narrow ridge that Saul Friedländer walks in his great narrative on the Holocaust. In this endeavor, he succeeds dramaturgically in staging, through a kind of kaleidoscopic narration, a *mise en scène* in which our knowledge about the end, and thus the teleological "guided tour" through the events, interlinks with its often paradoxical details to form a complex picture. In that picture, events as they really were, in their total massivity, impact on the reader, even as the elements separating from this incandescent core gain their own narrative right and due.

Saul Friedländer can take credit for having taken due account of the multiplicity of emergent constellations in the total narrative, and having effectively woven them together in a suitable manner into the fabric of the narration. That also holds when it comes to consideration of the differing narratives of the various European Jewries exposed to the Holocaust, due to their non-simultaneity and differing prehistories. Thus, for example, it is evident that the narrative of the German Jews centers essentially on the discriminations in the period 1933–9 in the Reich and the waves of emigration this generated – and this despite the fact that a substantial number of German Jews from 1941 on shared the fate of the Jews in eastern Europe. Like the others, they were also hurled into the vortex of the mass annihilation in the east. The ghetto in Łódź, the Fort in Kowno or the ghetto in Minsk are emblematic in this regard. However, their history as German Jews is ruptured there, broken off in a strange way. In any event, it is no longer narrated as such. Instead, it is absorbed within the comprehensive history of the destruction of European Jewry. But the narrative of the Jews of Poland is ostensibly focused on its history of suffering in the ghettos, until that is put to an end by industrial mass murder. The fact that their narrative largely focuses on the ghettoization is because so much was able to accumulate in that space in terms of duration of perception of the immediate realities and the future expectation, in order then to become historical material for the later narrative "re-telling." That is given ample testimony in diaries and other texts, and the tales of survivors. It gives rise to something like a Polish-Jewish master narrative of the Shoah. Somewhat similar, though quite different, is the impact of the accumulated writings of German-Jewish experience, which as "exile literature" has come to form a genre of its own. The mass of writings associated with this genre concentrate on descriptions of the experience of exile, so that the fate of the destruction of the German Jews transported to the east is eclipsed, as it were. The image, generated in retrospect, of the German Jews in the face of Nazism is by no means a pleasant fate, but nonetheless one that suffered perhaps less injury and murder. That image may well have been intensified by the fact that after the war, German Jews in the early period of reparations measures were granted restitution in one or another way. From an Eastern Jewish perspective, that acted to strengthen the view, in any case operative, that German Jews had been "privileged Jews." That perspectival tension may have been intensified even more by the fact that this constellation was also impacted by histories extending back into the nineteenth century of a tense Jewish-Jewish antagonism, the conflict-ridden relations between Western and Eastern Jewry. Added to this was a third Jewish experience that would appear to distance itself from evoking the Holocaust as Holocaust: namely the narrative of Soviet Jewry. The Soviet Jews had, after all, taken part mainly in the Soviet war effort against Nazi Germany, and were to that extent also bound up with the Soviet narrative of victory over the "Hitlerian fascism."

Although those Jews did not subordinate themselves to the previous official Soviet line which tended to ignore the Holocaust as a Holocaust of the Jews – this in order to integrate its associated events in the general Soviet narrative of victimhood – much of their most primary and profound history of experience contributed to giving priority to the emerging historical narrative of the history of the war, decreed from above, over the narrative of the Holocaust. To construct the Holocaust as secondary to the events of the war and its battles was not something exclusive solely to the Soviet construction of events. By and large, this was a general phenomenon, which was not broken through until the late 1970s and especially the 1980s and 90s via public discourse in the West. Only when seen from this high point in fresh perception does the Soviet special consciousness of the events appear in its singular peculiarity.

It was indeed during these two decades, that the Holocaust as Holocaust erupted into historiography and public awareness. From the vantage of such a time-bound perception, the present oeuvre of Saul Friedländer closes that window of perception that then was opening. To that extent, it is a comprehensive treatise of its time. It seeks a literary answer, not only to the question of the events he reconstructs, but also responds to the fundamental questions the Holocaust poses to humanity.

In his magisterial history of the destruction of European Jewry, Saul Friedländer does not just wish to describe and narrate. The book links the enterprise of a large-scale narrative with that of a historiographical purpose. This especially since his work in view of previous inquiry on the topic cannot stand alone. Ultimately it stands within an intertextual discourse with other works and their interpretations. In an extended introduction, Friedländer attempts something like a charting of his position. There he voluntarily lays out his perspective. And his perspective on the monstrous Event foregrounds the world view of antisemitism, though without, as in the case of Goldhagen, having to account for the respective concrete actions of the perpetrators as being driven by antisemitic motives in order to substantiate his thesis. There is indeed a difference between a concrete antisemitism that guides a person's actions and a culture impregnated with hostility towards Jews, which in certain constellations may suggest that it is quite natural to kill Jews only because they are Jews. The understanding that hovers over the entire mass of events of the Holocaust, namely that the Jews as authors of all conceivable manner of evil justifiably must be killed, permeates his presuppositions. One can sense it in the most minute ramifications of his implementation. This does not mean that one must ascribe great causal energy to the constellation and the circumstances necessary for it. But the Holocaust as the final genocide of European Jewry is simply unimaginable without that antisemitic impregnation, which otherwise does not necessarily have to take a fatal end, but in certain constellations can condense to a motivation to kill. In view of the self-evidential character of this perspective on things, it may be astonishing that this view is not perceived as a matter of course. What else is supposed to have led to the murder of the Jews other than the circumstance that they were Jews?

Yet this matter of course is not self-evident. In recent years, the popular books about the Holocaust that have been on bestseller lists, boasting quite phenomenal sales figures for this historical genre, tend to downplay the notion that animosity towards the Jews was the main reason behind the mass murder of European Jewry. The fact that the murdered Jews were Jews tends to be relegated to a kind of secondary reason. Such arguments are popular because they prefer to concentrate on what is material, on robbery and plunder, greed and economic forethought. Such human failings are understandable to all, since they are grounded after all on something like a negative anthropology of everyday experience that all can concretely grasp. Of course, the monstrous dimensions of the murder of the Jews may burst asunder all criteria of previous experience, those popular books would admit. But ultimately it is about an event which challenges our knowledge about the nature of evil in this world less than it calls upon us to search out specific reasons behind its execution – reasons which if possible transcend all notions of utility. The wish felt everywhere to create a Holocaust without Jews is in any case abiding.

Saul Friedländer's history of the Holocaust goes contrary to that trend. Instead of heightening eccentric and marginal phenomena to a point where they serve to explain everything, he concentrates on the essential events; those that were existential and those that guided action. In the process, he returns lived experience to the stage of events, front and center. His perception of the victims, which he utilizes more extensively despite all pluralism of perspectives, returns to imbue the events with that sharpness of personal experience which they have increasingly forfeited through the shifts of focus on matter more marginal. Ultimately, Friedländer is concerned to make visible once again what distinguishes the Holocaust against the backdrop of the still valid culture of the Enlightenment, all denials of this notwithstanding: erratic bewilderment.

*Notes*

1   Translated from the German by Bill Templer.
2   Saul Friedländer, *The Years of Extermination: Nazi Germany and the Jews, 1939–1945* (New York: HarperCollins Publishers, 2007), 197.
3   Saul Friedländer, *Nazi Germany and the Jews*, vol. I: *The Years of Persecution, 1933–1939* (New York: Harper Perennial, 1997).

# 4

# Saul Friedländer, Holocaust Historiography and the Use of Testimony

## Tony Kushner

Saul Friedländer's two-volume history of the Holocaust represents a landmark in the use of testimony, especially (though not exclusively) with regard to the victims.[1] The incorporation of testimony as one of the central features of such a narrative would have been unimaginable for many years after the Second World War. Indeed, the early histories of the "Final Solution" explicitly ignored and downplayed victim testimony. Typical was English historian Gerald Reitlinger's ambivalent comment that he had avoided using the testimony of the "hardy survivors" because they were "seldom educated men."[2] Such elitism reflected the state of Western historiography in the 1950s before the impact of the social history revolution and "history from below" movement. But there was also a specific dynamic at work which explains the downplaying of victim testimony within the representation of the Holocaust. With the existence of those who actively deny the Holocaust, historic and other evidence-based works on the subject bear the burden of having, at some level, to "prove'" the event. Thus, in the words of Reitlinger's French contemporary, Leon Poliakov, in his *Harvest of Hate* – one of the first coherent narratives of the Holocaust – "wherever possible, to forestall objections, we have quoted the executioners rather than the victims."[3]

Over half a century on from Reitlinger's and Poliakov's work, the desire for Holocaust victim testimony to have what might be labelled a legally valid "truth" has not gone away. Christopher Browning, for example, perhaps the most thoughtful, sensitive and convincing of historians of the destruction process since the 1980s, has rigorously evaluated the potential dangers (and advantages) of extensively utilising victim testimony in reconstructing the place of slave labor in the Holocaust. Only recently have historians started to give this neglected aspect of the Holocaust the attention it deserves and Browning has been at the forefront of rectifying this lacuna.[4]

Browning is more than aware of the different approaches to confronting victim testimony, including those from literary and cultural studies as well as psychology where the tendency has been to deal with it through detailed analysis of the individual. In contrast, Browning's methodology is to deal with testimony *en masse*. Browning has used material gathered from a variety of witnesses and taken at different times since 1945 for his sensitive case study of the slave labor camps in Starachowice. Such victim evidence was crucial to reconstruct the narrative of this camp complex as it is "rarely mentioned in surviving German documentation."[5] For Browning, in contrast to Reitlinger and Poliakov, this witness testimony is like any other historical source and needs to be dealt with both critically and imaginatively. To Browning, survivor testimony must not be treated as a "historian's 'silver bullet' that will answer all his questions and solve all his problems." Equally, however, Browning is insistent that "Claiming that survivor testimony must be accorded a privileged position not subject to the same critical analysis and rules of evidence as other sources [. . .] will not serve the cause of integrating survivor testimony into the writing of Holocaust history."[6] Browning's perspective suggests a more mature approach to the use of Holocaust testimony, neither apologetic nor possessing missionary zeal in arguing for its inclusion and normalization within history writing. Indeed, in his lecture essays *Collected Memories: Holocaust History and Postwar Testimony*, Browning is convincing in his argument, when confronting perpetrator evidence, that if used with subtlety, Eichmann's numerous writings and rewritings and interviews of his life, despite the obvious distortions, silences and self-justifications, can still be used with profit by the historian.[7]

In the case of survivor testimony, the potential problems for the historian are less blatant than those relating to the perpetrator. There may be silences emerging from the possible accusation of collaboration or the impact of later collective memories of the event shaping individual survivor narratives. But Browning argues that if the same points and details are raised by the survivors at different times, in different genres and in different circumstances, then the historian should feel comfortable with incorporating "concurring accounts" that have "proved relatively stable."[8] In short, they pass "the test" of being used as "reliable" evidence, and for Browning, a master of narrative history writing, with regard to the utilization of survivor testimony, "the historian needs accuracy, not just sincerity."[9]

Browning, I would suggest, is using the same methodology, albeit in a more sophisticated form, as that promoted by one of the key figures in the early collection of Holocaust survivor testimony – Richard Koebner of the Hebrew University, who worked closely from the late 1950s with Yad Vashem in Jerusalem and the Wiener Library in London. Koebner stated that "If I find only one piece of evidence, it does not mean anything to me; if I have ten records that is good; but if I have a hundred, then the evidence is conclusive."[10] Yet others today still cast doubt on such positivist approaches to testimony. In Peter Novick's polemical *The Holocaust and Collective Memory* he suggests that the memories of survivors are "not a very useful historical source." Novick then qualifies himself that "some may be, but we don't know which ones."[11] For some, this uncertainty of which is, or is not, a reliable survivor testimony is particularly dangerous due to the existence of those who actively seek to deny the Holocaust. In December 2008 Berkley Books, part of the Penguin Group (USA), at the last moment cancelled publication of a Holocaust memoir *Angel at the Fence* subtitled "The True Story of a Love that Survived." The author, Herman Rosenblat, was indeed a Holocaust survivor, but he fabricated the last days of his experiences in a satellite of the

Buchenwald concentration camp complex. Rosenblat wrote that his wife to be, a Jew in hiding, threw him apples over the camp fence and thereby enabled him to survive until liberation. In justifying this fictional addition to his life story, Rosenblat stated that "I wanted to bring happiness to people. I brought hope to a lot of people. My motivation was to make good in this world."[12] Others, however, feared that such embellishments only succeeded in giving ammunition to Holocaust deniers. Indeed, the withdrawal of *Angel at the Fence* is not an isolated example – in 2000 it was discovered that Deli Strummer, who had survived Theresienstadt, Auschwitz and Mauthausen, had falsely killed off her husband who, as she claimed in a 1988 memoir and a later educational video, had died in Dachau.[13] In this case, the postwar break up of her marriage to a fellow victim of the Holocaust was thus erased.

Walter Reich has suggested that there are certain themes that Holocaust survivors must try to avoid in their accounts, especially expressing feelings of anger and revenge. Equally, he argues, "they may also know there are themes they *should* emphasize." In particular, "The progression from trauma and atrocity to healing, hope, and renewal is a story-line that warms the heart of the audience that hears it." Reich adds that "The practice of showing upbeat endings could justifiably be called the Schindlerization of Holocaust testimony" and that filmmakers prefer story-lines that are "genuinely life-affirming" over those that "display permanently embittered and perhaps broken lives, to which audiences would react by trying to escape the movie theatre."[14] In this respect, it is not surprising that until its "exposure," a film of *Angel at the Fence* was due to go into production in 2009.[15]

Much earlier, Martin Gray had added an alternative ending to his story of survival in the Warsaw ghetto, claiming that he had escaped from Treblinka.[16] Gray responded to those who pointed out that he had neither been in nor escaped from Treblinka by asking "Does it matter?" Gray was insistent that what *did* matter was that the camp existed and that "some Jews should be shown to have been heroic."[17] In other, perhaps much rarer cases, some survivor accounts have proved to be totally fictitious, such as Binjamin Wilkomirski's *Fragments* (1996) and Misha Defonseca's *Misha: A Memoir of the Holocaust* (1997).[18]

These fabrications – total or partial – would seem to provide ammunition to Peter Novick's analysis that we simply do not know which survivor accounts to trust. But Browning in his forensic analysis of the testimony relating to the Starachowice camps is far more optimistic. There are, he believes, elements of the accounts of some of the survivors which are more suspect, especially the entry into Birkenau where, like in many survivor accounts, Mengele was present to carry out the selection.[19] In fact, and most unusually, no selection took place with the particular transport from Starachowice. In explaining this distortion in memory, Browning suggests that selection on the ramp by Mengele has "become one of the most broadly recognized archetypal episodes of the Holocaust, widely disseminated in both books and films."[20] In contrast, because of the marginalization of slave labor camps in representations of the Holocaust and even then the fact that "Starachowice was both small and obscure" within such camps, it is "virtually unknown" and thus not subject to the complications of later collective memory. Browning is thus convinced that:

> For the historian, this has the significant advantage that survivor memories of Starachowice are relatively pristine and uncontaminated by the later incorporation into individual memories of archetypal images broadly disseminated in popular consciousness.[21]

The slave labor camp experiences as narrated by the survivors can therefore be differentiated from the arrival at the notorious and infamous Birkenau. Whether Browning's differentiated approach, and his often statistical analysis of testimony is fully sustainable will be returned to later. But it is within the context of this heated and ongoing debate about the use (or otherwise) of Holocaust testimony that Saul Friedländer's remarkable narratives must be placed.

Friedländer's two books, especially the more recent, go beyond the question of whether the testimony of the survivor is trustworthy/accurate, or not. On one level, his work corresponds to changes within general historiography and approaches to the testimony of ordinary people, especially that within the oral history movement. In the 1960s and 1970s, when oral history as a form of social history emerged powerfully in both the Western academic and non-academic worlds, it faced snobbery and dismissal from many in the historical profession. The testimony collected was seen of little value as it related "only" to everyday life. Moreover, it was seen as suspect because it was somehow manufactured by those carrying it out and was therefore inherently unreliable or, alternatively, distorted by hindsight. The response from those in the oral history movement to such attacks was defensive – oral history projects should be based on large samples and if themes and details were constantly repeated by the interviewees then the evidence was regarded as sound and more "scientific."[22] In effect, the methodology outlined by Richard Koebner was being replicated.

By the 1990s, however, a more nuanced approach was emerging, typified by the work of Luisa Passerini in Italy and Paul Thompson and Raphael Samuel in Britain.[23] The possibility of oral history being used to reconstruct history from its unique source base of ordinary people's memories, recovering stories and episodes ignored or silent in the written archives, is not dismissed in new approaches and in this respect Browning's work on slave labor camps is a fine example of what can be recovered. But more and more the mythology within oral history and other forms of autobiographical and literacy practice is seen not as an inherent weakness of the source, but in fact a strength, telling of the identity and identity constructions of individuals both then *and now*. Methodologically, the emphasis has moved to the use of smaller samples dealt with in a manner in which subjectivity is valued and away from large scale projects with the implicit desire for representativity and statistically 'reliable' data. It has also moved away from the focus on specific events in individuals' lives and to a more inclusive "life story" approach.[24] It is this turn towards a critical engagement with the construction of individual testimony that divides its utilization by scholars today. At a more popular level, the dismissive approach of Peter Novick is less and less significant and testimony has come to the fore not only in historical works but also in museum displays – most extensively and prominently in the video interviews utilised by the Imperial War Museum in London in its permanent Holocaust exhibition which opened in 2000.[25] Testimony is also dominant in a range of documentary films, from Claude Lanzmann's *Shoah* (1985), in which it is presented in a "legal [. . .] framework [. . .] outside the courtroom,"[26] through to more illustrative approaches such as the Spielberg produced film directed by James Moll, *The Last Days* (1999) and Jon Blair's *Anne Frank Remembered* (2000). In the major BBC production, *Auschwitz*, written and produced by Lawrence Rees (2005), both approaches – personalizing the impact of the Holocaust on the victims and interrogating the perpetrators – were employed. Yet in spite of this "normalization" of testimony, we are still at an early stage of development of how we are to utilize it in representations of the Holocaust. How to deal with testimony in a constructive but critically engaging way requires, I would argue, far more attention and care.

Saul Friedländer points out in the introduction to *The Years of Extermination* that there are an "unusually large number of diaries (and letters) written during the events and recovered over the following decades."[27] It is the diary form of individual testimony, especially that of the victims, that predominates in Friedländer's narrative – indeed, there are only occasional uses of postwar accounts, whether in written or oral format. But Friedländer's point about the sheer quantity of material, including but beyond the diaries, does require further consideration. I have estimated that we now have, including all the oral and video history projects, contemporary documents such as diaries, reports and letters, and later printed and unprinted written accounts, something close to 100,000 testimonies of the Holocaust produced by the victims. This is simply unprecedented with regards to any other historical event.[28] There are, for example, in stark contrast, less than a hundred American slave narratives written before abolition and not that many more subsequently either written or recorded. John Blassingame's classic and exhaustively researched account *The Slave Community: Plantation Life in the Antebellum South* is based on seventy-six black autobiographies, forty-two of which were written after 1860.[29]

With regard to the Holocaust, the emphasis at present is still on what might be termed "rescue archaeology" – interviewing ageing survivors or persuading them to write down their experiences before they pass away. Thus in 2008, the New York-based Conference on Jewish Material Claims Against Germany launched a "race against time" so that survivors across the world would "commit to paper their experiences that have lived so vividly in their memories for more than 60 years" before it was too late.[30] Such a move is connected to a change noted by Annette Wieviorka, linked, since the last decades of the twentieth century, to the "Americanization" of the Holocaust where "Testimony given spontaneously, as well as testimony solicited by the needs of justice, were succeeded by the social imperative of memory. The survivor was now supposed to honor a 'duty to remember,' which could not morally be evaded."[31] This "moral duty" was not necessarily a straightforward process, logistics of geography and the resources to do so aside.[32] Some survivors, it has to be accepted, were and are simply reluctant to talk about or confront their past in any form of autobiographical practice – to them talking is far from therapeutic, indeed often quite the contrary. Yet it seems that the imperative, if for the best possible motives of remembering, is to continue to collect, without enough thought, or at times any thought whatsoever, of what is to be done with this mountain of material. In relation to future historiography, this is a crucial question.

Focusing again on Saul Friedländer's utilization of victim testimony in *The Years of Extermination*: as with his first volume, *Nazi Germany and the Jews: The Years of Persecution*, the author is explicit that the use of such material has a clear purpose. It is worth quoting at length Friedländer's justification in *The Years of Persecution*:

> In many works the implicit assumptions regarding the victims' generalized hopelessness and passivity, or their inability to change the course of events leading to their extermination, have turned them into a static and abstract element of the historical background. It is too often forgotten that Nazi attitudes and policies cannot be fully assessed without knowledge of themselves. Here, therefore, at each stage in the description of the evolving Nazi policies and the attitudes of German and European societies as they impinge on the evolution of those policies, the fate, attitudes and, sometimes the initiatives of the victims are given major importance. Indeed, their voices *are essential* [my emphasis] if we are to attain an understanding of this past. For it is their voices that conveyed both the clarity of insight and the total blindness of human beings confronted with an entirely new and utterly horrifying reality.

Friedländer concludes his justification of this inclusion by arguing that: "The constant presence of the victims in this book, while historically essential in itself, is also meant to put the Nazis' actions into full perspective."[33]

In *The Years of Extermination* Friedländer goes further, both in using such testimony and in providing a methodological framework for doing so. The extensive inclusion of personal accounts, especially of the victims, is initially justified in the introduction to this volume by stating that the "personal chronicles are like lightning flashes that illuminate parts of a landscape. They confirm intuitions; they warn us against the ease of vague generalizations. Sometimes they just repeat the known with an unmatched forcefulness."[34] But then Friedländer goes further than simply including the individual voice as a "trace left by Jews that bears witness to and confirms and illustrates their fate."[35] The diaries, he tells his reader at the beginning of his study, will have a "further role as well. By its very nature, by dint of its humanness and freedom, an individual voice suddenly arising in the course of an ordinary historical narrative of events such as these presented here can tear through seamless interpretation and pierce the (mostly involuntary) smugness of scholarly detachment and 'objectivity'." Here Friedländer provides an alternative perspective to the more detached and "scientific" use of testimony in the work of Christopher Browning:

> Such a disruptive function would hardly be necessary in a history of the price of wheat on the eve of the French Revolution, but it is *essential* [my emphasis again] to the historical representation of mass extermination and other sequences of mass suffering that 'business as usual historiography' necessarily domesticates and 'flattens'.[36]

It is the "disruptive function" of victim testimony that is so critical to the success of Friedländer's second volume. What I want to explore in the remainder of this chapter is the nature and extent of this disruptive function. It almost goes without saying that Friedländer, described most rightly as "the most astute, sophisticated and stylish historian of the Holocaust working in any language today,"[37] utilises the diary testimony deftly and with enormous sensitivity. The quotations he has selected are powerful and, as intended, often startling, evocative and moving. And Friedländer's *The Years of Extermination* goes beyond other historic writings that have extensive usage of victim testimony such as Martin Gilbert's *The Holocaust: The Jewish Tragedy* (1986), which is made up almost solely of such material and was pathbreaking in this regard.[38] Gilbert's "monumentally detailed" study was, as Lawrence Langer suggests, up to this point "the sole volume by a prominent historian to base its narrative almost exclusively on eyewitness accounts."[39] The difference in respect of victim testimony between Gilbert and Friedländer is that Friedländer allows space for multiple and often contradictory voices – he moves beyond the more simplistic approach of simply reproducing eyewitness accounts to show what happened. There is, for example, in Friedländer's work the space within his choice of testimony to reveal pessimism and optimism relating to the future of the Jews following particular events and episodes, moods that depend on the ideological perspective of the writer – sometimes relating to their religious beliefs or political allegiance – but also their individual personality and circumstances at that moment in time. Friedländer's narrative is thus multi-layered and complex and lacks the chronological smoothness of Gilbert's equally extensive work.

Indeed, differences in style, politics and belief systems amongst the diarists are acknowledged by Saul Friedländer in the early stages of *The Years of Extermination*:

> These diarists were a very heterogeneous lot. Klemperer was the son of a Reform rabbi. His conversion to Protestantism, his marriage to a Christian wife, clearly demonstrated his goal: total assimilation. Entirely different was Kaplan's relation to his Jewishness. A Talmudic education at the Yeshiva of Mir (and later, specialized training at the Pedagogical Institute at Vilna) prepared him for his lifelong commitment: Hebrew education.[40]

Friedländer then explores the turn of expression and tone of his major diarists, especially Klemperer with his "light ironic touch" and Kaplan with his
"emphatic style of biblical Hebrew."[41] Nevertheless, the treatment of the handful
of major diarists who will feature throughout *The Years of Extermination* (Victor
Klemperer, Chaim Kaplan, Emmanuel Ringelblum, Jochen Klepper, Dawid
Sierakowiak, Dawid Rubinowicz, Itzhok Rudashevski, Moshe Flinker and Anne
Frank) is still limited to a page and a half of the text at the end of the first chapter.[42] It is rare thereafter in this text that the reader encounters further authorial
intervention when the diaries and other forms of victim testimony are quoted.
It could be argued that these diary entries, exquisitely selected by Friedländer,
are so searing in their content and description, and so crucial in undermining
the euphemisms of Nazi discourse and the utter callousness of the bureaucratic
language of the "Final Solution," that they in effect "speak for themselves."

On one level this lack of intervention is justified and the author is simply
trusting the reader to draw their own implications from the diaries. Friedländer
often shows admirable restraint, other than to provide clarification and to take
the narrative beyond the confines of the testimony – for example when quoting
from the final diary entry of Egon Redlich, who in October 1944 was facing
deportation and assimilating the reality of what this meant. Redlich had a newborn son, Dan, to whom his diary was named. His diary entry reads "They send
small children, and their prams are left here." Friedländer comments that "For
Redlich sending the child and leaving the pram behind meant death. On the eve
of his deportation he had exchanged food to get a pram for his son." Permission
to take the pram on the transport allowed Egon Redlich an element of optimism,
but Friedländer adds that "Redlich and his infant son, Dan, were murdered on
arrival. Dan's pram, with tens of thousands of other baby carriages, probably
found its way back to the Reich."[43]

Yet I would suggest that it is important to take this testimony even more
seriously and to examine the literary strategies employed by its authors as they
attempted to convey what they saw, felt and experienced. Close reading of these
testimonies is needed not simply because the ones chosen by Saul Friedländer
have outstanding literary qualities, but because all autobiographical writings
require to be dealt with critically and imaginatively. In the hands of scholars and
those involved especially with the remembrance of the Holocaust, the testimony
of victims has become almost sacred. Indeed, those used by Gilbert have been
treated as such and incorporated into religious services to commemorate the
Holocaust.[44] More generally, as Eliane Glaser provocatively suggests, "As the last
generation of survivors dies out, we are encouraged to regard each particular
testimony with something approaching religious worship."[45] To "interrogate"
testimony for its narrative strategies – whether in diary or life story format – may
appear to be disrespectful and it is not an approach normally approved of by the
survivors themselves who often feel it somehow casts doubt on the authenticity of
their stories. One survivor, for example, responded to Glaser's analysis by stating
that "We don't want to be put on a pedestal," also acknowledging that survivors

may not always remember the same events in exactly the same way. Nevertheless he was convinced that "does not mean they did not witness the events they describe." In response to the issue of "bogus Holocaust memoirs," the survivor added that "Those who experienced the Shoah are familiar with what is credible and would have immediately identified such work for what it is."[46] In fact, those who seemed most reluctant to accept that Binjamin Wilkomirski's *Fragments* was not an authentic autobiography were child survivors who (understandably) believed that he had given voice to their neglected traumas.[47] I would argue strongly with regard to the testimony of Holocaust victims that we follow the analysis of Paul Thompson and Mary Chamberlain that "any life story, whether a written autobiography or an oral testimony, is shaped not only by the reworkings of experience through memory and re-evaluation but also always at least to some extent by art."[48] This is as true of contemporary diaries as it is of later testimony. The diary as a literary form is always constructed and one of its intriguing elements for the study and understanding of the Holocaust is how its daily, chronological sequence is challenged by the intensity of persecution. Everyday rituals and the structure of the day itself increasingly break down under the Nazi onslaught. The diary, as with Janusz Korczak's remarkable writing, can become more and more streams of consciousness where specific dates meld into one.[49]

To bring this discussion of the instrumentalization of Holocaust testimony to a close, Saul Friedländer utilises its diary form to superb effect in *The Years of Extermination*. It avoids the pitfalls of much Holocaust historiography when dealing with the dynamics of Nazi bureaucratic language and the parallel implementation of mass murder – Friedländer's readers can never forget what such policies actually meant in practice and how attitudes affected behaviour. There is never *any* danger of mistaking who the victims were. In this respect, the book succeeds in its objective of providing a narrative of the Holocaust that is "both an integrative and integrated history."[50] Yet by maintaining throughout a strong emphasis on chronology, powered by a nuanced intentionalist interpretation of the Holocaust, the use of testimony is still kept in relative harness. Victim testimony is utilised far more than simply as an illustrative device, as is achieved so remarkably in the Imperial War Museum's permanent exhibition.[51] But its disruptive function in *The Years of Extermination* is still restrained by the imperative to provide a clear narrative framework chronologically arranged by the incremental growth of Nazi persecution.

In Friedländer's account, the reader becomes familiar with his favoured diarists, especially the sublime writer, Victor Klemperer. But we do not always get to grips with the personal chronologies of these individuals and their particular imperatives to write and record. Their silences, for example, are almost inevitably passed over and the diaries are only brought into use when they relate to the wider narrative. To make testimony, whether in written, oral or video form, even more centre stage in representations of the Holocaust would, it might be argued, be to risk the loss of cohesion with regard to time and place. And if this is true of the sophisticated and multi-layered work of Saul Friedländer it is even more the case in the use of victim testimony in more popular forms such as museum displays, films, pedagogic initiatives and documentaries of the Holocaust. I would still put forward the case for a more qualitative approach and one that acknowledges the inherent messiness and almost untameable nature of individual testimony. Less, as Friedländer's *The Years of Extermination* so eloquently proves, can so often be more. In this respect, a brilliant example of providing a multi-layered narrative of the victim, if still restricted to the "years of extermination," is provided by Mark Roseman and his study of the German Jewish survivor, Marianne Ellenbogen, *The Past in Hiding*.[52] This work brings together oral and written testimony as well as diaries, letters and other contemporary records – Nazi and resistance – and postwar restitution documents to reconstruct her life story, especially that relating to the Second World War. Roseman produces what he has labelled a "detective story" to understand the processes "by which Marianne's past life regained shape in the present."[53] But in using testimony both more selectively and prominently, I would suggest that we must also allow in the future for its full complexity to be acknowledged, including (where possible) an acknowledgment of life before and, for the minority who were the survivors, "after" persecution.

Geoffrey Hartman, the founder and leading force of the Fortunoff Video Archive for Holocaust Testimonies at Yale University has reflected on its development since it was formed in 1979. Hartman concludes that "despite their many dimensions, the testimonies [collected] have generally been used too restrictively."[54] Historic overviews of the Holocaust produced in the early twenty-first century now integrate witness accounts as a matter of course – for example that of Deborah Dwork and Robert Jan van Pelt, which especially uses oral testimony.[55] Friedländer's *The Years of Extermination* is thus part of a wider inclusivity, although the testimony is handled with much more care and thought than in many other narratives.

Christopher Browning has argued for a pluralistic approach in which encouragement is given to "different scholars and different disciplines to explore the potential of survivor testimonies as creatively and extensively as possible." Whilst Browning's plea is hard to query, his supplementary comment that "Creating a coherent and as accurate as possible narrative from an array of differing perspectives and memories, while critically acknowledging the problems of such an endeavour [. . .] is what historians do" is more problematic.[56]

Annette Wieviorka states that "'The historian knows that all life stories are constructions but that these (re)constructions are the very armature, the vertebral column, of life in the present." Because of this, she argues:

> Faced with survivor testimony, historians find themselves in an impossible situation.
> [. . .] Each person has an absolute right to his or her memory, which is nothing other
> than his or her identity, his or her very being. But this right can come into conflict with
> an imperative of the historian's profession, the imperative of an obstinate quest for the
> truth.[57]

Christopher Browning, in his study of the Starachowice slave labor camp, has illustrated that it is still possible to integrate testimony into a "traditional" historical narrative through the extraordinary skills of a critical researcher. If testimony is to be used beyond such utilization, however, this will require the risk and acceptance of greater incoherence – one that Friedländer's *The Years of Extermination* only begins to confront.

It is significant that Saul Friedländer uses testimony largely in the form of diaries, enabling them, with some precision, to be placed in a chronology generated by the actions taken by the Nazis. Had life story, whether in written, oral or video format been the basis of *The Years of Extermination* his approach would have been deeply problematized. As Lawrence Langer, confronting the Yale Fortunoff Video Archive, notes, "the Holocaust has a different beginning for each witness."[58] If the focus shifts in emphasis from perpetrators to the victims then a straightforward chronology, always problematic in the first place because of the complexity of Nazi policies and local variations and initiatives, becomes obsolete. The chronology is further complicated if equal weight is given to the "now" as well as the "then" of survivor testimony. Indeed, confronting testimony, as Wierviorka maintains, is a major challenge, especially to historians. Yet, as she concludes, it is one worth facing, for "testimony contains extraordinary riches: the encounter with the human voice that traversed history and, in oblique fashion, not factual truth but the more subtle and also indispensable truth of an epoch and of an experience."[59] There is clearly a danger of chaos developing in narratives of the Holocaust if it is victim testimony led, rather than supplemented. Yet, it might be argued finally, this is how the years of extermination were experienced by the victims, and, for the minority who were survivors, it was a chaos from which they had to make sense of their lives thereafter.

## Notes

1   I would like to thank my colleague Dr Shirli Gilbert for her helpful comments on an earlier draft of this paper.
2   Gerhard Reitlinger, *The Final Solution: The Attempt to Exterminate the Jews of Europe 1939–1945* (London: Vallentine Mitchell, 1953), 531.
3   Leon Poliakov, *Harvest of Hate* (London: Elek Books, 1956 [1951]), xiv.
4   Christopher Browning, *Nazi Policy, Jewish Workers, German Killers* (Cambridge: Cambridge University Press, 2000), chapter 3.
5   Christopher Browning, *Collected Memories: Holocaust History and Postwar Testimony* (Madison: University of Wisconsin Press, 2003), 44.
6   Ibid., 43–4.
7   Ibid., chapter 1.
8   Ibid., 66, 82.
9   Ibid., 42, 82.
10  Kurt Ball-Kaduri, "Evidence of Witnesses, its Value and Limitations," *Yad Vashem Studies* 3 (1959): 79–90, here 89.
11  Peter Novick, *The Holocaust and Collective Memory – The American Experience* (London: Bloomsbury, 2000), 275.
12  Ewen MacAskill, "Publisher Scraps Tale of Holocaust Love," *The Guardian* (29 December 2009).

See also Elizabeth Day, "When One Extraordinary Life Story is Not Enough," *The Observer* (15 February 2009).

13  Libby Copeland, "Survivor," *Washington Post* (24 September 2000).
14  Walter Reich, "Unwelcome Narratives: Listening to Suppressed Themes in American Holocaust Testimonies," *Poetics Today* 27 (2006): 463–72.
15  MacAskill, "Publisher Scraps Tale."
16  Martin Gray, *For Those I Loved* (London: Bodley Head, 1972 [1971]).
17  Gitta Sereny, "The Men Who Whitewash Hitler," *New Statesman* (2 November 1979).
18  Alex Kasriel, "A Strange Tale of Holocaust Fakes," *Jewish Chronicle* (7 March 2008).
19  Geoffrey Hartman has commented that "every Auschwitz survivor seems to have gone through a selection by Mengele, as if he manned his post 24 hours a day." See his "Learning from Survivors: the Yale Testimony Project," in Hartman, *The Longest Shadow: In the Aftermath of the Holocaust* (Bloomington: Indiana University Press, 1996), 141.
20  Browning, *Collected Memories*, 83.
21  Ibid., 82.
22  Paul Thompson, *Oral History: The Voice of the Past* (Oxford: Oxford University Press, 1978, 3rd ed., 2000).
23  Raphael Samuel and Paul Thompson (eds), *The Myths We Live By* (London: Routledge, 1990).
24  Ibid., introduction.
25  Tony Kushner, "Oral History at the Extremes of Human Experience: Holocaust Testimony in a Museum Setting," *Oral History* 29 (2001): 83–94.
26  Aleida Assmann, "History, Memory and the Genre of Testimony," *Poetics Today* 27 (2006): 261–73.
27  Saul Friedländer, *The Years of Extermination: Nazi Germany and the Jews, 1939–1945* (London: HarperCollins, 2007), xxiv.
28  Donald Bloxham and Tony Kushner, *The Holocaust: Critical Historical Approaches* (Manchester: Manchester University Press, 2005), 16.
29  John Blassingame, *The Slave Community: Plantation Life in the Antebellum South* (New York: Oxford University Press, 1972).
30  Rachel Fletcher, "Race on to Save Shoah Memories," *Jewish Chronicle* (18 April 2008).
31  Anna Wieviorka, "The Witness in History," *Poetics Today* 27 (2006): 385–97, here 394.
32  It could be argued that this moral duty has always been present with survivors, although it has grown in intensity as the Holocaust has become ever more central in more universal discussions of ethics and human rights.
33  Friedländer, *The Years of Extermination*, 2.
34  Ibid., xv.
35  Ibid., xxv.
36  Ibid., xxv–xxvi.
37  By Michael Burleigh on the cover jacket of *Nazi Germany and the Jews*.
38  Martin Gilbert, *The Holocaust: The Jewish Tragedy* (Glasgow: Collins/Fontana, 1986).
39  Lawrence Langer, "Hearing the Holocaust," *Poetics Today* 27 (2006): 297–309, here 299.
40  Friedländer, *The Years of Extermination*, 63.
41  Ibid., 63.
42  Ibid., 63–4.
43  Friedländer, *The Years of Extermination*, 639.
44  Bloxham and Kushner, *The Holocaust*, 33.
45  Eliane Glaser, "Let's not Sentimentalise the Shoah," *Jewish Chronicle* (12 December 2008).
46  Rubin Katz letter to *Jewish Chronicle*, 19 December 2008.
47  Blake Eskin, *A Life in Pieces: The Making and Unmaking of Binjamin Wilkomirski* (London: Aurum Press, 2002).
48  Mary Chamberlain and Paul Thompson, "Introduction: Genre and Narrative in Life Stories," in Mary Chamberlain and Paul Thompson (eds), *Narrative and Genre* (London: Routledge, 1998), 1–22, here 4.
49  Janusc Korczak, *Ghetto Diary* (New York: Holocaust Library, 1978).
50  Friedländer, *The Years of Extermination*, xv.
51  Kushner, "Oral History at the Extremes of Human Experience."

52  Mark Roseman, *The Past in Hiding* (London: Allen Lane, 2000).

53  Mark Roseman, "Surviving Memory: Truth and Inaccuracy in Holocaust Testimony," *Journal of Holocaust Education* 8 (1999): 1–20, here 2.

54  Geoffrey Hartman, "The Humanities of Testimony: An Introduction," *Poetics Today* 27 (2006): 249–60, here 250.

55  Deborah Dwork and Robert van Pelt, *Holocaust: A History* (New York: Norton, 2002).

56  Christopher Browning, "Eschewing Good Guys and Bad Guys," *Patterns of Prejudice* 41 (2007): 524–6, here 526.

57  Wieviorka, "The Witness in History," 395–6.

58  Lawrence Langer, *Holocaust Testimonies: The Ruins of Memory* (New Haven: Yale University Press, 1991), 66.

59  Wieviorka, "The Witness in History," 6.

# 5

# Holocaust Perpetrators in Victims' Eyes[1]

## Mark Roseman

*"And they will ask, is this the truth?"*

"I reply in advance: No, this is not the truth, this is only a small part, a tiny fraction of the truth." Thus a quotation from Stefan Ernest's little-known "The Warsaw Ghetto," written in hiding on the "Aryan" side of Warsaw in 1943.[2] And thus begins Saul Friedländer's second volume, which places this quotation emblematically on the front paper, before the table of contents. More than any other historian of Nazi policy, Friedländer has succeeded in putting the victim center stage. Friedländer's choice of extract here not only gives prominence to the victims' voice, but at the same time reminds us of victims' doubts about their ability to capture the Holocaust's character and scope. Indeed, many of the difficulties which the Holocaust continues to pose to our understanding had, as Friedländer knows, already been identified by contemporaries as it was being lived through. Finally, with this epigrammatic announcement, Friedländer alerts us also to the way he will use victim testimony, namely, as part of a mosaic of vantage points, each offering a fragment of the whole.

Does Friedländer's magnum opus, then, give the lie to those historians, notably Raul Hilberg, who have seen victim testimony as offering little of value compared with the official perpetrator records? Has he succeeded in transcending the long division in Holocaust historiography between histories of the perpetrators and those of the victims? There is no doubting the power of the diaries and contemporary texts which enrich the pages of *The Years of Extermination*. But victim testimony is deployed above all to convey the consequences of Nazi policies and actions for those affected by them. Perhaps understandably, it is rarely used to explain why and how those policies came about in the first place. Is Hilberg therefore right that when it comes to understanding the perpetrators themselves, which he saw as his main task, the victims have little to offer?[3] This contribution seeks to test the limits of the victim-centered approach, by asking whether the victims can tell us much about the perpetrators themselves. Or do they, in so far as they talk about the perpetrators, in fact always tell us more about what it is to be a victim?

It is striking that despite the huge amount of research on the Holocaust there has been virtually no work on this question. This is a sign not only that historians of the Jewish experience and chroniclers of Nazi policy have often had very separate agendas, but also that much scholarly interest in the victims has called into question their ability to provide witness at all.[4] We have learned to see in narrative ruptures and gaps the only traces of inassimilable experience.[5] And Auschwitz, it has been argued, is the kind of place to which there can be no true witness.[6] It is hard to accept such absolutes when confronted with the diarists and chroniclers appearing in Friedländer's pages. But the question remains: can the victims offer insights into the perpetrators that we have not yet gained from other sources? Are they, by dint of their proximity to their tormentors, uniquely well qualified to observe? Or did their confinement to camps and ghettos in fact prevent them from assessing the murderous machinery in which they were caught? Does the extremity of the victims' predicament shed an incandescent light on all that lies before them, or must it blind them to everything but their own condition? Jean Améry, reflecting on his torture at the hands of the Gestapo, invoked insight and blindness in the same telling phrase: "Everything is self-evident, and nothing is self-evident as soon as we are thrust into a reality whose light blinds us and burns us to the bone."[7] Was it humanly possible for the victims to discern human motives in oppressors who were stamping them as inhuman?

To pose this question is not to claim there was only one victim experience, indeed the coexistence of striking commonalities and important distinctions is one of this essay's themes. Because so little research has been done, it is not possible to offer more than very tentative distinctions between different categories of observer – between the "privileged," and those less well-situated, for example, between young and old or between non-Jewish and Jewish victims. The present essay can also not offer anything more than the most rudimentary observations about the significance of different moments and places of observation. It is clear that Jews were best placed to make observations on their counterparts when they were working alongside them, but the character and duration of such Jewish labor varied enormously. Another key distinction is that between the contemporary observer and the later chronicler – a distinction acknowledged but not systematically explored here. However, the question of victim observations should never be reduced to discussions about memory. Whilst time and context affect what is and can be said, there is also in many cases striking persistence in testimony.[8] In any case, as in Friedländer's volume, many of the sources used in the present piece are contemporary diaries.

If there was no single victim experience, nor was there one perpetrator – indeed the term itself, which in the context of Holocaust research has come into common usage only relatively recently, is not one that many contemporaries used.[9] One of the questions of interest is how the victims delimited those who oppressed them – whom did they see as the core actors, and whom as the bystanders, and how were the two connected. Again, only the first forays through the undergrowth can be ventured in this essay.

> *"It should be obvious by now that these pages hardly deal with the Nazis."*

Thus, Ruth Klüger, in describing her childhood in Nazi Vienna. Klüger continues: "I didn't know any Nazis, but I knew the difficult neurotic people whom they oppressed."[10] One reason that we have not looked at victims' perceptions of perpetrators as much as we might is that in many victim accounts, the perpetrators are so often strikingly absent. So often we fail even to register this absence, which merely becomes part of the landscape of misery and devastation. In Dawid Sierakowiak's powerful adolescent diary of the Łódź ghetto, to take one example, we find, true enough, a few early encounters with Germans in 1939. But once the ghetto is formed, the Germans almost completely disappear from the story. A brief glimpse of a medical commission in April 1942 constitutes a rare exception: "Today the German medical commission visited our workshop. They are people from another world; our rulers, masters of life and death."[11]

In the case of more artful observers, particularly those writing in freedom with the opportunity to reflect, such absence is more self-consciously invoked. In Ruth Klüger's three vignettes of her life as a girl in Auschwitz, for example, guards appear only very late on, and then only in the distance.[12] Even a relatively privileged adult prisoner, such as the non-Jewish Spanish Communist Jorge Semprún, could note of much of his experience in Buchenwald that:

> There were the SS as well, naturally. But it was hard to catch their eye. They were so distant: lofty, above it all, beyond reach. Our eyes could never meet. They passed by, busy, arrogant, crisply outlined against the pale sky of Buchenwald and the drifting smoke from the crematory.[13]

These observations are a reminder that in many contexts and for considerable periods of time the Nazis were able to rule at a distance. Many victims had relatively little contact with Germans, sometimes only at the point of their deaths, sometimes not even then. This was a function of the spatial organization of camps and ghettos. Children in the ghettos, in particular, often went for long periods without any direct experience of their tormentors, as we learn from Sierakowiak, Mary Berg[14] and Yitskhok Rudashevsky.[15] This distancing also reflected the Nazi use of proxies. There was not a prisoner of the camps who did not "remember his amazement at the time," recalled Primo Levi, "the first threats, the first insults, the first blows came not from the SS but from other prisoners, from 'colleagues,' from those mysterious personages who nevertheless wore the same striped tunic that they, the new arrivals, had just put on."[16] Thus the key protagonists were obscured behind the system of brutality and savagery they had created.

But we should not see the perpetrators' absence merely as the product of a system that created distance. Sometimes, as Améry's reference to blinding light implies, it is because the perpetrators are (or remain in memory) such fearful presences that the victims were unable to focus on them. Hermann Langbein, a relatively privileged Communist prisoner in Auschwitz, was able to write his "People in Auschwitz" only after entering the Frankfurt court room of the "Auschwitz trial" in 1963 and seeing the once fearsome SS *Oberscharführer* Joseph Klehr, now aged, primitive and defending himself clumsily.[17] Simon Wiesenthal, too, writes of the liberating moment when he saw a brutal guard being interrogated by US officers after the war. That night, he lay on his bunk and "saw the trembling SS man – a contemptible, frightened coward in his black uniform. For years that uniform had been a symbol of terror."[18] Such moments of revelation, bringing the monsters to human scale, made writing possible.

Sometimes, when it was not directly fear that kept the perpetrators off the page, it was the fact that their behavior seemed so inexplicable that they could not really be discussed. In her Belsen diary, the Yugoslav Jewess, Hanna Lévy-Hass, struggled in late 1944 to keep her moral compass and learn for the future. She promised herself that she would "keep firmly in my mind everything that I have seen, everything that I have experienced and learnt, everything that human nature has revealed to me." And she went on:

> I shall judge each man according to the way he has behaved, or could have behaved, in these conditions that surround us. My opinion of him whether I respect him or not, or have an affection for him or not, will depend on how he reacted, or would have reacted, physically, psychologically and morally to the strain of these terrible years – the strength of character he displayed, how much tensions his nerves could bear [. . .].

What is noteworthy is that Lévy-Hass includes only the prisoners and the Kapos in her reflections. The Nazis are off the charts of this moral universe.[19] Of course, this is a question of moral evaluation, not of observation per se, something to which we must return, but as this passage implies, the difficulty of evaluating could inhibit any kind of description.

Ruth Klüger's declarative statement with which this section opens is moreover not the mere dictate of a restricted vantage point – it also represents her own choice of theme. The heart of her account, her story, is her predicament as survivor, and the relationship with her mother that both enabled her survival and burdened her survivorship. In other words, we should also recognize the narrator's agency in removing the perpetrator from her tale. Many contemporary chroniclers of the Holocaust wanted above all to record the fate of the Jewish people – that, and not the nature of their tormentors – was their story. They were, as David Roskies tells us, continuing the tradition of the precise communal chronicle in hard times that Simon Dubnow had instituted during the Russian pogroms and the First World War.[20] Nowhere is this approach more evident than in Hermann Kruk's magnificent chronicle of the Vilna ghetto.[21] Thus in an early entry after the German invasion (June 28, 1941), it is the breakdown of social cohesion in the bread queue, not the brutal Lithuanian policeman beating all comers, that excites him. People denounce each other and slander each other to the Lithuanian policemen, writes Kruk:

> He drives them away and is the only judge. Suddenly everything disappeared. In a few days, all those who hid under the guise of [international] solidarity have suddenly turned into animals ready to devour one another. The policeman has fun and abuses people. I feel as if the blood is draining out of me. I escape from the line and remain without bread.[22]

In line with Kruk's interest in the Jewish community and its ability to maintain solidarity under stress, the perpetrators who do receive lengthy descriptions are the Jewish police. In the Jewish militia, he writes, "[. . .] a unique ethic about the residents developed. You beat them, you steal from them, and you do any possible evil."[23] After a whole series of further such entries, he notes on 29 January 1942, "The Jewish police are more German than the Germans. The Germans once ordered furs taken. They took what they could, and it calmed down. But the Jewish police never rest."[24] Again, we are crossing here from observation to judgment, and again we must return to this, but we need to be aware how much Kruk is choosing what to put on the page. When he is summoned to meet the vicious Gestapo second-in-command, Franz Murer, it is the Jewish Council members who accompany him whom he describes. Murer is barely sketched in at all:[25]

*"They would have gladly hurled themselves upon us like beasts."*

Thus we learn much about the *victims* by noting where their vision is occluded or their gaze averted. But if the perpetrators' absence is striking in many accounts where we expect to find them, the reverse is also true:

The travelers saw a transport [of German soldiers] at the station, which looked with contempt and hatred at their enemies that already had found themselves in their net. They would have gladly hurled themselves upon us like beasts. Upon us who were responsible for the fact that they had had to leave their homes, to say good-bye to their parents, sisters and brothers. They had had to leave their wives, who had spasmodically sobbed, and their children, who did not let themselves be wrenched away from their arms, crying 'Papa, don't go away.' They see us now weak, broken and helpless. We had brought upon them this great disaster, we are those who had led nations to battlefield. If they had only been permitted to come near us, they would have devoured us with sadistic cruelty and would have broken our bones. Why should they be sent to fight distant enemies if they had right under their noses a more dangerous and more considerable enemy than were those they were led to meet. Let them be allowed to fight here; they would prove then what they were capable of.[26]

Seldom has the uncomprehending gaze across the railway tracks between the perpetrators and their victims been evoked with greater poignancy than in these pages, recovered from the ashes of Auschwitz long after their author had been murdered. Salmen Gradowsky, a Grodno Jew who had the misfortune to be included in one of the Auschwitz *Sonderkommandos*, wrote these notes in the extermination camp in 6 September 1944, recalling a train stop during his family's transport from the Kiełbasin labor camp to Auschwitz more than a year earlier. A German troop train had been stationed across the platform and he had seen the soldiers headed for the front, gazing across at the trucks full of Jewish transportees. His words remind us of the astonishing nuggets of insight we find buried among ashen silence. The seeming impossibility of recording observations only spurred witnesses on to the most extraordinary efforts to ensure their reflections were preserved.

What then do the victims see? To delve into victim accounts, be they contemporary or postwar, is to enter a different world from that which emerges from Nazi records, or much of postwar perpetrator testimony. Ubiquitous cruelty is its hallmark, expressed in far more than merely the execution of lethal orders. There were the countless speech acts, uttered not just in the camps but by figures at all levels of the agencies and administrations with which Jews had to deal. On 31 May 1942 seven German policemen from the Nazi Driver Corps visited the Kovno Jewish Council. "One of them, a high-ranking officer who had recently returned from the front," noted the Council's chronicler, Avraham Tory, "heaped insults and curses on the Jews: 'You are to blame for the war; just wait, the time will come when you'll eat grass.'"[27] "'The pits are always open and the bullets are always ready for the Jews,'" said Spiez, the political deputy of the military construction corporation, to engineer Yellin in September 1942.[28] A month later, the commandant of the labor camp at Palemonas came for a visit to the old municipality building "where he delivered derisive and hateful comments against the Jews. He said: 'When I need to kill even a hundred Jews, I do it with pleasure; I don't mind killing even a thousand Jews' and other 'gems' in this vein."[29] Behind such speech acts, Tory, as Gradowsky, perceived an army of men imbued with an implacable hatred of the Jew.

From speech acts to play. Not least because those observers who survived to write their diary or offer postwar testimony were more likely to have been privy to small-scale acts than large-scale murder, their accounts are as full of willful individual gestures of humiliation, sadism and torture as of the systematic execution of genocide. Even before the war had ended, those American readers who took the trouble could read in Mary Berg's diary of Warsaw ghetto life entries from 1941 about guards at the checkpoints who "when it is cold, open fire every so often to warm up. Or if they are bored they arrange entertainments, telling people to throw themselves down in the snow and pulling off peoples beards so that the snow is red with blood."[30] Far more than the narration of those perpetrators who were induced to give testimony, victims highlighted the extraordinary violence wrought against women, children and babies. David Boder, former head of the Department of Psychology and Philosophy at the Lewis Institute Chicago, traveled to Europe in 1946 armed with a cumbersome wire recording machine to preserve testimonies about what had been taking place. In August 1946, one of his interviewees, Nechamah Epstein, described the beginning of deportations from Warsaw to Treblinka:

Epstein: And they began [. . .] It was terrible. Many ran into the gates. They saw small children. They grabbed them by the legs and knocked them against the walls /enunciation not clear/. Boder: The Germans? Epstein: The Germans. The SS men. Grabbed [. . .] Boder: Knocked against what? Epstein: Against the walls. Boder: Oh, the walls. Yes?

Epstein: Against the walls. Then they took [. . .] They saw [. . .] The mothers saw what is being done to their children. They threw themselves out of windows. Boder: Hm.[31]

Boder's difficulty in following the story seems partly simple acoustic confusion. But if the translated transcript is a guide, it seems also clear that, at that point in time, there was no ready set of assumptions or knowledge that could enable the listener to follow such a narrative. What we are witnessing here is one of the early moments when the unbelievable became the world's knowledge. "Sadism and humiliation," noted Eva Hoffman, summing up the stories narrated to her as the child of Polish Jewish survivors, "Those were the distinctive horror marks of the Holocaust. The extravaganzas of cruelty that characterized Nazi behavior towards Jews: the bouts of brutal mockery and loutish laughter that accompanied the free-for-all massacres in eastern European villages – those, as much as the phantasmagoric statistics of death, gave the Nazi project of annihilation its uniquely grotesque character."[32] This was a very different account of the Holocaust to the rule-bound, process-oriented story emerging in much of the postwar historiography. Indeed, we might well say it is the world of observation that gives Daniel Goldhagen's animus its logic, even if it does not give his mono-causal explanation plausibility.[33]

The victims were struck not only by the extraordinary inhumanity of the *actions*, but also by the perpetrators' lack of inhibition and their engagement. The protagonists did not seem to be unwilling or even hesitant. On the contrary, account after account emphasized their willfulness, their energy, their buy-in. Jean Améry's torturers from the SS had not been philosophers, he wrote:

> But that did not mean that the evil they did to me was banal. To be sure, one could see them as blinkered bureaucrats of torture. But they were also much more than that – I saw it from the first in their faces – intent, not swollen from sexual-sadistic desire but focused in murderous self-realization. With all their souls they were committed to their task – to power and authority over spirit and flesh, an excess of unbounded self-aggrandizement.[34]

If the historical profession had paid proper attention to victim testimony, quite a bit of which was available from an early stage in the postwar period, certain ways of writing about the perpetrators should not have been possible. Améry's description of his torturers, noted earlier, in challenging the idea of banality explicitly opposed his experience to the then recently published account of Eichmann's trial in Jerusalem by Hannah Arendt, or at least to the way her "banality of evil" had popularly been understood. Perhaps in one sense his torturers had indeed been unthinking bureaucrats. But they had also been fully absorbed with their whole being in the sadistic project. Just as limp, when measured against the yardstick of victim testimony, was the widely shared view that a sworn, tiny cast of murderers had masterminded genocide in secret. While different victims might characterize the membership and institutional boundaries of the group of tormentors somewhat differently, and whilst many explicitly or implicitly distinguished between core groups of players, on the one hand, and wider circles of sympathizers or the indifferent, on the other, a common feature of victims' accounts was to note alongside the depth of commitment the breadth of players involved in their persecution.

From an officer in the Jewish police the Warsaw ghetto diarist Abraham Lewin heard a disturbing story that was "worth recording for future generations." Noting that in the early days of the July 1942 expulsions to Treblinka, elderly people were not transported but were taken to the Jewish cemetery and machine-gunned there, Lewin went on:

> On the fourth day of the expulsion, Saturday 26th July, a car drove to the Jewish cemetery and a middle-aged German woman with two young children got out. She took them inside the cemetery and led them to the place where our old people were being murdered. She wanted to show the children how the Jews were dying. A typical illustration of the character of this evil and brutal people. New Amalekites.[35]

If respectable middle-aged women were bringing their children to the site, that implied no boundaries at all to the acceptance of murder. It would be more than four decades after the war till historians accepted as a given the breadth of endorsement indicated in Lewin's vignette.[36]

### "He is definitely a pleader."

How did victims explain what they saw? Many accounts do not in fact offer much by way of explanation. Confronted with the mystery of human participation in such violence, most chroniclers chose to eschew speculation and to remain at the level of detailed description coupled with the occasional pithy epithet. The anxiety about being credible put a premium on objective observation. Contemporary chroniclers, from "official" diarists such as the Kovno ghetto's Avraham Tory to private diarists, thus saw their task as recording faithfully what was happening, and not speculating. Many, like Kruk and Ringelblum, hoped against hope they might have leisure in the postwar era to write a more analytical history.[37]

In the postwar period, this push towards objective description was often reinforced by the fact that survivors found they had to learn to suppress their emotions in the telling. As Helmut Peitsch and Nicolas Berg have observed for West Germany, the witnesses were under intense pressure in the postwar period to be dry and factual, if they wanted to avoid accusations of partiality. (Former soldiers and ex-Nazis were, by contrast, allowed to invoke as much pathos in their memoirs as they liked.)[38] This was partly because the propaganda and counter-propaganda from the First World War had created skepticism about atrocity stories, partly because of intolerance for "Jewish pleading," and partly because emotional or moral defense mechanisms kicked in, confronted with such suffering. Eva Hoffman, as a youngster in 1950s Poland, hearing her parents talk about their experiences, soon realized that such discussions did not belong in public discourse at all, remaining "the kind of secret one wraps in a cocoon of silence, or protects as one protects an injury."[39] And then, after emigrating to Canada, her parents met with something they hadn't encountered in Poland – "polite incredulity."[40]

Thus, although in wartime letters, particularly those sent to family in the face of imminent death, we quite often encounter angry calls for revenge, these are very rarely to be seen in chronicles for public consumption, and particularly not once we enter the postwar period.[41] Kalman Eisenberg, interviewed immediately after the war by David Boder, tried to find a tone to convey to his interlocutor the enormity of the actions committed by Willi Althoff in the Starachowice labor camps.[42] Althoff's pleasure in killing, his inventive sadistic games, forcing one prisoner to torture another, beg belief. But that was not called for in the postwar period. "The style of this interview appears especially full of somewhat artificial pathos," writes Boder on the transcript. "He is definitely a pleader." And, after Eisenberg has tried to describe Althoff's killing games, Boder cuts in: "All right. No more about general /?/ stories [. . .] /Tell me about/ your last days in the Lager."[43] As is well known, Elie Wiesel, too, learned to adapt to postwar expectations and made some striking adjustments to his text. Travelling to South America in 1954 he wrote his memoirs in Yiddish, for them to be included in the Yiddish series "Dos poylishe yidntum," published in Argentina. In describing the days and weeks after liberation, the Yiddish version runs: "Early the next day Jewish boys ran off to Weimar to steal clothing and potatoes. And to rape German girls [un tsu fargvaldikn daytshe shikses]. The historical commandment of revenge was not fulfilled." But in Stella Rodway's English rendition (and in the French edition that preceded the English one), the passage appears: "On the following morning, some of the young men went to Weimar to get some potatoes and clothes – and to sleep with girls. But of revenge, not a sign."[44]

Moreover, as Eva Hoffman has argued in a slightly different context, quite apart from such external pressures survivors themselves may well have implicitly rejected pat explanations, exercising "a kind of prohibition on the very quality of coherence."[45] In their astonishing Auschwitz memoirs, both Charlotte Delbo and Primo Levi explore what it was to be in a realm where no explanation was possible. Until well into her book, for example, Delbo deploys no adjectives at all to describe the SS. The very first qualifying word of any description in relation to them appears on page 66: "[T]all," a word which obviously offers no glimpse of their inner lives or qualities and no hint of judgment: "The SS women officers stride by – tall in their black capes, boots, high black hoods."[46] In using this strategy of withholding description, Delbo conveys the sense of the SS almost as natural forces, removed from human society, part of a landscape in which tormenting thirst is just as brutal a taskmaster. Primo Levi too, famously, describes a situation in which there is "no why."[47] When his *Ecce Homo* (the US title is *Survival in Auschwitz*) appeared in German, Levi found he had no direct message for his readers. Instead, he suggested, when invited to do so, that the edition contain a letter to his translator. In that letter he said that he did not hate the Germans and refused to judge an individual by dint of their membership of the collective. "But I cannot say I understand the Germans. Now something one cannot understand constitutes a painful void, a puncture, a permanent stimulus that insists on being satisfied." Levi concluded by hoping that the book's echo would help him understand the Germans and thus "placate the stimulus."[48]

*"Mitmn rosh in adome."*

In different ways, however, we do gain glimpses of victims seeking to make sense of those who were assaulting them. Understandably enough, many initially used past experience to try to get a handle on their tormentors. In practical terms, it was essential to make some kind of calculation of what the invaders were after and what they would do. In Poland, when the war started some Jews expected that the invaders from the West would behave as had their counterparts in the First World War. This hope faded fast, but many Polish Jewish communities were initially encouraged to think that bribery might buy off the persecutors. It often had in the past, and for brief periods, in some contexts, it did again. The Jewish ghetto policeman Calel Perechodnik remembered a small "action" in which the first gendarme on the scene, keen to milk the opportunity, promised reprieve to those who gave him their money. Otherwise they would be shot:

> Magical word, derszosyn, [erschossen] as if they would not be killed in an hour anyway. Magical because they all run quickly to him, give him all their money, tell him that they are ready to work eighteen hours around the clock only if they are not killed. They address him as *Unserer Gott*, and maybe they are right because he does indeed dispose of their lives.[49]

Elsewhere Perechodnik berated his countrymen who, remembering how to appease the Tsarist thugs, would go down on their knees and kiss the boots of their guards.

Yitskhok Rudaveshki, another of Saul Friedländer's sources, a young teenager in the Vilna ghetto, and, like many others his age, too young to be in a workshop, reported on the stories that his parents brought home. "If they meet some fool of a German who wants a cap," he noted on 13 September 1942:

> [T]he fellows make fun of him, they bring out a Jew and introduce him as the 'best cap-maker of Poland.' The German believes it. Then they tell him that this diligent Jew can make beautiful caps only when he receives a little food. He is persuaded. [. . .] When the time comes for delivery, he is simply told: 'Listen, do you have cigarettes? Give us cigarettes and you will have a delightful cap [this was written in quasi-German in the original].' Finally they make him a hat which looks like a blintz on him and he exclaims into the bargain, 'Jews are a capable people.' They add the sardonic blessing, 'mitmn rosh in adome.' [With his head in the ground.] 'It looks sometimes, the workers say, like a Jewish bazaar. They get along well with the Germans. 'Yankl,' shouts one tailor to

the other, 'measure this gentlemen for shrouds,' or "Please take him to the Taare bret, hurry up.'

But after narrating this story with relish, Rudashevski adds: "The truth is that all these stories are merely wishful thinking. People are actually afraid of the German. However, if it is possible to curse him, to play a trick on him, they do so whenever they can."[50]

There is much that we might dwell on in Rudashevski's tale – the particular position of the youngster, cut off from direct contact with the Germans; the role of Jewish labor in facilitating extended contact with the other side, one that frequently reinforced the sense that civilians were in on the murderous project too, but sometimes did not, though the civilians usually seemed oblivious to the enormity of what their country was doing; the strange interregnum that characterized the Vilna, Riga and Kovno ghettos during 1942–3, and the fact that even after the murderous ghetto clearances of late 1941 such moments of hope could still resurface. But the most important point is that Rudashevski here relates a collective fantasy, seeking to fit the new enemy into an older kind of story of the emperor with no clothes, the absurd ruler, whose pretensions might be both flattered and punctured. Clearly, there was much that was absurd about the newcomers; equally clearly they could not really be rendered safe as the idiotic oppressor. Probably most listeners had the same ambivalence as Rudashevski himself, sucking up the tales with relish, yet at the same time acknowledging their implausibility.

In similar vein, stories abounded of the Good German, some of which may be true, some of which we know were apocryphal. Perechodnik's report of the good Kreishauptmann in Mińsk Mazowiecki seems to be based on myth.[51] Rudashevski, too, recorded tales of Good Germans he had heard – including the "noble person" for whom his mother worked – but he continued, "The stories sound half like legends. Every ghetto Jew enjoys expanding, enriching such a story; people revel in them. Thus, for instance, they tell that a German tore the badges off a Jew's clothes, saying that badges will soon no longer be needed!" Once again, there was an explicit acknowledgement of the fantasy in this. "All these stories circulate among the people, or they change them, strengthen the impression, embellish them." Yet the idea that something about it was real was too strong to let go: "But the spark of truth exists. We are touched by the thought that among the Germans there are great numbers who sympathize with us, and feel their shame in our anguish."[52]

Beyond such everyday attempts to fit the perpetrators in some recognizable mold, the great communal ghetto chroniclers – the Kaplans, Kruks, Lewins, and Ringelblums – at times also sought to claim long-term parallels and continuities, as Lewin's earlier reference to "New Amalekites" suggested. For the most part, however, such invocations of traditional enemies of the Jewish people remained at the level of angry phrases. The more time passed, the more it was clear that the new threat exceeded all historical comparisons. Chaim Kaplan might, as Alexandra Garbarini has observed, cry out one minute that the plan for the ghetto clearances "could have been invented only by Satan." Within such a quasi-religious framework one could see continuity in the tribulations of the Jewish people, and those inflicting misery as merely the latest incarnations of an age-old evil. But Kaplan's sense that the current situation was radically different was evident when he continued: "In these two days the emptiness of the ghetto has been filled with cries and wails. If they found no way to the God of Israel it is a sign that He doesn't exist."[53] The thoroughness and completeness of the eliminatory enterprise had departed from all historical parallel.[54]

*"You should have seen their faces, they were not really human."*

If the Nazis did not fit the traditional mold, how, then, might they be understood? While Kaplan's reference to Satan can be seen as establishing a link back to Jewish experiences of persecution since biblical times, it can also be seen as removing the perpetrators from all recognizable human context and rendering them monstrous. The most common epithets in victim accounts for the perpetrators are, indeed, "devils" or, even more commonly, "beasts." "My most Sacred, beloved, worn-out, blessed, cherished Mother," an anguished Dawid Sierakowiak, trapped in the Łódź ghetto, scorched in the pages of his diary in September 1942, "has fallen victim to the bloodthirsty German Nazi beast!!!"[55] The "beasts" who carried out strip searches of the women in Mary Berg's house committee "did not leave until 2 a.m., carrying a scanty loot of a few watches."[56] "Outside, at work, the men are subject to bestial torments," noted the Communist Jew Lévy-Hass in her Bergen-Belsen diary in 1944, "The German beasts keep to their preferred method: terrible beatings and coarse, hysterical invective."[57] "'You should have seen their faces,'" Eva Hoffman's mother said to her young daughter sometime in the early 1950s. "'They were not really human.'"[58] As time went on in postwar accounts, this animal note was somewhat muted. The Lévy-Hass quotation above is my translation from the earlier German edition; it is noteworthy that the later English translation tames the "beasts" in the above quotation to "savages".[59] but even the reflective Primo Levi noted in his *The Drowned and the Saved*: "Almost all, but not all, had been deaf, blind and dumb: a mass of 'invalids' surrounding a core of ferocious beasts."[60]

As a figure of speech, the epithet "beast" served as a metaphor for inhumanity and a container for anger. It vividly captured behavior that seems unworthy of human beings, and offered a fitting counterpoint to frequent victim self-descriptions of being herded like cattle, or hunted like prey. That even such sophisticated observers as Primo Levi or such precise chroniclers as Avraham Tory should speak of beasts showed how powerfully this language expressed the experience of confronting humans who behaved so inhumanly. It was probably less the proximity to violent action that made such vocabulary unavoidable than being the victim or the potential victim of it oneself. In the memoirs of privileged non-Jewish political prisoners in the concentration camps, that is, those able to see their Nazi counterparts close-up but less directly the target of the most murderous measures, the language is often different. Here is Jorge Semprún, caught in the woods at Buchenwald, having made a trip with a colleague in the *Arbeitsstatistik*. Confronted by a member of the SS who threatens him with a weapon, Semprún (in his retrospective account, at least) "does not see the premonitory signs of death anywhere. [. . .] He is quite simply pitiful, this SS officer, as he tries to turn this incident into a tragedy, tries to look like the impalpable, voracious shadow of destiny."[61] "I look at the SS officer. I want to laugh. I want to call over to him: 'Drop your gun, old pal! You're too lightweight for the part!'"[62] Later we are introduced to a Hauptsturmführer Schwartz, a "sinister idiot."[63] But such devil-may-care tones are hard to find in Jewish accounts.

Renata Laqueur's Belsen diary offers a revealing transition from one state to the other. An educated German Jew who had sought refuge in Holland, she was interned initially in relatively privileged conditions. On the train from Holland to Belsen, the SS gave the group bread. Early diary entries from Belsen in March 1944 indicate that they were not beaten, though they were well aware that others were not being treated with the same restraint.[64] In this early period, Laqueur offered contextual explanation for the guards' behavior. She abjured the idea of postwar revenge. The guards should not be put behind barbed wire. Instead "Break up the camps and teach the people to live, instead of to order, to kick and to shoot."[65] "Ordering people about" [Kommandieren] she noted wryly, while observing their own Dutch barrack elder "is an infectious disease."[66] A day or two later, she observes an SS man with his Alsatian dog walking between the watch-towers: "What must such a man be thinking. Does he find it pleasant to stand guard over us? Does he know that we want to go home, and does he find it 'good' that we are held here against our will?"[67] Her reflections go on to reveal not only the space for empathy left when one was treated half-way as a human being, but also the way her knowledge of German culture facilitated telling snapshots of the kinds of characters she was dealing with at work – the sentimental, bawdy and greedy foremen, for example. But as the treatment in Belsen worsens, many of Laqueur's earlier imaginative flights disappear. She voices hatred, and calls the SS devils.[68] But if the epithet "beast" or "devil" was authentic on one level, it was on another clearly an expression of perplexity, of inability to make any human sense of the perpetrators at all. Symbolic of the way the distance, the power differential, and the degradation of their victims transmuted the perpetrators into beings from another planet is that simultaneously with their characterization as beasts, in many victim accounts they appear as almost supernaturally handsome. The soldiers marching "in shorts, with blue ties over naked torsos, with no shirts on, with automatic guns in their hands, and without hats. They were tall, blond and athletic."[69] At Auschwitz, Mengele, on the ramp, "impeccable in his uniform, a gold rosette gracing his lapel, his boots smartly polished,"[70] elsewhere SS officers "strutting in their sleek uniforms and polished boots."[71] Yet as Hermann Langbein noted, when reviewing survivor descriptions of some of the masters of life and death at Auschwitz, a glance at contemporary photos of many of the Auschwitz

"Gods" seldom warrants such exalted characterizations.[72] Instead, it was a sign that the beasts were like the Gods of antiquity, beings living on a different planet, following rules of behavior that were scarcely recognizable, rules that could spell the end, or occasionally, arbitrarily, survival, for ordinary mortals.

*"It seems, however, that he was not in any way excited by his job."*

I have argued thus far that the most powerful note in victim testimony lies in uncovering the breadth and depth of enthusiastic participation and human cruelty in the Holocaust. This view stands in some conflict with our sense of the Holocaust as a planned and centrally controlled phenomenon, even allowing for the degree of improvisation and regional initiative which we know the Nazi policy process incorporated. As a corrective to postwar historians' overemphasis on orders, on automaticity, and their description of a process operating almost without human agency except at the top, the victims' perspective is invaluable. But does it not also obscure our understanding of the Holocaust? For, however willful and spontaneous daily actions and outbursts may have been, and however enthusiastically endorsed such actions were, all of the perpetrators whom the victims encountered were in broad terms not acting under their own initiative. Most, as we know, would not have been killers had it not been for the Holocaust. Almost all of those who survived easily found their place in a very different postwar society. They were for the most part not monsters, monstrous though their deeds often were.[73]

The last part of this essay argues that alongside and sometimes modifying the powerful picture of agency and cruelty, victims in fact often offer much more subtle and differentiated views of the perpetrators. The term "beast" itself, for example, carried very diverse connotations of motive and agency, connotations that varied between observer, and sometimes between pages of the same diary or memoir. Sierakowiak's cry of despair about the "bloodthirsty German Nazi beast [in the singular]," captured not the animal-like individual but rather the system as a devouring machine. This use of "beast" to denote a collective, in which the individual perpetrator figured as the replaceable part of the whole, is quite common. Yitzhak Katzenelson, for example, referred to "that part of Europe occupied by the German beast. It resembles that devouring ogre of a thousand eyes, the Hydra of a thousand heads; in reality only one evil eye and one monstrous head." Katzenelson here wanted to make the point that everywhere under Nazi control the newspapers chanted in the same monstrous language.[74]

Where the term was explicitly applied to individuals, it was often used to describe sadistic behavior. Here is Lévy-Hass, talking in December 1944 about the new Aryan Kapos who have been put in charge in Belsen:

[. . .] the most terrible thing about them is they have the mentality of criminals of the worst kind. They are true creatures of the devil – the devil Kramer – and are no longer human. Cold, cruel sadistic – had I not seen with my own eyes the obscene delight they take in beating us, I would never have thought it possible. The Germans have made them what they are, have turned them into wild animals in human shape, and it is as though this makes them want to avenge themselves on us.[75]

A different kind of beast, also not uncommon, was the "correct" beast of prey. Avraham Tory, the assiduous chronicler of Kovno, describes a conversation with Keiffler, the deputy city governor, 6 January 1943:

A stranger, eavesdropping on this conversation, would think that we were faced with a well-mannered man showing great interest in friends whom he had not seen for a long time. In fact, Keiffler's questions are correct and to the point. But if the aforementioned imaginary stranger were to peer through the keyhole at the partners in this conversation, he would behold a weird scene: Keiffler stretching himself in his armchair, puffing smoke from his cigar, from time to time looking at Garfunkel and me with eyes full of disgust and contempt. At the same time, he would see both of us standing on our feet throughout the meeting anxiously following not only the drift of his questions but the tone of his voice, his facial expression, and his gaze penetrating the depth of one's soul. The stranger would realize then that this was not exactly a conversation between friends – that we stood in front of a beast of prey in human disguise, an aggressive, biting animal, eager to inflict pain.[76]

On 15 Feb 1943, we find another entry in Tory's chronicle, however, in which the term "beast" connotes far less independence of mind or volition. Tory described a senior Gestapo official who had just taken possession of articles from Jews recently murdered. "It seems, however, that he was not in any way excited by his job – not yesterday nor today. He has turned into a beast; perhaps he was born this way? Human feelings are alien to him. He completed his job and returned to the city."[77] At other times, again, "beast" stands in merely as a metaphor for an obsessive policy element. On February 24 1943 Tory noted new pressure to remove the non-working element from the ghetto, while he attempted to convince the authorities of the value of these Jews and the potential impact on morale of their removal. "The problem is that we are not dealing with people whose actions are guided by logic. We are dealing with wild beasts, with savages who are bent on killing, exterminating, and destroying Jews. Mass murder is their raison d'être."[78]

Thus the sadist, the fanatical ideologue, the cynical automaton, or the system as a whole might all be labeled as the "beast." These various incarnations had in common a lack of human empathy. Yet other than the sadist, most were not particularly animal-like, and some indeed exhibited explicitly rule-bound and dispassionate behavior. Beneath the common layer of ruthlessness and cruelty, such examples offer a first glimpse of the diversity, distinctness and precision of victim observation.

Victims were often not in a position clearly to distinguish between individual initiative and orders from behind the scenes, but they could observe what kind of factors might mitigate threats or excite responses. Those victims who experienced sustained contact with their German counterparts, above all through some kind of working relationship, particularly observed diversity and change, sometimes merely proving that not all Nazis, SS men or soldiers were alike, but sometimes allowing us access to larger patterns and processes. To take just one brief example, many diaries and memoirs talk about role-play in ways which have not yet been properly examined. Role-play might mean visibly enjoying the pleasure of lording it over others. At a meeting in January 1943, in which the Jewish representatives of the Kovno ghetto leadership met with a key German official, according to Avraham Tory: "Miller [the official] played the main part; he radiated contentment. His behavior gave the impression of a Polish aristocrat among his servants, who were deprived of any rights. He willingly accepted help in taking off his coat. He then accepted a lighted match offered to him to light a cigarette. He also asked for an ashtray [. . .]."[79] Playing a role also could mean acting very differently in private and in company. "It was quite theatrical," Tory noted a little later, "but this is how the German rulers usually present themselves. The Germans speak with us as humans quite often, but when they suddenly realize that the person they are talking to is simply a Jew, they raise their voices."[80] On another occasion, Tory noted:

> Miller's tone of voice was domineering and commanding. This is the accepted practice when speaking to Jews when there are two Germans or more in attendance. One to one they are not so dangerous. I often speak to Miller one to one; on such occasions our conversation is polite and to the point. But when Gilow or Keiffler is also present, Miller raises his voice to show how the Jews are to be spoken to.[81]

Tory was not alone in recognizing such drama. In Belsen, Lévy-Hass observed the "Gray Mouse," a female guard, getting into character.[82] Paul Neurath, in his little-known and recently published wartime sociology based on personal experiences at Dachau and Buchenwald camps in the 1930s, similarly observed differences between public and private behavior.[83] More research is needed to explore these observations. Is this merely the normal amplifying effect of an audience on communicative styles? Does it imply that privately many participants were less sold on their murderous enterprise than when acting as a collective? And how much mental separation was there between the protagonists and their assigned roles?

*"A small part, a tiny fraction of the truth."*

In the last fifteen years or so, the mainstream historiography of the Holocaust has moved closer to the victims' world and has also grown more conscious of individual action and agency at the level of the ordinary perpetrator.[84] By greater use of court records, for example, historians have been confronted with victim testimony, though court proceedings often dragooned and marginalized the victims in favor of other sources.[85]

At the same time, the victims' own perspective has widened as survivors participated in wider intellectual life. Sophisticated observers such as Jean Améry processed their own experiences in explicit debate with academic discussion of the Holocaust, as his remarks above responding to Arendt's notion of banality make clear.[86] As Charlotte Delbo was writing the second volume of her Auschwitz memoirs, it is clear that the My Lai episode in the Vietnam War was throwing up disturbing parallels.[87] And survivors trained as historians themselves, becoming often the most important figures shaping the historiography of the Holocaust. For some such "survivor historians," writing a professional history of the Holocaust meant above all devoting themselves to the perpetrator's own records. Raul Hilberg, who fled Nazi Vienna as a child, is the most famous exponent of this. But no historian has been more effective at integrating personal experience, professional training, and the voice of both victims and perpetrators than Saul Friedländer. Friedländer's opening quotation from Stefan Ernest invited us to take the victims seriously, to add them to the mosaic, and to recognize that the victims knew their ability to understand the whole was not a given.

Yet as this essay has suggested, there is yet more to mine from victim accounts. The detailed observations of actions and encounters which we find there offer a wealth of insights into the perpetrators themselves. And as this paper has also argued, historians have only barely begun to reflect on them.[88] Provided we build the difficulties of observation and understanding into our analysis, victims' testimony about their tormentors can shed light on the nature of their perpetrators as well as on their own predicament.

*Notes*

1   For their very helpful comments on the manuscript I would like to thank Roberta Pergher and Anna Hájková, as well as the participants in the conference on which this volume is based and at seminars at the US Holocaust and Memorial Museum Center for Advanced Holocaust Research, the Minda de Gunzberg Center for European Studies, Harvard University, and at the Universities of Toronto, Bielefeld and Munich where versions of this chapter were presented.
2   Ernest's fate is not known, but it is presumed he died in 1943.
3   Raul Hilberg, *Sources of Holocaust Research: An Analysis* (Chicago: I.R. Dee, 2001).
4   See Cathy Caruth, *Trauma: Explorations in Memory* (Baltimore: Johns Hopkins University Press, 1995), particularly the essay by Dori Laub.
5   Lawrence L. Langer, *Holocaust Testimonies: The Ruins of Memory* (New Haven: Yale University Press, 1991).
6   Giorgio Agamben, *Homo Sacer: Sovereign Power and Bare Life, Meridian* (Stanford: Stanford University Press, 1998).
7   Jean Améry, *At the Mind's Limits: Contemplations by a Survivor on Auschwitz and Its Realities* (Bloomington: Indiana University Press, 1980), 26.
8   On testimony see Christopher R. Browning, *Collected Memories: Holocaust History and Postwar Testimony* (Madison, WI: The University of Wisconsin Press, 2003); Devin Pendas, "Testimony," in Miriam Dobson and Benjamin Ziemann (eds), *Reading Primary Sources: The Interpretation of Texts from Nineteenth- and Twentieth-Century History Routledge Guides to Using Historical Sources* (London and New York: Routledge, 2008). Jürgen Matthäus, *Approaching an Auschwitz Survivor: Holocaust Testimony and Its Transformations* (New York: Oxford University Press, 2009).

9    Mark Roseman, "Beyond Conviction? Perpetrators, Ideas, and Action in the Holocaust in Historiographical Perspective," in Frank Biess, Mark Roseman, and Hanna Schissler (eds), *Conflict, Catastrophe and Continuity: Essays on Modern German History* (New York: Berghahn Books, 2007), 83–103.

10   Ruth Klüger, *Still Alive: A Holocaust Girlhood Remembered*, 1st English-language ed., *The Helen Rose Scheuer Jewish Women's Series* (New York: Feminist Press at the City University of New York, 2001), 52.

11   Dawid Sierakowiak, Alan Adelson, and Kamil Turowski, *The Diary of Dawid Sierakowiak: Five Notebooks from the Lódź Ghetto* (New York: Oxford University Press, 1996).

12   Klüger, *Still Alive*, 52.

13   Jorge Semprún, *Literature or Life* (New York: Viking, 1997), 23.

14   Mary Berg, *The Diary of Mary Berg: Growing up in the Warsaw Ghetto*, trans. Susan Lee Pentlin, new ed. (Oxford: Oneworld, 2006).

15   Isaac Rudashevski, *The Diary of the Vilna Ghetto, June 1941–April 1943* ([Tel Aviv]: Ghetto Fighters' House, 1979).

16   Primo Levi, *The Drowned and the Saved* (New York: Vintage International, 1989).

17   Hermann Langbein, *Menschen in Auschwitz*, new ed. (Vienna: Europaverlag, 1995), 15.

18   Simon Wiesenthal, *The Murderers among Us: The Simon Wiesenthal Memoirs* (New York: McGraw-Hill, 1967), 47.

19   Hanna Lévy-Hass, *Inside Belsen* (Brighton, Sussex and Totowa, NJ: Harvester Press; Barnes & Noble, 1982), 41–42, and see March 1945; again 1963–1945.

20   David G. Roskies, *Against the Apocalypse: Responses to Catastrophe in Modern Jewish Culture* (Cambridge, MA and London: Harvard University Press, 1984), 135.

21   See Barbara Harshav's comments about Kruk's magnum opus in Herman Kruk, *The Last Days of the Jerusalem of Lithuania. Chronicles from the Vilna Ghetto and the Camps, 1939–1944*, trans. Barbara Harshav (New Haven and London: Yale University Press, 2002), xxii.

22   Ibid., 50.

23   Ibid., 114.

24   Ibid., 187.

25   Ibid., 260–72.

26   Jadwiga Bezwinska and Danuta Czech, *Amidst a Nightmare of Crime: Manuscripts of Prisoners in Crematorium Squads Found at Auschwitz* (New York: H. Fertig, 1992), 91.

27   Avraham Tory, *Surviving the Holocaust: The Kovno Ghetto Diary*, trans. Jerzy Michalowicz (Cambridge, MA: Harvard University Press, 1990), 91.

28   Ibid., 135.

29   Ibid., 149.

30   Berg, *The Diary of Mary Berg*, 36–7.

31   http://voices.iit.edu/frames.asp?path=Interviews/&page=epste&ext=_t.html, accessed 6/18/2007.

32   Eva Hoffman, *After Such Knowledge: Memory, History, and the Legacy of the Holocaust* (New York: Public Affairs, 2004), 43.

33   Daniel Jonah Goldhagen, *Hitler's Willing Executioners: Ordinary Germans and the Holocaust* (New York: Knopf, 1996).

34   Jean Améry, *Jenseits Von Schuld und Sühne. Bewältigungsversuche eines Überwältigten*, 2nd ed. (Munich: Szczesny, 1966), 63.

35   Abraham Lewin, *A Cup of Tears: A Diary of the Warsaw Ghetto*. Edited and with an Introduction by Antony Polonsky (Oxford and New York: Basil Blackwell in association with the Institute for Polish-Jewish Studies, Oxford, 1988), 230.

36   The historian and Holocaust survivor Josef Wulf, confronted in the 1960s with the official history of Nazi policy as it was being formulated by the *Institut für Zeitgeschichte* in Munich, was one of the few historians in the West who rejected the Institute's tendency to separate the SS from the rest. Wulf did not directly rely on testimony and his insights reminds us that there were other ways to arrive at least at some of these conclusions – German military records or the diary or correspondence of a pastor might indicate the breadth of involvement in the Holocaust for example. But nothing conveyed the dispersal of energy, agency and cruelty as much as victim testimony. Nicolas Berg, *Der Holocaust und die westdeutschen Historiker: Erforschung und Erinnerung* (Göttingen: Wallstein-Verlag, 2003), 613.

37 On Ringelblum, see Samuel D. Kassow, *Who Will Write Our History?: Emanuel Ringelblum, the Warsaw Ghetto, and the Oyneg Shabes Archive, The Helen and Martin Schwartz Lectures in Jewish Studies* (Bloomington: Indiana University Press, 2007). On Kruk, see Harshav's comments in the introduction to Kruk, *The Last Days of the Jerusalem of Lithuania: Chronicles from the Vilna Ghetto and the Camps, 1939–1944.*

38 Berg, *Der Holocaust und die westdeutschen Historiker: Erforschung und Erinnerung*; Helmut Peitsch, *Deutschlands Gedächtnis an Seine Dunkelste Zeit: Zur Funktion der Autobiographik in den Westzonen Deutschlands und den Westsektoren von Berlin 1945 bis 1949* (Berlin: Ed. Sigma, 1990).

39 Hoffman, *After Such Knowledge*, 25.

40 Ibid., 83.

41 Zvi Bachrach, *Last Letters from the Shoah* (Jerusalem; New York: Devora Pub., 2004), 50–4.

42 That Eisenberg was not remotely exaggerating, we know from Christopher R. Browning, "Survivor Testimonies from Starachowice. Writing the History of a Slave Labor Camp," in *Collected Memories*, 37–59.

43 "Voices," http://voices.iit.edu/frames.asp?path=Interviews/&page=eisen&ext=_t.html.

44 Annette Wieviorka, *The Era of the Witness* (Ithaca, NY: Cornell University Press, 2006), 37. The English here comes from Wiesel's own translation in his memoir *All Rivers Run to the Sea*, 319–320. See also Wieviorka's comparison of the epilogue to the Yiddish edition, and to La Nuit. Wieviorka, *The Era of the Witness*, 38. Citing *Night*, 109. Wieviorka is herself responding to Naomi Seidman, 'Elie Wiesel and the Scandal of Jewish Rage', *Jewish Social Studies*, 3 (1996): 1–19, but offers a more generous and less accusatory interpretation.

45 Hoffman, *After Such Knowledge*, 15.

46 Charlotte Delbo, *Auschwitz and After* (New Haven: Yale University Press, 1995), 66.

47 Primo Levi, *Survival in Auschwitz*, trans. Stuart Woolf (New York: Collier Books, 1960), 27.

48 Cited in Levi, *The Drowned and the Saved*, 174.

49 Perechodnik, *Am I a Murderer? Testament of a Jewish Ghetto Policeman*, 76.

50 Rudashevski, *The Diary of the Vilna Ghetto, June 1941–April 1943*, 52. Abraham Lewin observed an encounter in which a German officer, who, against the general policy hitherto, had insisted on hats being removed in his presence, was made fun of by a series of young Jewish men ostentatiously repeatedly returning to fawn and remove their caps. Lewin, *A Cup of Tears*.

51 Perechodnik, *Am I a Murderer?*, 65 and note 133 with reference to ZIH testimonies. See also 9.

52 Rudashevski, *The Diary of the Vilna Ghetto*, 81–2.

53 Cited here from Garbarini's Ph.d. thesis: Alexandra Garbarini, "To 'Bear Witness Where Witness Needs to Be Borne': Diary Writing and the Holocaust 1939–1945" (UCLA, 2003), 100.

54 Roskies, *Against the Apocalypse*, 221–2.

55 Sierakowiak, Adelson, and Turowski, *The Diary of Dawid Sierakowiak: Five Notebooks from the Łódz Ghetto.*

56 Berg, *The Diary of Mary Berg*, 207.

57 My translation from Hanna Lévy-Hass, *Vielleicht war das alles erst der Anfang. Tagebuch aus dem Kz Bergen-Belsen, 1944–1945*, Rotbuch 191 (Berlin: Rotbuch Verlag, 1979), 14.

58 Hoffman, *After Such Knowledge*, 12.

59 Lévy-Hass, *Inside Belsen*, 10.

60 Levi, *The Drowned and the Saved*, 168–9.

61 Jorge Semprún, *What a Beautiful Sunday!* (San Diego: Harcourt Brace Jovanovich, 1982), 193.

62 Ibid., 198.

63 Ibid., 207.

64 Renata Laqueur, *Bergen-Belsen Tagebuch, 1944–1945*, 3rd ed. (Hannover: Fackelträger, 1995), 16.

65 My translation from ibid.

66 My translation from ibid., 17.

67 My translation from ibid.

68 Ibid., 45.

69 Boris M. Zabarko, *Holocaust in the Ukraine, The Library of Holocaust Testimonies* (London: Vallentine Mitchell, 2005), 29.

70 Miklós Nyiszli, *Auschwitz: A Doctor's Eyewitness Account*, trans. Tibere Kremer and Richard Seaver (New York: Arcade Publishing, 1993), 17.

71   Lilly Pancis, "Deportation to the East," in Gertrude Schneider (ed.), *Muted Voices: Jewish Survivors of Latvia Remember* (New York: Philosophical Library, 1987), 41–55, here 45.

72   Langbein, *Menschen in Auschwitz.*

73   Roseman, "Beyond Conviction?"

74   Katzenelson on 23 July 1943 in Alexandra Garbarini, *Numbered Days: Diaries and the Holocaust* (New Haven: Yale University Press, 2006), 73.

75   Lévy-Hass, *Inside Belsen*, 50.

76   Tory, *Surviving the Holocaust*, 176.

77   Ibid., 221.

78   Ibid., 238.

79   Ibid., 179.

80   Ibid., 181.

81   Ibid., 178.

82   Lévy-Hass, *Vielleicht war das alles erst der Anfang*, 36–7.

83   Paul Martin Neurath, *The Society of Terror: Inside the Dachau and Buchenwald Concentration Camps* (Boulder, CO: Paradigm Publishers, 2005).

84   There was of course from the very beginning an extensive Jewish scholarship in Poland and Israel that was much closer to the victims. To look at Philip Friedman's review of literature as early as 1949 is to be astonished by how much work had already been done; see Philip Friedman, "The European Jewish Research on the Recent Jewish Catastrophe," *Proceedings of the American Academy for Jewish Research* 18 (1949): 179–211.

85   See Devin Pendas' sensitive examination of the fate of the witness Simon Gotland in the Frankfurt Auschwitz trial, in Pendas, "Testimony." Victims had much greater autonomy in some of the earlier postwar trials in Allied hands, see Tomaz Jardim, "Die ersten Erhebungen von Nazi-Kriegsverbrechen in Mauthausen: Amerikanische Ermittler und die Befreiung des KZ," in *2008 Jahrbuch des KZ-Gedenkstätte Mauthausen* (Vienna: Austrian Ministry of the Interior, 2009) and "The Mauthausen War Crimes Trial and American Military Justice In Germany" (Diss., University of Toronto, 2009).

86   See page 87. The popular, one might almost say "banal," reading of Arendt's banality in reality did not do Arendt's own work justice. Though she is not always consistent in her usage, it is clear that she did not regard Eichmann's "banality" as precluding the kind of commitment or energy that Améry observed in his torturers. She was making a more profound point that a lack of deeper moral and intellectual anchoring enabled respectable citizens to go along with this horror.

87   Charlotte Delbo, *Auschwitz and After* (New Haven: Yale University Press, 1995), 179–80.

88   Amy Simon is currently researching a Ph.D. at Indiana University on Polish Jewish perceptions of perpetrators.

# 6

# Raul Hilberg and Saul Friedländer – Two Perspectives on the Holocaust[1]

## Michael Wildt

I

Raul Hilberg's *Destruction of the European Jews* and Saul Friedländer's two volumes *Years of Persecution* and *Years of Extermination* seem to represent two different, even contradictory historical approaches to the Shoah.

Hilberg began his Holocaust studies in exile, to be precise, under his two mentors, Hans Rosenberg and Franz Neumann. Both had emigrated as soon as the National Socialists had come to power, first to Britain and then to the USA. From 1938 Rosenberg, a historian, taught at Brooklyn College, New York, where his classes were attended by the young politics student Raul Hilberg after the war. Hilberg recalls in his memoirs that Rosenberg had a deeper and more lasting influence on him than any of the political scientists teaching at the College.[2]

Hilberg's family had managed to escape from Vienna to the USA in 1939, before the outbreak of the war. Having attended school in New York, Raul was drafted, aged eighteen, in 1944, sent to the European theatre of war and deployed in Bavaria in spring 1945. In the former headquarters of the National Socialist Party in Munich he discovered, by pure chance, several cases containing the private library of Adolf Hitler, which awakened his ambitions as a researcher – an anecdote that has been repeatedly reported in his recent obituaries.[3]

On his return to New York Hilberg continued his studies at Brooklyn College, taking part in Rosenberg's seminars on the rise of the nation state and the development of bureaucracy in Europe from the seventeenth to the twentieth century. A few years later Rosenberg's celebrated book *Bureaucracy, Aristocracy and Autocracy: The Prussian Experience 1660–1815* appeared, stressing the significance of the Prussian bureaucracy as a leading political group and raising the awkward question of how, seen from a secular point of view, the breakthrough of the National Socialists could have occurred, as Rosenberg himself explained after the war.[4] It was in Rosenberg's lectures, Hilberg wrote, that he "became aware of the concept of jurisdiction, that bedrock of the legal order, which appeared to be both the basis and the basic tool of the bureaucrats. These potentates were an unstoppable force. As administrators they would always follow precedent, but if need be they would break new ground, without calling attention to themselves or claiming a patent, trademark or copyright. The bureaucracy was a hidden world, an overlooked world, and once I was conscious of it I would not be deterred from prying open its shuttered windows and bolted doors."[5]

Franz Neumann, a lawyer, was first employed at the renowned Institute of Social Research, which had found refuge in the USA, and in 1936 became a lecturer in Public Law and Government at Columbia University, New York. His book *Behemoth: The Structure and Practice of National Socialism*, first published in 1942, was a brilliant, thoroughly documented analysis of the National Socialist regime that attracted a large circle of readers, in particular within the Roosevelt administration.

Neumann's book has been for Hilberg, as he wrote in his memoirs, one of the basic studies, which he has read several times:

> In a single, startling generalization he pointed out that under National Socialism the whole of German society was organized into four solid, centralized groups, each operating under a leadership principle, and each with legislative, administrative, and judicial powers of its own. These four hierarchies were the civil service, the army, industry, and the party. Operating independently of one another, without a legislature specifying their prerogatives, they coordinated their efforts with agreements that, in class, he caustically referred to as 'social contracts.' Here then I found a Nazi Germany that in its roots was anarchic, an organized chaos, but with the freedom to march into completely uncharted areas of action.[6]

Hilberg decided to write his Ph.D. thesis about the extermination of the European Jews under the auspice of Franz Neumann, who agreed but warned him in view of his academic career: "It's your funeral!"

The extermination of the European Jews was in fact a taboo during the intense period of the Cold War. "This has been some kind of a revolt," Hilberg admitted later in an interview, "a revolt against Germany, and against Jewry, too. Wherever I looked, nothing had been done, nothing had been written, nothing had been tried. I even regard myself to be the only one who is researching about the destruction of the Jews."[7] This stubbornness, even in times when being isolated und unnoticed, has distinguished Hilberg during his entire life. And it may be significant that an academic outsider has had the courage to approach this enormous task.

Neumann's analysis of the Nazi regime as a bureaucratic system which has been technically rational and destructive at the same time – no rule of law, but a rule of order, no state at all, but a "behemoth" – has shaped the conceptual framework of Hilberg's study:

> Basic was the immersion in destructive activity of the bureaucratic apparatus as such. As the process unfolded, its requirements became more complex and its fulfilment involved an ever larger number of agencies, party offices, business enterprises, and military commands. The destruction of the Jews was a total process, comparable in its diversity

to a modern war, a mobilization, or a national reconstruction. [...] The machinery of destruction, then, was structurally no different from organized German society as a whole; the difference was only one of function. The machinery of destruction *was* the organized community in one of its special roles.[8]

Hilberg wanted to detect the mechanism of this machinery of destruction. He has, therefore, taken a point of view looking from the perspective of the engineers of this machinery:

> I was convinced from the very beginning of my work that without an insight into the actions of the perpetrators, one could not grasp this history in its full dimensions. The perpetrator had the overview. He alone was the key. It was through his eyes that I had to view the happening, from its genesis to its culmination. That the perpetrator's perspective was the primary path to be followed became a doctrine for me, which I never abandoned.[9]

Does the perpetrator have the overview? Or, in adopting his point of view, are we only looking at the events from a specific perspective? In conjunction with Neumann's structuralist analysis Hilberg developed the image of the perpetrator as an administrative functionary. Restricted to their own part of the work process, receiving administrative instructions tailored to it and carrying them out correctly and conscientiously without feeling responsible for the whole – in short, regarding themselves as a small cog in a large mechanism beyond their control. This image corresponded not only to the justifications of numerous perpetrators, but also to the everyday experience of a bureaucratized society dominated by the division of labour. Mass murder was regarded as mechanized, industrial killing; the bureaucrat became the "unsentimental technocrat of power" (Hans-Ulrich Thamer), the cold, indifferent technician of death who kept his part of the great extermination machine in order and made optimal use of it without wasting one thought on the murderous purpose of the whole, let alone developing any moral scruples.

Hilberg's thesis of the bureaucratic course of the destruction of the European Jews is closely connected with his passion for archives and documents. "I knew that the more I looked, the more [...] I would find. When I was rewarded with a discovery, I experienced a sensation that is best known to my fellow pageturners. It is an excitement that still comes to me when I run a microfilm through a machine."[10] Thanks to his knowledge of bureaucratic processes the least conspicuous document meant something to him. Whenever he entered an archive, he once told me, he first ordered any available collection of documents – and more often than not found instructive material on the Shoah among them. "Because the destruction of the Jews was so decentralised, it required the participation of all those agencies that had the means to perform their share of the action at the moment when the need for their contribution arose. The spectrum of offices that were ultimately involved in the process is synonymous with the concept of

German government or the whole of Germany's organized society."[11] It was not testimonies or photos that represented the nucleus of the archive that Hilberg was looking for, but official documents.

And yet the question remains whether the perpetrators did not themselves impose a certain bureaucratic form on their activities in order to hide the emotions, the hatred, that drove them. If we read in Rudolf Höss's notes from his death cell about the flair for improvisation, the commitment and the organizational skill it took him to construct the concentration camp of Auschwitz against all odds, we realize that the "destruction machine," as Hilberg called it, needed committed engineers, mechanics and labourers to be kept going.

Hilberg does not fail to recognise this. The bureaucracy of extermination worked not only on the principles of instruction, least of all at the middle and upper levels. "Instead of unequivocal chains of command," Hilberg says, there were:

> conferences, suggestions, initiatives of all kinds, even arguments, and then perhaps a decision. Initiatives at all levels were the absolute prerequisite of the persecution of the Jews, be it the withdrawal of tenant protection, the setting up of ghettos in Poland, or the right of Jews to plead in court. All this was devised by bureaucratic perpetrators. They had not been ordered to have ideas. They brought their ideas to their superiors, hoping that their initiatives would result in the addition of some regulation or directive to the advancement of the policy of destruction [...]. By orders alone the Jews would never have been destroyed. What was needed was a will, a readiness, a train of thought and a consensus.[12]

## II

Saul Friedländer, born in 1932 in Prague, having survived the Holocaust in a Catholic residential school in France while his parents were murdered in Auschwitz, went a different way. His intention to write his books about the persecution and extermination of the European Jews stemmed from a debate between him and functionalist historian Martin Broszat in the mid-1980s. Broszat has emphasized a historicization of National Socialism by examining "the proximity and interdependence of its capacity for success and its criminal energy, of its mobilization for achievement and for destruction, of people's participation and dictatorship."[13] In his view it was not the case that all that happened during the National Socialist regime had served the inhuman aims of National Socialism to the exclusion of everything else. He suggested that the twelve years from 1933 to 1945 must not be hermetically sealed off from German history. "The fact that his epoch was in general one of infamy should not mean that its many social, economic, and civilizing forces and efforts at modernization must be deprived of their historical significance solely because of their connection with National Socialism."[14]

Friedländer objected that by treating National Socialism like any other epoch one ran the risk of relativizing the criminal character of the regime.[15] In his first, very cautious and understanding reply he did not deny the occurrence of such processes between 1933 and 1945, but he asked what made them relevant to the examination of the National Socialist era. "Where are the limits of 'comprehension,'" he queried. "Where does critical detachment come into play? There is no difficulty as far as the obviously criminal aspects of the Nazi era are concerned. But what about those *Wehrmacht* units that held the eastern front in 1944–5?"[16]

Friedländer insisted on a change of perspective after Auschwitz, while Broszat, with his plea for historicity, tried to separate the "non-criminal" areas from the criminal and did not mention Auschwitz and the destruction of the Jews by one word. Friedländer did not deny the existence of many different lines of action and historical subjects, but in his opinion the focus of investigation was altered by the Shoah. If one takes the murder of European Jews seriously as a "break in civilization," one is likely to define the Archimedean point of the twentieth century in a new way.

Friedländer was rightly angered by the fact that Broszat could only perceive this perspective as the point of view of the Jewish victims or as a "mythical memory" that undoubtedly had its justification and should be taken seriously by German historians, but nevertheless had no claim to scientific status. Why, he asked, should historians from the ranks of the persecutors be more qualified to handle the past in a detached manner than those from the ranks of the victims? Indeed, Friedländer suggests that Broszat's question as to whether there could be a fruitful tension between scientific insight and Jewish mythical memory – memory understood as being built "on the gradual coarsening of the historical, on forgetting the details and imponderables of history that are still familiar to contemporaries"[17] – may reveal a concern that the memory of the Jewish victims could eclipse the memory of Broszat's own German generation.[18]

Friedländer objected to Broszat's analysis – and began his own project: a history of the Shoah as an integrated history. As he put it twenty years later: "By means of an integrated history I wanted to prove the opposite: that it was possible to write the two histories in one comprehensive picture and to include the Jewish dimension in an integrated historical narrative."[19]

According to Friedländer the history of the Holocaust cannot be reduced to the "Final Solution," the decrees and measures of the Nazi regime, but has firstly to include the actions of all the institutions and groups in the occupied areas and allied states. Secondly, it is evident that in each period of the persecution process the Jewish perception and reaction has been an inseparable part of this history. Thirdly, an integrated history can improve the representation of events which occurred at the same time at different places in different contexts.[20]

Friedländer's study is characterized by the voices of Jewish individuals, which he integrated into his narrative, not only to illustrate the pain of nameless victims, but in particular to make the voices heard as those of sharp-eyed, arguing, reasonable, worrying, feeling individuals. Therefore letters, diaries and testimonies are important sources for Friedländer's book, whereas other Holocaust historians, and above all Raul Hilberg, depend mainly on the official documents of the Nazi regime:

> These diaries and letters were written by Jews of all European countries, all walks of life, all age groups, either living under direct German domination or within the wider sphere of persecution. Of course the diaries have to be used with the same critical attention as any other document, especially if they were published after the war by the surviving author or by family members. Yet, as a source for the history of Jewish life during the years of persecution and extermination, they remain crucial and invaluable testimonies.[21]

But Friedländer does not replace knowledge with memory as Martin Broszat once insinuated. On the contrary, Friedländer's kind of narration, the literary style of his historiography, succeeds to link memory and knowledge together, to weave a comprehensive texture in which all threads are still visible and yet the whole picture is to be seen.[22] There are caesuras in the narration – comparable to film cuts – followed by intensive analytical passages or short biographical sketches; they lead to changing dynamics which can carry the readers or open a wide horizon for them.

Friedländer himself reflected on the problem of an appropriate narrative of the Shoah in a recent essay. No general voice of the Holocaust, he says, can do justice to the interaction of the multitude of elements if these are presented side by side in the manner of a textbook. The alternative, therefore, is the sudden cuts and abrupt changes of perspective that are common in the cinema.[23] This assertion of Friedländer's can be developed further by recalling the impossibility of enclosing the twentieth century, with its catastrophic fractures, caesuras and crashes, within the great sweep of a weighty historiography looking backward with detached self-assurance.

Friedländer does not look "from above" to the bottom, from the level of anonymous structures to the innumerable small wheels of the machinery of destruction and finally to the victims. Instead, as Jan Philipp Reemtsma has put it, everything, everyone is in the game: acting people who knew about their freedom to act in every direction and who acted in this way.[24]

Even on the Jewish side agency constitutes an indispensable perspective:

> From the outset all the steps taken by individual Jews or Jewish groups to disrupt the efforts of the National Socialists represented an obstacle, however small it may have been, on the road to total extermination: whether bribing civil servants, police officers or informers, paying families to hide children or adults, escaping to the forests or the mountains, lying low in small villages or large cities, converting to Christianity, joining resistance groups, stealing food or doing anything else that led to survival. It was on this microlevel that the fundamental and continuous interaction of the Jews took place with the forces at work on the 'Final Solution'. It is on this microlevel that Jewish reactions and initiatives must be examined and integrated in a comprehensive history. At this microlevel a large proportion of the events is a history of individuals.[25]

## III

At first glance, it seems, therefore, that the two approaches have nothing in common; that Hilberg's structuralism and Friedländer's integrated history are different, even contradictory concepts of the historiography of the Holocaust. And yet they are both confronted with a problem which is usually neglected by most other Holocaust historians: the problem of finding a language, an idiom to write about the Holocaust.

When Alfons Söllner – in an interview in 1988 – asked Raul Hilberg about George Steiner's statement, according to which German is the only language to speak about the Holocaust, Hilberg agreed:

> Isn't it evident that one would miss the atmosphere, the feeling for what has occurred if one moves away from the German language? Writing protocol instead of *Niederschrift* sounds very different. Perhaps there's no solution to the dilemma, because if I use the term *Niederschrift* someone could accuse me of not writing *about* National Socialism but of writing in a National Socialist idiom. But by using the actually usual term protocol I missed the atmosphere then. And that's only an example for one word. This dilemma continues for the sentences and the whole mode of speaking.[26]

Hilberg denominated the difference subtly. Using contemporary terms does not necessarily mean writing in a National Socialist idiom. He himself, although trying to keep very close to the German original terms, has never been accused of writing about the destruction of the European Jews in the perpetrators' idiom. Although carefully camouflaged, Hilberg's emotions are still visible in his texts.

Friedländer, too, has this subtle sense for the problem of how to speak about the Holocaust. At the end of the famous Stuttgart conference in 1984 about the decision-making in the process of the "Final Solution," he drew the attention of the audience to the problem that debating the Holocaust in a scholarly manner cannot detract from the fact that what is being discussed is mass murder. Talking about mass murder in an abstract manner must necessarily cause a profound emotional dissonance. And even a sober scholarly language has to be considered as inappropriate and inadequate when debating about mass murder:

> I take as an example Mr Broszat's essay on the genesis of the Final Solution. It says here: On such and such a day the Lange Commando comes to Chelmno and starts to build facilities of mass executions. There are two parts here. On such and such a day the Lange Commando came to a town. And any specialist will ask himself immediately (and that is why we had this debate): Was it that day or the next? But that is normal, that is the normal scientific way. One asks: Was it Lange or somebody else? But then the sentence goes on: and starts to build facilities for mass executions. I know no other literature that contains such sentences. One comes to a place and one starts to build. That is normal and our brain normally continues in a normal, that is, neutral manner. It isn't possible to switch suddenly in the middle of a sentence from the neutral to the emotional. The

Lange Commando came on this day and started to build facilities for mass executions. In this sentence you have two worlds, and yet it's only one sentence.[27]

The question of the emotions in writing history, particularly the history of mass crimes, has exercised historians time and again. In an interview Friedländer warns us against piling horror scenes on horror scenes in order to achieve an emotional effect. In clear opposition to such an instrumentalized method of writing that uses emotions calculatedly to captivate the reader by means of the text, Friedländer traces the true emotions in history, without trying either to conceal or to instrumentalize them, but in order to make them known. Friedländer does not avoid the emotions; rather he confronts them and comes to terms with them. It is probably not a coincidence that he is one of the few historians who have intensively studied psychoanalysis and the nature of historical knowledge.[28]

In contrast, Raul Hilberg concentrates entirely on the official documents of the Holocaust. In his book *Sources of Holocaust Research: An Analysis* (2001) he once more unfolds his detailed knowledge of the administrative apparatus that carried out the extermination of millions of people, describing accurately the differences between laws, directives, decrees and orders of the German administration. Although Hilberg concentrates on the documents of the perpetrators, because he wants to demonstrate the process of destruction, the emotions and suffering do not disappear from his writing. The despair of Adam Czerniaków, President of the Jewish Council in Warsaw, who committed suicide in July 1942 after receiving the instructions of the Germans for the deportation of the Jews to the extermination camp of Treblinka and realizing that there was no way out, is also conveyed by the sober matter-of-fact language of Hilberg. And Hilberg's style becomes equally bitter and sarcastic when it comes to the perpetrators' own statements. More than any other historian Hilberg is a master at using the perpetrators' documents, without falling victim to their language or their rhetoric of legitimization.

Nevertheless, he advances some skeptical objections of principle to the memories of survivors. It is essential, he claims, that the survivors were not a random sample, in statistical and economic terms, of the Jewish communities that were destroyed. They differed in their physical condition, their social background and qualities such as a sense of reality, decisiveness or self-confidence, which allowed them to survive. Accordingly, their testimonies were not representative of the possible testimonies from Jewish communitiees in general. But even the reports as such were sometimes far from being an exhaustive reproduction of the events because the witnesses missed important details and were only able to remember certain things in retrospect.[29]

Hilberg's skepticism reiterates the objections that are often raised to Oral History. But it is difficult to see why the official sources he regards as valid and authoritative should not show the same shortcomings as the testimonies of survivors. In the official documents, too, there is a shortage of detail, the overview is lost and events are considered from the point of view of one institution, or indeed one bureaucrat. In both cases a scientific critique of sources is indispensable. And yet, the testimonies of survivors contain a specific, individual view of the events which makes them so valuable for historiography. It is only in them that we can recognize the experiences, the suffering, and the emotions of the persecuted that do not emerge from the documents of the persecutors. In them alone, too, do we realise that the victims were by no means passively suffering objects in the hands of their persecutors, but tried to escape the deadly situation, to make it more bearable or at least to preserve their own dignity. Friedländer's claim that at every stage of the persecution Jewish perceptions and reactions, whether collective or individual, were inseparable parts of the history is not refuted by reference to the inevitable murder.

"Up to this point," Friedländer writes, "the individual voice has been mainly perceived as a trace, a trace left by the Jews that bears witness to and confirms and illustrates their fate." But in his book these voices play a very different part. "By its very nature, by dint of its humanness and freedom, an individual voice suddenly arising in the course of an ordinary historical narrative of events [...] can tear through seamless interpretation and pierce the (mostly involuntary) smugness of scholarly detachment and 'objectivity.'"[30]

By including the voices of the persecuted as an indispensable element in his approach to the history of the Shoah, Friedländer not only widens the perspective, he arrives at an integrated history of the Holocaust. He also alters the position of the historian, who does not analyze world events with the presumption of the authorial narrator from a secure observation post, but rather exposes himself to what the voices talk about and how they talk about it. These events, says Friedländer, represent "a constant source of bewilderment – a bewilderment that arises on the first confrontation with the Shoah from the depth of one's own immediate understanding of the world, which determines the perception of what is 'normal' and what remains 'incredible': a reaction that occurs before knowledge arrives to suppress it."[31]

This approach to writing about the Shoah also changes the readers. In the reviews of *The Years of Extermination 1939-1945* Friedländer has been widely praised for making the voices of the victims heard. It is said that he does not describe a nameless suffering but the fate of concrete people. However justified the praise, it hides an important difference. Friedländer personally heard the voices of the persecuted people he brings back to life in his books. He recalls their tone and he knows what they said. We do not. Our knowledge of the Holocaust lacks this dimension of the survivor's memory. Friedländer often revisited the problem of how historiography changes when the witnesses, primarily the Jewish witnesses, are no longer alive. But – such is the art of writing history as Friedländer, perhaps above all others, achieved it – we will, when we read his books, be able to surmise what these voices are talking about:

Each of us perceives the impact of the individual voice differently, and each person is differently challenged by the unexpected 'cries and whispers' that time and again compel us to stop in our tracks. A few incidental reflections about already well-known events may suffice, either due to their powerful eloquence or their helpless clumsiness; often the immediacy of a witness's cry of terror, of despair, or of unfounded hope may trigger our emotional reaction and shake our prior and well-protected representation of extreme historical events.[32]

## IV

The differences between Hilberg's and Friedländer's perspectives on the Holocaust are evident. Emphasizing the role of the perpetrators as a "key" and the perpetrators' view as the "primary path," as Hilberg put it in his memoirs, is much different from Friedländer's approach to the Shoah as an integrated history. But both, Hilberg as well as Friedländer, agree on the dilemma posed by the question of how to speak about the Holocaust, how to find a language, an idiom to describe and analyze what has happened. Their answers are certainly different. Hilberg wanted to keep close to the original German terms, whereas Friedländer aims at making the voices of the persecuted Jews heard. Yet both had the sense that words are, if not inadequate, able to communicate only a fragmentary dimension of what has happened, and in the case of the persecution and extermination of the European Jews this epistemological insight is valid in a particular way.

When receiving the Peace Prize of the German Book Trade in 2007, Saul Friedländer said at the end of his acceptance speech, in which he had referred to the personal documents of his own family:

> Sixty years have elapsed since these voices and countless similar ones were heard. And yet, the passage of time notwithstanding, they touch us with an unusual power and immediacy that resonate far beyond the borders of the Jewish community and have moved vast segments and successive generations of Western society. In listening to these cries we are not facing some ritualized memory, nor are we being manipulated by commercial renditions of the events. Rather, these individual voices shake us due to the naïve unawareness of the victims regarding their fate while many around them knew the outcome and, at times, were involved in its implementation. Mainly, however, the voices of those facing extermination reach us to this very day precisely because of their utter helplessness, their innocence and the solitude of their despair. The voices reach us beyond all reasoning, as they tear apart and put in question ever anew the belief in the existence of a human solidarity.[33]

The history of the Shoah is, among other things, the history of the loss of certainty. With Auschwitz the promise of historical progress and self-perfectibility held out by modernity vanished and it was revealed what human beings were and are capable of. All the standards of civilization – legal justice, reason, morality, autonomy, self-determination – on which bourgeois society rightly prided itself failed the moment they would have been needed in the twentieth century. Not one boundary of civilization barred the mass murder; the dynamic of radicalism was only occasionally slowed down by the difficulties created by the National Socialists themselves. Even religion was unable to recognize the monstrous blasphemy of the apotheosis of the racist perpetrators, which would have made a determined resistance a downright Christian duty.

Hilberg was also very much aware of this break in civilization. Contrary to the current desire to overcome disagreements, to reconcile former opponents, for a certain non-Jewish-Jewish *oikoumene* in the historiography of the Holocaust, his life and work are pervaded by an infinite and incurable sadness. This sadness connects his own existence with the research topic that has become his central purpose and without which neither the one nor the other can be understood.

In his memoirs he quoted a letter about his book *Destruction of the European Jews* written in 1962 by Hans G. Adler, the survivor of Theresienstadt and author of important studies about the ghetto and the deportation of the German Jews. "Reading that thirty-year-old letter," Hilberg noted, "I felt as though Adler had peered directly into the core of my being." This is what Adler had written about Hilberg:

> No one until now has seen and formulated the total horrible process so clearly. [...] What moves me in this book is the hopelessness of the author, who was born in 1926, and who came to the United States before the war, surely from Germany to which he returned at the end of the war with the US Army. In 1948 Hilberg began his work. Therefore he already has the viewpoint of a generation, which does not feel itself affected directly, but which looked at these events from afar, bewildered, bitter and embittered, accusing and critical, not only vis-à-vis the Germans (who else?), but also the Jews and all the nations which looked on. At the end nothing remains but despair and doubt about everything, because for Hilberg there is only recognition, perhaps also a grasp, but certainly no understanding.[34]

Despite the necessary scholarly distance to the events, the imperative self-criticism, and the rationality there is still a horror, a dismay – in the German context Friedländer uses the term *Fassungslosigkeit* – which could neither be abolished nor enclosed. And it may be that by this sense for the inadequacy of idioms to talk about the Holocaust, even in a scholarly language, Hilberg and Friedländer have more in common than the first glance might suggest.

*Notes*

1  Translated from German by Ladislaus Loeb.
2  Raul Hilberg, *The Politics of Memory: The Journey of a Holocaust Historian* (Chicago: Ivan R. Dee, Chicago, 1996), 57.
3  Ibid., 56.
4  Hans Rosenberg, "Rückblick auf ein Historikerleben zwischen zwei Kulturen," in Rosenberg, *Machteliten und Wirtschaftskonjunkturen. Studien zur neueren deutschen Sozial- und Wirtschaftsgeschichte* (Göttingen: Vandenhoeck & Ruprecht, 1978), 11–23, here 21.

5   Hilberg, *The Politics of Memory*, 58.

6   Ibid., 62–3.

7   Harald Welzer (ed.), *Auf den Trümmern der Geschichte. Gespräche mit Raul Hilberg, Hans Mommsen und Zygmunt Baumann* (Tübingen: Edition diskord, 1999), 36.

8   Raul Hilberg, *The Destruction of the European Jews* (3rd ed.). (New Haven and London: Yale University Press, 2003), vol. 3, 1060–61.

9   Hilberg, *The Politics of Memory*, 61–2.

10  Ibid., 75.

11  Ibid., 68.

12  Raul Hilberg, *Gehorsam oder Initiative? Zur arbeitsteiligen Täterschaft im Nationalsozialismus.* Beitrag zum Internationalen Hearing, 23.-25. Oktober 1991, Frankfurt am Main, Arbeitsstelle zur Vorbereitung des Frankfurter Lern- und Dokumentationszentrums des Holocaust, Frankfurt am Main 1991.

13  Martin Broszat, "A Plea for the Historicization of National Socialism," in Peter Baldwin (ed.), *Reworking the Past: Hitler, the Holocaust and the Historians' Debate* (Boston, Beacon Press, 1990), 77–87, here 82.

14  Ibid., 87.

15  Saul Friedländer, "Some Reflections on the Historicization of National Socialism," in Baldwin (ed.), *Reworking the Past*, 88–101; cf. Jörn Rüsen, "The Logic of Historicization: Metahistorical Reflections on the Debate between Friedländer and Broszat," in Gulie Ne'eman-Arad (ed.), *Passing into History: Nazism and the Holocaust beyond Memory: In Honor of Saul Friedländer on His Sixty-Fifth Birthday* [*History & Memory* 9 (1997)]: 113–45.

16  Friedländer was alluding to Andreas Hillgruber's book, *Zweierlei Untergang*, published in 1986, in which Hillgruber explicitly adopted the point of view of a *Wehrmacht* officer who defended Germany against the Red Army in 1945 in full knowledge of the fact that this was facilitating the continuing murders by the regime.

17  Martin Broszat and Saul Friedländer, "A Controversy about the Historicization of National Socialism," *New German Critique* 44 (1988): 85–126, here 90.

18  Saul Friedländer, "Ein Briefwechsel, fast 20 Jahre später," in Norbert Frei (ed.), *Martin Broszat, der "Staat Hitlers" und die Historisierung des Nationalsozialismus* (Göttingen: Wallstein Verlag, 2007), 188–94, here 193.

19  Saul Friedländer, *Den Holocaust beschreiben: Auf dem Weg zu einer integrierten Geschichte* (Göttingen: Wallstein Verlag, 2007), 7.

20  Ibid., 11.

21  Saul Friedländer, *The Years of Extermination: Nazi Germany and the Jews 1939–1945*, vol. II (London: Harper Perennial, 2008), xxiv–xxv.

22  Cf. Steve Aschheim, "On Saul Friedländer," *History & Memory* 9 (1997): 11–46.

23  Friedländer, *Den Holocaust beschreiben*, 18.

24  Saul Friedländer and Jan Philipp Reemtsma, *Gebt der Erinnerung Namen: Zwei Reden* (Munich: C. H. Beck, 1999), 19.

25  Friedländer, *Den Holocaust beschreiben*, 14.

26  Raul Hilberg and Alfons Söllner, "Das Schweigen zum Sprechen bringen. Ein Gespräch über Franz Neumann und die Entwicklung der Holocaust-Forschung," in Dan Diner (ed.), *Zivilisationsbruch: Denken nach Auschwitz* (Frankfurt am Main: Fischer-Verlag, 1988), 175–200, here 193–4.

27  Quoted in Eberhard Jäckel and Jürgen Rohwer (eds), *Der Mord an den Juden im Zweiten Weltkrieg. Entschlußbildung und Verwirklichung* (Stuttgart: Deutsche Verlagsanstalt, 1985), 243.

28  See Saul Friedländer, *History and Psychoanalysis: An Inquiry into Possibilities and Limits of Psychohistory* (New York: Holmes & Meier, 1978).

29  Raul Hilberg, *Sources of Holocaust Research: An Analysis* (Chicago: Ivan R. Dee, 2001), 48–9.

30  Friedländer, *The Years of Extermination*, xxv–xxvi.

31  Friedländer, *Den Holocaust beschreiben*, 25–6.

32  Friedländer, *The Years of Extermination*, xxv–xxvi. As a result Hans Rolf Vaget described the concern for remembrance as the point of Friedländer's entire work; see Hans Rudolf Vaget, "Saul Friedländer und die Zukunft der Erinnerung," in Dieter Borchmeyer und Helmuth Kiesel (eds),

*Das Judentum im Spiegel seiner kulturellen Umwelten: Symposium zu Ehren von Saul Friedländer* (Neckargmünd: Edition Mnemosyne, 2002), 11–32.

33 Friedenpreis des Deutschen Buchhandels/Peace Prize of the German Book Trade 2007, ed. Börsenverein des Deutschen Buchhandels (Frankfurt am Main: MVB Verlag, 2007), 77.

34 Hilberg, *Politics of Memory*, 202–3.

PART II

*German Society and Redemptive Antisemitism*

# 7

# National Socialism, Antisemitism and the "Final Solution"

*Peter Pulzer*

It might seem strange, even perverse, to ask, more than sixty years after the event, about the connection between Nazi antisemitism and the Shoah. Yet the sources of Nazi ideology were numerous, the policy-making process of the Third Reich was unsystematic and both the means and ends of Nazi policies were subject to continuous disputes, personal rivalries and turf wars within the counsels of the régime. To this day there is less than complete certainty about who issued which order when, though I think we have got quite close to a plausible idea on this topic. Even more contentious – and it is here that Saul Friedländer's contribution is central to the debate – is the question of what motivated the perpetrators, the indirect collaborators, the bystanders and the resisters. How wide and how deep was support for Nazi antisemitism in general and for genocide in particular, both among the German population and in the rest of Nazi-occupied Europe?

The ideology of the Nazi movement had a number of sources which over-lapped, but need to be considered separately. The primary source was racism, a form of biological determinism that became increasingly influential in the late nineteenth century. It established a hierarchy of races in which the North-West European ("Aryan") nations occupied the highest rank. A second source related to, and derived from this doctrine was racial antisemitism. Antisemitism or Judaeophobia was, of course, much older, but it was the modern race-based variety without which Nazi policies and Nazi actions cannot be understood. A third source was cultural and social anti-modernism: a dislike of urban, especially metropolitan lifestyles, cosmopolitanism, political individualism, democracy in domestic politics and internationalism in foreign affairs. The fourth was a continental imperialism, first formulated by pre-1914 pressure groups like the Pan-German League and prominent in the debate on war aims during the First World War. The fifth was resentment at the outcome of that war, whether at the "stab in the back" in 1918 by civilian politicians who realized that the war was lost or at the terms of the Versailles Peace Treaty.

Interpretations of history and politics based on theories of racial superiority and inferiority were gaining in popularity before 1914 and even more in the 1920s. In Germany and Austria they acquired respectability through semi-academic circles, like the "political anthropologists" around Ludwig Woltmann and Ludwig Wilser and even more through best-selling charlatans like Houston Stewart Chamberlain, author of *The Foundations of the Nineteenth Century*. The appeal of such theories was not restricted to the German-speaking countries. In France and Britain they were useful in justifying imperialism; in the United States they served as an argument for racial segregation and restrictions on immigration. Not all nineteenth-century racialist publicists were antisemites. The founder of modern racial theorizing, Count Gobineau, was primarily interested in establishing the inferiority of the "Yellow" race to the "White" and of the "Black" to both; indeed he admired Jews – erroneously – for having preserved their racial purity: "[T]his is a powerful race, which merits all the respect that we owe to strength."[1] Later racialists, however, were almost without exception antisemites and an increasing number were primarily so. That was true particularly in Germany, where the recent creation of the empire had failed to solve questions of national identity, and in German Austria, where the traditional hegemony of the German-speaking group was threatened by non- and anti-German nationalisms.

The combination of racialism and antisemitism was all the more attractive to political agitators, since dislike and, indeed, hatred of Jews had long been embedded in the mentalities of many Europeans. Traditionally the motives for these sentiments had been religious and commercial; they were facilitated by laws that almost everywhere discriminated to a greater or lesser extent against Jews, whether in the form of ghettoization, or exclusion from certain occupations or forms of property ownership, and which therefore lent legitimacy to the treatment of Jews as separate and inferior. There were therefore few obstacles to a merging of inherited Judaeophobia and the newer racialism. Indeed the various categories of, and motivations for, Jew-hatred were never strictly separated. Religious rejection, economic resentment and racial prejudices could co-exist in the same person and the same movement. In the rhetoric of antisemitic agitators the various categories were frequently combined and muddled, which helped to maximize the appeal of the message of prejudice. However, for political movements whose starting point was the concept of race the distinctions were crucial. Hitler was in no doubt about this. He admired the Christian Social Mayor of Vienna, Karl Lueger, for his success in mobilizing a mass following with antisemitic slogans, but faulted him for his traditionalist Catholic and pro-Habsburg proclivities. Ideologically he identified with the other major figure of Austrian antisemitism, Georg von Schönerer, who was politically less successful, but understood the primacy of race. In so far as antisemitism was a factor in the popular appeal of Nazism, this lay *both* in the eclecticism with which it portrayed the Jew as the enemy, *and* in the insistence that the "Jewish Question" was a biological one.

The anti-modernist component of the Nazi movement's sources is more complex. It simply will not do to assert that Nazism is explained by a rejection of the modern world. Much in the armoury of the European far Right was highly modern. The idea of nationalism was modern, that of race, with its appeal to the authority of science, even more so. So was the political mobilization of the masses and the exploitation of mass media. Above all, both National Socialism and Italian Fascism proclaimed themselves to be agents of renewal, regeneration and rebirth. They were future-oriented as well as backward-looking, unlike other movements of the European far Right, such as the *Action Française* or the Austrian *Heimwehr*. What was anti-modern was firstly an aversion to the *avant-garde* in the arts and in some instances also the sciences, for example, theories of relativity or of quantum mechanics, but above all to the message of liberty, equality and fraternity and the entire legacy of the Enlightenment and of the French Revolution. The anti-Western and anti-Enlightenment outlook achieved a near-consensus among German nationalist thinkers in the second half of the nineteenth century. Heinrich von Treitschke, for instance, boasted of Germany's pioneering role in "overcoming the *Weltanschauung* of the eighteenth century"[2] and in 1914 no less a figure than Thomas Mann popularized the distinction between German culture and French civilization and between the German soul and French reason.[3] The rejection of Enlightenment values grew even more emphatic in the interwar period, intensified by the "Western" constitutions of the Weimar and Austrian Republics. The Catholic publicist Anton Orel saw in the newly established Austrian democracy no more than "our miserable Jew republic."[4] For Edgar Jung, one of the principal theorists of the "conservative revolution," "Versailles and Geneva [i.e. the League of Nations] are the symbols of the victory of 1789 [...] Weimar and Versailles are the guarantees of the Central European defeat and the Western European victory."[5] It should therefore not surprise us that Joseph Goebbels felt justified in telling the German people on the well-chosen date of 1 April 1933 that with the Nazi accession to power "the year 1789 is being expunged from history."[6] This disavowal of Liberal and Enlightenment values was not restricted to the German-speaking countries; according to the article 'La dottrina del Fascismo' in the *Enciclopedia Italiana* of 1932, Fascism rejected "the flabby, materialistic positivism of the nineteenth century, all Jacobin utopias [...] and universal concord."

The aesthetic conservatism of the Right was satirized by Carl von Ossietzky:

> When the conductor Klemperer takes different tempi from his colleague Furtwängler, when a painter uses a colour for a sunset that one cannot see in Lower Pomerania even in clear daylight, when one favours birth control, when one builds a house with a flat roof, when the physicist Einstein insists that the principle of the constant speed of light is valid only in the absence of gravity, [...], that is 'cultural bolshevism.' The democratic principles of the brothers Mann or a composition and Hindemith and Kurt Weill – that is 'cultural Bolshevism.'[7]

There was some difference in this respect between the National Socialist and Italian Fascist régimes; the latter being more willing to embrace aspects of modernism in both literature and design, and even in the Third Reich there were ambiguities and inconsistencies,[8] but the direction was unmistakable.

What marked much of Europe in the interwar period was a trend already noticeable before 1914, namely a disillusionment with the values and institutions of Liberalism. This put the concepts of democracy, equality before the law, international conciliation, market economics, aspirations to progress and faith in scientific rationality at a discount. While these beliefs affected only a minority of politicians, publicists and academic thinkers before the First World War, whether in Germany or elsewhere, they acquired near-hegemony in the 1920s and even more so after the Great Depression. In 1920 almost all European states had democratic or at least parliamentary constitutions. In 1938 this was true of only eleven out of twenty-seven, of which only one, Czechoslovakia, was a "post-Versailles" state. All the others had possessed firm and stable parliamentary institutions before 1914. The principles of national self-determination proclaimed by Woodrow Wilson had turned sour. The doctrine of nationalism, originally emancipatory and universalistic, had increasingly become an instrument of exclusion, intolerance, even persecution. More and more the nation came to be defined by who did not belong to it. Those who did not belong were in many cases the Jews, a people without territory who therefore fitted no blood-and-soil message and were suspect as agents of cosmopolitanism, economic and social mobility and subversion. Not all nationalists became antisemites or fascists, but one can see the connection. Thus the "Man from Mars," challenged to identify the dominant values of Europe in 1938, or even 1933, would have had to reply: authoritarianism, chauvinism, militarism and intolerance.

This was the context in which National Socialism gained power in Germany, with Adolf Hitler as chancellor. What was the causal connection between the ideological trends we have outlined and the practices of the régime between 1933 and 1945? There are three points to be made here by way of guidance. The first is that one did not have to be a Nazi to accept some or all of the political beliefs outlined above. This had both advantages and drawbacks for the NSDAP. It meant that its potential constituency was wide, well beyond its own core following, but also risked being shallow. The number of potential NSDAP sympathisers was therefore at all times much larger than the reliably committed. The second point is that, especially in the crisis years of 1930–3, many Germans might be tempted to support the NSDAP without paying any attention to the party's programmatic platform. They could be attracted by Hitler's charisma, by the prospect of strong leadership, by the hope of economic recovery or simply the conclusion that since all else had failed one might as well gamble on the unknown. Such motivations could produce a landslide in votes, but were not a secure basis for later support of the régime's more extreme policies. That leaves the third – the central question of this volume: where does antisemitism fit into all this?

The Nazis did not invent antisemitism, nor even racial antisemitism. German and Austrian antisemitism in its various guises has a long history, but as a phenomenon in modern politics, as an organized movement, with membership structures, candidates for public office and a newspaper and periodical press it dates from the 1870s.[9] It was then that formal civil equality for Jews was enacted (in Austria in 1867, in Germany in 1869) and a public sphere based on a mass electorate – one that could be mobilized against this civil equality – came into being in both Empires. While much of the new antisemitism took the form of expressive rather than instrumental politics, serving to articulate resentments and prejudices, rather than to propose real solutions to real problems, it created a continuity of associations, parties and personnel that reached into the twentieth century and in some instances beyond 1933. The link between all these bodies was a desire to reverse Jewish emancipation. The manifestos of almost all German antisemitic parties in the period of the Empire demanded the status of aliens for the Jewish population and either a quota for Jews, or their complete exclusion from certain professions, such as medicine, law, higher education and the civil service, and a ban on immigration. After 1918 even the Austrian Christian Social Party, whose antisemitism had up to then been primarily economic and cultural, joined the demand for alien status.[10] Often the calls consisted of quite unspecific slogans. Georg von Schönerer, the most extreme of Austrian antisemites, demanded "the removal of Jewish influence from all areas of public life,"[11] while the German Conservative Party committed itself in 1892 to "combat[ing] the widely obtruding and decomposing Jewish influence on our popular life."[12] In many ways this empty rhetoric was more influential than the explicit proposals of fringe parties, by simply spreading the notion that Jews *qua* Jews were different, inferior, undesirable and not entitled to the equal protection of the law. One therefore sees why it suited the Nazi party to combine the traditional inherited components of antisemitism with the racial variety. If the "Jewish Question" could be shown to be a biological one, then it could not be solved by conventional political means such as negotiation, compromise or rational argument within the framework of the law.

The uncompromising character of Nazi antisemitism and indeed of the Nazi attitude to the entire political process meant that its campaigning was inseparable from violence. The rhetoric of Nazism was filled with references to struggle and combat. Not for nothing were stormtroopers called stormtroopers. Nazi violence fitted the more polarized and extreme politics of the postwar period with its street terror and assassinations. It was, however, as much a cause as a symptom of the breakdown of a pacific civil society, since violence was as much the movement's *raison d'être* as a means to an end. Terror and violence directed against Jews came almost exclusively from the extreme Right, initially from the *Deutschvölkischer Trutz- und Schutzbund*, an offshoot of the Pan-German League, until it was banned in 1922; thereafter from the SA and other Nazi-affiliated bodies. Jews were not the only victims. Terror was also directed against the political Left, the Polish minority and some Catholic organizations; indeed in the final years of the Weimar Republic it was Communists, Social Democrats and trade unionists who were the principal targets.[13] In terms of threats and denunciations, however, it was the antisemitic message that was the most uncompromising and the most extreme. Anyone who doubts this needs only to turn to the references to "the Jew" (*der Jude*) and "Jewry" (*das Judentum*) in *Mein Kampf*, the *Völkischer Beobachter*, Goebbels's *Der Angriff* or Streicher's *Der Stürmer*.

The violence that the Nazi movement preached and practised was both a recruiting device and a prophecy. It based its justificatory appeal on the concept of the *Volksgemeinschaft* or national community, which had gained increasing popularity during and after the First World War. In its evocation of a patriotic spirit that transcended class, religion or other special interests the concept could be used in both an inclusive and exclusive sense.[14] In the mouths of democratic politicians it implied equal citizenship; employed by the Right and especially the Nazis it proclaimed separateness and discrimination. Assaults on Jewish citizens, calls for boycotts of Jewish businesses and vandalism directed at Jewish religious installations and cemeteries had a dual purpose: to intimidate the Jewish population and to proclaim that such acts were a legitimate and indeed praiseworthy way of strengthening the true, racially defined *Volk*: a form of "self-empowerment," to quote Michael Wildt's formulation,[15] that flourished all the more in the immediate aftermath of Hitler's assumption of power and, in an even more extreme form, in Austria after the *Anschluß*. Whereas in the late nineteenth century the nation had come to be defined by who did not belong to it, in the 1920s and 1930s it was *Volksgemeinschaft* that came to be defined in terms of outsiders (*Volksfremde*, aliens to the people) who could be humiliated, plundered and – ultimately – murdered.[16] It is this project of purging the nation's body of Jews to create a purified core that led Saul Friedländer to launch the concept of "redemptive anti-Semitism."[17] It constitutes a major contribution to our understanding of the place of Jew-hatred in the Nazis' palingenetic scheme and has found echoes in much of the subsequent literature. As reformulated by Dominick LaCapra, in a direct reference to Friedländer, the Jew "was a polluter or contaminant in the *Volksgemeinschaft* that had to be eliminated for the Aryan people to reach its purity and wholeness."[18] Giving an even greater reach to the Nazis' regeneratively-inspired destruction, Stephen Eric Bronner claims that "the pathological undertaking was universal in its intentions and the radicalism of its eschatological aims."[19] As with other Nazi slogans, however, it meant one thing to the faithful and something else to the man in the street. While for Hitler the concept entailed "the racial-social cleansing of the people's body" and was "a precondition for a racial-imperialist expansion of power," for "broad sections of the population, including the working class, it seemed to be credible and even attractive" as a metaphor for social reconciliation.[20]

So much for the character of Nazi antisemitism. The question remains: what role did it play as a vote-getter for the NSDAP, as a guarantee for its subsequent popularity or indeed as a glue for its cohesion? The evidence on this is sketchy and in part circumstantial. The greater the Nazis' electoral successes following the onset of the Great Depression, the more their campaign rhetoric concentrated on other, more promising themes. Antisemitism was also an obstacle to a firm alliance with big business. The Ruhr industrialist Emil Kirdorf was not alone in seeing the type of antisemitism preached by the Nazis, with its overtones of economic populism, as a threat to the rights of property.[21] In the course of his crucial two-and-a half-hour speech to the Industry Club of Düsseldorf on 26 January 1932 Hitler "did not utter the word 'Jew' once."[22]

For the state of opinion inside the Nazi movement we have one valuable set of documents: the 683 autobiographical essays of "little Nazis" collected in 1934 by the Columbia University sociologist Theodore Abel, of which 581 have survived. The essays were re-evaluated some forty years later by the political scientist Peter Merkl of Santa Barbara. They do not constitute a scientific sample; the respondents are self-selected and may have been encouraged, or discouraged, by the units to which they belonged. The authors do not, however, appear to have engaged in self-censorship to any significant degree. As Merkl notes, "They are astonishingly candid about their hatreds and their violence [...] They had won their battle for utopia and their hearts were filled with the urge to tell their stories exactly as they perceived them." Nor would they have had a motive to conceal their prejudices. It is a characteristic of those whom we think of as extremists that they regard their views as unexceptionable, indeed normal: "sincerity and self-righteousness are literally the hallmark of bigots of every stripe."[23] What then, do they reveal? Analyzing the total sample for antisemitic content, Merkl notes that 33.3 per cent volunteer no antisemitic opinions, while 12.9 per cent show a preoccupation with "the Jewish conspiracy," the remainder displaying various shades of prejudice.[24] These respondents were not average citizens or unattached swing voters, but men who had made a conscious decision to join a Nazi organization before 1 January 1933. Within these overall averages there were significant variations. Office-holders in the party held the strongest prejudices; the higher the rank held in the party, the SA or the SS, the stronger the antisemitism. "The prominence of the political antisemites in this area in spite of their patent mania clearly heralded the course of the Third Reich."[25] Another significant discriminator was age. The youngest recruits, those brought in by the Depression, were less ideologically formed and therefore less imbued with antisemitism than those who had been politicized by the traumatic years 1918–23, when they experienced defeat, attempted revolution, the Kapp *putsch*, inflation and the French occupation of the Ruhr. Many in that group had begun their political careers in other formations of the extreme Right, such as the *Deutschvölkischer Schutz- und Trutzbund*, the *Freikorps* and the various other racist parties that faded away in the course of the 1920s. What motivated the majority of Abel's respondents was the more general message of the NSDAP – hatred of or contempt for the "Marxist-liberal" Republic, revanchism, national rebirth, the leadership cult and *Volksgemeinschaft*. All of these beliefs were compatible with antisemitism and one can see why those who held them could either come to accept the validity of Nazi antisemitism or see no reason for rejecting it. The range of ideological preferences among Nazi followers does, however, also show that the leadership's own obsessions were not always the main reason for the loyalty of the régime's supporters or servants. This becomes important when we consider one of Friedländer's main themes, the question as to why the genocidal policies of the Third Reich appeared to command such widespread assent, or at least so little outright opposition.

No-one living in Germany from 1933 could be in any doubt about the antisemitic character and intentions of the régime. All the rhetoric and the violence of the previous years were intensified, now with impunity. Many of the régime's other aims were expressed in antisemitic terms. The "Law for the Restoration of a Professional Civil Service," designed to provide a blanket authority for a general purge, targeted Jews disproportionately, since civil servants with left-wing associations were in many cases also Jews. The book burnings, the closure of that ultimate flat-roofed monstrosity, the *Bauhaus*, and the exhibition of "degenerate art" were all proclaimed as blows against the "un-German," that is, Jewish spirit, although the works of Erich Kästner and Erich Maria Remarque were consigned to the flames along with those of Sigmund Freud and Albert Einstein. Nor did it matter that Walter Gropius, Ludwig Mies van der Rohe and most of the prominent German Expressionists, Cubists, Surrealists and followers of the "New Objectivity" movement were impeccably "Aryan." The identification of "Jewish" and "degenerate" was already a common trope in the Weimar years, and had been institutionalized by Alfred Rosenberg in 1928 in the *Kampfbund für deutsche Kultur* (Combat League for German Culture).[26]

One feature of the early Nazi years that Friedländer stresses is the apparent calm acceptance, whether by the population generally or by influential elite organizations, such as universities or the churches, of the escalating measures of discrimination – a "total collapse" that he describes as "more than unusual." Unusual, but not that surprising, given that antisemitism, even if of the non-Nazi type, was well embedded in these institutions and that non-conformist writers, Jewish or not, were hastening to flee abroad. "The concrete situation of the Jews," Friedländer argues, "was a litmus test of how far any genuine moral principle could be silenced."[27] It was, indeed, and the ease with which disemancipation went through strongly suggests that there had never been a consensus within German society in favour of the legal equality laid down by the law and, after 1919, the constitution. But the Nazi régime was about more than depriving Jews of their rights. What happened in 1933–4 was the abolition of the entire system of the rule of law and of constitutional restraints on the executive, the banning of all political parties except the NSDAP and the absorption (*Gleichschaltung*) of trade unions, professional organizations and leisure associations into Nazi front bodies. That, too, went through with scarcely a protest. All these acts were, apparently, an acceptable price for the prospect of better times.

That brings us to the central question that Friedländer poses, that of the reciprocal relationship between the régime's antisemitism and public opinion. Here it will be helpful to observe the chronology of Friedländer's two volumes, *The Years of Persecution* of the peacetime years up to 1939 and *The Years of Extermination* under the shadow of war – six years of escalating discrimination and enforced emigration, followed by six of genocide. While the majority of the population treated the end of legal equality with at best indifference, the more spectacular instances of arbitrariness and violence went down badly. The call to boycott Jewish shops could mean pressure to break old habits, an unreasonable demand in the minds of more than a few citizens. Victor Klemperer records that his neighbors simply patronized more distant Jewish shops and pretended not to notice others doing the same.[28] As late as 1937 the population of rural Bavaria was written off as "ideologically unteachable" in this respect.[29] *Kristallnacht* was an even greater propaganda failure, even in Austria where, as had been shown at the time of the *Anschluß*, the taste for street pogroms was stronger than in the "old *Reich*." Reporting to his superiors, SS-*Hauptsturmführer* Trittner noted that "acquaintance with the details had a depressing effect on the general mood, thereby counteracting the initially favorable reception of the overall action."[30] The evidence seems to support the conclusions of Friedländer and Kershaw that "the bulk of the population disliked acts of violence but did not object to the disfranchisement and segregation of the Jews"[31] and that "the largely negative attitude of the population, especially in South Bavaria to the open violence of Nazi thugs [. . .] was perfectly compatible with broad approval of the anti-Jewish legislation passed at the Nuremberg Party Rally in September 1935."[32] Indeed, once segregation had the cover of legality, the average citizen could consider himself absolved from responsibility for its consequences.

Nazi policies were not conducted in a vacuum, either before 1939 or after. They were accompanied by a pervasive and technically sophisticated campaign of propaganda, carried out via the press, cinema, posters, public exhibitions and indoctrination courses for anyone recruited into the party, party-affiliated organizations and the armed forces. The propaganda served a general purpose and a particular one. The general purpose was simply to mobilize support for the regime and emphasize "national rebirth," whether on the basis of economic recovery, foreign policy successes or the *Führer*'s charisma. The particular purpose was to create political solidarity by isolating the enemy. More than ever *Volksgemeinschaft* was to be defined in terms of who did not belong; race was the basis of the Nazi social utopia.[33] Eastern and southern Europeans did not belong there, non-Whites certainly did not, except for Japanese, who were promoted to the status of "honorary Aryans." Enemies within included Gypsies, homosexuals, the "congenitally disabled" and those "unworthy of life," as well as assorted "asocials" – vagrants, alcoholics, habitual delinquents, prostitutes and the "work-shy." Jews, too, were by definition "asocial," not members of the *Volksgemeinschaft*. But they were more than that: unlike vagrants, pickpockets or Jehovah's Witnesses they were an evil, destructive force, an existential threat through the power they wielded. The "Jewish Question," as invented by the Nazis, was not merely a subset of their wider racial fantasies; it was "the core of their worldview."[34] While Hitler's obsessions pointed the direction of the régime's anti-Jewish measures, these should not be laid at his door alone. The "Law for the Protection of German Blood and Honor" (that is, the Nuremberg Law) was the brainchild of Dr Gerhard Wagner, the head of the *Reich* Doctors' Union; the confiscation of Jewish property was the province of Hermann Goering; the *Kristallnacht* was initiated by Joseph Goebbels and the deportation programme came under the ægis of Heinrich Himmler and Reinhard Heydrich. None of them could have acted without Hitler's encouragement and approval, but the "Final Solution" was a collective enterprise.

With the outbreak of the war the ideological pressure escalated. It was aimed at three targets: a domestic audience, to justify the war and blame the Jews for it; a military audience, to neutralize any misgivings soldiers might have about their tasks; and, especially as Nazi rule spread over Europe, the populations of the conquered territories, to reconcile them to their occupied status. In each case we need to ask: did the intention lead to the desired effect? As far as the domestic audience is concerned, there are two further questions: how did Germans on the home front react to the still increasing isolation of Jews from everyday life? And what did they know about deportations and genocide? On isolation there are two sources, neither of them entirely satisfactory. There are the SD reports for the Nazi authorities on public attitudes and there are the records and recollections of Jews remaining in Germany after the outbreak of war. The introduction of the yellow star for Jews in 1941, a deliberately public act, is as good a test as any of German reactions. Some SD reports speak of strong public approval, others of mixed responses. Some Jews experienced further humiliations, others covert or overt moral support.[35] But who were the SD's enthusiasts? Party members or ordinary people? And how representative were the experiences of those Jews who recorded them?

On the implementation of the "Final Solution" the rulers of the Third Reich tried to be as secretive as possible – deportations from Berlin started from the obscure suburban station of Grunewald – but this was a hopeless undertaking, given the scale of the operation. Nor could the details of the genocide be kept secret. Visits to the front by relatives, conversations with soldiers on leave and letters from the front broke the conspiracy of silence. The leaders' rhetoric did not conceal much either. Neither Hitler nor Goebbels hesitated to use the word "exterminate" (*ausrotten*) in their public speeches and Hitler repeatedly reverted to the threat of "the destruction of the Jewish race" he had first uttered in his speech of 30 January 1939. The war was routinely presented both as a Jewish assault on Germany and as a necessary all-out conflict against "World Jewry." The war against the Soviet Union was repeatedly declared to be against "Jewish Bolshevism"[36]; Britain's declaration of war on 3 September 1939 was the work of "our Jewish-democratic world enemy"; the declaration of war against the United States in the wake of Pearl Harbor was directed personally against Franklin D. Roosevelt "and the circle of Jews surrounding him" who wished to subject Europe to "another Purim."[37] Preparing the German army in the west for the expected Allied invasion, the *Nationalsozialistischer Führungsoffizier* warned: "Who is coming? The plutocratic masses of World Jewry. The Anglo-American without a mask, no whit better than the Bolshevik."[38]

Once the war had broken out, propaganda for the home front intensified further, through feature films, newsreels and wall newspapers, of which the weekly "Word of the Week" (*Parole der Woche. Parteiamtliche Wandzeitung der NSDAP*), with a print-run of 135,000, was the most important. Jeffrey Herf, who has examined these media in detail, concludes:

During World War II anyone in Nazi Germany who regularly read a newspaper, listened to the radio or walked past the Nazi political posters between 1941 and 1943 knew of the threats and boasts of the Nazi regime to exterminate European Jews, followed by public assertions that it was implementing that policy.[39]

Yet how many times can someone be told something on a topic he is not all that interested in before it really sinks in? Herf's verdict is distinctly skeptical:

> The material presented here does not resolve the issue of what most Germans knew or thought about the Holocaust, how they responded to the radical anti-Jewish discourse and images churned out by Nazi propaganda or how widespread radical antisemitism was in the Third Reich. The beginning of wisdom in these matters is a certain restraint and much less certainty regarding what 'ordinary Germans' made of Nazi propaganda.[40]

Does this confirm Kershaw's verdict of a quarter century ago that the Shoah "was built by hate, but powered by indifference"?[41] That verdict is valid only with some qualification. No doubt the fate of the Jews was far from the minds of most German civilians. Once the war had broken out, certainly once the Third Reich was engaged in total war, they had other matters on their minds: were they going to be bombed, would their rations be honored, would their husbands or sons return unscathed from the Eastern front? But their "passive complicity"[42] was made much easier by the physical isolation and relentless moral denigration of Jews in the course of the preceding decade. If the Nazi propaganda machine failed to manufacture mass hatred of the Jews, it succeeded in the lesser but nevertheless adequate objective of convincing the majority of Germans that Jews were exempt from considerations of human sympathy.

What applied to the home front applied less to those wearing a uniform. While genocide was initially delegated specifically to the task forces (*Einsatzgruppen*) of the SS and the security police (*Ordnungspolizei*), the *Wehrmacht* became increasingly implicated in the crimes of the Third Reich. The uniformed services were predictably manned by males of the younger age groups, many of whom had been socialized since 1933 and had all undergone indoctrination courses of varying intensity. Not all army commanders or ordinary soldiers cared for this aspect of their duties and some were actively disgusted. Captain Hosenfeld, who appears briefly at the end of the film *The Pianist*, became convinced that the murder of the Jews was "an inextinguishable stain for which we shall have to bear responsibility,"[43] but many letters from the front are quite open about mass atrocities, in either a coldly matter-of-fact or a chillingly sadistic manner, whether the victims described are Jews, "bandits" (that is, partisans, often conflated with Jews) or hostages.[44] While some of this can be attributed to the brutalizing effect of war or the pressures of camaraderie, the frequent references to Jews in Nazi ideological terms, suggest that the propaganda campaign was more successful here than when directed at civilians.

For the Nazi leadership the war against "Jewish Bolshevism" was not just a

German, but a Europe-wide crusade. The populations of conquered countries were therefore also wooed on behalf of this cause, initially with some success, as shown by levels of recruitment to the Waffen-SS. Defeatism, the temptations of collaboration, a shared antisemitism and/or anti-Communism and personal envy or greed lured at least some in occupied Europe to follow the Nazi pied piper. The willingness of ordinary Frenchmen to denounce and discriminate against their neighbours and of the Vichy authorities to do the Nazis' dirty work has been well-documented.[45] In parts of eastern Europe, where hatred of Jews and of Communism was more deeply implanted – in Latvia, Lithuania, Slovakia, Romania and Ukraine – the Nazis found an even greater willingness to help in their genocidal enterprise. This initial collaboration, however, soon lost its attractions. In France the reality of the round-ups, not only of foreign Jews but also of French citizens, culminating in the horrors of the *Vélodrome d'Hiver* in July 1942, were decisive in turning public opinion. Even before that Dr Helmut Knochen, the head of the SD in France, was forced to admit the "slight – or totally lacking – comprehension" of "large portions of the population" for the requirement to wear the yellow star.[46] Another factor was that though Jews might be disliked, in occupied Europe the persecutor of the Jews was also the oppressor of the nation. As resistance movements began to form, the Germans' task became even more difficult. In June 1944, following the Allied landings in Normandy, the German commandant in Paris, General Karl Heinrich von Stülpnagel, opposed the deportation of the remaining 40,000 Jews on the grounds that this would "create disquiet among the hitherto placid population."[47] In the end 75,000 French Jews perished in the Shoah, but three-quarters of French Jews survived.[48]

Even in the East support for the "Final Solution" was less than universal. The massacres at Babi Yar were too much for many inhabitants of Kiev.[49] Gunnar Paulsson has calculated that at one time or another some 28,000 Jews, or one in twelve of the prewar Jewish population of Warsaw, survived on the "Aryan" side of the city,[50] which would not have been possible without considerable non-Jewish help. However honorable and courageous these individual acts were, they could not make much impact on the total number of the murdered. They do, however, raise the question of how wide and how deeply "redemptive antisemitism" had penetrated into European consciousness.

Both in *The Years of Extermination* and in his lecture Friedländer pleads for "an integrated history" of the Shoah, that is, one based on a counterpoint of the Third Reich's policy-making processes and developments that are "internal to the community of victims." Friedländer succeeds brilliantly at the task he has set himself. There is surely no book that records so graphically the hopes, fears, illusions and desperate measures that characterized the office-holders of official and unofficial Jewish organizations and of ordinary individuals – grandmothers, heads of families, even children – from France to Ukraine and from Hungary to the Netherlands and relates them to each turn of the ever-tightening screw of Nazi oppression. There is, however, another dimension to understanding what happened and why so much of the entire Nazi enterprise, including the conquest of much of Europe, economic recovery, the mobilization of the German population behind Hitler and the régime of the Third Reich, was so close to success. For Friedländer "redemptive antisemitism" explains not only the internal cohesion of the Nazi movement, but also its reach to all those whose support it needed: "For a regime dependent on constant mobilization, the Jew served as the constant mobilizing myth."[51] The content of Nazi propaganda seems to confirm this assertion. That Hitler not only launched the figure of the Jew as "the metahistorical enemy"[52] but believed in it cannot be doubted. From his first recorded reference to Jews on 16 September 1919 – demanding, as the "ultimate aim" of a government of national strength "the removal of the Jews altogether"[53] – to his Political Testament, composed just before his suicide, in which he named "Jewry" as "the real criminal of this murderous struggle," this obsession defined his entire outlook, however much it suited him to tone it down from time to time for tactical reasons. "The tenacity to which he held to his dogmatic belief [...] is truly striking."[54] That his belief was shared by most of his immediate entourage, by many SS, SA and party members as well as at least some of his "willing executioners" is also well documented. But does it explain why the NSDAP leapt from 2.6 per cent of the vote in 1928 to 37.2 per cent in 1932? And is this obsessional belief the whole explanation for charisma that the *Führer* was able to exude, and for "the hysterical adoration and blind faith of so many for so long, that well after Stalingrad, [...] countless Germans still believed in his promises of victory'?[55]

There are two reasons for qualifying these verdicts. The *first* is that Hitler, like any other mortal, was not a complete master of events. He was able to exploit and exacerbate resentments and grievances, but not to create them – whether at the collapse of 1918, the burden of reparations, the inflation of 1923 and the harshness of the currency stabilization, the fear of Communism, the contempt for democracy and, above all, the Great Depression. Contingency as well as intention determined the course of Nazi fortunes and, with it, the prospects for a "Final Solution." Would we be holding our conference if the New York stock market had not crashed in 1929? The *second* is that the appeal of the Nazi Party, both before and after 1933, was highly eclectic. Not everyone who supported the party or its régime at one time or another bought the whole package. Anyone with a conscientious disapproval of antisemitism could not have voted for the NSDAP, but such a person probably disapproved of other aspects of the party's aims, too. Among the remainder, whether inside or outside the borders of the Third Reich, antisemitism could easily have been a subordinate rather than a decisive motive for going along with Hitler. A Latvian member of the Waffen-SS or a Frenchman in the Vichy *milice* might well have been motivated by hatred of the Jews, but a Spanish recruit to the Blue Division? The role of anti-Communism, a major spur for many Nazi sympathizers, illustrates this ambivalence. For Hitler and his entourage, hatred of Bolshevism derived from their "redemptive antisemitism"; for others, such as the German, French or Hungarian conservative elites, or many

Catholic, Protestant or Orthodox clergy throughout Europe, the connection was as likely to be the other way round. Similar considerations would apply to a dislike of finance capitalism or parliamentary democracy.

Friedländer's *magnum opus* is a major contribution to the scholarly history of the twentieth century and to our understanding of the dynamics of genocide. It stresses the centrality of a particular ideology as the stimulus of the Shoah, an ideology whose components were far from new, but which were qualitatively intensified by the obsessional fanaticism of Adolf Hitler that was "at the core of Nazism's ideological universe." We can therefore agree that redemptive antisemitism was a necessary condition for the Shoah, but was it a sufficient one? In the mobilization of support or compliance was it an independent variable, or a dependent one? And what were the relative roles of design and contingency? These are questions to which we do not yet have definite answers.

## Notes

1    Michael D. Biddis, *Father of Racist Ideology: The Social and Political Thought of Count Gobineau* (London: Weidenfeld and Nicolson, 1970), 255.
2    Heinrich von Treitschke, *Deutsche Geschichte im neunzehnten Jahrhundert*, vol. 2. (Leipzig: Hirzel, 1982), 7.
3    Thomas Mann, "Gedanken im Kriege" [1914], in *Essays*, vol. 2: *Politische Reden und Schriften* (Frankfurt am Main: Fischer, 1977), 36.
4    Anton Orel, *Das Verfassungsmachwerk der "Republik Österreich" von der Warte der immerwährenden Philosophie aus und im Lichte von der Idee, Natur und Geschichte Österreichs geprüft und verworfen* (Vienna: Vogelsang Verlag, 1921), 30.
5    Edgar Julius Jung, *Sinndeutung der deutschen Revolution* (Oldenburg: Stalling, 1933), 42, 43.
6    Joseph Goebbels, *Revolution der Deutschen. 14 Jahre Nationalsozialismus: Goebbelsreden mit einleitenden Zeitbildern* (Oldenburg: Stalling, 1933), 155.
7    Carl von Ossietzky, "'Kulturbolschewismus,'" *Die Weltbühne* XXVII/16, 21 April 1931: 559–63, here 560.
8    Roger Griffin, *Modernism and Fascism: The Sense of a Beginning under Mussolini and Hitler* (Houndmills: Palgrave Macmillan, 2007).
9    Peter Pulzer, "Third Thoughts on German and Austrian Antisemitism," *Journal of Modern Jewish Studies* 4 (2005): 137–178, here 165–7.
10   Klaus Berchtold, *Österreichische Parteiprogramme 1868–1966* (Munich: Oldenbourg, 1967), 357.
11   Ibid., 203.
12   Peter Pulzer, *The Rise of Political Anti-Semitism in Germany and Austria*, rev. ed. (London: Peter Halban, 1988), 112.
13   Richard Bessel, *Political Violence and the Rise of Nazism: The Storm Troopers in Eastern Germany 1925–1934* (New Haven: Yale University Press, 1984), 74–80, 98–105.
14   Norbert Frei, *1945 und wir: Das Dritte Reich in Bewusstsein der Deutschen* (Munich: C. H. Beck, 2005), 107–25; Adelheid von Saldern, "Innovative Trends in Women's and Gender Studies of the National Socialist Era," *German History* 17 (2009): 84–112, here 85–6.
15   Michael Wildt, *Volksgemeinschaft als Selbstermächtigung. Gewalt gegen Juden in der deutschen Provinz* (Hamburg: Hamburger Edition, 2007), 370–4.
16   Ibid., 63–100; Dirk Walter, *Antisemitische Kriminalität und Gewalt. Judenfeindschaft in der Weimarer Republik* (Bonn: Dietz, 1999), 23–37, 244–56.
17   Saul Friedländer, *Nazi Germany and the Jews: Vol. I, The Years of Persecution, 1933–1939* (New York: HarperCollins, 1997), 73–112.
18   Dominick LaCapra, *Writing History, Writing Trauma* (Baltimore: Johns Hopkins University Press, 2001), 165.

19  Stephen E. Bronner, "Making sense of hell: three meditations on the Holocaust," *Political Studies* 47 (1999): 314–28, here 323.
20  Frei, *1945 und wir*, 119, 111, 114.
21  Henry A. Turner, *German Big Business and the Rise of Hitler* (New York: Oxford University Press, 1985), 90–8.
22  Ibid., 208.
23  P. H. Merkl, *Political Violence under the Swastika: 581 Early Nazis* (Princeton: Princeton University Press, 1975), 8, 9.
24  Ibid., 499.
25  Ibid., 503, 504.
26  Robert Cecil, *The Myth of the Master Race: Alfred Rosenberg and Nazi Ideology* (London: Batsford, 1972), 56.
27  Friedländer, *Nazi Germany and the Jews*, 60.
28  Victor Klemperer, *I Shall Bear Witness. The Diaries of Victor Klemperer 1933–1941* (London: Weidenfeld and Nicolson, 1998), 65.
29  Ian Kershaw, *Popular Opinion and Dissent in the Third Reich: Bavaria 1933–1945* (Oxford: Oxford University Press, 1983), 245.
30  Herbert Rosenkranz, *Verfolgung und Selbstbehauptung: Die Juden in Österreich 1938–1945* Munich: Herold, 1978), 162.
31  Friedländer, *Nazi Germany and the Jews*, 164.
32  Kershaw, *Popular Opinion*, 1983, 239.
33  Michael Burleigh and Wolfgang Wippermann, *The Racial State: Germany 1933–1945* (Cambridge: Cambridge University Press, 1991), 44–197.
34  Ian Kershaw, *Hitler, the Germans and the Final Solution* (New Haven: Yale University Press, 2008), 4.
35  Friedländer, *Nazi Germany and the Jews*, 251–5, Kershaw, *Hitler, the Germans and the Final Solution*, 218–9; Klemperer, *I Shall Bear Witness*, 414–20.
36  Christopher Browning, *The Origins of the Final Soution: The Evolution of Nazi Jewish Policy, September 1939–March 1942* (Lincoln, NE: University of Nebraska Press, 2004), 216–24.
37  Saul Friedländer, *The Years of Extermination: Nazi Germany and the Jews 1939–1945* (New York: HarperCollins, 2007), 278–9.
38  Peter Lieb, *Konventioneller Krieg oder NS-Weltanschauungskrieg? Kriegsführung und Partisanenbekämpfung in Frankreich 1943/44* (Munich: Oldenbourg, 2007), 138.
39  Jeffrey Herf, *The Jewish Enemy: Nazi Propaganda during World War II and the Holocaust* (Cambridge, MA: Harvard University Press, 2006), 15, 267.
40  Ibid., 275.
41  Kershaw, *Popular Opinion*, 1983, 227.
42  Otto D. Kulka and Aron Rodrigue, "The German Population and the Jews in the Third Reich," *Yad Vashem Studies* 16 (1984): 421–35, here 434.
43  Wilm Hosenfeld, *"Ich versuche jeden zu retten": Das Leben eines deutschen Offiziers in Briefen und Tagebüchern* (Munich: Deutsche Verlags-Anstalt, 2004), 714.
44  Friedländer, *The Years of Extermination*, 208–14.
45  Michael R. Marrus and Robert O. Paxton, *Vichy France and the Jews* (New York: Basic Books, 1981), 73–196, 343–56, 365–72.
46  Adam Rayski, *The Choice of the Jews under Vichy: Between Submission and Resistance* (Notre Dame, IN: University of Notre Dame Press, 2005), 74; also Marrus and Paxton, *Vichy France and the Jews*, 234–40).
47  Lieb, *Konventioneller Krieg*, 410.
48  Rayski, *The Choice of the Jews under Vichy*, xiii.
49  Friedländer, *The Years of Extermination*, 537.
50  Gunnar S. Paulsson, *Secret City: The Hidden Jews of Warsaw 1940–1943* (New Haven: Yale University Press, 2002), 224–5.
51  Friedländer, *The Years of Extermination*, xix.
52  Ibid., 657.
53  Eberhard Jäckel and Axel Kuhn, *Hitler: Sämtliche Aufzeichnungen 1905–1924* (Munich: Deutsche Verlags-Anstalt, 1980), 89–90.

54   Kershaw, *Hitler, the Germans and the Final Solution*, 89–91.
55   Friedländer, *The Years of Extermination*, 657.

# 8

# Speaking in Public About the Murder of the Jews: What did the Holocaust Mean to the Germans?

*Nicholas Stargardt*

On 3 August 1941, the Catholic Bishop of Münster, Clemens August Count von Galen, used his pulpit in the Lamberti church to preach a public sermon against the murder of psychiatric patients in German asylums. Disclosing all he knew of the killing of patients, Galen warned about what would happen to the old, the frail, and wounded war veterans, "if you establish and apply the principle that you can kill 'unproductive' human beings." Galen's sermon made a significant local impression. It was read out in diocesan churches in the Münsterland, and the Royal Air Force (RAF) dropped copies of it in leaflet form more widely.[1] A month later, Galen received an anonymous letter of praise for this courageous stand. The letter-writer went on to remind Galen of what was happening to German Jews, even to highly patriotic ones like himself, concluding: "Only the senseless wish, the mad hope, that somewhere a helper will stand up for us incited me to address this letter to you. May God bless you!" Galen neither replied in private, nor uttered a word in public about the persecution of the Jews. Instead, he went on preaching patriotic war sermons against the Bolshevik threat menacing Germany in the east.[2]

Three other Catholic bishops, Conrad Gröber, Archbishop of Freiburg, Wilhelm Berning of Osnabrück and Konrad Count von Preysing of Berlin, did have a record of intervening on behalf of Jewish converts to Catholicism, but they too failed to speak out. In November 1941, all three were responsible for drafting a pastoral letter of protest against the government's treatment of the Church, but in it they carefully avoided any reference to the Jews. Preysing at least went on try-ing to persuade his fellow Catholic bishops to do something, culminating in 1943 in confidential discussion of a petition against the "deportation of non-Aryans in a manner that is scornful of all human rights," but the episcopate undertook noth-ing. The Protestant Churches' record of public activity was equally supine. Only one leading German cleric protested against the murder of the Jews: Theophil Wurm, the Bishop of Württemberg and an outspoken leader of the Confessing Church, wrote a *private* letter to Hitler in July 1943. Those looking for moral guidance from their spiritual leaders were left without any direction.

The failure of the Churches in almost every country occupied by Germany was all the more profound because they were virtually the only civic bodies that continued to enjoy an independent existence. Their abandonment of the Jews lies at the heart of Friedländer's book: it is central to his story of Europeans' destruction of their own cultural heritage. Conservative Catholicism was also a devotional world Friedländer had come to know intimately during the war, when his parents entrusted him to the care of the Sisters of the Sodality in Montluçon. In the 1970s, he revisited this period of his childhood in a moving self-analysis, probing the depth of his own childhood desire to belong, to move from the ranks of the persecuted Jewish minority to the "compact invincible majority"; exploring the deep spiritual appeal of the cult of the Virgin Mary to a boy who had lost his parents.[3]

What had happened to his own absent parents was something Paul did not learn until eighteen months after liberation: intended by now for the Jesuits, he was fortunate in finding a spiritual counsellor in the order who was determined that the young disciple should know and understand what had happened at Auschwitz. Friedländer reverted to his original name, joined the *Irgun* and emigrated to Israel. That Paul – now Saul – Friedländer would become a historian, let alone *the* contemporary historian of the Holocaust, was not foreseeable – but perhaps his own need to know was. This is what singles him out amongst his peers: a refusal to stop at the often technically demanding challenge of establishing the relationship between ideologies, policies and killings – those complex contours of the external, causal history of the Holocaust; he needed to know what it meant in personal terms too.

Since then Friedländer has consistently argued that we need to understand the Holocaust in its emotional and psychological as well as its historical dimensions, and it is this more than anything else which makes the two volumes of Friedländer's *Nazi Germany and the Jews* such a monumental achievement. Friedländer achieves his narrative feat of integrating perpetrators and victims, critics and bystanders within his history by adopting the structure of a chronicle, unfolding it six months at a time. He charts the careful adjustments in German law and policy, but the central narrators, who animate the chronicle and give it the yardstick of individual humanity, are Jewish diarists: Victor Klemperer in Dresden, Etty Hillesum and Anne Frank in Amsterdam, Moshe Flinker in Brussels, Mihail Sebastian in Bucharest, Dawid Sierakowiak in Łódz and Yiskhok Rudashevski in Vilna. Sebastian wonders what has happened to his brother in Paris in June 1940, when he expects the French defeat to "find release in one long pogrom." For Klemperer, the same events saw a visit from a widow in deep mourning, thoughtfully bringing him the socks, shirts and underpants which had belonged to her recently killed soldier husband. Nothing better conveys the enormous scale of these events, or their duration, than this sense of time passing so slowly, as some of the same motifs and actors come around again and again: German occupation officials pleading against having to house or feed any more deportees; Himmler trying to prevent the Security Police and the SS from becoming corrupted by the business of mass murder; German firms snapping up Jewish assets in order to gain a toehold within major Dutch companies.

The structure of the chronicle also allows Friedländer to shift the balance from instigation to process and social impact. This is a major historiographic shift: for decades, historians have been interested principally in the moment of decision to murder, whether this was the decision on high by Hitler, or those numerous decisions of reserve policemen in the field, famously debated by Daniel Goldhagen and Christopher Browning in the 1990s. The defining moment which turned men into perpetrators matters to Friedländer too, but one of his major achievements has been to avoid any fetishisation of the moment of killing, by exploring the multiple ways in which individuals enacted the chain of decisions across a whole continent.

In the first volume, Friedländer traced how a minority of Germans were attracted to antisemitic violence, while the majority retreated into civil cowardice. In part, this tale continues in the second volume. By focusing on the expectations, knowledge and calculations of those affected on every side and at all levels, Friedländer paints the most varied and vivid, but cumulatively also the bleakest group portrait of a Europe in which the guardians of its heritage abandoned both their own values and a core part of its Judeo-Christian moral foundation. From the antisemitic leadership of the Polish Catholic Church, which openly welcomed the ghettoization of the Jews, to the studied indifference of the Communist resistance, non-Nazi and even anti-Nazi organisations in occupied Europe simply shrugged off any humanitarian responsibility as they focused their efforts on their own sectional interests.

With the genocide placed in these pan-European dimensions, the multitude of non-Nazi or even non-German institutions and actors who told themselves at the time that they were choosing the lesser evil becomes a crucial part of the story of isolation and destruction: in every sense, the Jews had nowhere to go. This story of abandonment yields the full significance of the Holocaust for European culture and society. For Friedländer, the Holocaust touched everyone – and he applies this rule unflinchingly to the Jewish elites as well. Where postwar commemoration in Israel focused on the ghetto fighters in Warsaw and Białystok and more recent Holocaust studies have searched out examples of cultural, or "spiritual," resistance, Friedländer refuses to find any redemptive consolation. Rather, he insists on stripping away all those historical alibis and myths built up to convince postwar Europeans that they had not been tainted by their experience of German occupation.

Beneath the tale of Europeans' unheroic and self-absorbed behaviour, with its manifold calculations of immediate threat and comparative advantage, there is another and jarringly different one. This is the story of a far more radical antisemitism, which, Friedländer contends in the pages of *The Years of Destruction*, hardened until it encompassed the majority of German society, wedded to their *Führer* and his war against the Jews. As he puts it:

> Hitler was surrounded by the hysterical adoration and blind faith of so many, for so long, that well after Stalingrad [. . .] countless Germans still believed in his promises of victory. [. . .] A metahistorical enemy demanded, when the time for the decisive struggle arrived, a metahistorical personality to lead the fight against those forces of evil. [. . .]

As the struggle reached its critical phase, at the height of the war, to lose faith in Hitler meant only one outcome: the prospect of horrendous retaliation at the hands of 'Jewish liquidation squads,' in Goebbels's words. Robbing the Jews contributed to the upholding of the *Volksstaat*; murdering them and fanning the fears of retribution became the ultimate bond of *Führer* and *Volk* in the collapsing *Führerstaat*.[4]

This is a view which Friedländer first developed in 1982 in a short essayistic book called *Reflets du Nazisme*, and it has remained central to his interpretation ever since. What is at stake here, as he puts it, is not Hitler's psycho-biography, but "why tens of millions of Germans blindly followed him to the end, why many still believed in him at the end, and not a few, after the end."[5]

This question is crucial to Friedländer's enterprise. He does not simply ascribe generalised nihilistic, destructive urges to Hitler. That has long been popular in all the wrong places. The notion that Hitler and Goebbels wanted to kill the German people when they finally killed themselves has provided one of the oldest alibis amongst conservative German nationalists: if they could paint themselves as Hitler's final victims, they could also proclaim themselves innocent of his crimes.[6] Such slipshod special pleading is anathema to Friedländer: on the contrary, the antisemitism of the conservative nationalist elites provides a powerful line of continuity across the work. For Friedländer, all the destructive impulses are concentrated relentlessly, and almost solely, upon the Jews. Hitler's rants about the Jews are not just the ravings of one possessed – though they are that too – but more ominously proffered an enticing promise to redeem the German nation by purging it of all the Jewish influences which had allegedly led to defeat in 1918. This thesis of "redemptive antisemitism" as "*the mobilising myth of the regime*" is Friedländer's distinctive interpretative contribution. And it provides the unifying arch joining the two volumes of his history of *Nazi Germany and the Jews* into a single *magnum opus*.[7]

How can we test the propensity of "ordinary Germans" to embrace the radical antisemitic violence of the regime during the war? There are examples of ordinary soldiers, like the one Friedländer quotes writing home from Brest-Litovsk in June 1942, describing the shooting of 1,300 "men, women and children" in the pits outside town and speculating with macabre irony that "if the war goes on much longer, the Jews will be turned into sausage and served to Russian war prisoners and to the Jewish specialised workers [. . .]."[8] Friedländer has a sharp eye for how new genocidal social norms and personal virulence shaped each other in wartime Germany. Yet, there is something missing, which he was careful to chart in volume one, culminating in his magisterial account of the 1938 pogrom: the many who saw but did not take part in what was being done to the Jews by an active minority, and who watched with resigned disgust, curiosity, indifference or even shame. What happened inside this majority during the war? Did they go on disapproving or go on adapting, as they learned to accept the impotence of their reactions to the 1938 pogrom, the tens of thousands of shootings in Poland in 1939 or the millions executed in full view in the Soviet campaigns of 1941 and

1942? Were Germans living in a society constantly catching up with the import of its own actions, with people looking for moral guidance to deal with the latest breach of their previous moral codes?

In volume one, Friedländer approached these questions from this cultural point of view; in volume two, he simplifies the problem by looking for a more unifying and uniform German reaction to what was being done. As a result, his depiction of the range of public reactions in wartime Germany and his overall argument are much more hard-hitting: Friedländer is arguing that the Germans continued fighting the war because the chief effect of feelings of responsibility for the genocide was to deepen and strengthen the current of radical antisemitism. In the end, we are told, it was not just Hitler but the German people who were waging war principally against the Jews.

Most of what we know about German responses to the Holocaust comes from the reports on public opinion collected by different sections of the regime, principally the Security Service of the SS (the SD). The SD received local reports from which it compiled national weekly summaries, a selection of which was first published by Heinz Boberach in 1965, followed in 1984 by the complete national series.[9] Other scholars have gone back to the original – often more inflected – reports from the localities (and enough survived the great destruction of regime files of 1945 to leave a complex regional patchwork), and also supplemented them with the reports of other agencies, such as state prosecutors, the Nazi Party, or, in the final months of the war, the *Wehrmacht*. Thanks to a project headed by Otto Dov Kulka and Eberhard Jäckel, we now have an extraordinarily rich compilation of these different kinds of local and national reports on popular attitudes to the Jews, which provides by far the most detailed picture to date, and on which Saul Friedländer and other recent scholars have been able to draw.[10]

Several things emerge clearly from this remarkable scholarly endeavour. First, knowledge of the murder of the Jews was both widespread and detailed; second, because it was essentially private knowledge, transmitted by rumour, listening to enemy radio or reported by eyewitnesses, it was both uncontrollable and people had to fall back on their own resources in order to work out what it meant. Thirdly, and this is perhaps the most significant clue for historians, there was a crucial time gap between learning about the murder of the Jews – which was contemporaneous with the mass shootings of 1941 and 1942 – and it becoming a major topic of conversation in public: this did not happen until 1943.

To give but one example, in the summer and autumn of 1943 Himmler gave SS *Standartenführer* Paul Blobel the daunting task of locating and erasing the traces of the millions of Jews and Red Army prisoners shot in the occupied Soviet Union. With his small staff, Blobel's *Sonderaktion* 1005 was meant to be entirely secret.[11] Nonetheless, by October 1943, astonishingly accurate news was circulating about it. As the SD reported from the Lower Franconian towns of Bad Neustadt and Münnerstadt, people surmised that the *Führer* had had "the Jews dug up again and burned, so that in the event of a further retreat in the east, no propaganda material should fall into the hands of the Soviets like that at Katyn, etc."[12]

Unlike many of the original executions, there were no crowds of camera-toting soldiers to witness these clean-up operations.[13] To safeguard the secret, the teams of concentration camp prisoners assigned to dig up and burn the bodies were themselves shot by their SS guards once their work was done.[14] Presumably, it was the SS personnel themselves who directly or indirectly brought the news back to Germany, and so it would not be surprising if regions like Lower Franconia, famous for their Nazi sympathies, were the first to hear.

There was a media context to this: the BBC had been broadcasting allegations of genocide against the Jews during the second half of 1942, to which Goebbels decided that, rather than refute the allegations, the only feasible response was to mount counter-allegations, confusing international opinion and diverting attention in Germany elsewhere.[15] The result came in mid-April 1943, with the much-trumpeted exhumation of the corpses of Polish officers massacred by the NKVD (*Narodnyy Komissariat Vnutrennikh Del*) at Katyn, all carefully documented by an international commission, photographed at close-quarters and showcased in the German media for the following seven weeks, to illustrate the evils of the Jewish-Bolshevik enemy.[16]

News transmitted by rumour operated at two levels: first was the information itself, in this case something that was meant to be a closely-guarded secret; second, and equally as important for its news-worthiness, was how people framed its significance. As they pieced together what they knew, they tried to supply missing bits of information and logical links. So, they suggested that the action to exhume and burn the corpses of the Jews – which was actually underway – was the result of an enquiry about the whereabouts of the Jews once resident in the Reich which the Red Cross had passed on from the "Feindmächte" to the "*Führer.*" Although there was no basis for this surmise, it would have made sense to people who knew that enemy radio had been broadcasting allegations of genocide in the past year. Such speculative piecing together of gobbets of knowledge is typical of a society where none of this was public information, but a lot of people had seen or heard something. It has its parallels in the way that news about the murder of the Jews spread within the Nazi elite by word of mouth: even in Paris, the German administration learned of it from colleagues arriving from the east.

This spread of information had complex patterns and eddies. It is quite possible that there were people in Lower Franconia who were completely outside the loop. Mass shootings had taken place right across the eastern front and had drawn hundreds of thousands, perhaps even millions, of German witnesses. Yet, as relatives and friends chatted on trams and trains and in shopping queues about what they had heard, it was possible to have knowledge without incurring responsibility. Hitler might prophesy the destruction of the Jews with increasing frequency, but he did not make the policy of mass murder public or ask the German people to approve it. Auctions and markets selling Jewish property brought furniture and clothing whose origins were readily known into German homes. But in many contexts, Germans referred to the annihilation of the Jews in a piecemeal fashion, trying not admit to themselves the enormity of what was underway, as if, by not linking it to Hitler's "prophesies" or the oft-repeated threat of "Perish Judah," they could lessen their own culpability. Whether they were soldiers observing the shootings, railway men running the deportation trains, or local government officials making sure that keys to apartments were handed over before their occupants left, people simultaneously hid behind their functionally circumscribed roles in the division of labor that mass murder involved and passed their little nuggets of knowledge into the general private circulation of social information. In the official silence about the actual murder of the Jews, people often strove not to take responsibility for their knowledge, their foreboding about what they already wanted not to know both provoking and curbing their own curiosity.[17]

Extraordinarily accurate knowledge almost always went hand in hand with inferential fiction. OSS investigators in Italy overheard stories circulating amongst German prisoners of war about the death camps, even before the first of them – Majdanek – was liberated. They told of death by mass electrocution as well as mass gassing. Curiosity drove men to broach the taboo subject of what actually happened in these secret locations. And in the mistakes, or the correct details incorrectly understood, such as references to the pillars of corpses – actually formed by people fighting in the darkness of the gas chamber to reach the remaining oxygen near the ceiling – we are reminded how fragmentary even piercingly accurate information was.[18]

There is, of course, something odd, even paradoxical, about relying on the reports of the secret police to discern the contours of public opinion, as if modern dictatorships had not also tried to preclude its very formation. Even if people had felt able to express independent views, would not the secret police censor its own reports in order to please the dictatorship? In this respect, the German SD *Stimmungsberichte* are remarkably different from the *svodki* produced by the NKVD under Stalin: where the NKVD reports often become entangled within the ideological language of the regime, recasting local disputes in order to conform to the language of Bolshevik social hygiene, with its notions of degeneracy and corruption, as well as the Stalinist language of "enemies" and "wreckers," to the point where the original cultural contours become blurred and indistinct, this is not the case with the SD.[19] Operationally, it seems to have enjoyed a remarkable independence: its reporting functions were not mixed up with day-to-day policing like the NKVD, and, although Goebbels complained when the reports on morale got bad and the circle of those who were permitted to read the reports became more restrictive, no-one seems to have prevented the SD from relaying bad news. It is hard to imagine Stalin being told that his broadcasts were prompting widespread criticism, but this was relayed to Hitler – and his response was not to execute the messenger but to stop broadcasting.[20] Goebbels, who read the reports in order to gauge the reception of his propaganda spin and to see how to recalibrate the German media in the coming weeks, complained in his diary that the SD had an in-built tendency to exaggerate, rather than to minimise, the scale of social discontent. He was probably wrong in the immediate sense of how critical Germans were capable of being during the war years, but he was almost certainly right in the larger sense that the SD itself did not have any way of knowing quite what such a litany of criticisms and complaints meant. Given that one of the primary purposes of the reports was to act as the early warning system to a regime which believed that Germany had lost the First World War because of a collapse of civilian morale, it was hardly surprising if it was over-sensitive to symptoms of discontent in the present war.

To be sure, the SD had its own agenda; its hostility to the Churches leading it to emphasise any anti-Nazi or humanitarian strains of criticism, whilst passing in silence over those conservative or *völkisch* sermons and pastoral letters which supported the regime. These were areas where the reporting was also influenced by the SD's desire to influence policy. But the SD reports also show every awareness of dealing with a far more complex and opinionated, post-liberal society than their Soviet counterparts: they expected remnants of Weimar civil society to continue to operate at an informal level, and they distinguished regularly between what was being said in working-class, religious, and oppositional circles.

By the spring and summer of 1943, the SD had considerable discontent to report. The destruction of the Sixth Army at Stalingrad and the mass air raids on the cities of the Ruhr industrial region began in a year in which the news kept getting worse. Spontaneous discussion in public about "what we did to the Jews" was most widespread in the wake of heavy bombing raids on German cities, and it is clear that some kind of moral and political equivalence was being made between the two sets of events. This link first appeared sporadically in 1942 after the first "1,000 bomber raid" on Cologne, but it became far more common with the onset of the mass bombing campaign, starting with the raids against Essen in March 1943. The Hamburg fire-storm of 27 July and the mass evacuations which followed all over northern and western Germany that summer and autumn meant that evacuees spread their tales and anxieties to the sheltered south and east of the country, bringing tales of "terror bombing" to East Prussian, Swabian, Austrian and Bavarian small towns and villages.[21]

So, in early September 1943, it was said that Frankfurt and Fürth were being spared from the general "reckoning" because the Jews wanted to regain their houses in these "exceptionally Jewish cities" after the war.[22] When Frankfurt was nonetheless targetted, people in the small Bavarian town of Bad Brückenau were deeply affected by the tales told by the evacuees from Frankfurt (to their west) and Schweinfurt (to their southeast). In "their mood of deep pessimism and growing fatalistic apathy" they now saw the bombing of Frankfurt as "retaliation to the nth degree for the Jewish action of 1938."[23] Under the immediate impact of the Hamburg raids, the inhabitants of Ochsenfurt were wondering whether Würzburg would be next. While some claimed it was being spared because "in Würzburg no synagogues were burned," others warned "that now the airmen would come to Würzburg too, given that the last Jew recently left Würzburg." For good measure, he was even reported to have "declared before his deportation that now Würzburg would also receive air raids."[24] From Hamburg to Bavaria,

Germans spoke about the Allied bombing as "retaliation" for Germany's treatment of the Jews. In Rothenburg ob der Tauber, local Nazi officials confirmed that "One often hears the opinion amongst national comrades that the terror attacks are a consequence of the measures carried out against the Jews."[25]

Why was the genocide seen as equivalent to the bombing of German civilians and why were they seen as causally linked? With the onset of the RAF's raids on the Rhineland and the Ruhr, Goebbels had toured their cities, rousing packed auditoriums in Essen and Dortmund with his promises of retaliation against England.[26] On 5 June 1943, Goebbels had promised a Party rally massive "retaliation" against the British people. It was they who "would have to pay for the bill marked up by its leaders by order of those Jews who instigated and spurred them into their bloody crimes."[27] Within weeks of its fire-bombing on 29 May 1943, in which 3,000 had died, Wuppertal became a new *lieu de memoire*. In Zella-Mehlis, near Weimar, the armament workers had begun to sing a new song, adding their own voices to the clamour for revenge for the "terror bombing" which Goebbels had orchestrated in the media:

> The Reckoning: The day is coming to avenge the crime of Wuppertal most bitterly
> And it will break upon you in your towns in a hail of iron.
> You murderers, you knew no pain as fire took this city
> And you slew the child at his mother's breast, the father and the grandpa.
>
> That whips us on to hate most wildly and relentlessly,
> For you and all Jewish races bear the stigma of the Wupper.
> The dead call for vengeance! And we stand firm to our word
> And build weapons that will deliver the hard answer for this murder.[28]

Through the spring and summer of 1943, the Nazi regime promised "retaliation" for the bombing and there was every reason for Germans to believe that they were still powerful enough to deliver it. In the Rhineland and Westfalia, people disregarded the Catholic Church's preaching against vengeance and fantasized about the scale of the retaliation which would be launched against England.[29] But the longer it was delayed, the more the Security Police reports on public opinion registered high levels of anxiety about when the promised retaliation was actually going to come, and when the "miracle weapons" would be deployed which would turn the war into a German victory. Throughout that spring and summer, the military censors' reports traced the waves of panic and pessimism which swept across the Rhineland and the Ruhr. They also reported the mixed emotions with which soldiers at the front responded to the news; with the anxieties of men from the affected cities about the fate of their families vying with a more widespread frustration amongst the troops that the homefront lacked their unshakeable resolve and determination to fight on.

In 1943, rumours of Jewish "retaliation" expressed a particular sense of helplessness, as well as bitter disappointment at the failed promise of German retaliation against England. Even when the RAF and USAAF were in fact sustaining very heavy losses, to many German civilians they appeared omnipotent. In the cities this manifested itself in urban myths that greatly flattered and exaggerated the accuracy of Allied targeting. When both airforces, and especially the British, were having great difficulties delivering their payloads within the prescribed three-mile radius of the target, Berliners often imagined that they were deliberately targeting particular streets, and particular neighbourhoods which they wished to punish. It is this same underlying current of naked vulnerability which animated the rumours about what particular Jews had said before their deportation or whether particular cities had burned or spared their synagogues in 1938. This means that we cannot take these SD and Nazi Party reports as direct commentary or a proxy plebiscite on the "Final Solution." Rather, the "measures carried out against the Jews," as the SD euphemistically called them, appear as one step in a cycle of what Germans saw as mutually destructive escalation.

But what was the dynamic of this imagined relationship in Germany between the war and the murder of the Jews? These same kinds of source material have been interpreted in completely divergent ways. In Saul Friedländer's view, the Holocaust and the fear of Jewish revenge were bound to one another in an exclusive vicious circle which fed radical antisemitism and kept Germans fighting the war. But this misses two key features of these sources: first, their deeply pessimistic character casts them as moments of despair, not rallying cries; and second, their principal point of reference is not the Jews but the Germans. For this reason, Ian Kershaw, David Bankier and Frank Bajohr tend to interpret these comments within a framework of generalised defeatism: far from spurring Germans on to last-ditch efforts to resist, as Friedländer contends, they see the home front as convinced that the war was lost. Following the lead of Martin Broszat, they date this defeatism from Stalingrad onwards, in other words from exactly the period that Germans started comparing the air raids on German cities to the murder of the Jews. Instead of finding an ever more radical and murderous antisemitism within German society at large, Ian Kershaw and Peter Longerich have read the same sources as suggesting that Germans were largely indifferent to the fate of the Jews.[30]

I think it is clear that these sources only tell us about how Germans discussed the genocide as an accomplished fact. In 1941 and 1942, when the greatest number of eyewitnesses brought back news of the mass shootings in the east, and when consent or opposition to the killing might have altered its outcome, there was nothing like the public discussion of mass murder to be found in 1943 and 1944. Earlier, the murder of the Jews was almost always discussed in relation to the specific circumstances of particular killings, as if this could insulate the narrators from acknowledging their full genocidal dimensions. It took a convinced opponent of the Nazi regime to make the conscious connection between the rumours from the east and Hitler's repetitions of his famous prophesy about world war bringing the annihilation of the Jews. For, in 1941 and 1942, it did not look as if anyone else could bring Germans to account for these deeds: they were simply an inconvenient, deeply embarrassing fact of the war, whose full meaning was best left unexplored.[31]

The more people bemoaned the consequences, in 1943 or 1944, of how they had treated the Jews, the more they were forced to recognise that the deportations and mass shootings already lay in the past. Mass murder was no longer a matter of present intention, but of ineradicable past actions, which Germans had to take into account as they formed their expectations of what was happening to them now and what might happen next. I would agree with Saul Friedländer that the Jews mattered intensely here, but I think the relationship was not only the binary one of perpetrator and victim. And it was the progress of the war, rather than the Holocaust, which provided the escalatory logic and dynamism to German responses. In 1943–5, these conversations reported among Germans were not primarily preoccupied with the fate of German or European Jews, but, rather, with Jews as a power in the global scales of world war. Goebbels may have read the SD reports as a critique of official propaganda, but at a deep level he had clearly succeeded in establishing sturdy axioms of common sense in which Anglo-American "plutocracy," and with it the bombing war, were being driven by Jewish interests. This at least was not a matter of indifference to most people, and possessed a dynamism which the German occupation of Budapest brought into the open. German civilians eagerly watched what was happening to the Jews. When the Allies stopped bombing the Hungarian capital in March, people concluded that keeping the Jews in a ghetto in the city had created an effective human shield.[32] As one report from Bad Brückenau ran:

> Many national comrades consider that the Jewish Question has been solved by us in the stupidest of ways. They say quite openly that in this respect Hungary has learned from our mistake; and our cities would surely remain intact, if we had herded the Jews into ghettos at that time. And then we would have at our disposal a real threat and means to retaliate.[33]

The escalatory logic here is unmistakable, made still more explicit in a string of letters to Goebbels that summer urging the regime to execute Jews in retaliation for Allied air raids against German civilians. It also bears the mark of desperation, of falling faith in the *Luftwaffe* and civil defence.[34] But, as Victor Klemperer found out, Goebbels' orchestration of the Jew as the true protagonist in the war provided a focus for the fears and disorientation felt by people who were not Nazis and who would have been horrified at the idea of shooting Jewish hostages. The nice factory foreman, a fellow veteran of the First World War who had sympathised with Klemperer on 12 March 1944 for having lost his academic job just because he was Jewish, turned a week later to the idea of Jewish "billionaires" as he cast about helplessly to give Klemperer a reason for the latest, senseless American bombing of Hamburg. For people like him, the abstract idea of a foreign "Jewish plutocracy" offered an explanation which cut across their personal liking for individual German Jews. To make sense of the ferocity of the aerial onslaught on the civilian population, the "terror bombing" required a conspiracy by an enemy who was filled with an implacable hatred of Germans and Germany.[35]

The Nazi regime had always claimed that Germany's enemies were reducible to a world Jewish conspiracy, and its response to the defeat at Stalingrad and mass bombing of German cities had been to launch a new antisemitic campaign of unprecedented proportions. At its centre lay the Jew, the single and unitary image of all Nazi propaganda in the last two years of the war.[36] The problem which surfaces again and again in public responses to the war in Germany is that people spoke about Jews in two separate but connected contexts: foreign, overseas Jews as the organizing power of the Allied coalition, and Jews executed, principally, in the east. It was the link between the two, but also the possibility of separating them which preoccupied German society and stimulated inadvertent admissions in public of what people knew about the Holocaust.

So, the mass graves of Poles and Ukrainians unearthed first at Katyn and later Vinnitsa in 1943 were a strange, double-edged propaganda weapon: they reminded Germans of what they had seen or heard of the mass shootings conducted by their own side in the east;[37] and they summoned humanitarian sympathies for people, Poles and Ukrainians, whom Germans had been taught were *Untermenschen*. Faced with Katyn and the RAF's Bomber Command, a kind of consensus emerged that extreme measures were simply unavoidable in this war. So:

> A large section of the population sees the elimination of the Polish officers [at Katyn] [. . .] even the radical wiping out of a dangerous opponent, as something that cannot be avoided in the war. People say that one could place the bombing of the German cities by the English and Americans and in the end also our own exterminatory struggle against Jewry on the same level.[38]

Others, especially anti-Nazi Catholics and Protestants, took the opposite point of view and warned that Germany had merited divine retribution for their murder of the Jews, and "If these murders are not bitterly avenged against us, then there is no longer any divine justice!" But the critical churchmen in North Westfalia were also said to have warned that "On account of these barbaric methods, a humane conduct of war by our opponents is no longer possible. The Jewish press's outbreaks of rage and its exterminatory tendencies is said to be the natural reaction."[39] Here the humanitarian and religious objections came close to the nationalist and secular ones: what did moral restraint have to do with total war? In other words, even those most preoccupied with German guilt, also saw themselves caught up in an escalating international conflict whose only logic was the abandonment of moral restraint – and, from their point of view, the bombing of German civilians by the British and Americans provided evidence that this was really so, long before the Red Army reached German territory.

"National comrades" with fewer self-critical reservations about the German conduct of the war reached the same conclusion more swiftly – as the Security

Service paraphrased it, "that 'total war' is understood by the national comrades as the ruthless deployment of all means that lead to a swift victory, that moral arguments play no part on the other side and achieve nothing on ours, and that a ruthless application of the same means in retaliation to the [air] attacks is the only correct answer."[40] Some could not see why they should sympathise with the Poles at all, while others concluded that their side should learn from the Soviets how to be truly ruthless and effective in pursuit of their national interest: as a very well-read armaments worker in Friedberg was overheard saying: "The Russians know exactly what they want. They are completely annihilating a class of the population because they don't like it. They think everything through to the end and don't stop in the middle like us!"[41] Hitler may have endlessly told his generals that there was no place for "sentimentality" in this war, but now this moral conclusion was becoming commonplace.

What all this reveals is that by 1943, "Jewish retaliation" was seen both in the way the regime portrayed it – as the logical outcome of Jewish control of the Allied war effort – and, in a way that the regime condemned as "defeatist," namely as retribution or revenge for "our own exterminatory struggle against Jewry." The fact that a largely religious minority continued to insist upon the immorality of a completely nationalized ethics meant also that a sense of guilt remained available as soon as it looked as if outside powers were going to call Germans to account.[42] When the Americans reached Aachen in September 1944 they found a population which expected to be collectively punished for what had been done to the Jews.[43] In the meantime, the fear of Jewish retaliation and knowledge of what Germans had done to the Jews fed upon one another, creating a general framework for understanding and, increasingly, accepting that the war was one of national survival.[44]

This was a logic of escalation, but if Germans were already overwhelmingly defeatist, why would they have wanted to continue and escalate the war, let alone to use Jews as human shields? The one thing which Saul Friedländer and Martin Broszat agreed about was that the Germans continued fighting the war out of *fear*. Broszat may have insisted on the inward denazification of German society after Stalingrad and Friedländer on its conscious collusion in the Holocaust, but they each posit a logic of pure *fear*. For the one, fear was fanned by Nazi terror; for the other by the threat of Jewish revenge. But was fear enough? What could Germans *hope* for during these years, and did their hopes play a part in their responses to the Holocaust?

Despite the vast amount of research on Nazi Germany, we do not know how the Germans were able to go on fighting a world war until they were utterly defeated: indeed the findings of military and socio-political history pull in opposite directions. Social and political historians generally agree that most Germans knew the war was lost by 1943: Martin Broszat and Ian Kershaw established a consensus position which dates this realisation to the news of the Sixth Army's destruction at Stalingrad; some, like Joachim Szodrzynski and Richard Evans, to the bombing of Hamburg six months later.[45] Yet, the *Wehrmacht* continued to fight on into 1945 without any repetition of the mass desertions, military strikes or mutinies which befell Austrian and German armies in 1918.[46] Given that these were mass conscript armies, whose ties to the home front were never severed – indeed, every delay in the military post led to acute anxieties and plummeting morale – it is not conceivable that both the military and the social historians can be right.

Stringing together all the instances of "poor morale" in the SD reports would encourage one to see an unbroken line of defeatism. The evidence the Allied psychological war experts gathered from their interrogations of German prisoners of war tends in the opposite direction. Even in February 1945, there were many German prisoners who were willing to argue with their British and American interrogators and try to convince them that Germany was winning the war. Far more widespread was the conviction that Germany could not afford to lose it. "Germany must not lose this war" was an admonition so endlessly reported from prisoners of war of all social origins, religious affiliations and political hues that the British and American psychological warriors were forced to accept that there were some tenets which had an axiomatic status. When confronted with even openly anti-Nazi German prisoners insisting that German must not and would not lose the war, the leading British psychological war expert Henry Dicks was at a loss to explain it and took refuge in an empty, exasperated phrase – "the German capacity for repressing reality." From his interrogator's desk on the Italian front, the novelist Klaus Mann expressed his bafflement at the intransigence of his erstwhile fellow countrymen rather better in a letter to his literary editor: "Why don't they finally stop? What are they waiting for, the unfortunates? This is the question which I don't just keep on asking you and me, but also each of them."[47]

Writing late in 1944, Klaus Mann could not know that the findings of other members of the Psychological Warfare Branch were about to change. Between January and late March 1945, the confidence of the German prisoners they were interrogating went into free-fall: whereas 62 per cent said that they trusted the *Führer* in January, only 21 per cent did by the end of March. Even fewer now believed that Germany was winning the war (44 per cent in January, down to 7 per cent by the end of March), or possessed secret weapons (47 per cent in January, down to 9 per cent by the end of March).[48] But what is striking for the historian is how *late* in the war this happened – that is, not until the Red Army had reached the Oder and British and Americans the Rhine. And evidence of desertion tends in the same direction: most German prisoners taken on the southern and western fronts up to this point surrendered in groups of fewer than ten. There was not yet any collapse, no mass breaking of ranks heralding the onset of mass defeatism.

This evidence, provided by soldiers who had just endured battle and capture and had seen the enormous material superiority enjoyed by the British and Americans, is important because it offers an alternative perspective which the internal reports of military censors and the SD – obsessed with the danger of a "stab in the back," – did not have. The Nazi regime knew that grumbling and defeatism were not the same thing, but it did not know how long "good behaviour" could withstand "bad morale." Historians have found themselves in a similar position.

If defeatism did not begin to take hold until *after* the summer of 1944, and possibly not until the Soviet offensive of January 1945, then we have to rethink how we periodize German morale in the Second World War. In particular, we need to part with the conventional chronology, with its single great turning-point around Stalingrad, preceded by a first period of easy victories and followed by a second period of unremitting defeats. The first signs of "defeatism" appeared much earlier, when the *Wehrmacht* was forced to retreat from Moscow in November 1941, while the Ardennes offensive of December 1944 brought one last great upsurge in expectations. This suggests that we ought to treat the long years from the end of 1941 to late 1944 as a separate, open-ended – and key – middle phase of the war, in which confidence in *Blitzkrieg* was gone but defeat did not yet appear as the only possible outcome. This was also the period in which mass murder became genocide.

And this brings me back to the Jews and the bombing. Talk about "Jewish retaliation" surfaced when people felt most vulnerable, and its repetition marks out a string of low points. But its repeated occurrence does not, however, make it a continuous state of mind. It might just signify the troughs in rapidly oscillating civilian morale, whose recovery and peaks can be measured by the resurgence of other motifs, such as "new weapons" or the prospects of a separate peace with the Western powers: and the last time "new weapons" generated much excitement was in December 1944 during the temporary success of the Ardennes offensive; hopes for a separate peace lasted even longer – right up to Roosevelt's death on 22 April 1945. It is the presence of such hopes which is probably the key to understanding morale and the willingness to continue the war in the west as well as the east.

I think what we are dealing with here is a popular state of mind and not just the product of regime propaganda. We know that war exacerbated social conflicts in Germany, between evacuees and their hosts, between the bombed out and those sheltered from air raids, between working-class families from the industrial cities and farmers in the southwest and Austria. We know too from personal diaries and family letters how much the war disrupted family life, creating deep personal rifts between soldiers and civilians within families, which were hard to bridge after the war.[49] For exactly these reasons, it is all the more remarkable that these ways of understanding the war penetrated so deeply into popular common sense, and cut across all of the social divides and conflicts between soldiers and civilians, and differences of region, religion, class, and gender. What we see in the rumours about Allied retaliation for the murder of the Jews is a snapshot of the way a whole culture understood the war. Even the moral discord about how to respond – with religious humanitarians warning that Germans had invited divine as well as Allied retribution, and pragmatic nationalists urging the government to wage as ruthless a war as its enemies – in fact dwelt upon the same issues, the same view of international relations and tended to reinforce their common stock of associative ideas about who the war was being fought against and what Germans had to expect.

This cultural common sense showed the long-term influence of Nazi propaganda, but it also proved remarkably resistant to the regime's efforts at short-term manipulation. David Bankier, Jeffrey Herf and others have charted the deluge of antisemitic propaganda during the war.[50] But the interesting thing is that even as Germans unhesitatingly took up Goebbels' epithet of "terror bombing" and made it their own, they also refused to accept each and every invocation of it by the regime. For, when the RAF carried out the "dam-buster" raids on the Ruhr in May 1943, the media immediately reached for its familiar headlines of "Jewish terror bombing": indeed, breaching the Möhne and Eder dams did cause catastrophic flooding of the Ruhr valley with a death toll of over 5,000. To the regime's surprise, however, Nazi Party and state agencies immediately reported a wave of criticism and incomprehension about how the bombing of a legitimate strategic target could be confused with "Jewish terror." On the contrary, Party officials warned the propaganda ministry:

> The population is very critical of two things: 1) The destruction of the dam walls is an extraordinary success for the English and the distortion of a legitimate attack on a militarily significant installation into a pure terror attack is not understood and 2) in connection with the preceding, the singling out of a Jew [as the responsible party] is incomprehensible.[51]

And someone wise-cracked that "if we have failed to attack installations of this sort in England because we had to await the brainwave of a Jew, then our responsible men should get the cost of their training back." In other words, "terror bombing" could not be attached to any air-raid Goebbels chose: when the "English" performed legitimate military strikes, they were not seen as carrying out a "Jewish" act. People readily absorbed terms like "terror attacks," *Mordbrenner*, *Luftgangster*, *Luftpiraten* into their daily conversations, letters and diary entries, but just because they attached real meaning to them, they were also discriminating about how they applied them. In popular common sense only limitless violence, the pure terror of mass attacks on civilians merited the term "Jewish terror."[52]

The fact that people continued to keep such distinctions alive, on occasion in spite of Goebbels' propaganda, also fed their hopes that England and America could – perhaps – be saved from Jewish influence, and prised away from their Soviet alliance. Not only Hitler, Himmler, Goebbels and Goering intermittently discussed the possibilities of a "separate peace" in the west. This hope surfaces increasingly in private diaries and public opinion reports also – and it was, of course, a hope shared by the conservative circles of the resistance. They hoped that peace in the west would allow the *Wehrmacht* to win the war in the east. If only Britain and America would rid themselves of Jewish influence. As Goebbels was cranking up the antisemitic propaganda in the spring of 1943, Hitler con-fided to him how he hoped to use antisemitism to drive a wedge between "the Churchill regime" and the English people.[53] Indeed, in June 1943, the NSDAP Kreisleiter for Bad Neustadt felt moved to warn his bosses in Nuremberg that party propaganda about growing antisemitism in England and the USA raised hopes which could all too easily be disappointed: "National comrades are always ready to hang great hopes on such phenomena. I myself know from my own experience that in Neustadt/Aisch people are talking eagerly about how this hostility to the Jews in the enemy countries will probably lead to a revolution and [their] collapse."[54] Behind such hopes lay a longer tradition of Anglophilia, which the Nazis had carefully nurtured, using the radical social criticism of A. J. Cronin's novels and George Orwell to feed a sense of their blood brothers across the North Sea awaiting their liberation from an antique monarchical-aristocratic government and – of course – Jewish finance.[55] By 1944, helpful citizens were sending proposals to the propaganda minister for leaflets asking the English and American "worker" why he was letting himself be duped into fighting for the Jews.[56] At least half-expecting such efforts at enlightenment to fail, Dr A. D. Börner, a Party member from Hamburg, pointed out to Goebbels that the Germans were too educated to be understood by the English-speaking world: "We Germans, however, are used to speaking to an educated population. [. . .] These preconditions are not met by the wretched level of the English-speaking peoples. So we risk speaking over their heads." Leaflets would have to address the exploited English workers and soldiers "in the manner of drumming something into someone slow on the uptake and which he only grasps with difficulty."[57]

As German hopes gradually shifted from winning the war to forcing a stale-mate and a negotiated settlement with the Western Allies, in order to concentrate the whole power of the *Wehrmacht* against the Red Army, so the paradox emerged that ever more extreme methods were required to achieve increasingly limited aims. From this perspective, the German propensity to see the war in apocalyptic terms was not at all incompatible with rational appraisal. It was this paradoxical quandary which made people talk so much and so openly about the Holocaust. At each step during the second half of the war, as they recalibrated their expecta-tions in order to fit fresh circumstances, people kept looking for a way out of the apocalyptic prospect confronting them: the chances of a *de*-escalation and of a separate peace in the west increasingly seemed to offer the only chance to stave off defeat, and so made the issue of how many moral boundaries had already been crossed a pressing one, worth risking the wrath of the authorities to talk about in public places. These were dilemmas shared even by Germans who were not Nazis and who disapproved of much of what the regime stood for: because they knew how the war had already been fought and what had already been done, by 1943 they too came to share the most profoundly nationalist of Hitler's core beliefs: his conviction that Germany faced encirclement and destruction. The ways in which people talked about the murder of the Jews almost always expressed both their fear and the hope that such a fate could somehow be avoided.

All this suggests that it is not really possible to write "an integrated history of the Holocaust" which brackets the rest of the war out of the story. On the contrary, if we want to understand what sense Germans made of the murder of the Jews, then we need to bring the war back in and recognise that there was no longer a common frame of reference shared by Jews and Germans. It was not knowledge of the events which separated them, but, rather, the profound nationalization of meaning. During the war, Germans were already relativizing the Holocaust against their own suffering in self-pitying ways which promised to have a fertile postwar future. Herein lies a key asymmetry between Jewish and German responses: for the Jews, the Holocaust shaped their understanding of the war; for Germans, the war framed their understanding and response to the murder of the Jews. Their respective positions were marked by huge asymmetries not only of power, but also of empathy and identification. At a profound emotional level, they were not talking about the same events.

I would agree with much of Saul Friedländer's reading of Hitler's key role and relentless drive to destroy, but I think we have a long way to go before we will have a similar level of clarity about German society as a whole. Just as continued trust in Hitler's leadership does not show that Germans ascribed the same significance to the Jewish threat that their leader did, so there is no reason to suppose that a whole nation was gripped by the same nihilistic embrace of the power of destruction itself which was such a prominent element in Hitler's own thinking. There is a major problem that still needs to be explained here: how do we account for the willingness of Germans to go on fighting a war they knew was being prosecuted by genocidal means. Perhaps, we need to think about what Germans hoped for as well as what they feared in this war. We need to move beyond the contours of Nazi propaganda and consider the transformative potency of German nationalism, as well as its specifically Nazi ideological variant, and contemplate a ruthless escalation of ideas grounded on national self-defence as well as on the drive to conquer. But this is a discussion among friends; and none of it makes the moral abyss any less deep, or the Holocaust less central.

## Notes

1    Peter Löffler (ed.), *Clemens August Graf von Galen: Akten, Briefe und Predigten 1933–1946*, vol. 2 (Mainz: Matthias Grünewald-Verlag, 1988), 878; Michael Burleigh, *Death and Deliverance: "Eithanasia" in Germany c. 1900–1945* (Cambridge: Cambridge University Press, 1994), 176–8 and 217.

2    Saul Friedländer, *The Years of Extermination: Nazi Germany and the Jews, 1939–1945* (London: Weidenfeld & Nicolson, 2007), 303, citing Löffler, *Clemens August Graf von Galen*, 910–11.

3    Saul Friedländer, *When Memory Comes* (New York: Farrer Straus Giroux, 1979), 120–2.

4    Friedländer, *The Years of Extermination*, 657–8.

5    Ibid., 656–7; Saul Friedländer, *Reflections of Nazism: An Essay on Kitsch and Death* (Bloomington: Indiana University Press, 1993), 131–4.

6    On the cultural history of German "victimhood" in the 1950s, see Robert G. Moeller, *War Stories: The Search for a Usable Past in the Federal Republic of Germany* (Berkeley: University of California Press, 2001; Hanna Schissler (ed.), *The Miracle Years: A Cultural History of West*

*Germany, 1949-1968* (Princeton, NJ: Princeton University Press, 2001); Bill Niven (ed.), *Germans as Victims: Remembering the Past in Contemporary Germany*, (Basingstoke: Palgrave Macmillan, 2006); for more moderate conservative continuities in Sebastian Haffner, *The Meaning of Hitler*, Cambridge, MA, 1983, and also Joachim Fest, *Der Untergang: Hitler und das Ende des Dritten Reiches* (Reinbek: Rowohlt, 2002), turned by Fest, Bernd Eichinger and Oliver Hirschgiebel into the feature film *Der Untergang* in 2004.

7   Friedländer, *The Years of Extermination*, 288.

8   Ibid., 426; citing Walter Manoschek (ed.), *"Es gibt nur eines für das Judentum – Vernichtung": Das Judenbild in deutschen Soldatenbriefen 1939-1944* (Hamburg: Hamburger Edition, 1997), 58.

9   The first, path-breaking study was Marlis Steinert, *Hitlers Krieg und die Deutschen: Stimmung und Haltung der deutschen Bevölkerung im Zweiten Weltkrieg* (Düsseldorf: Econ-Verlag, 1970; Heinz Boberach (ed.), *Meldungen aus dem Reich: Auswahl aus den geheimen Lageberichten des Sicherheitsdienstes der SS 1939-1944* (Neuwied: Luchterhand, 1965); Heinz Boberach (ed.), *Meldungen aus dem Reich: Die geheimen Lageberichte des Sicherheitsdienstes des SS 1938-1945*, vols. 1-17 (Berlin: Pawlak, 1984). The first forays into these sources for what they reveal about the murder of the Jews were: Ian Kershaw, "The Persecution of the Jews and German Popular Opinion in the Third Reich," *Leo Baeck Institute Year Book* 26 (1981): 261-89; Ian Kershaw, *Popular Opinion and Political Dissent in the Third Reich: Bavaria, 1933-1945* (Oxford: Clarendon Press, 1983); Ian Kershaw, "German Public Opinion during the 'Final Solution': Information, Comprehension, Reactions," in Asher Cohen, Joav Gelber and Charlotte Wardi (eds), *Comprehending the Holocaust*, (Frankfurt am Main: Lang, 1989), 145-58; Hans Mommsen, "What Did the Germans Know about the Genocide of the Jews?," in Walter H. Pehle (ed.), *November 1938: From "Reichskristallnacht" to Genocide* (New York: Berg, 1991), 187-221; Lawrence Stokes, "The German People and the Destruction of the European Jews," *Central European History* 6 (1973): 167-191. Research was widened by David Bankier, *The Germans and the Final Solution: Public Opinion under Nazism* (Oxford: B. Blackwell, 1992); Frank Stern, *The Whitewashing of the Yellow Badge: Antisemitism and Philosemitism in Postwar Germany* (Oxford: Pergamon, 1992); Robert Gellately, *The Gestapo and German Society: Enforcing Racial Policy, 1933-1945* (Oxford: Clarendon Press, 1990); Robert Gellately, *Backing Hitler: Consent and Coercion in Nazi Germany* (Oxford: Oxford University Press, 2001); Patrick Wagner, *Volksgemeinschaft ohne Verbrecher: Konzeption und Praxis der Kriminalpolizei in der Zeit der Weimarer Republik und des Nationalsozialismus* (Hamburg: Christians, 1996), especially 304-11 and 316-28. For a compilation of *Wehrmacht* reports from the home front in 1944-5, see Wolfram Wette, Ricarda Bremer and Detlef Vogel (eds), *Das letzte halbe Jahr: Stimmungsberichte der Wehrmachtpropaganda 1944/45* (Essen: Klartext-Verlag, 2001).

10  Otto Dov Kulka und Eberhard Jäckel (eds), *Die Juden in den geheimen NS-Stimmungsberichten, 1933-1945* (Düsseldorf: Droste, 2004). Other recent contributors are: Frank Bajohr and Dieter Pohl, *Der Holocaust als offenes Geheimnes / Die Deutschen, die NS-Führung und die Alliierten* (Munich: C. H. Beck, 2006); Peter Longerich, *"Davon haben wir nichts gewußt!" Die Deutschen und die Judenverfolgung 1933-1945* (Munich: Pantheon, 2006); Nicholas Stargardt, "Rumors of Revenge in the Second World War," in Belinda Davis, Thomas Lindenberger and Michael Wildt (eds), *Alltag, Erfahrung, Eigensinn. Historisch-anthropologische Erkundungen* (Frankfurt am Main: Campus Verlag, 2008), 373-88.

11  Yitzhak Arad, *Belzec, Sobibor, Treblinka: The Operation Reinhard Death Camps* (Bloomington: Indiana University Press, 1987), 170-8.

12  Kulka and Jaeckel, *Die Juden in den geheimen NS-Stimmungsberichten*, 3652, SD Außenstelle Bad Neustadt, Bericht ("I-Bericht – Allgemeine Stimmung und Lage"), 15.10.1943, StA Wü; SD-Hauptaußenstelle Würzburg Nr. 14: "Der Führer hätte daraufhin die Juden wieder ausgraben und verbrennen lassen, damit bei einem weiteren Rückzug im Osten den Sowjets kein Propagandamaterial wie das bei Katyn usw. in die Hände fallen würde."

13  See Ernst Klee, Willi Dressen and Volker Rieß (eds), *"The Good Old Days": The Holocaust as Seen by its Perpetrators and Bystanders* (New York: Free Press, 1991); Dieter Pohl, *Nationalsozialistische Judenverfolgung in Ostgalizien 1941-1944: Organisation und Durchführung eines staatlichen Massenverbrechens* (Munich: Oldenbourg, 1996); Dieter Pohl, "The Murder of the Jews in the General Government," in Ulrich Herbert (ed.), *National Socialist Extermination Policies:*

*Contemporary German Perspectives and Controversies* (New York and Oxford: Berghahn Books, 2000), 83–103; Thomas Sandkühler, *"Endlösung" in Galizien: der Judenmord in Ostpolen und die Rettungsinitiativen von Berthold Beitz 1941–1944* (Bonn: Dietz, 1996); Thomas Sandkühler, "Anti-Jewish Policy and the Murder of the Jews in the District of Galicia, 1941/42," in Herbert (ed.), *National Socialist Extermination Policies*, 104–27; and, on the significance of Holocaust photography in Germany more generally, Habbo Knoch, *Die Tat als Bild: Fotografien des Holocaust in der deutschen Erinnerungskultur* (Hamburg: Hamburger Edition, 2001).

14    Shmuel Spector, "Aktion 1005 – Effacing the Murder of Millions," *Holocaust and Genocide Studies* 5 (1990): 157–73.

15    On the British, see Martin Gilbert, *Auschwitz and the Allies* (London: Mandarin, 1981), 42–7; Bernard Wasserstein, *Britain and the Jews of Europe, 1939–1945* (London and Oxford: Clarendon Press, 1977), 173; on Goebbels, see Willi A. Boelcke (ed.), *Wollt Ihr den totalen Krieg? Die geheimen Goebbels-Konferenzen 1939–1943* (Munich: Deutscher Taschenbuch-Verlag, 1969), 409–13.

16    See Joseph Goebbels, *Die Tagebücher*, ed. Elke Fröhlich, vol. 2/8 (Munich: K. G. Saur, 1993), 119; Steinert, *Hitlers Krieg und die Deutschen*, 255–6; Longerich, *"Davon haben wir nichts gewusst!-"*, 267–81; Bajohr and Pohl, *Der Holocaust als offenes Geheimnis*, 69–70 and 102–3.

17    See Klaus Latzel, *Deutsche Soldaten – nationalsozialistischer Krieg? Kriegserlebnis – Kriegserfahrung 1939–1945* (Paderborn: Schöningh, 1998), 203–5; Jörg Friedrich, "'Die Wohnungsschlüssel sind beim Hausverwalter abzugeben': Die Ausschlachtung der jüdischen Hinterlassenschaft," in Jörg Wollenberg (ed.), *"Niemand war dabei und keiner hat's gewußt": Die deutsche Öffentlichkeit und die Judenverfolgung 1933–1945* (Munich and Zurich: Piper, 1989), 188–203 and Heiner Lichtenstein, "Pünktlich an der Rampe. Der Horizont des deutschen Eisenbahners," in ibid., 204–23.

18    David Bankier, "German Public Awareness of the Final Solution," in David Cesarani (ed.), *The Final Solution: Origins and Implementation* (London: Routledge, 1994), 215–27.

19    See Lewis Siegelbaum and Andrei Sokolov, *Stalinism as a Way of Life* (New Haven: Yale University Press, 2000), e.g. documents 40, 95, 117 and 118; Sarah Davies, *Popular Opinion in Stalin's Russia: Terror, Propaganda and Dissent, 1934–1941* (Cambridge: Cambridge University Press, 1997).

20    On Hitler's retreat, see Ian Kershaw, *Hitler. 1936–1945: Nemesis* (London: Penguin, 2000), 565–6; on Goebbels' frustration with the "defeatist" tone of the SD reports, see Longerich, *"Davon haben wir nichts gewußt!"*, 290; on the character of the SD apparatus and its reporting in general, see Boberach (ed.), *Meldungen aus dem Reich*, 1, 11–40; Michael Wildt, *Generation des Unbedingten: Das Führungskorps des Reichssicherheitshauptamtes* (Hamburg: Hamburger Edition, 2002), especially 239–51 and 378–91.

21    See Bankier, *The Germans and the Final Solution*, 148; Kulka and Jäckel, *Die Juden in den geheimen NS-Stimmungsberichten*, 3592, Regierungspräsident Schwaben, Bericht für Mai 1943 ("Monatsbericht (Lagebericht)"), Augsburg, 10.06.1943; 3571, SD Außenstelle Bad Brückenau III A 4, Bericht ("Stimmung und Lage"), Bad Brückenau, 22.04.1943; 3647, SD Außenstelle Schweinfurt, Bericht ("Lagebericht III A 4 – Allgemeine Stimmung und Lage"), Schweinfurt, 06.09.1943, StA Wü; SD-Hauptaußenstelle Würzburg Nr. 22; 3661, NSDAP Kreisschulungsamt Rothenburg/T., Bericht ("Weltanschaulicher Lagebericht"), Rothenburg/T., 22.10.1943, StA Nü; NS-Mischbestand Gauleitung Nr. 83; 3693, SD Außenstelle Schweinfurt III A 4, Bericht ("Lagebericht"), Schweinfurt, o.D. [1944], 1944 StA Wü; SD-Hauptaußenstelle Würzburg Nr. 22; 3573, SD Außenstelle Schweinfurt III A 4, Bericht, ("Lagebericht III A 4 – Allgemeine Stimmung und Lage"), Schweinfurt, 16.04.1943, StA Wü; SD-Hauptaußenstelle Würzburg 22.

22    Kulka and Jäckel, *Die Juden in den geheimen NS-Stimmungsberichten*, 3648, SD Hauptaußenstelle Würzburg III A 4, Bericht ("Allgemeine Stimmung und Lage"), Würzburg, 07.09.1943, StA Wü; SD-Hauptaußenstelle Würzburg Nr. 37: "ausgesprochener Judenstädte." For a different interpretation, reading these sources as expressing moral indifference, see Ian Kershaw, *Popular Opinion and Political Dissent*, 369 and Longerich, *"Davon haben wir nichts gewußt!"*, 284–7.

23    Kulka and Jäckel, *Die Juden in den geheimen NS-Stimmungsberichten*, 3708, SD Außenstelle [Bad Brückenau] III A 4, Bericht ("Stimmung und Lage"), Bad Brückenau, [2?].04.1944, StA Wü; SD-Hauptaußenstelle Würzburg Nr. 12: "Sehr pessimistische Stimmung und zunehmend fatalistische Gleichgültigkeit, stark beeinflußt durch Äußerungen und Schilderungen der

hier zahlreich eingetroffenen Frankfurter und Schweinfurter Bombengeschädigten. Vielfach zu hörende Meinung, daß Terrorangriffe besonders auf Frankfurt xfache Vergeltung für Judenaktion 1938 seien."

24   Kulka and Jäckel, *Die Juden in den geheimen NS-Stimmungsberichten*, 3628, SD Außenstelle Würzburg, Bericht ("Allgemeine Stimmung und Lage"), Würzburg, 03.08.1943, StA Wü; SD-Hauptaußenstelle Würzburg 23; 3718, SD Außenstelle Lohr III A 4, Bericht, ("Allgemeine Stimmung und Lage"), Lohr, 15.05.1944, StA Wü; SD-Hauptaußenstelle Würzburg Nr. 19: "da in Würzburg keine Synagoge gebrannt habe"; others warned "daß nunmehr auch die Flieger nach Würzburg kämen, da vor kurzer Zeit der letzte Jude Würzburg verlassen habe" and "vor seinem Abtransport erklärt, daß nun auch Würzburg Luftangriffe bekommen werde."

25   Kulka and Jäckel, *Die Juden in den geheimen NS-Stimmungsberichten*, 3661, NSDAP Kreisschulungsamt Rothenburg/T., Bericht ("Weltanschaulicher Lagebericht"), Rothenburg/T., 22.10.1943, StA Nü; NS-Mischbestand Gauleitung Nr. 83.

26   See Ralf Blank, "Kriegsalltag und Luftkrieg an der 'Heimatfront'," in Jörg Echternkamp (ed.), *Das Deutsche Reich und der Zweite Weltkrieg*, 9/1, *Die deutsche Kriegsgesellschaft 1939 bis 1945* (Munich: Deutsche Verlagsanstalt, 2004), 433–41.

27   Jeremy Noakes (ed.), *Nazism, 1919–1945: A Documentary Reader*, vol. 4, *The German Home Front in World War II* (Exeter: University of Exeter Press, 1998), 500.

28   Boberach (ed.), *Meldungen aus dem Reich*, 5426 and 5432, 2 July 1943: "Vergeltung:

> Es kommt der Tag, wo das Verbrechen von Wuppertal sich bitter rächt und ihr auf euern Länderflächen im Eisenhagel niederbrecht. Ihr Mörder trugt nicht Schmerzen in dieser Stadt und Feuersnot sogar das Kind am Mutterherzen schlugt ihr samt Greis und Vater tot. Das peitscht uns auf, auch nun zu hassen, mit wildester Verbissenheit, weil ihr mit allen Judenrassen das Schandmal von der Wupper seid. Die Toten rufen, sie zu rächen! Und wir stehn fest zu unserem Wort und bauen Waffen, die einst sprechen die harte Antwort auf den Mord."

29   Boberach (ed.), *Meldungen aus dem Reich*, 18 October 1943, 5885–7.

30   Kershaw, *Popular Opinion and Political Dissent*, 369, and Kershaw "German Public Opinion during the 'Final Solution'"; Longerich, *"Davon haben wir nichts gewußt!"*, 284–7; Friedländer, *The Years of Extermination*, 211–12; 293–96; 399–400; 510–20; 634–6; 643–44; Bajohr and Pohl, *Der Holocaust als offenes Geheimnis*, 66; Bankier, "German Public Awareness of the Final Solution," 221–2.

31   Karl Dürkefäldens, in Hans Dollinger (ed.), *Kain, wo ist dein Bruder? Was der Mensch im Zweiten Weltkrieg erleiden mußte – dokumentiert in Tagebüchern und Briefen* (Munich: List, 1983), 141: 12 June 1942.

32   Kulka and Jäckel, *Die Juden in den geheimen NS-Stimmungsberichten*, 3716, SD Außenstelle Bad Brückenau, Bericht, 8.5.1944, StA Wü; SD-Hauptaußenstelle Würzburg Nr.12.

33   Kulka and Jäckel, *Die Juden in den geheimen NS-Stimmungsberichten*, 3716, SD Außenstelle Bad Brückenau, Bericht ("Stimmung und Lage"), 08.05.1944, StA Wü; SD-Hauptaußenstelle Würzburg Nr. 12.

34   See Bundesarchiv, R55/570, 571, 577 and 578; also Nicholas Stargardt, "Opfer der Bomben und der Vergeltung," in Lothar Kettenacker (ed.), *Ein Volk von Opfern? Die neue Debatte um den Bombenkrieg 1940–45* (Berlin: Rowohlt, 2003), 56–71; and Stargardt, "Rumors of Revenge in the Second World War."

35   See Klemperer, *To the Bitter End: The Diaries of Victor Klemperer 1942–45* (London: Weidenfeld & Nicholson, 1999), 289 and 291: 12 and 19 Mar. 1944, and his *The Language of the Third Reich: LTI – Lingua Tertii Imperii: A Philologist's Notebook* (London: Athlone Press, 2000), 172–81.

36   David Bankier, "German Public Awareness of the Final Solution," 219–21; Jeffrey Herf, *The Jewish Enemy: Nazi Propaganda during World War II and the Holocaust* (Cambridge, MA: Belknap Press, 2008).

37   Boberach (ed.), *Meldungen aus dem Reich*, 26 July 1943, 5530ff.: "daß auch von uns alle gegnerischen Elemente im Osten, vor allem die Juden, ohne Rücksicht ausgemerzt worden seien. Dabei spielen Erzählungen von Soldaten und anderen im Osten eingesetzter Personen eine große Rolle."

38    Kulka and Jäckel, *Die Juden in den geheimen NS-Stimmungsberichten*, 3571, SD Außenstelle
      Bad Brückenau III A 4, Bericht ("Stimmung und Lage"), Bad Brückenau, 22.04.1943, StA
      Wü; SD-Hauptaußenstelle Würzburg 12: "[. . .] sieht ein großer Teil der Bevölkerung in der
      Beseitigung der polnischen Offiziere – wie bereits im vorhergehenden Bericht erwähnt – eben
      die radikale Aus[löschung] eines gefährlichen Gegners, wie es im Krieg nun einmal [nicht] zu
      vermeiden ist. Man könne auf dieselbe Linie die Bombenangriffe der Engländer und Amerikaner
      auf die deutschen [Städte] und letzten Endes auch unseren eigenen Vernichtungskampf gegen
      das Judentum setzen." See also reports 3567, 3568, 3570, 3574, 3589.
39    Kulka and Jäckel, *Die Juden in den geheimen NS-Stimmungsberichten*, 3604, NSDAP Parteikanzlei
      II B 4, Bericht für 6.6.-12.6.1943 ("Auszüge aus Berichten der Gauleitungen u.a. Dienststellen"),
      München, 12.06.1943, BArch; NS 6/415: "Wenn diese Ermordungen sich nicht bitter an uns
      rächen würden, dann gäbe es keine göttliche Gerechtigkeit mehr!" and "Aufgrund dieser bar-
      barischen Methoden sei auch eine humane Kriegsführung unserer Gegner nicht mehr möglich.
      Die Wutausbrüche der jüdischen Presse und ihre Vernichtungstendenzen sei die natürliche
      Reaktion."
40    The original German text is: "daß der 'totale Krieg' von den Volksgenossen als rücksichtsloser
      Einsatz aller Mittel zugunsten eines raschen Sieges verstanden wird, daß moralische Argumente
      in diesem Krieg auf der Gegenseite keine Rolle spielen und von unserer Seite aus nichts helfen,
      und daß eine rücksichtslose Anwendung der gleichen Mittel, in der Vergeltung der Angriffe die
      einzige richtige Antwort sei."
41    Kulka and Jäckel, *Die Juden in den geheimen NS-Stimmungsberichten*, 3572, SD Außenstelle
      Friedberg III A 4, Bericht ("Stimmung und Lage") Friedberg, 23.04.1943, StA Abg; NSDAP Gau
      Schwaben, SD Unterabschnitt Schwaben 2/1: "Die Russen wissen ganz genau was sie wollen.
      Die vernichten eine Schicht der Bevölkerung vollkommen, weil sie ihnen nicht paßt. Sie denken
      alles bis zum Ende und hören nicht in der Mitte auf wie wir!"
42    For both Catholics and Protestant objections to Nazi inhumanity, see Kulka and Jäckel, *Die
      Juden in den geheimen NS-Stimmungsberichten*, 3604, NSDAP Parteikanzlei II B 4, Bericht
      für 6.6.-12.6.1943 ("Auszüge aus Berichten der Gauleitungen u. a. Dienststellen"), München,
      12.06.1943, BArch; NS 6/415.
43    Bankier, "German Public Awareness of the Final Solution," 216, based on American Intelligence
      reports from the 12th Army Group.
44    As a farmer in the Schwerin district put it succinctly in the spring of 1944: "Der jetzige Krieg,
      der aus dem Kampf verschiedener Weltanschauungen gegen einander zu einem Ringen der
      germanischen Welt mit der jüdischen Welt geworden ist, hat in manchen Menschen erst das
      Wort Germanentum zu einem Begriff werden lassen." Kulka and Jäckel, *Die Juden in den
      geheimen NS-Stimmungsberichten*, 3713, SD Abschnitt Schwerin, Bericht ("Zum Bericht des
      SD-Abschnittes Schwerin"), Schwerin, 04.04.1944, BArch; NS 6/407.
45    Martin Broszat (ed.), *Von Stalingrad zur Währungsreform: Zur Sozialgeschichte des Umbruchs in
      Deutschland* (Munich: Oldenbourg, 1988); Ian Kershaw, *The "Hitler Myth": Image and Reality in
      the Third Reich* (Oxford: Oxford University Press, 1987), ch. 8; Kershaw, *Hitler*, 2, 556–7; Joachim
      Szodrzynski, "Die 'Heimatfront' zwischen Stalingrad und Kriegsende," in *Hamburg im "Dritten
      Reich"*, ed. Forschungsstelle für Zeitgeschichte in Hamburg (Göttingen: Wallstein-Verlag, 2005),
      633–85; Richard J. Evans, *The Third Reich at War, 1939–1945* (London: Allen Lane, 2008),
      449–50 and 463–6.
46    Michael Geyer, "Endkampf 1918 and 1945: German Nationalism, Annihilation, and Self-
      Destruction," in Alf Lüdtke and Bernd Weisbrod (eds), *No Man's Land of Violence: Extreme
      Wars in the 20th Century* (Göttingen: Wallstein-Verlag, 2006), 35–68; Richard Bessel, *Nazism
      and War* (New York: Modern Library, 2004), 169–81; Richard Bessel, *Germany, 1945: From War
      to Peace* (London: Simon & Schuster, 2009); on German resistance on the western front, see
      Klaus-Dieter Henke, *Die amerikanische Besetzung Deutschlands* (Munich: Oldenbourg, 1995).
47    Rafael A. Zagovec, "Gespräche mit der 'Volksgemeinschaft'. Die deutsche Kriegsgesellschaft
      im Spiegel westalliierter Frontverhöre," in Jörg Echternkamp (ed.), *Das Deutsche Reich und
      der Zweite Weltkrieg*, 9/2, *Die deutsche Kriegsgesellschaft 1939 bis 1945* (Munich: Deutsche
      Verlagsanstalt, 2004), 289–381, here 289, citing Klaus Mann, letter to his New York publisher
      Fritz Landshoff from the end of 1944, in *Der Wendepunkt: Ein Lebensbericht* (Reinbek bei
      Hamburg: Rowohlt, 2001), 649: "Warum hören sie nicht endlich auf? Worauf warten sie, die

Unglückseligen? Dies die Frage, die ich nicht nur Dir und mir, sondern auch jenen immer wieder stelle."

48  Zagovec, "Gespräche mit der 'Volksgemeinschaft,'" 347, 357–8.

49  Birthe Kundrus, *Kriegerfrauen: Familienpolitik und Geschlechterverhältnisse im Ersten und Zweiten Weltkrieg* (Hamburg: Christians, 1995), 261 and 271; Jill Stephenson, "'Emancipation' and its Problems: War and Society in Württemberg, 1939–45," *European History Quarterly* 17 (1987): 345–65, here 358–360; Jill Stephenson, *Hitler's Home Front: Württemberg Under the Nazis* (London and New York: Hambledon Continuum, 2006); Gerda Szepansky (ed.), *Blitzmädel, Heldenmutter, Kriegerwitwe. Frauenleben im Zweiten Weltkrieg* (Frankfurt am Main: Fischer-Taschenbuch-Verlag, 1986); Neil Gregor, "A Schicksalsgemeinschaft? Allied bombing, Civilian Morale, and Social Dissolution in Nuremberg, 1942–1945," *Historical Journal* 43 (2000): 1051–1070.

50  Bankier, *The Germans and the Final Solution*; Herf, *The Jewish Enemy*.

51  Kulka and Jäckel, *Die Juden in den geheimen NS-Stimmungsberichten*, 3595, NSDAP Parteikanzlei II B 4, Bericht für den 23.5.-29.9.5.1943 ("Auszüge aus Berichten der Gauleitungen u.a. Dienststellen"), München, 29.05.1943, BArch; NS 6/415: "Die Bevölkerung kritisiert zwei Dinge sehr stark: 1) Die Zerstörung der Talsperren ist ein außerordentlicher Erfolg der Engländer und die Umfälschung des berechtigten Angriffs auf eine kriegswichtige Anlage in einen reinen Terrorangriff wird nicht verstanden und 2) im Zusammenhang mit vorstehenden ist die Heraushebung eines Juden durchaus unverständlich"; see also Boberach (ed.), *Meldungen aus dem Reich*, 30 May 1943, 5285 and 5290.

52  Norbert Krüger, "Die Bombenangriffe auf das Ruhrgebiet im Frühjahr 1943," in Ulrich Borsdorf and Mathilde Jamin (eds), *Überleben im Krieg. Kriegserfahrungen in einer Industrieregion 1939–1945* (Reinbek bei Hamburg: Rowohlt, 1989), 88–100, here 91.

53  Joseph Goebbels, *Die Tagebücher*, in vols 9 and 15, ed. Elke Fröhlich *et al.* (Munich: K. G. Saur, 1993–2006), 8 May 1943.

54  Kulka and Jäckel, *Die Juden in den geheimen NS-Stimmungsberichten*, 3606, NSDAP Kreisleitung Bad Neustadt/Aisch, Bericht für Juni 1943 ("Weltanschaulicher Bericht"), Neustadt/Aisch, 17.06.1943, StA Nü; NS-Mischbestand Gauleitung Nr. 81: "Die Volksgenossen sind immer gleich bereit, an solche Erscheinungen zu große Hoffnungen zu knüpfen. Ich selbst weiß aus Erfahrung, daß man in Neustadt/Aisch schon fleißig davon spricht, daß diese Judengegnerschaft in den Feindländern wahrscheinlich zu einer Revolution und zum Zusammenbruch führen wird."

55  Gerwin Strobl, *The Germanic Isle: Nazi Perceptions of Britain* (Cambridge: Cambridge University Press, 2000), 141–50.

56  Bundesarchiv, R55, 578, Bl 210, Hans Humel, Direktor der Staatl. Ingenieurschule in Kaiserslautern, to Reichsminister Goebbels, 25 October 1944; R55/577, Bl. 35–6, Friedrich Schauer, Rechtsanwalt am Landgericht, Freiburg im Breisgau, to Reichsminister Goebbels, 10 November 1944.

57  Bundesarchiv, R 55/ 577, Dr AD Börner, Hamburg, to the Reichsminister for Propaganda, 3 December 1944: "Wir Deutschen sind aber gewöhnt zu einem gebildeten Volke zu reden. [. . .] Diese Voraussetzungen treffen für das kümmerlich Niveau der englisch sprechenden Völker nicht zu. Daher kommen wir in Gefahr, bei ihnen an Hirn und Herz vorbeizureden." And "in der Kunst, jemandem, der eine lange Leitung hat, etwas einzutrichtern, was er schwer begreift [. . .]."

# 9

# An "Indelible Stigma": The Churches between Silence, Ideological Involvement, and Political Complicity[1]

## Christian Wiese

*We will not [. . .] be capable of 'thinking the Shoah,' albeit inadequately, if we divorce its genesis, and its radical enormity from theological origins.*

GEORGE STEINER[2]

I

Saul Friedländer's multi-layered and thought-provoking history of the perse-cution of the German Jews between 1933 and 1939 and the genocide of the European Jews during the Second World War is distinguished by a wealth of characteristics that make it a masterpiece of today's Holocaust historiography. It is, in many respects, a conclusion and at the same time it breaks new ground, opening up new challenges and questions. Entitled *The Years of Persecution* and *The Years of Extermination*, the two volumes of his encompassing *magnum opus* about *Nazi Germany and the Jews* provide nothing less than a masterly synthesis resulting in a comprehensive, discerning reconstruction of the National Socialist Jewish policy in the different phases of the Third Reich. It illuminates, in a most impressive and painfully clear manner, the ideological motives and political developments that led to the unprecedented event of the Shoah. As Gulie Ne'eman Arad aptly put it: "This work embodies a lifetime of travail, to remember, understand and represent that which tempts forgetfulness, resists clarity and defies narration."[3] Many elements that contribute to the masterly quality of his account have already been praised and critically discussed in the literature: the differentiated ideological-critical elucidation of the phenomenon of "redemp-tive antisemitism" within the wider horizon of the development of "modern antisemitism" in Europe; the broad European perspective on the destruction of the Jews, which opens the view of the entire landscape of collaboration, abandon-ment of solidarity and political impotence in the war years; the interconnection of the history of ideology, perpetrator history and victim history; the "integrative" narrative strategy with which Friedländer tries "to name the nameless, to echo the voices of the speechless, of those who were silenced because, only because they were Jews, and to reclaim them for history,"[4] and through which, based on the memories and witness statements of the victims and the survivors of the Shoah, he makes visible the dimensions of the maelstrom of destruction that engulfed Jewish life in Europe during the war years; the theoretical clarity with which questions of memory and insight into the limits of the representation of the Shoah are made into the yardstick of his understanding;[5] and not least the attempt, perhaps unparalleled in any other history of the Shoah, to combine an ethos of dispassionate historical matter-of-factness with reverence for the enormity of the historical object, for the *tremendum* that is beyond human understanding and historical systematising, the effort to preserve, for all the necessary historical distance, that "initial sense of disbelief" that Holocaust historiography is always tempted to "eliminate" or to "domesticate."[6]

One element of this "disbelief" – apart from the stress on the "singularity of the Nazi project,"[7] the unprecedented nature of the crime itself and the incomprehensibility of the suffering connected with it – is the horror of the historian at the breakdown of any humanity, particularly in German society after 1933, but also in the rest of war-torn Europe. Despite all historical explanation there remains the incomprehensibility of the absence of any effective resistance against the discrimination and destruction practised on the Jewish minority; the shocking lack of solidarity and simple humaneness; the abrogation of moral standards rooted in Christianity or in secular traditions of enlightenment, human rights and liberalism through the brutalisation of politics that went beyond all historical experience; or the silence and profound involvement of the intellectual and religious elites. This horror, which casts a radical doubt on the very foundations of European culture, is described by Friedländer as follows:

> Not one social group, not one religious community, not one scholarly institution or professional association in Germany and throughout Europe declared its solidarity with the Jews [. . .]; to the contrary, many social constituencies, many power groups were directly involved in the expropriation of the Jews and eager, be it out of greed, for their wholesale disappearance. Thus Nazi and related anti-Jewish policies could unfold to their most extreme levels without the interference of any major countervailing interests.[8]

Reflections about the centuries-old Christian tradition of Jew-hatred and the obvious moral and political failure of the Churches before and during the period of National Socialism run like a *leitmotiv* through all parts of Friedländer's account of the Shoah and are more prominent than in most other comprehensive studies of the Third Reich and the genocide.[9] This indicates the importance he attributes to this aspect in trying to explain the catastrophic erosion of fundamental categories of humanity, compassion and respect for the value of life. Thus the remarkable achievements and challenges of his work include the historical precision, analytical force and moral intensity with which he has woven the complex theme of the role of Christianity in the creation of modern antisemitism and the concrete involvement of the Churches in the National Socialist Jewish politics in his narrative. The striking centrality of this aspect in Friedländer's account is a result of the fact that this topic – beginning with his documentation about *Pius XII and the Third Reich*, dedicated to "the memory of My Parents Killed at Auschwitz,"[10] and his detailed study of Kurt Gerstein[11] – had troubled him for decades. As his own painful journey of remembering in *When Memory Comes* shows, this theme is deeply anchored in his biographical experience: in the memories of the historian who, after having been baptised while being hidden in a French monastery, "had passed over to Catholicism, body and soul" and who, after the war, rediscovered his Jewishness in conversation with a Catholic priest who spoke to him "of the lot of the Jews with [. . .] much emotion and respect."[12] Apart from that, however, the important role of the Churches in his interpretation of the Shoah can also be traced back to the fact that its analysis can serve to discuss decisive aspects of Holocaust research: the nature of Nazi antisemitism as opposed to the tradition of Christian Jew-hatred in Europe; the question of the anchoring of Nazi ideology in German society; the problem of complicity mainly among the intellectual elites; the causes of the lack of dissent and resistance against the criminal character of the regime; and the role of Christian prejudices as a motive for collaborating with the Jewish policy of the Nazis in many regions of occupied Europe.

The comments which follow trace Friedländer's analysis, reflecting it in the wider context of the current research on antisemitism and the Holocaust and in particular the exploration of the role of the Churches in Nazi Germany, and trying to initiate a discussion between these often separated research areas. Special importance is attributed to a critical comparison with Daniel J. Goldhagen's controversial views regarding the nature of Nazi antisemitism and the contribution of Christianity as well as the Churches to the destruction of European Jewry. It will be seen that Friedländer's attempt at interpretation is strongly motivated by the striving for differentiation and justice in historical judgement without alleviating the horrifying extent of Christianity's and the Churches' involvement. Attention will also be paid to the way the Churches responded to the fateful historical effects of Christian Jew-hatred, their collusion with modern antisemitism and the role of theology and the Churches in the discrimination, disenfranchisement, persecution, abandonment and murder inflicted on a large proportion of European Jews. This critical investigation, above all in Germany, became a fundamental element of theological self-reflection after 1945 and has grown worldwide into a central characteristic of the reorientation of Christian self-understanding in the course of the Jewish-Christian dialogue since the 1970s and 1980s. The recognition of the horrifying dimension of responsibility shared by Christians and the Christian Churches for the crimes of the Shoah – accomplished initially by a few theologians who exposed themselves to the shock of the 'break in civilisation' represented by Auschwitz and to the profound challenge it poses to their own tradition – became the foundation on which the dialogue between Christianity and Judaism rests at present. The process of the recognition and the historically correct elucidation of the historic guilt of Christianity has advanced the awareness that Christian tradition's fundamentally anti-Jewish orientation and the repression and distortion of Jewish self-understanding in the history of Christian Europe – including the "catastrophic violence"[13] against Jews connected with this – have caused infinite suffering and belong to the history of the murderous antisemitism of the Nazis. As a result the Churches, while still at risk of falling back into the traditional stereotypes of their theology and practice, have advanced part of the way to overcoming the deeply rooted 'teaching of contempt' (Jules Isaac) for Judaism. However, this is not a matter of learning processes strictly within Christianity, but a joint confrontation of history by Jews and Christians. Without the challenge, the contradiction, the encouragement of a readiness to engage in dialogue – and the patience of Jewish interlocutors – the discourse about causes, forms and consequences of Christian antisemitism and the critical examination of those elements in Christian theology hostile to Jews and to Judaism could not have acquired the dynamic and the intensity that has been in evidence since the 1980s. The profoundly disturbing recognition that the genocide occurred in a heartland of Christian Western culture – which from a purely Christian perspective is a cause for extreme shame and dismay – has become a shared Christian and Jewish challenge and a motive for a reflection, carried out in a dialogue about the human condition, religion and ethics after Auschwitz.

## II  CHRISTIAN ANTISEMITISM AND MODERN ANTISEMITISM: CONTINUITIES AND DISCONTINUITIES

> Christianity is a religion that consecrated at its core and, historically, spread throughout its domain a megatherian hatred of one group of people: the Jews. It libelously deemed them – sometimes in its sacred texts and doctrine, to be Christ-killers, children of the devil, desecrators and defilers of all goodness, responsible for an enormous range of human calamities and suffering. This hatred – Christianity's betrayal of its own essential and good moral principles – led Christians, over the course of almost two millennia, to commit many grave crimes and other injuries against Jews, including mass murder. The best-known and largest of these mass murders is the Holocaust.[14]

This passage, quoted from Daniel J. Goldhagen's book *A Moral Reckoning*, is characteristic of a range of attempts to go beyond a historical analysis of the concrete part played by theology and ecclesiastical politics in the persecution and destruction of European Jewry and to raise the ethical question of how the Churches handled their share of the responsibility for the Shoah. With the Catholic Church as an example, it represents a type of historical interpretation – practiced by Jewish and non-Jewish researchers alike – that assumes the unequivocal complicity of Christianity with genocide[15] and an undeniable continuity between religious forms of Jew-hatred, modern antisemitism in the second half of the nineteenth century, and the racial antisemitism of the Nazis. In his massive attack on the Roman Catholic Church, which evolved from a review of recent writing about the problematic role of Pope Pius XII during the

Shoah, Goldhagen postulates the existence of an "eliminationist antisemitism" that was deeply rooted in Church history. This ideology did not demand the mass murder of Jews and was even capable of expressly rejecting violent solutions. Nevertheless, based on the political dimension of the centuries-old religious demonization of Jews and Judaism, it "was, however unintended, compatible with or implied eliminationist solutions, including perhaps extermination"[16]: "Anti-Semitism led to the Holocaust. Anti-Semitism has been integral to the Catholic Church. The question of what the relationship is between the Church's anti-Semitism and the Holocaust should be at the center of any general treatment of either one."[17]

Goldhagen's critique of the Catholic Church begins with an assessment of the tradition of Christian Jew-hatred as a fundamental theological and ethical failure at the heart of Christianity and a detailed reconstruction of the Church's historical guilt up to the time of the Shoah. It continues by accusing the Church of a lack of repentance and critical self-reflection after Auschwitz, and it ends by demanding a radical reorientation of the Church's theological traditions. Ultimately, it is an explication of the moral subtext of his no less controversial book *Hitler's Willing Executioners*. In placing the antisemitic ideology at the centre of his explanation of the Shoah Goldhagen claims that the Nazis' policy of annihilating the Jews can be traced back to a certain type of "ubiquitous demonizing, racial anti-Semitism"[18] which dominated the ideas of German society and its elites, including the Churches, to such an extent that the overwhelming majority of Germans became willing, enthusiastic followers of National Socialism, among whom it was easy to recruit the real murderers. Using the police battalions that took part in the mass murders in east Europe, the labour camps and the death marches towards the end of the war, he analyzes the motives of the perpetrators – with the result that a willing, indeed enthusiastic readiness to murder, an inclination to humiliate the victims and sadism without end was a characteristic feature of German society. The obsessive "eliminationist" antisemitism, which in his view was responsible for this, dated back to the Middle Ages and the Early Modern period; in Germany it had acquired a dominant political and cultural significance by the nineteenth century.[19] There were several interrelated types of "eliminationism." The first was the moderate, liberal type of the progressive forces, who regarded the Jews in Germany as an alien element, but one that was capable of becoming assimilated and truly German by accepting German culture in general and Christianity in particular. This amounted to an elimination of the Jews by assimilation and conversion. The second type of "eliminationism" was the more radical antisemitism of those nationalists who wanted to restore the situation that had pertained in Germany before the Jews were emancipated and granted equal rights. The even more extreme third type was represented by those who wanted to drive out the Jews, as the medieval rulers of western and central Europe had done. Finally Goldhagen describes in great detail the murderous type of "eliminationism," which had developed into the antisemitism of the Nazis in the twentieth century. According to Goldhagen almost the entire German nation, whether passively or actively, willingly participated in the project of the destruction of the Jewish people because German society was totally steeped in this variant of antisemitism, which he distinguishes from the others but nevertheless portrays as an expression of the same "eliminationist" mindset. The Christian tradition as well as the Protestant and Catholic Churches in Germany play a central part in Goldhagen's contention that the antisemitism of the Nazi period was an "axiom of German culture" and "just a more accentuated, intensified, and elaborated form of an already broadly accepted basic model."[20] He claims that Christian culture had turned the Jews into a "central cultural symbol," in fact "the symbol of all that was awry in the world"[21] – a structure that had persisted throughout the transformations and intensifications of Christian prejudice. He recognizes historical change in the cultural and ideological manifestations of Jew-hatred and he grants that antisemitism in its extreme racial and *völkisch* form has invalidated traditional Christian elements – such as the hope of limits on violence extended to Jews by salvific history. However, he interprets it as a mere modernization of a Manichaean construction and a demonization of Judaism created by Christianity. The question with which Goldhagen confronts the Churches, despite the many deficiencies and the lack of historical differentiation and intellectual distance in his judgement,[22] is whether there is indeed *one* continuous line from traditional Christian Jew-hatred – which is already discernible in texts of the New Testament, by way of medieval Jew-hatred, Luther's anti-Jewish diatribes, the ambivalent judgements on Judaism during the Enlightenment period and the nationalism of German romanticism – to modern antisemitism, and whether the history of Jewish suffering all the way to the Shoah was not a direct consequence of Christian ideas about Judaism. As long as the Churches fail to admit this truth, Goldhagen says, the road to a genuine change of direction and a reconciliation between Judaism and Christianity will remain barred.[23]

The heated public debate about Goldhagen's portrayal of Catholicism[24] indicates the problematic nature of his moralising passion. But, at the same time it reveals the challenge that the determination of the relationship of Christian Jew-hatred and modern antisemitism, including its destructive consequences, represents for the Churches. It shows, as well, how strong the temptation is to evade recognition of guilt and the failure of theology and the Churches by pointing out the author's careless historical mistakes. An exemplary expression of this attitude is the document *We Remember: A Reflection on the Shoah*, published in 1998 by the "Holy See's Commission for Religious Relations with the Jews," which can be read as a precise counter-thesis to Goldhagen's point of view (or, as we shall see, to Saul Friedländer's analysis). This statement solemnly condemns all forms of antisemitism, demanding, in the face of the Shoah's "unspeakable tragedy," a "moral and religious memory and, particularly among Christians, a very serious reflection on what gave rise to it." But it consistently avoids mentioning any guilt on the part of the Church and, by drawing a sharp dividing line between anti-Judaism and antisemitism, as well as placing a strong emphasis on Catholic objections to the policies of the Nazis, finally arrives at the thesis: "The *Shoah* was the work of a thoroughly modern neo-pagan regime. Its antisemitism had its roots outside Christianity and, in pursuing its aims, it did not hesitate to oppose the Church and persecute her members also." Even the concession that religious stereotypes of Christians could have prevented the development of Christian sensitivity to the persecution of the Jewish minority ends with an apologetic interpretation, which claims that ultimately it was not the Church as an institution, but at the most "some Christians" who had incurred the guilt of hostility towards Jews and Judaism and "indifference" to the fate of the hard-pressed Jewish people. In contrast, "many" Christians and Christian functionaries are mentioned as having saved Jews.[25] This half-hearted examination by the Catholic Church of its own past caused bitter disappointment. It was sharply criticized not only by Jewish authors but also by Christians engaged in the dialogue with Judaism.[26] This suggests that Christian self-reflection had long since arrived at much more radical conclusions, leaving such a trivialization of theological anti-Judaism – which should have been overcome in the entire *oikumene* a long time ago, at least in official proclamations – far behind.

Christian theology cannot wish to retract the reflections about the shared responsibility of Christianity for the Shoah that have been aired in different variants all over the world by both the Catholic and the Protestant Churches[27] without reversing the process of a profound renewal of the definition of the relationship of Judaism and Christianity and demolishing the very foundation of a still extremely sensitive dialogue. "Remembering the Shoah," as the study *Christen und Juden III* of 14 March 2000 by the Council of the Evangelical Church in Germany has it, "for all Christians means the insight that it is the consequence and culmination of a relationship with Judaism that has been misdirected for almost two thousand years."[28] In its reply to the Vatican's document *We Remember* the International Jewish Committee for Interreligious Consultations issued a warning against an uncritical separation of "anti-Judaism" and "antisemitism," and demanded an honest recognition of the link between both phenomena despite all the justifiable historical distinctions:

> The implication that while Christians have been guilty of anti-Judaism antisemitism is a contradiction of the teaching of the Church is dubious and it is unfortunate that it is put forward in generalities that could well mislead many for whom this document is intended. There was indeed a change in the main emphases of antisemitism in the late nineteenth century from a religious basis to a more secular prejudice with a pseudo-racialist base. However can it be said that the latter was not influenced by the long centuries of Church conditioning? [. . .] Thus the statement that this was 'an anti-Judaism that was essentially more sociological and political than religious' plays down the fact of the unbroken line of Christian anti-Judaism/antisemitism and its impact throughout Europe. After all, the Jew was still the deicide and the traditional anti-Jewish stereotypes were not changed or renounced and were absorbed into the new antisemitism. The Catholic attitude toward the Jews was unchanged and its influence cannot be excluded. This is why the suggestion of a complete dichotomy between 'anti-Judaism'

and 'antisemitism' is misleading. One shades into the other. It was Christian anti-Judaism that created the possibility of modern pagan antisemitism by delegitimizing the Jews and Judaism. [...] It is true that the National Socialist regime adopted a pagan ideology which rejected the Church – although this did not mean that all Churchmen and believers rejected National Socialism. It may be noted that Hitler, Himmler and the other Nazi leaders were all baptized Christians who were never excommunicated. The same is true of the vast apparatus of killers, the product of Christian Europe. The Church is not accused of direct responsibility for the Shoah but of its legacy of sixteen centuries of conditioning which had created an environment in which a Shoah became possible and many Christians would feel no compunction in collaborating.[29]

The controversy about the historical effect of Christian antisemitism and the shared responsibility of the Churches for the Shoah is not restricted to Christianity's internal discourse. It also plays a decisive part in the current dialogue between Christians and Jews and it leads to very different judgements even among Jewish dialogue partners. This is corroborated by a look at a fiercely disputed passage of the declaration *Dabru Emet: A Jewish Statement on Christians and Christianity*,[30] drafted by a group of Jewish scholars in 2000 and signed in the USA by more than 200 rabbis and intellectuals. The document was intended by its initiators to respond to changes in the attitude of the Churches towards Judaism in past decades and to dispel the reservations within the Jewish public against active participation in the Christian-Jewish dialogue. A central thesis of the document tries to counteract the construction of a direct line of continuity between Christian Jew-hatred and the Holocaust and to make appropriate historical distinctions:

Nazism was not a Christian phenomenon. Without the long history of Christian anti-Judaism and Christian violence against Jews, Nazi ideology could not have taken hold nor could it have been carried out. Too many Christians participated in, or were sympathetic to, Nazi atrocities against Jews. Other Christians did not protest sufficiently against these atrocities. But Nazism itself was not an inevitable outcome of Christianity. If the Nazi extermination of the Jews had been fully successful, it would have turned its murderous rage more directly to Christians. We recognize with gratitude those Christians who risked or sacrificed their lives to save Jews during the Nazi regime. With that in mind, we encourage the continuation of recent efforts in Christian theology to repudiate unequivocally contempt of Judaism and the Jewish people. We applaud those Christians who reject this teaching of contempt, and we do not blame them for the sins committed by their ancestors.

Unlike *We Remember* this passage aims not at an exoneration of Christianity but at a discerning treatment of historical reality. There is no doubt that the text is based on the results of recent historical debates, which it reflects at least in hints. This does not alter the fact that the authors are not historians and that both individual statements and the intention of the passage as a whole are highly problematic shorthand, if only in response to the genre of a theological explanation.

The authors themselves realized this and anticipated the criticism of some Jewish commentators who feared that the formulations concerning antisemitism might be used by Christians to avoid the painful confrontation with Christian historical guilt. They argued that what was intended was something completely different, that is, a fair assessment of history which recognized that Christianity included some central values that contained the potential for resistance against the Nazi ideology and in some cases had actually led to solidarity with the persecuted Jews. This negation of the unavoidable involvement of Christianity in the crimes of the Nazis, they claimed, provided the basis for a Jewish-Christian dialogue by indicating the possibility of overcoming Christian anti-Judaism. Michael Signer in particular also stressed the pedagogical and psychological function of the passage: to suggest topics for a dialogue that will enable Christians to "discover" the anti-Judaism of their own tradition and to "choose" an alternative route. By acknowledging the rescue of Jews by Christians, recognizing the attempts of post-1945 Christian theology to reject the contempt for Judaism and the Jewish people, and refraining from accusations against contemporary Christians the document had been intended not to promote "forgiveness" but to provide an answer to Christian "metanoia" that would encourage greater efforts to reform the relations of Christians with Judaism.[31] Not least, Jewish interpreters such as David Rosen have engaged in hermeneutical reflections about the particular context of *Dabru Emet*, stressing that the entire explanation is not addressed to Christians but must be understood in the context of a debate between Jews in the USA which is strongly affected by the awareness of the connection between Christian Jew-hatred and the Shoah: "Of course, if this had been a Christian statement, then we would have expected some extensive soul searching and greater acknowledgement of the sin of Christian antisemitism. But *Dabru Emet* is a Jewish statement that is explicitly directed at Jews. The Jewish community does not need persuading as to the case of Christian historic guilt and responsibility for antisemitism – on the contrary! As a modern Jewish leader in the dialogue with Christianity has put it, the Jewish community often tends to indulge in a 'triumphalism of pain.'"[32]

Insofar as *Dabru Emet* aims above all to counteract the monolinear identification of Christianity, antisemitism and the Shoah in the American-Jewish context, it requires not only a general historical commentary but also an intensive critical exegesis of both the overall structure and individual formulations of the text. This shows that the reflection about the shared responsibility of Christianity for the Shoah not only oversimplifies the historical discourse but in part misses the point and therefore holds more dangers than opportunities. At first sight the text contains several elements that – considered in isolation – even seem to have structural similarities to the Vatican document *We Remember*, despite the completely different motivation. The radical thesis "Nazism was not a Christian phenomenon," which would be historically incorrect without recourse to differentiated reflections about the interplay of Christian and non-Christian elements in modern antisemitism and the receptivity of Christian theologies to

Nazi ideology, does not, in principle, preclude the disastrously trivial interpretation implied in the view that antisemitism has "its roots outside of Christianity." The next sentence – "Without the long history of Christian anti-Judaism and Christian violence against Jews, Nazi ideology could not have taken hold nor could it have been carried out" – implies the sharing of responsibility by Christianity. However, owing to its linguistic structure, which suggests a rather passive effect of Christian discourse about Judaism, Christianity fails to articulate what a Christian reception must urgently stress in a self-critical way: that Christian theology and the policy of the Churches, as well as a widespread social mentality determined by demonizing stereotypes of the "alien" dangerous Jew, actively and often consciously, prepared the ground for the National Socialist policy of disenfranchisement and – a few exceptions apart – contributed to the fate of the Jewish minority through consistent desolidarization and quiet surrender. It is true that the text of *Dabru Emet* refers to a violent relationship between Christians and Jews and does not deny the participation of Christians in the "atrocities" of the Nazis. However, with its rather simplistic use of language and argument it is unable to counter the suppression of the concrete historical affinity of anti-Jewish thought patterns and the National Socialist ideology by documents such as *We Remember*. At any rate, a Christian reception would have to state unequivocally that the unprecedented monstrosity of the crime was "not only, albeit primarily, the first, German nightmare of European history, but also the real culmination of a European fantasy of destruction sown by Christians."[33] It would also have to become clear that a wealth of historical writing demonstrates the extent to which anti-Jewish theology and racial antisemitism could mutually influence and reinforce each other; and that the spectrum of Christian guilt and shared responsibility for the Shoah extended from active ecclesiastic and theological complicity to the failure even of those in the resistance movement against the Nazi regime who were Christian-motivated to feel, let alone to express solidarity with the persecuted Jews. Not least, it would be necessary to name the phenomenon of a racially infected antisemitic current within the Church – say, the Protestant 'German-Christian' theology, whose radical representatives aimed to conquer the Church for National Socialism and who tried to cleanse Christianity of all Jewish traces.[34] Without a detailed historical commentary analyzing and naming the guilt and the responsibility in concrete terms, the text of *Dabru Emet* is, at the very least, liable to be misunderstood and prone to apologetic interpretations. Its fundamental message intervenes in a historically controversial debate about the structural involvement of the Christian Churches in the National Socialists' racial antisemitism and their shared responsibility for the Shoah, and it seems to put an end to this debate by the apodictic sound of its main argument. However, what is indispensable for the unfolding of a common Christian-Jewish horizon of understanding in respect of this central question is precisely an open discourse about historical reciprocities and differences.

In any case the historical facts revealed by the research into antisemitism and the Holocaust are much more complex than *Dabru Emet* – arising as it does from the context of the attempts at a religious dialogue – is able to explain. The proposition "Nazism was not a Christian phenomenon" initially only articulates a historical distinction that is also frequently supported by Jewish scholars, but it can be weighted in different ways. The historical classification and interpretation is often determined as soon as the controversial question is raised of whether or not to make a conceptual and functional distinction between "anti-Judaism" and "antisemitism" and further types of Jew-hatred. In today's historical research the term "antisemitism" is frequently applied to all the periods and varieties of Jew-hatred, while distinguishing, say, "religious," "political" or "racial" antisemitism. However, the clear distinction between "anti-Judaism" and "antisemitism" is classic and still widespread. It can claim that the term "antisemitism," used as a self-description, did not appear till the second half of the nineteenth century. As is well-known, the term was originally intended to indicate that the antisemites were not concerned with religious prejudice, or the conflict between Christians and Jews, but with the allegedly objective contrast between the "Aryan" and the "Semitic race." According to this distinction, "anti-Judaism" was a theological concept directed against Judaism based on the conviction that the Jews had been driven out of their country as a punishment for allegedly murdering the Son of God. Consequently, they were now living scattered and deprived of rights – as a sign of the truth of Christianity – among the nations, while the status of being Chosen had been transferred to the Church as the "new Israel."

The distinction between "anti-Judaism" and "antisemitism" is said to be susceptible to the trivialization of religious Jew-hatred and frequently inclined to overlook the concrete political dimension of theological issues. It can be argued that theological anti-Judaism has never been a 'purely theological' phenomenon, but has always influenced the concrete political relations with the Jewish minority through its images and myths, be it directly or by imprinting a mentality that regarded the persecution, disenfranchisement and violent treatment of Jews as a matter of course and justified. Religious, cultural and political-social or economic reasons have always been closely interwoven, and theological ideas about Jews and Judaism never failed to have a concrete existential effect on the objects of those ideas. That is why Goldhagen warns against a distinction between anti-Judaism and antisemitism, which in his view "is itself founded on a fiction, a sanitized account of the Church's so-called anti-Judaism," and assumes an indissoluble connection between them.[35] His theses, therefore, lead to the question of whether there is such a thing as an "eternal Jew-hatred" that has pervaded the history of the Western world since the beginning of Christianity and assumed in Germany, in particular, "eliminatory" features until the catastrophe occurred between 1933 and 1945; or whether it is necessary to assume clear ruptures and transformations which endowed Jew-hatred with a completely new quality. The long-standing question about the influence of Christian antisemitism on later racial or Nazi antisemitism has, however, been the topic of intense disagreement, with historians providing very different answers.[36] Hannah Arendt, for example, in *The Origins of Totalitarianism* demanded, precisely with reference to the Shoah a strict distinction between the murderous hatred of modern antisemitism since the nineteenth century and the traditional Christian Jew-hatred. She regarded the hypothesis of the continuity of an "eternal antisemitism" of Christian provenance as absurd.[37] George L. Mosse, in his *The Nationalization of the Masses*, made a similar argument, stating that the Nazis, like the intellectual "forefathers" of racial antisemitism in general, completely changed the character of anti-Jewish prejudice by secularising, albeit not abandoning the "basic form" of Christian anti-Judaism.[38] Michael Burleigh echoes this interpretation when he argues that Christianity's "fundamental tenets were stripped out," even though "the remaining diffuse religious emotionality had its uses."[39] In contrast to this line of argument Leon Poliakov – like Raul Hilberg in his seminal book *The Destruction of the European Jews*[40]– in the Preface to his comprehensive *The History of Antisemitism* argues that "antisemitism" must be understood as an ancient phenomenon which has remained unchanged, not in its forms of expression, but in its essence.[41] And Lucy Dawidowicz in her portrayal of the Shoah likewise traces modern racial antisemitism to "Haman's advice to Ahasuerus," even though she is aware that it has more recent roots in the nineteenth century: the German variant of modern antisemitism was "the bastard child of the union of Christian antisemitism with German nationalism."[42] Other historians such as Steven T. Katz contradicted this assumption of an essential continuity between Christian and National Socialist antisemitism and – without trivializing the dehumanization and demonization of the Jews by Christian theology – pointed out that Christian thinking was able to live with contradictions, including the continuing existence of Judaism despite its alleged divine "rejection," or defer the resolution of the contradiction to the end of history. On the other hand, secular racist ideologies raised the "solution of the Jewish Question" to the level of a human task and thus aimed to disenfranchise and expel, and in their extreme *völkisch* form destroy the Jews.[43] It is true that Katz too notes a "decisive element of continuity" – the construction of the "otherness of Jews" – but unlike Goldhagen he concludes that the Shoah was "not primarily a consequence of traditional antisemitism." Instead it resulted from the "Aryan myth," together with its counter-myth of the biologically inferior and destructive character of the Jews and its dualistic outlook that explained the course of Western history, including the social, political and intellectual conflicts of the time, with reference to the alleged German-Jewish racial differences.[44]

The dissension in both Christian and Jewish historiography concerning the evaluation of the precise historical connection between the centuries-old ecclesiastical tradition of Jew-hatred and the murderous antisemitism of the Nazis shows that this is one of the most complex and controversial questions not only of the critical self-reflection of Christendom after the Shoah but also of the history of antisemitism. The distinction between the two phenomena always balances on a ridge between a necessary historical differentiation and an improper trivialization of what seems to be a 'merely theological' anti-Judaism. The argument that the latter – the theological antagonism to Judaism – essentially belongs to Christianity but must not be made responsible for antisemitism and the Shoah, was and is to this day one of the most common strategies for avoiding a confrontation with the historical guilt of Christian theology and the Churches. However, the theoretical differentiation between racial, political, economic or cultural antisemitism and theological anti-Judaism that aims at a precise historical understanding of anti-Jewish motives and causes is meaningless and irresponsible unless it serves as an instrument of critical analysis, precluding the trivialization of 'merely' anti-Judaistic images of Judaism by leaving the political implications out of account.[45] It is necessary to recognize the interplay between the two phenomena and to examine in concrete terms the way in which Christian elements continued to be active in antisemitism and how closely models of anti-Judaistic and antisemitic thought have been linked in recent history.[46] Christian self-reflection needs to acknowledge historical research into antisemitism that asks very precise questions about the continuing effect of traditional theological thought patterns in the new, often secular contexts of the nineteenth and twentieth centuries. Renowned scholars such as Yehuda Bauer and, above all, Saul Friedländer have unequivocally contradicted both the separation of anti-Judaism and modern antisemitism and Goldhagen's simplistic thesis of continuity. They have demanded a clear analysis of both the differences and the connections between the different forms of antisemitism before the Nazi era and the genocidal antisemitic ideology of the Nazis. Bauer pleads for a differentiated approach that recognizes the special position of antisemitism in the Nazi ideology, but at the same time bears in mind its connection with the racist and nationalist programme for rearranging the map of Europe and takes the new murderous dimension of Nazi antisemitism seriously. He describes the "latent or overt nonmurderous antisemitic attitudes in the general population" as a consequence of a Christian antisemitism "that had sought to dehumanize the Jews for many centuries," but was never "translated into a genocidal program" by Christian society. It was not directly responsible for the Nazi persecution, but it had a disastrous effect on the development of hateful mentalities and, as an antisemitic consensus, "prevented any serious opposition to the Nazis once they had decided to embark on the murder of the Jews."[47] And Friedländer, who does not regard Goldhagen's teleological reconstruction of the continuity of an "eliminationist" antisemitism as worthy of a detailed refutation and rejects it with a laconic remark,[48] suggests that "the majority of Germans, although undoubtedly influenced by various forms of traditional antisemitism and easily accepting the segregation of the Jews, shied away from widespread violence against them, urging neither their expulsion from the Reich nor their physical annihilation."[49]

Friedländer's extremely helpful, sophisticated interpretation of the relationship between Christian Jew-hatred and modern antisemitism is part of his comprehensive analysis of the specific character of Nazi antisemitism. In the first volume of *Nazi Germany and the Jews* his starting point is a differentiated connection between traditional and modern motives, according to which the biological-racist antisemitic ideology of the Nazis did, indeed, use traditional antisemitic images and stereotypes, but radicalized them. With its fantasies of being under threat as well as its visions of the exclusion, disfranchisement and expulsion of the Jews the Nazi ideology decisively went beyond the general anti-Jewish resentment that had been rife at the end of the nineteenth century and especially after the First World War. In opposition to the separation of the two phenomena Friedländer stresses the relevance of two aspects for the new radical racial antisemitism: "the survival of traditional religious anti-Semitism and the related proliferation of conspiracy theories in which the Jews always played a central role."[50]

That radical antisemites could invoke Christian Jew-hatred as a matter of course is, in his view, a result of the *longue durée* of the perhaps most deeply rooted prejudice in Christian Europe, that is, the fact that "in dogma, ritual, and practice, Christianity branded the Jews with what appeared to be an indelible stigma. That stigma had been effaced neither by time nor by events, and throughout the nineteenth and the early decades of the twentieth centuries, Christian religious anti-Semitism remained of central importance in Europe and in the Western world in general."[51] At the same time Friedländer contradicts the analysis of those Jewish historians for whom the "rootedness" and the "very permanence of Christian anti-Judaism" represents the only foundation of all forms of modern antisemitism. In so doing he refers not to Goldhagen, but to Jacob Katz's argument that modern antisemitism is merely "a continuation of the premodern rejection of Judaism by Christianity, even when it [modern antisemitism] renounced any claim to be legitimized by it or even professed to be antagonistic to Christianity." Friedländer considers this interpretation "excessive,"[52] but agrees in principle with the assumption that modern antisemitism is unimaginable without the profound influence on European societies of the religious antagonism to Jews and Judaism. He believes that the murderous racial antisemitism that led to an unprecedented crime in Nazi Germany possessed a new quality in comparison to traditional Jew-hatred. He aptly calls this "redemptive anti-Semitism" because it made the redemption of "Germanness" and the Aryan world dependent on liberation from the Jews and was therefore consistently inclined to racial struggle and strategies of extermination. Based on this premise, Friedländer assumes a dual connection between anti-Judaism and modern antisemitism which is decisive for a differentiated evaluation of the historical impact of Christian elements right up to the Shoah. One aspect which will be discussed later concerns the specific contributions of Christian theologians and Church leaders who expressed opinions about antisemitism and the situation of the Jewish minority in Germany against the background of their theological and political convictions. At this point, however, the most important aspect is Friedländer's conviction that the tradition of Christian Jew-hatred, with its language, its images and its construction of the Jews as the "others" in European civilization, formed the background and the indispensable arsenal of the more radical and by now really "eliminationist" forms of modern antisemitism. In Friedländer's very precise and felicitous words:

[. . .] the very notion of 'outsider' applied by modern anti-Semitism to the Jew owed its tenacity not only to Jewish difference as such but also to the depth of its religious roots. Whatever else could be said about the Jew, he was first and foremost the 'other,' who had rejected Christ and revelation. Finally, perhaps the most powerful effect of religious anti-Judaism was the dual structure of the anti-Jewish image inherited from Christianity. On the one hand, the Jew was a pariah, the despised witness of the triumphal onward march of the true faith; on the other, from the Late Middle Ages onward, an opposite image appeared in popular Christianity and in millenarian movements, that of the demonic Jew, the perpetrator of ritual murder, the plotter against Christianity, the herald of the anti-Christ, the potent and occult emissary of the forces of evil. It is this dual image that reappears in some major aspects of modern anti-Semitism. And, its threatening and occult dimension became the recurrent theme of the main conspiracy theories of the Western world.[53]

Nevertheless, although according to Friedländer the "centrality of the Jews" in the "phantasmic universe" of paranoid racial antisemitism can be explained "only by its roots in the Christian tradition,"[54] the spread of a radical variant of this ideology, which led to the murderous antisemitism of the Nazis, represents a new phenomenon that contradicts simplistic assumptions of continuity. The specifically German contribution to this ideology cannot be understood simply in terms of a long-standing "eliminationist" spirit of Jew-hatred, as Goldhagen claims, but must be related to the concrete political conditions within German society, in particular the social and economic crises after the First World War. In Friedländer's view it consists in the development of a radical current of racial antisemitism which "emphasized the mythic dimensions of the race and the sacredness of Aryan blood."[55] This "redemptive anti-Semitism" represents a novel mutation of racially motivated Jew-hatred which hoped for an intellectual, moral and physical redemption of the "Aryans" by cleansing both the individuals and society of the "decomposing" presence of the Jews. Friedländer discusses two types of racial antisemitism. One is based on the results of pseudo-scientific research in the late nineteenth century, such as in the areas of racial biology, social Darwinism and eugenics, the other on a "decidedly religious vision" where "the struggle against the Jews is the dominant aspect of a worldview in which other racist themes are but secondary appendages."[56] The second type arose from the fear of "miscegenation," the apprehension about a Jewish infiltration of German society and the dream of a German rebirth, which would be the result of liberation from the Jews by expulsion or something worse. The distinguishing marks of the new quasi-religious ideology were the assertion of the biologically inferior and destructive character of the Jews and a dualistic outlook that explained the course of Western history, including the social, political and intellectual conflicts of the time, in terms of the alleged Germanic-Jewish racial difference. Friedländer's convincing portrayal of the National Socialist variant of racial antisemitism integrates the elements of continuity and discontinuity in the German ideology through the ages. The combination of Christian Messianic hopes and traditional anti-Jewish motives had already given rise to an enormously powerful Jew-hatred, which now was joined – and not only in Germany – by modern pseudo-science and the mystical Messianic promise of the redemption of the "Aryan race" from contamination by the Jewish counter-race. This account recalls Friedländer's interpretation of National Socialism as a pseudo-religious ideology in his early writings.[57] In addition it shows strong affinities with Uriel Tal's studies of the type of radical *völkisch* antisemitism that logically developed into a religion which, despite remaining utterly dependent on Christian antisemitism for its success, also turned against Christian religion's Jewish origins and demanded the programmatic Germanization and "de-Judaization" of Christianity.[58]

The critical question one must ask Friedländer is whether it is possible to plausibly reconstruct the way in which this ideology spread among the German population and the extent to which it actually impinged on the events of the Nazi era.[59] The decisive factor, for Friedländer, is the interaction of the fears and hopes of a crisis-shaken population with what has been described by many historians as a perception of the Jews as the alien, threatening "Other" of German society. In any case, his portrayal of "redemptive antisemitism" is much more convincing than Goldhagen's thesis of a pathological eliminatory norm affirmed over centuries by the majority, if not the whole, of German society. Friedländer does not claim that "redemptive anti-Semitism" was a ubiquitous conviction, but based on the history of the late nineteenth and early twentieth centuries he describes how it gained ground – particularly in the Weimar years – in parts of the public sphere in Germany. "Redemptive antisemitism" thus becomes a key concept for understanding not only the Nazi ideology as such but also the enormous attraction it had for the German elites (including the Protestant and Catholic Christian Churches) and the population as a whole. By combining the old Christian antisemitic prejudices and the social-Darwinistic theses of modern science with Messianic hopes and expectations, National Socialism created a powerful instrument for its struggle for the approval of the German people. At the same time it should be noted that racial antisemitism, including the variant of "redemptive antisemitism" – albeit already in evidence, above all among the intellectual elites, before the Nazis came to power – was a marginal phenomenon initially rejected even by convinced representatives of a nationalistic antisemitism that was widespread in the Churches.[60] Friedländer notes that the general approval of the antisemitic measures of the Nazi regime up to 1938, which aimed at the exclusion of the Jews from German society and which pressed ahead fast with their dispossession and stigmatization, was ultimately based on the proliferation of a non-radical, non-murderous Jew-hatred among the German population. In parallel, thanks to an intensive propaganda campaign, the Nazis managed to convert "redemptive antisemitism" rapidly from the quasi-religious belief of a small minority into an opinion which – assisted by the current "moderate" antisemitism – was accepted by more and more people. Friedländer offers no explicit explanation as to how this rapid transformation occurred, but the portrayal of the development itself seems more than plausible.

As far as the relationship between continuity and change in antisemitism in the nineteenth and early twentieth centuries is concerned, Friedländer's interpretation ultimately produces a certain synthesis between two interpretative models found in recent research into antisemitism. These have arrived at rather different evaluations of the significance of religious elements in the context of "modern" variants. One model, which stresses the political and social prerequisites and contexts of antisemitism, interprets "modern antisemitism" in Germany as the expression of a crisis in modern liberal bourgeois society and culture, in which everything frightening and contradictory was projected onto the Jews, who appeared as a dangerous alien power and from whom Germany had to be liberated, at least by restricting or abolishing their civil rights. Initially the religious tradition of Jew-hatred does not seem to play a special part in this form of antisemitism, whose function as the "cultural code" of a secular, anti-liberal, anti-democratic and anti-pluralist ideology which turned the Jewish minority into a symbol of the crises of the liberal capitalist economic order cannot be overlooked.[61] Therefore, at first glance, in an age of increasing secularization the political, social and economic causes of antisemitism appear much more significant than religious thought patterns that are patently unable to explain the novelty of modern antisemitism. However, the current leaning towards cultural history and history of mentalities, which places greater emphasis on the long continuity of Jew-hatred in the Christian West, rightly stresses that the Jewish minority could become a symbol of hatred because Jews have always been negative symbols, embodiments of the "Other," and because the traditional stereotypes and religious prejudices also remained effective under increasingly secular conditions. Images and myths of a religious kind about Jews and Judaism, such as charges of deicide and ritual murder or fantasies of well poisoning and host desecration, were deeply anchored in the collective consciousness even after the Enlightenment and far into the twentieth century and could be activated for racially motivated campaigns of hatred. At the level of images and stereotypes, therefore, we must assume a strong connection between Christian anti-Judaism and "modern antisemitism."[62]

Research based on the history of mentality, even though it regards the religious tradition of anti-Judaism as the lasting foundation of the changing forms of Jew-hatred, also starts from important differences between religious anti-Judaism and antisemitism. However, it describes precisely how the religious myths were able to remain effective because they were modernized and appeared in new clothes. Thus the charge of ritual murder in the nineteenth century was transformed into the image of Jewish "Mammonism," materialism, or Jewish "bloodsucking" (capitalism) and the accusation of "deicide" into the claim of the dangerous alien and demonic qualities of Judaism, which was considered to be capable of any and every crime against non-Jewish society. This "rational" antisemitism, as it claimed to be, was altogether more consistent than the traditional Jew-hatred because the "Jewish question" had to be "solved" in one way or another. However, research into the ecclesiastical history of the nineteenth and twentieth centuries not only proved that the modernized forms of Jew-hatred preserved many traditional motifs and stereotypes of anti-Judaism, but at the same time irrefutably demonstrated that parts of both Protestant and Catholic theology in Europe were influenced by the transformations of Jew-hatred at any one time and that racism and *völkisch* ideas penetrated deep into ecclesiastical life – above all in Germany in the last phase of the Weimar Republic and during the "Third Reich." This was possible chiefly because one of the fundamental structures of anti-Jewish discourse was preserved despite all modernization: Judaism served throughout as a counter-image to self-understanding. Conservatives and liberals, orthodox Christians and radical critics of religion, *völkisch* nationalists and early socialists all regarded Judaism as the antithesis of their aims – as unbelievers, as representatives of capitalism, as enemy of the world, as counter-race. That is why Nazism's strategic "usurpation and colonization of Christian theology, especially its antisemitism," was so successful in the 1930s;[63] conversely, this is the reason why Christian anti-Judaism remained compatible with political forms of Jew-hatred and why there were reciprocal influences and partly an adoption of racial antisemitism by the Church. Friedländer also described this process in his work, at the same time revealing perspectives for further research.

## III  FRIEDLÄNDER'S INTERPRETATION OF THE SILENCE AND COMPLICITY OF THE CHURCHES: PERSPECTIVES

The clarity and perspicacity of Friedländer's interpretation of the continuity and discontinuity between religious Jew-hatred and Nazi antisemitism is equalled in his account of the concrete involvement of the Christian Churches in the Shoah: their theological contribution to the antisemitic discourse of the 1930s and 1940s; their assent to the disfranchisement of German Jewry; their political failure in the face of the dramatic and murderous intensification of the Jewish policy of the Nazis from the pogrom of November 1938 and the outbreak of the Second World War; and their general inability to respond to the genocide in a way that would have corresponded to the ethical claims of Christianity. Here, as before, a brief comparison with Goldhagen's interpretation will be instructive. It is not surprising that Goldhagen, in *Hitler's Willing Executioners*, talks about the "moral bankruptcy of the German Churches"[64] and devotes a large space in his arguments to their share of the ideological and political responsibility for the Shoah, since he believes Christian antisemitism to have been the nucleus of the "eliminationist" ideology of the Nazis and the attitude of the Churches emblematic for the entire German people. The "attitude of the Churches serves as a crucial test for evaluating the ubiquity and depth of eliminationist antisemitism in Germany,"[65] he asserts, and the detailed reasons he gives for his view that both the Protestant and the Catholic Church not only kept silent when Jews were discriminated against, persecuted, driven out of their homes, deported and murdered[66] – as if all moral commands had been cancelled and Jews were not part of humanity – but "cooperated wholeheartedly" in the Nazis' murderous policies,[67] supply the proof of his book's fundamental thesis:

> If the ecclesiastical men, whose vocation was to preach love and to be the custodians of compassion, pity, and morality, acquiesced or looked with favour upon and supported the elimination of the Jews from German society, then this would be further and particular persuasive proof of the ubiquity of eliminationist antisemitism in Germany, an antisemitism so strong that it not only inhibited the natural flow of the feeling of pity but also overruled the moral imperatives of the creed to speak out on behalf of those who have fallen among murderers. As studies of the Churches have shown, it cannot be doubted that antisemitism did succeed in turning the Christian community – its leaders, its clergy, and its rank and file – against its most fundamental tradition.[68]

Friedländer's analysis is much more cautious and discerning, but its moral force is by no means less than that of Goldhagen, who carried his judgement even further by adding an accusing gesture in *A Moral Reckoning*. On the contrary, the softer and subtler tone of Friedländer's examination of the silence and ideological complicity of the Churches, based on a detailed study of the relevant research, not only produces a more differentiated and nuanced image, but in its sober clarity confronts the reader at least as forcefully with the frightening insight into the full dimension of the moral and political failure of the Christian Churches in Germany and in the whole of Nazi-occupied Europe. Friedländer's comprehensive judgement, despite its differentiation and the fact that it is sometimes articulated in the form of questions rather than apodictic assertions, is no less drastic than Goldhagen's. In his view no Christian self-reflection after the Shoah can avoid the realization that the role of the Christian Churches "was, of course, decisive in the permanence and pervasiveness of anti-Jewish beliefs and attitudes in Germany and throughout the Western world."[69] This was all the more the case because the Christian faith continued to exert a strong influence within German society – despite the often hostile attitude of the NSDAP to the Christian tradition and the organized Church – and because it was precisely this deeply rooted religious anti-Judaism that made many Christians receptive to the antisemitic propaganda of the Nazis, facilitated their assent to anti-Jewish measures and calmed their conscience over the discrimination and persecution inflicted on the Jewish minority. Without wishing to generalize, Friedländer arrives at some fundamental conclusions which challenge European Christianity. First, they concern the pervasiveness of Christian antisemitism, that is, the "stigmatizing intrinsic to Christian dogma or tradition," which did not entail a uniform eliminationist ideology, as Goldhagen assumes, but which in their often very different forms and nuances "found their way into the minds and hearts of tens of millions of believers, Protestant or Catholic" and "offset any urges of compassion and charity, or even fuelled aggressive antisemitism."[70] Second, they refer to the fatal, shocking silence in the face of the Jews' sufferings and the Nazis' genocidal intentions: "Although some sporadic protests by some Catholic bishops or Protestant religious leaders did take place, the vast majority of Protestant and Catholic authorities remained publicly silent in the face of the deportations of the Jews and the growing knowledge of their extermination."[71] Unlike Goldhagen, Friedländer does not insinuate that the Christian Churches actively assented to the genocide as an ultimate fulfilment of their obsessive eliminationist fantasies, but rather establishes the connection between the silent abandonment of the Jews to the National Socialist Jewish policy and the ingrained culture of anti-Jewish resentment in the form of a question, which he leaves unanswered and therefore to be further investigated in detail:

> None of this [the pervasiveness of the different forms and degrees of antisemitism within the European society], of course, was new either in Europe or in other parts of the Christian world, but the question that surfaced and surfaces repeatedly in our context is stark: What was the contribution of such a religious anti-Jewish culture to the passive acceptance, sometimes to the occasional support, of the most extreme policies of persecution, deportation, and mass murder unfolding in the midst of Europe's Christian populations?[72]

Apart from the clarity and even-handedness of these general observations, Friedländer's interpretation of the attitude of the Churches is characterized above all by three features that are of central significance for a convincing analysis of Christianity's role in Nazi Germany and during the Shoah, be it in ecclesiastical history or in Holocaust historiography: firstly, the way he examines the attitude of the Churches in the context of intellectual elites, instead of isolating them, and reveals the diversity of ideological motives which – apart from antisemitism – secured their approval of National Socialism;[73] secondly, the comparative perspective with which Friedländer surveys Protestantism and Catholicism as well as the German and European Churches: his brief comments about the contradictory position of French Catholicism between complicity with the antisemitic policy of the Vichy government and occasional protests in the name of humanity,[74] the virulent Jew-hatred of the Romanian Orthodox Church, the extreme exclusionary antisemitism of Polish Catholicism, the attitude of the Churches in Ukraine, Slovakia, Hungary, Croatia and Lithuania, as well as the half-hearted protests of the Dutch Hervormde Kerk against the deportation of the Jews contain the elements of a map of the Churches' shared responsibility for the Shoah, which need further detailed research in a systematic comparative fashion;[75] thirdly, the differentiated awareness of diverse voices and currents within the Protestant and the Catholic Church: this is combined with a moderate judgement which dispenses with the agitation and sensationalism of many a public debate in recent years and thereby discourages apologetic reactions on the part of the Churches as much as it does exaggerated accusations against them.

This characteristic strikes a particularly welcome note in Friedländer's judgement on the attitude of Catholicism and the role of Pius XII during the Shoah. This is a topic that is highly charged with emotion due to its uncritically apologetic interpretation by a large proportion of Catholic historiography and the inaccessibility of decisive documents in the archives of the Vatican, on the one hand, and to uncommonly polemical accounts, on the other hand, and which is therefore in urgent need of an open, sober and objective debate.[76] Friedländer's contribution consists not so much in the discussion of new details, but rather in the discriminating consideration of the fundamental ambivalence of the Catholic Church. This concerns primarily the attitude of the Catholic Church in Germany to National Socialism in general, which was distinguished, at least in theory, by a greater distance from the regime than in the case of Protestantism; however, this distance was "uniquely determined by Church interests" and did not produce any solidarity with the persecuted Jewish minority, but at most some scepticism about possible anti-Christian implications of racial antisemitism or with an eye on assaults on Jewish converts to Catholicism.[77] Although the Catholic Church was, according to Friedländer, "more immune to Nazi theories than its Evangelical counterpart," its members and its clergy were so strongly conditioned by "traditional religious anti-Judaism" that there was no question of resistance to the persecution of the Jews, particularly as the Catholic Church shied away from conflict with the regime and "displayed unwavering loyalty toward both Führer and fatherland."[78] A special part is played in Friedländer's interpretation, however, by the obvious contrast between the deliberate silence – even in the face of the deportations and the growing awareness of the mass extermination of Jews in eastern Europe from the early 1940s – and the readiness of German Catholics to resist the euthanasia programme of the Nazis.[79] While he sees a clear indication in the extent to which the majority of the Catholic leaders approved of disfranchisement, exclusion and expulsion, unlike Goldhagen he traces the silence about the genocidal development of the Nazis' Jewish policy during the war back, not to an "eliminationist" tendency within Christian Jew-hatred, but to a mixture of moral indifference, political strategy and the lack of ethical guidance by the Vatican.[80]

As one would expect, this aspect – the role of the Vatican and Pius XII during the Shoah – plays a central part in Friedländer's account, particularly in the context of the search for explanations of the motives of the bystanders during the genocide. However, in the introduction to *The Years of Extermination* Friedländer consciously puts his interpretation forward with the reservation that "the historian's inability to get access to the Vatican archives represents a major constraint [. . .]. I shall deal with the Pope's attitude as thoroughly as present documentation allows, but historians face an obstacle that could have been yet has not been eliminated."[81] This remark, a distant echo of his caveat in *Pius XII and the Third Reich*,[82] articulates what Steven Aschheim has characterised as Friedländer's "ongoing desire for some kind of future redeeming explanation"[83] and his profound disappointment at seeing his hopes of obtaining sources that would allow a more historically precise judgement still unfulfilled after four decades. At the same time the restraint of his judgement reflects the methodological cautiousness of the historian, aware of the provisional and incomplete nature of his interpretation. However, the "agonizing questions" about the "reasons for his [the Pope's] silence in the face of the systematic extermination of the European Jews," which already haunted him in 1964,[84] have lost none of their significance for him. The opportunity for a theologically pronounced condemnation of Nazi antisemitism by the unpublished encyclical *Humani Generis Unitas*,[85] which was destroyed by the death of Pius XI in 1938, and the election of Pius XII on 2 March "inaugurated a new phase of Catholic appeasement of Hitler's regime"[86] and, despite growing tensions due to the racial objectives of the Nazis and their infringements of the domains of Catholic autonomy in Germany, led to the total abandonment of the Jews on the part of the highest religious and moral authority in Europe. Friedländer explains this above all by the political strategy of the Pope, connected with his conservative attitude and his hope that the Nazi regime would form an effective defence against the advances of Soviet Bolshevism in Europe. He points out, however, that this consideration did not prevent the Pope from publicly condemning the euthanasia programme, lamenting the suffering of the Polish civilians during the war and intervening with the Nazi regime by the diplomatic route, while *"not one such diplomatic intervention dealt with the overall fate of the Jews."*[87] Friedländer formulates the motives of this silence in the form of questions: Was the Pope convinced that the Nazis would simply ignore such interventions? Was he afraid of reprisals against converted Jews the Catholic Church was trying to protect? Was he concerned about the safety of the Jews who had gone under cover in Italy? Was he afraid of attacks on Catholics in Germany or an occupation of the Vatican? Was he hoping to be able to help the Jews better in secret than by public protest?[88] Friedländer grants that a combination of these motives, which have been quoted in defence of Pius XII, may well have played a part, and he rejects the opinion of some historians that in the 1940s the traditional anti-Judaism of the Pope had turned into an anti-Bolshevist antisemitism: "There is no specific indication," he writes, "that the Pope was anti-Semitic or that his decisions during the war stemmed, be it in part, from some particular hostility toward Jews." Yet, contrary to his feelings for the Polish Catholics and the German people, "it does not seem that Pius XII carried the Jews in his heart."[89] However, Friedländer unequivocally contradicts the apologetic position of the official Catholic Church (which is also reflected in *We Remember*), according to which the Pope's silence was connected with the intention of making secret rescue missions of the Church in Italy easier.[90] Ultimately, Friedländer blames this silence on the Pope's concern about the counter-productive consequences of a public intervention and a certain fatalism in view of the inevitability of the fate of the Jews. Many of Friedländer's questions are indeed likely to remain open until the Vatican allows access to all those documents that would help us reconstruct the Pope's motives and decision processes in those fateful years of war and genocide. What distinguishes his interpretation is the impressive combination of historical judgement with a truly breathtaking passage in which he reminds the Church of its own standards and confronts it with a question that neither future historical research nor the self-reflection of the Church will be able to evade:

In more general terms, if the Catholic Church is merely considered as a political institution that has to calculate the outcome of its decisions in terms of instrumental rationality, then Pius's choice may be deemed reasonable in view of the risks entailed. If, however, the Catholic Church also represents a moral stand, as it claims, mainly in moments of major crisis, and thus has to move on such occasions from the level of institutional interests to that of moral witnessing, then of course Pius's choice should be assessed differently. What we do not know and have no way of knowing – and there lies the core of the issue – is whether for Pius XII the fate of the Jews of Europe represented a major crisis situation and an anguishing dilemma or whether it was but a marginal problem that did not challenge Christian conscience.[91]

Protestantism is not spared the question about the motivation of its silence and the task of serious soul-searching, even though Friedländer devotes far less attention to it than he does to Catholicism. In comparison to recent historiography his judgement is again unequivocal and discerning, but at the same time surprisingly reticent and general. Nevertheless, he leaves no doubt that the "traditional alliance between German Protestantism and German nationalist authoritarianism"[92] rendered all currents of the Protestant Church, including the Confessing Church especially susceptible not only to an affinity to National Socialism but also to various forms of antisemitism. The penetration of racial antisemitism into parts of Protestant theology and the Church in the form of the "German Christians" – whose programme of the "dejudaization" of Christianity appears to Friedländer as a "Sisyphean task"[93] – is mentioned, as is also the "omnipresence of antisemitism in most of the Evangelical Lutheran Church," particularly in the "neutral" regional Churches.[94] In Friedländer's view it is quite uncontentious, and in need of no further explanation, that these two currents, each in its own way, contributed to the acceptance by the German population of the National Socialist persecution of the Jews. He is much more interested in the results of historical research since the 1980s that has applied a fundamental criticism to the idealizing myth created after 1945, according to which the Confessing Church, as part of its fight against the ideology of the "German Christians" also resisted the racial policy of the Nazi regime. He largely follows the convincing theses of Wolfgang Gerlach, stressing the shocking realization of the extent to which the Confessing Church, conditioned by the antisemitism prevailing also among its adherents, kept silent about the fate of the Jews and, apart from the efforts of a few individuals, denied them its solidarity.[95] The Confessing Church rejected racial antisemitism, intervened – albeit often half-heartedly – on behalf of "non-Aryan Christians" and resisted at considerable risk the National Socialist *Gleichschaltung* of the Protestant Churches; but, as Friedländer puts it, in the words of Richard Gutteridge, there "was no disavowal of anti-Semitism as such, including the Christian type, but merely of the militant Nazi version without even an oblique reference to the plight of the Jews themselves."[96] Even where a hint of solidarity with the persecuted Jews is visible, as in the reflections of the Freiburg Circle or in the objections of the Protestant Bishop Theophil

Wurm against the deportations and mass murders in 1943, Friedländer detects a fundamentally antisemitic mentality that was prepared to stop short only of murder, but considered discrimination and disenfranchisement legitimate.[97] Even Dietrich Bonhoeffer's solitary, courageous attitude, which cost him his life, was not devoid of the theological ambivalence towards Judaism that curtailed an effective resistance against antisemitism.[98]

Friedländer's account of the Protestant Churches reveals in particular how much a dialogue between ecclesiastical history, research into antisemitism and Holocaust research is needed and how these disciplines can enrich each other. His unavoidably brief reference to Protestant antisemitism, which is distinguished by an awareness of the diversity and heterogeneity of ideological and political motives, raises numerous questions that play a significant part in the current discourse about the shared responsibility and guilt of German Protestantism for the Shoah and are still far from having been conclusively answered. They demand a more precise, more detailed and still more differentiated exploration of the concrete relationship between those theologies infected by anti-Judaism or antisemitism and the National Socialist ideology; the attitude of different ideological currents within the Nazi movement towards Christianity and in particular towards the aspirations within Protestantism to combine Christianity, National Socialism and racial thinking; the significance of non-racial anti-Jewish attitudes for the inconceivable measure of indifference to the suffering of the Jewish minority on the part of Protestant theologians and Church leaders, as diagnosed by Friedländer; and the role of antisemitism in the political contradictions of the resistance against Hitler with reference to the so-called "Jewish question." In this context it may be asked whether the category of "silence," which is so strikingly foregrounded by Friedländer, suffices to comprehend the entire dimension of the failure of the Protestant Churches, or whether it would be necessary to place more emphasis on the very high degree of theological and political involvement and complicity.

Research carried out in the past decade confirms Friedländer's careful distinctions between different forces, currents and motivations in German Protestantism, while suggesting new details and theoretical approaches that could add greater depth of focus to his own picture of the landscape of Protestant antisemitism.[99] Based on the still growing amount of literature on this theme, it is possible to identify at least three main anti-Jewish tendencies within Protestantism, which Friedländer has also observed. However, they are in need of a more precise and focused analysis with regard to their effect in the context of National Socialist Jewish policy, which can only be indicated in outline here.

Friedländer does not devote a great deal of space to the phenomenon of an "anti-Judaistic" current, found in particular among liberal, progressive Protestants, which argued its case in mainly theological terms. The political dimension of this current, which cannot easily be recognized at first sight, resides in the counter-productive relationship between its image of Judaism and its otherwise positive democratic attitude. The liberal Protestantism of the nineteenth century and the Weimar period was committed to comprehensive civil rights and as a rule rejected antisemitic demands as something inhuman. But the majority of its representatives, even while arguing for the rights of Jewish citizens, continued to pass traditional judgements about the Jewish religion in their work as scholars. This ambivalence prevented the development, on theological foundations, of a tradition of tolerance and dialogue with Jews. The self-understanding and the social, religious and cultural reality of the current, living Jewish community was of little interest to them – it was a relic from an age long past, which they wanted to disappear because it seemed incompatible with a unified national German identity.[100] The diagnosis of the disastrous effect of this anti-Judaism, above all on the educated middle class, stands even if one feels bound to agree with Kurt Nowak that "in the Protestant landscape of the 1920s" it could be difficult "to find another group that defended the legitimate place reserved for Jewish citizens in the modern development of German society with anything like the human and political directness displayed by the cultured law-abiding Protestants."[101] However, it is necessary to mention in the same breath the political relevance of the anti-Judaist stereotypes that prevailed, without being given further thought, beyond 1933 in liberal Protestant theological and religious studies. The far-reaching silence of liberal Protestants and their inner emigration in the face of *völkisch* antisemitism and the systematic disenfranchisement and persecution of the Jews are certainly connected with the fact that in the Nazi era, when justice and humanity were at stake, their anti-Jewish theology offered no ready criteria for an awareness of the solidarity of Christians and Jews.[102] What they overlooked was that even seemingly politically neutral theological judgements were capable of being exploited for antisemitic purposes and that it was impossible to pass down a "doctrine of contempt," that is, theological images of the alienness and inferiority of Judaism, and at the same time stand up to antisemitic slander effectively and showing solidarity. Fighting antisemitism effectively would have meant entirely abandoning the negative stylization of Judaism and identifying with the Jews. The Church, instead of declaring that the Gospel had defeated Judaism, should have realized that any attack against Jews and Judaism was an attack against its own roots – its own identity. But in Germany in 1933 – let alone in the Shoah years – even the liberal forces within Protestantism were a long way from such a sense of solidarity.

The second current was that of conservative political and cultural antisemitism, which Friedländer places at the centre of his analysis and which, as he demonstrates, even permeated the Confessing Church. Theological and political motives were closely linked insofar as Judaism was being fought as the counter-image of the idea of an authoritarian national society built on Christian foundations; thus the systematic political and social disenfranchisement of Judaism was demanded.[103] The starting point was the outlook of the Prussian court chaplain Adolf Stoecker, who regarded the Jews as representatives of the revolutionary democratic ideas of 1789 and who claimed that an anti-Christian Jewish culture was undermining "Germanness."[104] The movement was guided by the ideal of the conservative "Christian state" in which there was no room for an "alien" religious identity such as the Jewish. In conjunction with the cultural pessimism of the *fin de siècle*, as Fritz Stern has described it,[105] this combination of conservative Protestantism, authoritarian nationalism, anti-democratic resentment and an antisemitism that was becoming increasingly susceptible to racist ideas in the decades up to 1933 played a decisive role in moulding theology and the Church with their image of modern "subversive" Judaism. This type of antisemitism, convincingly analyzed by Robert P. Ericksen, for which theological arguments had become marginal, made an astonishing impact in the Weimar period, creating among the Protestant majority a disastrous discourse of hatred, which effectively prepared the ground for the widespread social acceptance of the persecution of the Jewish minority by the Nazis.[106]

The third current – which Friedländer described rather casually as the radical minority position of a racially infected antisemitic strand within German Protestantism – has perhaps received the greatest attention from researchers in recent years. It included in particular the "German-Christian" theology, whose radical representatives wanted to conquer the Church on behalf of National Socialism and who intended to cleanse Christianity of all Jewish traces.[107] The theology of one of the better-known representatives of this current, the Jena New Testament scholar Walter Grundmann, may be called a Christian-antisemitic form of National Socialist thought before 1933. He called the strategy by which he intended to refute the verdict of the "Judaization" of Christianity pronounced by *völkisch* ideologues such as Alfred Rosenberg the "de-Judaization of religious ecclesiastical life." In 1938 in Eisenach he founded the "Institut zur Erforschung und Beseitigung des Einflusses des Judentums auf das deutsche kirchliche Leben" [Institute for the Study and Eradication of Jewish Influence on German Church Life], whose history has recently been illuminated in Susannah Heschel's brilliant study *The Aryan Jesus*. By documenting the large number of renowned theologians who contributed to the project of interpreting the Christian faith as being separated from Judaism by an unbridgeable gulf and "liberating" it from its Jewish roots, Heschel demonstrates that this was not a marginal and negligible phenomenon,[108] but the expression of an extremely virulent current within German Protestantism in the late 1930s and early 1940s, whose theological radicalization was internally related to the genocidal policy of the Nazis during the Second World War. The institute "carried out its program of eradicating the Jewish within Christianity precisely while the Jews of Europe were being deported and murdered."[109] The concept of the "Aryan Jesus," who unavoidably found himself in a racial conflict with Judaism and was crucified because he had rejected Judaism, combined religious anti-Judaism and racial antisemitism to form an intellectual structure in which the two elements mutually confirmed each other: for example, Grundmann stressed the Jews' collective responsibility for the crucifixion of Jesus and in the same context talked about the eternal Jewish hatred of Christianity up to the point where it was threatening Germany, the latest victim of a Jewish world conspiracy. This construction secured the historic right of the Germans to fight Judaism.[110] The idea of the "Aryan Jesus" removed the most important foundation of Christian resistance against antisemitism: the solidarity of Jesus with his Jewish people. And if the aim of Jesus was the destruction of Judaism, neither were any strategies of destruction that Christianity legitimized to be ruled out as a matter of principle. Therefore Doris Bergen was right to speak of an "ecclesiastical final solution," while Susannah Heschel argued that through such a theology the destruction of Judaism was being raised to an "*imitatio Christi*."[111]

This is, of course, much more than just silent assent to the regime's measures or lack of solidarity, as in the case of the Confessing Church or of cultural Protestantism, but clearly a conscious theological legitimation of the National Socialist persecution of the Jews. Against this background the statement in *Dabru Emet*, which recalls the arguments of *We Remember* – "If the Nazi extermination of the Jews had been fully successful, it would have turned its murderous rage more directly to Christians" – seems somewhat simplistic and misleading. The intention is indeed to point out a potential community of Jews and Christians based on a shared fate in the face of the National Socialist *Weltanschauung* and to indicate the extent to which the "de-Judaization" of Christianity missed the very essence of the Christian tradition. However, to construct a deadly threat for the Christians on that basis would be a historical speculation that could be used only too readily in order to blur the boundaries between the victims of the Shoah and the society of perpetrators. The historical interpretation of the relationship between National Socialism and Protestantism remains contentious and in flux.[112] Despite all the tensions between the neo-pagan inclinations of part of the National Socialist leadership and parts of the Christian Churches, one must not overlook the undeniable affinities and common interests precisely where Judaism was concerned. In order to justify its Manichaean fantasies of being threatened by the "World Jewish Conspiracy," racial antisemitism used the ideologization and politicization of the Christian Churches, whose traditional anti-Judaism and whose reception of antisemitic thought "could comfortably and advantageously be combined with the racial image of the Jews as enemies and destroyers of the Christian Protestant German people's state."[113] The solidarity of the Churches, with a few exceptions, belonged to the National Socialist state. This was expressed by a methodical strategy, not only of a political but also of a theological kind, of the withdrawal of solidarity – albeit at different levels of intensity – and a distancing from the Jewish tradition and the Jewish elements of Christianity. This must also have hidden the fear that National Socialism might accuse Christianity of being "judaized." However, the Churches did not derive from it a sense of solidarity and even less the awareness of fundamentally missing their own Jewish roots as a result of their antisemitism. Even if it was only a minority that advocated the complete "Aryanization" of Christianity, it cannot be denied that this was the logical consequence of the general abandonment of solidarity with the Judaism and the Jews that prevailed in the majority of Protestantism at the time. The claim of a potential community of fate therefore is only a fiction without any corresponding solidarity in the ideas and behaviour of the overwhelming majority of Christians. The historical fact is that the European Jews fell victim to an unprecedented genocide, while after 1945 decades were still to pass before the Churches began to recognize the inhumane consequences of their refusal of solidarity and to come to terms with Elie Wiesel's thesis that "in Auschwitz it was not the Jewish people who died but Christianity."[114]

\*\*\*

"What is the value of religion, and in particular of Christianity, if it provides no defense against brutality and can even become a willing participant in genocide?" This question, with which Doris Bergen confronts the reader in the introduction to her book *The Twisted Cross*,[115] could be a secret *leitmotiv* of Saul Friedländer's reflections on the involvement of Christianity (through its tradition of stigmatizing Judaism) and the Christian Churches (through their silence and their theological and political complicity) in the history of the unprecedented genocide of the Jews. In an age of ongoing genocides this theme – beyond the role of the Christian Churches in enabling, motivating, or failing to prevent mass violence against the European Jews – raises universal issues of the relationship between religion and barbaric violence, as well as the potential of religions to counteract inhumanity.[116] Friedländer's dispassionate and, at the same time, urgent analysis of the shared responsibility of theology and the Church for the Shoah can also be read as a paradigmatic encounter with this profoundly troubling theme. Over and above his masterly contribution to the history of the Shoah and genocide, he confronts religious thought as such with the question of the "value of religion" in the present. For the Christian Churches one element of this reflection could lead to a resistence of the temptation of apologetics concerning the past and an engagement, with greater historical honesty, in a self-critical dialogue with those disastrously influential theological thought patterns that belong to the heritage of Christianity and have been among the causes of its failure in the face of the inhumanity of the Nazi regime. The mixture of Friedländer's inexorable insistence on historical truthfulness and his differentiated judgement, which takes account of the different shades and nuances, at any rate, seems suited to break through the compulsion to deny or relativize historical guilt.[117]

*Notes*

1   Translated from the German by Ladislaus Löb.
2   George Steiner, "Through that Glass Darkly," reprinted in Steiner, *No Passion Spent: Essays 1978-1996* (New Haven: Yale University Press, 1996): 328–47, here at 336
3   Gulie Ne'eman Arad, "Paucis Verbis," in Ne'eman Arad (ed.), *Passing into History: Nazism and the Holocaust beyond Memory: In Honor of Saul Friedländer on His Sixty-Fifth Birthday* (Special Issue of History & Memory 9 [1997]) (Bloomington: Indiana University Press, 1997): 7–8, here 7.
4   Ibid.

5 On memory and the problem of the representation of the Holocaust in Friedländer's work see Saul Friedländer, "Introduction," in Friedländer (ed.), *Probing the Limits of Representation: Nazism and the "Final Solution"* (Cambridge, MA and London: Harvard University Press, 1992), 1–21; Friedländer, *Memory, History, and the Extermination of the Jews of Europe* (Bloomington: Indiana University Press, 1993); particularly illuminating is Steven E. Aschheim, "On Saul Friedländer," in Ne'eman Arad (ed.), *Passing into History*, 12–46; and see the contributions of James E. Young (47–58) and Carlo Ginzburg (353–63) in the same volume; Karolin Machtans, "History and Memory: Saul Friedländer's Historiography of the Shoah," in Martin L. Davies and Claus-Christian Szejnmann (eds), *How the Holocaust Looks Now: International Perspectives* (Basingstoke: Palgrave Macmillan, 2007), 199–207.

6 Saul Friedländer, *The Years of Extermination: Nazi Germany and the Jews, 1939–1945* (New York: HarperCollins, 2007), xxvi.

7 Friedländer, *Memory, History, and the Extermination of the Jews*, 107.

8 Friedländer, *The Years of Extermination*, xxi.

9 However, Michael Burleigh, *The Third Reich: A New History* (Basingstoke and Oxford: Macmillan, 2000), includes substantial reflections on the Nazi approach to Christianity and the Churches as well as on Protestant and Roman Catholic responses to Nazism and antisemitism.

10 Saul Friedländer, *Pius XII and the Third Reich: A Documentation* (London: Alfred A. Knopf, 1966).

11 Saul Friedländer, *Kurt Gerstein: The Ambiguity of Good* (London: Weidenfeld & Nicolson, 1969).

12 Saul Friedländer, *When Memory Comes* (New York: Farrar, Straus, Giroux, 1979), 120 and 138; see Sidra DeKoven Ezrahi, "See Under: Memory: Reflections on *When Memory Comes*," in Ne'man Arad (ed.), *Passing into History*, 364–75.

13 For the importance and continuity of Christian violence against Jews in Germany from the early modern period to the Shoah, see Helmut Walser Smith, *The Continuities of German History: Nation, Religion, and Race across the Long Nineteenth Century* (Cambridge: Cambridge University Press, 2008), chapter 3; for the concept of "catastrophic violence," see particularly 7; 75–7; 83; 101–3.

14 Daniel J. Goldhagen, *A Moral Reckoning: The Role of the Catholic Church in the Holocaust and Its Unfulfilled Duty of Repair* (London: Abacus, 2002), 9.

15 According to Goldhagen, ibid., 149, the genocide was "one logical, though not the only logical or an inevitable, policy extension of the antisemitism they had propagated and the earlier eliminationist policies they had supported. Even if the churchmen disapproved of this most extreme eliminationist punishment, their antisemitism was such that it was hard to rouse themselves in sympathy for the Jews."

16 Ibid., 32. Equally drastically, Karl Jaspers drew a line of continuity from Martin Luther to Auschwitz, claiming – in view of Martin Luther's infamous anti-Jewish recommendation to the authorities in 1543: "What Hitler has done, had been recommended by Luther, with the exception of the murder in gas chambers"; see Karl Jaspers, "Die nichtchristlichen Religionen und das Abendland," in Jaspers, *Philosophie und Welt: Reden und Aufsätze*, 2nd ed. (Munich: Piper, 1963), 156–66, here 162.

17 Goldhagen, *A Moral Reckoning*, 49. Goldhagen emphasizes, of course, that he could have written the same moral verdict on the Protestant churches and that his analysis is meant to be "exemplary" for the German and European churches in general (34).

18 See Daniel J. Goldhagen, *Hitler's Willing Executioners: Ordinary Germans and the Holocaust* (London: Abacus, 1997), 442.

19 See the argument of chapter 1, in ibid., 27–48.

20 Ibid., 32.

21 Ibid., 67.

22 For the discussion on Goldhagen's book see Julius H. Schoeps (ed.), *Ein Volk von Mördern? Die Dokumentation zur Goldhagen-Kontroverse um die Rolle der Deutschen im Holocaust* (Hamburg: Hoffmann & Campe, 1996); Yisrael Gutman, "Goldhagen – His Critics and His Contribution," *Yad Vashem Studies* 26 (1998): 329–64; Robert A. Shandley (ed.), *Unwilling Germans? The Goldhagen Debate* (Minneapolis: University of Minnesota Press, 1998); Geoff Eley (ed.), *The "Goldhagen Effect": History, Memory, Nazism – Facing the German Past* (Ann Arbor: University of Michigan Press, 2000); Yehuda Bauer, *Rethinking the Holocaust* (New Haven and London: Yale University Press, 2001), 93–111.

23   See the chapter "Repairing the Harm," in Goldhagen, *A Moral Reckoning*, 243–372.
24   See John K. Roth, "Goldhagen and the Moral Reckoning," *Menora* 14 (2003): 71–5; Olaf Blaschke, "Hitlers willige Katholiken?: Goldhagens Moralpredigt gegen die katholische Kirche aus der Sicht eines anderen Kritikers ihres Antisemitismus," *Zeitschrift für Geschichtswissenschaft* 50 (2002): 1099–1115; Olaf Blaschke, "Goldhagen und Hitlers willige Katholiken zwischen Sensationshascherei und Wirklichkeit. Ein ernstes Themenfeld droht zu verbrennen," *Menora* 14 (2003) 163–93; Julius H. Schoeps (ed.), *Goldhagen, der Vatikan und die Judenfeindschaft* (Berlin: Philo, 2003); Ronald J. Rychlak, "Goldhagen vs. Christianity," in Patrick J. Gallo (ed.), *Pius XII, the Holocaust and the Revisionists: Essays* (Jefferson, NC: McFarland&Co, 2006), 167–80.
25   See http://www.vatican.va/roman_curia/pontifical_councils/chrstuni/documents/rc_pc_chrs-tuni_doc_16031998_shoah_en.html; the document responds to the question, "Did Christians give every possible assistance to those being persecuted, and in particular to the persecuted Jews?," in a way that distorts historical reality and seems clearly motivated by apologetics: "Many did, but others did not. Those who did help to save Jewish lives as much as was in their power, even to the point of placing their own lives in danger, must not be forgotten. During and after the war, Jewish communities and Jewish leaders expressed their thanks for all that had been done for them, including what Pope Pius XII did personally or through his representatives to save hundreds of thousands of Jewish lives. Many Catholic bishops, priests, religious and laity have been honoured for this reason by the State of Israel."
26   See the response of the International Jewish Committee on Interreligious Consultations (http://www.jcrelations.net/en/?item=1016); as a critique of the document's unhistorical character from a historian's point of view, see Michael R. Marrus, "We Remember: The Vatican and the Holocaust in Historical Context," in Judith H. Banki and John T. Pawlikowski (eds), *Ethics in the Shadow of the Holocaust: Christian and Jewish Perspectives* (Franklin, Wisconsin: Sheed & Ward, 2001), 117–33. For critical comments from a Catholic theologian involved in Catholic-Jewish Dialogue, see John T. Pawlikowski, "The Vatican and the Holocaust: Putting 'We Remember' in Context," *Dimensions* 12 (1998): 11–6. The United States Catholic Conference implicitly contradicted the Vatican document in its 2001 statement "Catholic Teaching on the Shoah: Implementing the Holy See's *We Remember*": "Christian anti-Judaism did lay the groundwork for racial, genocidal anti-Semitism by stigmatizing not only Judaism but Jews themselves for opprobrium and contempt. So the Nazi theories tragically found fertile soil in which to plant the horror of an unprecedented attempt at genocide" (cited in http://www.bc.edu/research/cjl/meta-elements/texts/cjrelations/resources/documents/catholic/NCCB_Shoah_teaching.htm#A Word on the Present Document). As a comparison to the apology of the French episcopate in 1997, see Patrick Henry, "The Art of Christian Apology: Comparing the French Catholic Church's Apology to the Jews and the Vatican's "We Remember," *Shofar* 26 (2008) 87–104. Goldhagen, *A Moral Reckoning*, 90 accuses the Catholic Church of erecting "an iron curtain between the Church's own virulent antisemitism and the virulent antisemitism that led the Germans and those who helped them to persecute and then slaughter Jews."
27   See the documents in Rolf Rendtorff and Hans H. Henrix (eds), *Die Kirchen und das Judentum*, vol. 1: *Dokumente von 1945–1985* (Paderborn and Munich: Bonifatius and Gütersloher Verlagshaus, 1988); Henrix and Wolfgang Kraus (eds), *Die Kirchen und das Judentum*, vol. 2: *Dokumente von 1986–2000* (Paderborn: Bonifatius, 2001).
28   Ibid., vol. 2, 862–932, here 898.
29   International Jewish Committee for Interreligious Consultations, "Response to Vatican Document 'We Remember: A Reflection on the Shoah'" (cited in http://www.bc.edu/research/cjl/meta-elements/texts/cjrelations/resources/documents/jewish/response_We_Remember.html).
30   For the text of the declaration, see http://www.jcrelations.net/en/?item=1014; for the genesis of the document as well as the public discussion on its different elements, see the contributions in Rainer Kampling und Michael Weinrich (eds), *Dabru Emet – Redet Wahrheit: Eine jüdische Herausforderung zum Dialog mit den Christen* (Gütersloh: Gütersloher Verlagshaus, 2003); Erwin Dirschel (ed.), *Redet Wahrheit – Dabru Emet: Jüdisch-christiches Gespräch über Gott, Messias und Dekalog* (Münster: Lit, 2004); Hubert Frankemölle (ed.), *Juden und Christen im Gespräch über "Dabru Emet – Redet Wahrheit"* (Paderborn: Bonifatius, 2005). As a more comprehensive commentary on the entire document, see Tykva Frymer Kensky, David Novak, Peter

Ochs, David Fox Sandmel and Michael A Signer (eds), *Christianity in Jewish Terms* (Boulder, CO: Westview Press, 2000).

31  See Michael A. Signer, "Some Reflections on Dabru Emet" (http://www.jcrelations.net/en/?item=781).

32  David Rosen, "*Dabru Emet*: Its Significance for the Jewish-Christian Dialogue" (http://www.bc.edu/bc_org/research/cjl/articles/rosen.htm).

33  Ekkehard Stegemann, "Theologie zwischen Antisemitismuskritik und alten Vorurteilen," in Christina Tuor Kurth (ed.), *Neuer Antisemitismus – alte Vorurteile?* (Stuttgart et al.: Kohlhammer, 2001), 199–215, here 200.

34  See Peter von der Osten-Sacken (ed.), *Das mißbrauchte Evangelium: Studien zu Theologie und Praxis der Thüringer Deutschen Christen* (Berlin: Institut für Kirche und Judentum, 2002).

35  Goldhagen, *A Moral Reckoning*, 104.

36  See, for example, Gavin Langmuir, *Toward a Definition of Antisemitism* (Berkeley: University of California Press, 1990), 57–99; Paul Lawerence Rose, *Revolutionary Antisemitism in Germany from Kant to Wagner* (Princeton: Princeton University Press, 1990); John Weiss, *Ideology of Death: Why the Holocaust Happened in Germany* (Chicago, Ivan R. Dee, 1996).

37  Hannah Arendt, *The Origins of Totalitarianism* (New York: Harcourt, Brace and Company, new ed. with added prefaces, 1978), xi–xvi; 3–120; and see Hannah Arendt, "Approaches to the German Problem," *Partisan Review* 12 (1945): 93–106, here 96: "Nazism owes nothing to any part of the Western tradition, be it German or not, Catholic or Protestant, Christian [. . .]."

38  George L. Mosse, *The Nationalization of the Masses: Political Symbolism and Mass Movements in Germany from the Napoleonic Wars through the Third Reich* (New York: Howard Fertig, 1975), 80.

39  Burleigh, *The Third Reich*, 256.

40  See Raul Hilberg, *The Destruction of the European Jews*, vol. 1, 3rd ed. (New Haven and London, Yale University Press, 2003), 1–27.

41  Leon Poliakov, *The History of Antisemitism*, vol. 1: *From the Time of Christ to the Court Jews* (Philadelphia: University of Pennsylvania Press, 2003), 0000.

42  Lucy Dawidowicz, *The War Against the Jews: 1933–1945* (London: Weidenfeld and Nicolson, 1975), 23.

43  See Steven T. Katz, *Kontinuität und Diskontinuität zwischen christlichem und nationalsozialistischem Antisemitismus* (Tübingen: J. C. B. Mohr, 2001), esp. 43–5.

44  Ibid., 41–3 and 59–61. For the "Aryan Myth," see Leon Poliakov, *The Aryan Myth: A History of Racist and Nationalist Ideas in Europe* (New York: Barnes and Noble Books, 1996).

45  For research on Protestant antisemitism, see, e.g., Marikje Smid, "Protestantismus und Antisemitismus 1930–1933," in Jochen-Christoph Kaiser and Martin Greschat (eds), *Der Holocaust und die Protestanten: Analysen einer Verstrickung* (Munich: Kaiser, 1988), 38–72 and Heinz E. Tödt, "Die Novemberverbrechen 1938 und der deutsche Protestantismus: Ideologische und theologische Voraussetzungen für die Hinnahme des Pogroms," *Kirchliche Zeitgeschichte* 2 (1989): 14–37. The conceptual distinctions are based on the assumption that the varied manifestations and motives of Protestant Jew-hatred cannot simply be understood with the aid of the concept of antisemitism but have to be interpreted by using different conceptual categories. In contrast to racial antisemitism, whose biologist-determinist views do not permit the Jews to escape their alleged racial characteristics, "anti-Judaism" aims explicitly at "the rejection of Judaism as a non-Christian religious community on biblical and theological grounds" (Smid, "Protestantismus und Antisemitismus," 41). In contrast to this, the most common type of social and cultural Jew-hatred was characterized by moral, social and cultural distance from the Jewish minority, but could also adopt both racial and religious elements; see Marikje Smid, *Deutscher Protestantismus und Judentum 1932/1933* (Munich: Kaiser, 1990), 200–1. Tödt, "Die Novemberverbrechen 1938," 32 assumes a "synergy of anti-Jewish attitudes" and argues that these ideal-typical motives never existed in their pure form but interacted and reinforced each other. The differentiation between "anti-Judaism" and "antisemitism," I would argue, is only meaningful as an instrument that contributes to a critical analysis of theological traditions (such as parts of cultural Protestantism in Germany) which, although actively rejecting antisemitism in the political realm, continued to pass on anti-Jewish theological images of Judaism without reflecting upon their political impact; see Christian Wiese, *Challenging Colonial Discourse:*

*Jewish Studies and Protestant Theology in Wilhelmine Germany* (Leiden and Boston: Brill Publishers, 2005).

46   See, for example, Leonore Siegele-Wenschkewitz, "Mitverantwortung und Schuld der Christen am Holocaust," in Siegele-Wenschkewitz (ed.), *Christlicher Antijudaismus und Antisemitismus: Theologische und kirchliche Programme Deutscher Christen* (Frankfurt am Main: Hain, 1994), 1–26.

47   Bauer, *Rethinking the Holocaust*, 105.

48   Friedländer, *Nazi Germany and the Jews*, 387 n. 53: "An interpretation of the events assuming the widespread presence in German society at large, throughout the modern era, of an 'elimination-ist anti-Semitism,' craving the physical annihilation of the Jews, is not convincing on the basis of the material presented in this study."

49   Ibid., 4.

50   Ibid., 82–3.

51   Ibid. Similar is the interpretation by Philippe Burin, *From Prejudice to the Holocaust: Nazi Anti-Semitism* (New York and London: The New Press, 2005), who emphasizes the "internal diversity and the relative novelty of Nazi-Judeophobia" (6), but also the "extent to which the new [antisemitic] discourse in fact substantially perpetuated the Christian tradition of stigmatizing the Jews" (20). Similarly, Peter Pulzer writes in the introduction to the revised edition of his classic study on antisemitism: "I am more strongly convinced than I was when I wrote the book that a tradition of religiously-inspired Jew hatred [. . .] was a necessary condition for the success of antisemitic propaganda, even when expressed in non-religious terms and absorbed by those no longer religiously observant"; see Peter Pulzer, *The Rise of Political Antisemitism in Germany and Austria*, 2nd ed. (Cambridge, MA: Harvard University Press, 1988), xxii. Pulzer, Burrin and Friedländer thus display an affinity to the influential current within Holocaust historiography that tends to see the Holocaust as the culmination of religiously inspired antisemitism. Historians and theologians – some Jewish, others Christian – such as Victoria Barnett, Doris Bergen, Susannah Heschel, David Kertzer, Franklin Littell, John Pawlikowski, and Robert Wistrich have made major contributions to this part of Holocaust studies.

52   Friedländer, *Nazi Germany and the Jews*, 83. The quotation from Katz is to be found in Jacob Katz, *From Prejudice to Destruction: Anti-Semitism 1700–1933* (Cambridge, MA: Harvard University Press, 319). Katz continues: "No anti-Semite, even if he himself was anti-Christian, ever forwent the use of those anti-Jewish arguments rooted in the denigration of Jews and Judaism in earlier Christian times." See the similar argument in Burin, *From Prejudice to the Holocaust*, 24.

53   Friedländer, *Nazi Germany and the Jews*, 84. According to Burrin, *From Prejudice to the Holocaust*, 32–4, the religious element was particularly important in Germany, for example, in contrast to France: this was due to the traditional alliance between throne and altar as well as to the fact that "right from the start, nationalism had been influenced by Christian religiosity"; secondly, it was a result of the confessional tensions in Germany which reinforced the inclination to strive for a *völkischen* religiosity that promised to fulfil the hope for a political and religious unity of the German nation. The movements of the "German Christians" or the neo-pagan "German Believers" bear witness to the "strength of the aspiration to endow the Germans with a single common religion of an ethnic or ethnoracist culture"; both movements embraced traditional religious prejudices, but their antisemitism was "a far cry from the traditional Christian anti-Judaism."

54   Friedländer, *Nazi Germany and the Jews*, 85.

55   Ibid., 86.

56   Ibid., 86–7.

57   See Saul Friedländer, *L'Antisémitisme nazi: histoire d'une psychose collective* (Paris: Editions du Seuil, 1971); Saul Friedländer, *Reflections of Nazism: An Essay on Kitsch and Death* (New York: Harper & Row, 1984).

58   See Uriel Tal, "Religious and Anti-Religious Roots of Modern Anti-Semitism," in Tal, *Religion, Politics and Ideology in the Third Reich: Selected Essays*, ed. Saul Friedländer (New York: Routledge, 2004), 171–90; and see Uriel Tal, *Christians and Jews in Germany: Religion, Politics and Ideology in the Second Reich, 1870–1914* (Ithaca, NY and London: Cornell University Press, 1975), 223–89.

59  As a critical assessment of Friedländer's concept of "redemptive antisemitism" see Peter Pulzer, Review of Friedländer, *Years of Extermination, The Times Literary Supplement,* 2 January 2008.

60  See Geoff Eley, "What Are the Contexts for German Antisemitism?," *Studies in Contemporary Jewry* 13 (1997): 100–132, here 122; and see the chapter on "Eliminationist Racism" in Walser Smith, *The Continuities of German History,* 167–210.

61  See Shulamit Volkov, "Antisemitism as a Cultural Code: Reflections on the History and Historiography of Antisemitism in Imperial Germany," *Leo Baeck Institute Yearbook* 23 (1978): 25–46.

62  See Christhard Hoffmann, "Christlicher Antijudaismus und moderner Antisemitismus. Zusammenhänge und Differenzen als Problem der historischen Antisemitismusforschung," in Siegele-Wenschkewitz (ed.), *Christlicher Antijudaismus und Antisemitismus,* 293–317.

63  Susannah Heschel, *The Aryan Jesus: Christian Theologians and the Bible in Nazi Germany* (Princeton: Princeton University Press, 2008), 8.

64  Goldhagen, *Hitler's Willing Executioners,* 107. See his detailed analysis within the context of his chapter on "Eliminationist Antisemitism," particularly 107–14.

65  Ibid., 434.

66  See ibid., 436–7: "Throughout the period of Nazi rule, as the government and people of Germany were subjecting the Jews of Germany and those of the conquered countries to an increasingly severe persecution that culminated in their physical annihilation, the German Protestant and Catholic churches, their governing bodies, their bishops, and most of their theologians watched the suffering that Germans inflicted on the Jews in silence. No explicit public word of sympathy for the Jews, no explicit public condemnation or protest against their persecution issued from any of the authoritative figures within the churches [. . .]."

67  Ibid., 111.

68  Ibid., 434–5. The reason for this is the fact that "even in the Christian Churches, racist antisemitism overlay, and to a large extent, replaced the traditional religious enmity to Jews" (436).

69  Friedländer, *The Years of Extermination,* 55. See ibid., 190–1: "The anti-Jewish measures were accepted, even approved, by the population and the spiritual and intellectual elites, most blatantly so by the Christian Churches. What was tacitly approved by the French Church was explicitly welcomed by the Polish clergy, enthusiastically supported by part of German Protestantism, and more prudently so by the remainder of Christian churches in the Reich. Such religious support for or acceptance of various degrees of anti-Jewish persecution helped of course to still any doubts, particularly at a time when among most Europeans the influence of the Churches remained considerable and their guidance was eagerly sought."

70  Ibid., 575.

71  Ibid., 574. Friedländer emphasizes that "a clear distinction was systematically established between the tiny minority of converted Jews and the quasi totality of the 'ordinary' Jews" (ibid.). He acknowledges that some Christian institutions took risks in hiding Jews, however not without pointing out that "proselytism and conversion were major, albeit very elusive elements in granting such help, particularly in the hiding of children. In some places conversion may have been considered essential for better camouflage, but generally it was an aim in itself. This of course changes the historical assessment of Christian assistance, notwithstanding risk, compassion, or charity" (ibid., 577); this remark is especially significant given Friedländer's own biographical experience.

72  Ibid., 576.

73  See the depiction of the Churches' response to Nazism in the chapter "Consenting Elites, Threatened Elites," in Friedländer, *Nazi Germany and the Jews,* 41–72, esp. 41–9. The comparison of the Churches' attitude towards the regimes's early anti-Jewish measures to that of other academic elites reveals that they shared important ideological positions (such as a conservative or radical brand of nationalism, anti-modernism, anti-liberalism, and anti-Bolshevism), but that the Churches were distinguished by specific interests which informed their ambivalence towards some elements of radical Nazi antisemitism: "The Jews as Jews were abandoned to their fate, but both the Protestant and Catholic churches attempted to maintain the pre-eminence of such fundamental beliefs as the supersession of race by baptism and the sanctity of the Old Testament" (59).

74   See Friedländer, *The Years of Extermination*, 112–4; 419–21; see Richard H. Weisberg, "Differing Ways of Reading, Differing Views of the Law: The Catholic Church and its Treatment of the Jewish Question during Vichy," in *Remembering for the Future*, vol. 2 (2001), 509–30.

75   See Friedländer, *The Years of Extermination*, 24–6; 124–6; 167–8; 184–7; 213; 228–30; 242; 410–1; 534–8; 619–20; 640. Some elements of a comparative representation can be found in Kevin P. Spicer (ed.), *Antisemitism, Christian Ambivalence, and the Holocaust* (Bloomington, Indiana University Express, 2007) and in books and articles devoted to the different national Churches, but an overall systematic representation is lacking; as an analysis of Polish Catholicism, see Ronald Modras, *The Catholic Church and Antisemitism: Poland 1933–1939* (Chur: Harwood Academic Publishers, 1994).

76   Among the wealth of literature on this topic and the debate surrounding it, see Guenter Lewy, *The Catholic Church and Nazi Germany* (London: Weidenfeld & Nicolson, 1964); John F. Morley, *Vatican Diplomacy and the Jews during the Holocaust, 1939–1943* (New York: Ktav, 1980); John S. Conway, "Catholicism and the Jews," in Otto D. Kulka and Paul R. Mendes-Flohr (eds), *Judaism and Christianity under the Impact of National Socialism* (Jerusalem: The Historical Society of Israel, 1987), 435–451; Sergio Minerbi, *The Vatican and Zionism* (New York: Oxford University Press, 1990); Harry J. Cargas (ed.), *Holocaust Scholars Write to the Vatican* (Westport, Conn: Greenwood Press, 1998); John Cornwell, *Hitler's Pope: The Secret History of Pius XII* (New York: Viking Press, 1999); Michael Phayer, *The Catholic Church and the Holocaust, 1930–1965* (Bloomington: Indiana University Press, 2000); Goldhagen, *A Moral Reckoning*; Susan Zuccotti, *Under His Very Windows: The Vatican and the Holocaust in Italy* (New Haven: Yale University Press, 2000); David I. Kertzer, *The Popes against the Jews: The Vatican's Role in the Rise of Modern Antisemitism* (New York: Alfred A. Knopf, 2001); Randolph A. Braham (ed.), *The Vatican and the Holocaust: The Catholic Church and the Jews during the Nazi Era* (New York: Columbia University Press, 2000); Carol Rittner and John K. Roth (eds), *Pope Pius XII and the Holocaust* (Leicester: University of Leicester Press, 2002).

77   Friedländer, *Nazi Germany and the Jews*, 46 and 47–8.

78   Friedländer, *The Years of Extermination*, 57–8. Friedländer does not intend to provide a more detailed comparative analysis of the character of Catholic antisemitism in Germany in this context; recent research, however, has shown that Catholicism, despite the more traditional character of its antisemitism, was by no means immune to the temptation of a racist radicalization of its anti-Jewish attitude or free from affinities to Nazi-ideology in general. For the history of Catholic antisemitism in nineteenth- and early twentieth-century Germany, see Olaf Blaschke, *Katholizismus und Antisemitismus im Deutschen Kaiserreich* (Göttingen: Vandenhoeck & Ruprecht, 1999); Donald J. Dietrich, "Modern German Catholic Antisemitism," *Christian Jewish Relations* 18 (1985): 21–35; Gerhard Besier, "Anti-Bolshevism and Antisemitism: The Catholic Church in Germany and National Socialist Ideology 1936–37," *Journal of Ecclesiastical History* 43 (1992): 447–56; Donald J. Dietrich, "Catholic Theology and the Challenge of Nazism," in Spicer (ed.), *Antisemitism, Christian Ambivalence, and the Holocaust*, 76–101; Robert Michael, *A History of Catholic Antisemitism: The Dark Side of the Church* (London: Palgrave Macmillan, 2008), esp. 193–204.

79   Friedländer, *The Years of Extermination*, 302–3.

80   Ibid., 515–6; 570–1.

81   Ibid., xxiii.

82   Friedländer, *Pius XII and the Third Reich*, xxii–xxiii; 238.

83   Aschheim, "On Saul Friedländer," 13.

84   Friedländer, *Pius XII and the Third Reich*, xv. "How was it conceivable that at the end of 1943 the Pope and the highest dignitaries of the Church were still wishing for victorious resistance by the Nazis in the East and therefore seemingly accepted by implication the maintenance, however temporary, of the entire Nazi extermination machine?"(237).

85   See Friedländer, *Nazi Germany and the Jews*, 251. See Georges Passelecq and Bernard Suchetzky (eds), *The Hidden Encyclical of Pius XI* (New York: Harcourt, Brace & Company, 1997); Michael R. Marrus, "The Vatican on Racism and Antisemitism, 1938–39: A New Look at a Might-have-been," *Holocaust and Genocide Studies* 11,3 (1997) 378–395; Frank J. Coppa, "The Papal Response to Nazi and Fascist Anti-Semitism: From Pius XI to Pius XII," in Joshua D. Zimmerman (ed.), *Jews in Italy under Fascist and Nazi Rule, 1922–1945* (Cambridge: Cambridge

University Press, 2005), 265–86; Frank J. Coppa, "Between Anti-Judaism and Anti-Semitism: Pius XI's Response to the Nazi Persecution of the Jews: Precursor to Pius XII's 'silence'?," *Journal of Church and State* 47 (2005): 63–89; Frank J. Coppa, "Pope Pius XI's Encyclical 'Humani Generis Unitas' against Racism and Anti-Semitism and the 'Silence' of Pope Pius XII," *Journal of Church and State* 40 (1998): 775–95.

86   Friedländer, *The Years of Extermination*, 58.

87   Ibid., 568 (emphasis in the original).

88   Ibid., 569–72.

89   Ibid., 571.

90   Ibid., 572. For the question regarding the Pope's involvement in rescue operations, see Zucotti, *Under His Very Windows*, 307–8. According to her, Pius XII must have known about those activities, but was never personally involved; nor did he approve or forbid such operations. For the Pope's silence see also Frank J. Coppa, "Between Morality and Diplomacy: The Vatican's 'Silence' during the Holocaust," *Journal of Church and State* 50 (2008): 541–68.

91   Friedländer, *The Years of Extermination*, 573.

92   Friedländer, *Nazi Germany and the Jews*, 44.

93   Ibid., 327; for their racist programme see Friedländer, *The Years of Extermination*, 161–2.

94   Ibid., 56.

95   See Wolfgang Gerlach, *And the Witnesses Were Silent: The Confessing Church and the Persecution of the Jews* (Lincoln and London: University of Nebraska Press, 2000); and see the slightly contrasting views of Victoria Barnett, *For the Soul of the People: Protestant Protest against Hitler* (New York and Oxford: Oxford University Press, 1992), 122–54.

96   Richard Gutteridge, "German Protestantism and the Jews in the Third Reich," in Kulka and Mendes-Flohr (eds), *Judaism and Christianity Under the Impact of National Socialism*, 251–70, here 238; see Friedländer, *Nazi Germany and the Jews*, 190.

97   See Friedländer, *The Years of Extermination*, 300–1; 512–3; 515–7; see Gerlach, *And the Witnesses Were Silent*, 194–205; 210–4.

98   Friedländer, *Nazi Germany and the Jews*, 45–6; Friedländer, *The Years of Extermination*, 575; for the discussion on Bonhoeffer, see William J. Peck, "Theology and Politics in Bonhoeffer's view of Judaism," *Christian Attitudes on Jews and Judaism* 30 (1973): 13–7; Ruth Zerner, "Dietrich Bonhoeffer and the Jews: Thought and Actions, 1933–1945," *Jewish Social Studies* 37 (1975): 235–50; Eberhard Bethge, "Dietrich Bonhoeffer und die Juden," in Heinz Kremers (ed.), *Die Juden und Martin Luther – Martin Luther und die Juden: Geschichte, Wirkungsgeschichte, Herausforderung* (Neukirchen-Vluyn: Neukirchener Verlag, 1985), 211–48; Andreas Pangritz, "Dietrich Bonhoeffers theologische Begründung der Beteiligung am Widerstand," *Evangelische Theologie* 55 (1995): 491–520; Kenneth C. Barnes, "Dietrich Bonhoeffer and Hitler's Persecution of the Jews," in Robert P. Ericksen and Susannah Heschel (eds), *Betrayal: German Churches and the Holocaust* (Minneapolis: Fortress Press, 1999), 110–28; Hans-Walter Krumwiede, "Dietrich Bonhoeffers Kampf gegen die Judenvernichtung durch den Nationalsozialismus," *Kirchliche Zeitgeschichte* 13 (2000): 59–91; Stephen R. Haynes, "Bystander, Resister, Victim: Dietrich Bonhoeffer's Response to Nazism," in Donald J. Dietrich (ed.), *Christian Responses to the Holocaust; Moral and Ethical Issues* (Syracuse, NY: Syracuse University Press, 2003), 99–118; Victoria J. Barnett, "Dietrich Bonhoeffer's Relevance for post-Holocaust Christian Theology," *Studies in Christian-Jewish Relations* 2 (2007): 53–67.

99   For a historiographical survey, see Robert P. Ericksen and Susannah Heschel, "The German Churches and the Holocaust," in Dan Stone (ed.), *The Historiography of the Holocaust* (London: Palgrave Macmillan, 2004), 296–318, and see the different contributions in Ericksen and Heschel (eds), *Betrayal*.

100  As an analysis of the attitude of Liberal Protestantism from a contemporary Jewish perspective, see Christian Wiese "The 'Religion of the Future': The Conflict between Wissenschaft des Judentums and Liberal Protestantism 1900 to 1933," *Jewish Studies Quarterly* 7 (2000): 367–98.

101  Kurt Nowak, *Kulturprotestantismus und Judentum in der Weimarer Republik* (Göttingen: Wallstein, 1993), 35.

102  See Friedrich-Wilhelm Graf, "'Wir konnten dem Rad nicht in die Speichen fallen.' Liberaler Protestantismus und 'Judenfrage' nach 1933," in Kaiser and Greschat, eds, *Der Holocaust und die Protestanten*, 151–85.

103   For the history of the impact of this type of antisemitism, see Christian Wiese, "Vom 'jüdischen Geist.' Isaak Heinemanns Auseinandersetzung mit dem akademischen Antisemitismus inner-halb der protestantischen Theologie in der Weimarer Republik," *Zeitschrift für Religions- und Geistesgeschichte* 46 (1994): 211–34.

104   See Martin Greschat, "Protestantischer Antisemitismus in Wilhelminischer Zeit: Das Beispiel des Hofpredigers Adolf Stoecker," in Günter Brakelmann and Martin Rosowski (eds), *Antisemitismus: Von religiöser Judenfeindschaft zur Rassenideologie* (Göttingen: Vandenhoeck & Ruprecht 1989), 27–51.

105   See Fritz Stern, *The Politics of Cultural Despair: A Study in the Rise of the Germanic Ideology* (Berkeley: University of California Press, 1961).

106   Robert P. Ericksen, *Theologians under Hitler: Gerhard Kittel, Paul Althaus, and Emanuel Hirsch* (New Haven: Yale University Press, 1987).

107   See Doris Bergen's excellent study *Twisted Cross: The German Christian Movement in the Third Reich* (Chapel Hill: The University of North Carolina Press, 1996).

108   According to Heschel, *The Aryan Jesus*, 3, the movement "eventually attracted between a quarter and a third of Protestant church members"; Bergen, *Twisted Cross*, 2–3 likewise disputes the mar-ginality of the movement. And see Manfred Gailus, *Protestantismus und Nationalsozialismus: Studien zur nationalsozialistischen Durchdringung des protestantischen Sozialmilieus in Berlin* (Cologne et al.: Böhlau, 2001).

109   Heschel, *The Aryan Jesus*, 16.

110   See, for example, Walter Grundmann, *Der Gott Jesu Christi* (Weimar: Verlag der Deutschen Christen, 1936).

111   Bergen, *Twisted Cross*, 142; Susannah Heschel, "Theologen für Hitler: Walter Grundmann und das 'Institut zur Erforschung und Beseitigung des jüdischen Einflusses auf das deutsche kirch-liche Leben,'" in Siegele-Wenschkewitz (ed.), *Christlicher Antijudaismus und Antisemitismus*, 125–70, here 000.

112   See the reinterpretation of the complex and diverse relationship of the Nazi elite towards Christianity in Richard Steigmann-Gall, *The Holy Reich: Nazi Conceptions of Christianity, 1919-1945* (Cambridge: Cambridge University Press, 2003); the author challenges the conven-tional view, apparently partly shared by Friedländer, that Nazism was basically an anti-Christian movement, and argues that, despite the blatant paganism of some Nazi leaders, there was a much stronger affinity with what he calls the "positive Christianity" of a majority of the Nazi elite. See also Klaus Scholder, "Judaism and Christianity in the Ideology and Politics of National Socialism," in Kulka and Mendes-Flohr (eds), *Judaism and Christianity under the Impact of National Socialism*, 183–95; for the paradoxical nature of Nazi anti-Christianism and Nazism's character as a political religion, see Philippe Burrin, "Political Religion: The Relevance of a Concept," in Ne'eman Arad (ed.), *Passing into History*, 321–49.

113   Smid, "Protestantismus und Antisemitismus 1930–1933," 66.

114   See Rolf Rendtorff, "Auschwitz als Anfechtung des Christentums: Elie Wiesels Botschaft für Christen nach Auschwitz," in Rendtorff, *Christen und Juden heute: Neue Einsichten und neue Aufgaben* (Neukirchen-Vluyn: Neukirchner Verlag), 94–111.

115   Bergen, *Twisted Cross*, xii.

116   See Doris Bergen, "Religion and Genocide: A Historiographical Survey," in Dan Stone (ed.), *The Historiography of Genocide* (London: Palgrave Macmillan, 2008), 194–227; Omer Bartov and Phyllis Mack (eds), *In God's Name: Genocide and Religion in the Twentieth Century* (New York: Berghahn, 2001).

117   For the question about guilt in the discourse on the Shoah, see Dan Diner, "On Guilt Discourses and Other Narratives: Epistemological Observations," in Ne'eman Arad (ed.), *Passing into History*, 301–20.

# "The Ethics of a Truth-Seeking Judge": Konrad Morgen, SS Judge and Corruption Expert[1]

## Raphael Gross

In his second volume of his *Nazi Germany and the Jews*, Saul Friedländer refers to a person I would like to discuss more closely: SS judge Konrad Morgen (1909–1982).[2] Morgen embodies one of Friedländer's central themes, the ideological motivation and moral dimension of Nazi crimes, or, to be more precise, the thinking of men who in one form or another became intimately involved in these crimes. What was their scope of action, and how were their biographies judged, especially when these biographies proved to be ambiguous or at least ambivalent? Friedländer already pursued this topic when analyzing the complex course of SS officer Kurt Gerstein's life.[3] In the following discussion I will consider key postwar actions and statements of the two men, in the hope of illuminating their decisions and inner motives from a fresh perspective.

Konrad Morgen is mentioned by Saul Friedländer in the context of the central role he played as the "corruption expert" of Reichsführer-SS Heinrich Himmler. In his notorious speech on 6 October 1943 at Posen Himmler had demanded, with much rhetoric, "an utterly clear solution" to the "Jewish Question" (which he explicitly stated to be the mass murder especially of Jewish women and children) while at the same time stressing the "decency" of his SS men. At the core of Himmler's speech, which consisted of a mixture of high praise and the threat of draconian punishment, was the citation of a catalogue of virtues with a special emphasis on "decency." "Decency" in this context referred above all to the men not gaining personal advantage from the murder of the Jews. Friedländer quotes from Himmler's long speech at the point when he states that the SS men have no right to profit from their victims and that they must not take "even one fur, even one watch, even one Mark or cigarette."[4] While Reichsführer-SS Heinrich Himmler let himself be carried away by such rhetorical flights of fancy his SS men – as he himself knew best of all – were busy not only murdering people but also robbing them. Thus Friedländer explains the context of Himmler's speech as follows:

As a matter of fact, while the Reichsführer was both praising and threatening, an inquiry commission headed by SS investigating judge Konrad Morgen, had uncovered widespread corruption and unauthorized killings of political prisoners (mainly Poles and Russians) at the very center of the extermination system, in Auschwitz. Rudolf Höss was relieved of his command (but transferred to a more elevated position in Berlin); others also had to leave: the head of the political section, Maximilian Grabner; the head of the

Kattowitz Gestapo, Rudolf Milner; even one of the chief physicians [. . .] Friedrich Entress (who also specialized in phenol injections into the hearts of inmates in the infirmary of the main camp), and smaller fry.[5]

Konrad Morgen was the child of an engine-driver and grew up in Frankfurt am Main.[6] There he attended the Liebig *Oberrealschule* and, after having passed his university entrance examination (Abitur), he first worked at the banking house of S. A. Goldschmid. He subsequently studied law at the universities of Frankfurt, Rome and Berlin, as well as in The Hague and Kiel. We have documentary evidence from his estate, dated 3 May 1937, in the form of an account, written by Morgen himself, detailing his "political development":

> The ignominy of the lost war began to burn in me as soon as I started to think about things. I therefore started quite early to concern myself with the external enemies of the German people. [. . .] While abroad I got to know the irreconcilable hatred of our enemies. [. . .] I became a member of the university section of the Deutsche Volkspartei since my family was quite close to this party. Fairly quickly I became the head of the university section and got to know the leading members of the party.

After having lost confidence in the effectiveness of the "Volkspartei youth section" he resolved to "vote exclusively National Socialist in future." This is followed by an interesting passage which was meant, it seems, to explain his late entry into the NSDAP by referring to the "nobility" of his stance:

> The reason for not deciding to become a member of the NSDAP straightaway was mainly based on the thought that it was ethically not justifiable to change straightaway from one camp [. . .] to the next. As much as it seemed essential to me to courageously draw a line [under my past] by resigning [from the party] tactfulness equally did not allow me to go beyond that. In April 1933 I became a member of the NSDAP and the SS. Here I also did not push myself forward, but rather saw my task as fulfilling my duty to the letter whilst keeping back with modesty.

Regarding his religious views he writes, fully in accordance with the line then dominant in the SS:

> I had already left the church approximately 10 years ago. Religion to me was in an irreconcilable conflict with the findings of the natural sciences, church dogma was too narrow for the modern world and I was deeply conscious of the socially divisive [*volkszersplitternd*] and stultifying [*machtlähmend*] activities of the churches. I therefore believed that I could not in conscience justify staying in this organization. Resolving to leave [the church] was my own personal and completely independent decision.[7]

Let us now turn to Morgen's professional career: on 1 April 1939 he started his first appointment as a judge at the *Landgericht* (regional court) in Stettin.

Following a disagreement regarding the stance he took in a particular court case he was removed from the judiciary; at the outbreak of war he served in the Waffen SS until, in 1940, he was transferred to Munich to the position of SS judge. Such irregularities, it seems, were linked less to his political views than to his confrontational personality.[8] However, exactly this character trait – being part of the "SS virtues" he displayed – may have predisposed him to work for Himmler as his willing servant in the latter's internecine battles within the SS. At least in some reports a character trait becomes discernible which makes him appear to be less conforming than others. This becomes clear in a testimonial, dated 2 September 1939, provided by the president of the *Oberlandesgericht* in Frankfurt: "It must also be stressed that he is always inclined to view problems critically and to put forward his opinion emphatically."[9] The report continues: "Dr Morgen possesses a distinct sense of honour and is an upright, decent person. [. . .] There have been no doubts about his political reliability."[10] From 1 January 1941 he was employed at the *SS-und Polizeigericht VI* (SS and Police Court) in Cracow. In 1942 Himmler again removed him from his post and, having been demoted from lieutenant to private, he was sent to the eastern front.[11] In this instance he had come into conflict with other judges – according to his own testimony "because I, as presiding judge [*Vorsitzender*], had acquitted a defendant involved in a racial issue who had admitted his guilt; because of this I was accused of sabotaging an order of the Reichsführer."[12] But Morgen believed that the "real reason" for his demotion – and there are good reasons to agree with him here – was his work as investigator in several serious cases of corruption involving a considerable number of high-ranking SS men. In May 1943 Himmler personally entrusted him again with the task of fighting corruption and he was transferred, having been restored to his old rank, to the *Reichs-Kriminal-Polizeiamt* (criminal investigation department) in Berlin. Apparently he was suddenly again important for Himmler in the fight against corruption in the concentration camps and, above all, in the internecine fights between the Nazi Party elites struggling for supremacy in Germany. From now on he was mainly occupied with the high profile case of the former concentration camp commander at Buchenwald, Karl Koch, whom, after complex investigations, he was finally able to incriminate to such an extent that he was executed in the grounds of Buchenwald concentration camp only one week before the end of the war. The eagerness Konrad Morgen displayed in uncovering crimes of corruption was certainly extraordinary and no doubt led to many of his SS colleagues becoming hostile towards him. The exact number of criminal procedures instigated by Morgen can so far not be ascertained, but it might well have been over 700. In his postwar publication *Der SS Staat* (1946), which received much attention, Eugen Kogon stated that Morgen's investigative methods were in themselves murderous – a claim that was also supported by a witness statement.[13] The background to these brutal methods is as follows: when Karl Koch, after long investigations, could finally be taken into custody, Morgen's most crucial witness for the prosecution, a certain *SS-Hauptscharführer* Köhler, was found dead in his cell. Morgen then tried to prove that this was a murder ordered by Koch. To demonstrate that this was so it is said that Morgen gave small doses of the poison which had been found in the stomach of the deceased to four Soviet prisoners of war. These four men then reportedly died in the presence of Morgen and several other witnesses and in this way Morgen acquired important evidence against Koch. After the war Morgen was prosecuted for this crime but the case never came to a conclusion and it cannot be demonstrated that Kogon actually reported the circumstances correctly.[14]

From the autumn of 1944 onwards, Morgen was the Chief SS Judge of Cracow, making him also responsible for the Auschwitz extermination camp, where he prosecuted cases such as the smuggling of dental gold (after discovery by the German customs authorities) and theft, corruption, grievous bodily harm, and murder. On 8 August 1946, when questioned as a defense witness at Nuremberg, he explained under oath that:

> I thought that this happened for reasons of camouflage, so that on the surface one could not distinguish these camps, the extermination camps, from the other labor camps or the concentration camp itself. For me as a soldier it was simply incomprehensible that this was done to the reputation of the SS, which had after all nothing to do with this extermination.[15]

On 9 March 1964 Konrad Morgen gave a detailed statement on the twenty-fifth day of the Auschwitz trial in Frankfurt am Main. I shall return to this later.[16]

## II

The case of Konrad Morgen never gained much public attention but it plays a central role in the international bestseller *Die Wohlgesinnten* (2008) by Jonathan Littell, which received controversial reviews, and in a new German novel by Volker Harry Altwasser (*Letzte Haut*, 2009). In contrast the story of the SS officer Kurt Gerstein (1905–45), who was responsible for the delivery of Cyclone B gas but who also told neutral observers about the mass murder in German extermination camps immediately after having witnessed these events, was brought to wide public attention by Rolf Hochhuth in his play *Der Stellvertreter* (premiered in Berlin in 1963). In this essay, we cannot examine the highly complex biographies of these two SS men at this point. Moreover Saul Friedländer has already provided us with an impressive portrait of Kurt Gerstein which, at best, I could only retrace here. But I would like to take a closer look at these biographies to allow us to discern the inner attitude of these two men, within the limited way such knowledge is available to historians, as well as to see how these two people were judged.

Even after his death Kurt Gerstein – and this is confirmed by Saul Friedländer's final remarks in his portrayal of Gerstein – was not fully rehabilitated by the *Spruchkammergericht* (a civilian court responsible for the denazification process in postwar Germany) in Tübingen after the war with regard to his conduct as an SS officer. I quote the relevant passage as set out in Friedländer's publication:

> By making known those extermination measures to prominent personalities in the Evangelical Church and to members of the Dutch Resistance Movement with the request that they bring them to the notice of the public throughout the world, and in rendering useless two shipments of prussic acid, Gerstein committed acts of resistance, which, had his actions been discovered would have placed him in very great jeopardy. However, in view of the appalling scale of the crimes committed, his behaviour, [. . .] cannot exonerate him altogether from sharing the responsibility, but can only contribute toward earning him a more lenient verdict. After his experiences in the Belzec camp, he might have been expected to resist, with all the strength at his command, being made the tool of an organized mass murder. The court is of the opinion that the accused did not exhaust all the possibilities open to him and that he could have found other ways and means of holding aloof from the operation. It is incomprehensible and inexcusable that, as a convinced Christian [. . .] he allowed himself to be used [. . .] as an agent passing orders to the Degesch Company. [. . .] [I]t must have been utterly clear to him that he, as an individual, was in no position to prevent these extermination measures, or by rendering useless trifling quantities of the prussic acid supplied, to save the lives of even some of the persons concerned. Accordingly, taking into account the extenuating circumstances noted [. . .] the court has not included the accused among the main criminals but has placed him among the 'tainted.'[17]

Saul Friedländer comments on this verdict by asking which criterion one could use to discern genuine resistance in a totalitarian system, considering that such resistance would of necessity have had to be ambiguous. He believes such a criterion is "that of the danger incurred. There were many Germans who put forward the argument that they had resisted within the system to explain away their participation in Nazi activities. Yet how many of them demonstrated their will to resist by committing acts which, had they been discovered, would have cost the perpetrators their lives? Kurt Gerstein was one of these people."[18]

In contrast to Saul Friedländer's analysis, the actions of the deeply religious SS man Kurt Gerstein received no mercy in the Spruchkammer case after the war and he was, as we have seen, classified as "tainted" (*belastet*). The consequence of this was that his surviving dependants not only were refused the payment of an inheritance, his widow also had to pay the high court costs. In the estate of Kurt Morgen a much more positive assessment by a *Spruchkammergericht* headed by *Justizoberinspektor* Mayer can be found:

> The person concerned was an SS judge most probably from 1941 onwards. At the beginning of the war SS courts were instituted which have to be regarded as proper courts analogous to courts martial [*Kriegs- und Feldgerichte*] as well as to the courts set up by the air force or the navy; they dealt with all those offences and crimes which the military penal code [*Strafgesetzbuch*] regards as subject to prosecution and punishment.

The person concerned was tasked almost exclusively with investigating capital crimes – cases that are pursued in every civilized state. It could not be demonstrated that in carrying out his duties he was guilty of perversion of justice or the suppression of law [*Rechtsunterdrückung*]. On the contrary, he especially sought out SS men for prosecution and brought them to justice. Doing so he maintained to the utmost the ethics of a truth-seeking judge and carried out the duty of a conscientious representative of the law. The court was therefore convinced that he, as an SS judge, cannot be called to account. To the contrary, the *Kammer* (court) has become convinced that the person concerned not only showed courage when pursuing the above mentioned cases against the highest-ranking SS officers but that he also actively resisted by doing so, as violence was an essential part of SS activity, especially in the concentration camps. And the person concerned fought forcefully against such violence by intervening energetically so that from 1942 he succeeded in breaking the violence perpetrated in Buchenwald, leading – according to statements by the witness Miller – to circumstances improving considerably. It is not disputed either that the person concerned suffered disadvantages as a direct consequence. In the case of the Schutz Polizist he was compulsorily transferred immediately after the case, in other cases he had to reckon with the possibility that SS men might murder him secretly as was most probably the case with *Oberscharführer* Köhler. He thus put his life at risk and pursued the path of a judge with determination.[19]

For these reasons the court assigned Morgen to the group of the exonerated.

Neither in the case of Konrad Morgen nor in that of Kurt Gerstein do these judicial assessments remain the last, definitive ones. Although the judgment on Gerstein was confirmed in another court case, finally, in 1965, *Ministerpräsident* Georg Kiesinger reassigned him to the group of the exonerated.[20] In the decades after Konrad Morgen's acquittal several preliminary proceedings were undertaken against him, but all of them were discontinued without coming to any conclusions. In Frankfurt am Main proceedings against Morgen accusing him of the attempted murder of four Russian prisoners of war were stopped on 29 March 1961.[21] Another set of preliminary proceedings relating to Morgen's alleged participation in the deportation and murder of Hungarian Jews was stopped as late as 6 March 1972. In his estate there can even be found a notification of suspension regarding another preliminary investigation which was only discontinued because Morgen had died in the meantime.[22] Despite this, Morgen's assessment of himself and that of the public remained quite positive. A report in the *Stuttgarter Nachrichten* in 1950 is typical of those times, regarding both style and content:

Having served as an SS judge during the war, Morgen stayed true to his sense of justice [*Recht*] and decency [*Sauberkeit*]. Everywhere he went he followed the trail of crime and greed of the higher and highest-ranking SS officers, secretly checked their bank accounts and [searched] their homes and sent one after another to jail. Among the 700 criminal proceedings there are twelve death sentences imposed on the worst of those he brought down: amongst them the commander of Buchenwald, Koch.[23]

Several other newspaper cuttings in Morgen's estate demonstrate how he himself was presented as a man of the resistance: "The *SS-Untersuchungsrichter* Dr Konrad Morgen, who was formerly accused of being one of the main culprits, has been reassigned to the group of the exonerated. Dr Morgen was a *Sturmbannführer* in the SS but was able to prove membership of the Hildebrand resistance group, whose aim was to eliminate Hitler and put an end to the Nazi tyranny."[24] Whenever there were negative assessments of him Morgen was only too eager to put himself in a positive light, as numerous letters in his estate show. Thus he wrote to the editor in chief of the *Deutsche Volkszeitung* after it had published a critical article about him: "Even in the blackest hours of those dark years I never completely lost the belief that the honesty of my actions [undertaken] for the sake of humanity and a higher law would finally be recognized and supported by well-meaning people."[25]

## III

According to his own account Kurt Gerstein joined the SS after learning that mentally ill people had been murdered in Grafeneck and Hadamar; therefore "I decided to at least try to have a closer look at these ovens and [death] chambers."[26] Although this reasoning – as well as a few other points in Gerstein's complex and complicated biography – has not remained undisputed, it is nevertheless certain that before joining the SS Gerstein had been arrested twice by the Gestapo: first on 24 September 1936, because he had systematically distributed pamphlets of the Confessing Church to top civil servants and ministers of state. This first arrest led to his exclusion from the NSDAP in October 1936. But subsequently Gerstein nonetheless continued with his attempts to spread his Christian views, for instance by publishing a slim brochure entitled *Um Ehre und Reinheit* (On Honour and Purity) dealing in the main with Christian sexual ethics.[27] In July 1938 he was arrested for the second time and spent six months in the concentration camp at Welzheim until a Gestapo officer released him. Although he tried to come to some kind of arrangement with the regime, his relationship to the Nazi state remained at all times ambivalent, to put it mildly.[28] After having witnessed the murder of Jews on 19 August 1942 in Treblinka with his own eyes he approached Baron von Otter, the secretary of the Swedish embassy in Berlin, the following evening in a sleeper car. Otter later also confirmed that the following report by Gerstein was correct:

> Still under the fresh impression of those horrific experiences I told him [Otter] everything, asking him to report this straightaway to his government and the allies since every day of delay would cost thousands or tens of thousands of lives. [. . .] I again met Herr von Otter in the Swedish embassy. [. . .] I tried to report the same matter to the papal nuncio in Berlin. There I was asked if I were a soldier. Subsequently they refused to have any further conversation with me and I was asked to leave the embassy of His Holiness.[29]

In his book Saul Friedländer carefully documented and, as far as possible, also verified from sources further moving attempts by Kurt Gerstein to bear witness. He stressed that Gerstein told so many people about his experiences that this bordered on carelessness and one gets the firm impression that Gerstein was on a deeply moral, political mission – albeit a futile one – to inform and to warn, above all, those in neutral countries but that he at the same time attempted to soothe his own deep feelings of guilt; summing up, Friedländer states that Gerstein "looked forward to death as a certainty; he may indeed have longed for it as an escape from intolerable and irresolvable conflicts."[30] Both during his service as an SS officer as well as after the end of the Nazi regime it is without doubt the case that Gerstein was deeply affected and distressed by the murders he witnessed – although that did not prevent the *Spruchkammergericht*, as mentioned above, from classifying him as one of those who were incriminated.

Regarding Konrad Morgen there is no documentary evidence whatsoever from the period of the Nazi regime which would indicate anything like resistance, although after the war, as we have seen, he impressed the *Spruchkammergericht* with his later reports to such an extent that it even acknowledged his "active resistance." Even his doctoral dissertation "Kriegspropaganda und Kriegsverhütung" (War Propaganda and War Prevention), submitted in 1936, which he later claimed had not found favour with the Party, fitted well into the "visions of peace" as repeatedly propagated by the National Socialists before the outbreak of war – or, as Morgen put it: "Peace, too, is surrounded by a thoroughly Nordic aura."[31] Through his work as a corruption expert within the ranks of the SS he became intimately involved in the internecine struggles for power amongst members of the SS elite and – as became evident when he was temporarily demoted – he was not always sufficiently protected by Himmler's or Hitler's backing.[32] In view of his massive attacks – especially on Koch – it can certainly be said that he was not reluctant to make powerful and dangerous enemies within the system. But then, what was his aim in this regard? To offer resistance or to create the "decent" type of SS Himmler kept talking about? [33]

Surely Konrad Morgen could claim that he represented a certain National Socialist idealism. But did this really lead him into conflict with the SS? Apparently, as the above mentioned quotations show, even in 1946 he was still convinced that the SS was a thoroughly good organization.[34] To be sworn to the ideals and virtues of the "*Volk*" was a ritual common to the Party and the SS. Amongst the documents in Morgen's estate is his own NSDAP identity card containing a preface by Hitler dated 9 January 1927, which reads as follows:

In everything act as if the fate of your people rested on your shoulders alone and do not expect from others anything you are not prepared to deliver or do yourself, always be an example to your comrades! As leader be tough [against yourself] in your fulfilment of duty, resolved to do the necessary, helpful and good to your subordinates, never petty when judging human weaknesses, generous in recognizing the needs of others and modest with regard to your own! Never get drunk! [. . .] Always fulfil your duties regarding the movement and remember that the greatest work can only be done by human beings when they are ready to subordinate their own ego for the sake of the greater common good and necessity. In all this be the [kind of] example to your fellow members of the Party and the community [*Volk*] you wish them to emulate. See even in the least of your fellow Germans [*Volksgenosse*] someone of the same blood to whom fate has bound you irretrievably on this earth and therefore hold the lowest-ranking road sweeper of your people in higher regard than any king of a foreign land. [. . .] When you are fighting for the NSDAP you are fighting for your people.[35]

Beyond the inherent cynicism and "völkisch" particularism of Hitler's exhortation, it possessed, within its own framework of values, a moral drive certainly perceived as idealism by Nazis such as Morgen – who both before and after 1945, in many respects thus himself embodied the ideal of the decent SS man as envisaged by Himmler.

There is, then, a crucial space separating Kurt Gerstein's moral shock and horror at the Nazi state's ongoing mass murder campaign, as articulated both in the war years and in the short postwar phase before his alleged suicide, from the stance maintained by Konrad Morgen. This becomes particularly clear with consideration of one key document: the long interrogation of Morgen in Frankfurt on 9 March 1964,[36] which was both of considerable importance in the information it offered the prosecutors and revealed feelings and values maintained by Morgen of central significance in the present context. Morgen began his response to the Auschwitz-trial interrogators as follows:

My investigations regarding the concentration camp in Auschwitz were triggered by a field post parcel. [. . .] That is to say it contained three lumps of gold. [. . .] The gold in question was high carat dental gold which had been melted down in a primitive way. There was one very large lump, perhaps the size of two fists, the other was considerably smaller, the third one rather insignificant [in size]. But still, these amounted to a considerable number of kilograms. Before I started further proceedings I began to think about the whole thing. First of all it was the audacity of the perpetrator – at that point unknown to me – which stumped me. This case seemed to be one of utter stupidity. But the longer I thought about it the more I began to believe that this way of thinking underestimated the perpetrator. It was after all like this: as there were hundreds of thousands of field post parcels the chances were quite low that this dangerous consignment would be the one to be seized and discovered. A trait of rather shifty primitivity and unscrupulous recklessness seemed to me to predominate in this perpetrator, [an assumption] which in the course of my later investigations in Auschwitz would prove to be correct.[37]

In the following he describes how he traced this "shifty primitivity" and the various other discoveries he made in the course of doing so:

A further consideration sent shudders down my back: for a [kilogram] of gold consists of 1,000 grams. I knew that the dental facilities at concentration camps were charged with collecting gold retrieved from the burnt corpses and sending it on to the Reichsbank. And a gold crown – that's only a few grams. 1,000 grams or several thousand grams represent the death of several thousand people. But not everyone has gold crowns, especially in those rather poorer times when only a certain fraction [of the population had them]. Therefore one had to multiply this figure – according to one's estimate whether every twentieth or fiftieth person had gold crowns in their mouths – with that figure, and thus the confiscated consignment represented the equivalent of twenty-thousand, fifty-thousand or hundreds of thousands of corpses.[38]

At this point Morgen displays for the first time a trace of empathy with the victims of these SS men: "A harrowing thought. But the really incomprehensible thing about it was that the perpetrator was able to put aside such amounts without being detected."[39] Thus, in the very next sentence, he immediately relativizes his feelings for the victims. In the following we shall take a detailed look at his report, which – apart from containing horrific facts and his astonishingly strong emphasis on so-called "Jewish collaboration" – demonstrates how his feelings seem to work throughout in a similar fashion.

That's how I found myself standing one morning on the station at Auschwitz. [. . .] Auschwitz was a small town with a through station and marshalling yard, somewhat similar to Bebra. [. . .] People disembarked there as if it were the most ordinary thing in the world – the young were jolly, the older ones sullen [and] worn out. [. . .] I started with the beginning of the end, the ramp at Birkenau. The ramp looked like any other ramp at any freight yard. [. . .] I therefore asked my guide and companion how things worked. He explained to me how the camp would be informed from the station about a transport, most often of Jews, immediately before its arrival at Auschwitz. Then the doors of the carriage would be opened, the new arrivals would have to get out und put down their luggage. Men and women would have to line up separately and then, he said, they would be asked about any rabbis [present in the group]. Rabbis and other important Jewish personalities would be selected straightaway, [then] taken to the camp [and to] a separate hut which they had all to themselves. [. . .] After that, one would ask [them] about any specialists the camp needed – for it was connected to large industrial com-panies – these would then be selected first. And the remainder would be grouped into those who were fit for work and those who were not. Those who could work would then march to the camp at Auschwitz, would there be received as regular prisoners, receive clothing and be divided [into work groups]. The other group would have to get into a lorry – no names would be taken – which would drive straight to the gas chambers at Birkenau. [. . .] Starting at the ramp we followed the track of the death transports to the Birkenau camp, which was a few kilometres away. Behind it was the so-called 'Kanada' compound where the belongings of the victims were checked, sorted, and re-utilised. [. . .] And then, behind that, there were the crematoria. [. . .] In the yard there was – one cannot call it anything else – a pack of Jewish prisoners wearing yellow stars, with their Kapo, who carried a long truncheon – they straightaway began to circle around us. They were constantly circling around there, always on the alert for any orders and ready to catch the eye [of any commanding officer]. And I suddenly realized: they are behaving like a pack of Alsatians. And then and there I said as much to my companion who laughed at that and said, yes, that was their job. [. . .] And along this corridor there were many rooms without any furnishings whatsoever, bare, devoid of everything, [with] cement floors. The only noticeable and at first inexplicable thing was that in the center there was a cross-barred shaft reaching up to the ceiling. At first I had no explanation for this until I was told that through an opening in the roof gas – in its chrystalline form, i.e., Zyklon B – could be poured into these death chambers. So until this moment the prisoner did not suspect anything and then, of course, it was too late. [. . .].[40]

So far the rather sober description by Morgen which leads up to the real aim of his investigation:

After having seen these external facilities and SS men somehow not having made an appearance at all I was of course interested to take a look at and get to know the SS men who were administering the whole operation there and kept it going. I was then allowed to cast a quick glance into the so-called guardroom *and it was here that I suffered for the first time a real sensation of shock* [my emphasis, RG]. You know that a military guardroom in all armies of the world is marked by Spartan simplicity. There is [usually] a desk, placards [on the wall], some plank beds for those about to be relieved, a desk and a telephone. But this was different. It was a low-ceilinged, quite dim room and in it there was an odd collection of couches. And on those couches a few, mostly lower-ranking, SS men were lounging about in a picturesque manner, dozing away, their eyes glazed over. I had the impression that they must have had a lot of alcohol the night before. Instead of a desk there was a huge cooking range, as used in hotels, where four or five young girls were busy making potato pancakes. They were obviously Jewish, very beautiful, oriental beauties, with fiery eyes, who did not wear prison clothing but normal, rather coquettish civilian dress. And these were offering those potato pancakes to their lords and masters who were lounging and dozing around, feeding them and asking in a concerned manner whether more sugar was needed. [Pause]. Nobody took any notice of me or my companion – who was after all a captain [*Hauptmann*].[41] No-one saluted, nobody was bothered at all. And I thought I could not trust my ears: these female prisoners and the SS men addressed each other with the familiar 'du.' I must have looked rather aghast at my companion. He merely shrugged and said: 'The men have had a hard night. They had to deal with the transports.' [Pause] Then I took action and got the whole of the SS crematorium commando to stand to attention in front of their lockers and started a search. And exactly as I had thought – a lot of stuff then began to appear: gold rings, coins, chains, small necklaces, pearls, [cash in] roughly all the currencies of the earth. In some cases just a few 'souvenirs' as the person in question said, in another case a small fortune. What I had not expected however was that from one of the lockers there tumbled the sexual organs of a freshly slaughtered bull. At first I was completely flabbergasted and could not think of what these might be used for. Until the man whose locker it was blushed (yes, really, such things did happen) and confessed that one got hold of this stuff to refresh one's own sexual potency. [Pause] So, after I had carried out this search and thus caught out the whole crematorium commando, I questioned them and then that day was over.[42]

At this point in his account, Morgen took some time to dwell on a purported episode of *nearly enacted* resistance. More precisely: on ruminations, in the course of this purported near enactment, over where the act itself would lead – followed by new, contradictory insight regarding "a possible path for proceeding." The passage casts particularly sharp light on the specific moral framework within which Morgen seems to have consistently operated, both during the Nazi years and after; it thus merits citation at considerable length:

At the end of this sleepless night I had to accept that this system could only be fought and destroyed from outside. And I believed I had to try and do so. [Pause] It occurred to me that some time previously I had talked to a *Kriminalkommissar* (detective superintendent) who served in the border district close to Switzerland, in Constance, and who in the course of our discussion had told me about the many ways of crossing the border, saying [that there were] streets with houses where the front door was on the German side while the back door opened to Swiss territory. I thought I [could] find these border-crossing locations. I issued [myself] a ticket and a marching order [which was headed] 'court martial investigation Vienna' from Vienna and then on to Constance and then travelled all the way without stopping. Approximately 36 hours later I was approaching my destination. In the meantime I had calmed down to the extent that I was able to envisage the forthcoming events and firmly believed that I would succeed in crossing the border and I asked myself what exactly would happen [once I was] on the other side. Surely there would be an interrogation, one would be passed on from one authority to the next one up. And while I was trying to imagine this in detail – the questions, my answers – I realised all of a sudden that my account and my talk would sound so incredible and inconceivable to an outsider, especially a neutral one, that I would not be believed. Certainly the question [would be asked]: did you yourself see a gassing, have you seen a corpse or a prisoner who has been beaten? And I would have to say in all honesty: no. But I tore myself away from this thought and imagined the opposite: if it all goes well, if they believe you, what happens then? The Swiss government would do nothing that was certain. But most probably they would make me face the press and I would make statements. The consequence of that would be that the war propaganda against Germany would be immensely revved up. And I had to tell myself, after everything I had seen: in the event of a total collapse, a complete victory over Germany the victorious powers would, on the basis of what had happened, annihilate the whole of the German people and – so I thought – draw and quarter each and everyone. [Pause] And to initiate something like this and be responsible for it, that was beyond my strength. "The German *Volk*," that's truly a great concept but it's made up of many individuals. And I now thought of my nearest and dearest. First of all, of my parents who had sacrificed much to make it possible for me to study and whom I knew to be dear and decent people who did not deserve such a fate. I further thought of my comrades whom I had left behind at the Russian front barely three months ago. At that time I was a member of the regiment SS-Germania, which consisted largely of Danes,

Belgians, Dutchmen and Norwegians, volunteers, young idealists who had openly told me that they were no National Socialists but that now the point had come when it was essential to defend European culture and fight against the upsurge of Bolshevism and who, inadequately armed, fighting against a superior power, obeying non-sensical orders to hold the line, as – soldiers know all that from the Russian front – the division was sacrificed and who still suffered death for their ideals. Those, too, did not deserve this. And then I realised, no matter from which angle I looked at the issue, that only disaster would result from such action, and consequently I returned to Berlin.

On my journey I calmed down even more. And while I was thinking – at first with hatred, contempt and abhorrence – of these henchmen [*Henkerknechte*] in Auschwitz but also of the prisoners who had let themselves be used, I tried to put myself in their position. It is one of the prominent traits of human beings, of life in general, that one adjusts to circumstances and grasps at every straw for the chance of survival. And therefore one could not resent the prisoners on account of this, one could not hold it against the whole of mankind just as one could not do so with regard to these SS men or the whole of the German people. [Pause]

And based on this insight I suddenly saw a possibility of how to proceed. Where the highest of legally protected interests, life, no longer counts for anything, is dragged through the mire, massively annihilated, all other legally protected interests, whether property, loyalty, or whatever else, must also crumble and lose their value. And therefore – and of that I had already convinced myself – those people who had been asked to carry out these tasks, would, of necessity, have to become criminals. And it was exactly my task, and the penal code gave me the opportunity to do so, to prosecute these crimes, namely those that had not been ordered. And that's what I then did.[43]

# IV

If we assume that this account of Morgen's planned but not executed border crossing into Switzerland corresponds to the truth, then it is of special interest what he says with regard to the moral scruples which in the end kept him from deserting. His moral feelings of duty, his feelings of "loyalty" are all attached in the first place to his family, his comrades and the German people.[44] The victims' fate suddenly did not weigh on him as heavily after those 36 hours had passed. He behaves like an employee who rants and raves against his boss but then calms down quite quickly. He minimises any possible feelings of guilt regarding the victims – or does not allow them to arise in the first place – by remembering the victims essentially as co-perpetrators both here and at other points (especially when interrogated during the Nuremberg trials on 7 August 1946): the Jewish women as lascivious and willing servants of the guards and the Jewish guards as members of an aggressive horde resembling dogs. In Kurt Gerstein's case the exact opposite is apparent: in his reports there are more SS perpetrators and more Jewish victims than is historically verifiable. At one point in his famous report he even speaks of 25 million victims.[45] Morgen might have felt appalled for a moment or two about what was happening in Auschwitz – but these feelings were apparently not as deep as his feelings of loyalty and solidarity with the German people. While Morgen's outrage about the misdeeds of the guards and other SS officers appears genuine, his outrage about the murder of the Jews seems to have a comparatively minor quality and is, perhaps, only simulated in retrospect. We cannot possibly discern the truth in this matter. But Morgen seems unable at any point to imagine himself being a member of another group – for him there is only his "*Volk*." Everything else is rather abstract. His moral feelings and utterances seem more typical of something which one might call a specific type of "particular National Socialist morality" which produced moral emotions. Inside Nazi society there was pressure on each member of the "*Volksgemeinschaft*" – restricted to those defined as "Aryan" – to share these moral emotions and express the appropriate feelings of anger, disgust, revulsion, guilt, etc., on a massive scale. And this is exactly the kind of framework in which Konrad Morgen expresses his feelings even after the war: now he of course condemns the mass murders in Auschwitz. He does so because after the war he either had to do so or because he really does abominate these crimes. His real feelings of outrage however, his feeling of shock as he calls it, remain completely focused on the "indecencies" in his own "Aryan" ranks, and, more abstractly, on the "*Schande*" (disgrace) brought upon the SS and the German *Volk* by these crimes. It is impossible to say whether prior to 1945 he was indignant at all about the murder of the Jews or just exclusively about the corrupt circumstances in which these murders were committed: it is possible that the corruption disturbed him so much that it motivated him to flee in the half-hearted way he did. At any rate, after 1945 he continued to vigorously defend SS values, as we have demonstrated, and tried to exonerate the SS from their crimes in the extermination camps by blaming others for having committed them or claiming the unjust rule of law during the Nazi era was responsible for what the SS men did.

Perhaps it was exactly this steadfast loyalty to the German people and to the SS who had remained "decent" that ultimately motivated the *Spruchkammergericht* after 1945 to finally discover in him a resistance fighter. It was quite unproblematic to feel empathetic with his fight against corruption within the Nazi state. In contrast it seemed the courts were unable to show any sympathy with Kurt Gerstein, the man who had worked in a completely unorthodox manner and was truly affected by those German crimes. Why was that so?

I think here it is important to understand National Socialism not as a system beyond morality but as a movement which made a great effort to implement a system of moral feelings which were to be shared and, indeed, mutually exactable.[46] When investigating National Socialism we are confronted not only with a horrific system and practice of politics but also with a certain mentality. And the latter is much less restricted to the years between 1933 and 1945 than other elements of Nazism. Echoes of what one might call "Nazi morality," that is, of a system of moral feelings forced through with much vigour and shared by many Germans, can be discerned in varying degrees to this very day. They are particularly noticeable in the immediate postwar years when the court judgements on Morgen and Gerstein were passed. The more or less subtle influence of Nazi mentality and *"völkisch"* attitude most probably prevented Kurt Gerstein – as Saul Friedländer has demonstrated – from being recognized as a hero of the German resistance. It is indeed possible that, despite everything, the court saw in him a kind of traitor, since he had betrayed the most crucial state secrets to foreign diplomats and members of the resistance abroad. On the other hand it was possible for Konrad Morgen, with his story of having been an "active resistance fighter," to be exonerated from any kind of incrimination with Nazi crimes. Let us recall again what happened: although in his account at the Nuremberg trials he explicitly defended the "reputation of the SS" he was able to present himself to the court as an active resistance fighter because of his role in the investigation of crimes of corruption. The difficulty of classifying his case correctly shows the urgency needed to investigate more closely the transition from Nazi Germany to the pos-war era against the background of a moral history which still needs to be written. This juxtaposition of two Nazi biographies – evaluated in the postwar years in astonishingly different ways – demonstrates, we hope, how urgent this need really is.

*Notes*

1 This article was translated from the German by Gabriele Rahaman. The author would like to thank Werner Konitzer, Werner Renz (Fritz Bauer Institut), Christine Wern (Jewish Museum Frankfurt), Joel Golb, Birgit Erdle and Daniel Wildmann (Leo Baeck Institute London) for their input.

2 Saul Friedländer, *The Years of Extermination: Nazi Germany and the Jews, 1939–1945* (London: Weidenfeld & Nicolson, 2007), 544. The Fritz Bauer Institut owns the *Nachlass* of Konrad Morgen. In addition it holds documents regarding Konrad Morgen collected by the historian Karsten Raabe for the purpose of serving as background material for the novel by Volker Harry Altwasser, *Letzte Haut* (Berlin: Matthes & Seitz, 2009).

3 Saul Friedländer, *Kurt Gerstein oder die Zwiespältigkeit des Guten*, 2nd ed. (Munich: C. H. Beck, 2007, 1st ed. 1968). Although the following publications appeared after Friedländer's volume: Pierre Joffroy, *L'espion de Dieu. La passion de Kurt Gerstein* (Paris: Grasset, 1971); Pierre Joffroy, *Der Spion Gottes. Kurt Gerstein – ein SS-Offizier im Widerstand* (Berlin: Aufbau-Taschenbuch-Verlag, 1995) and Jürgen Schäfer, *Kurt Gerstein – Zeuge des Holocaust. Ein Leben zwischen Bibelkreisen und SS* (Bielefeld: Luther-Verlag, 1999), it seems to me, despite the amendments of many details in these publications, that the central questions raised by Saul Friedländer are still by far the most significant for our understanding of Gerstein's contradictory personality.

4 Friedländer, *The Years of Extermination*, 544. The sentence from Himmler's speech that precedes this one was not quoted by Friedländer: "Wir hatten das moralische Recht, wir hatten die Pflicht gegenüber unserem Volk, dieses Volk, das uns umbringen wollte, umzubringen." ("We had the moral right, we had the duty to our people to kill this people who wanted to kill us") as quoted in: Bradley Smith und Agnes F. Peterson, *Heinrich Himmler. Geheimreden 1933 bis 1945 und andere Ansprachen* (Frankfurt am Main: Propyläen-Verlag, 1974), 18.

5 Friedländer, *The Years of Extermination* 544. In *Das Dritte Reich und die Juden* (Munich, C. H. Beck, 3rd ed. 2007), 927, fn. 13 and 14 Saul Friedländer refers to the following literature: Raul Hilberg, "Auschwitz and the 'Final Solution'," in Yisrael Gutman and Michael Berenbaum (eds), *Anatomy of the Auschwitz Death Camp* (Bloomington: Indiana University Press, 1994), 373–9; Hermann Langbein, *Menschen in Auschwitz* (Vienna and Munich: Europaverlag, 1999),

373–9; in addition see the following: "The Morgen Commission," in Rebecca Wittmann, *Beyond Justice: The Auschwitz Trial* (Cambridge, MA: Harvard University Press 2005), 160–90; James J. Weingartner, "Law and Justice in the Nazi SS: The Case of Konrad Morgen," *Central European History* 16 (1983): 276–94. For a revisionist portrayal, see Hans Hoffmann, *"Hast du diese Tötungen befohlen?"*. *SS-Richter und ihre Ermittlungen in den KZ*, (Bad Harzburg: Hoffmann, 1997).

6   This and the following are based on affidavits contained in the *Nachlass* of Konrad Morgen, 03.
7   All quotations in this paragraph are taken from: Lebenslauf des Gerichtsrefendars Dr Konrad Morgen, 3.5.1937, in: Nachlass Konrad Morgen, 03, Schriften, Aufzeichnungen, Korrespondenz.
8   The *"Dienststrafverfügung"'* of 2 April 1939 and extensive correspondence on this conflict are located in: Nachlass Konrad Morgen, Schriften, Korrespondenzen, 02.
9   *Nachlass* Konrad Morgen, 03, Schriften, Aufzeichnungen, Korrespondenz.
10  *Nachlass* Konrad Morgen, 03, Schriften, Aufzeichnungen, Korrespondenz.
11  On the independent jurisidiction of the SS courts established on 17 October 1939 see: Bianca Vieregge, *Die Gerichtsbarkeit einer "Elite." Nationalsozialistische Rechtsprechung am Beispiel der SS- und Polizei-Gerichtsbarkeit* (Baden-Baden: Nomos, 2002); also: Wolfgang Scheffler, "Zur Praxis der SS- und Polizeigerichtsbarkeit im Dritten Reich," in Günther Doeker and Winfried Steffani (eds), *Klassenjustiz und Pluralismus, FS Ernst Fraenkel* (Hamburg: Hoffmann & Campe, 1973), 224–36.
12  *Nachlass* Konrad Morgen, 03. Eidesstattliche Erklärung vom 28. Januar 1947, 3.
13  Eugen Kogon, *Der SS-Staat, Das System der deutschen Konzentrationslager* (Munich: Kindler, 1974 [1st ed. 1946]), 325–6.
14  Raul Hilberg relies completely on witness statements by Eugen Kogon and therefore assumes that Konrad Morgen had the four Soviet prisoners of war murdered in order to convict Koch. Cf.: Raul Hilberg, *Die Vernichtung der europäischen Juden*, vol. 2 (Frankfurt am Main: S. Fischer, 1990), 970. But – when being interrogated by Dr. Krüger on 22 August 1950 at the Spruchkammergericht – Kogon relativised his earlier incriminating testimony to such an extent that it was not sufficient enough for the court to issue a negative assessment of Morgen. A copy of the interrogation record may be found in *Nachlass* Konrad Morgen, 03.
15  Cf. his statement in: *Nürnberg: Der Prozess gegen die Hauptkriegsverbrecher vor dem Internationalen Gerichtshof. Nürnberg 14. November 1945–1. Oktober 1946*, vol. 20 (Nürnberg: Internationaler Militärgerichtshof, 1948), 531–63, here 552. In order to protect the SS from accusations of being involved he again maintained regarding the Auschwitz extermination camp: "[When I said] 'extermination camp Auschwitz' I did not mean the concentration camp. That did not exist there. I meant a special extermination camp close to Auschwitz called 'Monowitz'" (545).
16  Vernehmung des Zeugen Konrad Morgen, 25. Verhandlungstag 9.3.1964, in: *Der Auschwitz-Prozeß. Tonbandmittschnitte, Protokolle, Dokumente*, ed. Fritz Bauer Institut and die Staatliches Museum Auschwitz-Birkenau. Digitale Bibliothek Nr. 101 (DVD-Rom) (Berlin: Zenodot Verlagsgesellschaft, 2004), 5.553–5.693.
17  Saul Friedländer, *Counterfeit Nazi – The Ambiguity of Good* (London: Weidenfeld & Nicolson, 1969), 225–6.
18  Ibid., 227.
19  *Nachlass* Konrad Morgen, 03, Spruchkammer der Interniertenlager Ludwigsburg, 24.6.1948.
20  Cf. Schäfer, *Kurt Gerstein*, 19.
21  On Konrad Morgen see Weingartner, "Law and Justice in the Nazi SS," *passim*.
22  Staatsanwaltschaft Frankfurt am Main, Aktenzeichen 4 Js 767/58 und 4 Js 402/70.
23  *Nachlass* Konrad Morgen, 03, Abschrift – Stuttgarter Nachrichten Nr. 218 v. 19.9.1950.
24  *Nachlass* Konrad Morgen, 03, Zeitungsausschnitt, ohne Ort, ohne Datum. Blf Stuttgart, 25. Juni 1950r (Eig. Bericht).
25  *Nachlass* Konrad Morgen 03, letter by Konrad Morgen to the editor in chief of the *Deutsche Volkszeitung* dated 15 October 1964.
26  This is the wording in Kurt Gerstein's report, written on 4th May 1945 in Tübingen, reprinted in "Dokumentation zur Massenvergasung" (Bonn: Bundeszentrale für Heimatdienst, 1962), 5.
27  Friedländer, *Kurt Gerstein*, 56. Kurt Gerstein (ed.), *Um Ehre und Reinheit* (Hagen: Selbstverlag, n.d. [but with a preface dated 1936 signed by Kurt Gerstein "Hagen, Im Mai 1936"]) with two texts by Kurt Gerstein: "Im Kampf um Ehre und Reinheit," 13–22; and "Unser Weltbild," 22–8.

28 On his attempted arrangement with the Nazis see: Schäfer, *Kurt Gerstein*, 121–52.

29 Gerstein, "Dokumentation zur Massenvergasung," 9 and 10.

30 Friedländer, *Counterfeit Nazi*, 179.

31 Konrad Morgen, *Kriegspropaganda und Kriegsverhütung*, vol. 4: *Wesen und Wirkungen der Publizistik. Arbeiten über die Volksbeeinflussung und geistige Volksführung aller Zeiten und Völker* (Leipzig: Noske, 1936), 108.

32 Weingartner, "Law and Justice in the Nazi SS," 286, points out that Morgen became involved in the conflicts of the SS hierarchy.

33 Rebecca Wittmann points out that Morgen sometimes even went against the orders of his superiors, but was never reprimanded for this; see *Beyond Justice*, 308: "It is quite telling that Morgen was not punished for his direct disobedience to one of the highest officials of the SS. We already know that no-one was ever punished for refusing to follow his or her orders; presumably, Morgen was reprimanded for doing his duty with too much zeal and without any proper order from Berlin. This was also the standard Morgen himself applied in investigating the guards at Auschwitz."

34 Wittmann, *Beyond Justice*, 172 also comes to the conclusion: "Morgen [at the Auschwitz trial – RG] defended the laws of the SS, arguing that individual and sadistic murder 'was beneath a true German; and despite everything that everyone says about them, despite everything that happened, the SS never ordered or demanded such cruelties. On the contrary.'"

35 NSDAP – Ausgabe 1935; Personal-Ausweis Konrad Morgen; Mitgliedsbuch Nr. 2536236; Eingetreten: 1. Mai 1933; Vorwort von Adolf Hitler München, 9. Januar 1927, pp. 4/5. Nachlass Konrad Morgen, Fotos, Dokumente.

36 Vernehmung des Zeugen Konrad Morgen, 25. Verhandlungstag, 9.3. 1964 in *Der Auschwitz-Prozeß. Tonbandmittschnitte, Protokolle, Dokumente*, 5.553–5.693.

37 Ibid., 5.557–5.558.

38 Ibid., 5.558–5.559.

39 Ibid., 5.559.

40 Ibid., 5.560–5.567. Part of the report quoted here has been replicated in Hermann Langbein, *Menschen in Auschwitz* (Frankfurt am Main: Ullstein, 1980), 336–7; however, exactly those points at which Morgen during his interrogation tries systematically to blame the Jews for their own extermination are not quoted there.

41 Morgen at that time held the rank of *SS-Hauptsturmführer*.

42 *Der Auschwitz-Prozeß. Tonbandmittschnitte, Protokolle, Dokumente*, 5.567–5.570.

43 Ibid., 5.575–5.579.

44 On the function of "loyalty" in National Socialism cf. Raphael Gross, "'Loyalty' in National Socialism: A Contribution to the Moral History of the National Socialist Period," *History of European Ideas* 33 (2007): 1–16.

45 As quoted in Friedländer, *Counterfeit Nazi*, 111–12: "The figures given on the radio by the British Broadcasting Co. are not correct; in actual fact, the total number of people involved was 25,000,000!"

46 For literature, see: Raphael Gross and Werner Konitzer, "Geschichte und Ethik. Zum Fortwirken der nationalsozialistischen Moral," *Mittelweg* 8, 4 (1999), 44–67; Werner Konitzer, "Antisemitismus und Moral. Einige Überlegungen," *Mittelweg* 14, 2 (2005) 24–35; Raphael Gross. "Der Führer als Betrüger: Moral und Antipositivismus in Deutschland 1945/1946 am Beispiel Fritz von Hippels," in Anne Klein et al. (eds), *NS-Unrecht vor Kölner Gerichten nach 1945* (Cologne: Gesellschaft für Christlich-Jüdische Zusammenarbeit Köln, 2003), 23–35; Raphael Gross, "Zum Fortwirken der NS-Moral: Adolf Eichmann und die deutsche Gesellschaft," in Raphael Gross and Yfaat Weiss (eds), *Jüdische Geschichte als Allgemeine Geschichte. Festschrift für Dan Diner zum 60. Geburtstag* (Göttingen: Vandenhoeck & Ruprecht, 2006), 212–31; Raphael Gross, "Moral und Gott im NS," in Martin Treml and Daniel Weidner (eds), *Nachleben der Religionen. Kulturwissenschaftliche Untersuchungen zur Dialektik der Säkularisierung* (Munich and Paderborn: Fink, 2007), 176–87. And see Raimond Reiter, *Nationalsozialismus und Moral. Die "Pflichtenlehre" eines Verbrecherstaates* (Frankfurt am Main et al.: Lang, 1996); Claudia Koonz, *The Nazi Conscience* (Cambridge, MA: Belknap Press, 2003); Harald Welzer, *Täter. Wie aus ganz normalen Menschen Massenmörder werden* (Frankfurt am Main: Fischer-Taschenbuch-Verlag, 2005), 48–67.

## PART III

*Mass Killing and Genocide*

# 11

# Mass Killing and Genocide from 1914 to 1945: Attempting a Comparative Analysis

*Alan Kramer*

This chapter is an attempt at a comparative, transnational analysis, as a way of transcending the "germanocentric" or only selectively comparative approach that has characterized the discussion of Germany's "special path" (*Sonderweg*) from the authoritarian militarism of the Wilhelmine empire to the genocidal Third Reich.

Saul Friedländer has stressed the role of ideology in the motivation for the genocide of the Jews, both for Hitler and for "the vast majority of Germans." Crucially, he suggests that the Jew had the "essential mobilizing function" and acted as the bond between Hitler, the "providential leader," and his people. The Jew "represented evil per se" in the three central "suprahistorical salvation creeds": the purity of the racial community, the "crushing of Bolshevism and plutocracy," and "the ultimate millennial redemption."[1] There is broad consensus among historians that antisemitism was Hitler's ideological obsession. However, the research of Ian Kershaw and others has shown that antisemitism was not the main reason why ordinary Germans followed Hitler – either before or after 1933. The compliance of perpetrators with orders to carry out genocidal acts was founded in a range of motivations, of which antisemitism was only one. Complicity, indifference, and passivity on the part of bystanders and the broader population are even less susceptible to explanation by religious concepts such as redemption. Yet ideology, in a broader sense, was undeniably important: pseudo-scientific concepts such as racial hygiene and the need to "cleanse" the nation, vulgarized Darwinist clichés on "the survival of the fittest," and eugenics, all facilitated the justification of mass murder. Alongside ideology, certain cultural factors, above all military culture, were decisive. The latter included military training, traditions, and institutional memory. The experience of war radicalized military culture in several stages, and it "licensed barbarism."[2] The paranoid world view was another cultural factor that could predispose military and political leaders to commit mass killing and genocide.

This chapter aims to locate the Nazi genocide of the Jews within a broader synchronic and diachronic context, and ask whether Friedländer's concept of "redemptive antisemitism" is a useful analytic tool to examine the relationship between ideology and mass killing.

"Mass killing and Genocide from 1914 to 1945" sounds rather like the revival of an old idea, the "Second Thirty Years War" of which Winston Churchill wrote immediately after the Second World War. It implies a continuum, indeed direct continuities from one war to the next.[3] On three grounds, this could be considered problematic. First, there are several aspects that do not fit this neat chronology of thirty years. Some scholars justifiably see the German war against the Herero in Southwest Africa, 1904 to 1907, as a case of genocide. While it is very difficult to prove a continuity from German colonial warfare to "absolute destruction" in the First World War and the Holocaust, still less a causal connection, it is plausible to speak of Nazi racial warfare that evolved against the background of colonial precedents and drew at least in part on a discourse of colonial war.[4]

If we go beyond the borders of Germany we can extend the time-frame to the 1890s: the genocide of the Armenians carried out by the Young Turk regime in 1915 was anticipated by the mass killing of some 100,000 Armenians under the *ancien régime* of Sultan Abdülhamid II in the 1890s. Already in the period 1912–14, the Young Turk leadership aimed to replace the multi-ethnic and multi-confessional character of the Ottoman Empire with Turkish ethnic nationalism and Islamism. In secret meetings of the Young Turk central committee with the so-called "Special Organization" in the spring and summer of 1914 "population-technical" measures were called for, with the aim of the "liquidation of non-Turkish settlements in strategically important positions which are in contact with foreign interests." By the end of 1914, 1,150,000 people, mainly Greeks, had been deported.[5] During the course of 1915–16, at least one million Anatolian Armenians were killed or perished during their expulsion from their homes. Other Christian populations, above all the Assyrians in Anatolia and Mesopotamia, were likewise the victims of "systematic extermination."[6] After Turkey's defeat in the First World War and occupation by Greek forces, the Young Turk leader Mustafa Kemal created a new movement that remobilized the nation and launched a military offensive, forcing the Greek army back to the coast. The culmination of the push for ethnic redistribution was reached in September 1922, with the burning of Smyrna and the expulsion of the remaining Greek population of Anatolia (and the reciprocal Greek expulsion of Muslims to Turkey). The elimination of the Armenian, Assyrian, and Greek populations was an integral part of the Young Turk "struggle for independence" and the reinvention of the Ottoman Empire as the Turkish nation.[7] Modern (and modernizing) ideologies of nationalism, race, and the pseudo-scientific discourses of hygiene and purity, held out the nationalist utopia of an ethnically "pure" Turkish state. Yet after the early 1920s Turkey was conspicuous by its abstention from further international conflict. It is, moreover, not possible to construct any real learning process by which other states emulated the Turkish example in launching genocides.

The mass violence in Spain that erupted with the civil war in 1936 flatly contradicts the assumptions of the "Thirty Years War" thesis: Spain was neutral in the First World War. It is, of course, possible to argue that the struggle was rooted in the ideologies that had arisen in the First World War. Yet in 1936, neither fascism nor communism was more than a fringe group. There were far stronger roots, some of which went back at least to the nineteenth century: the conflict between secularism and the Church, between democracy and authoritarianism, the social conflict over land reform, and the fact that the Spanish military had had a long tradition in the nineteenth century of intervening in politics.[8] With the memory of a world empire lost in the nineteenth century, the experience of recent colonial warfare was crucial: the defeats imposed on the Spanish army in Morocco in 1909 and 1921 were perceived as humiliating "disasters," and led to the radicalization and brutalization of military culture in the 1920s. The Nationalist army perceived its campaign as a new "Reconquest" to "redeem" degenerate Spain from the foreign forces of atheism and communism.[9]

So if we cannot speak of a Second Thirty Years War in Germany and Europe, a definable historical epoch can nevertheless be established in the half-century from the 1890s to 1945. This was the era in which imperialism reached its apogee: the modernization of warfare converged in a dynamic of destruction with the growth of modern nationalism, producing ethnically based and political violence that culminated in genocidal killing. That tendency was far stronger in authoritarian states engaged in nation-building, or nation reconstruction, than in democratic states with established national traditions, although democratic states were by no means immune to the dynamic of destruction or ideological vogues such as eugenics.

This is not to deny that earlier historical epochs have seen mass killing that resulted in the annihilation of entire peoples. Leaving aside the wars of antiquity and the prehistorical periods, in the modern era, above all, colonial expansion by "advanced" powers produced mass death in indigenous societies. However, it is highly problematic to apply the term "genocide" to these earlier conflicts. The wars of the British settlers against the Native Americans and the nineteenth-century frontier wars of the USA were not intended to annihilate, but to drive the indigenous population out of the settlement areas and break their resistance. The contact between colonial settlers and native peoples could lead inadvertently to mass death through diseases to which the latter were not resistant; the appropriation of land deprived them of their means of existence, and the conquests were inherently brutal and violent, as were often the responses of the displaced. Yet neither this expansion in North America, nor the earlier Spanish conquests of Central and South America, can be placed in the same category as twentieth-century genocide, because the essential conditions, the genocidal intent and the central will of the state (or state-like organizations), were absent.[10]

The second point is that we self-evidently need to differentiate the processes between nations. Italian militarist nationalism glorified war no less than its counterpart in Germany, and Italy turned to Fascism ten years before Germany. Yet in terms of the dynamic of destruction Italy followed a different path to Germany both in the First World War and the Second World War. The German army killed some 6,500 Belgian and French civilians during the invasion of summer 1914, in a series of mass executions that outraged world public opinion and greatly damaged Germany's standing with the neutral countries. The "German Atrocities," as they became known, resulted partly from the pathological fear (almost invariably groundless) that civilians had engaged in fighting, and partly from orders issued by senior officers to expect such civilian resistance and execute "innocent" civilians to ensure the safe passage of troops by intimidating the people.[11] Nothing analogous occurred in the Habsburg territory conquered by the Italian army.

Another obvious distinction was in the history of antisemitism. Although theological antisemitism was not unknown in Italy, antisemitism did not become state policy until 1938; indeed, many Jews were members of the Fascist party, 230 Jews had participated in the march on Rome in 1922, and there was even a Jewish minister of finance under Mussolini.[12] That is not to say that Fascism was free of racism. Mussolini and his generals eagerly collaborated with the Nazi demands to deport Jews to the death camps.[13] Moreover, the military and the regime were obsessed with the notion of "racial improvement" through colonial war. This was not even the invention of the Fascist regime, as one might assume, but a continuation from the Liberal era (above all with the invasion of Libya in 1911). The consequences were the forgotten history of the 100,000 Libyans killed in the course of "pacification" during the years 1923 to 1932, and the several hundred thousand Ethiopians killed from 1935 to 1942. In neither case was this a genocide, but by any standards it was racist mass killing that pointed in the direction of genocide. It challenges the thesis of German singularity, the *Sonderweg* from near-total war in the First World War to total war and genocide in the Second.

Thirdly, while there are lines of continuity which one can trace from 1914 to 1945, there are also discontinuities, breaks, and radically new departures. In order to determine whether the continuities or the discontinuities were stronger, it is useful to compare Germany with other nations.

## ALLIED WARFARE AND MASS KILLING

It is therefore necessary to ask whether states such as Britain, America, or Russia engaged in policies of mass killing and genocide. From the First to the Second World War there was an immense progression in the dynamic of destruction, with a terrible increase in non-combatant loss of life. Whereas civilian deaths accounted for something over one-third of the war dead in the First World War, civilian deaths in the Second World War amounted to almost two-thirds (and if the mass death of Soviet and German prisoners of war is counted, well over two-thirds were non-combatants).[14] There were two main causes for this dramatic shift: the revolution in the technology of war, primarily aerial warfare, and the revolution in ideology, primarily racial warfare. Together they totally removed the distinction between civilians and soldiers, between "home" and "front." As Ian Kershaw has written, the Second World War was "a *popular* war in the sense of the full involvement of the peoples of Europe in the fighting, and the suffering."[15] This being a global war, the peoples of Asia were equally involved in the fighting and suffering.

In fact, it was not German, but Allied warfare that showed a linear continuity from the First to the Second World War. The tendency towards total war was already apparent in the Allied naval blockade in the First World War. The policy was to try to deprive Germans, including civilians, of seaborne imported goods. In the 1920s German nationalist propaganda produced the death toll of 730,000 civilians as a result of the blockade, which is to this day often uncritically repeated.[16] Jay Winter, an expert in demographic history and the First World War, has calculated 478,500 "excess civilian war-related deaths in Germany."[17] Clearly, countless vulnerable civilians, especially working-class women and children, suffered owing to malnutrition and hunger. In fact, the Allied blockade was not the only, and probably not the main, cause of the hardship, which was due also to the other effects of war, among them the food priority enjoyed by the army, the lack of farm labor and draft animals, the poor administration of food supply, and profiteering and hoarding by farmers and middlemen.[18] In any case, the main intention of the British navy in its planning for blockade was to provoke the numerically inferior German navy into battle; the prime goal of economic warfare, which would only become effective in the long term, was to prevent raw materials and other essential imports from reaching the German armaments industry and the armed forces. Blocking the import of food evolved into an important part of economic warfare. However, since Germany was dependent on seaborne imports for only between ten and twenty per cent of its food, the British navy's intention of starving the population could never be realized, because import substitution, exploitation of occupied territories, and a switch away from high meat consumption would have prevented, and to some extent did prevent, starvation.[19]

Intention, as we see, was neither a necessary nor a sufficient condition of mass death. In the Second World War the Allies repeated the blockade, but this time Germany was better prepared, partly by autarky policy and an improved rationing system, above all through the exploitation of occupied Europe, at the cost of widespread hunger even in rich countries like France, and deliberate starvation of the people of eastern Europe.[20]

Aerial warfare was a different matter. The low level of civilian casualties from aerial bombardment during the First World War was due less to the observance of the laws of war than to the fact that the technology was in its infancy. By 1918, however, the potential of aerial warfare for mass destruction was recognized by thinkers such as the Italian Giulio Douhet, and it has been realized in almost every war since then. In the interwar years the British used aerial warfare against civilians in Iraq, as did the Italians in Abyssinia, and the Germans practised it in Spain. In the Second World War, the Germans, applying the lessons of Douhet, bombed Warsaw in 1939 and Rotterdam in 1940 to terrorize the population into a quick surrender.

However, it was the democratic states which took the logic of annihilation through air war to its extreme conclusion. The British bombing of German cities, starting in 1941, razed half of Hamburg in 1943, and Anglo-American aircraft destroyed the historic heart of Dresden in 1945. While German bombs killed some 60,000 British civilians, British and American bombing killed ten times as many Germans. It was no paradox that the Nazi leadership had eagerly looked forward to aerial bombardment with German civilians as the victims. At the height of the Allied bombing campaign Hitler welcomed it, saying that the less the people had to lose, the more fanatically they would fight.[21] The American strategic air war against civilian targets culminated in the fire-bombing of Tokyo and the destruction of Hiroshima and Nagasaki with nuclear weapons in 1945. It would be unhistorical to deny or relativize the appalling suffering of the victims of the Allied air war. On the other hand, Jörg Friedrich, in calling the Allied bombing of Germany a "continuous mass extermination," thus indirectly equating it with Nazi genocide, was engaging in a glib provocation in order to sell his book *Der Brand*.[22] There was no genocidal intention on the part of the Allies; the enormous effort made by the British and the Americans to feed the hungry Germans and rebuild the economy as soon as fighting ended is ample proof.[23] But it was a close-run thing: if the war in Europe had continued into August 1945 there is no doubt that the American air force would have dropped the first nuclear bombs on German cities.

The fact that industrialized mass killing from the air did not descend into genocide shows that the dynamic of destruction could be stopped. There could even be a learning process that worked in favour of humanity. Conditions in Britain's concentration camps in the South African War (1899–1902), with the death of almost 28,000 Afrikaner civilians, mainly women and children, and at least 20,000 usually forgotten Africans, scandalized world public opinion. Above all, it mobilized liberal opinion in Britain itself; a report by Emily Hobhouse and the denunciation by the parliamentarian Henry Campbell-Bannerman of British "methods of barbarism" received wide public attention and enforced the improvement of camp conditions, reducing the death rate.[24] Although the British interned enemy civilians in both world wars, there was no repeat of the mass death of internees. In warfare, the British and French armies in the First World War emulated the German dynamic of destruction; the last months of the war saw the massive deployment of British and French artillery to destroy everything (including entire French villages) in the relentless Allied advance towards the German frontier. However, the ultimate end of Britain's version of industrialized mass killing was defeat of the enemy's armed forces, not the annihilation of its entire society and culture.[25] British and American land warfare operations in the Second World War were partly conditioned by the horror at the mutual mass slaughter in the trenches of the First World War: massive air power and artillery deployment against enemy combatants, with mobility provided by tanks, ensured there was no repeat of the Somme. The same learning process applied also to German non-combatants: although civilians caught in battle zones could fall victim to the indiscriminate and overwhelming fire-power of long-distance weapons, German prisoners of war and the civilian population were generally spared violence so far as possible during the invasion. The reaction of German

civilians to the American invasion was in general one of "incredulous amazement" at the unexpected "decent" and humane conduct of the GIs, especially in
contrast with the terror unleashed by the *Wehrmacht* and the Nazi regime on its
own citizens in the last months of the war.[26]

## SOVIET POPULATION POLICY, REPRESSION, AND MASS KILLING

The Soviet invasion in eastern Germany was another matter. But given the traumatic history of Soviet Russia, the conduct of its troops in Germany was hardly
surprising. Starting in 1914 Russia experienced a seven-year nightmare of war,
revolution, and civil war. Above all in the civil war civilians were targeted, and
there was widespread ethnic violence. In the Terror the Bolsheviks at various
stages aimed to "exterminate" the bourgeoisie, the kulaks, and the Cossacks; the
Whites encouraged their soldiers and the peasants to take vengeance on the Jews.
Hundreds of thousands were killed; the death toll during the civil war was ten
million (military and civilian victims, including those who died of hunger and
disease), at least five times greater than the number of Russian soldiers killed in
the First World War. This epidemic of violence not only devastated Russian and
east European society; it also militarized the Bolshevik party, and produced a
"readiness to resort to coercion [. . .] [and] summary justice."[27] The attempt by
the revolutionary state to destroy all the cultural institutions of the old regime
lent legitimation not only to Stalin's rule by terror, but also to mass mobilization
for cultural revolution and what amounted to a second revolution.

The cultural revolution of 1927 to 1930 radicalized the techniques of violence
and to some extent even ethnicized the vision of the enemy. There were no longer
just "class enemies," but also "kulaks," "Cossacks," "social aliens," and "enemies of
Soviet power." They were to be deported, imprisoned, executed, or sent to labor
camps. As the paranoid fantasy of Stalin and his helpers suspected plots and
sabotage by foreign agents everywhere in the Soviet Union, ethnic minorities
were removed from border areas and the cities. By 1938 more than 350,000 had
fallen victim to Stalin's national policies, which amounted to "ethnic cleansing."[28]
Surviving kulaks, whether still in camps or "rehabilitated," were still suspected
in 1937 of being a counter-revolutionary "fifth column," preparing to support a
capitalist-fascist invasion.[29] Stalin's policy of collectivization and "dekulakiza-
tion" in the early 1930s caused the starvation deaths of probably 7 or 8 million
people, of which 4 to 6 million were in Ukraine. Although some historians
have spoken of a genocide of the Ukrainian people, there is no evidence of an
ethnically-defined policy of mass murder: non-Ukrainian grain-growing areas
were as badly affected by the consequences of harvest failure, famine, and the
Soviet policy of denying aid to the affected rural areas and even denying the
existence of famine. Ukrainians in urban areas suffered hunger like every other
nationality, but were not picked out for specially harsh treatment. This was

therefore neither genocide, nor mass killing, although there can be no doubt that the Soviet state was responsible for mass death through criminal negligence. That, plus the long silence of Soviet archives, helps to explain why it was in many ways as traumatic for the collective memory of Ukrainians as the Holocaust was for Jews, and why the debate about how to assess its place in history has been so impassioned.[30]

Excluding those victimized as members of national minorities, approximately one million people held guilty of political offences, as well as common criminals, were executed between 1921 and 1953; of the 2.6 million persons sentenced to jail, camps, or internal exile in the period from 1934 to 1945, probably 2 million died prematurely during deportations and in labor camps, penal colonies, and prisoner of war camps. Based on modern research in the former Soviet archives, they are considerably lower than the figures commonly used in the popular discourse on Stalinism, which derive from the politically inspired guesses by Conquest, Solzhenitsyn, and others.[31] Polemical exaggerations are unnecessary: the execution of up to 1.5 million people for political reasons, and the regime's responsibility for the premature death of at least 10 million people, were a man-made hell which can be compared, although not equated, with the murderous policies of the Nazi regime.

In the war, the terror was extended to the territories annexed by the Soviet Union between 1939 and 1941: at least 380,000 people were deported from Poland and other eastern European countries, or possibly up to one million on some estimates from Poland alone.[32] Soviet policy towards Poland in 1939 to 1941, although it was not genocidal, was not much less destructive than German policy. The Soviets executed 4,000 officers at Katyn in 1940. Altogether the Soviet secret police killed 33,000 officers, political leaders and intellectuals in the eastern borderlands, while tens of thousands died as a result of the deportations. The intention was to deprive Poland of independent leadership by eliminating its military and political elite.[33]

The brutal measures of ethnic redistribution during the war and in the immediate postwar years, carried out by both the Stalinist regime, and by non-communist regimes such as the Czechoslovak government, with the initial agreement and later acquiescence of the Western democracies, were a response to the experience of Nazi occupation, but also the product of home-grown policies. They were not without precedent in prewar Soviet and prerevolutionary Russia. Stalinist social engineering aimed to create ethnically homogenous spaces, but also to fill the insatiable demand for forced labor. In the inherently violent process entire civilizations were uprooted: more than three million Soviet citizens, including 1 million Volga Germans and at least 470,000 Ingush, Chechens, Crimean Tatars, and other "suspect" minorities, were deported to central Asia between 1941 and 1944. Almost one-quarter of the Ingush and Chechen population perished. Ethnic hatred practically became state doctrine at the end of the war. In a campaign of annihilation against Ukrainian partisans, more than 150,000 Ukrainians were killed and 200,000 deported. In the newly reconquered

Baltic republics the Soviets arrested and deported hundreds of thousands; in Lithuania alone 20,000 people were executed by the Soviet secret police and 240,000 – more than one-tenth of the population – were jailed or deported.[34] Between 120,000 and 200,000 Hungarians were deported from present-day Hungarian territory, plus a further 50,000 Hungarians from annexed areas. The ethnic Hungarian population of Yugoslavia was terrorized and expelled, and about 15–20,000 were executed.[35]

It might be argued that the Stalinist policies of forced population transfer and mass terror hardly required Nazi precedent or inspiration. Without the experience of Nazi racial-biological warfare, however, it is hard to imagine the qualitative leap to the policies of ethnic collective punishment, backed by popular desire for revenge, that raged across all of eastern and central Europe, including both Stalinist and democratic regimes. Inevitably, the foremost victims were Germans. Countless captured German soldiers were shot on the spot, despite repeated orders from senior commanders to stop the practice. In total, 1,100,000 out of 3.1 million German prisoners died in Soviet captivity, but since this figure includes the many men captured at the end of the war, it conceals the much higher death rate for Germans captured during the war, of whom as many as 90 per cent died in 1941 and 1942, and 70 per cent in 1943.[36]

As the war ended, millions of Germans were forced to leave their homes in territories that were allocated to Poland and Russia, and expelled to the west in circumstances of great cruelty; according to the official West German documentation 75,000 to 100,000 civilians were killed in the first few weeks of the Soviet occupation.[37] At least 7.5 million Germans fled or were expelled from the territories that would become Poland; over 3 million German speakers fled or were expelled from newly restored Czechoslovakia, for the time being still a democracy. Many more fled or were expelled from east, east-central, and southeast Europe. An estimated 380,000 ethnic Germans from eastern Europe were deported to labor camps in the Soviet Union in late 1944 and early 1945; as many as 100,000 may have died as a result of the harsh conditions of transport and hard labor.[38] Ethnic minorities were not the only victims of Stalinist rule. Discipline in the Red Army was even more ruthless than in the German army: 175,000 Soviet soldiers were executed for disobedience, cowardice, or desertion.[39]

## GERMAN WARFARE AND GENOCIDE FROM THE FIRST TO THE SECOND WORLD WAR

German warfare from 1914 to 1945 differed from Allied warfare not so much in radicalizing the conduct of war, but rather because it manifested a break in continuity by 1939 in turning to wars of annihilation which denied enemy peoples the right to existence. This was just becoming visible at the end of the First World War as a radical dystopian vision. As the German army collapsed in August 1918, General Karl von Einem, commander of the Third Army, wrote in a private letter that he expected the Allies to inflict the same kind of destruction on Germany with which it had devastated the occupied territories: "Hatred of us unites our enemies ever more firmly, and their will to annihilate has grown stronger than ever. [. . .] May God let our grandchildren experience a flourishing Germany at the end of their lifetime."[40] Kurt Riezler, the former political adviser to chancellor Bethmann Hollweg, had an equally apocalyptic vision in 1918: "Slavery for 100 years. The dream of world power gone forever. The end of all hubris. The scattering of Germans throughout the world. Fate of the Jews."[41] These outlandish fantasies were a nightmare projection onto the enemies of Germany's own utopian vision of the absolute subjugation or destruction of the enemy. German victory in the east, marked by the Treaty of Brest-Litovsk, and the enthralling vision of a vast eastern empire had turned the heads of usually rational military leaders. General Hans von Seeckt talked in May 1918 of the ambition to take Tiflis and oil-rich Baku, the cotton-fields of Turkestan, and then "knock on the gates of India."[42] At the end of August 1918 Lieutenant-General Wilhelm Groener, who was soon to succeed Erich Ludendorff as quartermaster-general, stated in a speech to officers in occupied Kiev: "Ukraine is at present nothing other than an extended German economic region," and demanded the early conquest of Baku and Turkestan. These territorial goals were not only to feed the war machine in the short term; they were long-term ambitions for imperialist expansion.[43] The experience of conquest and occupation and the dream of empire transformed the meaning of the terms "*Volk*" and "*Raum*," which were reinterpreted through the lens of "scientific" racism. "*Ostforschung*" (research on the east) provided the scholarly legitimation, and the Nazis were able to turn the collective memory of the primitive chaos of the east into their vision of a racial utopia in the coming empire.[44]

Such utopian thought and its negative counterpart left strong traces in German military and nationalist culture. One was in the politics of catastrophe: large parts of the officer corps, the bourgeois parties, and the foreign ministry campaigned to reject the peace treaty and provoke the Allies into the resumption of war. This would cause mutinies in the Allies' armies, mass strikes, and revolution; international catastrophe would offer the chance for Germany to tear up the treaty and create a new world order. The interwar period was not so much a peaceful interlude or a break in continuity; rather, it formed an essential bridge between two violent periods.

However, the "brutalization" thesis, the idea that the experience of the First World War brutalized both the men who fought in it and entire societies, making political violence acceptable, and leading to Fascism, can be consigned to the realm of myth.[45] The vast majority of returning soldiers in 1918 wanted peace; time and again, militarists from General von Seeckt to Hitler complained bitterly at the predominant pacifism, or fear of war, of the Germans down to 1939. Hitler's popularity reached its peak in 1938, because the people regarded him as the leader who had won diplomatic triumphs without war, not, *pace* Friedländer, because of antisemitic policy. However, one crucial pillar of the bridge was the emergence after the war of the *Freikorps* and other extreme right-wing nationalist groups which unleashed a historically new quality of violence in German politics. It was thus not war in general, but the interpretation of defeat and revolution that was the decisive factor. Partly, this militarist nationalism was the response to the utopian dreams of the socialist left; anti-Bolshevism coalesced with antisemitism and hostility to the new democratic state. Legitimated by the rhetoric of violent hatred that spoke of annihilating selected internal enemies, this emerged before the end of the war in view of the impending defeat. As navy Lieutenant Commander B. von Selchow said on 6 September 1918 in conversation with a leading admiral: "One year ago some of us believed we could win the war if men like Max Weber were put up against the wall. But today, all that is too late." Just a few days after the armistice, on 15 November, von Selchow noted, after seeing a number of Jews and deserters, "For the Jews the time will come, too, and then woe to them!"[46] Motivated by the promise of colonial settlements and hatred of Jews, Slavs, and Bolsheviks, the *Freikorps* spread fear and terror; the "Baltic *Landwehr*" killed more than 3,000 people in May-June 1919 in Riga alone, and several hundred more in other towns. The three hundred assassinations committed in Germany by members of right-wing terrorist groups between 1919 and 1923 were a visible sign of the new quality of political violence. The brutality of the *Freikorps* in the Baltic in early 1919 anticipated the violence against noncombatants during the invasion of Poland twenty years later.

The Kapp-Lüttwitz putsch of 1920, spearheaded by *Freikorps* units, which almost succeeded in crushing democracy, had the goal of returning Germany to an authoritarian-military state, in defiance of the Allies, via the violent suppression of the labor movement. It was evidence of utopian thinking on the part of the incompetent leaders of the putsch, a continuation of the "dreamland" in which Germany found itself after the armistice in 1918, as the Protestant theologian Ernst Troeltsch wrote, "where everyone, without grasping the conditions and real consequences, could portray the future in fantastic, pessimistic or heroic terms."[47] Less well-known but equally significant eruptions of ideologically motivated violence were the massacre by regular troops under General Lüttwitz of over 1,100 Berlin workers, including women and children, in March 1919, and several other cases of brutal repression of left-wing risings across Germany.

Another pillar in the bridge was the memory of heroic deeds in the world war and in the *Freikorps* fighting, kept alive in a macabre cult of sacrifice and death by means of innumerable cheap publications and commemorations.[48] It was one of the Republic's fatal errors to overestimate the loyalty of the armed forces, to fail to democratize them, and allow them to create myths about the "unvanquished" army and the "stab in the back." In short, the failure of "cultural demobilization," not only by military and conservative elites, but by the Republican leadership itself, was a major factor.[49]

The continuities in the history of antisemitism appear to be obvious. The growing tensions during the First World War produced the first spike in the history of antisemitism in twentieth-century Germany, marked by the "Jew census" in the army in 1916 and the spread of antisemitic ideology in right-wing parties after

1918. The election successes of the Nazi party in the years 1930 to 1933 showed that one-third of the German electorate supported a party which stood for violent racism, although several other political issues were more important in mobilizing voters and the support of the army and political and business elites. Although Hitler played down antisemitic rhetoric for tactical reasons in the years 1930 to 1933, Nazi propaganda against the Jews by his subordinates continued unabated. The struggle against the Jews was a constant of Hitler's politics from 1920, and the pseudo-religious nature of his ambition was one of its features, evident for example in a speech in Munich on 18 December 1926, when he claimed that "Christ had been the greatest precursor in the struggle against the Jewish world enemy [. . .]. The task that Christ had started he [Hitler] would fulfill."[50] Yet when we examine the decisions leading to the genocide of the Jews, it is not the continuities between the First and the Second World War, but the discontinuities which are most striking. In the First World War and the Weimar Republic the state attempted to prevent the spread of antisemitism; acts of antisemitic violence during the Republic were the work of extremists opposed to the state. By contrast, in the Third Reich antisemitism was raised to the status of state doctrine. Above all, the intention of genocide was not part of traditional antisemitism, nor even a part of the policy of the Third Reich, until the decision was taken in 1941.[51]

Michael Wildt's important recent study suggests that the successive waves of antisemitic actions, 1933 to 1939, were more significant than has been hitherto acknowledged. The Nazi leadership's radical rhetoric unleashed a dynamic in which antisemitic mobs felt "empowered" to vent their rage in a myriad of incidents to create the *Volksgemeinschaft* by violent exclusion. While the mass violence of the November pogrom 1938 ("Crystal Night") was deliberately fomented, the actual measures were the result of local initiatives from below. The unleashing of "empowering" emotions of hate was thus possibly a crucial link between 1933 and the perpetration of genocide.[52]

The history of the Nazi regime reveals a triad of continuity, learning process, and radical discontinuity. Hitler and the Nazi movement embarked on the total radicalization of these crucial elements deriving from Germany's experience in the First World War and postwar political violence, as well as older racist and imperialist ideas, to create the essence of the Nazi state, as Saul Friedländer has written: "a regime of constant mobilization, a war on the internal enemy, *Lebensraum* as the link between space and race, and social engineering culmi-nating in genocide."[53] Notwithstanding the vast dimensions and brutality of Stalinist population policy and the extent of the collateral violence and death, Nazi population policies were of another category entirely.

In some ways the genocidal process of the Nazi regime resembled that of the Armenian genocide, but the similarities are due more to common patterns of political pathology than conscious emulation. It was certainly the case that the Nazi regime, like the Young Turk regime in 1915, constructed its Jewish victims as the "enemy," associated them with perceived foreign enemies, and used provocation to justify eradication. The comparison between the two genocides may throw light on one of the questions relating to the origins of the judeocide. Christopher Browning has argued that the Nazi leadership decided on genocide in the euphoria of victory. Was there not rather a close relationship between military setbacks and genocidal decisions? The shock of the Ottoman Empire's defeat by the Russian army in the Caucasus in January 1915 and the real fear of Russian invasion prompted accusations of Armenian betrayal and subversion. The ensuing deportations and massacres of Armenians, starting in February 1915, were ordered by the ruling Committee for Union and Progress as a means to "eliminate the internal danger."[54] There is a similarity in this regard also with the genocide of the Herero, on which the German army embarked, as Isabel Hull has argued, after suffering military setbacks.[55] As Friedländer has shown, the Nazi decision to murder the Jews arose in late 1941 from the growing sense of foreboding, after the first military setbacks, that the Soviet Union was not going to be a pushover, and that the United States would soon join the war. Hitler's self-fulfilling prophecy of January 1939 should be seen in this light: it was now becoming a *world* war. In that context, too, the Nazis "working towards the Führer" knew they had passed the moral point of no return in the incremental radicalization of mass murder that was developing on the eastern front.[56]

It would therefore be incorrect to deduce a linear continuity in the development of genocidal policy from the start of war in 1939. Certainly, from the first day of the invasion of Poland in September 1939, the German army acted with extreme violence against the population and prisoners of war. The frequently nervous German soldiers feared "*francs-tireurs*," or Polish resistance fighters, who would attack "treacherously," according to the troops' prewar training; entire villages were burned down on suspicion, and thousands of civilians were murdered. Yet while the military conduct resembled that of 1914, even in vocabulary, the racist mobilization of violence from below was a historically new phenomenon in German warfare in 1939: the *Einsatzgruppen* were assisted by the militia of the *Volksdeutscher Selbstschutz*, recruited from the resentful German minority in Poland. Motivated by the desire for vengeance and Nazi racial ideology, the militiamen killed 20,000 Poles and Polish Jews, often in arbitrary actions characterized by extreme brutality and torture. There was widespread military violence against Jews, not only because they were thought to be the ringleaders of subversion, but also because of many soldiers' antisemitic prejudice, drummed into them by years of Nazi propaganda, and their experience of violent attacks on Jews in Germany.[57] This ocurred fully two years before the decision for genocide was taken, in other words, there was an outline agreement that a genocidal war was to be conducted.

Yet there were distinctions between 1939 and 1941. In 1939 the army mainly assisted by arresting members of the Polish elites and male Jews, and handing them over to the *Einsatzgruppen* for executions; it also participated directly, especially in the killing of those suspected of armed resistance. It was in fact the army that put an end to the lynch-type murders by the *Volksdeutscher Selbstschutz* in November 1939. The killings were more on the scale of 1914 than of 1941: the army and the *Einsatzgruppen* were responsible for executing 16,336 civilians in the space of eight weeks.[58]

In 1941 the army played a more active role, cooperating with the perpetrators and participating along with the SS in genocide.[59] Planning for the new war that began with Operation Barbarossa, the invasion of the Soviet Union in June 1941, went far further than even the radical transformation of occupied Poland had suggested. Now the colonial vision of "germanizing" parts of the conquered Soviet Union envisaged the enslavement of a part of the population and the elimination by one means or another of the Jews and the elites. In addition, leading Nazi officials and the army leadership reached consensus in January-February 1941 that the territory to be invaded would be forced to provide a food surplus to feed Germany; in the process 30 million inhabitants would be killed or starve to death.[60] This amounted to the planning of a vast war crime, a starvation strategy perpetrated for economic reasons, underpinned by the ideology of racism. Nazi warfare was thus inseparable from the policies of genocide.[61]

Policy for the killing of non-combatants was deliberately radicalized; it was prepared before the invasion of the Soviet Union by criminal orders, notably the "Commissar Order" and the "Decree on Military Justice." The latter stated on 13 May 1941 that there would be "no compulsion to prosecute *Wehrmacht* personnel for actions committed against enemy civilians, even if the act is also a military crime or offence."[62] In other words, the "barbarization of warfare on the eastern front," of which Omer Bartov has so persuasively written, was not entirely the result of the harsh conditions of fighting in Russia.[63] The reason given in the decree for the decriminalization of military crime was precisely the memory of the First World War in its Nazi interpretation: "In judging such acts at every stage it must be brought into consideration that the collapse in the year 1918, the later period of suffering of the German people, and the fight against National Socialism with its countless bloody sacrifices paid by the movement, were due to the Bolshevik influence [. . .]." Victory against "Bolshevism," which was synonymous with expunging the humiliating defeat of 1918, would be gained by allowing all means of combat, including against defenceless captured soldiers and civilians. The "Commissar Order" of May 1941, which laid down that Soviet "political commissars," whether military or civilian, were to be executed upon capture, arose from Hitler's speech to the armed forces commanders on 30 March 1941. The fundamental idea was that the coming war would be a "struggle between two ideologies," that the "Jewish-Bolshevist system" had to be wiped out: "We must forget the concept of comradeship between soldiers. A communist is no comrade before or after battle. This is a war of extermination."[64] The army was a willing accomplice. Army commander-in-chief Field Marshal von Brauchitsch told top commanders on 27 March: "The troops have to realize that this struggle is being waged by one race against another, and proceed with the necessary harshness."[65]

The last remnants of the army's traditional moral and legal codes, which had led some generals to protest at the "atrocities" against the civilian population in

1939, had thus disappeared by summer 1941. The result was the collaboration of the army in almost all aspects of Nazi genocide, although the actual mass killing was usually carried out by the *Einsatzgruppen* in the field and the SS in the death camps. But the genocide of the Jews has to be seen in the broader context of the radicalization of warfare. The army had no compunction in the mass killing of those alleged to be partisans: partly because of the historical "memory" of the fight against "*francs-tireurs*" in 1914, above all because of the nature of Nazi warfare. Hundreds of thousands of real and imagined partisans were killed, many of whom were soldiers stranded behind the lines who had thrown away their weapons; and civilians. For example, the regular army in the central area alone killed 63,257 Soviet partisans or partisan suspects by 1 March 1942.[66] In Belarus, German forces killed about 345,000 people in suppressing "partisans" from 1941 to 1944, of whom no more than one in ten was actually a partisan. In total, 1.6 or 1.7 million of the prewar population of Belarus of 10.6 million perished or were killed.[67]

What conclusions can be drawn in relation to the question of continuities from earlier German history? The mass killing and genocidal policies of Nazi Germany cannot be explained without the experience and memory of the First World War and the interwar years, which was a constant reference point for Nazi leaders and army officers, in a way that colonial warfare clearly was not. Yet it was equally clearly not the result of linear continuity, still less of a causal relationship. The scale of the mass killing and genocide renders that argument void.. The evolution of mass killing and genocide from the 1900s to 1945 thus reveals a twisted path of continuities and discontinuities. While Nazi mass killing and genocide bore some obvious similarities to the ethnically based and political violence of other authoritarian states engaged in nation-building projects, from the crusading, redemptive violence of the Spanish Civil War, to the "cleansing" of suspect populations in the Soviet Union, Nazi policies were *sui generis*: radically distinct from German warfare of earlier periods, and from Allied warfare.

Parallels could be seen between the concept of the "redemptive antisemitism" of Hitler and the Nazis, as used by Friedländer, and the Young Turk ambition to create an ethnically pure Turkey as a modern state, the Italian nationalist goal of "redeeming" the supposedly Italian Habsburg territories, and the Stalinist utopia of the socialist society purified of all opposition, peasants, bourgeoisie, and ethnic minorities. "Redemptive antisemitism" was a prominent feature of Poland's violently antisemitic Endek party in the 1930s, led by Roman Dmowski; to Polish nationalists and the Catholic church, Jews were a backward, alien minority that blocked Poland's path to becoming a modern national state.[68] Yet in none of these cases was "redemption" the dominant element in ideology, and in the Italian case the "redemptive" mission did not lead to genocide. Hitler's occasional use of the rhetoric of religious redemption was not the dominant mobilizing ideology for Nazism; it was simply one trope alongside several others. The Nazi project of colonization of the better parts of eastern Europe plus a vast programme of ethnic redistribution was one essential factor. A secularized social-Darwinist view can be identified as an equally powerful constant of Nazi ideology. A paranoid world view was a common pattern among the perpetrators of mass violence, whether in the German army in 1914, or in Stalin's Soviet Union.[69] Christopher Browning's study of police reservists in the Nazi genocide pointed to a mix of peer-group pressure, military discipline, and antisemitic propaganda. For *Wehrmacht* personnel engaged in rounding up or shooting Jews, the motivations were, in addition to these, the (pseudo-) military rationale of anti-partisan warfare, real belief in the propaganda stereotypes of the Bolshevik-Jewish menace, comradeship (as Thomas Kühne has persuasively argued), or the sheer pleasure in danger-free killing which can result from the barbarization of men in war.[70] Dominick LaCapra has pointed to the perpetrators' "carnivalesque glee [. . .] [in] involvement in outlandish transgression [. . .] [and] in the suffering of others that doesn't seem to be intelligible from any rational point of view."[71] Few of the above motivations can be identified in the cases of Polish, Lithuanian, or Ukrainian killers of Jews in the pogroms instigated under German occupation: against a background of pre-existing antisemitism they were motivated mainly by a spirit of revenge for "Judeo-Bolshevik" oppression, and the desire for plain material gain; however, the quasi-religious aim of "redemption" appears to be absent.[72]

Although the concept of "redemptive antisemitism" is one plausible explanation of the personal motivations of Hitler and his immediate close followers, it is therefore not broad enough to bear the weight of the multiple roots of the Nazi policies of genocide and the actions of the perpetrators. It is also too vague to explain why, if the physical elimination of all Jews in the world would lead to the salvation of Germany (or the world?), the all-powerful Nazi regime allowed several hundred thousand Jews to escape abroad before 1941. Self-evidently, it cannot explain the motivations for the closely related policies of genocide of Sinti and Roma, the mass killing of "racially inferior" Germans, the eradication of the Polish elite, or the mass killing of Soviet prisoners of war. That Jews appeared to pose a far more dangerous threat to Germany than any other group, and that the judeocide therefore stood at the top of Nazi priorities, is beyond question, but it is also best explained in the context, and as the extreme culmination, of a transnational dynamic of destruction, a half-century of mass killing and genocide by authoritarian states engaged in nation-building or national reconstruction.

*Notes*

1    Saul Friedländer, *The Years of Extermination: Nazi Germany and the Jews, 1939–1945* (New York: Harper Collins, 2007), xx.

2    "Licensing barbarism" is the apt title Ian Kershaw gave chapter 6 in his *Hitler 1936–1945: Nemesis* (London: Allen Lane, 2000); see also chapter 3.

3    Hans-Ulrich Wehler, *Deutsche Gesellschaftsgeschichte*, vol. 3: *Von der "Deutschen Doppelrevolution" bis zum Beginn des Ersten Weltkriegs 1849–1914* (Munich: C. H. Beck, 1995), 1168; Eric Hobsbawm, *Age of Extremes: The Short Twentieth Century, 1914–91* (London: Michael Joseph, 1994); Arno Mayer, *Why Did the Heavens not Darken? The "Final Solution" in History* (New York: Pantheon, 1988). Mayer explicitly compares the Thirty Years War with the period 1914–45.

A stimulating discussion of the concept is to be found in Jörg Echternkamp, "1914–1945: Ein zweiter Dreißigjähriger Krieg? Vom Nutzen und Nachteil eines Deutungsmodells der Zeitgeschichte," in Sven Oliver Müller and Cornelius Torp (eds), *Das Deutsche Kaiserreich in der Kontroverse* (Göttingen: Vandenhoeck & Ruprecht, 2009), 265–80. Winston S. Churchill, *The Second World War*, vol. 1: *The Gathering Storm* (London: Cassell, 1949 (1948)), ix.

4    Isabel V. Hull, *Absolute Destruction: Military Culture and the Practices of War in Imperial Germany* (Ithaca and London: Cornell University Press, 2005). Rejecting causality and a German *Sonderweg*, but affirming the need to take seriously the possibility that Nazi Germany's war in the east drew ideologically on the "colonial imagination," is Jürgen Zimmerer, "'Kein Sonderweg im 'Rassenkrieg'. Der Genozid an den Herero und Nama 1904–08 zwischen deutschen Kontinuitäten und der Globalgeschichte der Massengewalt," in Müller and Torp (eds), *Das Deutsche Kaiserreich in der Kontroverse*, 323–40.

5    Hans-Lukas Kieser and Dominik J. Schaller, "Völkermord im historischen Raum 1895–1945", in Hans Lukas Kieser and Dominik J. Schaller (eds), *Der Völkermord an den Armeniern und die Shoah. The Armenian Genocide and the Shoah* (Zurich: Chronos, 2002), 11–80, here 19–21.

6    Hannibal Travis, "'Native Christians Massacred': The Ottoman Genocide of the Assyrians during World War I," *Genocide Studies and Prevention* 1 (December 2006): 327–71, here 336. "Systematic extermination" was the description by the German ambassador to Constantinople in 1915; American diplomats concurred.

7    Hasan Kayali, "The Struggle for Independence," in Reşat Kasaba (ed.), *The Cambridge History of Turkey*, vol. 4: *Turkey in the Modern World* (Cambridge: Cambridge University Press, 2008), 112–46; cf. Alan Kramer, *Dynamic of Destruction. Culture and Mass Killing in the First World War* (Oxford: Oxford University Press, 2007), ch. 4.

8    Cf. Roger Chickering, "The Spanish Civil War in the Age of Total War," in Martin Baumeister and Stefanie Schüler-Springorum (eds), *"If you tolerate this . . ." The Spanish Civil War in the Age of Total War* (Frankfurt: Campus, 2008), 28–43; on anti-clerical violence, Catholic mobilization, and the relationship between Catholicism and Fascism, see Mary Vincent, "The Spanish Civil War as a war of religion," in ibid., 74–89.

9    Sebastian Balfour, "Colonial War and Civil War: The Spanish Army of Africa," in Baumeister and Schüler-Springorum (eds), *"If you tolerate this . . ." The Spanish Civil War in the Age of Total War*, 171–85.

10    Cf. Boris Barth, *Genozid. Völkermord im 20. Jahrhundert. Geschichte, Theorien, Kontroversen* (Munich: C. H. Beck, 2006), 33–6.

11    John Horne and Alan Kramer, *German Atrocities 1914: A History of Denial* (London and New Haven: Yale University Press, 2001).

12    Richard Bosworth, *Mussolini's Italy: Life Under the Dictatorship* (London: Allen Lane, 2005), 415.

13    MacGregor Knox, "Das faschistische Italien und die 'Endlösung', 1942/43," *Vierteljahrshefte für Zeitgeschichte* 55 (2007): 53–92.

14    Jay Winter, "Demography of the War," in Ian C. B. Dear (ed.), *The Oxford Companion to the Second World War* (Oxford and New York: Oxford University Press, 1995), 289–92, here 290.

15    Ian Kershaw, "War and Political Violence in Twentieth-Century Europe," *Journal of Contemporary European History* 14 (2005): 107–23, here 110.

16    Belinda J. Davis, *Home Fires Burning: Food, Politics, and Everyday Life in World War I Berlin* (Chapel Hill and London: University of North Carolina Press, 2000), 184; Avner Offer, *The First World War: An Agrarian Interpretation* (Oxford: Clarendon, 1991 [1989]), 81; Holger H. Herwig, "Total Rhetoric, Limited War: Germany's U-Boat Campaign, 1917–1918," in Roger Chickering and Stig Förster (eds), *Great War, Total War: Combat and Mobilization on the Western Front* (Washington, DC and Cambridge: German Historical Institute and Cambridge University Press, 2000), 189–206, here 189.

17    Jay Winter, "Surviving the War: Life Expectation, Illness, and Mortality Rates in Paris, London, and Berlin, 1914–1919," in Jay Winter and Jean-Louis Robert (eds), *Capital Cities at War: Paris, London, Berlin 1914–1919* (Cambridge: Cambridge University Press, 1997), 487–523, here 517, fn 34.

18    For a recent restatement of the argument that the blockade represented a "British policy of annihilation" of the German civilians, see Dirk Bönker, Ein *"German Way of War?* Deutscher

Militarismus und maritime Kriegführung im Ersten Weltkrieg," in Müller and Torp (eds, *Das Deutsche Kaiserreich in der Kontroverse*, 308–22.

19   Hew Strachan, *The First World War*, vol. 1: *To Arms* (Oxford: Oxford University Press, 2001), 397.

20   Rolf-Dieter Müller, "The Mobilization of the German Economy for Hitler's War Aims," in Bernhard R. Kroener, Rolf-Dieter Müller and Hans Umbreit (eds), *Germany and the Second World War*, vol. 5: *Organization and Mobilization of the German Sphere of Power*. Part I: *Wartime Administration, Economy, and Manpower Resources, 1939–1941* (Oxford: Oxford University Press, 2000), 405–785; Christian Gerlach, *Kalkulierte Morde. Die deutsche Wirtschafts und Vernichtungspolitik in Weißrußland 1941 bis 1944* (Hamburg: Hamburger Edition, 1999).

21   Jörg Friedrich, *Der Brand. Deutschland im Bombenkrieg 1940–1945* (Munich: Propyläen, 2003 [12th ed.]), 407.

22   Ibid., 115.

23   Alan Kramer, *The West German Economy 1945–1955* (Oxford and Providence: Berg, 1991).

24   Bill Nasson, *The South African War 1899–1902* (London: Arnold, 1999), 220–24, 281, 283.

25   Alan Kramer, *Dynamic of Destruction: Culture and Mass Killing in the First World War* (Oxford: Oxford University Press, 2007).

26   Klaus-Dietmar Henke, *Die amerikanische Besetzung Deutschlands* (Munich: Oldenbourg, 1995), 963. Henke emphasized that the American, and by analogy the British, conquest of Germany, was "predictable, correct, and in principle humane – 'soft.'" Ibid., 26.

27   Sheila Fitzpatrick, *The Russian Revolution* (Oxford: Oxford University Press, 1982), 64.

28   Jörg Baberowski and Anselm Doering-Manteuffel, *Ordnung durch Terror. Gewaltexzesse und Vernichtung im nationalsozialistischen und im stalinistischen Imperium* (Bonn: Dietz, 2006), 49–58.

29   Lynne Viola, *The Unknown Gulag: The Lost World of Stalin's Special Settlements* (Oxford: Oxford University Press 2007).

30   Bernd Bonwetsch, "Der GULAG und die Frage des Völkermords," in Jörg Baberowski (ed.), *Moderne Zeiten? Krieg, Revolution und Gewalt im 20. Jahrhundert* (Göttingen: Vandenhoeck & Ruprecht, 2006), 111–44, here 126–31. Robert Conquest, writing of a Soviet policy of genocide, stated an exaggerated death toll of a total of 14.5 million peasants as victims of collectivization, including 5 million Ukrainians: *The Harvest of Sorrow. Soviet Collectivization and the Terror-Famine* (London: Hutchinson, 1986), 306. Some Ukrainian publications and the Ukrainian Congress Committee of America speak of 7 to 10 million Ukrainian victims of a policy of genocide. Cf. Bonwetsch, "Der GULAG," 126–30.

31   Stephen G. Wheatcroft, "Ausmaß und Wesen der deutschen und sowjetischen Repressionen und Massentötungen," in Dittmar Dahlmann and Gerhard Hirschfeld (eds), *Lager, Zwangsarbeit, Vertreibung und Deportation. Dimensionen der Massenverbrechen in der Sowjetunion und in Deutschland 1933 bis 1945* (Essen: Klartext, 1999), 67–109, here 84–7.

32   Pertti Ahonen, Gustavo Corni, Jerzy Kochanowski, Rainer Schulze, Tamás Stark, and Barbara Stelzl-Marx, *People on the Move: Forced Population Movements in Europe in the Second World War and Its Aftermath* (Oxford and New York: Berg, 2008), 74.

33   Malgorzata and Krzysztof Ruchiniewicz, "Die sowjetischen Kriegsverbrechen gegenüber Polen: Katyn 1940," in Wolfram Wette and Gerd G. Ueberschär (eds), *Kriegsverbrechen im 20. Jahrhundert* (Darmstadt: Wissenschaftliche Buchgesellschaft, 2001), 356–69, here 356–7.

34   Baberowski and Doering-Manteuffel, *Ordnung durch Terror*, 84–8. For the higher estimate of 900,000 deported Ingush, Chechens, Tatars, and others, see Ahonen et al., *People on the Move*, 220, fn. 50.

35   Ahonen et al., *People on the Move*, 77–9.

36   Rüdiger Overmans, "Das Schicksal der deutschen Kriegsgefangenen des Zweiten Weltkrieges," in *Das Deutsche Reich und der Zweite Weltkrieg*, vol. 10: *Der Zusammenbruch des Deutschen Reiches 1945*, part 2: *Die Folgen des Zweiten Weltkrieges*, ed. Rolf-Dieter Müller on behalf of the Militärgeschichtliches Forschungsamt (Munich: Deutsche Verlags-Anstalt, 2008), 379–507, here 404–5. See also his discussion of the problems of the statistics, ibid., 502–03.

37   Manfred Zeidler, "Die Tötungs- und Vergewaltigungsverbrechen der Roten Armee," in Wette and Ueberschär (eds), *Kriegsverbrechen im 20. Jahrhundert*, 419–32, here 422 and 429.

38   Ahonen et al., *People on the Move*, 122–3. The figures are from the publication of the German

Federal Ministry for Expellees, Refugees and War Victims, *Documents on the Expulsion of the Germans from Eastern Central Europe*, Bonn, 1958. Cf. also Hans Lemberg, "Das Konzept der ethnischen Säuberungen im 20. Jahrhundert," in Dahlmann and Hirschfeld (eds), *Lager, Zwangsarbeit, Vertreibung und Deportation*, 485–92, here 490.

39   Jörg Echternkamp, "Im Kampf an der inneren und äußeren Front. Grundzüge der deutschen Gesellschaft im Zweiten Weltkrieg," in *Das Deutsche Reich und der Zweite Weltkrieg*, vol. 9 part 1: *Politisierung, Vernichtung, Überleben*, ed. Jörg Echternkamp on behalf of the Militärgeschichtliches Forschungsamt (Munich: Deutsche Verlags-Anstalt, 2004), 1–92, here 49–51.

40   Letter 31 August 1918, Karl von Einem, *Ein Armeeführer erlebt den Weltkrieg. Persönliche Aufzeichnungen des Generalobsteren v. Einem* ed. Junius Alter (Leipzig: Hase & Koehler, 1938), 430.

41   Kurt Riezler, Diary entry 1 October 1918, cited in Holger H. Herwig, *The First World War. Germany and Austria-Hungary 1914–1918* (London: Arnold, 1997), 433.

42   Lieutenant-General von Seeckt, the German chief of the Turkish general staff, letter 2 May 1918, in Helmut Otto and Karl Schmiedel (eds), *Der erste Weltkrieg. Dokumente* (Berlin: Militärverlag der DDR, 1983 [1977]), 296.

43   Speech by Lieutenant-General Wilhelm Groener, chief of staff of the army group Kiev, to the education and press officers of the army group, late August or early September 1918, in ibid., 314–16.

44   On *Ostforschung* see Michael Burleigh, *Germany Turns Eastwards: A Study of Ostforschung in the Third Reich* (Cambridge: Cambridge University Press, 1988); on the perception of the primitive chaos of the east see Vejas Gabriel Liulevicius, *War Land on the Eastern Front. Culture, National Identity, and German Occupation in World War I* (Cambridge: Cambridge University Press, 2000); idem, "Von 'Ober Ost' nach 'Ostland'?," in Gerhard P. Groß (ed.), *Die vergessene Front. Der Osten 1914/15. Ereignis, Wirkung, Nachwirkung* (Paderborn: Schöningh, 2006), 295–310. On the concepts "*Nation*" and "*Volksgemeinschaft*" between the First and the Second World Wars see Sven Oliver Müller, *Deutsche Soldaten und ihre Feinde. Nationalismus an Front und Heimatfront im Zweiten Weltkrieg* (Frankfurt am Main: S. Fischer, 2007), 29–84.

45   This was argued above all by George L. Mosse, *Fallen Soldiers: Reshaping the Memory of the World Wars* (New York and Oxford: Oxford University Press, 1990).

46   Cited in Michael Epkenhans, "Die Politik der militärischen Führung 1918: 'Kontinuität der Illusionen und das Dilemma der Wahrheit'," in Jörg Duppler and Gerhard P. Groß (eds), *Kriegsende 1918. Ereignis, Wirkung, Nachwirkung* (Munich: Oldenbourg, 1999), 217–33, here 232.

47   Ernst Troeltsch, *Spectator-Briefe*, 26 June 1919 (Tübingen: J. C. B. Mohr, 1924), 69.

48   Boris Barth, *Dolchstoßlegenden und politische Desintegration. Das Trauma der deutschen Niederlage im Ersten Weltkrieg 1914–1933* (Düsseldorf: Droste, 2003), 258–66, 544–47.

49   Ibid., *passim*; see Vanessa Ther, "Constructs of war – representation and evaluation of the republican press of the Weimar Republic 1918–1920," Ph.D. thesis, University of Dublin, 2010. On "cultural demobilization" see John Horne, "Kulturelle Demobilmachung 1919–1939. Ein sinnvoller historischer Begriff?," in Wolfgang Hardtwig (ed.), *Politische Kulturgeschichte der Zwischenkriegszeit 1918–1939* (Göttingen: Vandenhoeck & Ruprecht, 2005), 129–50.

50   Cited in Saul Friedländer, *Nazi Germany and the Jews*, vol. 1: *The Years of Persecution, 1933–1939* (London: Weidenfeld & Nicolson, 1997), 102.

51   Saul Friedländer, *The Years of Extermination: Nazi Germany and the Jews, 1939–1945* (New York: Harper Collins, 2007), 272–88, esp. 282–88.

52   Michael Wildt, *Volksgemeinschaft als Selbstermächtigung. Gewalt gegen Juden in der deutschen Provinz 1919 bis 1939* (Hamburg: Hamburger Edition, 2007).

53   Ibid., xix–xx, 287–88.

54   Taner Akçam, *Armenien und der Völkermord. Die Istanbuler Prozesse und die türkische Nationalbewegung* (Hamburg: Hamburger Edition, 1996), 59. Available evidence shows that the government was not formally involved in the decision.

55   Hull, *Absolute Destruction, passim*.

56   Cf. Friedländer, *Years of Extermination*, 261–328.

57   Cf. Wildt, *Volksgemeinschaft*.

58    Christopher Browning, *The Origins of the Final Solution: The Evolution of Nazi Jewish Policy, September 1939–March 1942* (Lincoln: University of Nebraska Press, 2004), 29.
59    Jörg Echternkamp, "Im Kampf an der inneren und äußeren Front," 58.
60    Gerlach, *Kalkulierte Morde*, 44–76; Rolf-Dieter Müller, "Das Scheitern der wirtschaftlichen 'Blitzkriegstrategie,'" in *Das Deutsche Reich und der Zweite Weltkrieg*, vol. 4: *Der Angriff auf die Sowjetunion*, ed. Horst Boog, Jürgen Förster, Joachim Hoffmann, Ernst Klink, Rolf-Dieter Müller and Gerd. R. Ueberschär (Stuttgart: Deutsche Verlags-Anstalt, 1983), 936–1029, here 989–96.
61    Christian Gerlach, *Kalkulierte Morde*, 17.
62    Facsimile of the decree in *Verbrechen der Wehrmacht. Dimensionen des Vernichtungskrieges 1941–1944*. Exhibition catalogue, ed. Hamburger Institut für Sozialforschung (Hamburg: Hamburger Edition, 2002), 47.
63    Omer Bartov, *The Eastern Front, 1941–1945: German Troops and the Barbarisation of Warfare* (London: Macmillan, 1985).
64    Cited from the Halder diaries in Jürgen Förster, "Operation Barbarossa as a War of Conquest and Annihilation," in Militärgeschichtliches Forschungsamt (ed.), *Germany and the Second World War*, vol. 4: *The Attack on the Soviet Union* (Oxford: Clarendon, 1998 [Stuttgart, 1996]), 481–521, here 497.
65    Förster, "Operation Barbarossa," 485.
66    Gerlach, *Kalkulierte Morde*, 875.
67    Ibid., 957–8, 1158.
68    Richard J. Evans, *The Third Reich in Power, 1933–1939* (London: Allen Lane, 2005), 606–07. Friedländer does not acknowledge the "redemptive" element in Dmowski's antisemitism; cf. *The Years of Extermination*, 26.
69    On the paranoid racist ideology of the Nazis, see, for example, Evans, *The Third Reich in Power*, 604–05. On the paranoid world view of militarist nationalists in Germany in 1914, see Horne and Kramer, German Atrocities 1914, ch. 4.
70    Christopher Browning, *Ordinary Men: Reserve Police Battalion 101 and the Final Solution in Poland* (New York: Harper, 1993); Thomas Kühne, *Kameradschaft. Die Soldaten des national-sozialistischen Krieges und das 20. Jahrhundert* (Göttingen: Vandenhoeck & Ruprecht, 2006).
71    Dominick LaCapra, *Writing History, Writing Trauma* (Baltimore: Johns Hopkins University Press, 2001), 168.
72    The most notable example is the massacre at Jedwabne in July 1941. Jan T. Gross, *Neighbors: The Destruction of the Jewish Community in Jedwabne, Poland* (Princeton, NJ: Princeton University Press, 2001). For some other cases, see Friedländer, *The Years of Extermination*, 221–25.

# 12

# Redemptive Antisemitism and the Imperialist Imaginary[1]

## A. Dirk Moses

## 1 INTRODUCTION

Saul Friedländer's concept of "redemptive antisemitism" has become as classic as the book in which he first presented it in 1997.[2] Eclipsing rival formulations like "eliminationist antisemitism", "chimerical antisemitism," and "revolutionary antisemitism," it is a ubiquitously-cited reference point for commentators on Nazi Germany, and it is unlikely to be supplanted by new terms such as Jeffrey Herf's striking "radical antisemitism."[3] Peter Pulzer spoke for many when he wrote:

> That the ideological driving force behind Hitler and his hard-core entourage was "redemptive antisemitism" is a proposition we can accept. No other explanation can tell us why the Holocaust was pursued with such relentless, escalating and ultimately counterproductive thoroughness, or why the Nazi leadership appeared to be convinced that Jews commanded the agenda of both Soviet Bolshevism and British and American capitalism.[4]

What is more, the concept has been taken up by those who study Israel and the Middle East. Paul Landau, the French author of *Tariq Ramadan and the Muslim Brotherhood*, wrote that Hamas's ideology is suffused by a "millenarian and redemptive anti-Semitism," a move that links the Palestinian Islamists to Nazis in the manner of the recent interventions by Herf, Matthias Künzel, and Paul Berman.[5]

It is a testimony to Friedländer that others find his ideas useful to approach contemporary issues such as the Middle East. It is also fitting, perhaps, in view of Friedländer's signing, along with other Hebrew University of Jerusalem luminaries, of a letter to the *New York Review of Books* in 1973, protesting against diplomatic pressure on Israel to return the territories it conquered in 1967 in exchange for peace. Doing so, they argued, would make it "easier for them ['the Arabs'] to attack Israel." Despite Israel's peaceful intentions, it was constantly threatened: "For this fourth time since 1948, we have seen our country besieged and attacked, our friends and relatives killed; we have been the target of terror on a world-wide scale." Without mentioning the Palestinians, their claim to self-determination, or the incipient Jewish settlement of the so-called "occupied territories," the signatories affirmed Israel's right to exist in the community of nations: "The cause of organizing a peaceful world is based on the right of all peoples to free existence and harmonious national self-expression and self-government. These rights cannot be denied to Israel and its people."[6] And yet they were by "present governments of the Arab states" which "go to any length to destroy the existence of Israel." Similar fears are being expressed today by the advocates of the "Islamofascism" thesis: contemporary Islamism at once borrows anti-Jewish themes from Nazism and represents an analogous threat. The catastrophic conclusion to which prominent scholars like Künzel, Herf, Berman, and Benny Morris come is that a "second Holocaust" is imminent.[7]

Saul Friedländer was working on the Holocaust at about the time he signed that letter. His famous memoir about his childhood and youth in Nazi-occupied Prague and France, and later emigration to Israel a few weeks after its establishment, appeared only a few years later.[8] In other words, intense anxiety about the survival of Israel as a Jewish state and autobiographical reflection on escaping the Nazis who murdered his parents coincided temporally with his historical scholarship. Can it be coincidental that the homologies between his political and historical analyses are so striking: European Jews, a tiny minority, isolated and friendless in a hostile Europe; Israel, a small nation surrounded by enemies, virtually alone in a hostile world? The Holocaust clearly had lessons to teach. Now, as then, the answer to Jewish survival was the same: the readiness of gentile society, whether Christian-European or Arab-Muslim, to accept Jews as they were.

An important publication that foreshadowed his two-volume magnum opus was an article in *The Jerusalem Quarterly* in 1976. Entitled "The Historical Significance of the Holocaust," it is a critique of historiographical attempts to subsume the Holocaust under concepts like totalitarianism, fascism, and economic exploitation.[9] Instead, the singularity of the Holocaust is asserted on the basis of the special Nazi motivation that set it off from previous genocides: "Thus, although there are precedents for an attempt at total physical eradication, the Nazi exterminatory drive was made unmistakably unique by its motivation." This motivation was distinguished by its totality and absoluteness – the intended murder of *all* Jews – unlike the relative and pragmatic aims of destruction directed towards Slavs and "Gypsies." Moreover, the genocide of the Jews was suffused with a millenarianism that transcended pragmatic concerns: it was driven by "a fundamental urge and a sacred mission, not a means to other objectives." Although he did not yet use the term "redemptive antisemitism" – Friedländer then referred to "murderous anti-Semitism, which was fueled by an element of true insanity" – he was surely heading in the direction of that formulation.[10]

That the Nazi project possessed a "redemptive" character was a claim already being made by Friedländer's slightly older colleague at the University of Tel Aviv, Uriel Tal (1926–1986). An expert in political theology and antisemitism, he wrote about the Nazis' "redemptive political messianism."[11] Behind them both loomed the older figures of Eric Voegelin, Jacob Talmon, Norman Cohn, and Jacob Taubes, who had written extensively about political messianism and political religion decades earlier.[12] Joined by Yehuda Bauer (the same age as Tal), Friedländer and Tal were at the forefront of the attempt to assert the world-historical character of the Holocaust on the basis of the mythic and redemptive structure of Nazi antisemitism. This move sought to establish antisemitism as the fundamental explanatory concept not only for the Holocaust but for Nazism as well, challenging the then fashionable theories of fascism and totalitarianism.

The world-historical nature of the phenomena was not based solely on the total and absolute nature of Nazi antisemitism. It was also entailed by the special status of the victims: Jews, the representatives of Western civilization. Their intended destruction was therefore not a regulation genocide, but rather a nihilistic attack on the monotheistic values that the Nazis sought to transvalue: "God, redemption, sin and revelation."[13] Not for nothing does Dan Diner refer to the Holocaust as a "profound civilizational break."[14]

This cohort has succeeded brilliantly in advancing its project. If Tal is now largely forgotten due to his premature death and unpopular application of the political messianism paradigm to Israeli politics in the 1980s,[15] Bauer and Friedländer have become celebrated historians in the Western academy, especially in Germany, where they are regarded with prophetic reverence as living representatives of the destroyed Jewish past in Europe, symbols of Jewish rebirth in the Holy Land.[16] Whereas the Holocaust once rated only a few lines in textbooks on twentieth-century history, it now features prominently: the Holocaust as the negative telos of modernity.[17]

This cohort has also seen off rival paradigms along the way. In the 1970s, Friedländer took on Geoffrey Barraclough's "post-liberal" prioritization of the social and economic factors over the political and ideological ones, that is, antisemitism, in Nazi Germany.[18] A decade later, in a well-known exchange, he disposed of Martin Broszat's advocacy of a similar social and national "historicization."[19] Tal ensured there could be no confusion between the Holocaust and genocide, and others distinguished antisemitism from racism.[20] Diner then rebuked Götz Aly and Susanne Heim for their attempt to reimpose an economistic paradigm on the Holocaust, a critique reiterated recently by Natan Sznaider in his review of Aly's depiction of the Nazi state as a project motivated less by antisemitism than imperial plunder and racist redistribution.[21] Whilst some scholars have insisted that modernity, technology and bureaucracy lay at the heart of Nazism and the Holocaust, this cohort has replied that antisemitism is not a derivative or secondary phenomenon, but is a variable in its own right, independent, indeed primary.[22]

The reasons for this success lie in the cogency of the arguments. For all that the Nazi treatment of Jews shares with their other victims – a commonality that I myself have been wont to stress – these scholars have been able to show that the nature of the prejudice, the fears, the anxieties, and the fantasies about Jews were distinctive in significant ways. Leaving aside the theological and political question of whether notions of "specialness" or "uniqueness" should be then invested in these differences, the centrality of "the Jews" as a counter-race to "Aryans" in Nazi thought is a proposition whose analytical significance is readily apparent to anyone who studies the sources. It is no surprise, therefore, that scholars from different traditions, like the philosopher Philippe Lacoue-Labarthe, have come to the same conclusion without reading Tal, Friedländer, or Bauer. By studying Heidegger's Nazi sympathies, he determined that "the extermination of the Jews [. . .] is a phenomenon which follows *essentially* no logic (political, economic, social, military, etc.) other than a spiritual one, degraded as it may be." Accordingly, the genocide of European Jewry should be distinguished from other genocides.[23]

Plausible as this position is, however, it seems caught on the horns of a temporal dilemma. How can one insist on the historical *novum* of the Holocaust while invoking the *tradition* of antisemitism, even in its most radical instantiation? Are Friedländer and his cohort substituting one continuity – antisemitism – for others such as imperialism? That the answer to this question can be answered affirmatively is suggested by books like Jeremy Cohen's *The Friars and the Jews: The Evolution of Medieval Anti-Judaism*, which purports to identify the origins of genocidal antisemitism in the "original vision of Europe's *judenrein*" entertained by thirteenth-century Christian monks.[24] Invoking traditions of antisemitism thus embeds the Holocaust diachronically into a narrative of steadily intensifying anti-Jewish feeling with the Holocaust as effectively its possible, if not logical outcome. Leaving aside the fact that casting the Nazi project as an exclusively Gentile (German)-Jewish story omits other victims of the Nazis, whose targeting and suffering is a necessary inclusion in any adequate account of the Nazi regime, we are confronted with a temporal *aporia* regarding its continuity and rupture with European traditions. That the historical mind has reached the limits of its temporal horizon with the Nazi project is indicated in the ambivalence of various terms used to describe the salient intellectual context: conservative revolutionaries, reactionary modernism, redemptive antisemitism, and so forth. How can the tension between tradition and revolution be negotiated satisfactorily? And where do European Jews fit in?

The problem with this debate about continuities between Nazism, the Holocaust, and preceding events is that it implies a linear process in which discrete causal chains determine later events. Such a conception of history leads to nonsensical distinctions, such as whether colonialism *or* antisemitism *or* World War I are the principal "continuities" for the Holocaust. Setting the First World War against colonialism as an enabling context, for instance, misses the point that the former was a clash of imperial powers in which colonies were among the most strategically significant assets at stake; indeed, that the war was fought with methods hitherto reserved for "natives": the machine gun, gas, aerial bombing, and the general "barbarization of warfare" in which civilians often became fair game. Not for nothing did the belligerents invoke the classical colonial rhetoric of barbarism and savagery to accuse one another of outrages and excesses, especially when the Allies used their non-European colonial troops against the Germans on the western front.[25] Furthermore, however brutalizing the war experiences may have been, had they not long been common in the colonies? The war in effect reproduced colonial experiences in Europe.[26]

Metaphors of transfer, continuity and even knowledge-exchange are too linear and mechanical. They imply the circulation of discrete units of information or motivation that are transferred here or there, but miss the mediating dimension of interpretation and application. The solution to our temporal conundrum, then, is to re-imagine the role of human agency in historical processes. I proceed as follows. First, I suggest that an alternative temporal concept, namely the "political imaginary," offers historians a more fruitful way to integrate human agency with historical processes. Secondly, I show how an imperialist political imaginary functioned in sections of the German political class between the 1890s and 1930s. Then I see how Adolf Hitler utilized this imaginary for his own purposes. In this way, I hope to offer an intellectually more satisfying approach to relating National Socialism and the Holocaust to world history without subsuming antisemitism and the Holocaust beneath a generic concept.

## 2 POLITICAL IMAGINARIES

Imaginaries, whether about gender, the social, the political, or nature, have become commonplace in the titles of scholarly books and articles over the past twenty years or so. But what are they and why can "the political imaginary" help us think more satisfactorily about broader patterns and processes? It is not entirely clear what the origin of the concept is – some suggest it lies in Jacques Lacan's *imaginaire* – but the earliest and most systematic elaboration is by Cornelius Castoriadis in his book, *The Imaginary Institution of Society*. Disillusioned with structuralist Marxism in the 1970s and keen to revive the voluntarist dimensions of social protest and change from the 1960s, he developed the notion of the "social imaginary" as the symbolic, generative matrix within which people imagine their social world and constitute themselves as political subjects.[27] It comprises the background assumptions about reality that makes daily praxis possible. It is not a set of ideas; it is what makes the formation and articulation of ideas possible. As Charles Taylor puts it, the imaginary is a pre-theoretical sense of human surroundings, "carried in images, stories, and legends"; it underlies and enables the repertoire of actions available for any particular society.[28] Deeper than the immediate "background" understanding needed to interpret social life, the imaginary is also temporally constituted, because social interpretation necessarily entails a narrative of the collective "becoming" of the primary social group, for example, the nation, standing internationally in history. A culture's sense of moral order is also part of the social imaginary – which lends it the revolutionary potential prized by Castioradis.[29]

Castoriadis's project was explicitly political. Given that history was the realm of determinacy, the heteronomy of causal relations, the unsteered unfolding of events, how can people become authors of their own destiny by imagining radically different life worlds? As the pre-political and sub-ideological basis of human communicative togetherness that is never exhausted by any particular social or political formation, the social imaginary is a potential source of critique, of novelty, even revolution. Imaginative praxis, based on the tropic nature of language – that is, the surplus meaning inherent in words, which allows official meanings to be challengeable – can serve as a resource with which to inaugurate a new society. Freedom subsists in the fact that this act of imagination cannot be deduced logically or causally from the previous actions of events.

The conception of human freedom as rupturing the heteronomy of the historical process is very important when we consider Hitler's political imaginary below. Also important will be Castoriadis's French contemporary Gilles Deleuze who, though not attracted to the notion of the imaginary, also conceived of history as the realm of determination and of philosophy as the possibility of freedom; in his case, when history is interrupted by sublime moments of condensation, that is, revolutionary moments in which pure events erupt into the flow of historical events. And, like Castoriadis, he thought that reinterpretation of the past was a radical act of politics because, following Nietzsche, it could inaugurate an "untimely" – unexpected and unpredicted experience and reality. Such moments occur in particular when "pure events," as he conceived them, overwhelm our interpretive capacities to understand what has occurred. Existing frameworks need to be discarded and we find ourselves in a new horizon of possibilities.[30] We can observe how traumatic historical experiences inaugurate learning processes that, in the name of freedom from history's "terror," lead to revolutionary politics. Unfortunately, Castoriadis and Deleuze were incorrect in thinking that such a catastrophic sensibility has to be on the Left.

## 3   EUROPEAN CULTURAL IMAGINARY

The central dimension of the European social and political imaginary in the 100 years after 1850 was imperial and colonial. Edward Said drew attention to the imperialist nature of the modern imaginary when he noted that empire depended on a "structure of attitude and reference."[31] Politics could not be conceived except in terms of binaries like colonizer and colonized, occupier and occupied; or as the economist Max Sering (1857–1939) put it at a pro-colonial policy discussion in 1907, "Here, the maxim counts that whoever does not want to be the hammer will become the anvil,"[32] closely echoing Thucydides' Athenian justification of empire: "[I]t was not we who set the example, for it has always been the law that the weaker should be subject to the stronger. Besides, we believe ourselves to be worthy of our position."[33] Hitler, we will see below, made exactly this argument in foreshadowing his version of German empire in Europe.

This harkening to antiquity should also make us question the postulated modernity of the imperialist imaginary. Customarily, the imperialist imaginary is thought to have originated in the period of intense European imperial and colonial expansion followed by intra-European wars characterized by genocide. In fact, it was suffused with medieval beliefs about violent relations among different peoples, beliefs based on the Old Testament and antique legends, such as the destruction of Carthage, Melos, and Troy. These myths showed that migration and settlement, the divine mission of particular people, and the merciless slaughter or dispersion of others accorded with destiny or divine will. They percolated into the heroic sagas of many European clans, tribes, and peoples – legends of indigenous pasts, safeguarded by warriors and endless violence.[34]

Taylor argues that a modern social and economic imaginary of individualism and social contract replaced this early modern imaginary based on "hierarchical division into types," natural domination, the priority of the communal and divine order.[35] But such images persisted "nonsynchronically," as Ernst Bloch would put it. They could be activated *against* the modern imaginary in destructive ways at moments of crisis, as we will see with Hitler. Moses Finley's observation of the Athenian empire of antiquity could apply to paranoid political leaders milennia later: "[A] reassertion of the universal ancient belief in the naturalness of domination."[36] Where Bloch attributed the persistence of such myths to the crises of declining premodern social classes, I would argue that they were generally accessible and available cultural resources.[37]

Just as importantly, imaginaries framed how politics was imagined at all. European powers distinguished between their active historical agency, which spread civilization through colonialism on the one hand, and the passive objects of their endeavours, the colonized, waiting to be enlightened and modernized on the other. Such a worldview was necessarily racist because it presumed the inherent, indeed often biological superiority of the European colonizers over non-Europeans, as well as their inherent right to dominate other peoples. At the very least, the Europeans were *Kulturvölker* (peoples of culture) and most non-Europeans were *Naturvölker* (people of nature).[38]

Nowhere was the imperialist imaginary more apparent than in the contemporary fascination with the global spread of European empires and settlers, and the consequent "disappearance" of the "natives." The German Darwinians noted, and some even welcomed, this disappearance, and such observations were usually comparative in nature.[39] After his extensive travels around the British Empire, English radical and later politician Charles Dilke proclaimed with some satisfaction in his best-selling *Greater Britain* that: "The Saxon is the only extirpating race on earth. Up to the commencement of the now inevitable destruction of the Red Indians of Central North America, of the Maories [sic], and of the Australians by the English colonists, no numerous race had ever been blotted out by an invader."[40] Writing twenty years later, Theodore Roosevelt, the future US president, was equally entranced by the "spread of the English-speaking peoples." Having moved to North America, they were natural conquerors whose destiny was "to grasp literally world-wide power."[41] Part of this "race history," as he put it, was the superiority of their "race characteristics," which meant that:

"The English had exterminated or assimilated the Celts of Britain, and they substantially repeated the process with the Indians of America."[42] Both Dilke and Roosevelt compared the British conquering and settling prowess favourably with the Iberian powers, whose colonists had disastrously intermarried with the Indians of the Americas and even been expelled by them on occasion. Madison Grant was equally blunt in his assessment of racial history: "No ethnic conquests can be complete," he wrote, "unless the natives are exterminated and the invaders bring their own women with them," lest they be racially absorbed.[43]

German commentators felt they could learn from the Anglo-American experience, and possessed no illusions about the violence of conquest. Thus one author, in the pages of the German Colonial Society's journal, answered the question of what the authorities should do with the survivors of Herero genocide by looking to America. He approvingly noted the earlier "policy of extermination" (*Politik der Vernichtung*) against the "Red Skins," followed by one of protective reservations.[44] Support of colonialism did not have to approve of genocide, but even "scientific" colonialism regarded the fate of "dying races" with equanimity.[45] The liberal Bernard Dernburg, the German-Jewish first state secretary of the Colonial Office from 1907 to 1910, was a reformer who opposed genocidal policies towards Germany's African subjects. However, he noted in similar terms that:

> It cannot be doubted that some aboriginal tribes, like some animals, will have to disappear in the civilization process ["*in der Zivilisation untergehen müssen*"] if they are not to degenerate and become wards of the state. We are fortunate in our German colonies that we are not too heavily burdened by such elements. But the history of colonization of the United States, surely the greatest colonial project that the world has ever seen, had as its first act, the virtually complete extermination ["*Vernichtung*"] of the aborigines.

He was happy to report that if destruction marked the old style of colonization, the new style relied on conserving the native population and exploiting the land's resources scientifically.[46] In this vein, thirty years later, the anthropologist Richard C. Thurnwald (1869–1954), Professor of Ethnology, Race Psychology, and Sociology at the University of Berlin, defended his plans for a "scientific" exploitation of future Nazi-governed African colonies by comparing them with previous colonialisms: "My proposal is, in any event, more humane than the practice of the Americans when they largely exterminated the Indians, and the Australians when they made sport of shooting the blacks, as well as the violent deportations of the Russian communists."[47]

The question that German academic elites were asking was: how do we compete, indeed, survive in an international system of states and empires in which we are such late starters? One consequent anxiety was biopolitical. British settler colonies – the USA, Canada, and Australia – had become home to millions of German settlers who rapidly assimilated at the expense of global *Deutschtum*. Writing in 1905, the Pan-German leader Ernst Hasse commented explicitly on Dilke's and Roosevelt's celebration of the Anglo-Saxon expansion, warning of

German vulnerability abroad.[48] This anxiety about biopolitical strength recurs consistenly among liberals and conservatives.[49] Max Weber and later Carl Schmitt observed enviously that those Anglo-Saxons knew how to retain their national homogeneity. In Australia, "the immigration of Chinese is banned," wrote Weber, comparing them to "the Poles [who] are even more dangerous due to the possibility of mixing and of bringing down German culture."[50] The political imaginary of a zero-sum game struggle between peoples was virtually ubiquitous, framing the analysis of sophisticated intellectuals. Decades later, Hitler made challenging Anglo-Saxon word hegemony, coded as Jewish domination, the keystone of his political program.[51]

Another anxiety was land and imperial competition. The competition among core states for resources and geopolitical advantage was registered by anyone with an interest in global affairs, such as Professor Dietrich Schäfer in 1907:

> Our colonial policy does not deal with the will or lack or will of individuals. We are standing amid a gigantic movement that has all nations in its grasp, and in which we must participate if we want to avoid being overrun. [. . .] The earth is being given away; we must seize land ["*Besitz ergreifen*"] that is still on offer and that is useful and necessary for us.[52]

Lessons were offered by rival powers. The geographer Friedrich Ratzel (1844–1904) gained his interest in continental expansion and control from his visit to the United States, where he met the famous historian Frederick Jackson Turner. Likewise, Max Sering travelled in the US and Canada, where he too admired the American settlers. He drew specifically German conclusions in the book, *Die innere Kolonisation im östlichen Deutschland*, in which he regarded eastern Europe as a frontier equivalent for settlement, as did his colleague Gustav Schmoller and many others.[53] Not for nothing did Pan-German leaders like Ernst Hasse come to see the east rather than Africa as the destiny of the German Empire. The fascinating circulation of notions of continental expansion and German expansion eastwards occurred in a hyper-imperialist context; that is what makes it meaningful.

This context determined the self-understanding of Germany in the international system. Paul Rohrbach (1869–1956) was typical in taking a consistent anti-British, anti-French, and anti-imperial line in the 1920s and 1930s, praising the nationalist movements of colonial peoples seeking independence from the established European powers. As the historian Eric Kurlander shows in his book on German liberals and the Nazis, Rohrbach claimed to recognize equally the rights of all "oppressed" peoples, be they German, Indian, Arab, or African. According to this common view, Germany was a young nation that, like these non-Europeans ones, had to cast off the yolk of Anglo-French world domination. For this reason, he defended Japan's occupation of China and Southeast Asia in the mid-1930s as a reaction to Anglo-Saxon imperialism and American economic warfare, though he thought Germany's allies had an obligation to respect the rights of sovereign nations.[54]

Later, in the Weimar Republic, eugenicists also felt the compulsion to "catch-up" with Western rivals. It was "absolutely necessary to create a scientific center for anthropology, human heredity, and eugenics in Germany," noted leaders of the Kaiser-Wilhelm Gesellschaft, "since Sweden, the United States, and England have gone ahead with work in this area, in particular because these inadequacies and dilettante efforts in this area have to be countered."[55] As we shall see below, Hitler, too, wanted both to counter the Germany's enemies and perfect their imperial policies.

This is also the context for the truculent reaction of humiliated Germans to the Treaty of Versailles, which sliced territory off Germany's eastern and western borders and entrusted its African colonies to its colonial rivals. German complaints that world politics remained imperial and colonial, despite the post-colonial rhetoric of the League of Nations, were borne out by statements of British politicians who regarded their ex-German African trusts as de facto annexations unaccountable to any foreign body. Germany had been relegated to the second rung of European powers or worse while Britain and France continued, in effect, to rule much of the world.[56]

The imperialist imaginary was also readily apparent in the mutual penetration of antisemitism and colonial racism at the end of the nineteenth century. Contrary to the conventional view that these two racisms represent entirely distinct "continuities" to the Holocaust, recent research has shown how they became rhetorically intertwined and impossible to disentangle entirely. The social location of this intersection between colonial racism and antisemitism is the right-wing milieu of the Pan-Germans.[57] Their understanding of a future German European empire in the twenty years before the First World War was influenced by contemporaneous discussions about German colonialism in Africa and the Pacific; and it is entirely possible that the reverse was also the case.[58] Upset by the success of Jewish integration into German society, they became obsessed with racial mixing, which they called "bastardization," a problem that they thought led to the destruction of the Roman Empire. Their ideal of a "tribal empire" (*Stammesreich*) in Europe posited a racially pure utopia of German rule over Slavs.[59] Radical *völkisch* ideology was the nexus that explains Pan-German imperialism, the drive for living space on the continent, ethnic cleansing, and a "progressive" belief in social engineering/welfare, from Hasse – and Heinrich Class (president of the Pan-German League from 1908 to 1939) – to Hitler.[60]

German rule over Africans provided the model of racial subjugation, segregation, and oppression. For instance, in the 1890s these anti-Semites demanded that Jews be placed under a special alien law at the same time as they advocated that Africans be subject to a separate "native law." They defended Carl Peters – the German colonial adventurer whose brutal treatment of the locals in German East Africa scandalized sensibilities at home – by insisting that European norms of war could not apply to Africans, who effectively occupied another moral universe.[61] Above all, the understanding of the Jewish presence in Germany occurred in the context of a race-conscious worldview in which conquest and colonization of foreign peoples, hierarchies of civilization, progress and decline, survival and extinction were central elements.[62]

## 4 JEWS AND COLONIAL RULE IN THE ANTISEMITIC IMAGINATION

For all these similarities and mutual imbrications, an important distinction between colonial racism and antisemitism was the fact that Jews were *in* Germany and doing well. This spatial difference inverted the framing dichotomy of colonizer-colonized in Germany. Especially during the First World War, antisemites coded events in terms of Jewish success and non-Jewish German suffering, indeed, as Jewish domination over non-Jewish Germans. Already during the 1912 national elections, right-wing Germans had decried supposed Jewish control of the "red" and "gold" internationals. In Austria, they complained that Jews owned more than 50 per cent of banks and held 80 per cent of the key positions in that sector. The development of capitalism was regarded as a Jewish imposition, a "control system" over gentiles.[63] During the war, the military, in particular, complained about shirking and profiteering by Jews. Ludendorff levelled an accusation that would be common during the Weimar Republic:

> They acquired a dominant influence in the "war corporations" [. . .] which gave them the occasion to enrich themselves at the expense of the German people and to take possession of the German economy, in order to achieve one of the power goals of the German people.[64]

In other words, many Germans regarded themselves as an "indigenous" people who were being slowly colonized by foreigners, namely Jews. The cult of indigeneity was signalled by the *völkisch* obsession with "ancient German tribes" whose virtues of simplicity and honesty were contrasted with the decadent civilization of the French and British. The trend to identify with "Aryans" participated in this cultural phenomenon, eventually locating their origin not in India but in northern Europe.[65] This ideology culminated in the "blood and soil" rhetoric of the Nazis, who idealized the peasant rooted in the land. Nomadic peoples like Arabs and Jews were parasites, whereas settlers, such as "Nordic" colonists in North America, spread civilization and advanced humanity.[66] If settlers were mobile as well, they eventually became agriculturalists and rooted in the soil. Ironically, the environmentalist racialism prevalent in Germany speculated that Jews could not be part of the *Volkskörper* because their racial characteristics had been formed by another geographical environment.[67] Applying the North American term of "nativism," Jeremy Cohen identifies this reaction already in the medieval period in Christian Germany.[68] It is a nativism that justifies colonial expansion by coding its movement as productive and that of "nomads" – and sedentary Slavic peasants – as parasitic.

The anxiety about "colonization" by Jews was compounded after the First World War when the Rhineland was occupied by French troops from Africa. Not only had Germany been forcibly decolonized by its imperial rivals (and recolonized by its rivals under the mandate system), now they had imposed "inferior" black troops on the country. Germany was now the colonized, not the colonizer.[69] Right-wing Germans launched a massive propaganda campaign against the "black disgrace" of the occupation, replete with lurid tales of rapes and violence against local women. In thrall to conspiracy theories, they believed the occupation was an international plot to contaminate Germans with "inferior blood." Foreign Minister Adolf Köster spoke for many when he complained that "the German *Volkskörper* was facing permanent annihilation on his western front."[70] In effect, the occupation was a policy of genocide, as Hitler believed in *Mein Kampf*:

> It was and is the Jews who bring the negro to the Rhine with the same concealed thought and clear goal of destroying, by the bastardisation which would necessarily set in, the white race which they hate, to throw it down from its cultural and political height and in turn to rise personally to the position of master.[71]

His sense of panic about Jewish rule was palpable. Jews, as a "foreign people," had erected a "tyranny" over Germany, and now enslaved, through the stock exchange and media, but also via cultural life and the state, the Weimar Republic.[72] His arguments that Jews had infiltrated the ruling strata by intermarriage were echoed by other writers, like *Sippenforscher* Heinrich Banniza von Bazan, who deplored Jewish emancipation and the "flood" of immigration from Poland. "It looks like a planned dividing up of all German cultural areas. Four sons enter the four university faculties, another becomes an artist, while the daughter disports herself as the wife of the pastor." This integration did not bode well for Germany. "Since the collapse of the German people after the world war, [Jewish] domination over the political fate of the nation became totally naked. A racially alien strata developed that arrogated to itself the power to codetermine the welfare and direction of the German people." As a result, by the Nazi seizure of power in 1933, "some 2.5 million residents had Jewish blood coursing through their veins."[73]

Not unlike the Pan-German leader, Heinrich von Class, Hitler's "indigenous" response at this perceived colonization and foreign rule was to expel the colonists and establish an autarkic economy, that is, to preserve its "national character" by removing it from "international finance control," that is, from Jewish hands.[74] Otherwise the fate that met other peoples in the past awaited Germany: "Carthage's fall is the horrible picture of such a slow self-earned execution of a nation."[75] Time was short. The perceived Jewish colonizer was pressing its rule over the world: "The British Empire is slowly becoming a colony of the American Jews!"[76]

## 5  HITLER AND SELF-CONSCIOUS IMPERIALISM

Surveying the wreck of German empire in the 1920s, Hitler concluded, on the basis of his eclectic reading and exposure to the new discipline of geopolitics with its concepts of continental domination and *Lebensraum* (living space), that Germany's future lay in a European empire. Here, too, he followed in the steps of the Pan-Germans, who had advocated annexation and ethnic cleansing in east-central Europe during the First World War. Past empires – Greek, Persian, Mongol, Aztecs, Inca, and Spanish – were part of Hitler's historical repertoire. He was especially interested in the Roman Empire, whose success he attributed to its absorption of Aryan blood by its ruling strata. The destruction of that empire was – here he followed the Pan-German view – caused by racial intermixing. Christianity, with its pernicious doctrine of racial equality, was to blame. A Jewish invention as well, Bolshevism performed the same corrosive, levelling function.[77]

Traumatized by Germany's loss in the First World War and convinced that Germans faced extinction, Hitler consciously applied the perceived lessons of world history imagined imperialistically and without sentimentality. In his hands, he fantasized, Germany would never again be open to internal colonization by a foreign people (Jews), at the mercy of foreign powers, or vulnerable to the labor movement that he thought had stabbed the army in the back.[78] Applying these lessons meant founding an autarkic continental empire – "a great Germanic empire" – eradicating opposition, depopulating superfluous Slavs, and settling its border regions with "Aryan" colonists.[79] The Indian intellectual Ashis Nandy has drawn attention to the conscious nature of this project, which was not mechanically repeating patterns but radicalizing them:

> The industrialized, scienticized, technological violence Europe had tried outside Europe. In Europe, there was at most you could say trench warfare, but that was not self-conscious. Even in World War I, the killings in places like Flanders were not self-conscious exercises, as was Nazism; outside Europe it was often a self-conscious enterprise. Nazis, with Teutonic thoroughness, brought that experience to work within Europe; they applied to Europe what Europe had done outside Europe.[80]

This German Empire would not be formed "in a fit of absence of mind," then, but deliberately in light of world history. Hitler drew on an ancient imperialist imaginary to make sense of Germany's place in the world:

> We have the so-called white race that, since the collapse of antiquity, has over around 2,000 years taken on a leading position in the world. I cannot understand the economic dominance of the white race over the rest of the world unless I relate it closely to a political dominance that the white race has possessed naturally for hundreds of years and that it has projected outwards. Think of any area; consider India: England has not won India with justice and law but without regard for the desires, aspirations or laws of the natives, and it has when necessary maintained its dominance with the most brutal

measures (*Rücksichtslosigkeit*): just like Cortez or Pizarro claimed Central America and the northern states of South America not on the grounds of some legal basis but out of the absolute, inherited feeling of dominance of the white race. The settlement of the North American continent succeeded just as little from some democratic or international conception of legal claims, but out of a sense of justice that is rooted only in the conviction of superiority and with that the right of the white race.[81]

World history did not yield examples of peaceful economic conquest, especially British history: "no nation has more carefully prepared its economic conquest with the sword with greater brutality and defended it later on more ruthlessly than the British."[82] The British Empire, he thought, was not based on the professed humanitarian ideals of its apologists, but on ruthless exploitation. Its wealth stemmed from the "capitalist exploitation of 350 million slaves."[83] In effect, Hitler was observing what Partha Chatterjee later called "the rule of colonial difference," in which the postulated equality of colonial subjects is forever deferred by the ruler's racist judgement that they are not sufficiently mature for self-government.[84] Of course, if Indians and Hitler concurred in decrying British hypocrisy, they differed in their assessment of European domination. Long rule in India had inculcated in the British a racial arrogance and born-to-rule mentality that Hitler wished Germans to emulate.[85] His imperial commissars in Ukraine should act like viceroys.[86]

Hitler has been interpreted as being, in principle, against far-off colonies, but a careful reading of his texts shows that he admired how the British could use many of their colonies for *both* settlement and resource exploitation. The problem with Germany's African colonies was that their harsh climate and economy was ill-suited to North American- or Australian-style settler colonialism.[87] They were dominated by capitalists rather than settlers. A *völkische Boden-* and *Raumpolitik* (folkish land/ground and space policy) for Germany must be based, therefore, on contiguous territory in eastern Europe. Germany needed to colonize this space as it had so successfully in the past.[88] Dismissing the Western rhetoric of civilizational uplift and local autonomy as brazen hypocrisy, Hitler enjoined ruthless exploitation in the manner in which he thought the West actually governed their colonial possessions.[89] He wanted an extractive empire like the British had in India, but also settler colonies like North America, supplemented by outright plunder. In Hitler, the imperial models of centuries of human history congealed into a single, total, imperial fantasy of genocidal conquest, colonization, and exploitation. The Nazis turned the ubiquitous ideology of colonial rule into ruthless expansionism by emphasizing its exploitative dimension over any meliorative counter-discourses. Nazism's *raison d'être* was imperial expansion.[90] The purpose was not just to challenge the "Judeo-Bolshevism" of the Soviet Union, but also to secure continental hegemony for the ultimate showdown with the United States, whose awesome economic power Hitler had begun to appreciate only after writing *Mein Kampf*.[91]

To trivialize these fantasies as hapless groping for orientation or as *post facto* legitimations of conquest, as critics of the continuity thesis have, misses the point about the framing function of the imperialist imaginary.[92] The rise and fall of empires and concomitant extinction of peoples was constitutive of the global political gaze, as we saw with Dilke, Roosevelt, and Thurnwald. These were not marginal figures but popular writers, national leaders, and intellectuals. This gaze meant that when senior bureaucrats, academics, and Nazis gathered in 1934 to plan the Nuremberg laws they were inspired less by the intermarriage ban in the former German colonies than by such bans in North American states.[93]

## 6 REDEMPTIVE ANTISEMITISM

How can we understand this particularly disturbing learning process? The imperial, indeed, genocidal history of humanity lay before Hitler, as for his contemporaries like Oswald Spengler, who also expounded on the rise and fall of civilizations, for interpretation and guidance. That much seems clear. But why the catastrophic and, indeed, apocalyptic conclusions drawn by Hitler? Recall that Castoriadis and Deleuze regarded history as the realm of heteronomous determination, the almost mechanical unfolding of events stymieing human freedom. Spengler's rigid historical philosophy is a case in point, with its pessimistic conclusion that Western culture was dying because it had reached the stage of over-cultivated civilization. His cyclical theory was pessimistic because of its maudlin acceptance of long-term, inevitable developments that cultured men had to stoically bear.[94]

Hitler, by contrast to those of *bildungsbürgerliche* sensibility, was a revolutionary who would not accept the cards that history and world events had dealt the German people. He wanted to assert that people's freedom against its destiny by an act of radical imagination. The First World War had been an "event" in the Deleuzean sense, rupturing received categories of political and historical interpretation, opening up the political and imaginative space for revolutionary activity in the name of rival projects of human freedom, whether Bolshevik or racist.

National Socialism was experienced as "national liberation" by many Germans, who wanted to rid the country of parliamentarism and "Jewish social democracy"; in other words, to replace modern political imaginary of the social contract and liberalism represented by "the Jew" with a premodern one of hierarchy and order embodied by National Socialism – though of course with ultra-modern techniques. The natural order would be restored after the disorder of modern German politics. There would be a "rebirth of our racial life force," as Walter Gross, the Nazi Party's Department for Racial Matters, put it. Max Wundt, too, wrote of "rebirth," linking it to his "unshakeable faith in the liberating mission of the Führer."[95] The question, then, is less about "continuities"[96] than the "caesura" that Lacoue-Labarthe discerns in the Nazi project, the quasi-aesthetic attempt to "*fiction*" a new beginning in light of a disastrous past, to effect a "violent *abortion* of [the old] Germany in its frenzied attempt to appropriate itself as such (to identify itself) and to step into the light of history."[97] Only a radical gesture of political imagination and action could inaugurate and vouchsafe the national-racial German project by rupturing the temporal flow of events that had conspired to prevent German "becoming." Enduring for a thousand years, it would defeat its enemies – and time itself.[98]

What of "redemptive antisemitism"? In light of the imperialist imaginary, it is worth exploring the broader context in which the political emotions associated with redemptive violence develop: after all, violence is a core implication of redemptive antisemitism. In view of the colonial metaphors that suffused not only the Nazi imperial project but also its framing of the Jewish presence in Germany, that context has to be the imperial imaginary. Frantz Fanon's writings on violence and nation liberation are a good starting point because he was sensitive to colonialism's psychological effects and legacies. Evicting the settlers and their state was insufficient, he noted, because the subjectivity cultivated under occupation, a subjectivity that internalized racist stereotypes, would endure. True liberation required the violent, indeed, fatal attack on the European colonizer; it was therapeutic because it destroyed the inferiority complex of the subaltern habitus. As Sartre put it in his famous introduction to Fanon's *The Wretched of the Earth*: "[T]o shoot down a European is to kill two birds with one stone, to destroy the oppressor and the man he oppresses at the same time: there remains a dead man, and a free man; the survivor, for the first time, feels a *national* soil under his foot."[99] Here is liberation that is genuinely redemptive because it is cathartic: an expression of freedom from the past, implying revenge, and of self-fashioning in the present and future; "it is man recreating himself," as Sartre wrote.[100] Or as Tsenay Serequeberhan puts it, "[I]t is only when the colonized appropriates the violence of the colonizer and puts forth his own concrete counterviolence that he reenters the realm of history and human historical becoming."[101] For the Nazis and their supporters, destroying the "Jewish spirit" and its bearers, "the Jews," was necessary for the birth of a new Germany, a Germany inhabited by now racially conscious citizens that had transcended the bitter class divisions of the Weimar years, an imperial Germany that would protect itself from inner and outer enemies. An imperial country that had been thwarted by the Jewish colonizer whose international system held Germany in its thrall, Germany could now embark on its destiny.[102]

Needless to say, Germany was not in fact being colonized by Jews as Algeria was by the French. And there are obvious and significant differences between Fanon's and Hitler's project that space limitations prevent me from elaborating here. But if we are interested in political subjectivities, as we must be when the focus of redemptive antisemitism is on the perpetrators, then the stories they tell themselves are centrally important – especially if they are paranoid.[103] The *consciousness* of the Nazis needs to be invested with analytical weight, rather than being ascribed to *any* particular "continuity."[104] For all the differences between the Nazis' antisemitism and anti-colonial "nativist" violence, then, the tendency to hold members of the "occupying" group *collectively* guilty is striking. So is the totality of the ambition. Fanon wrote that "Liberation is the total destruction of the colonial system"[105]; Hitler also aimed at total destruction of the Jews who, in his view, ran the corrupt world and Weimar systems that were on the brink of destroying the Germans.

Perhaps, Fanon and Friedländer can be linked in another way, as well, namely regarding the status of the victims. Where Friedländer, Tal, and others postulated the uniqueness of the Holocaust in part because Jews incarnated Western civilization, Fanon condemns that civilization for perpetrating colonialism on the rest of the world: "The West saw itself as a spiritual adventure. It is in the name of the spirit, in the name of the spirit of Europe, that Europe has made her encroachments, that she has justified her crimes and legitimized the slavery in which she holds four-fifths of humanity."[106] For Friedländer, the Nazis are nihilist opponents of the West, for Fanon they embody its pathologies in the most virulent way. What the imperialist imaginary shows is that genocidal racism and imperial conquest transcend any particular civilization – which is far more disturbing. Sartre clearly sided with Fanon, deriding the Western justifications of empire as "the strip tease of our humanism" and an "ideology of lies."[107] As much as he opposed antisemitism, he would have equally opposed German Jews who participated in the German imperial project, like the jurist Max Fleischmann who, at the 1910 *Kolonialkongress* in Halle, denounced "mixed-marriages" in the colonies by appealing to the "racial consciousness" (*Rassenbewusstsein*) of Europeans.[108] To this extent, Friedländer, Tal and others are correct to note that Jews at least participated in Western civilization, indeed represented its origins.

Speaking on behalf of Europeans, Sartre proposed an antidote: decolonizing the self by rooting out the settler lurking in each of us.[109] He was not the first to advance such an idea. After Arab rioting in 1929, Hans Kohn, the famous historian of nationalism and, like Friedländer, Jewish native of Prague, abandoned Palestine for the USA, accusing Zionism-in-practice of colonial tendencies in relation to the Palestinian Arabs; there had been no "serious effort to obtain the agreement of the people, to negotiate with the people that live in the country," he wrote, and consequently they had perpetrated atrocities against Jews that were "typical of a colonial uprising." Echoing the revisionist Zionist Vladimir Jabotinsky – though critically – he observed that the only way for the settlement to endure was "on the basis of our ability to defend ourselves, internal militarization, and outwardly directed inflammatory rhetoric." Unlike Sartre, however, his decision was undertaken *in the name* of humanism, which he called "a moral spiritual movement" that was pacifist as well as liberal.[110] Seen in this light, Sartre's advice participates in the Manichean either/or logic of colonialism that Fanon had so carefully exposed. Kohn's was a vision of an alternative moral order, rooted in a non-imperialist imaginary whose calling into consciousness the twentieth century has shown to be as urgent as ever; the willingness to forgo collective redemption at the expense of others.

*Notes*

1   Thanks are extended to Paul Betts, Yotam Hotam, Eric Kurlander, Neil Levi, Dan Stone, and Lorenzo Veracini for very helpful comments on earlier drafts. All the usual qualifications apply. I am grateful, as well, to the editors for the invitation to the conference in Brighton at which parts of this chapter were aired.

2   Saul Friedländer, *The Years of Persecution: Nazi Germany and the Jews, 1933–1939* (New York: Harper Perennial, 1998).

3   Daniel J. Goldhagen, *Hitler's Willing Executioners: Ordinary Germans and the Holocaust* (New York: Knopf, 1996); Gavin Langmuir, *Toward a Definition of Antisemitism* (Berkeley: University of California Press, 1996); Paul Lawrence Rose, *Revolutionary anti-Semitism from Kant to Wagner* (Princeton: Princeton University Press, 1990); Jeffrey Herf, *The Jewish Enemy* (Cambridge, MA: Harvard University Press, 2006).

4   Peter Pulzer's review of Saul Friedländer, *The Years of Extermination: Nazi Germany and the Jews, 1939–1945* (London: Weidenfeld and Nicolson, 2007) in *The Times Literary Supplement*, 2 January 2008.

5   Paul Landau, "Hamas and Islamic Millenarianism: What the West Doesn't Recognize," 8 January 2008: http://www.worldpoliticsreview.com/articlePrint.aspx?ID=1481; Matthias Künzel, *Jihad and Jew-Hatred: Islamism, Nazism, and the Roots of 9/11* (New York: Telos Press Publishing, 2007); Jeffrey Herf (ed.), *Anti-Semitism and Anti-Zionism in Historical Perspective* (London: Routledge, 2007); Paul Berman, *Liberalism and Terror* (New York: W. W. Norton, 2003).

6   "Two Statements on the Mid-East War", *New York Review of Books*, 15 November 1973: http://www.nybooks.com/articles/9681?email. A responding letter by Daniel J. Amit, also of the Hebrew University, addressed to Jacob Talmon, accuses him of having produced "propaganda worthy of having been written in the office of I. Galili, Minister of Information, with the assist-ance of some of your cosignatories"; Amit, "The Mideast War: A Reply," *New York Review of Books*, 29 November 1973: http://www.nybooks.com/articles/9663. See also Saul Friedländer and Mahmoud Hussein, *Arabs and Israelis: A Dialogue* (New York: Holmes and Meier, 1975).

7   Benny Morris, "This Holocaust Will be Different," *Jerusalem Post*, 18 January 2007.

8   Saul Friedländer, *When Memory Comes*, trans. Helen R. Lane (New York: Farrar, Strauss, Giroux, 1979). It was first published in French in 1978. Before turning to academia, he had worked for the Jewish Agency.

9   Saul Friedländer, "The Historical Significance of the Holocaust," *Jerusalem Quarterly* 1 (1976): 36–59. Reprinted in Yehuda Bauer and Nathan Rotenstreich (eds), *The Holocaust as Historical Experience* (London and New York: Holmes and Meier, 1981), 1–23.

10  Ibid., 2–4, 15.

11  Uriel Tal, *Religion, Politics and Ideology in the Third Reich*, foreword Saul Friedländer (London: Routledge, 2004), 179, 87. This book collects Tal's essays from the 1970s and 1980s.

12  Jacob L. Talmon, *Political Messianism: The Romantic Phase* (London: Secker and Warburg, 1960); Eric Voegelin, *Die Politische Religionen* (Stockholm: Berman-Fisher, 1939); Norman Cohn, *The Pursuit of the Millennium: Revolutionary Millenarians and Mystical Anarchists of the Middle Ages*, rev. ed. (Oxford: Oxford University Press, 1970 [1957]). Jacob Taubes, *Abendländische Eschatologie* (Munich: Matthes and Seitz, 2007). On Taubes, see Joshua Robert Gold, "Jacob Taubes: 'Apocalypse From Below,'" *Telos*, no. 134 (Spring 2006): 140–56.

13  Uriel Tal, "Forms of Pseudo-Religion in the German *Kulturbereich* Prior to the Holocaust," *Immanuel* 3 (1973/74): 68–73. This line of reason is also pursued by Philippe Lacoue-Labarthe, *Heidegger, Arts and Politics*, trans. Chris Turner (Oxford: Blackwell, 1990), 37.

14  Dan Diner, *Beyond the Conceivable: Studies on Germany, Nazism, and the Holocaust* (Berkeley: University of California Press, 2000), 3

15  Uriel Tal, "The Foundations of Political Messianism in Israel," *The Jerusalem Quarterly*, no. 35 (Spring 1985): 36–55.

16  Friedländer won the Peace Prize of the German Book Trade in 2007, and his views are regularly sought in newspaper interviews, for example, "'Heute interessiert mich Walser nicht mehr'", *Der Tagesspiegel*, 13 October 2007. In 1998, Bauer spoke before the German *Bundestag* on the occasion of the annual commemoration of the Victims of National Socialism: http://www.bundestag.de/geschichte/gastredner/bauer/rede.html.

17 Regarding the pedagogical marginalization of the Holocaust, Friedländer cites Gerd Korman, "Silence in the American Textbooks," *Yad Vashem Studies* 8 (1970): 182–202.

18 Friedländer, "The Historical Significance of the Holocaust," 4–6; Friedländer, "From Anti-Semitism to Extermination: A Historiographical Study of Nazi Policies toward the Jews and an Essay in Interpretation," *Yad Vashem Studies* 16 (1984): 1–50.

19 Martin Broszat, "A Plea for the Historicization of National Socialism," in Peter Baldwin (ed.), *Reworking the Past: Hitler, The Holocaust, and the Historians' Debate* (Boston: Beacon Press, 1990), 77–87; Friedländer, "Some Reflections on the Historicization of National Socialism," in ibid., 88–101.

20 Uriel Tal, "On the Study of the Holocaust and Genocide," *Yad Vashem Studies* 8 (1979): 24–46; Steven T. Katz, "The Holocaust: A Very Particular Racism," in Michael Berenbaum and Abraham J. Peck (eds), *The Holocaust and History: The Known, The Unknown, The Disputed, and The Reexamined* (Bloomington, IN: University of Indiana Press, 1998), 56–63.

21 Götz Aly and Susanne Heim, *Vordenker der Vernichtung: Auschwitz und die deutsche Pläne für eine neue europäische Ordnung* (Frankfurt a/M: Fischer, 1993); Dan Diner, "Rationalization and Method: Critique of a New Approach in Understanding the 'Final Solution,'" *Yad Vashem Studies* 26 (1994): 71–108; Natan Sznaider, "Review of Götz Aly, *Hitler's Volksstaat: Raub, Rassenkrieg und nationaler Sozialismus*," *H-German*, H-Net Reviews, May 2005: http://www.h-net.org/reviews/showrev.cgi?path=202471121350466.

22 An excellent analysis of these debates is by Dan Stone, *Constructing the Holocaust: A Study in Historiography* (London: Vallentine Mitchell, 2003); Stone, *History, Modernity, and Mass Atrocity: Essays on the Holocaust and Genocide* (London: Vallentine Mitchell, 2006).

23 Lacoue-Labarthe, *Heidegger, Art and Politics*, 37.

24 Jeremy Cohen, *The Friars and the Jews: The Evolution of Medieval Anti-Judaism* (Ithaca, NY: Cornell University Press, 1982), 17.

25 John Horne and Alan Kramer, *German Atrocities, 1914: A History of Denial* (New Haven: Yale University Press, 2001), 223

26 Hugh Ridley, "Colonial Society and European Totalitarianism," *Journal of European Studies* 3 (1973): 147–59, here 159.

27 Cornelius Castoriadis, *The Imaginary Institution of Society*, trans. Kathleen Blamey (Cambridge; Polity, 1987).

28 Charles Taylor, "Modern Social Imaginaries," *Public Culture* 14 (2002): 91–124, here 106. In that sense, I am supplementing the current scholarly focus on the German "colonial fantasies" and an "imperialist imagination": Susanne Zantop, *Colonial Fantasies: Conquest, Family, and Nation in Precolonial Germany, 1770–1870* (Durham: Duke University Press, 1997); Sara Friedrichsmeyer, Sara Lennox, and Suzanne Zantop (eds), *The Imperialist Imagination: German Colonialism and Its Legacy* (Ann Arbor: University of Michigan Press, 1998).

29 Charles Taylor, "What is a 'Social Imaginary?,'" in Charles Taylor (ed.), *Modern Social Imaginaries* (Durham: Duke University Press, 2004), 23–30, here 27–8.

30 Deleuze defines the pure event as that part of every event that escapes its own actualization. Pure eventness in this sense is the highest object of historical thought. It is what must be thought from an historical point of view, but at the same time that which can never, or never exhaustively, be thought since it is only given to us through what actually happens. See Gilles Deleuze, *The Logic of Sense*, trans. Mark Lese and Charles Stivale, eds, Constantin Boundas (London: Athlone Press, 1990).

31 Edward Said, *Culture and Imperialism* (London, 1993), 10.

32 Max Sering, in *Schmoller, Dernburg, Delbrück, Schäfer, Sering, Schillings, Brunner, Jastrow, Penck, Kahl über Reichstagsauflösung und Kolonialpolitik*, offizieller stenographischer Bericht über die Versammlung in der Berliner Hochschule für Musik am 8. Januar 1907, ed. Kolonialpolitschen Aktionskomite (Berlin: Dr. Wedekind, 1907), 25.

33 Thucydides, *Peloponnesian War*, trans. Richard Crawley, rev. and intro., T. E. Wick (New York: The Modern Library, 1982), 1.76.

34 Len Scales, "Bread, Cheese and Genocide: Imagining the Destruction of Peoples in Medieval Western Europe," *History* 92 (2007): 284–300.

35 Taylor, "Modern Social Imaginaries," 94–8.

36 Moses I. Finley, "The Athenian Empire: A Balance Sheet," in Peter D. A. Garnsey and Charles R.

Whittaker (eds), *Imperialism and the Ancient World* (Cambridge: Cambridge University Press, 1978), 103–26, 306–10, here 125.

37    Ernst Bloch, "Nonsynchronism and the Obligation of its Dialectics," *New German Critique* 11 (1977): 22–38. This article was originally published in 1932.

38    Marcia Klotz, "Global Visions: From the Colonial to the National Socialist World," *European Studies Journal* 16 (1999): 37–68; Richard Grove. *Green Imperialism: Colonial Expansion, Tropical Island Edens and the Origins of Environmentalism, 1600–1860* (Cambridge: Cambridge University Press, 1995).

39    For example Georg Gerland, *Über das Aussterben der Naturvölker* (Leipzig: Friedrich Fleischer, 1868).

40    Charles Wentworth Dilke, *Greater Britain: A Record of Travel of English-Speaking Countries During 1866 and 1867* (London: MacMillan, 1868), 308–9.

41    Theodore Roosevelt, *The Winning of the West*, Vol. 1. (New York: G. P. Putnam's Sons, 1889), 4.

42    Ibid., 11–2.

43    Madison Grant, *The Passing of the Great Race* (New York: Scribners, 1916), 65.

44    Rittmeister a. D. von Simon, "Wie wird sich die Zukunft der Eingeborenen in SW Afrika gestalten müssen?," *Zeitschrift für Kolonialpolitik, Kolonialrecht und Kolonialwirtschaft* 8 (1906): 855.

45    On "dying races," see Patrick Brantlinger, *Dark Vanishings: Discourse on the Extinction of Primitive Races, 1800–1930* (Ithaca: Cornell University Press, 2003).

46    Dernberg in Kolonialpolitschen Aktionskomite, *Schmoller, Dernburg, Delbrück*, 8.

47    Richard C. Thurnwald, "Die Kolonialfrage," *Jahrbuch für Nationalökonomie und Statistik*, no. 145 (1937), 83. For a recent study on Thurnwald, see Kevin S. Amidon, "'Diesmal fehlt die Biologie!': Max Horkheimer, Richard Thurnwald, and the Biological Prehistory of German Sozialforschung," *New German Critique* 104 (2008): 103–37.

48    Ernst Hasse, *Das Deutsche Reich als Nationalstaat* (Munich: J. S. Lehmann's Verlag, 1905), 132–3.

49    Sebastian Conrad, "Globalization effects: mobility and nation in Imperial Germany, 1880–1914," *Journal of Global History* 3 (2008): 43–66.

50    Quoted in ibid., 59; Carl Schmitt, *The Crisis of Parliamentary Democracy*, trans. Ellen Kennedy (Cambridge, MA: MIT Press, 1988), 90, fn. 6.

51    Adam Tooze, *The Wages of Destruction: The Making and Breaking of the Nazi Economy* (London: Penguin, 2007), xxiv.

52    Dietrich Schäfer in Kolonialpolitschen Aktionskomite, *Schmoller, Dernburg, Delbrück*, 20, 22; see also Erik Grimmer-Solem, "The Professors' Africa: Economists, the Elections of 1907, and the Legitimation of German Imperialism," *German History* 25 3 (2007): 313–47.

53    Max Sering, *Die innere Kolonisation im östlichen Deutschland* (Schriften des Vereins für Sozialpolitik, vol. 56, 1893); see also Robert Nelson (ed.), *German, Poland, and Colonial Expansion to the East: 1850 Through the Present* (New York: Palgrave MacMillan, 2009).

54    Eric Kurlander, *Living with Hitler: Liberal Democrats in the Third Reich* (New Haven: Yale University Press, 2009).

55    Peter Weingart, "German Eugenics between Science and Politics," *Osiris*, 2nd series, 5 (1989): 26–84, here 263.

56    A. Edho Ekoko, "The British Attitudes towards Germany's Colonial Irredentism in Africa in the Inter-War Years," *Journal of Contemporary History* 14 (1979): 287–307, here 289; Marcia Klotz, "The Weimar Republic: A Postcolonial State in a Still-Colonial World," in Eric Ames, Marcia Klotz, and Lora Wildenthal (eds), *Germany's Colonial Pasts* (Lincoln and London: University of Nebraska Press, 2005), 135–47.

57    See the still seminal work of Geoff Eley, *Reshaping the German Right: Radical Nationalism and Political Change after Bismarck* (New Haven: Yale University Press, 1980).

58    Dennis Sweeney, "The Racial Economy of *Weltpolitik*: Imperialist Expansion, Domestic Reform, and War in Pan-German Ideology, 1894–1918," unpublished manuscript. See also Dennis Sweeney, *Work, Race, and the Emergence of Radical Right Corporatism in Imperial Germany* (Ann Arbor: University of Michigan Press, 2009).

59    Elisa von Joerden-Forgey, "Nobody's People: Colonial Subjects, Race Power and the German State, 1884–1945" (Ph.D. dissertation, University of Pennsylvania, 2005), 434–44; Elisa von Joeden-Forgey, "Race Power, Freedom, and the Democracy of Terror in German Racialist

Thought," in Richard King and Dan Stone (eds), *Hannah Arendt and the Uses of History: Imperialism, Nation, Race, and Genocide* (Oxford and New York: Berghahn Books, 2007), 21–37.

60    Eric Kurlander, *The Price of Exclusion: Ethnicity, National Identity, and the Decline of German Liberalism, 1898–1933* (New York: Berghahn Books, 2006).

61    Christian Stuart Davis, "Colonialism, Antisemitism, and Germans of Jewish Descent in Imperial Germany, 1884–1912" (Ph.D. dissertation, Rutgers, State University of New Jersey, 2005), 14, 29, 104, 135–203. For the German racial order in Southwest Africa, see Jürgen Zimmerer, *Deutsche Herrschaft über Afrikaner*, 3rd ed. (Münster: Lit, 2004).

62    von Joeden-Forgey, "Nobody's People," 12.

63    George L. Mosse, *The Crisis of the German Ideology* (London: Weidenfeld and Nicolson, 1964), 142.

64    Friedländer, *The Years of Persecution*, 74–82. In fact, Jews were over-represented in the German armed forces: Werner Angress, "The German Army's 'Judenzählung' of 1916," *Leo Baeck Institute Yearbook* 23 (1978): 117–35.

65    Klaus von See, "Kulturkritik und Germanenforschung zwischen den Weltkriegen," *Historische Zeitschrift* 245 (1987): 343–62; Klaus von See, "Der Arier-Mythos," in Klaus von See, *Ideologie und Philologie: Aufsätz zur Kultur- und Wissenschaftsgeschichte* (Heidelberg: Universitätsverlag, 2006), 9–53.

66    Mosse, *The Crisis of the German Ideology*, 67–71; Clifford R. Lovin, "Blut und Boden: The Ideological Basis of the Nazi Agricultural Program," *Journal of the History of Ideas* 28 (1967): 283–84.

67    David T. Murphy, "Familiar Aliens: German Antisemitism and European Geopolitics in the Inter-War Era," *Leo Baeck Institute Yearbook* 43 (1998): 175–191, here 181.

68    Cohen, *The Friars and the Jews*, 260–1.

69    Jared Poley, *Decolonization in Germany: Weimar Narratives of Colonial Loss and Foreign Occupation* (Bern: Peter Lang, 2005).

70    Christian Koller, "Enemy Images: Race and Gender Stereotypes in the Discussion on Colonial Troops," in Karen Hagemann and Stefanie Schüler-Springorum (eds), *Home/Front: The Military, War and Gender in Twentieth-Century Germany* (Oxford and New York: Berg, 2002), 139–57, here 145–7.

71    Adolf Hitler, *Mein Kampf* (New York: Reynal and Hitchcock, 1940), 448–9.

72    Ibid., 426–33.

73    Heinrich Banniza von Bazan, *Das deutsche Blut im deutschen Raum: Sippenkundliche Grundzüge des deutschen Bevölkerungswandels in der Neuzeit* (Berlin: Alfred Meßner Verlag. 1937), 92–3.

74    On Class, see Mosse, *The Crisis of the German Ideology*, 220–5; Helmut Walser Smith, *The Continuities of German History: Nation, Religion, and Race across the Nineteenth Century* (New York: Cambridge University Press, 2008), 206–10, 222.

75    Hitler, *Mein Kampf*, 380, 969.

76    Adolf Hitler, *Monologe im Führer-Hauptquartier, 1941–1945*, ed. Werner Jochmann (Hamburg: Albrecht Knaus, 1980), 305.

77    Adolf Hitler, *Hitler's Table-Talk, 1941–1945*, intro. Hugh R. Trevor-Roper (Oxford: Oxford University Press, 1953), 78.

78    Timothy W. Mason stresses that Hitler blamed the labor movement in particular; see Mason, "Die Erbschaft der Novemberrevolution für den Nationalsozialismus," in Mason, *Sozialpolitik im Dritten Reich: Arbeiterklasse und Volksgemeinschaft* (Opladen: Westdeutscher Verlag, 1977), 15–41.

79    Wendy Lower, *Nazi Empire-Building and the Holocaust in Ukraine* (Chapel Hill, NC: University of North Carolina Press, 2005).

80    Ashis Nandy, "The Defiance of Defiance and Liberation for the Victims of History: Ashis Nandy in Conversation with Vinay Lal," in Vinay Lal (ed.), *Dissenting Knowledges, Open Futures: The Multiple Selves and Strange Destinations of Ashis Nandy* (Delhi: Oxford University Press, 2000), 21–93, here 57.

81    Adolf Hitler, *Hitler Reden und Proklamationen, 1932–1945, Vol. 1 Triumph (1932–1938)*, ed. Max Domarus (Würzburg, 1962), 74–5.

82    Hitler, *Mein Kampf*, 189.

83    Hitler, *Hitler's Table-Talk, 1941–1945*, 193; see also Johannes H. Voigt, "Hitler und Indien," *Vierteljahrshefte für Zeitgeschichte* 19 (1971): 33–63.

84    Partha Chatterjee, *The Nation and Its Fragments* (Princeton: Princeton University Press, 1993).

85    Dan Stone, "Britannia Waives the Rules: British Imperialism and Holocaust Memory," in Dan Stone, *History, Memory and Mass Atrocity* (London: Mitchell Vallentine, 2006), 174–95.

86    Alexander Dallin, *German Rule in Russia, 1941–1945*, 2nd ed. (London: MacMillan, 1981 [1957]), 103.

87    Adolf Hitler, *Hitlers zweites Buch: Ein Dokument aus dem Jahr 1928*, intro. Gerhard L. Weinberg, foreword Hans Rothfels (Stuttgart: Deutsche Verlags-Anstalt, 1961), 100.

88    Adolf Hitler, *Hitler's Words: Two Decades of National Socialism, 1923–1943*, ed. Gordon W. Prange, intro. Frederick Schuman (Washington DC: American Council on Public Affairs, 1944), 26–7.

89    Ibid., 353.

90    Woodruff D. Smith, *The Ideological Origins of Nazi Imperialism* (New York and Oxford: Oxford University Press, 1986), 231.

91    Philipp Gassert, *Amerika im Dritten Reich* (Stuttgart: Steiner, 1997); Tooze, *Wages of Destruction*, 10.

92    Birthe Kundrus, "Kontinuitäten, Parallelen, Rezeptionen: Überlegungen zur 'Kolonialisierung' des Nationalsozialismus," *Werkstattgeschichte* 43 (2006): 45–62, here 60–1.

93    Claudia Koonz, *The Nazi Conscience* (Cambridge, MA: Belnap Press of Harvard University Press, 2003), 172–6.

94    Oswald Spengler, *Der Untergang des Abenlandes: Umrisse einer Morphologie der Weltgeschichte*, 2 vols. (Munich: Beck Verlag, 1918–22).

95    Both quotations in Tal, "Of Structures of Political Theology and Myth," 49, 59.

96    Smith, *The Continuities of German History*.

97    Lacoue-Labarthe, *Heidegger, Art, and Politics*, 75–82 (emphasis in the original).

98    See Neil Levi, *Modernism, Dirt, and the Jews* (New York: Fordham University Press, forthcoming); Neil Levi, "'Judge for Yourselves!': The Degenerate Art Exhibition as Political Spectacle," *October* 85 (1998): 41–64.

99    Jean-Paul Sartre, "Preface," in Fanon, *The Wretched of the Earth*, 22 (emphasis in the original).

100   Ibid., 21.

101   Tsenay Serequeberhan, *The Hermeneutics of African Philosophy* (New York: Routledge, 1994), 71.

102   There is further discussion in A. Dirk Moses, "Empire, Colony, Genocide: Keywords and the Philosophy of History," in Moses, *Empire, Colony, Genocide: Conquest, Occupation and Subaltern Resistance in World History* (New York: Berghahn Books, 2008), 34–40.

103   Alon Confino, "Fantasies about Jews: Cultural Reflections on the Holocaust," *History and Memory* 17 (2005): 296–322, here 297, 317.

104   Cf. Ranajit Guha, *Elementary Aspect of Peasant Insurgency in Colonial India* (Durham: Duke University Press, 1999), who argues that consciousness of peasant insurgents has been ignored by historiography, which consistently reduces it to an expression of some larger story.

105   Frantz Fanon, *Towards the African Revolution*, trans. Haakon Chevalier (London: Penguin, 1970), 105.

106   Fanon, *The Wretched of the Earth*, 313.

107   Sartre, "Preface," 24–5.

108   Cornelia Essner, "'Border-line' im Menschenblut und Struktur rassistischer Rechsspaltung," in Micha Brumlik, Susanne Meil, Susanne, and Werner Renz (eds), *Gesetzliches Unrecht: Rassistisches Recht im 20. Jahrhundert* (Frankfurt: Campus, 2005), 27–64, here 40–2. Also see Jürgen Zimmerer, "Von Windhuk nach Warschau. Die rassische Privilegiengesellschaft in Deutsch-Südwestafrika – ein Modell mit Zukunft?," in Frank Becker (ed.), *Rassenpolitik in den deutschen Kolonien* (Stuttgart: Franz Steiner Verlag, 2004), 97–123.

109   Sartre, "Preface," 24.

110   Christian Wiese, "The Janus Face of Nationalism: The Ambivalence of Zionist Identity in Robert Weltsch and Hans Kohn," *Leo Baeck Institute Year Book* 51 (2006): 103–30, here 119.

# 13

# Murder amidst Collapse: Explaining the Violence of the Last Months of the Third Reich

## Richard Bessel

In the last chapter of *The Years of Extermination*, Saul Friedländer devotes only a few pages to the murders that accompanied the dissolution of the Nazi concentration-camp empire and the collapse of the "Third Reich."[1] Given the scale of the story that is told in the previous 600 pages, it may be understandable that these killings appear almost as a footnote to the campaigns of mass murder that had unfolded over the previous four years – campaigns that resulted in the extermination of the great majority of Europe's Jewish population. The dreadful crimes of the final months of the Nazi regime did little to change the nature or scope of that campaign of extermination, and might even be characterized as an afterthought, had any real thought been involved. They also differed substantially from what went before due to the chaotic context of the murders, which claimed the lives not just of tens of thousands of Jews who up to that point had survived against the odds but also of thousands of foreign labourers of other nationalities, prisoners of war, inmates of German prisons and German soldiers and civilians. These murders were neither a return to the isolated attacks on Jews in Germany before the outbreak of war, nor did they comprise a well-organised campaign of extermination. Both symptom and consequence of the disintegration of a vicious dictatorial regime, their story does not fit easily with narratives which assume a clear, targeted and ideologically driven campaign of Nazi genocide during the Second World War – unless, perhaps, one accepts Daniel Goldhagen's view of a German culture saturated by an "eliminationist antisemitism" that inspired the treatment meted out to Jews on the death marches of early 1945.[2] Thus while the argument that antisemitic ideology lay at the heart of everything done by the Nazi regime serves well when explaining the persecution of the Jews during the 1930s and the campaigns of extermination from the outbreak of war through 1944, it may be less convincing with regard to what occurred during the first four months of 1945. Yet it is where phenomena are most difficult to explain that they can be most illuminating, and the very difficulty of trying to place this violence within an interpretative framework makes the orgy of murder amidst the collapse of Nazi Germany an important place to seek insights into a regime that was willing and able to launch a campaign of genocide that extinguished the lives of millions of Europe's Jews.

The attempt to explain the last outburst of murder by the Nazi regime must begin with context. That context is framed by one overwhelming fact: in 1945

Germany became the first country in modern history to experience total defeat. It did so amidst an eruption of violence that was without parallel in modern European history. Nazi Germany ended not with a whimper but a bang. It should be remembered – although it often is forgotten – that the last months of the Second World War in Europe were the bloodiest. The greatest losses of the *Wehrmacht* arose from the fighting of the final months of the war, and the lion's share of the casualties – although by no means all of them – were taken by the German armies facing east. Whereas in the west the resistance of the *Wehrmacht* to the advance of the Allied armies crumbled during April 1945 (but not before!), on what remained of the "eastern front" the fighting remained incredibly intense to the bitter end. The result was massive destruction and loss of life. In the first five months of 1945 alone, German military deaths were greater than they had been in 1942 and 1943 put together.[3] Indeed, in January 1945 the number of German military casualties reached its absolute peak, with over 450,000 dead in that single month; and in each of the three months that followed, the number of German dead exceeded 280,000. (That was far greater than the roughly 185,000 *Wehrmacht* soldiers who died in January 1943, the month of the German defeat at Stalingrad.) The numbers of wounded and injured – at a time when German medical facilities, both military and civilian, were in a state of collapse – were even greater. The losses suffered by the Red Army probably were larger still. Altogether, during the first four months of 1945 Germany was the epicentre of probably the greatest killing frenzy in the history of the modern world.

The final military campaigns resulted not only in astronomical numbers of dead and injured. They also led to the loss of large swathes of German territory, as entire regions were overrun by Allied armies, cut off from one another, and overwhelmed by vast numbers of homeless refugees. Cities and towns were declared "fortresses," to be defended to the last – a tactic that could not stave off defeat and succeeded only in ensuring even greater destruction.[4] At the same time, the bombing campaign against German cities reached its peak. During the last months of the war – as Nuremberg and Magdeburg (in January 1945), Dresden and Pforzheim (in February), and Swinemünde and Würzburg (in March) were destroyed, as the Luftwaffe no longer was able to offer any significant resistance to British and American air attacks, and as all of Germany's cities were within range of Allied bombers – a greater tonnage of bombs was dropped on Germany and a greater number of Germans were killed daily as a result than ever before.[5] Furthermore, during the final months of the war not only were bombers flattening German cities, but fighter planes were strafing the rural population as Allied armies closed in on the Reich – causing Germans to hide in forests during daylight hours to avoid being shot.[6] Throughout the country, an orderly existence became impossible as people found themselves in a sea of death and destruction.

The now unhindered Allied bombing campaign had catastrophic effects on Germany's infrastructure – most importantly on the transport infrastructure – and that in turn had catastrophic consequences for the supply of fuel and food.[7] Together with the loss of what had been eastern Germany in the wake of the massive offensive unleashed by the Red Army on 12 January 1945, this spelled disaster for the provisioning of the civilian population. During early 1945 (as millions of hungry refugees were fleeing the Red Army and streaming west-wards into what remained of Germany) anxious discussions took place among the civil and military leadership of the Nazi regime about the consequences of the loss of eastern regions – East and West Prussia, the "Wartheland," Silesia, Pomerania and the Courland – which had comprised more than 30 per cent of the agricultural land at Germany's disposal.[8] Hinrich Lohse, Nazi Party *Gauleiter* of Schleswig-Holstein, Reich Commissar in the Baltic and "Reich Defence Commissar," summed up these discussions with the observation that "we no longer can prevent that the people go hungry, only that they starve."[9] In the event, while Germans faced hunger in the last months of the war, it was their prisoners who faced starvation. If there were any food to be had, the people dumped into desperately overcrowded concentration camps in early 1945 certainly would not be at the front of the queue.

As the German economy collapsed, the Nazi regime no longer was able to shape events, save attacking individuals still within its grasp. The destruction of the country's infrastructure meant that the already inadequate provisioning of the concentration camps and prisons largely broke down; the collapse of medi-cal services and social-welfare provision meant that the German victims of the bombing and fighting were left to depend largely on their own resources; and the erosion of public order during the last months drove the Nazi police state to lash out against foreign labourers who appeared to pose a growing threat of crime, as well as against "racial comrades" who dared to admit out loud that the war was lost. In the chaos that enveloped Germany in early 1945, desperation, framed by an apocalyptic ideology that glorified violence, fuelled the murder of foreign labourers, concentration-camp inmates and allegedly "defeatist" members of their own "racial community."

Nowhere was this awful process more apparent than with regard to the concentration camps. The most terrible chapter in the history of the Nazi con-centration camps (as distinct from the extermination camps, whose sole purpose had been to kill human beings) was that which occurred during the last months of Nazi rule. The German military collapse created huge problems for the opera-tion of the camps, and led to the worst conditions and highest death rates seen in them during the entire war. In the east, following the Soviet offensive launched in mid-January 1945, and in the west as the Americans, British and Canadians crossed the Rhine and streamed eastwards, camp after camp was approached by the advancing Allied armed forces. The Germans, keen to cover their tracks, evacuated camps and prisons in order to prevent inmates being freed by the Allied armies. Whereas in some cases – for example, from Natzweiler in Alsace and from Herzogenbusch in the Netherlands in late 1944 – the evacuations were undertaken well before Allied armies drew near and took place in reasonably good order, in others they were sudden and chaotic.[10] When the *Wehrmacht's* eastern front buckled under the massive Soviet offensive of January 1945, tens of thousands of prisoners were evacuated hastily from Auschwitz, Stutthof (near Danzig) and Groß Rosen (about 60 kilometres southwest of Breslau); from Auschwitz camp complex alone an estimated 56,000–58,000 were removed once the evacuation commenced there on 17 January.[11] Some of the prisoners, already gravely weakened by ill-treatment, malnutrition and disease, were put onto trains in the dead of winter and transported (sometimes in open coal wagons) without food or sanitary facilities; trains filled with prisoners bound for camps in the Reich or the Czech Protectorate (Mauthausen, Buchenwald, Bergen-Belsen, Ravensbrück, Sachsenhausen, Theresienstadt) sometimes were made to turn back from camps which already were overflowing and which refused to accept any more evacuees; terrible scenes occurred at railway stations where prisoners were shot or beaten to death.[12] Others, the majority, faced even worse, as they were forced onto what became death marches, often without any particular end to the trek in sight, on which thousands lost their lives.

Within what was left of the Nazi concentration-camp empire, already horrible conditions deteriorated further as food supplies diminished and the numbers of prisoners increased. In January 1945, when the evacuations from Auschwitz, Groß Rosen and Stutthof began as the Red Army advanced, the concentration camps in the Reich recorded 714,211 prisoners (511,537 men and 202,674 women, of whom roughly 200,000 were Jews); this was nearly 200,000 more than they had held during the previous summer.[13] Of the prisoners in the camps in January, somewhere between 200,000 and 350,000 died during the winter and early spring of 1945: Martin Broszat estimated in the 1960s that "at least a third of the over 700,000 prisoners registered in January 1945 died on the exhausting evacuation marches, in the transport trains which wandered about for weeks, and (above all) in the completely overcrowded reception camps during the months and weeks immediately before the end of the war"; more recently, Yehuda Bauer has estimated that as many as half the prisoners may have died.[14]

Forcing ill and undernourished prisoners to criss-cross the country from one camp to another proved an ideal means to spread disease and increase the numbers of dead. In Buchenwald, where large numbers of evacuees had arrived from Auschwitz and Groß Rosen in early 1945, nearly 14,000 people died between January and the beginning of April.[15] In Dachau and its satellite camps, where the influx of evacuees from the east also led to massive overcrowding, more than 13,000 prisoners died during the first four months of 1945, many falling victim to a typhoid epidemic.[16] In Mauthausen (near Linz, in Upper Austria), which was the first concentration camp to have been established outside the borders of the "old Reich" and which also received evacuees from Auschwitz and Groß Rosen in early 1945, the highest monthly death rates of the camp's entire existence were recorded from January to April 1945 – some four times the mortality rates over the preceding nine months; roughly 45,000 prisoners died there between the onset of winter in 1944–5 and the beginning of the following summer.[17] Particularly horrific were conditions in the Mittelbau-Dora camp complex near Nordhausen in Thuringia, where prisoners had been forced to work in vast underground tunnels assembling, among other things, V-1 flying bombs and V-2 rockets.[18] During the last months of the war some 60,000 prisoners, many of whom were evacuees from Auschwitz and Groß Rosen, were sent to Mittelbau-Dora. Between mid-January and mid-February 1945 the number of prisoners at the main Mittelbau-Dora camp increased by 50 per cent; housing provision was primitive; death due to undernourishment and disease was common; and the camp administration reacted to the worsening conditions by stepping up the terror: in March 1945 150 prisoners were hanged.[19] It was the crumbling of the concentration-camp system against the background of military defeat, rather than its efficient operation, that led to the greatest cruelty and the highest numbers of deaths.

Examination of what occurred in the camps during the final months reveals a variety of conflicting motives and considerations, which led to murder in some cases and not in others. As Allied armies approached the camps and plans were made for their evacuation, increasing concern was expressed that – as was stipulated in a detailed evacuation order for Auschwitz drafted in late December 1944 – "no prisoner must fall into the hands of the enemy alive."[20] While similar phrases had been used before, in the last weeks of the Reich they were translated into action: from January 1945 instructions were issued by senior SS and police officers for a number of camps to liquidate prisoners who were ill, unable to work or unfit to set out on the marches. At Auschwitz, where as many as 58,000 prisoners were evacuated between 17 and 21 January, nearly 9000 mostly ill prisoners remained behind – to be killed shortly thereafter by an SS unit.[21] As the front drew nearer, the responses to an increasingly desperate situation themselves became increasingly desperate, as the head of the Gestapo, Heinrich Müller, instructed camp commanders at the end of January 1945 that political prisoners regarded as dangerous (resistance fighters, etc.) also be killed. Some SS and police chiefs went even further, urging that prisoners generally be killed to reduce the population in the camps and thus mitigate problems of overcrowding and insufficient numbers of guards.[22] In some instances, these instructions had their deadly effect; in others, however, sometimes because there was insufficient time to carry out massacres before Allied troops arrived, they did not. While the treatment of those in the camps and those forced onto the death marches often differed according to their place in the Nazis' racial hierarchy (and the various groups of prisoners kept separate according to nationality and category), the mounting chaos meant this was not always strictly the case. As the SS killed thousands of concentration-camp prisoners during the final weeks, the weak and those unable to work tended to be the main targets, and the massacres committed by SS men at Palmnicken (in East Prussia, in January 1945) and Gardelegen (in Saxony-Anhalt, in April 1945) were motivated among other things by a desire to be rid of their weakened prisoners in order to facilitate their own flight from rapidly advancing enemy troops.[23] According to Gabriele Hammermann, towards the end of the war the SS, both its leadership in Berlin and its personnel running the camps, often acted from tactical considerations "despite racist axioms."[24] As the

SS empire crumbled, the coherence of its murderous campaign against allegedly inferior peoples crumbled with it.

As Nikolaus Wachsmann has shown, it was not only the captives in the concentration camps who faced deteriorating conditions and brutal evacuations in early 1945. Once the Red Army began its January offensive, the German authorities had to decide what to do with the roughly 35,000 inmates held in prisons and gaols in the east of the Reich.[25] Death rates among prison inmates forced onto marches were not so high as among the much larger numbers of people evacuated from the concentration camps. However, conditions were awful enough: thousands of prisoners were herded, mostly on foot, towards penal institutions in central and western Germany in freezing weather, without proper clothing or shoes and without sufficient food (sometimes without food at all). Here too the breakdown of the Nazi regime resulted in even greater violence and inhumanity than its smooth functioning had done previously.

How can we explain this? The war was lost; Allied armies were rapidly closing in; the bureaucratic structures of the Nazi state and the coherence of its military were breaking down; the reach of the government in Berlin was shrinking rapidly. And the killing continued amidst the chaos. Some insights are offered by Yehuda Bauer in his seminal article on the death marches of early 1945:

> Faced with conflicting signals from above, in the context of an increasingly chaotic situation, the camp commanders were left to fend for themselves. No psychological or ideological-psychological sketches on a comparative basis exist for the various camp commanders, but the general impression is that of weak, brutal despots who at the last minute tried to save their own hides. We do not know of even one camp commander who died defending his post – they all either ran or hid, or both. In the situation just described, this personal element had a sometimes-decisive influence on the final outcome: only in one camp, Ohrdruf, not far from Buchenwald, were the inmates murdered on the eve of liberation. Elsewhere, they were either left alone to starve to death or die of typhus and typhoid; others were marched off. Only token resistance was offered by the SS when Allied troops came to liberate the camps.[26]

This was neither systematic murder, nor was it a straightforward expression of fanatical devotion to the Nazi cause and Nazi ideology. Certainly the creation of the camps, the recruitment of their personnel and the functions they served up to the last months of Nazi rule involved making a criminal, racist ideology real. Yet what occurred during the final months was not simply a continuation of what had gone before. Rather it was a result of the simultaneous persistence and decomposition of the Nazi racial state, an expression of both "racist axioms" and tactical considerations resorted to by desperate, guilty men. The actions carried out by the crumbling institutions and personnel of the Nazi regime in its final months were shaped as much by the mounting chaos as by the ideological imperatives that originally had set the machinery of mass murder in motion.

Similar explanations may be put forward for the actions of Germany's police who, like the concentration-camp and prison guards, participated in this final wave of murder. In part this followed from directives from above: in the autumn of 1944, Himmler had instructed local police commanders that, "should the uncertainty at the front continue or even grow," the "danger" this posed was "to be removed," that is, prisoners were to be "fetched from the gaols and liquidated."[27] Local commanders did as Himmler wished. In Cologne, for example, the Gestapo began selecting foreign prisoners for execution in late October 1944, and the killings continued until the beginning of March 1945. In the last weeks of the war, people whose court cases still were pending were executed. Altogether hundreds of prisoners were hanged in the courtyard of the Cologne Gestapo headquarters. The killings continued until the Americans reached the city, and the last of the planned executions, scheduled for 4 March, was called off only because of the heavy bombing that had taken place the night before.[28] Although in some instances German police moderated their behaviour as Allied armies approached, in others they continued to murder prisoners even as Allied artillery shelled the towns in which they were working.[29]

As Germany's final defeat drew nearer, imprisoned foreign labourers were increasingly likely to become targets of police violence. This too owed as much to the breakdown of the Nazi regime as it did to ideological commitment. As communication between Berlin and the rest of the country grew more difficult with the breakdown of telephone and postal networks, local police effectively had greater latitude when responding to real and imagined threats. On 6 February Ernst Kaltenbrunner, the last chief of the Reich Security Main Office, decreed that heads of police offices throughout the Reich themselves could decide "about special treatments with regard to crimes deserving death." Local Security Police commanders were granted wide discretion with regard to executing foreign workers. How they were expected to apply this discretion was made brutally clear: "From all police offices [I] expect the highest state of readiness, responsibility, robust action, no hesitation. Ruthlessly eliminate any defeatism in one's own ranks with the harshest measures."[30]

There is little doubt that many members of the police forces behaved as Kaltenbrunner wished. In the Ruhr region, where huge numbers of foreign workers were living in a bombed-out industrial landscape, police repeatedly resorted to deadly violence as Allied armies approached in early 1945. By that time, controls over foreign labourers were eroding; there was little to keep them busy in factories where fuel and supplies no longer were available; and hungry gangs of foreign workers, emboldened by the imminent defeat of their erstwhile masters, were roaming the streets. Not surprisingly, hundreds landed in Gestapo and police gaols, often for theft of food and for looting, and many were murdered.[31] Such behaviour was by no means confined to the Ruhr. During the last couple of months of the war, police across Germany went on the rampage against "community aliens." Throughout the territory remaining under German control, prisoners were selected, transported to isolated places of execution, shot and dumped in mass graves. This was not simply a response to orders emanating from the centre; it persisted even where no direct link remained with the Nazi leadership in Berlin – for example, in Schleswig-Holstein, which had been cut off from Berlin at the end of March and where the Gestapo and SS continued to murder prisoners.[32] It has been estimated that more than ten thousand people were executed in this way during the last months of the war; roughly 90 per cent of the victims were foreigners, the majority of them labourers from Eastern Europe.[33] The remainder were a few German Jews who had managed to survive the deportations to death camps, Communist resisters and Germans who for some reason or other were considered suspicious.

Does this mean that the agents of the crumbling Nazi police state murdered because they were told to, because they were allowed to, because they wanted to, or because they resorted to violence in an increasingly hopeless situation? It is not easy to disentangle the motives of those who took up Kaltenbrunner's call for "the harshest measures." Many things combined to fuel this wave of murder at the eleventh hour: prejudice against eastern Europeans whose behaviour may have appeared to confirm racist stereotypes; hatred of people whose country-men were pounding Germany into the ground; grudges and thirst for revenge; a radicalization of German police during wartime; fear of possible uprisings and what the prisoners might do once Germany was defeated; and a feeling among members of the Gestapo and SS, who saw little future for themselves in a postwar world, that they might as well take as many people down with them as possible. Clearly race-thinking was important here: the foreigners most frequently tar-geted – generally from eastern Europe, branded as criminal, often ragged and in ill health, disorderly and constituting an apparent threat to Germans now that the Nazi state was disintegrating – were of precisely those groups that the racist regime had targeted for years. At one level, this last outburst of Nazi violence can be regarded, as Ulrich Herbert has observed, "as the epitome of National Socialist racial insanity and of the thinking and behaviour of its proponents."[34] Its perpetrators often were men who had developed their skills in Nazi-occupied eastern Europe – many of the commanders of the Security Police responsible for the wave of murder within Germany in early 1945 had been heads of Security Police squads in the east (for example, in the General Government in Poland)[35] – and now were employed to "strike immediately and brutally" to shore up the home front in the final struggle.[36]

Yet to ascribe this violence solely or necessarily to "racial" motives may be to overlook important aspects of what brought it about. The violence and terror in areas still under German control in early 1945 were aimed not just against prisoners and foreign labourers who found themselves in the wrong place at the wrong time, but against German "racial comrades" as well. As we know, *Wehrmacht* "justice" treated those accused of desertion and cowardice with remarkable severity. Altogether some 15,000 members of the *Wehrmacht* were executed for desertion and more than 20,000 were executed altogether, largely during the final months of the war. (By contrast, a mere 18 German soldiers had been executed for desertion and 48 altogether in the First World War, and only one American soldier and no British soldiers were executed for desertion during the Second World War.)[37] In the final months of the Nazi regime, as inevitable defeat loomed while the German leadership refused to countenance surrender, heightened terror was employed not only against regular troops and members of the *Volkssturm* militia to maintain discipline and prevent military units from falling apart; it also increasingly was aimed at the civilian population as Allied armies drove into Germany. In mid-February the Reich Justice Minister, Otto Thierack, decreed that summary courts martial be set up in areas threatened by Allied occupation; their competence extended to any actions "which threaten German fighting strength or determination to fight."[38] For the military, on 9 March a "Führer Decree" ordered the establishment of "Flying Courts Martial of the Führer," consisting solely of officers and with their own execution squads;[39] in reality these courts martial were little more than roving death squads, and *Wehrmacht* officers who might be tempted to act responsibly and protect the men under their command by ordering tactical retreat were themselves threatened with execution. The summary courts martial liberally handed out death sentences – sentences that often were carried out immediately. Lists of the executed were publicized in the newspapers, to make clear what was in store for anyone who "avoids doing his duty in the decisive hour of his people."[40] Not just soldiers and militia members fell victim; local mayors, government personnel and ordinary citizens who displayed a willingness to surrender also were rewarded for their efforts with execution.[41] As the "Third Reich" neared its end, German soldiers and civilians willing to give up the fight had more to fear from their own regime than they did from the enemy.[42]

The spectre of 1918, when Germany's armies supposedly had been "stabbed in the back" and suffered defeat and dishonor as a result, was never far from the minds of Adolf Hitler and the Nazi (and military) leadership. Although they fully realized in 1945 that Germany was headed for catastrophic defeat, they were determined that that defeat would be "honourable" – that Germany would go down fighting heroically rather than give up, in order to set an example for future generations who might again take up the struggle.[43] A repetition of November 1918 was to be prevented through violence and terror; Germans who appeared "defeatist," who sought to avoid fighting and dying in the futile final battles, were to be hunted down and killed. Their deaths were to be public, to make clear to anyone else with "defeatist" thoughts what might be in store for them. As Günter Grass recalled more than 60 years later, in the interview in which he revealed his membership, as a 17-year-old, in the Waffen-SS, "the first dead that I saw were not Russians, but Germans. They were hanging from the trees, many of them were my age."[44]

The fact that the remnants of the Nazi regime were striking out in all directions suggests that this violence, including the murder of Jews during the last months of the "Third Reich," was rooted not just in antisemitic ideology. It also sprang from motives that simultaneously drove the violence aimed against foreign labourers, "defeatist" German civilians and soldiers during the weeks and months before

Germany's surrender. Although the treatment aimed at Jews remained more deadly than that aimed at any other ethnic group, it was a product not just of murderous antisemitism but also of the general decomposition of a regime whose capacity for systematic, organised and targeted action was becoming more limited by the day but whose residual capacity for violence remained frighteningly powerful.

The murderous rampages during the last months of the "Third Reich" were both facilitated and exacerbated by the destruction of Germany's infrastructure. Communication – which was necessary for the regime to maintain its grip on the population – became increasingly difficult. Services that people in developed industrial societies take for granted – the postal service, telecommunications, railways, local public transport, gas and electricity supply, running water and food distribution – largely ceased to function. Civil administration and the police, as well as military units, increasingly were cut off from the central authorities, from one another, and from the people they were meant to rule. Functionaries in local government or Party offices, in charge of camps or in police stations increasingly were left to their own devices. As Gabriele Hammermann has concluded in her recent examination of the death marches, "[a] decisive characteristic of the evacuations was indeed the collapse of vertical command structures": "[w]ithout institutional control the members of the SS on the ground got unlimited authority and the possibility to decide on life and death."[45] Thus "the decrees of the top leadership of the Nazi regime formed only a framework within which the subordinate authorities, especially the senior SS and police officers, the Gauleiter and the camp commanders *in situ* made their decisions."[46]

Unlike what had occurred over the previous twelve years, the savagery let loose during the first four months of 1945 was not facilitated by the tight control of the Nazi regime over German society. Instead, it was facilitated by the breakdown of order, which crippled the machinery of government but left a willingness and indeed desire to commit violence in utter disregard for the lives of individual human beings. The horrors of the death marches and the terrible conditions in vastly overcrowded concentration and transit camps during early 1945, as well as the terror meted out to German soldiers and civilians and to foreign labourers during the last months of the Reich, were consequences of a willingness, when the opportunity arose, to exercise almost unlimited power over others together with a fundamental disrespect for basic human values. After twelve years of Nazi rule, violence had become second nature to the regime and its representatives; in the end violence was all that it had left to offer.

The murder and mayhem that unfolded within what was left of Nazi-occupied Europe during the first five months of 1945 should cause us to re-assess the explanatory power of the racial paradigm, which has come to dominate scholarly investigations of Nazi Germany over the past couple of two decades. No one can deny that racism lay at the centre of the Nazi "worldview" and informed the intentions of the Nazi leadership and the policies of the Nazi regime. Furthermore, the racial paradigm no doubt has been a necessary corrective to the class-based, Marxist-influenced approaches which informed many studies of Nazi Germany during the 1960s and 1970s, studies which sometimes displayed an extraordinary blindness with regard to the applied racism of the Nazi regime and the campaigns of mass murder that it undertook.[47] However, racist intentions do not sufficiently explain murderous actions; reference to racist, antisemitic ideology provides a necessary but insufficient answer to questions about what led to the violence of the Nazi regime, particularly in its dying days.

This is the problem that lurks behind the brief concluding section of *The Years of Extermination*: that an explanatory framework which works well for the calculated, deliberate murder of the Jewish population in Nazi-occupied Europe is less satisfactory when it comes to the violence that accompanied the disintegration of the Nazi regime. As the regime crumbled, as the power and control of the Berlin authorities disintegrated along with Germany's infrastructure, those lower down the hierarchy – in the camps, gaols, police stations and army units – effectively were handed almost limitless power over those in their grip.[48] They could become, as a *Wehrmacht* captain who had been charged with setting up a summary court martial in Soltau announced in mid-April 1945, "lord over life and death of everyone."[49] Their actions on the ground no longer were dictated by their superiors; as institutional controls crumbled, they were left increasingly to their own, often murderous devices. They may have been guided by a general acceptance of racist Nazi ideology, but their actions also were the product of a self-mobilization, which, as Alf Lüdtke has pointed out for a different context, "imbues a sense of domination to those who actively participate in subjugating others."[50] A cumulative radicalization of the Nazi regime was overtaken by the personal radicalization of fearful, angry, and desperate individuals who found themselves in a position to dispense deadly violence, in a society which had come to be characterized by chaos, brutality and the "loss of any standard for dealing with human lives."[51] As the Nazi regime disintegrated, an ill-defined sense of nationalism and desperation combined with short-lived but virtually unlimited possibilities for self-mobilization and subjugating others. While the Nazi dictatorship crumbled, the essence of Nazism remained: violence. Violence had always been at the core of Nazism; the citizen of Nazi Germany was not so much the person who might participate in politics (for meaningful political participation largely had ceased to exist) as the person who could engage in and profit from violence against others. In the last terrible months of the Nazi regime, this became true in a more direct, immediate sense than ever before. The blood-soaked events of early 1945 were the last chapter of a comprehensive "assault on the roots of civilization,"[52] by a regime that denied the worth of the individual and under whose rule normative constraints on barbarous behaviour had dissolved amidst dictatorship and war.

*Notes*

1    Saul Friedländer, *The Years of Extermination: Nazi Germany and the Jews 1939–1945* (London: Weidenfeld & Nicholson, 2007), 648–52.

2    Daniel Jonah Goldhagen, *Hitler's Willing Executioners. Ordinary Germans and the Holocaust* (London: Abacus, 1996), 327–71. Goldhagen concludes that "these German guards of [. . .] the [. . .] death marches, these ordinary Germans, knew that they were continuing the work that had begun and had been to a great extent already accomplished in the camp system and in the other institutions of killing: to exterminate the Jewish people" (371).

3    Rüdiger Overmans, *Deutsche militärische Verluste im Zweiten Weltkrieg* (Munich: Oldenbourg, 1999), 265–6.

4    See Richard Bessel, *Germany 1945: From War to Peace* (London: Simon & Schuster, 2009), 38–42.

5    Between January and April 1945 the British and Americans delivered more than a quarter of all the bomb tonnage that they dropped on Germany during the entire war; the bombing reached its peak in March 1945, with 133,000 tonnes of bombs dropped in a single month. See Jörg Friedrich, *Der Brand. Deutschland im Bombenkrieg 1940–1945* (Munich: Propyläen-Verlag, 2002), 107, 168; L. F. Ellis and A. E. Warhurst, *Victory in the West. Vol. II. The Defeat of Germany* (London: Her Majesty's Stationary Office, 1968; reprinted Uckfield: East Sussex Naval and Military Press, 2004), 219–28.

6    For example, in the Eifel region in January 1945. See Bundesarchiv-Militärarchiv (=BA-MA), RW 4, Nr. 722, f. 42: Chef OKW to the Chef des NS-Führungsstabes – Wehrmacht, "Reiseeindrücke im Eifelgebiet (Kreise Bitburg – Prüm)", Berlin, 29 Jan. 1945.

7    See Alfred C. Mierzejewski, *The Collapse of the German War Economy, 1944–1945. Allied Air Power and the German National Railway* (Chapel Hill and London: University of North Carolina Press, 1988), 162–76.

8    BA-MA, RW 4, Nr. 703, f. 133: WFSt, "Notiz für Staatssekretärbesprechung am 17.2.1945," "Betr.: Maßnahmen zur Verbesserung der Ernährungslage," 16.2.1945. See also BA-MA, RW 4, Nr, 712, ff. 4–7: [WFSt], 14.2.45.

9    Quoted in Gabriele Stüber, *Der Kampf gegen den Hunger 1945–1950. Die Ernährungslage in der britischen Zone Deutschlands, insbesondere in Schleswig-Holstein und Hamburg* (Neumünster: Wachholtz, 1984), 36.

10   Stanislav Zámecnik, *Das war Dachau* (Frankfurt am Main: Fischer-Taschenbuchverlag, 2007), 361–3.

11   Sybille Steinbacher, *Auschwitz. A History* (London: Penguin Books, 2005), 125–7. See also Andrzej Strzelecki, "Der Todesmarsch der Häftlinge aus dem KL Auschwitz," in Ulrich Herbert, Karin Orth and Christoph Dieckmann (eds), *Die nationalsozialistischen Konzentrationslager. Entwicklung und Struktur* (Göttingen: Wallstein-Verlag, 1998), vol. 2, 1093–1112; Andrzej Strzelecki, *The Evacuation, Dismantling and Liberation of KL Auschwitz* (Oswiecim: Auschwitz-Birkenau State Museum, 2001).

12   Zámecnik, *Das war Dachau*, 362–3.

13   On 15 August 1944 the total had stood at 524,286: 379,167 men and 145,119 women. See Martin Broszat, "Nationalsozialistische Konzentrationslager 1933–1945," in Martin Broszat, Hans Buchheim, Hans-Adolf Jacobsen and Helmut Krausnick (eds), *Anatomie des SS-Staates* (Munich: Deutscher Taschenbuch Verlag, 1967), vol. 2, 11–133, here 132; Daniel Blatman, "Die Todesmärsche – Entscheidungsträger, Mörder und Opfer," in Herbert, Orth and Dieckmann (eds), *Die nationalsozialistischen Konzentrationslager*, vol. 2, 1063–92, here 1066–7. Friedländer discusses this in *The Years of Extermination*, 648–52.

14   Broszat, "Nationalsozialistische Konzentrationslager 1933–1945," 132–3; Yehuda Bauer, "The Death-Marches, January-May 1945," *Modern Judaism* 3 (1983): 1–21, here 2. See also Jan Erik Schulte, *Zwangsarbeit und Vernichtung. Oswald Pohl und das SS-Wirtschafts-Verwaltungsamt 1933–1945* (Paderborn: Schöningh, 2001), 405.

15   Harry Stein, "Funktionswandel des Konzentrationslagers Buchenwald im Spiegel der Lagerstatistiken," in Herbert, Orth and Dieckmann (eds), *Die nationalsozialistischen Konzentrationslager*, vol. 1, 167–92, here 186–7.

16   Gabriele Hammermann, "Das Kriegsende in Dachau," in Bernd A. Rusinek (ed.), *Kriegsende 1945. Verbrechen, Katastrophen, Befreiungen in nationaler und internationaler Perspektive* (Göttingen: Wallstein-Verlag, 2004), 27–53, here 27.

17   Michel Fabréguet, "Entwicklung und Veränderung der Funktionen des Konzentrationslagers Mauthausen 1938–1945," in Herbert, Orth and Dieckmann (eds), *Die nationalsozialistischen Konzentrationslager*, vol. 1, 193–214, here 202, 209.

18 Broszat, "Nationalsozialistische Konzentrationslager 1933–1945," 132; Jens-Christian Wagner, *Produktion des Todes, Das KZ Mittelbau-Dora* (Göttingen: Wallstein-Verlag, 2001), 201–8.
19 Ibid., 272–3.
20 Quoted in Gabriele Hammermann, "Die Todesmärsche aus den Konzentrationslagern 1944/1945," in Cord Arendes, Edgar Wolfrum and Jörg Zedler (eds), *Terror nach Innen. Verbrechen am Ende des Zweiten Weltkrieges* (Göttingen: Wallstein-Verlag, 2006), 122–148, here 124.
21 Ibid., 131.
22 Ibid., 128.
23 Blatman, "Die Todesmärsche," 1088; Hammermann, "Die Todesmärsche," 134–5, 139–40. For details of the massacres at Palmnicken and Gardelegen, see Reinhard Henkys, "Ein Todesmarsch in Ostpreußen," *Dachauer Hefte* 20 (2004), 3–21, and Diana Gring, "Das Massaker von Gardelegen," *Dachauer Hefte* 20 (2004): 112–26.
24 Hammermann, "Die Todesmärsche," 129.
25 Nikolaus Wachsmann, *Hitler's Prisons: Legal Terror in Nazi Germany* (New Haven and London: Yale University Press, 2004), 323–38.
26 Bauer, "The Death-Marches," 6.
27 Quoted in Gabriele Lotfi, *KZ der Gestapo. Arbeitserziehungslager im Dritten Reich* (Stuttgart and Munich: Deutsche Verlags-Anstalt, 2000), 292–3.
28 Ibid., 295.
29 For example, as American artillery was shelling Hemer (on 9 April) and Iserlohn (on 11 April) at least 13 foreign prisoners (who had been caught stealing food or looting) were executed. See ibid., 309.
30 Quoted in ibid., 277–8.
31 See Ulrich Herbert, *Hitler's Foreign Workers: Enforced Foreign Labour in Germany under the Third Reich* (Cambridge: Cambridge University Press, 1997), 370–4; Bernd A. Rusinek, "'Maskenlose Zeit'. Der Zerfall der Gesellschaft im Krieg," in Ulrich Borsdorf and Mathilde Jamin (eds), *Überleben im Krieg. Kriegserfahrung in einer Industrieregion 1939–1945* (Reinbek bei Hamburg: Rowohlt, 1989), 180–94, here 190–1. See also Gerhard Paul, "'Diese Erschießungen haben mich innerlich gar nicht mehr berührt' Die Kriegsendeverbrechen der Gestapo 1944/45," in Gerhard Paul and Klaus-Michael Mallmann (eds), *Die Gestapo im Zweiten Weltkrieg. "Heimatfront" und besetztes Europa* (Darmstadt: Wissenschaftliche Buchgesellschaft, 2000), 552–62.
32 See Gerhard Paul, *Landunter. Schleswig-Holstein und das Hakenkreuz* (Münster: Westfälisches Dampfboot, 2001), 298–300.
33 Paul, "'Diese Erschießungen haben mich innerlich gar nicht mehr berührt,'" 543, 561.
34 Herbert, *Hitler's Foreign Workers*, 374.
35 For example, at the end of 1944 the former head of the Security Police in Warsaw, the *SS-Standartenführer* Dr Ludwig Hahn, took command of the Security Police in Münster; at the beginning of February 1945 the *SS-Standartenführer* Rudolf Batz, who had headed the Security Police in Cracow, arrived to command the Security Police in Dortmund. See Lotfi, *KZ der Gestapo*, 278.
36 The quotation is from Walter Albath, the head of the Security Police in Düsseldorf, in late January 1945. See ibid., *KZ der Gestapo*, 277.
37 Steven R. Welch, "'Harsh but Just'? German Military Justice in the Second World War: A Comparative Study of the Court-Martialling of German and US Deserters," *German History* 17 (1999): 369–99, here 389. See, generally, Manfred Messerschmidt and Fritz Wüllmer, *Die Wehrmachtjustiz im Dienste des Nationalsozialismus. Zerstörung einer Legende* (Baden Baden: Nomos, 1987); Stephen G. Fritz, *Endkampf: Soldiers, Civilians, and the Death of the Third Reich* (Lexington, KY: University Press of Kentucky, 2004), 116–39; Norbert Haase, "Justizterror in der *Wehrmacht* am Ende des Zweiten Weltkrieges," in Arendes, Wolfrum and Zedler (eds), *Terror nach Innen*, 80–102.
38 Manfred Overesch, *Das III. Reich 1939–1945. Eine Tageschronik der Politik, Wirtschaft, Kultur* (Düsseldorf: Droste, 1983), 582.
39 Hans Vrobel, *Verurteilt zur Demokratie. Justiz und Justizpolitik in Deutschland 1945–1949* (Heidelberg: Decker & Müller, 1989), 95.
40 *Pommersche Zeitung*, 27 Feb. 1945, printed in Instytut Historii Uniwersitetu Szczecinskiego, ed., *Stettin 1945–1946: Dokumente – Erinnerungen* (Rostock: Hinstorff Verlag, 1995), 29–31.

41   See, for example, Hans-Erich Volkmann, "Südwestdeutschland und das Ende des Zweiten Weltkrieges," *Freiburger Universitätsblätter* 34, no. 130 (Dec. 1995): 30–35, here 34. In Breslau the fanatical Nazi Gauleiter, Karl Hanke, ordered the execution of the city's deputy mayor, Wolfgang Spielhagen, at the end of January 1945 for reputedly voicing opposition to the Silesian capital being declared a "fortress" city. See Sebastian Siebel-Achenbach, *Lower Silesia from Nazi Germany to Communist Poland 1942–49* (Basingstoke and New York: Macmilan, 1994), 61,

42   Michael Geyer, "Endkampf 1918 and 1945. German Nationalism, Annihilation, and Self-Destruction," in Alf Lüdtke and Bernd Weisbrod (eds), *No Man's Land of Violence: Extreme Wars in the 20th Century* (Göttingen: Wallstein-Verlag, 2006), 36–67, here 61.

43   See Bernd Wegner, "Hitler, der Zweite Weltkrieg und die Choreographie des Untergangs," *Geschichte und Gesellschaft* 26 (2000): 492–518; Hans Mommsen, "The Indian summer and the collapse of the Third Reich: the last act," in Hans Mommsen (ed.), *The Third Reich between Vision and Reality: New Perspectives on German History 1918–1945* (Oxford and New York: Berg, 2001), 109–27, here 119; Geyer, "Endkampf 1918 and 1945," 54–5.

44   "Warum ich nach sechzig Jahren mein Schweigen breche. Eine deutsche Jugend: Günter Grass spricht zum ersten Mal über sein Erinnerungsbuch und seine Mitgliedschaft in der Waffen-SS," *Frankfurter Allgemeine Zeitung*, 12 Aug. 2006, no. 186, 33.

45   Hammermann, "Die Todesmärsche," 142. The same point is made by Diana Gring in her examination of the massacre at Gardelegen in April 1945, "Das Massaker von Gardelegen," 121, where she speaks of the "detachment of the upper from the middle and lower levels of authority, that is, the displacement of hierarchical command structures and the absence of central control."

46   Hammermann, "Die Todesmärsche," 124.

47   This has been stated forcefully by Michael Burleigh and Wolfgang Wippermann in *The Racial State. Germany 1933–1945* (Cambridge: Cambridge University Press, 1991), 306–7: "The Third Reich was intended to be a racial rather than a class society. This fact in itself makes existing theories, whether based upon modernisation, totalitarianism, or global theories of Fascism, poor heuristic devices for a greater understanding of what was a singular regime without precedent or parallel."

48   This point is made in Hammermann, "Die Todesmärsche," 139.

49   "Herr über Leben und Tod Aller." Quoted in Willy Klapproth, *Kriegschronik 1945 der Stadt Soltau und Umgebung, mit Beiträgen zur Kriegsgeschichte 1945 der Süd- und Mittelheide* (Soltau: Stadtverwaltung, 1955), 34. A few days later this summary court martial sentenced to death three soldiers for desertion and one civilian for making defeatist statements while drunk; the sentences were carried out immediately. See Klapproth, *Kriegschronik*, 70.

50   Alf Lüdtke, "Explaining forced migration," in Richard Bessel and Claudia B. Haake (eds), *Removing Peoples: Forced Removal in the Modern World* (Oxford: Oxford University Press, 2009), 13–32, here 29.

51   Reinhard Henkys, *Die nationalsozialistischen Gewaltverbrechen. Geschichte und Gericht* (Stuttgart and Berlin: Landeszentrale für politische Bildungsarbeit, 1964), 166.

52   Ian Kershaw, *Hitler 1889–1936: Hubris* (London: Penguin Books, 1998), xxx.

# 14

# Opportunistic Killings and Plunder of Jews by their Neighbors – a Norm or an Exception in German Occupied Europe?

## Jan T. Gross

I would like to shed light in this paper on the killings and plunder of Jews by local people in German-occupied Poland – crimes that occurred on the periphery of the Holocaust. In terms of numbers of Jewish victims, this was a very small fraction of the total killed by the Nazis. The loot that remained in local hands – *not* equally insignificant, primarily because of the housing stock which was taken over by local residents – was also only a small fraction of the Jewish wealth that had been plundered. But as mysteries pertaining to the Holocaust abound, it is precisely these marginal phenomena – adversarial interaction between Jews and their fellow citizens in occupied societies – which were catapulted decades later into the center of preoccupation for national historiographies and have attracted extraordinary public interest both in eastern and in western Europe.

I use the anachronistic east/west distinction simply as a marker for radically different regimes of occupation imposed by the Nazis to the west and to the east of Germany. Despite all the differences – whether in France, the Low Countries, or in Poland – the relationships between indigenous populations and the Jews during the war remain a live issue, drawing a lot of attention from the mass media, public intellectuals and professional historians: as if they were some centerpiece of what had happened during the war in general. It might be a marginal issue in the historiography of the Shoah but, judging by public and professional attention, it is a "sticky" one – that is, one that cannot be easily avoided – as far as European societies under occupation are concerned.

To address this subject, one needs to contend with yet another sort of marginality, due to sources at historians' disposal. In the eastern European context – in addition to depositions taken in courts, which after the war tried a number of perpetrators of such crimes – for the most part the evidence comes from personal accounts by Jewish survivors. But such information, when provided by Jews during the war, has often been viewed with incredulity.

In part this was a perverse consequence of the "unbelievable" radicalism of Nazi policies. "Disbelief," I am quoting now from an essay by Geoffrey Hartman, "touched the survivors themselves [...]. [T]wo phrases stand out in their testimony: 'I was there' and 'I could not believe what my eyes had seen.' The second phrase is not purely rhetorical. Appelfeld writes: 'Everything that happened was so gigantic, so inconceivable, that the witness even seemed like a fabricator to himself.'"[1] (I can testify to this bafflement with the outsized scale of events reported by witnesses, from personal experience: It took me four years and a pure, lucky, coincidence to realize that Szmul Wassersztajn's concluding paragraph describing the crime in Jedwabne was not an exaggeration or a figure of speech but a pretty faithful description of what had happened.)[2] When we add a generally demeaning stereotype of Jews in the European Christian cultural tradition we can appreciate why Jewish sources were *a priori* treated with deep ambivalence.

The Israeli-French historian, Renée Poznanski describes a "generalized skepticism of high functionaries of the Foreign Office." "As a general principle," she characterizes the state of mind in British government circles, "Jews have a tendency to exaggerate the severity of persecution to which they are subjected."[3] A weighty point of view when held by those who controlled the most important propaganda vehicle broadcasting into occupied Europe – the BBC. In order to ensure the effectiveness of war propaganda, their concern was not to exaggerate any claims and *especially* those pertaining to the persecution of Jews – the latter, in order not to give plausibility to a German argument that the war was being waged by the Allies on behalf of and in the interest of the Jews.

Again, from east to west, from the Gaullist *France-libre* broadcasts to radio programs authorized by General Sikorski's Polish government in exile, those trying to beef up anti-Nazi resistance in their home countries were anxious not to emphasize the victimization of the Jews, lest they render plausible the Nazi arguments that Jews were pulling all the strings in London (and, it goes without saying, in America as well), fearing to go against the predominant antisemitic mood of public opinion in countries under occupation. There should not be any "privileged" victims in France, and *discretion* in Jewish matters is advised, Gaullist leadership was warned by its rapporteurs from across the Channel. The Polish prime minister, General Sikorski, was bluntly told by his underground commanders that he should cut expressions of sympathy for the Jews from radio broadcasts, because they made a bad impression in Poland.

*Pace* idiosyncratic views of the British Foreign Office, or reasons why the plight of the Jews was de-emphasized in European countries under occupation – as far as the Anglo-Saxon study of the war is concerned, the original direct culprit may have been none other than Raul Hilberg, the doyen of Holocaust historiography. We are all indebted to him and will be forever merely standing on his shoulders, but he dismissed victims' personal narratives as unreliable as they were – from his point of view – irrelevant.

He was interested in the German machinery of mass murder and demonstrated how its functioning can be pieced together from documentation generated by *institutional* participants in the process. And once the subject opened up, historians, for some time, were primarily interested in the perpetrators – naturally, a story to be dug up in the German archives rather than in memoirs of surviving Jews.

## EVALUATING INDIVIDUAL DEPOSITIONS

Other things being equal (even though they never are), the problem of availing ourselves of "testimony," of eye-"witnessed" accounts, about the Holocaust derives, it seems to me, from processing the evidence according to ordinary procedures and linguistic usage of categories employed. When we take in hand an eye-"witness" account of a Holocaust victim we mentally place it in a familiar context: we read it as a statement from an injured party. There is a victim and a victimizer in the scenario and we hear in the narrative the victim's side of the story; presumably – one side of the story. And where there are "sides," or, if you will – parties to a conflict – then we expect to hear from one party only partial truth.

It takes a moment and a *prise de conscience*, to realize that the vocabulary we employ – "victim," "testimony," or "witness" – puts a deceptive frame on our thinking. The "semantic heredity" of such concepts leads us astray, because there is no advocacy in the narratives of Holocaust victims and they do not make revindications.[4] I know that we should not naïvely accept an author's stated intentions as the one and only guide to the reading of a text, but they should not be discarded out of hand, either. We must remember, therefore, that Jewish testimonies about the Shoah have been *deliberately* written in order to provide an *exact* account of the catastrophe. This is evidenced in numerous memoirs and journals kept by Jews at the time. The same intention informed collective efforts such as the "*Oneg Shabbat*" initiative by Emanuel Ringelblum in the Warsaw ghetto,[5] or the daunting work of the archivists from the ghetto in Kovno; or, for example, Herman Kruk's extraordinary chronicle *The Last Days of the Jerusalem of Lithuania* from Vilnius.[6]

Since it appeared impossible to save the mass of Jewish people methodically annihilated in the Nazi-organized killing process, a sense of obligation grew among the Jewish record-keepers (they say so explicitly and repeatedly) that they must at least preserve the evidence of the very process of destruction. Thus revealed, future readers cannot dismiss authors' intentions lightly. Clearly their aim was to produce an account of what happened, not to embellish the story. If anything the record keepers' difficulty was the reverse – the reality surrounding them was such an exaggeration of everything people were accustomed to in the course of everyday life that their concern could only be whether posterity would be capable of believing in what had really happened, the record as it were.[7]

And then there was the flip-side of the same concern: In virtually all Holocaust-era diaries – detailed, unique, specific to the place and reflecting the vagaries of each author's individual destiny – one finds a common theme – a recurring line: "Whatever we may have foreseen and written about many times," (I am quoting from Herman Kruk's entry of 28 October 1942), "it is all hardly a fraction of the actual situation." One cannot grapple with the surrounding reality, the diarists all seem to be saying, it cannot be fully communicated.

Holocaust memoirists labored against enormous odds, most strikingly against their own incredulity at what was happening around them. Their predicament was bewildering: nobody will believe us if we say it how it was and yet we can at best only tell a fraction of what has actually happened. Did they have any need or inducement to exaggerate or embellish their narratives? I think not. Rather, their one and only ultimate satisfaction – a hopeless task, we know – could come from being able to say to themselves as readers of what they have left us: "Yes, that's exactly what happened." They left carefully crafted, deliberately assembled, meaningful documents of the epoch, which deserve to be treated as such. In order to make sense of our century's dark times we should read their testimony as it was conceived – one line at a time.[8]

Personal testimonies may have finally entered the mainstream of Holocaust historiography with the most recent grand synthesis, Saul Friedländer's *The Years of Extermination* (published in 2007), where the author draws on such material abundantly. He takes a radical stand with respect to individual testimonies when he writes in the introduction:

> By its very nature, by dint of its humanness and freedom, an individual voice suddenly arising in the course of an ordinary historical narrative of events such as presented here can tear through seamless interpretation and pierce the (mostly involuntary) smugness of scholarly detachment and 'objectivity'. Such a disruptive function would hardly be necessary in a history of the price of wheat on the eve of the French Revolution, but it is essential to the historical representation of mass extermination and other sequences of mass suffering that 'business as usual historiography' necessarily domesticates and 'flattens' … The goal of historical knowledge is to domesticate disbelief, to explain it away. In this book, I wish to offer a thorough historical study of the extermination of the Jews of Europe, without eliminating or domesticating that initial sense of disbelief.[9]

So far it has been a struggle to fend off criticisms, which easily dismiss writing on the basis of personal documents as not properly grounded and providing merely anecdotal evidence. In the meantime, for an entire spectrum of interesting subjects (the fate of Jews hiding on the so-called "Aryan" side, or resistance in provincial ghettos, for example), almost no other empirical evidence is available. The task before us then, is to figure out how to obtain a reliable understanding of a general phenomenon (in my case: killings and plunder of Polish Jews by their fellow citizens) on the basis of personal statements, which, by their very nature, offer only episodic and discrete information.

## HOW JEWS WERE MURDERED IN THE COUNTRYSIDE OF THE KIELCE VOIVODESHIP

One should note that killings and plunder of the Jews were intimately related activities during the war. In "almost all crimes [of murder that I am going to talk about below] "plunder of Jews took place as well, and was one of the predominant motives."[10] I will now draw on court depositions from cases where killings of Jews were tried after the war in order to analyze the phenomenon.

Ever since the story of the murder in Jedwabne was debated in Poland, historians of the Holocaust began to study court cases prosecuted after the war on the basis of the 31 August 1944 decree of the provisional Polish government (it's customary to refer to them now in a shorthand, as the so-called "August" cases).[11] The decree provided for criminalization of broadly conceived aid and assistance furthering German occupiers' goals to the detriment of Polish society. Occasionally, the murder of Jews was prosecuted under this law as well. Some two decades after the war, all the "August" cases from court districts around the country were conveniently assembled in one archival collection under the custody of the Main Commission for Investigation of Hitlerite Crimes.[12] Today, they are in the holdings of the Institute of National Memory.

I'll draw here on a very useful contribution of two historians who examined all the "August" cases in the Kielce voivodeship containing evidence about murders of Jews by the Poles in the countryside of this region. Altogether about 250 people were brought to justice there for the alleged involvement in the murder of several hundred Jews. The authors, Alina Skibinska and Jakub Petelewicz, complemented their knowledge acquired from archival readings with interviews conducted in the area.

A historian of the Holocaust would immediately understand that this is a source which reveals only a "tip of the iceberg" of the phenomenon under study – partly due to a reluctance of prosecutorial authorities after the war to bring such cases to court.[13] But most importantly this is a body of evidence from which Jewish voices are (almost) entirely absent. These were not cases brought by Jews. The Jews that appear in these depositions had been murdered. There were no Jewish witnesses left to testify about the killings.

On the other hand this material – even though affording us only a partial insight – represents the entire collection of a certain kind of evidence bearing on the issue. So, with respect to it we cannot be accused of a sample bias. By itself, this does not yet answer satisfactorily whether we can obtain a reliable general portrait of what happened (there could have been a bias on the part of prosecutorial authorities bringing the cases – for example one would still have to know more about the ecology of the crime to make sure that all murder episodes have not clustered in some small sub-region of the area, or if the entire region can be considered "typical" with respect to this kind of crime and similar to the rest of Poland). To allay doubts on this last point, I will mention a single statistic from a recent study of another region, *rzeszowszczyna* (around the city of Rzeszow) where murders of Jews by local Poles are documented in at least 110 locations.[14] In any case, taking all of the evidence of a particular kind under consideration is always a good practice.

We need to keep in mind what is at stake here and what kind of question we are bringing to the evidence at our disposal. Essentially we want to be able to adjudicate between two interpretations of the phenomenon of murder and plunder of Jews by their fellow Polish citizens during the war. One would simply be that "stuff happens": people get killed during the war. There was a lot of violence all around and so it got privatized at times – banditry was rampant and people lost their moral bearings. There is always "scum" in society and one should not generalize on the basis of isolated cases – in short, this was deviant behavior. Or else, it wasn't. In order to find out I suggest that we must read the content of the cases to understand what actually happened.

I am now going to quote extensively from the above mentioned article describing numerous murders of Jews hiding in the Kielce countryside, by the Polish population. I have spliced together fragments of text scattered over several pages, in a continuous narrative:

> Killings by shooting [...], with an axe, or using a wooden pole [...] were accompanied by acts of physical and psychological cruelty towards Jews who had been caught: women were raped, people were beaten, pushed around, cursed and verbally humiliated. The accused [i.e. the alleged perpetrators of crimes against the Jews] [...] were peasants, [Polish] dark-blue policemen from outposts closest to the site of murder, members of various guerilla organizations who were frequently the very peasants living during the day in their villages, rather than staying in forest detachments. In many cases (*w bardzo wielu sprawach*) the accused held some position or function in the local officialdom: village heads, deputy village heads, district heads, employees of district office, members and commanders of local fire brigades, members of the village guard. [...] They were, without exception, of Roman-Catholic denomination, grown men in general, without prior criminal records. [...] They had stable family lives, wives and children. Some of them were members of the Communist party (PPR) or worked in the People's Militia (the police force) after the war. [...] By virtue of their functions at least a part of them belonged to the local elite in the countryside [...].
>
> Women had often witnessed and observed what had happened. They belonged to passive crowds, which carried the killings with the hands of a few of their most active participants. [...] One could even venture a proposition, based on depositions from witnesses and the accused, that there were many active participants and observers in almost all of these crimes. [...] As far as murders perpetrated in villages we can even speak about an aggressive, criminal crowd, where a few people play an initiating and leading role, while everybody else, by witnessing their crime provide at the same time a background, and a 'moral' alibi for the crime committed.
>
> In a certain sense the entire village takes part in it, with a different degree of involvement or witnessing, and after the war the entire village keeps in its collective unconscious and memory events that then took place with its participation. This anonymous crowd constitutes an extremely important element for the analysis of this phenomenon. Its presence allows the diffusion of responsibility for the crimes committed and in a certain way, silently gives permission to do what had been done to the Jews.
>
> [In numerous files] we read detailed descriptions of the crimes, during which victims and perpetrators talked to each other. Jews defended themselves, begged and appealed to the conscience and pity of the killers ('After this man was killed this little boy stood

up and said to everybody present: Poles, spare my life, I am not guilty of anything, it is my misfortune that I am a Jew'). They tried to bribe the perpetrators with what they still had and thus save their lives ('We were playing cards when somebody dropped in and said that a Jew had been caught [...]. I went out doors. In front of the house stood a group of people and Moshek begged to be let go. He was with his little son, and they cried. [...] This little Jew said: "give them boots, daddy, maybe they'll let us go"'). Crimes were perpetrated against individuals known, often by name, against neighbors, against local folks.

A special category of perpetrators were the functionaries of the [Polish] dark-blue police [...], in their majority prewar employees of the state police. Policemen implicated in crimes against the Jews were heads of families, typically with several children at home. Their material status was usually rather good. [...] In their actions against the Jewish population one notices a large element of freedom and independence from the superior German authorities. [...] In the cases at hand there was not a single instance in which apprehended Jews were escorted back to a ghetto or to a police station – which would also mean death for them. They are usually killed right away or in a neighboring forest, and local peasants are ordered to bury the corpses [...].

The direct motive to commit the majority of murders and denunciations of Jews hiding in the countryside was the desire to plunder them, to take over their belongings, which were imagined to be considerable. This was a pernicious consequence of the stereotype of Jewish wealth. [...] Peasants imagined that by killing these people, they would get hold of their riches. One should suppose, that in a psychological sense the fact that hiding Jews were paying for shelter and food – often paying very high prices (by local standards), reinforced the belief that they had lots of money, which could be taken from them with impunity. Indirectly, the same motive was underlying murders of Jews who no longer could pay those giving them shelter [...]. People were getting rid of them, just as they were getting rid of Jews who had witnessed crimes committed earlier.

In over a dozen closely researched cases there is mention of characteristic and telling facts which accompanied the crime. After finishing, peasants gathered in the apartment of one of the participants to drink vodka, as if to celebrate their joint deeds with a meal, to divide the spoils and probably also to decompress [...]. [According to] depositions of the accused Wladyslaw Dusza: 'After they were thrown into a ditch [and] their clothes were taken off [...] we went to the apartment of Pawlik Wladyslaw, who invited us for supper and served us vodka.' [...] In the deposition of the accused Stawiarski [we read] 'After we drank vodka the mother of Jozef Dusza announced, speaking to us, that she is making for her son a wedding, she said so because the Jewesses were already delivered to the police station, and her son before taking them there, used to visit one of the Jewesses.'

The above summary does not represent *my* reading of the evidence from the files of "August" cases tried in the Kielce district court. It has been provided by two young Polish historians. It offers a composite image, and all the enumerated elements certainly could not be found in every episode they took under scrutiny. But it is nevertheless abundantly clear that any concept of deviance would have to be stretched beyond capacity to encompass the kind of behavior that Skibinska and Petelewicz have described.

Instead, we can note multiple ways in which killings of Jews by peasants in the Kielce countryside were sanctioned socially. Regular members of the community took part in them, not miscreants or "marginal" people easily identifiable in rural society. Indeed, the local elite's participation bestowed upon these crimes a kind of official imprimatur. Killings were carried out openly, often publicly, drawing crowds of onlookers, and, to quote from an article by an American legal scholar, "open criminality implicates all who know of the conduct and fail to act."[15] All in all the analogy which comes to mind as characteristic of the social atmosphere associated with the deed is that of a lynching as a collective experience.

Direct perpetrators of these crimes, the most active participants, as far as one can tell, remained members of local communities in good standing (as was mentioned earlier, some joined the Communist Party and the People's Militia after the war). In almost every file, there are group affidavits signed by inhabitants of the village where murder took place, "vouching for the good and honorable character of the accused [...]. This is proof," Skibinska and Petelewicz observe, "that the village was in solidarity with the accused and that in the consciousness of its inhabitants there was no need to prosecute or to expiate in any way for the crime."[16] In the conclusion of their article the authors finally draw on interviews they conducted in the region sixty years after the events. They note an "almost total lack of interest in the fate of murdered Jews," and that "if any emotion could be found [in conversations] it was of disapproval directed towards the victims." Given the deep religiosity of the peasants they wonder why obligations vis-à-vis other human beings derived from Christian ethics were never invoked.[17]

## A CLOSE-UP OF A MURDER SCENE

I propose now to visit a murder scene, in the village of Gniewczyn, in another part of the country – a large village of 5,000 inhabitants split administratively in two. In May 1942, a group of local notables including two village heads, a commander of the voluntary fire brigade, and half a dozen other associates, ferreted out several Jewish families hiding in the vicinity.[18] Men, women, and children – 16 persons altogether – were brought to the house of the Trinczer family which was centrally situated in the village, not far from the church. The captured Jews were held there for several days in two rooms separated by a small kitchen. One of the rooms was turned into a torture chamber. Women were raped there, while men were subjected to water torture to make them reveal the whereabouts of goods left with friendly peasants, goods on which they drew to pay for food and shelter while in hiding. Once the torturers obtained the desired information their emissaries visited peasant households demanding the surrender of "Jewish rags," lest the Gestapo be informed.

The word got around in Gniewczyn that the Jews were being forced to give up what remained of their belongings. One of the women managed to run away from the torture house, but was caught by her pursuer, an acquaintance with whom she went to school, who dragged her by the hair back across the village. Her mother, who earlier avoided the dragnet, showed up the next morning kneeling on the steps to the church to beg the priest for the lives of her daughter and grandchildren. But he declined to help.

After a few days, when the torturers concluded that they had all available Jewish property, they called the gendarmes. The Germans came to the village, where they were fed well. The Jews were then taken into the courtyard, ordered one by one to lie face down on the ground and everyone, beginning with the small children, was shot dead.

We owe this detailed description to an eyewitness, a boy 14 years old at the time, who wrote up the story now, after, he says, all the main protagonists had died. But for his narrative, which appeared in the April 2008 issue of the Catholic monthly *Znak*, a historian's inquiry revealed only one trace of this mass murder in printed sources – a note in the registry of German crimes kept by the earlier mentioned Commission, stating that 16 Jews were murdered in 1942 in the house of Leib Trinczer by gendarmes who came from a nearby town. That it was a crime for which local Poles were responsible, a well known fact in the entire community, there was no mention at all.[19]

The close-up of the Gniewczyn murder scene foregrounds two phenomena of which one is well known and the other is a speculation. Memory of wartime atrocities against the Jews is very well preserved (and passed on from generation to generation) in the Polish countryside. Journalists and scholars stumble upon it every time they take the trouble to make an inquiry. Reporters who went early to Jedwabne, before it became the site of a national scandal, got local folks to speak un-self-consciously about it. Ethnographic studies conducted in the countryside on other, related, subjects – by Alina Cala in the 1980s, or Joanna Tokarska-Bakir in 2006, for example – also revealed the same, almost inadvertently.[20] I believe that the reason is that these occurrences were quite common and therefore quasi-"normal" (and simultaneously also rare events with "significance" that ever took place there), and thus they remained a subject of conversations for years to come at local gatherings.

The second significant aspect of the murder revealed in this close-up is the role torture played in the Gniewczyn crime. I suspect that torture was ubiquitous in peasant-Jewish encounters. One reads about brutalization of Jewish victims in numerous depositions. To quote one more example from a study by historian Jan Grabowski, who more than anyone has contributed to our knowledge of the phenomenon:

A certain Marian Haba sought shelter in Cholerzyn (a village not far away from today's Krakow international airport in Balice). He remained in hiding, in the village, until the locals heard a rumor that Haba had gold stashed in the area. A 'Blue' policeman summoned a while later by the peasants, said: 'When I arrived in the village, I saw not a human being but a shapeless form. People told me they had killed the Jew because he was said to have buried five kilograms of gold.[21]

Yet historians, as a rule, did not pay much attention to such details, focusing on the fact of the murder instead.

But if indeed, when time and circumstances permitted, local folks applied themselves to force the Jews to reveal where their mythical "gold" had been stashed (there is plenty of evidence that rape of women and beatings were a common occurrence),[22] we get a better understanding of a troublesome element of Jewish wartime memory, which comes up in conversations with survivors and in their written testimonies – that the Poles (or Ukrainians, or Lithuanians, as the case may be) were "worse than the Germans." This attitude is often viewed by Polish historians or Polish media as proof of prejudice that leads Jews to absolve the Germans from responsibility for the Holocaust and blame it on the Poles instead. Why would it be so? If it is not a myopic, prejudiced, reconstruction of what happened – what does it mean?

My hypothesis, so far, had been that it was a manifestation of a sense of betrayal, and therefore of Jewish moral suffering at the realization of being under murderous assault by people they knew, by their neighbors. This is probably true, as far as it goes, but it may be as well that death at the hands of neighbors was literally very painful.

## THE SIGNIFICANCE OF "THICK DESCRIPTION"

Much of the evidence about killings or denunciations of Jews by peasants in the Polish countryside consists of uncorroborated personal testimony from survivors, their relatives, or acquaintances. It is typically brief and notes the facts without many details. Much of the time it is second-hand information, for example knowledge that was sought out and acquired, after the fact, by a concerned family member. Thus, the body of evidence is not "systematic" in any sense of the word; and it has not been part of any "record." Strictly speaking, we should, therefore, abstain from generalizing observations – such as whether peasant killings of Jews ought to be considered a normal occurrence or deviant behavior – on the basis solely of what we can find about the *frequency* and *distribution* of these crimes.

We can pose such questions only because frequency is sufficiently high and distribution sufficiently broad to preclude an easy refutation that these were isolated episodes in strictly confined areas. But the heart of the argument has to be made on the basis of a "thick description." Wherever evidence provides an opportunity we have to reconstruct *how* these murders were conducted and then, if a number of detailed narratives would indeed exhibit concurring social characteristics, we can make a leap towards a general understanding of the phenomenon.

It is so because a society with a common past and shared customs and institutions has a degree of internal coherence. One should view it as analogous to a text or a system, rather than a quilt stitched together from randomly assembled pieces. As a result, practices and attitudes engaging fundamental values (those concerning life and death, for example) must be intelligible across society – beyond the confines of any local community. Hence, even in the absence of firm knowledge about the distribution and frequency of peasant murders of Jews, *we can still tell whether they were an accepted social practice* from close analysis of a discrete number of episodes which demonstrate *how* such crimes were perpetrated. Given the character of these murders (that they were open, widely discussed public events) and given the identity of people involved, which is documented in detail (that these were regular folks, including members of local elites), a "thick description" of localized community events yields knowledge about behavior in peasant society at large.

## CHANGE IN SOCIAL NORMS CONCERNING JEWISH PROPERTY

Let me now move to the question of plunder, which, as I already mentioned, is intimately related to the killings of Jews by their neighbors. We must be aware that we are operating at the very end of a long food chain here. Real massive plunder took place as a result of state action in western Europe and Germany proper, where Jews were solidly middle class and had substantial wealth which had been taken over through a long process of Aryanization, forced emigration, outright confiscation and also deportation and killings. "Throughout the twelve years of the Third Reich," writes Saul Friedländer, "looting of Jewish property was of the essence. It was the most easily understood and most widely adhered-to aspect of the anti-Jewish campaign, rationalized, if necessary, by the simplest ideological tenets."[23] The Third Reich benefited most from the plunder of Jewish wealth, but Vichy France, for example, tried to get its cut as well. This is, therefore, not a uniquely east European story, though the "hands on" aspect of it is.

Mass killings in the Podlasie region, of which the murder in Jedwabne was but one episode, were accompanied by the widespread and thorough plunder of Jewish property. It would be more difficult to name townspeople who *did not* plunder Jewish houses while their inhabitants were being incinerated in a large barn on the outskirts of Radzilow, an eyewitness to the murders told a journalist sixty years later. Everybody seemed to be in the streets grabbing what they could. In the well-known diary of Dr Zygmunt Klukowski from Szczebrzeszyn – in another part of the country – we read how "a lot of [peasants with] wagons came from the countryside and stood waiting the entire day for the moment when they could start looting, [as rumors had it that Jews would be 'resettled' on that day]. News keeps reaching us from all directions about the scandalous behavior of segments of the local population who rob emptied Jewish apartments. I am sure our little town will be no different."[24] Symbolically most evocative were the calls of pogrom organizers in the hamlet of Wasilkow, "who were running around and screaming: 'Don't break anything, don't rip it up, all this is already ours'" ('*nie lamac niczego, niczego nie rozrywac, to wszystko i tak jest juz nasze*').[25]

Whether or not we quote evidence from three or from thirty-three incidents, we are confronted with a discrete number of episodes and we remain, epistemologically, on the ground of "anecdotal" (as opposed to "systematic") evidence. In order to overcome the inherently incomplete character of data we must keep asking *how* things were done in order to get a general understanding of *what* happened. We can get it by analyzing, in detail, the character of the crimes committed, as well as by reading people's minds, so to speak, wherever a record of conversations has been preserved.

Let me offer a few examples. In her memoirs, Chaja Finkelsztajn reports how (just as the mass killings were unfolding in her native Radzilow) someone suggested that she turn over whatever she still had, since together with her family she will certainly be killed. It was only right – Chaja's interlocutor argued without malice – for the good people who knew the Finkelsztajns to get these possessions, or else the killers would be rewarded.[26] To a Jewish man trying to find a hiding place with a peasant acquaintance near Wegrow, the latter's son-in-law said matter-of-factly: "Since you are going to die anyway, why should someone else get your boots? Why not give them to me so I will remember you?"[27] Miriam Rosenkranz had a moment of déjà vu during the pogrom in Kielce "when the horror of the ghetto came back to me and this scene when I worked with sorting down [feathers] and we were about to go back to the ghetto, and they were saying that that's the end, that they were deporting us for sure, and then this [Polish] woman acquaintance looked at my feet, [and the following exchange took place] 'Really, you could leave me your boots Missy.' 'But Mrs Joseph, I am still alive.' 'Well, I wasn't saying anything, only that those are nice boots.'"[28]

What we are eavesdropping on by listening to these exchanges are truly out-of-the-ordinary ideas. These snippets of conversations are built on an inversion of important principles regulating people's lives in common. The message – addressed to a Jewish interlocutor with the expectation of a voluntary surrender of property by a Jew to a Polish person – is embedded in a recast understanding of private property rights as well as the norm of goodwill binding people living in close proximity to one another.

Until these conversations took place, local people viewed the right to private property as inviolable. The only occasion when they felt it might be suspended, *when claims could be made legitimately to surrender what people rightfully owned*, would be to relieve extreme hardship, which befell some other members of the community – an act of goodwill, sustaining reciprocity for times when extreme hardship would in turn fall on them.

How is it that three different people, on three different occasions, happened to articulate exactly the same very unusual thought about a matter of fundamental importance in the life of a community (one could quote more similar exchanges as they caught the attention of Jewish interlocutors and were later recorded)?[29] I find it implausible that such a convergence of ideas inverting the meaning of private property and neighborly obligation, as far as the Jews were concerned, was purely coincidental. I am alluding here to the assumption that practices and important beliefs in society are interconnected and must be congruent. In other words, what is routine and accepted as a matter of fact in one of its segments could not be totally negated in another (at a minimum, the burden of proof would rest with those presuming the existence of such discrepancies). Thus, to my mind, this anecdotal evidence (and it would remain "anecdotal" even if we quoted ten, or fifteen such episodes) is an indication of a shift in *shared* views concerning acceptable behavior towards the Jews.

It may seem that I am grasping at straws here, but it is important to recognize ways of argumentation portraying plunder of Jews for what it was – namely a social practice, rather than a "criminal" or a deviant behavior of some rogue individuals. That plunder was widespread and sanctioned by norms is revealed precisely by the form of reference to it coded in language.

We find an echo of this shift in normative expectations not only among individuals speaking about interpersonal relations, but in "institutional" evaluations concerning relationships between groups, such as an early report of the underground sent to the London government in exile, indicating that Jews were non-responsive to Polish (that is, Catholic) fellow citizens' approaches to take their goods, even though it was clear that otherwise everything would only end up in German hands.[30] Evidently, by not consenting to be plundered by their neighbors, Jews were somehow favoring Germans over Poles. Thus the stakes were rising: a recalcitrant Jew, unwilling to surrender his or her boots to a Polish acquaintance was not only unfriendly, but, implicitly, also unpatriotic.

Conversely, when retail Jewish commercial property and real estate was ordered by German decrees into "Aryan" trusteeship – an opportunity for enrichment, which was taken up with eagerness by Polish lawyers, for example – this was also defended by suggestions that members of the corporation were rescuing this wealth from German hands. A line which at least the main underground publication, *Biuletyn Informacyjny*, was not buying, as it warned the legal profession in an article of 19 July 19 1940 that such behavior was objectionable. (But *Biuletyn Informacyjny* was an exceptional publication, where not a single line with antisemitic overtones was published throughout the occupation.)[31] Since the practice of "Aryanization" was continent-wide, Poland was not the only place where similar arguments had been advanced.

Finally there is the more familiar story of blackmail, known in Polish historiography as *szmalcownictwo*. It was primarily an urban phenomenon, and it affected most, if not all, Jews hiding on the Aryan side (that is, outside the ghettos).[32] Some people engaged in extortion ad hoc, spontaneously, when opportunities arose. In Jewish recollections we read about being approached in a public place – a street, a train station, or a streetcar – by strangers who signaled that they recognized them as Jewish and would not leave until paid off with some handout that had to be produced right away. This was opportunistic crime by amateurs, who could be shaken off rather easily. One young man, fresh out of high school, thus described his actions and motivation: "On the corner of Koszykowa and Mokotowska streets I bumped into two Jews unknown to me and I decided to impersonate a Gestapo agent. My idea was to get some money from them, because I know that Jews always have a lot of money."[33]

Then there were young ruffians who operated openly, often in packs. Near the entrance points to the Warsaw ghetto crowds of young men were milling, looking for Jews who might be attempting to sneak out, by removing their yellow star armband once they found themselves outside the walls. The great chronicler of the Jewish ghettos, Emmanuel Ringelblum, complained that nobody bothered these hoodlums whose ostentatious demeanor, after all, was about sending their fellow Jewish citizens to death.[34] And then there were "professionals" who carefully staked out their prey and then tried to bilk trapped Jews of all their material resources over a period of time.

Jan Grabowski consulted files from Nazi courts which prosecuted corruption in the German occupation administration and military personnel stationed in Poland. He found there a number of cases against gangs of extortionists including, alongside Polish participants, also German policemen or soldiers. It was of course Nazi policy to hunt after Jews who escaped from the ghettos, but not as a private initiative involving extortion. Enterprising Poles, impersonating German officials were also, in the eyes of the Gestapo, objectionable.

Criminal investigations of these cases provided unique insight into the functioning of predatory gangs. One of Grabowski's important findings, for instance, was that among 240 people accused of blackmailing Jews by the Warsaw German district courts between 1940 and 1943, only 20 had criminal records from before the war.[35] This put a hole in the conventionally accepted view that the *szmalcownicy* were primarily regular criminals, who simply took on a newly available, well remunerated, line of work.

Eventually, the Polish Underground State issued and carried out a number of death sentences against extortionists. But its actions came late, starting at the end of 1943, and, in practice, affected individuals who also spied upon or endangered patriotic conspiratorial networks. Grabowski concludes his study with a sobering comment, noting that "[s]zmalcownicy who did not have any contact with the underground or with the Germans did not have to fear punishment from underground authorities."[36]

Where do we go from here? Let me conclude this discussion of plunder with a few snippets of conversation, followed by views articulated in important underground memoranda. A certain Jozef Gorski, an upper-middle-class real estate owner from central Poland, writes in his memoirs about the Holocaust (he uses the term *zaglada* which is more or less synonymous) the following:

> [A]s a Christian I could not not feel compassion [double negative in the original] with my fellow human beings [...] but as a Pole I looked at what was happening differently

[…]. I considered Jews to be an internal enemy […] so I could not help feeling glad that we are getting rid of this enemy and, what's more, not with our own hands but thanks to the deeds of another, external, enemy. […] I could not hide satisfaction when I rode through our little towns, and saw that there were no more Jews […]. Asked by Thurm [a local German official with whom he was on this occasion]: *Sehen die Polen die Befreiung von den Juden als ein Segen an?* [Do Poles perceive being liberated from the Jews as a blessing?] I replied *Gewiss* [Of course] being sure that I was expressing the opinion of the overwhelming majority of my fellow nationals.[37]

And Gorski was reading the minds of his fellow nationals correctly. Some variation of a ditto – "we'll have to put up a monument to Hitler for having gotten rid of the Jews" – was overheard in private conversations all over Poland. We have testimony to this effect not only from Jews who were successfully "passing" as Aryans and later recounted what they saw and heard in their wartime milieus, but from numerous Polish witnesses as well.

Given such a widespread consensus of opinion in society it is no wonder that highly placed functionaries of the Polish Underground State advised the government in exile in London about a looming "Jewish problem." The official position of the government had been that all changes resulting from decisions taken by the occupier(s) with respect to matters involving geographical boundaries, citizenship rights and status, property confiscations – all purported legal changes, in other words – were null and void. But London was warned, repeatedly, from the home country that the matter was not as simple as it may have seemed. Return to the *status quo ante* and resumption by Jews of their economic role from before the war was an impossibility, reported Roman Knoll, the head of the Foreign Affairs Commission in the apparatus of the Government Delegate [underground civilian administration in occupied Poland]. The non-Jewish population had taken over Jewish positions in the social structure, he wrote in 1943, and this change is final and "permanent in character […]. Should Jews attempt to return en masse [rumors and exaggerated estimates circulated about the numbers of Jews who had managed to escape into the Soviet interior] people would not perceive this as a restoration but as an invasion, which they would resist even by physical means."[38]

In July 1945, another distinguished politician of the London-affiliated underground, Jerzy Braun, conveyed his observations about the growing antisemitism in Poland: "Today there is no place for a Jew in small towns and villages. During the past six years (finally! [emphasis in original]) a Polish third estate has emerged which did not exist before. It completely took over trade, supplies, mediation, and local crafts in the provinces […]. Those young peasant sons and former urban proletarians, who once worked for the Jews, are determined, persistent, greedy, deprived of all moral scruples in trade, and superior to Jews in courage, initiative, and flexibility. Those masses […] will not relinquish what they have conquered. There is no force which could remove them." It was understandable that Jews who survived the onslaught but could not return to their hometowns "leave ruined and broken telling the rest of the world that Poles are antisemites."

But what they take for antisemitism, Braun concludes, "is only an economic law, which cannot be helped."[39]

Truth be told, the majority of Polish peasants came into possession of Jewish property because Jews all over Europe, and *ipso facto* in Poland, had been killed by the Germans. Some peasants helped their luck and most liked what happened. But their involvement in these crimes was opportunistic. I am arguing for recognition that when the opportunity arose, they were not shy to take it.

## A NORM, NOT AN EXCEPTION

Plunder of Jewish wealth was a continent-wide affair. It took place from the Atlantic Ocean in the west, to as far east as German armies reached in their campaign against the USSR and was accompanied by opportunistic behavior on the part of the local population (despite the locals also being subject to exploitation by Nazi conquerors). Peasants from eastern Europe were not the only ones who acted in this manner. Accordingly, token Jews returning to their hometowns after the war, from Salonika to Prague, were made unwelcome by former neighbors already comfortably ensconced in their old apartments and jobs.

In 1943, in occupied France, for example, in anticipation of German defeat, various associations were formed to protect the interests of those Frenchmen who had acquired the so-called "Aryanized" Jewish property. Such associations continued to exist, albeit under new names, after the liberation. They defended their constituencies fiercely against the restitution of Jewish businesses or apartments to their rightful owners. "Those who bought Jewish property protected French interests," the association argued. "By buying property that the Germans threatened to liquidate, the purchasers 'preserved a precious inheritance for the national economy.'" Thus framed – stripping the Jews of their assets was cast as responsible and patriotic behavior. Little wonder that in April of 1945, hundreds of demonstrators went to the streets of Paris crying "Death to the Jews," and "France for the French."[40]

The story of the plunder of Jewish assets occasionally reaches large circulation press when Swiss banks are challenged to produce lists of dormant accounts or national museums are forced to return stolen Jewish paintings acquired through bona fide art dealers. However, its significance is not in being a momentary focus of journalistic zeal, but the very fabric of what Saul Friedländer identifies as the broad consent to the Nazi-organized Holocaust by institutions and people in occupied Europe. "Not one social group, not one religious community, not one scholarly institution or professional association in Germany and throughout Europe declared its solidarity with the Jews (some of the Christian churches declared that converted Jews were part of the flock, up to a point); to the contrary, many social constituencies and power groups were directly involved in the expropriation of the Jews and eager, be it out of greed, for their wholesale disappearance. Thus *Nazi and related anti-Jewish policies could unfold to their*

*most extreme levels without the interference of any major countervailing interests"*
(author's emphasis).[41]

## Notes

1   Geoffrey H. Hartman, "The Book of Destruction," in Saul Friedländer (ed.), *Probing the Limits of Representation: Nazism and the Final Solution* (Cambridge, MA: Harvard University Press 1992), 318–34, here 326–7.

2   My book *Neighbors: The Destruction of the Jewish Community in Jedwabne, Poland* (Princeton: Princeton University Press, 2001), which created quite a stir after it was published in Poland, took off from the deposition of Szmul Wasersztajn, who witnessed the crime committed against Jedwabne Jews by their Polish neighbors. Wasersztajn's testimony was preserved in the archives of the Jewish Historical Institute in Warsaw. I quote it *in extenso* on pages 16 through 20 of the Princeton edition.

3   Renée Poznanski, *Propagandes et persecutions. La Resistance et le "problème juif" 1940–1944* (Paris: Fayard, 2008), 144.

4   Or, perhaps, they do but in a fundamental sense, so that what was to be expunged from the face of the earth – the victim, the crime, and the memory of the crime – gets saved from oblivion.

5   See Samuel D. Kassow, *Who will Write Our History?: Emanuel Ringelblum, the Warsaw Ghetto, and the Oynes Shabes Archive* (Bloomington: Indiana University Press, 2007).

6   Herman Kruk, *The Last Days of the Jerusalem of Lithuania: Chronicles from the Vilna Ghetto and the Camps, 1939–1944* (New Haven and London: Yale University Press, 2002).

7   "However the war may end," I am quoting from Primo Levi's account of an SS man's scornful warning, "we have won the war against you; none of you will be left to bear witness, but even if someone were to survive, the world will not believe him [...] even if some proof should remain and some of you survive, people will say that the events you describe are too monstrous to be believed"; see Primo Levi, *The Drowned and the Saved* (New York: Random House, 1989), 12. Many a Jewish memoirist knew this without an SS man's reminder.

8   I am drawing in this passage on my article "One Line at a Time," *Poetics Today* 27 (2006): 425–429.

9   Saul Friedländer, *The Years of Extermination: Nazi Germany and the Jews, 1939–1945* (New York: HarperCollins, 2007), xxv, xxvi.

10  Alina Skibinska and Jakub Petelewicz, "Udzial Polakow w zbrodniach na Zydach na prowincji regionu swietokrzyskiego," *Zaglada Zydow. Studia i materialy* 1 (2005): 114–47.

11  For excellent examples of such studies see Pawel Machcewicz and Krzysztof Persak (eds), *Wokol Jedwabnego*, 2 vols. (Waszawa: Instytut Pamieci Narodowej, 2002), and four issues of the yearly *Zaglada Zydow. Studia i materialy*, a publication put out since 2005 by the Center for Holocaust Studies at the Institute of Philosophy and Sociology of the Polish Academy of Science, in Warsaw.

12  With the exception, probably due to oversight, of such cases tried in the Cracow district courts, which remain in local archives.

13  For a discussion of the rationale for adopting such a stance by Communist judiciary see the interview with Professor Andrzej Rzeplinski in *Gazeta Wyborcza* of 19 July, 2002, and also his "Ten jest z ojczyzny mojej? Sprawy karne oskarzonych o wymordowanie Zydow w Jedwabnem w swietle zasady rzetelnego procesu," in Machcewicz and Persak (eds), *Wokol Jedwabnego*, vol. I, 353–459. See also Jan T. Gross, *Fear: Anti-Semitism in Poland after Auschwitz – an Essay in Historical Interpretation* (New York: Random House, 2006), 52–57.

14  Dariusz Libionka, "Zaglada domu Trinczerow – refleksje historyka," *Znak* 4 (2008): 119–51, here 150.

15  Scott Horton, "Justice after Bush. Prosecuting an Outlaw Administration," *Harper's*, December 20, 2008, 51.

16  Skibinska and Petelewicz, "Udzial Polakow w zbrodniach na Zydach na prowincji regionu swietokrzyskiego," 128.

17  Ibid., 142. One should note, parenthetically, that the Catholic Church maintained its institutional presence in the Polish countryside throughout the German occupation. A local priest was then,

and remains to this day, a spiritual guide and moral beacon for inhabitants of the countryside. A full account of the phenomenon of peasant murders committed on Polish Jews must involve, therefore, a query about how the Catholic Church as an institution acquitted itself of its responsibilities.

18 Tadeusz Markiel, "Zaglada domu Trinczerow," *Znak* 4 (2008): 119–51.

19 Libionka, "Zaglada domu Trinczerow – refleksje historyka," 148. The GKBZH communiqué provides 14 names of the victims, listing also their age, including two one-year-old babies, as well as a three- and a ten-year-old child.

20 Alina Cala, *The Image of the Jew in Polish Folk Culture* (Jerusalem: Magnes Press, Hebrew University, 1995); Joanna Tokarska-Bakir, *Legendy o krwi. Antropologia przesadu* (Warszawa: WAB, 2008).

21 Jan Grabowski, *Rescue for Money: Paid Helpers in Poland, 1939–1945* (Jerusalem: Yad Vashem, 2008), 38.

22 On recurrent rape of Jewish women see Jan Grabowski, *"Ja tego Zyda znam!" Szantazowanie Zydow w Warszawie, 1939–1943* (Warszawa: Wydawnictwo IFiS PAN, 2004), 50–52.

23 Friedländer, *The Years of Extermination*, 497.

24 Zygmunt Klukowski, *Dziennik z lat okupacji zamojszczyzny*, Ludowa Spoldzielnia Wydawnicza, Lublin, 1958, entry of 13 April, 1942.

25 Machcewicz and Persak (eds), *Wokol Jedwabnego*, vol. 2, 358.

26 Extensive excerpts of Chaja Finkelsztajn's memoirs are translated into Polish and printed in Machcewicz and Persak (eds), *Wokol Jedwabnego*, vol. 2, 263–317. The episode is recounted ibid., 305.

27 Shraga Feivel Bielawski, *The Last Jew from Wegrow: The Memoirs of a Survivor of the Step-By-Step Genocide in Poland* (New York: Praeger, 1991), 72.

28 David Sztokfisz, *'Al Betenu she-harav = Fun der horuver-heym (About our House Which was Devastated) [Sefer Kielce]* (Tel Aviv: Irgune yots'e Kilts be-Yisra'el uva-tefutsot, 1981), 200.

29 See, for example, Grabowski, *Rescue for Money*, 20–21.

30 "Frequently Jews prefer to have their goods confiscated by the Germans rather than to give them to Poles for use for some time" – the quote is from an underground situation report for the period of 15 October through 20 November sent from occupied Poland to the government in exile in London, quoted by Dariusz Libionka, "'Kwestia zydowska' w Polsce w ocenie Delegatury Rzadu RP i KG ZWZ-AK w latach 1942 – 1944," paper presented at a conference "Les Juifs et la Pologne, 1939–2004," 13–15 January, 2005, Bibliothèque Nationale de France, Paris.

31 For the best analysis of this phenomenon see Jan Grabowski, "Polscy zarzadcy powierniczy majatku zydowskiego. Zarys problematyki," *Zaglada Zydow* 3 (2007): 253–60. For reference to the article in *Biuletyn Informacyjny*, see 259.

32 "There is literally not a Jew 'on the surface' or 'under the surface' who has not had something to do with them [the *schmalzowniks*] at least once or more than once, who has not had to buy himself off for a sum of money" (Emmanuel Ringelblum, *Polish Jewish Relations During the Second World War* (Jerusalem: Yad Vashem, 1974), 123).

33 Jan Grabowski, *"Ja tego Zyda znam!" Szantazowanie Zydow w Warszawie, 1939–1943* (Waszawa: Instytut Filozofii i Socjologii Polskiej Akademii Nauk, 2004), 32.

34 Ringelblum, *Polish Jewish Relations*, 128.

35 Grabowski, *"Ja tego Zyda znam!"*, 45.

36 Ibid., 55. Grabowski ends his book with a paradoxical finding that "punishment [if there was any], was meted out against [Polish] extortionists usually by German courts and police who objected to impersonations of Gestapo agents and pulling into this business the Wehrmacht and the police personnel" (ibid., 130).

37 Jozef Gorski, "Na przelomie dziejow," *Zaglada Zydow* 2 (2006): 288–91.

38 Dariusz Libionka, "'Kwestia zydowska' w Polsce w ocenie Delegatury Rzadu RP i KG ZWZ-AK w latach 1942 – 1944" (see fn. 30).

39 Ibid.

40 Maud S. Mandel, *In the Aftermath of Genocide: Armenians and Jews in Twentieth-Century France* (Durham and London: Duke University Press, 2003), 58–59; see, also, Renée Poznanski, *Jews in France During World War II* (Hanover and London: Brandeis University Press, 2001), 464–7.

41 Friedländer, *The Years of Extermination*, xxi.

# PART IV

*Perspectives*

# 15

# No End in Sight? The Ongoing Challenge of Producing an Integrated History of the Holocaust

## Doris L. Bergen

Perhaps others, too, first opened Saul Friedländer's book, *The Years of Extermination*, with a mixture of excitement and unexpected trepidation.[1] Dazzling in its insights and convincing in its approach, volume one of *Nazi Germany and the Jews*, subtitled *The Years of Persecution, 1933–1939*,[2] shaped a generation's thinking and teaching about the Holocaust in countless, profound ways. The fear was not that the second volume would disappoint: anyone who had heard Saul Friedländer speak about it publicly or privately knew it would be a masterpiece of research and reflection. A different and, in retrospect, no doubt unrealistic concern presented itself: would this new book somehow manage to finish the work to which so many scholars and thinkers had devoted and continued to devote their efforts and energy?[3] Would Friedländer have done it all, producing the very thing against which he and others had repeatedly and insistently warned: closure?[4]

This worry, itself a tribute to Friedländer's skills as a historian and wisdom as a thinker and writer about the Holocaust, was nevertheless unfounded. Although it is everything anticipated and more, the book is not and of course cannot be everything. Rather than containing or concealing the complexity of the Shoah, Friedländer's magisterial synthesis reveals its boundless scope, opening the subject out to expose issues and implications that even his approach cannot and could not fully incorporate. Among its many achievements, the book provides a framework and a guide to the ongoing project of producing a history of the Holocaust that is "integrative" and "integrated" in the fullest sense of the words.[5] The remarkable power of Friedländer's work of integration is evident in its limitations as well as in its successes. Both can be seen if we consider four concepts central to the structure and arguments of the book: chronology, agency, solidarity and religion.

## 1 CHRONOLOGY

Chronology is the major organizing principle in *The Years of Extermination*. Readers of Friedländer's personal account, *When Memory Comes*,[6] with its layering of experience and its jarring moves from wartime Europe to Israel decades later and back again, might have expected something else, a thematic arrangement or even some structure that tied broad historical developments to the rhythms of individual lives. Likewise, Friedländer's influential work *Reflections of Nazism: An Essay on Kitsch and Death*,[7] or the edited volume, *Probing the Limits of Representation*,[8] might have suggested a more theoretically self-conscious organization for his magnum opus, something startlingly innovative or disarmingly unfamiliar. Instead, we get dates: a book divided into three parts – "Terror (Fall 1939—Summer 1941)," "Mass Murder (Summer 1941—Summer 1942)" and "Shoah (Summer 1942—Spring 1945)" – each further broken down into chapters: "May 1940—December 1940," "December 1941—July 1942," "October 1943—March 1944" and so on. This strict attention to chronology is more what one would expect from the diplomatic historian Gerhard Weinberg,[9] or perhaps from Raul Hilberg, whose classic work, *The Destruction of the European Jews*, in fact is much less chronological in structure than is Friedländer's book.[10]

This simple tool – putting things in order – proves to be a powerful conceptual device for an integrated history. By using chronology, Friedländer is able to link experiences and observations of individual Jews in Europe and elsewhere with decisions and actions of those who wielded more power: the German leadership, institutional and individual collaborators and so-called ordinary people. Gerhard Weinberg has often pointed out that history is lived looking forward but written looking back.[11] That insight is embedded in Friedländer's chronological approach and the switching of perspectives it allows. How else could he represent and even in some measure reproduce the uncertainty, delusion, knowledge and misjudgement that made up the world of the targets and victims of Nazism? One of the accounts that provides a thread of lived experience throughout the book and exposes the deadly intersections of the private and the political on the Nazi German timeline, involves Lilli Jahn, a Jewish doctor and mother of five in Immenhausen. In October 1942, Jahn's "Aryan" husband, who was having an affair with a gentile woman, divorced her. The timing could not have been worse. Exactly a year earlier, transports of German Jews to the east for killing had begun, and by late 1942, only Jews married to Christians remained legally in Germany. Jahn's response was defiant or perhaps uninformed: she advertized for patients, using her professional title and name, absent the requisite "Sara." Denounced and arrested, she was murdered in Auschwitz in June 1944.[12]

Friedländer's focus on chronology allows him to integrate what are often known as the intentionalist and functionalist positions in ways that again are reminiscent of the very different work of Gerhard Weinberg. Was Hitler central? Both historians insist he was and demonstrate the driving force of his ideology. Did the war and contingency play key roles in shaping events? Absolutely. In Friedländer's words: "We do not know, of course, at what point Hitler started harboring the project of immediate extermination; this much, however, is certain: The timing of Hitler's decisions was a matter of circumstances; the decisions as such were not."[13] By the end of 1941, Friedländer shows, Hitler's impulse had spawned a tangled network of vested interests:

If before the attack [on the Soviet Union] the Reich had no choice but to win in order to escape eradication, how vastly more compelling the argument must have appeared after six months of mass murder on an unprecedented scale. The increasing number of Germans from all segments of society involved in all aspects of the extermination campaign knew perfectly well, as did the party elite, that they were now accomplices in crimes of previously unimagined scope; victory or fighting to the end were the only options left to their leader, their party, their country – and themselves.[14]

Integrating the war was not Friedländer's primary goal, but his decision to organize his book chronologically and the concerns, even obsessions, of the Jewish diarists who are his main informants reveal the omnipresence of the war in the Shoah as experienced by its victims. As Alexandra Garbarini observes in her study of Jewish diaries during the Holocaust, gathering and reflecting on the news was one way people sought to create meaning out of suffering.[15] For Jews in Europe, the war was a matter of life and death, and the diarists on whom Friedländer draws understood that urgency. Friedländer opens the book with Victor Klemperer, professor of Romance languages in Dresden, who responded to the news on 1 September 1939 with thoughts of suicide:

The young butcher's lad came and told us: There had been a radio announcement, we already held Danzig and the Corridor, the war with Poland was under way, England and France remained neutral. I said to Eva, then a morphine injection or something similar was the best thing for us, our life was over.[16]

The war is present in Friedländer's analysis, but its unforeseen consequences and direct impact on the fate of Jews, individually and collectively, merit further attention. Whether in camps, in hiding, or passing as gentiles, Jews all over Europe grasped a fact that eluded Allied planners at the time and observers since: military developments, whether the start of a Red Army counter-offensive in December 1941, the landing of Allied troops in North Africa in late 1942, or the stalling of the Soviet advance outside Warsaw in August 1944 – the results of decisions taken with little or no concern to their wellbeing – had immediate and enormous implications for them, even if they had no way to know what those might be. From his hiding place in Warsaw in 1943, the erstwhile ghetto policeman Calel Perechodnik, one of Friedländer's witnesses but not cited on this point, described how he and his bunker mates responded to news of the Italian surrender:

The same thought came to our minds: We longed for the end of the war, prayed for its early termination, and at the same time, trembled at the thought that the war would end. Where would we go then? With whom would we celebrate?[17]

By mid-1944, Herman Kruk, one of Friedländer's most-cited diarists, understood that every moment counted. Kruk, a Warsaw librarian in the Vilna ghetto and later prisoner in a labor camp in Estonia, wrote on 23 July 1944:

> Yesterday was a day of some tension. Today new rumors are spreading: the men will be castrated, the women sent to Königsberg. [. . .] Since the latest events on the eastern Front, since the assassination attempt on H., since Estonia and the entire Baltic has been surrounded, our situation seems to be coming to a head. We are so upset, our nerves choke us, and every day is superfluous. Everything is more and more irritating. We count not just the days, but the hours and minutes: any minute we may get out of hell. When I write about it, I can hardly believe it.[18]

Kruk was shot by the Germans and his body burned, in September 1944, one day before Red Army units reached the area.

A diarist not included by Friedländer, a young and decidedly apolitical intellectual, learned to pay attention to military developments and to see connections between the fate of French Jews, like herself, and all victims of Nazi German warfare. In her entry from 15 February 1944, Hélène Berr recorded what she heard from a co-worker at the *Union Génerale des Israélites de France*, who had just returned from Drancy. "Convoys" were sent east, Berr wrote, with sixty people in each sealed cattle-wagon, little food and no toilets. The Germans, Berr concluded, "have one aim, which is extermination."[19] Berr then reported on another conversation, with a Frenchman, who had seen Soviet POWs in German captivity:

> Typhus took hold and hundreds dropped dead each day. Each morning the Germans went round with guns finishing off those who were no longer able to stand up. So the sick, trying to avoid this fate, used to get themselves propped up by their healthy comrades. The Germans used their rifle butts to smash the hands of the men holding their comrades upright. The sick fell to the ground, they piled them onto carts, stripped them of their boots and clothing, hauled them to a pit, unloaded them *with pitchforks* and threw them into the pit alongside the corpses. A sprinkling of quicklime, and that was that.[20]

Berr's journal, interrupted by her arrest on 27 March 1944, ends with her response: "*Horror! Horror! Horror!*"[21] She died eight months later in Bergen-Belsen.

As Berr's entry reveals, a chronological frame that encompasses the war allows, perhaps demands, integration of non-Jewish targets of Nazi German killing. This project of integration extends in many directions. In May and June 1940, during the attack on France, Germans murdered between one and four thousand black French soldiers. On Hitler's instructions, the *Wehrmacht* had been deluged with propaganda that focused on France's use of native troops from its colonies and played on stereotypes of Africans as savages. In most cases, German officers ordered the execution of all black prisoners, and even when individual soldiers initiated the murders, they had their superiors' tacit approval. As Raffael Scheck has shown, these killings blur the familiar distinction between the "racial" war of annihilation in Germany's east and the supposedly normal war fought in the west.[22] They also underscore one of Friedländer's points: we cannot understand the Holocaust without examining the crucial events of 1939, 1940 and 1941.

Paying attention to "Hitler's African victims" (the phrase is Scheck's) complicates but need not decenter the role of antisemitism. Indeed, the combination of racist propaganda, scapegoating linked back to defeat in the "Great War" and accusing victims of slaughter of conspiring against Germany prefigured the "war against the Jews" that Jeffrey Herf identifies after the invasion of the Soviet Union in June 1941.[23]

The last year of the war constitutes another point where Friedländer's chronological approach might be stretched. One of his insights involves the momentum of Nazi killing. Mass murder and annihilation of Jews, he shows, increased antisemitism – it is easier to hate those one has destroyed – and added to Hitler's power by underlining the myth of his invincibility and omniscience. Friedländer demonstrates the dynamic of destruction in masterful strokes that reveal its force for the perpetrators of violence, the witnesses, the beneficiaries and enablers, and the targets. One thing we might contemplate is the nature and reverberations of that momentum itself. Might a closer look at that dynamic help explain some otherwise puzzling aspects of World War II and the Holocaust?

By the end of 1943, most of the Jews within Germany's reach had been killed, and in the eyes of the Germans, those still alive in Europe were nothing but an accident or temporary convenience; in essence they were already dead. The killers remained, however, thousands of experts in mass murder, skilled and hardened by years on the job. Many of them had plied their trade against more than one target group: SS killers had dumped Gypsies into Jewish ghettos all over Poland, and the Order Police who shot Jews into mass graves also massacred Red Army commissars, inmates of mental hospitals and Gypsies (Roma and Sinti). Franz Stangl, commandant of the killing centers of Sobibor and Treblinka, had started his career in the murderous "euthanasia" (T-4) program; so had Christian Wirth, his predecessor at Treblinka, and many others. The gas chambers at Auschwitz that were first used to kill Soviet POWs had been expanded and perfected as instruments for murdering Jews.

By 1944, men who had spent the previous years hunting and killing Jews had almost done themselves out of a job. During the last two years of the war, the rate of murdering Jews actually fell, with brief spikes for the slaughter of Jews from Hungary. In search of ways to continue to earn the promotions, rewards and power that their expertise had brought, the killers turned to the remaining targets. Thus, as soon as transports of Jews from Hungary to Auschwitz ceased in the late summer of 1944, camp personnel busied themselves with murdering those Roma and Sinti inmates who had been allowed to languish during the preceding hectic months and with rounding up and killing the Jews in Łódź, the last remaining ghetto in occupied Poland. German retreats westward through Belorussia and north through the Italian peninsula were marked by horrific brutality against local populations. Stangl, Wirth and others who had killed Jews at Chelmno, Treblinka, Sobibor, Belzec and elsewhere moved on, when those sites closed, to fight partisans and civilians of all kinds in areas still in German hands. Men who had solved every "problem" through total destruction were unlikely to unlearn that lesson merely because their problems were now called "bandits" not Jews.[24]

As the Germans retreated, they evacuated camps and killing centers and marched the remaining inmates in guarded columns away from the ever-advancing front. Throughout late 1944 and early 1945, trails of half-dead prisoners made their way through the Polish, German and Czech countrysides. For the guards, their enfeebled, starving charges remained the ticket towards home and safety. Meanwhile, Nazi authorities and activists introduced draconian measures against accused deserters and traitors in the German military, more than 20,000 of whom were shot over the course of the war, most of them in its last months. The SS and police also executed defeatist German civilians as the Allies advanced.[25] The "all or nothing" Nazi mentality and the years of war eventually made all lives, including German lives, cheap.

Evident in this last phase of the war is the contagion of killing, the way that the notion of a "Final Solution of the Jewish question" generated "final solutions" in a spiral of violence that fed on self-interest and cowardice as well as fanaticism and ruthlessness. The surge in prosecutions of men on charges of violating Paragraph 175 in early 1945 in Hamburg did not reflect a new-found passion for Nazi homophobia.[26] Rather it suggests that some policemen judged it safer to remain at home "fighting vice," even as the bombs fell, than to take their chances at the front, where casualty rates were mounting to heights unprecedented for the Germans.

## 2 AGENCY

Friedländer handles the subject of Jewish agency in the Holocaust with empathy and dignity. He uses the diaries and letters of Jews all over Europe to show them trying to do something, never passive, sometimes fatalistic but somehow actively so. In the Netherlands, Etty Hillesum fell in love, engaged in a variety of sexual affairs and insisted on courage and strength: "We left the camp singing," she wrote in September 1943, on a postcard thrown from the train that brought her to her death at Auschwitz.[27] Just to remind us of these astonishing individuals and their lives and efforts under the immense pressure of destruction is a major achievement. Friedländer has a knack for finding the telling moment, the action or scene that carries a world of meaning. At one point he depicts the nine elderly survivors of the Babi Yar massacre who assembled outside the Old Synagogue in Kiev:

> Nobody dared to approach or leave food or water for them, as this could mean immediate execution. One after another the Jews died until only two remained. A passerby went to the German sentry standing at the corner of the street and suggested shooting the two old Jews instead of letting them also starve to death. 'The guard thought for a moment and did it.'[28]

In that sketch, we see both the insistence of human agency on the part of Jews marked for destruction – and, in the case of those people, who in the eyes of everyone around them were already dead – its doomed futility.

Friedländer's insistence on Jewish agency is neither heroic, pathetic nor merely ironic. It is a resounding assertion of life, will and freedom, including the freedom of historical actors to do and be things quite different from what we who come after may desire and expect of them. Friedländer shows us people who participated in processes of destruction, who endangered and betrayed others, who occupied the moral terrain Primo Levi famously called "the gray zone."[29] In late 1943, the mother of Cordelia Edvardson chose her "Aryan" husband over her teenaged daughter, whom she abandoned to her fate as she was shipped to Theresienstadt.[30] Friedländer shows us these wrenching acts, not to pass some easy judgement or relativize radical evil but to remind us of the complexity of human life, the ferocity of genocidal destruction and the impossibility of avoiding compromise under such conditions.

The many powerful reminders of both the potency of human agency and its severe limitations for victims of the Shoah point to something remarkable yet unremarked by Friedländer. Rather than pleading powerlessness or begging for understanding for their failings, a surprising number of Jewish diarists claim a high degree of agency, indeed often wildly exaggerate the power or room to manoeuvre they had, in tormented efforts to expose their own implication in the processes of destruction. According to Raul Hilberg, before his suicide, Adam Czerniaków wrote a note in which he said of the German request that he organize removal of the orphans from the Warsaw ghetto to be sent to Treblinka: "They want me to kill the children with my own hands."[31]

This tendency to claim agency, indeed insist on it, contrary to all the evidence, is even more pronounced in Holocaust memoirs, where themes of failure, wrong decisions and responsibility abound. Adina Szwajger, a young Jewish doctor in the Warsaw ghetto in 1942, agonized throughout her memoir about administering lethal injections to a group of children in the ghetto hospital, to spare them from torment at German hands.[32] In July 1943, she helped her husband Stefan, who was in hiding in a greengrocer's cellar in Mokotow, to get a place in the "Hotel Poland" as part of a group escaping to Hungary. But the scheme was a trap, and Szwajger's husband, like all the others, ended up on a transport to Auschwitz. When she saw prison lorries, Szwajger wrote: "I knew beyond doubt, that it was all over. And that I had done it to him, with my own hands. Although he had wanted it, if not for me he wouldn't even have known that this could be his escape from life."[33]

Central to the memoir of Olga Lengyel from Transylvania is her insistence that the deaths of her loved ones at Auschwitz were somehow her fault. "*Mea culpa*," she declared in the first line of her book, "my fault, *mea maxima culpa!* I cannot acquit myself of the charge that I am, in part, responsible for the destruction of my own parents and of my two young sons."[34] Separated from her husband and father upon arrival at the camp, Lengyel stood on the ramp with her mother and two sons. The SS "selector" sent the younger boy with the children and elderly but paused before the older boy, who was almost twelve, Lengyel wrote, and "big for his age." Assuming children and old people would be spared the worst, Lengyel urged her son and mother to go to the left. In her words, "I had condemned Arvad and my mother to death in the gas chambers."[35]

Perhaps one more example will suffice. Henry Friedman spent most of 1943 hidden in the loft of a barn in eastern Poland with his mother, younger brother and school teacher. A teenager at the time, he remembers voting to have the baby to which his mother was about to give birth killed in order to increase the rest of the group's chances of survival. With the help of the woman who hid them, this was done.[36] Rather than point to the obvious: the complete desperation of the situation, his absolute powerlessness and total dependence on the Ukrainian woman who sheltered them in terribly dangerous conditions (she was having an affair with the local police chief, a notorious hater and hunter of Jews), Friedman claimed responsibility, even casting the decision in terms of a vote – the hallmark of freedom. His younger brother Isaac, Friedman maintained, does not remember voting and denies any input in the decision. By mentioning his brother's conflicting memory of the event, Friedman highlighted his own choice, not only to remember but to speak of his role. "I'm no hero," Friedman insisted throughout his memoir – and announced in its title.

Such assertions of agency, far out of proportion to any possibility of acting freely or exercising power, draw our attention to another phenomenon: the contrasting, predictable and even more typical claims of powerlessness in postwar accounts from the killers. "I had no choice," Franz Stangl, veteran of the T-4 killings of disabled people and commandant of Sobibor and Treblinka, maintained again and again during his interviews with the journalist Gitta Sereny.[37] "I was a victim; I was forced; someone else would have done it if I had not" – these refrains run through the statements of Rudolf Höss, Adolf Eichmann and the many of their counterparts and subordinates who came before courts and tribunals, agreed to interviews or made statements in public or private.[38] People like the physician Friedrich Menecke, who consigned thousands of people to death under the program code-named 14f13 while enjoying his dessert, wielded immense and deeply corrupting power, what Henry Friedlander has called "the drug of power over others."[39] Yet precisely such people later pleaded absolute powerlessness: they were only cogs in the machine, they maintained. In short, claims of agency after the fact seem to be inversely related to the amount of power held at the time: the more powerful the individual, the less agency they admit; the less powerful the person, the more she or he insists on bearing responsibility not only for her or his own fate but for the suffering and death of others.

This phenomenon points in at least two directions. Study of the perpetrators, an inquiry already well advanced and characterized by sophisticated and detailed analyses – one could mention the important work of Christopher Browning, Karin Orth, Sybille Steinbacher, Michael Wildt and Edward Westermann,[40] and still only be at the start of an illustrious list – might gain from more concerted attention to that "drug of power over others" – related to the killers' euphoric high analyzed elsewhere by Saul Friedländer under the label "Rausch" – and its sudden transformation into a quite different drug, a numbing sedative of retreat into powerlessness. How and at what point did this change occur – if it was a change? In *The Drowned and the Saved*, Primo Levi observes that the question of the perpetrators' motivations is of perennial interest, at least in part because it cannot be answered on the basis of the killers' own reflections. They lie, he points out, and their lies are precisely most convincing when they believe them themselves. Perhaps taking up the issue of perpetrators' motivations – in the Holocaust and also in other cases of genocide and extreme violence – from the angle of power and retreat into powerlessness could provide a way to understand how tensions and contradictions coexisted in the mentality of the perpetrators – normalcy and extraordinary violence; traditional ethics and radical evil – and even were necessary to create professional mass murderers who were also "ordinary" people.[41]

The inflated claims of agency on the part of victims and survivors lead to a very different but interconnected line of inquiry. How do such assertions of responsibility – personal, moral, universal in scale – fit into accounts of the Holocaust? What functions did and do they serve? What windows might they open into the mental world of targets of extreme violence, at the time of the assault and after, as they marshal and present their memories to others? At one level, expressions of shame and guilt and acts of self-criticism reflect the Shoah's crushing force: a devastation that cut into the very sense of self, with its pernicious methods of divide and conquer and its cunning proclivities at creating "self-service hells" where the worst suffering is what a person does to herself.[42] Whatever the purpose of such claims for those who made them, for readers of their words these assertions of agency lead back to the unending trauma of the Holocaust, a horror magnified by the degree to which perpetrators managed to shift blame onto their victims.

At another level, we might interpret unrealistic claims of agency on the part of survivors as an expression of what is misleadingly referred to as "survivor guilt" – a sense of the arbitrariness of one's survival and perhaps unworthiness compared to the many who were murdered. Here the claims of agency with regard to wrong decisions and destructive actions intersect with a widespread refusal to take credit for one's own survival. It was just chance, we read in account after account and hear in interview after interview, when survivors are confronted with the common question: how did you manage to survive against all odds? As usual, Primo Levi put his finger on the point. In a system of radical and contagious evil, he wrote, it was impossible to survive without compromise.[43] Acts of compromise might be as small and, viewed in retrospect, as insignificant as Levi's decision to share some water he found with his friend Alberto and no-one else. What difference would it have made, after all, if he had tried to distribute this meagre treasure more widely? Nevertheless, according to Levi, a sense of having failed contributed to some kind of shame, no doubt related to the loss of self-worth reported by so many victims of violence.

Perhaps the fixation on a moment of failure provides both a way to grapple with the sense of the compromised self and a way to contain the destruction. Victims agonize over their own responsibility precisely because at some level they know it was limited and they at least can hope for an understanding on the part of their listeners and interlocutors that, their protestations notwithstanding, they were not to blame. The perpetrators, by contrast, cannot admit agency or confront their power without removing themselves from the circle of humanity they so brutally assaulted. This recognition constitutes Stangl's moment of truth in his conversations with Sereny: the glimpse that through what he did and more significantly, what he became, he forfeited his place in human society. In Sereny's view, this flash of awareness killed him.[44]

Might the overblown claims of agency in survivors' accounts be understood in part as an effort to insist on their humanity, to demand acknowledgement of moral autonomy, even under the most horrific circumstances? By pointing to her role in the death of her mother and son, Olga Lengyel positioned herself, even on the platform at Auschwitz, in that arbitrary selection between immediate death and a chance at survival, as an agent, a person who knew right from wrong, although she could not discern in the moment the correct course of action. By telling how she ended the lives of a group of children in the Warsaw ghetto in September 1942, Adina Szwajger presented herself then and later as a fully human person, capable of profound love and loyalty, conscious of the difficulty, indeed impossibility of doing the right thing in a situation where there was no right choice, but nevertheless deciding herself how to act and acting, not as a victim or a pawn but as a person, despite everything, still capable of partaking in the universal moral law that gave Immanuel Kant such cause to marvel. In other words, might we understand the paradox of agency, of claims of power on the part of the powerless, as an existential statement, a rejection of retreat into passivity and the release from responsibility such a retreat would entail?

It may be instructive to consider Hilberg's analysis of the Jewish Councils in this light. By insisting on their failure, by depicting them as part of the machinery of destruction, Hilberg demands that Jewish leaders be viewed as agents and not passive victims. His very act of criticizing their participation in the German program of assault on Jews dignifies them with the assumption that they too were historical and moral actors, certainly limited in what they could know, see, or do, but nevertheless part of the human community.[45]

In the effort to integrate Jewish sources into the history of the Holocaust, Friedländer draws on wartime diaries, to the almost complete exclusion of memoirs written after the fact. The decision to use diaries is somewhat surprising for the author of a memoir, founder of the journal *History and Memory* and guide and inspiration to a wealth of investigations across the disciplines around issues of memory. Friedländer's decision is understandable when seen in light of his exchange with Martin Broszat in the 1980s and his effort to produce a synthesis that is both compelling and methodologically beyond reproach. Diaries give an immediacy and urgency to his account and at the same time underscore its chronological momentum. But Friedländer's choice to exclude memoirs or at least strictly limit their use points to an area still "unintegrated" in this history: postwar Jewish accounts.

As anyone with even cursory knowledge of Holocaust studies and Holocaust commemoration knows, the decades since the 1980s have witnessed a plethora of efforts to gather what are usually called "Holocaust testimonies." There are projects of every size and scale, from the Fortunoff Archives at Yale, to the massive, international Spielberg program "Survivors of the Shoah," to local efforts in towns and cities across the United States, like the interviews with survivors from South Bend, Indiana featured in the film "The People Next Door."[46] There are also private initiatives, accounts collected and recorded by students in courses on the Holocaust, by the grandchildren of survivors, by amateur historians and journalists. A few of these interviews – by now there must be hundreds of thousands of them worldwide, on audio- and videotape, stored digitally, or preserved as written transcripts – have been excerpted in published works or incorporated into documentary films.[47] Some of them have been analyzed with great insight by experts in various fields: the literary scholars Lawrence Langer and Shoshana Felman, the psychiatrist Dori Laub, the sociologist Henry Greenspan and others.[48] But for the most part historians steer clear of them or use them cautiously and sparingly. Earlier accounts are more honest, Na'ama Shik asserts in her insightful study of Jewish women's experiences in Auschwitz;[49] as the so-called Mengele effect indicates, survivors' accounts decades after the fact are shaped by what they have read and heard in the meantime. Can an integrated history of the Holocaust incorporate such imperfect and incomplete memories, and is there any value to making the effort?

The answer, I think, is "yes." Issues of agency and related questions about shame and dignity in the face of victimization take on different dimensions when memoirs and other accounts, such as interviews generated after – even long after – the events remembered are brought into consideration. Had Primo Levi somehow been able to keep a diary in Auschwitz, it would no doubt have included brilliant insights as well as telling details. But would it have had the breadth of vision of his memoir, *Survival in Auschwitz* (*Se questo è un uomo*),[50] published in 1958, or the depth of wisdom of *The Drowned and the Saved*, written forty years after the war? It seems impossible, if for no other reason than, as Levi pointed out, being inside the camp was not always the best vantage point for observing the camp.[51] We need memoirs to provide insight and open cracks through which we might catch glimpses of matters unspoken or unthinkable in earlier sources, for example, as Stacy Hushion has argued, on the issue of sexual violence.[52]

## 3 SOLIDARITY

For European Jews, Saul Friedländer demonstrates throughout his book, the Nazi assault crushed any possibility of solidarity, if it ever existed. At most, small groups of the like-minded managed to come together around shared interests and principles: bands of Zionist youth in some ghettos, pairs of Italian Jews in Auschwitz (most famously Primo Levi and his friend Alberto), ersatz families of Hungarian Jewish women on the death marches. But the destruction of Jewish communities and Jewish cohesion was brutal and complete. We see it over and over in Friedländer's narrative: French Jews betrayed foreign Jews; Jews of different political persuasions fought bitterly in the Vilna ghetto; police and elites in the ghettos exploited and abused those without privilege; German Jews lorded it over Dutch Jews at Westerbork. There are counter-examples: the Bielski partisan group in Belorussia, described by Nechama Tec and now the subject of a Hollywood movie;[53] persistent bonds between friends and families, but on the whole these exceptions underscore Friedländer's sobering observation. Oppression, in the words of Joan Ringelheim, does not make people better; it makes them oppressed.[54]

Friedländer's insight about solidarity is a major contribution to the understanding of the Holocaust and one only a history that integrates Jewish sources could achieve. But there is more to be known here, too. How does one measure solidarity? Elizabeth Strauss has suggested one approach: by considering the situation of the elderly in the ghettos.[55] In general, work on the ghettos – long neglected as sites of destruction – promises to develop in further detail and nuance the breakdown (and perhaps maintenance) of solidarity and its implications. Amos Goldberg's response to *The Years of Extermination* hints that perhaps Friedländer has been too quick or too general in his conclusion that the Holocaust meant the total collapse of Jewish solidarity.[56] Might Friedländer's integration of Jewish sources in the form of individual voices serve to disembody not only the individuals but the collective?

Friedländer's focus on Jewish solidarity provides a model that could help elucidate developments within and between other European populations during World War II. Examination of the situation of Roma and Sinti in camps and ghettos may reveal dynamics similar to what Friedländer shows. Otto Rosenberg, a Sinto born in 1927 and raised in Berlin, described in his memoir the assault on family ties he experienced and observed in Marzahn from 1936 to 1942 and subsequently in the Auschwitz "Gypsy family camp," Buchenwald, Bergen-Belsen and elsewhere.[57] Solidarity between Gypsies and the much more numerous Jewish inmates of major ghettos – Warsaw, Łódź, and Lublin – is hardly to have been expected, and we know that Gypsies were invariably on the first lists for transport out of the ghetto for killing.[58] Zygmunt Bauman's influential analysis of the Jewish ghetto leadership and its practices of "save what you can" reveals how, under the pressure of Nazi assault, the effort to preserve as many lives as possible for as long as possible compelled members of the Jewish Councils to implicate themselves more and more deeply in the machinery of destruction.[59] Perhaps there is more to be learned about the role that decisions about Roma and Sinti played, not only in quashing any solidarity between Jews and Gypsies (or even negating its possibility), but in contributing to the collapse of Jewish communal cohesion.

Shame is a bitterly isolating sentiment, and as Primo Levi has pointed out, it is often those nearest the "victim-end" of the "gray zone", that is, the people with relatively little or no power or control over their own fates, let alone the lives and deaths of others, who paradoxically agonize most over their actions and inactions towards others.[60] Then too, according again to Levi, there is "the shame of the world," a sense among victims and witnesses to extreme victimization (he gives the example of Red Army soldiers who arrived at Auschwitz in January 1945) of being ashamed to be alive, ashamed to be human when human beings are capable of wreaking such terrible destruction on one another and of existing amid such horror.[61]

Friedländer's insight about the centrality of solidarity to the process of destruction, that is, about Jewish solidarity as a site, perhaps the central site, of interaction in an integrated history of the Holocaust, leads to reflections on shame. That nexus in turn might be expanded to open up analysis of postwar treatment of Jews in Europe and beyond. Jan Gross has already embarked on this difficult project. Towards the end of *Neighbors*, his searing examination of the murder of the Jews of Jedwabne in July 1941 by gentile Poles, Gross provides an account from Karolcia Sapetowa, a former nanny who sheltered two Jewish children from March 1943 until the end of the war. Her neighbors were uneasy, Sapetowa recalled, because they knew the children were in her home and they understood that if the Germans discovered them, the entire village could be punished. At first she was able to appease the villagers with gifts or promises, but increasingly they pushed her to get rid of the children. "Don't kill us yet today," the little girl and boy would beg her. Desperate, Sapetowa said, she "got a brilliant idea":

> I put the children on a cart, and I told everybody that I was taking them out to drown them. I rode around the entire village, and everybody saw me and they believed, and when the night came I returned with the children.[62]

What does it tell us, Gross adds after quoting Sapetowa's testimony, that residents of a Polish village could sleep in peace only when they were convinced that their neighbour, with her own hands, had just drowned two children? And what, Gross implies, does the breakdown of moral order evident in Sapetowa's account portend for the years ahead? His subsequent book, *Fear*, tackles that question, revealing the cruel ways that the destruction of Polish Jewry served to create antisemitism and produce pogroms after the war, most notably at Kielce in 1946, where efforts to remove the last remaining or returning Jews constituted not only an attempt by Polish gentiles to retain the Jewish properties and positions they had grabbed during the war, but a bid to erase the victims of their own crimes and silence the witnesses of their own witnessing of mass murder.[63] It seems likely that related reactions occurred elsewhere in the wake of the Holocaust, perhaps in Hungary and Slovakia where, as Holly Case demonstrates, during the war, Jews were pawns in contests over territory.[64]

## 4 RELIGION

It is gratifying but not surprising to see the amount of attention Friedländer devotes to religion in *The Years of Extermination*. Gratifying because too often the role of Christian leaders and church people is ignored or generalized as "silence"; not surprising because Friedländer has proven elsewhere to be such an astute and careful observer of Christianity in the Nazi era.[65] In the first volume, Friedländer analyzed German church leaders as elites who bridged the gap between the Nazi leadership and the rank and file, and served to legitimate National Socialism and its attacks on Jews. In the second volume, Christian leaders are seen enabling genocide in concrete ways: preaching hatred of Jews in Poland, turning away would-be converts from Judaism in Germany; and killing and inciting killers in Croatia and Hungary, where in 1944, Father Kun exhorted shooters of Jews, "In the name of Christ – fire!"[66]

Friedländer's treatment of the Churches provides powerful ways to think about Christianity and the Holocaust beyond the tired trope of silence. This insight too can be extended to open investigations of religion and genocide in other settings,[67] and also to examine neglected aspects of the Holocaust. What roles did church leaders and Christians play in the second phase of the program to murder the disabled in Nazi Germany, the so-called 14f13 program? And what about forced abortions and infanticide committed against slave laborers and their babies in the last years of the war?[68] Many of those pregnancies were terminated and infants killed in hospitals run by the Catholic and Protestant Churches: is a systematic examination of their members and leaders possible? Daniel Goldhagen and others have contrasted the protests by Christian leaders against killings of disabled people in the so-called T-4 or "Euthanasia" program in 1941 with the "silence" of the Vatican and other Christian institutions regarding murder of Jews. But rather than a contrast, viewing programmes of killing together may suggest patterns of responses and actions that are more of a piece. Gerhard Weinberg has pointed out that Pius XII had information from reliable sources about at least five programmes of killing organized and carried out in Nazi Germany or under Nazi German leadership: murders of the disabled beginning in 1939, Polish intellectuals in 1939, Serbian Orthodox Christians beginning in 1941, Jews starting that same year; and the newborn babies of slave laborers, many of them from Ukraine, in 1943 and after.[69] In each case the Vatican's response was to say as little as possible. And yet the Pope was not incapable of action: in 1944 he wrote to British diplomats requesting that black troops not be used in the occupation of Rome.[70]

Friedländer's awareness of religion and his focus on solidarity mean he also offers glimpses into the religious responses of Jews in the face of destruction. We read of Zalman Gradowski from Lona, near Białystok, member of a Sonderkommando at Birkenau, who said Kaddish for the dead after each gassing.[71] And we find the anguished cries of an "anonymous adolescent" in Łódź in August 1944:

Is it not a shame to be a man on the same earth as the Ger-man? [. . .] Oh, God in Heaven, why didst thou create Germans to destroy humanity? [. . .] Why will you not punish, with all your wrath, those who are destroying us? Are we the sinners and they the righteous? Is that the truth? Surely you are intelligent enough to understand that it is not so, that we are not the sinners and they are not the Messiah![72]

It must still be possible to learn more about Jewish religious responses to the Shoah in all their variation. In her study of diaries in the Holocaust, Garbarini shows the endless range of possibilities. Where persecution and misery led Chaim Aron Kaplan in Warsaw to lose faith in a divine order and seek meaning and justice in rational, historical analysis, his French contemporary Lucien Dreyfus, a "bourgeois, acculturated west European Jew," moved in the opposite direction, away from belief in the values of Western civilization and towards deeper religiosity.[73]

Perhaps religion was both a source of continued solidarity and a major site of its breakdown, a duality evident in the response of the Romanian Jewish writer, Mihail Sebastian. Sebastian, another of Friedländer's diarists, observed Yom Kippur in Bucharest in October 1943:

I fasted, and I went to the synagogue in the evening to hear the sound of the shofar. Reading over someone's shoulder, I tried to intone the *Avinu Malkenu*. Why? Do I believe? Do I want to believe? No, not even that. But it is as if, in all these unthinking gestures, there is a need for warmth and peace.[74]

By then Sebastian's once large group of prominent gentile friends, among them Mircea Eliade, had not only abandoned him to isolation and poverty; they had become involved with the Iron Guard and embraced a vicious antisemitism.

Religion plays a further role in Friedländer's analysis, in the familiar guise of "political religion." "Modern society," Friedländer concludes, "does remain open to – possibly in need of – the ongoing presence of religious or pseudo-religious incentives within a system otherwise dominated by thoroughly different dynamics." Nazism, he maintains, "confronts us with some kind of 'sacralized modernism,'" a "mass craving for order, authority, greatness, and salvation" that Hitler proved uncannily able "to grasp and magnify."[75] Elsewhere, Friedländer has explicitly linked his interpretation of Nazism to the concept of "political religion" in the sense used by Eric Voegelin, Norman Cohn, Karl Dietrich Bracher, James Rhodes, Uriel Tal and many others.[76] Given the chronological momentum that drives Friedländer's analysis in *The Years of Extermination*, it comes as something of a surprise to find he invokes at the end a timeless, abstract, pseudo-/political religious force as a key explanatory device. Here too his chronological approach may provide clues to a more complex argumentation that differentiates between layers and stages of religious input in the Holocaust that intersected and diverged from time to time and place to place: religion as motivation, rationalization, radicalization, justification, normalization, vindication, camouflage and more.[77]

With *Nazi Germany and the Jews*, Saul Friedländer provides a model, a histori-cal and moral agenda, a set of themes and a method for integrating Jewish sources into the history of the Holocaust. His chronological framework, concepts of agency and solidarity, and attention to religion offer ways to continue the ongoing project of integration. Perhaps most important, Friedländer sets a tone for the endeavour. Clear and unflinching, neither sentimental nor cold, he never loses the "initial sense of disbelief." In his authority, elegance and economy of style, Friedländer is not so different from the author of another magisterial work on the Holocaust: Raul Hilberg.

Friedländer chose not to address his own experiences in *The Years of Extermination*. Perhaps this decision too was influenced by the exchange with Broszat and Broszat's insinuation that Jews were bound to "a ritualized, almost historical-theological remembrance" and could not write scientifically about the Holocaust.[78] Friedländer's first volume, published in 1997, opened with a direct response to this charge:

> Most historians of my generation, born on the eve of the Nazi era, recognize either explicitly or implicitly that plowing through the events of those years entails not only excavating and interpreting a collective past like any other, but also recovering and confronting decisive elements of our own lives.[79]

And further: "For my generation, to partake at one and the same time in the mem-ory and the present perceptions of this past may create an unsettling dissonance; it may, however, also nurture insights that would otherwise be inaccessible."[80]

Unmentioned in the second volume, Friedländer's biography nevertheless has a place here too. Born in 1932 in Prague, he fled with his parents to France in 1939. By July 1942, terrified by news of round-ups in Paris, Elli and Jan Friedländer decided to put their son into hiding. A French Catholic friend sub-sequently arranged for him to be taken into Saint-Béranger, a boarding school of the Sodality in Montluçon. In September 1942, Friedländer's parents tried to cross the border to Switzerland, but Swiss officials refused them entry, and they ended up in Rivesaltes and then on a transport to the east, where they were murdered, something their son, by then twelve and a half years old, would learn only when the war had ended.[81]

Absent from *The Years of Extermination*, Friedländer's parents are never-theless present, through the achievement of their beloved and brilliant son, and in his carefully documented account of the Swiss treatment of Jewish refugees. According to the directive signed by Swiss Federal Councillor Eduard von Steiger on 4 August 1942 and enforced by Heinrich Rothmund's Police Division, "*Political refugees were not to be sent back but 'persons who have fled purely on racial grounds, for example Jews, cannot be considered political refugees'*" (emphasis in original)."[82] Elsewhere, Friedländer has indicated that he learned border guards sometimes showed lenience if Jewish adults were accompanied by children.[83]

Friedländer's 1979 memoir anticipates themes central to his subsequent "integrative and integrated history" – the inescapability of chronology and its links to the impossibility of knowledge for the targets of annihilation; Jewish agency in the Holocaust, with all its layers of powerlessness and "choiceless choices"; solidarity and the force of destruction that crushed even the most intimate ties between people; and the surrounding and conflicting roles of religion, in particular Christianity. At the same time, Friedländer's words about his past, translated from the French in which he wrote them, interrupt and disrupt analysis in precisely the way he identifies in the introduction to *The Years of Extermination*:

> By its very nature, by dint of its humanness and freedom, an individual voice suddenly arising in the course of an ordinary historical narrative of events such as those presented here can tear through the seamless interpretation and pierce the (mostly involuntary) smugness of scholarly detachment and 'objectivity.'[84]

In autumn 1942, Saul Friedländer, then a ten-year-old known as Paul-Henri Ferland, ran away from his school and found his parents in a nearby hospital, where his father was being treated for an illness. "There are certain memories that cannot be shared," Friedländer writes, "so great is the gap between the meaning they have for us and what others might see in them."[85] Yet he made an eloquent attempt:

> I was sitting on my mother's lap, with my arms around her neck, weeping. [. . .] My father and mother spoke in turn. They assured me endlessly that we would not be separated long. Meanwhile, it was absolutely necessary that I return to Saint-Béranger. No, I wouldn't be going with them: they couldn't tell me why, but it was better that way. [. . .] A phone call had been made to Saint-Béranger. Madame Chapuis and Madame Robert arrived soon afterward, if I remember rightly. I had to leave. My mother put her arms around me, but it was my father who unwittingly revealed to me the real meaning of our separation: he hugged me to him and kissed me. It was the first time that that timid father of mine had ever kissed me. Nothing was definite yet; others had risked taking their children with them. My parents had put me in a safe place, but here I was, a runaway who had gone straight back to them, unable to bear being separated. Could I be dragged away from them a second time? I clung to the bars of the bed. How did my parents ever find the courage to make me loosen my hold, without bursting into sobs in front of me?
> It has all been swept away by catastrophe, and the passage of time. What my father and mother felt at that moment disappeared with them; what I felt has been lost forever, and of this heartbreak there remains only a vignette in my memory, the image of a child walking back down the rue de la Garde, in the opposite direction from the one taken shortly before, in a peaceful autumn light, between two nuns dressed in black.[86]

*Notes*

1   Saul Friedländer, *Nazi Germany and the Jews, 1939–1945: The Years of Extermination* (New York: HarperCollins, 2007).

2   Saul Friedländer, *Nazi Germany and the Jews*, vol. 1, *The Years of Persecution, 1933–1939* (New York: HarperCollins, 1997).

3   The somewhat anxious question about what would remain for subsequent scholars of the Holocaust is captured in the title of a session at the German Studies Association annual meeting in 2008 in Minneapolis, with papers by Alon Confino, Dan Stone, and Amos Goldberg and comment by Doris Bergen: "Holocaust Interpretation after Friedländer's Magnum Opus".

4   For discussion of issues related to closure, see Saul Friedländer, "Trauma, transference and 'working through'," *History & Memory* 4 (1992): 39–55. On the impossibility of achieving closure and the urgency of avoiding redemptive claims, see Lawrence L. Langer, *Holocaust Testimonies: The Ruins of Memory* (New Haven and London: Yale University Press, 1991). In a nuanced assessment of Langer, Dominick LaCapra concedes that, "One may agree with the view that the Holocaust is, in a manner than would have to be further differentiated, 'a communal wound that cannot heal.'" But he cautions against Langer's "very strong interpretation," a position that at least hints at "the rather levelling if not ahistorical idea of all modern history as holocaust or trauma"; see Dominick LaCapra (1994), *Representing the Holocaust: History, Theory, Trauma* (Ithaca and London: Cornell University Press, 1994), 187–203, particularly 195–6. Also instructive are LaCapra's postulations on the merits of "a broader theoretical awareness of possibilities" and how it might "enable a more modulated response to problems of analysis and judgment" (213) as well as his related discussion of Friedländer on closure (205–23). See also the discussion culminating in this conclusion: "Working through the past in any desirable fashion would thus be a process (not an accomplished state) and involve not definitive closure or full self-possession but a recurrent yet variable attempt to relate accurate, critical memory-work to the requirements of desirable action in the present"; see Dominick LaCapra (1998), *History and Memory after Auschwitz* (Ithaca and London: Cornell University Press, 1998), 42.

5   See Friedländer, *The Years of Extermination*, xv: "The history of the Holocaust should be both an integrative and an integrated history."

6   Saul Friedländer, *When Memory Comes*, trans. from French by Helen R. Lane (New York: Farrar, Straus and Giroux, 1979).

7   Saul Friedländer, *Reflections of Nazism: An Essay on Kitsch and Death*, trans. from French by Thomas Weyr (New York: Harper and Row, 1984).

8   Saul Friedländer (ed.), *Probing the Limits of Representation: Nazism and the "Final Solution"* (Cambridge: Harvard University Press, 1992).

9   Gerhard L. Weinberg, *A World at Arms: A Global History of World War II* (New York: Cambridge University Press, 1994); see also the essays in Weinberg (1995), *Germany, Hitler and World War II* (New York: Cambridge University Press, 2005).

10  Raul Hilberg, *The Destruction of the European Jews* (New Haven, CT: Yale University Press, 1961, rev. ed. 2003).

11  See, in particular, Gerhard L. Weinberg, *Visions of Victory: The Hopes of Eight World War II Leaders* (New York: Cambridge University Press, 2005), 2–3.

12  Friedländer, *The Years of Extermination*, 338–9, 517–8, 639.

13  Ibid., 287.

14  Ibid., 288.

15  Alexandra Garbarini, *Numbered Days: Diaries and the Holocaust* (New Haven and London: Yale University Press, 2006).

16  Victor Klemperer, *I Will Bear Witness: A Diary of the Nazi Years, 1933–1941*, trans. from German by Martin Chalmers (New York: Random House, 1998), 306 (entry from 3 September 1939). Quoted in Friedländer, *Years of Extermination*, 1.

17  Calel Perechodnik, *Am I a Murderer? Testament of a Jewish Ghetto Policeman*, ed. and trans. from Polish by Frank Fox (Boulder, CO: Westview, 1996), 187.

18  Herman Kruk, *The Last Days of the Jerusalem of Lithuania*, ed. and introduced by Benjamin Harshav; trans. from Yiddish by Barbara Harshav (New Haven and London: Yale University Press, 2002), 697–8.

19  *The Journal of Hélène Berr*, trans. from French by David Bellos (Toronto: McClelland and Stewart, 2008), 258.

20  Ibid., 262, emphasis in the original.

21  Ibid., emphasis in the original.

22  Raffael Scheck, *Hitler's African Victims: The German Army Massacres of Black French Soldiers in 1940* (New York: Cambridge University Press, 2006).

23  Jeffrey Herf, *The Jewish Enemy: Nazi Propaganda During World War II and the Holocaust* (Cambridge: Belknap Press of Harvard University Press, 2006).

24  A brief but incisive analysis of the vested interests of career killers appears in Gerhard L. Weinberg, "Crossing the line in Nazi genocide: On becoming and being a professional killer." Occasional paper, Center for Holocaust Studies, University of Vermont, 1997, 9–10.

25  Stephen Fritz, *Endkampf: Soldiers, Civilians, and the Death of the Third Reich* (Lexington: The University Press of Kentucky, 2004).

26  See John C. Fout, "The Fate of Gays in the Wehrmacht in World War II." Paper presented at the annual meeting of the German Studies Association, Chicago, 1995.

27  Friedländer, *The Years of Extermination*, 182–3, 376, 408; quotation on 599.

28  Ibid., 259–60.

29  Primo Levi, *The Drowned and the Saved*, trans. from Italian by Raymond Rosenthal (New York: Vintage, 1989), 36–69.

30  Friedländer, *The Years of Extermination*, 519.

31  Hilberg speaking in Claude Lanzmann (1985), *Shoah*. 566 minutes. DVD edition, American zone: New Yorker Video, #51003. See also Claude Lanzmann, *Shoah: An Oral History of the Holocaust* (New York: Pantheon, 1985), 190.

32  Adina Blady Szwajger, *I Remember Nothing More*, trans. from Polish by Tasja Darowska and Danusia Stok (New York: Simon and Schuster, 1990), 52–8.

33  Ibid., 135.

34  Olga Lengyel, *Five Chimneys: The Story of Auschwitz* (New York: Howard Fertig, 1983), 1.

35  Ibid., 15–6.

36  Henry Friedman, *I'm No Hero: Journeys of a Holocaust Survivor* (Seattle and London: University of Washington Press, 1999), 25–7.

37  Gitta Sereny, *Into that Darkness: An Examination of Conscience* (New York, Vintage, 1983), e.g.: 22, 134.

38  In his last statement, Adolf Eichmann wrote, "I am not the monster I am made out to be [. . .] I am the victim of a fallacy." Quoted in Hannah Arendt, *Eichmann in Jerusalem: A Report on the Banality of Evil* (New York, Viking, 1963), 248.

39  On Mennecke and 14f13, see Henry Friedlander, *The Origins of Nazi Genocide: From Euthanasia to the Final Solution* (Chapel Hill and London: University of North Carolina Press, 1995), 145–50. Excerpts from Mennecke's letters to his wife in Jeremy Noakes and Geoffrey Pridham (eds), *Nazism: A Documentary Reader*, vol. 3: *Foreign Policy, War and Racial Extermination* (Exeter: University of Exeter Press, 1988, rev. ed. 1997), 436–7.

40  Christopher R. Browning, *Ordinary Men: Reserve Police Battalion 101 and the Final Solution in Poland* (New York: HarperCollins, 1992); Karin Orth, *Das System der nationalsozialistischen Konzentrationslager. Eine politische Organisationgeschichte* (Hamburg: Hamburger Edition, 1999); Sybille Steinbacher, *"Musterstadt" Auschwitz. Germanisierungspolitik und Judenmord in Ostoberschlesien* (Munich: K.G. Saur, 2000); Michael Wildt, *Generation des Unbedingten. Das Führungskorps des Reichssicherheitshauptamtes* (Hamburg: Hamburger Edition, 2002); Edward Westermann, *Hitler's Police Battalions: Enforcing Racial War in the East* (Lawrence: University Press of Kansas, 2005).

41  This seeming contradiction between normalcy and monstrosity is at the heart of the controversial novel by Jonathan Littell (2008), *The Kindly Ones*, trans from French by Charlotte Mandell (New York: Harper, 2008). Reviewed by Daniel Mendelsohn, "Transgression," *New York Review of Books*, vol. 56, no. 5 (26 March 2009): 18–21.

42  Jan Kott refers to Jean-Paul Sartre's postwar play, *No Exit*, in which "the dead in hell are surprised not to see torturers. Hell is organized like a self-service cafeteria [. . .] an economy of man-power or devil-power. The customers serve themselves." See Kott, "Introduction" (trans. from Polish by Michael Kandel) to Tadeusz Borowski, *This Way for the Gas, Ladies and Gentlemen*, trans. from Polish by Barbara Vedder (New York, Penguin, 1976), 22.

43  Levi, *The Drowned and the Saved*, esp. the passage in "Shame," 78–85.

44  Sereny, *Into that Darkness*, 362–5.

45  Instructive here is the chapter on "The Jewish Leaders" in Raul Hilberg, *Perpetrators, Victims, Bystanders: The Jewish Catastrophe, 1933-1945* (New York: HarperCollins, 1992), 105–17.

46  *The People Next Door: A Story of Holocaust Survival* (1998), Golden Dome Productions for The Kurt and Tessye Simon Fund for Holocaust Remembrance, 37 mins.

47  For example, see the book based on Living Testimonies, an archive of videotaped interviews with Holocaust survivors in Montreal, Yehudi Lindeman (ed.), *Shards of Memory: Narratives of Holocaust Survival* (Westport, CT and London: Praeger, 2007); and the film *Spell Your Name*, Sergey Bukovsky, dir. (2006), based on interviews from the USC Shoah Foundation with Holocaust survivors in Ukraine.

48  Langer, *Holocaust Testimonies*; Shoshana Felman and Dori Laub, *Testimony: Crises of Witnessing in Literature, Psychoanalysis, and History* (New York and London: Routledge, 1992); Henry Greenspan, *On Listening to Holocaust Survivors: Recounting and Life History* (Westport, CT: Praeger, 1998).

49  Na'ama Shik, "Infinite Loneliness: Some Aspects of the Lives of Jewish Women in the Auschwitz Camps According to Testimonies and Autobiographies Written Between 1945 and 1948," in Doris L. Bergen (ed.), *Lessons and Legacies VIII: From Generation to Generation* (Evanston, IL: Northwestern University Press, 2008), 125–56, here 129.

50  Primo Levi, *Survival in Auschwitz*, trans. from Italian by Stuart Woolf (New York: Simon and Schuster, 1993).

51  See Levi, *The Drowned and the Saved*, 17–7: "For knowledge of the Lagers, the Lagers themselves were not always a good observation post: in the inhuman conditions to which they were subjected, the prisoners could barely acquire an overall vision of their universe."

52  Stacy Hushion, "Silence and Noise: Representations of Sexual Violence in Holocaust Survivors' Writing," unpublished paper, University of Toronto, 2008.

53  Nechama Tec, *Defiance: The Bielski Partisans* (New York and Oxford: Oxford University Press, 1993); movie *Defiance*, Edward Zwick, dir., starring Daniel Craig, 2008.

54  Joan Miriam Ringelheim, "Women and the Holocaust: A Reconsideration of Research," in Carol Rittner and John K. Roth (eds), *Different Voices: Women and the Holocaust* (New York: Paragon House, 1993), 373–418, here 375.

55  Elizabeth Covington Strauss, Ph.D. dissertation (in progress), "The Elderly in the Ghettos: A Study of Łódź and Vilna, 1939–44." University of Notre Dame.

56  Amos Goldberg, "The History of the Jews during the Holocaust: A Cultural Perspective". Paper presented at the annual conference of the German Studies Association, Saint Paul, 2008.

57  An example is the following passage: "I was always alone. My mother was in the KZ at Ravensbrück. And my father and my brother Waldemar were at Bialystok in a KZ, and my brother Max in the KZ Neuengamme. I was only together with granny, and that only for part of the time. And I believe that it was all for the best that I was alone. I did not have to make allowances for anybody. What I wanted to do, that I decided for myself and did it too. That was one reason why I survived." Ulrich Enzenberger, *A Gypsy in Auschwitz / Otto Rosenberg, as told to Ulrich Enzenberger*, trans. from German by Helmut Bögler (London: London House, 1999), 86. For an overview of Nazi measures against Sinti and Roma, see Sybil H. Milton, "'Gypsies' as social outsiders in Nazi Germany," in Robert Gellately and Nathan Stoltzfus (eds), *Social Outsiders in Nazi Germany* (Princeton: Princeton University Press, 2001), 212–32.

58  Adam Czerniaków, head of the Warsaw Jewish Council, noted on 17 June 1942: "It is reported that the Gypsies are to be deported from the ghetto. Thus I will not be an emperor of Ethiopians any more." Raul Hilberg, Stanislaw Staron and Josef Kermisz (eds), *The Warsaw Diary of Adam Czerniakow: Prelude to Doom*, trans. from Polish by Stanislaw Staron and the staff of Yad Vashem (Chicago: Ivan R. Dee, 1979), 368.

59  Zygmunt Bauman, *Modernity and the Holocaust* (Ithaca: Cornell University Press, 1989), esp. 117–50.

60  See Levi, *The Drowned and the Saved*, 77: "On a rational plane, there should not have been much to be ashamed of, but shame persisted nevertheless."

61  Ibid., 85–6: "And there is another, vaster shame, the shame of the world. [. . .] The just among us, neither more nor less numerous than in any other human group, felt remorse, shame, and pain for the misdeeds that others and not they had committed, and in which they felt involved, because they sensed that what had happened around them and in their presence, and in them,

was irrevocable. Never again could it be cleansed; it would prove that man, the human species – we, in short – had the potential to construct an infinite enormity of pain, and that pain is the only force created from nothing, without cost and without effort." Cf. the reference to Red Army soldiers on 72–3.

62   Testimony from the Jewish Historical Institute, Warsaw (ŻIH 301/579), quoted in Jan T. Gross, *Neighbors: The Destruction of the Jewish Community in Jedwabne, Poland* (Princeton: Princeton University Press, 2001), 108.

63   Jan T. Gross, *Fear: Anti-Semitism in Poland after Auschwitz: An Essay in Historical Interpretation* (New York: Random House, 2006). Also useful on this matter is Michael C. Steinlauf, *Bondage to the Dead: Poland and the Memory of the Holocaust* (Syracuse: Syracuse University Press, 1997).

64   Holly Case, "Territorial Revision and the Holocaust: Hungary and Slovakia during World War II," in Bergen (ed.), *Lessons and Legacies*, 222–44.

65   Saul Friedländer, *Kurt Gerstein, The Ambiguity of Good* (New York: Alfred, 1969); Saul Friedländer, *Pius XII and the Third Reich: A Documentation* (New York: Alfred A. Knopf, 1966).

66   Friedländer, *The Years of Extermination*, 641.

67   See Doris L. Bergen, "Religion and Genocide: A Historiographical Survey," in Dan Stone (ed.), *The Historiography of Genocide* (Houndmills and New York: Palgrave Macmillan, 2008), 194–227.

68   On forced abortions for slave workers, see Gabriella Hauch, "Zwangsarbeiterinnen und ihre Kinder. Zum Geschlecht der Zwangsarbeit in den Hermann Göring Werken/Linz, in Oliver Rathkolb (ed.), *NS-Zwangsarbeit. Der Standort Linz der "Reichswerke Hermann Göring AG Berlin", 1938–1945*, vol. 1. (Vienna: Böhlau, 2001), 355–448.

69   Gerhard L. Weinberg, "Pius XII in World War II," presentation at the University of Notre Dame, 2006.

70   Ibid.

71   Friedländer, *The Years of Extermination*, 581.

72   Ibid., 631.

73   Garbarini, *Numbered Days*, 79.

74   Mihail Sebastian, *Journal, 1935–1944: The Fascist Years*, trans. from Romanian by P. Camiller, introduction by Radu Ioanid (Chicago: Ivan R. Dee, 2000); excerpted as "Diary. Friends and Fascists," *The New Yorker* (2 October 2000), 107–13; entry from 11 October 1943 on 113.

75   Friedländer, *The Years of Extermination*, 657.

76   Martin Broszat and Saul Friedländer, "A Controversy about the Historicization of National Socialism," *New German Critique* 44 (1988): 85–126, here 109.

77   For some of the possibilities, see Susannah Heschel, *The Aryan Jesus: Christian Theologians and the Bible in Nazi Germany* (Princeton: Princeton University Press, 2008).

78   For Broszat's remarks about the contrast between "mythical memory" and scientific history, see "A Controversy about the Historicization of National Socialism," 101. Of considerable interest is Dominick LaCapra's discussion, "Reflections on the Historians' Debate," in LaCapra, *Representing the Holocaust*, esp. 57–63. Friedländer does not mention the exchange with Broszat in *The Years of Extermination*, although he foregrounded it in public talks before the book appeared (in his keynote address at the Lessons and Legacies conference at Claremont McKenna in October 2007 and at the University of Toronto in March 2007).

79   Friedländer, *The Years of Persecution*, 1.

80   Ibid.

81   Friedländer, *When Memory Comes*, 3, 30–31, 70–71, 77–80, 88–90, 133–4.

82   Friedländer, *The Years of Extermination*, 448.

83   Friedländer, *When Memory Comes*, 85.

84   Friedländer, *The Years of Extermination*, xxv–xxvi.

85   Friedländer, *When Memory Comes*, 85.

86   Ibid., 85–88.

# 16

# Towards an Integrated History of the Holocaust: Masculinity, Femininity, and Genocide

*Zoë V. Waxman*

In her memoir first published in Polish in 1967, Halina Birenbaum, a young Jewish girl in the Warsaw ghetto, describes the final moments of her father before his deportation to Treblinka:

> During these terrible minutes, a hurricane of blows fell on his already bent shoulders. Jewish police surrounded him and tried to herd him to the train. My father attempted to defend himself, to appeal. He shielded himself with his arms from the blows, tried to evade them, but was helpless against their brute force; he crouched down still further, but finally moved obediently to the wagons [. . .] I saw my father for the last time as he walked, bent and helpless under the police blows. [. . .] He was 47 years old.[1]

This desperate scene was reenacted in a myriad of different ways throughout the hundreds of ghettos of eastern Europe. The words of a young girl forced to watch as her beloved father was taken to an unknown fate speak for themselves and in many ways need no additional commentary. However, one might also enquire as to the fate of Halina and the rest of her family. In fact, while her father was being dragged to his death, her mother – a "sickly little woman, who suffered from frequent attacks of gall-stones"[2] – had managed to summon up every last vestige of strength and drag Halina and her brother away from the crowd of Jews being herded onto the cattle trucks to a series of hiding places. Rightly, perhaps, Birenbaum's memoir makes for uncomfortable reading. While it is in many ways written as a testament to the overwhelming strength, ingenuity, and love her mother displayed in the face of such appalling suffering, it also tells the story of the disintegration of a family – in particular, the mental and physical collapse of her father who became "so upset and terrified that he was incapable even of thinking of escape."[3]

It is tempting to minimize the role of Halina's father and instead valorize the response of Halina's mother. Indeed, many writers have done just that. However, as historians, we need to do more. We need to explore and understand the different ways in which the Jews responded to the destruction that was unfolding. In order to do that, and to begin to appreciate the heterogeneity of the victims of the Holocaust, we need to look more closely at the various factors which influenced the nature of that response – and that includes gender. Of course, gender alone is not enough: social, cultural, national, economic, religious and political differences all had an impact on the experiences of Jews during the Holocaust – as did age and familial circumstances. The Jewish victims cannot be treated as a homogenous entity. Some were religious, some secular, some Zionist and others assimilated or politically uninterested. While some Jews were poor and lived in small villages, others were more prosperous and lived in major cities. Nevertheless, gender as a category of analysis has tended to be at a discount – either ignored or downplayed by most writers, who have focused on other themes. In this essay I hope to suggest why that may be a mistake.

In particular, I want to suggest that Saul Friedländer's work provides both a provocation and a justification for a gendered approach to the Holocaust. For although he does not explicitly address gender – nor use it as a necessary category of analysis – nonetheless his approach necessitates taking gender seriously. Friedländer is surely right to argue that a truly integrated history of the Holocaust must go beyond "a recounting of German policies, decisions, and measures,"[4] to understand the experiences of the victims. For example, Friedländer reminds us that:

> At each step, in occupied Europe, the execution of German measures depended on the submissiveness of political authorities, the assistance of local police forces or other auxiliaries, and the passivity or support of the local populations. [. . .] It also depended on the willingness of the victims to follow orders in the hope of alleviating German strictures or gaining time and somehow escaping the inexorable tightening of the German vise.[5]

It is my contention that just such an "integrated" history of the Holocaust is one that takes gender seriously. As I shall show gender remains important in times of war and struggle and is an important influence on people's actions and decision-making. The gendered expectation that the Germans would not hurt women and children meant that many families were unable to recognize the direness of their predicament until it was too late. At the same time, Friedländer's work warns of the limits of a gendered analysis: "[A]ny influence the victims could have on the course of their own victimization was marginal."[6] Ultimately, of course, men and women were subjected to the same fate. Nonetheless, his determination to explore the experiences of the victims makes his disregard of gender surprising.

Taking gender seriously means recognizing when gendered expectations become redundant. It also means not just looking at gender in terms of femininity but also at masculinity and the plethora of biological and cultural roles and meanings it entails. While there is now a rapidly growing literature – appearing from the mid- and late-1990s onwards – looking at the specificity of women's Holocaust experiences,[7] research on masculinity and the Holocaust has largely restricted itself to the domain of the perpetrators.[8] In this essay, I do not wish to argue that either gender suffered more, or worse still behaved better or more heroically,[9] but rather that men and women not only might have had different experiences, but also might have experienced life under Nazism in different ways.

This seems particularly important because of the central role of gender in prewar Jewish family life. In both eastern and western Europe, family life before the outbreak of World War II revolved around specific gender roles. For the most part European Jewish life followed the bourgeois model, with women being responsible for maintaining the home and bringing up children, leaving men to participate in economic and professional life.[10] The exception was the less prosperous eastern Europe, where Jewish women needed to participate in outside work in order to support their families – for example, as shopkeepers, seams mistresses, and peddlers. In religious families too, women shouldered more financial responsibility to allow their men to pursue full-time Torah studies and communal responsibilities.[11] Ultimately, however, uniting European Jewish family life, whether middle or working class, urban or shtetl, secular or religious, was the fact that women were primarily viewed in maternal or wifely terms and men as figures of authority.[12] It was this intricate web of meanings and experiences that made up the gendered system of Jewish life and through this gendered system that the Holocaust was experienced.

Whilst the Nazis' overriding aim was the comprehensive mass murder of Jewish men, women, and children it is important to understand what the feminist researcher Joan Ringelheim has termed the "complex relationship between anti-Semitism [. . .] and sexism prior to and during the Holocaust."[13] In other words, although the antisemitism of the Nazis was premised on a monolithic hatred of the Jews it nevertheless saw Jewish men and Jewish women as different and as such accorded them different treatment. Women were viewed primarily in terms of their ability to bear children. The institutionalized and deep-rooted sexism of National Socialism – which extended to both Aryan and non-Aryan women[14] – is essential to understanding the unfolding of the genocide that ensued. As Raul Hilberg writes, "the Final Solution was intended by its creators to ensure the annihilation of all Jews [. . .] yet the road to annihilation was marked by events which specifically affected men as men and women as women."[15] For example, while Aryan women were encouraged to bear children for the future of the race and were prohibited from having abortions or sterilizations, those deemed "racially inferior" were forced to undergo abortions and sterilizations to prevent them from giving birth to future generations of "racial degenerates."[16] As Jewish children were regarded as enemies of the Reich, being pregnant became a crime. However, as if to show how contradictory attitudes towards gender can be, at the same time, the handful of Germans who refused to take part in the massacres in the early years of the war mostly did so because they could not come to terms with the idea of murdering women and children. That this was overcome in the death camps – deemed by Heinrich Himmler to be an efficient means of overcoming the revulsion of the physical act of killing – reveals the extent of the Nazis' antisemitic ideology. Nonetheless, even in Auschwitz – which functioned as both a concentration and death camp – gender was not irrelevant. Women, for example, were more likely to be sent straight to the gas chambers either because they came with small children or because they were not deemed capable of hard labor.[17] Being visibly pregnant also meant an immediate death sentence.[18]

At Majdanek, Halina Birenbaum was only spared thanks to her mother's efforts to make her look older. Her cherished mother, however, went straight to her death.

As this suggests, although German policy was driven by antisemitism, it would be illogical to believe that the Nazis had managed to invent a means of attack that transcended gendered thinking. From the outset the Nazis did distinguish between men and women. Believing that Jewish men presented the greatest threat they at least initially focused their efforts on the persecution of them. Jewish men, for example, were not only more likely to be arrested and imprisoned, but suffered public humiliation during the so-called "beard actions" when their facial hair was publicly shaved off. They were also murdered as part of the systematic targeting of community leaders. In the Łódź ghetto, for example, all the original members of the *Judenrat* with the exception of Chaim Rumkowski met their deaths in this way. As Nechama Tec recognizes, by targeting Jewish men the Nazis presumed themselves to be effectively quashing Jewish political opposition – an essential prerequisite to the goal of mass murder.[19] This gave Jewish women the ultimately misguided idea that they would be spared and there was a widespread belief that it was only men who faced real danger. In 1939, Calel Perechodnik, a member of the Warsaw ghetto police, wrote: "I thought that nothing would happen to women and particularly to children, and, besides, the war was to end shortly."[20]

Such a preconception had important consequences for the behavior of both sexes. Jewish men were encouraged to flee to Soviet-occupied eastern Poland to escape the approaching German army, while others responded to the request made by the Polish government for all young men to join the Polish army and were either killed in battle or captured and interned in German POW camps. In contrast, few women fled, not only because they believed they were in no immediate danger, but also because there were seldom enough financial resources to allow whole families to escape and women were more likely to take responsibility for elderly parents and small children.[21] The precarious situation of many of these women cannot be overestimated. Unless women were able to secure employment – and women were less likely than men to have employable skills and therefore were employed at lower rates than men – they would be unable to feed their families. Families headed by lone women were amongst the poorest in the ghetto and were among those most likely to suffer deportation.[22] As such it is particularly significant that of the estimated 300,000 Jews who went east, most were men. However, women soon discovered that they were not immune from Nazi brutality and humiliation. As well as being forced to clean the streets – and often in their underwear – they were also selected for hard labor and were subjected to sexual humiliation at the hands of their overseers.

The men who stayed behind were faced with a special German decree issued in October 1939, making work by Jewish men mandatory. A large number of men disappeared at this time after having been abducted for forced labor outside of the ghettos. Raul Hilberg argues that more men were killed in the early years of the war both because of these grueling labor assignments and also because they were killed in the first mass murders in the USSR and Serbia.[23] In December 1939 Dr Emmanuel Ringelblum, who initiated the clandestine *Oneg Shabbat* archive in the Warsaw ghetto, observed: "The women and children are left behind. A major problem for the entire country – the flight of the dynamic, working stratum."[24] By the end of October 1939 there were 164,307 men in Jewish Warsaw (46 per cent) compared with 195,520 women (54 per cent). Of those aged between sixteen and fifty-nine, the ratio expanded to 44:56 per cent, and among twenty to twenty-nine-year olds, women made up 65 per cent of the ghetto's population.[25] Ringelblum instructed the young journalist and translator Cecilya Ślepak to conduct research into "the Jewish woman in Warsaw in September 1939 and up to the end of 1941," paying particular attention to how women – from different social and economic classes – were forced to cope alone in the early days of the war.[26] During the winter and spring of 1942, Ślepak interviewed seventeen women about their prewar life, the siege and bombardment of Warsaw, and their incarceration in the ghetto and subsequent struggle to survive. Some of her questionnaires and notes were discovered with Ringelblum's diary after the war in the ruins of the ghetto.[27] Ślepak found that the women experienced a strong degree of traditional gender role reversal as circumstances conspired to make them become the primary breadwinners and defenders of the family.[28] For example, because men were forced to avoid being found outside during daytime hours the task of standing for hours in dangerous food lines as well as the procurement of employment and the ordeal of negotiating with both the Jewish and German authorities for the return of property, or immunity from deportation, also fell to women – who were on occasion brutally beaten for their efforts.[29] Adam Czerniaków, head of the Warsaw ghetto *Judenrat*, went so far as to write in his diary that he feared "a revolt by women."[30] Ślepak actually interpreted this inversion of gender roles positively. She was impressed by women's capacity to adapt to their new situation and hoped it would continue after the war:

> Women's individuality, so long hemmed in by ethical-cultural norms, has now become [a source of dynamic strength]. The particular circumstances of our socioeconomic life have impelled the Jewish woman to positions in the fight for life that are far more prominent than those occupied by women of other nationalities. The Jewish woman has penetrated into almost every aspect of life. In many areas she has acquired a dominant position and has become the positive factor in the formation of our new economic and moral reality. In her individual and communal activity she brings forward many models of behavior from the past; however, with a subtle and amazing sense of intuition she adapts this experience to new conditions, thus achieving very positive results. It is important to remember that the Jewish woman wants more than to simply 'endure'. She also wants to construct the foundations for the future socioeconomic rebirth [of our people]. Therefore we see the drive to acquire skills and professions [. . .] But the influence of the Jewish woman is also in the moral sphere. She is imparting a ray of hope and courage into our dull and dark life, a touch of humanity and [. . .] even of heroism.[31]

While this cannot be said to be representative of all female experience – particularly the women from the poorer echelons of ghetto society who found themselves in dire straits – and probably says more about the intellectual, social and moral concerns of Ślepak herself, it does contrast sharply with the experiences of men during these times. Unable to fulfill their traditional role of defender of the family, men found it particularly difficult to adapt to their bare-bones existence. In the Warsaw ghetto Chaim Kaplan noted that "important proprietors now attend to their household's needs, returning home laden with foodstuffs; in one pocket – a loaf of bread; in another pocket – an onion. [. . .] Authority has vanished; nobility has passed."[32] Other men could not even help with household tasks. Vladka Meed, who was a teenager in the Warsaw ghetto, describes the collapse of her father:

> He was not only helpless but a broken, dejected man who could not take care of his family. He was undernourished, run down; he got pneumonia and died. In contrast, my mother was someone who did not give up. Internally she was a strong person. Somehow she had the strength to keep our home spotless without soap. By keeping the place clean, she was fighting diseases, especially typhus.[33]

Despite their best efforts, men had to face the hard fact that they could no longer protect their families. For example, 27-year-old Calel Perechodnik joined the ghetto police in the hope that his position would protect his wife Anka and their two-year-old daughter Alúska from deportation. However, he was later to find them amongst 8,000 other Jews being herded into cattle cars for deportation to Treblinka.[34] In contrast Ringelblum wrote of "Women's power to endure. The main breadwinners [. . .] When [the man is picked up for hard labor] the woman does not give up. She runs after [the kidnappers], screams and pleads [. . .] she is not afraid of soldiers. She stands in endless queues – some of them are taken off to work."[35] Given this climate it is hardly surprising that survivors such as Birenbaum record their disillusionment with their fathers and disappointment in their inability to protect them. She writes, "Of the family, only my mother behaved courageously, without giving way to panic. She alone could control herself, comfort the rest of us and devise new ways of saving our lives."[36]

This description of course reflects Birenbaum's gendered expectation that, despite everything, her father should have done more to save the family. And indeed that gendered expectation is noteworthy and widely shared by the authors of other testimonies. As this suggests, not only was gender experienced but writers looking back on it tend to emphasize it in a way often ignored by historians. For example, although we know that in the face of the German occupation women were ultimately unable to provide their children with the nourishment and sense of security they required, as we have seen in the memoirs, they nevertheless take pains to stress the endurance of the maternal role under adversity. Gender is certainly crucial to survivors when understanding their experiences in the context of their families and wider communities. Indeed, it can be argued that the need to emphasize the centrality of gendered roles actually comes in part from the desire to reassure readers that despite everything those gendered roles remained intact. In other words that even in crisis gender held fast.

Nonetheless, contemporary diaries written in the ghettos of eastern Europe tell a rather different story, revealing the extent to which gendered boundaries were threatened by the hardships and uncertainties of ghetto life. Gender remained important, but previous norms were challenged. On 22 September 1942 *The Chronicle of the Łódź ghetto* recorded that:

> Here in the ghetto, after three years of war, the concept of the family has been erased from the lexicon, with a few exceptions. Any remaining illusions on the subject were completely dispelled after the deportation [. . .]. Instead of families, there are only 'family housing collectives' where all food commodities are weighed and doled out to family members, where strong family members deprive weaker ones of their food and set the stage for interminable family quarrels and conflicts.[37]

Diaries written in the ghettos of eastern Europe reveal the extent to which the hardships and uncertainties of ghetto life both strengthened and destroyed previously taken for granted familial bonds. Families became extended as relatives who lived outside the ghetto were forced to move in with those who lived inside the ghetto walls. At the same time, the overcrowding in the ghettos also meant that people had to live with strangers. Those unluckier still were forced to wander the streets. The strain of unsatisfactory shelter was made worse by the fact that the Jews were being purposely starved to death. Entire families could be found in the streets begging for food. In Warsaw, the Jews were allocated a mere 300 calories per day. Many of the ghetto diaries and memoirs suggest that it was men who felt the hunger more acutely. In her study of the Łódź ghetto Michal Unger argues that women "exercised superior self-restraint; dividing their bread into daily portions, while many men frequently consumed several days' bread in one sitting."[38] It is, however, difficult to evaluate to what extent this was the case. Certainly – judging by many of the ghetto diaries – women were perceived to need less food. Either on account of their physiology or socialization many women were accustomed to eating less than their male relatives. For example, Sara Zyskind writes of the Łódź ghetto:

> Hunger was now stalking the ghetto [. . .]. Mother and I didn't feel the shortage of food so much, for even in good times we had eaten sparingly, but Father, with his healthy appetite, suffered badly from hunger pangs. Mother tried hard to supplement his diet, salvaging every grain of barley or crumb of bread to make an additional meal. To disguise the terrible taste of the rotten potatoes we were now receiving, she grated them finely and made fritters out of them. When Father discovered her hidden culinary talents, he responded with good-humored praise.[39]

Not all families resolved the shortage of food so harmoniously. In her memoir of the Łódź ghetto Sara Selver-Urbach describes hearing "people fighting over bread, their screaming voices bursting out of the open window."[40] Even in her own family, which Selver-Urbach stresses never fought over food, they were reduced to weighing out their rations. She writes:

> Only people who participated in the weighing out of provisions in the presence of their whole family know what took place at those times: sharp, suspicious glances directed at the scales, mingled with shame and anger at having reached such a horrible degradation.
>
> I relate these events with a heavy heart because we too, we too, started weighing our food. At first, we tried to justify this new step by claiming that the weighing would ensure an accurate and fair apportioning of our rations, so that no one could be wronged. Still, in our family, we never fought over our food, neither during the weighings of rations nor prior to it [. . .].
>
> But I could not be blind to the naked truth, at least where I was concerned. For I coveted greatly my own portion, and the weighing secured every gramme that was justly mine. A burning shame sweeps over me when I think back to those weighings, and I am consumed with remorse lest I was partial, here and there, to myself and added an extra crumb of bread to my portion when it was my turn to weigh the food, though I know I would restore such a crumb on the very next occasion. And yet, this blot, this disgrace, will always remain with me, this shame at having had to lead such an inner struggle.[41]

Other witnesses make oblique references to family members stealing each other's food. Also in Łódź, Dawid Sierakowiak wrote in his diary that if his father and sister had not regularly eaten the food that should have gone to his mother she would not have grown so weak.[42] Sierakowiak records that his "tiny, emaciated mother gave up her life by giving away her food" because she "valued family more than herself."[43] In contrast he reserves particular scorn for his father who not only steals his wife's bread but also that of his son and daughter. Again in Łódź, an unknown girl wrote in her diary: "I ate all the honey. I am selfish [. . .]. I'm not worthy of my mother who works so hard [. . .] I eat everything that lands near me."[44]

Of course, these familial problems – serious as they were – became all but irrelevant in the summer of 1942 with the liquidation of the ghettos. The pace and violence of the deportations left practically no-one in its wake. Men, women, and children were all summoned to an unknown fate – the concentration and death camps. In Warsaw, between 22 July 1942 and 21 September 1942 approximately 265,000 Jews were herded into sealed, overcrowded cattle trucks and sent to the Treblinka death camp. On average 5,000 to 7,000 people were deported in a single day, with the figure sometimes swelling to 13,000. An additional 11,580 Jews were sent to forced-labor camps, and more than 10,000 were murdered in the ghetto's streets.[45] Approximately a million and a half Jewish children were murdered during the Holocaust. Even the most astute of ghetto chroniclers were ill-prepared for the scale and brutality of the operation. On arrival at the camps – where men were separated from women – the deportees were to experience such a depth of cruelty and deprivation that any remaining family ties were severely challenged.[46]

And yet, survivors such as Halina Birenbaum, often stress that they could not have survived without the support of those close to them. At Majdanek, after the realization that her mother had been taken away from her, Halina's sister-in-law tells her: "'From now on I am your mother, do you understand that?,'"[47] and until her death lavishes on Halina the love and care she once gave to Halina's brother.

The extent to which the experience of the Holocaust challenged, subverted and changed notions of gender and familial identity and role consequently demands further exploration. To what extent did the Nazi attack on the Jewish family affect masculinity as well as femininity? How were fathers affected as well as mothers by not being able to save their children? Elie Wiesel has written that: "The failure of my father and of all he symbolized long made me fear having a child."[48] While research has rightly been concerned with women's experiences of motherhood in the early postwar years – for example, regarding fears about fertility and the challenges of raising children in the absence of parents and grandparents[49] – fatherhood has received far less attention. While women had to endure the physical demands of pregnancy and the strain of caring for their children in difficult and uncertain circumstances, men had to overcome feelings of guilt at not being able to protect their families and reinvent traditional versions of paternity in the void left by the destruction of European Jewry. This important area of experience demands further research.[50]

As I have argued, gender was an important organizing principle for both Jewish men and Jewish women before, during, and after the Holocaust. Prior to the outbreak of World War II, Jewish family life was heavily structured along traditional gendered lines with men responsible for protecting their families and women in charge of domestic life. However, anti-Jewish legislation made the fulfillment of these socially constructed gender roles all but impossible and irrevocably transformed family life. As antisemitic policies became genocidal in their intent, gender structures were placed still more under pressure – and threatened to collapse altogether. Nonetheless, even in Auschwitz gender was still real and was still experienced as real. No account of the experiences of Jewish men and women during the Holocaust can afford to ignore that truth. When it comes to the testimonies of survivors, although gender as we understand it today undoubtedly operated very differently in 1930s and 1940s Europe, it nonetheless remains an important arbiter of experience. A truly integrated history of the Holocaust therefore, is also a history of gender in the Holocaust.

*Notes*

1   Halina Birenbaum, *Hope is the Last to Die: A Personal Documentation of Nazi Terror*, trans. David Welsh (New York: Twayne, 1967), 31.
2   Ibid., 22.
3   Ibid., 28.
4   Saul Friedländer, *The Years of Extermination: Nazi Germany and the Jews 1939–1945* (London: Weidenfeld and Nicholson, 2007), xv.
5   Ibid.

6    Ibid., xii–xxiv.

7    See for example, Brana Gurewitsch (ed.), *Mothers, Sisters, Resisters: Oral Histories of Women Who Survived the Holocaust* (Tuscaloosa: University of Alabama Press, 1998); S. Lilian Kremer, *Women's Holocaust Writing: Memory and Imagination* (Lincoln: University of Nebraska Press, 1999); Dalia Ofer and Lenore J. Weitzman (eds), *Women in the Holocaust* (New Haven, CT: Yale University Press, 1998); and Zoë Waxman, "Unheard Testimonies, Untold Stories: The Representation of Women's Holocaust Experiences," *Women's History Review* 12 (2003): 661–77.

8    For example, Christopher Browning, *Ordinary Men: Reserve Police Battalion 101 and the Final Solution in Poland* (New York: HarperPerennial, 1993).

9    As Joan Ringelheim has noted: "oppression does not make people better; oppression makes people oppressed"; see Joan Ringelheim, "Women and the Holocaust: A Reconsideration of Research," in Carol Rittner and John K. Roth (eds), *Different Voices: Women and the Holocaust* (New York: Paragon House, 1993), 374–418, here 387).

10   Paula E. Hyman, *Gender and Assimilation in Modern Jewish History* (Seattle: University of Washington Press, 1995).

11   Paula E. Hyman, "Gender in the Jewish Family in Modern Europe," in Ofer and Weitzman (eds), *Women in the Holocaust*, 25–34.

12   Margarete Myers Feinstein, "Absent Fathers, Present Mothers: Images of Parenthood in Holocaust Survivor Narratives," *Nashim: A Journal of Jewish Women's Studies and Gender Issues* 13 (2007): 155–82, here 161.

13   Joan Ringelheim, "Thoughts about Women and the Holocaust," in Roger S. Gottlieb (ed.), *Thinking the Unthinkable: Meanings of the Holocaust* (New York: Paulist Press, 1990), 141–9, here 145.

14   For example, Hitler stated that: "The Nazi Revolution will be an entirely male event" (cited in Claudia Koonz, *Mothers in the Fatherland: Women, the Family and Nazi Politics* (New York: St. Martin's Press, 1987), 56). On the question of Nazi attitudes towards women, see also Gisela Bock, *Zwangssterilisation im Nationalsozialismus. Studien zur Rassenpolitik und Frauenpolitik* (Opladen: Westdeutscher Verlag, 1986).

15   Raul Hilberg, *Perpetrators, Victims, and Bystanders* (New York: Harper Collins, 1992), 126.

16   Gisela Bock, "Racism and Sexism in Nazi Germany: motherhood, compulsory sterilization and the state," in Rittner and Roth (eds), *Different Voices*, 161–86.

17   The data supplied by Danuta Czech regarding transports to Auschwitz-Birkenau suggests that more women than men were immediately sent to the gas chambers (Danuta Czech, *Auschwitz Chronicle 1939–1945* [New York: Henry Holt and Company, 1990]). However, it should be noted that while some women sacrificed their lives to accompany their children to their deaths, other women attempted to distance themselves from their children in the uncertain hope of survival. See the description of one young mother provided by Tadeusz Borowski, *This Way for the Gas Ladies and Gentlemen*, trans. B. Vedder (Harmondsworth: Penguin, 1967), 43.

18   As Ellen Fine writes: "Being a mother directly affected the chances for survival; being a father did not"; see Ellen Fine, "Women Writers and the Holocaust: Strategies for Survival," in Randolph L. Braham (ed.), *Reflections of the Holocaust in Art and Literature* (New York: City University of New York, 1990), 79–98, here 82.

19   Nechama Tec, *Resilience and Courage: Women, Men, and the Holocaust* (New Haven, CT: Yale University Press, 2003).

20   Calel Perechodnik, *Am I a Murderer? Testament of a Warsaw Jewish Ghetto Policeman* (Boulder, CO: Westview, 1996), 7.

21   On women's ability to care for their children, see Renée Fodor, "The Impact of the Nazi Occupation of Poland on the Jewish Mother-Child Relationship," *YIVO Annual of Jewish Social Science* 11 (1956/57): 000–000, here 270–2.

22   Dalia Ofer, "Cohesion and Rupture: The Jewish Family in East European Ghettos during the Holocaust," in Peter Y. Medding (ed.), *Coping with Life and Death: Jewish Families in the Twentieth Century* (Studies in Contemporary Jewry, XIV) (New York: Oxford University Press, 1998), 143–65.

23   Hilberg, *Perpetrators, Victims, and Bystanders*, 126–30.

24   Emanuel Ringelblum, *Diary and Notes from the Warsaw Ghetto: September 1939–December 1942*, Yisrael Gutman, Yosef Kermisz and Israel Shacham, eds, (Jerusalem: Yad Vashem and Ghetto Fighters' House, 1993 [Hebrew]), 15.

25   Samuel Kassow, *Who Will Write Our History? Emanuel Ringelblum, the Warsaw Ghetto, and the Oyneg Shabes Archive* (Bloomington, IN: Indiana University Press, 2007), 241.

26   Yad Vashem Archives (YVA), M.10.AR.1/128.

27   In March 1944, Ringelblum and his family, together with sixty other people, were discovered in hiding and taken to the Pawiak prison in Warsaw where they were executed. Ślepak and her children died in Treblinka in the summer of 1942.

28   On this type of role reversal, see Sara R. Horowitz, "Memory and Testimony of Women Survivors of Nazi Genocide," in Judith R. Baskin (ed.), *Women of the Word: Jewish Women and Jewish Writing* (Detroit, MI: Wayne State University Press, 1994), 258–82; Sara R. Horowitz, "Gender, Genocide and Jewish Memory," *Prooftexts* 20 (2000): 158–90.

29   Lenore J. Weitzman and Dalia Ofer, "Women in the Holocaust: Foundations for a Gendered Analysis of the Holocaust," in M. Sachs-Little (ed.), *Women in the Holocaust: Responses, Insights and Perspectives. Selected Papers from the Annual Scholars' Conference on the Holocaust and the Churches 1990–2000* (Pennsylvania: Merion Westfield Press International, 2001), 1–34, here 7.

30   Adam Czerniakow, *The Warsaw Diary of Adam Czerniakow*, Raul Hilberg, Josef Kermisz and Stanislaw Staron, eds, (New York: Stein and Day, 1979), 162.

31   Cited in Kassow, *Who Will Write Our History*, 243.

32   Cited in Raquel Hodara, "The Polish Jewish Woman From the Beginning of the Occupation to the Deportation to the Ghettos," *Yad Vashem Studies* 32 (2004): 397–432.

33   Vladka Meed, *On Both Sides of the Wall*, trans. B. Meed (Tel Aviv: Hakkibutz Hameuchad, 1973), 8.

34   Perechodnik, *Am I a Murderer?*

35   Ringelblum, *Diary and Notes from the Warsaw Ghetto*, 51.

36   Birenbaum, *Hope is the Last to Die*, 18.

37   Lucjan Dobroszycki (ed.), *The Chronicle of the Łódź Ghetto, 1941–1944*, trans. R. Lourie et al (New Haven: Yale University Press, 1984), 236.

38   Michal Unger, "The Status and Plight of Women in the Lodz Ghetto," in Ofer and Weitzman (eds), *Women in the Holocaust*, 123–42, here 136.

39   Sara Zyskind, *Stolen Years*, trans. M. Insar (New York: Signet, 1981), 26.

40   Sarah Selver-Urbach, *Through the Window of My Home: Memories from Ghetto Lodz*, trans. S. Bodansky (Jerusalem: Yad Vashem, 1971), 77.

41   Ibid., 77–8.

42   Dawid Sieakowiak, *The Diary of Dawid Sierakowiak: Five Notebooks form the Łódź Ghetto*, trans. Kamil Turowski, ed. Alan Adelson (London: Bloomsbury, 1997), 220.

43   Ibid., 219–20.

44   Unger, "The Status and Plight of Women in the Lodz Ghetto," 123–42. Unger describes women's ability to fashion meals out of meager food rations. For example, they would transform ersatz coffee into ersatz cake and turn potato peelings into ersatz soup dumplings (ibid., 134–5).

45   Zoë V. Waxman, *Writing the Holocaust: Identity, Testimony, Representation* (Oxford: Oxford University Press, 2006), 39–44.

46   Ibid., 146–150.

47   Birenbaum, *Hope is the Last to Die*, 93.

48   Elie Wiesel, *And the Sea is Never Full*, trans. Marion Wiesel (New York: Alfred A. Knopf, 1999), 43. At the same time it should be noted that it was in the concentration camps that Wiesel was able to form a strong bond with his previously distant father; see Elie Wiesel, *Night*, trans. Stella Rodway (New York: Bantam Books, 1960).

49   See Atina Grossman, "Trauma, Memory and Motherhood: Germans and Jewish Displaced Persons in Post-Nazi Germany, 1945–1949," *Archiv für Sozialgeschichte* 38 (1981): 215–39; Atina Grossman, "Victims, Villains, and Survivors: Gendered Perceptions and Self-Perceptions of Jewish Displaced Persons in Occupied Postwar Germany," *Journal of the History of Sexuality* 11 (2002): 291–318; Atina Grossman, *Jews, Germans, and Allies: Close Encounters in Occupied Germany* (Princeton: Princeton University Press, 2007); and Robert G. Moeller, *Protecting Motherhood: Women and the Family in the Politics of Postwar West Germany* (Berkeley: University of California Press, 1993), 33.

50   For a rare treatment of this issue, see Myers Feinstein, "Absent Fathers, Present Mothers," *passim*.

# 17

# The History of the Holocaust: Multiple Actors, Diverse Motives, Contradictory Developments and Disparate (Re)actions

## Wolf Gruner

Many people, including historians, have fallen for the assumption that the Holocaust was a singular phenomenon that escapes any explanation or logic. Yet, this would also be true for other genocides perpetrated by human beings. As the German Heinrich Vierbücher wrote in 1930 about the mass murder of the Armenians in Turkey: "Annihilation of an entire nation with the conscious slaughter of women and children – to this progress the past was not "ripe" [. . .]. After trying to comprehend, using explanations such as the lust for murder, ravenousness, religious hatred, imperiousness and ignorance, we are left with so much which is still inconceivable that the tragedy of 1915 seems to us to have been the bloodiest and most atrocious mystery in history."[1]

Many identify a widespread radical antisemitism among the German population as the main cause for the Holocaust. Yet recent research reveals that some ordinary Germans demonstrated more anti-Jewish furore than Nazi activists, while some antisemitic Nazi party members showed opposition or even resistance. Hence, history has probably been much more complex. For a fuller understanding of the destruction of European Jewry by the Third Reich, a historical account needs to be established which integrates a more in-depth analysis of the perpetrators and their motives, the institutions involved, their relationships, including previously overlooked dependencies and contradictory developments, as well their impact on the Jewish population in different regions and localities.

In both of his widely acclaimed books on *Nazi Germany and the Jews*, Saul Friedländer masterfully depicts the persecution and the extermination of the Jews in Germany and other European countries.[2] While researchers started to discuss the Holocaust as a multi-causal phenomenon in the 1990s, Friedländer emphasizes the overwhelming importance of antisemitism in his impressive and colourful two-volume account. For Friedländer a "redemptive antisemitism" drove all Hitler's politics, whether the quest for war, *Lebensraum* or the people's community – the *Volksgemeinschaft*. As the Jews were perceived to constitute the ultimate and fatal danger to the Aryan race and the German People, the imagined fear of racial degeneration, the need to fight against the Jews and the religious belief in racial redemption dominated the Nazi worldview.[3] With this approach, Friedländer is not alone. After the so-called structuralist wave of interpretations since the 1980s, which have sought to locate the origins of the radicalization within the institutional struggle of Nazi German society, we now see a trend backwards to more intentionalist views of the Holocaust, as well as the belief in antisemitism – which already dominated the decades after the war – as the most important cause for persecution and murder.[4]

Those interpretations, however, fail to explain the crucial point as to how Nazism transformed Germans into mass murderers. Neither antisemitism nor racism or eugenics were German inventions, but were discussed in a world context during the 1920s and 1930s, as can be seen with the impact of California sterilization laws on the Nazi plans in 1933.[5] For Friedländer, the German peculiarity which distinguished it from antisemitic movements in other European countries and ultimately led to the Holocaust, resulted from Hitler's "redemptive antisemitism," his tight bonds with all strata of German society, the political exploitation of antisemitism after 1933 and the impact of the war. Yet, are these sufficient arguments to explain the unexplainable, to comprehend why so many Germans participated in mass crimes?

On what kind of motives did the perpetrators predominantly act? Provoked not least by Goldhagen's absolute claim of an "eliminationist antisemitism" as the sole motivation of the perpetrators, historians accomplished a great deal of new biographical studies since the 1990s. Research on the top Nazi echelons intensified, with studies on Hitler[6] and his party's entourage, such as SA-leader Ernst Röhm[7] and the head of the SS, Heinrich Himmler,[8] but also on the members of his government; for example, the Reich Minister of the Interior, Wilhelm Frick, and the Reich Minister of Economy, Hjalmar Schacht.[9]

Most of those studies tend to cloud previously held impressions. While Hitler was involved in almost all anti-Jewish decisions, for example the anti-Jewish laws, the pogroms and the deportations, as Peter Longerich has demonstrated,[10] the dictator did not always act as the most radical person. By contrast, he often decided upon a moderate solution for pragmatic political reasons. Moreover, research on the conservative members of Hitler's government introduced rectifying elements in the image of the driving political forces after 1933. Studies on Hjalmar Schacht, the Reich Minister of Economy 1934–7 and on Lutz Graf Schwerin von Krosigk, the Reich Minister of Finances 1932–45, blew apart the traditional and somewhat apologetic notion that the exclusion of the Jews from Germany's economy was driven by the Nazis alone and only started after the conservative non-Party members were dismissed from the government in 1938. Both cabinet members developed anti-Jewish initiatives on their own.[11] This could have been by no means a surprise, because – based on their Pan-German *völkisch* beliefs – most rightwing conservatives shared many goals with the National Socialists, including the prominent vision of creating a Greater Germany by annexing neighbouring territories, expelling the Jews and reuniting all Germans in one powerful Reich.

The second most notable group within the Nazi hierarchy, the leadership of the Security Police and the Security Service of the SS, also drew scholarly attention. While Hans Safrian and Yaakov Lozowick focused on the actions of the main personnel of the SS and its Security Service in their studies (for example, organization of deportation and mass murder) rather than on their motives,[12] Michael Wildt investigated the staff of the Reich Main Security Office in a collective biography.[13] Individual biographies were published on Müller, Heydrich, Best, Eichmann and others such as Odilo Globocznik, the former Vienna *Gauleiter* and later notorious Higher SS- and Police leader in the Lublin district of the General Government.[14]

Concentrating exclusively on the role of the top echelons of the Nazi Party and/or on the SS, one tends to neglect both the complexity of the persecution and the broad contribution of state administrations to it. Over the last two decades, the examination of public institutions involved in the persecutions, such as tax offices, labor offices, welfare institutions and local governments has pointed to a wider and more complex set of factors and motives, beyond pure ideological reasoning, for people to discriminate against Jews. Moreover, at the local level, the persecution of the Jews was shaped and radicalized by the activities of those agencies and their personnel rather than by national laws and/or the propaganda of the Nazi party.[15] This holds true even for the developments in occupied Poland or the Netherlands.[16]

While Friedländer, in his second volume, colorfully describes the life of oppressed Jews in ghettos in occupied Poland, he allocates no space to identify those people or agencies responsible for ghettoization, forced labor or expropriation. In this view, persecution seems to be produced by an abstract anti-Jewish force, supposedly the Nazi Party, yet seldom by a concrete institution or people. The range of institutions involved in all the different territories needs to be analyzed, not for a structuralist approach which perceives radicalism as evolving from conflict and competition, but in order to understand their individual impact on the formation of the "twisted road to Auschwitz."

Many historians today agree that the German army played a hitherto underestimated role in the massacres of Jews and other groups during the invasion of the Soviet Union. Yet, before, during and after this military campaign the *Wehrmacht* introduced the first anti-Jewish measures in the occupied territories, whether in Poland, the Soviet Union or western Europe, restricting the access of the Jews to their property, segregating them from the rest of the society and forcing them to perform hard manual labor.[17] If institutions such as the German army were so actively involved and were able to exert such a strong influence on the course of the persecution, we must analyze their personnel and their motives. Fortunately, first comparative biographical accounts of several army generals and lower ranking commanders surfaced, as well as studies on their attitudes and motivations during the war against the Soviet Union.[18]

However, anti-Jewish activists such as those found in the German *Wehrmacht* existed in all public institutions as well as in the private sector. Recently, business history has provided us with interesting insights regarding Germany's leading staff of private companies and banks and their activities, such as the expelling of Jewish employees and the taking over of property in Germany and the annexed territories.[19] Ulrich Herbert und Michael Wildt tried to locate the origin of the widespread radicalism in a so-called generation of soberness and uncompromisingness. This generation was born around 1900 and would have compensated for the missed opportunity to fight in the First World War with anti-Jewish rigor.[20] This observation is certainly true for parts of the SS elite and particularly for the top echelon of the Reich Main Security Office. On the contrary, many (including the most radical) civil servants and many officials of local institutions had been born during the 1880s and 1890s. Thus, they had been socialized differently under the monarchy and had fought in the First World War.[21]

If Nazi ideology alone or a particular generational socialization does not provide sufficient explanation of the fact that so many different men and women actively participated in the persecution, what is it that attracts people with diverse beliefs and socialization to discriminate against one group and to commit mass crimes? To answer this question, a more systematic discussion based on more biographical data is needed in the future. In my view, the administrative personnel are the key to understanding why and how the anti-Jewish persecution unfolded in the Third Reich. Establishing proper biographical accounts of the leading staff involved in different facets of the persecution of the Jews would provide a base from which to compare individual socialization, aims and experiences in order to unearth motives and interests that informed the decisions and actions of the perpetrators.

Moreover, an in-depth analysis of the perpetrators' careers is desperately needed in order to understand how people became involved in and adapted to crimes. First, a systematic examination of more leading figures of the Third Reich and of their institutional careers will reveal that some of them were highly active in developing and introducing anti-Jewish measures in various places and territories. For example, after serving as the "Reich Commissar for the Reintegration of the Saar territory" (1935–8), Joseph Bürckel applied his experiences as Reich commissar and *Reichsstatthalter* in Austria after the annexation (1938–40), as the head of the civil administration of the German army during the occupation in Moravia (spring 1939) and after 1940 as the head of the civil administration of the German army in occupied Lorraine and as the *Reichsstatthalter* of the *Westmark*.

Secondly, studies of the subordinate actors are equally important. They cannot be seen as executors of central decisions only, because they often developed their own discriminatory practises. Recently, the lives and careers of civil servants of institutions such as the German Foreign Office have started to be investigated.[22] As a long-term result of the Browning-Goldhagen controversy regarding the issue of "ordinary men" versus "willing executioners,"[23] we have gained new information about the participation of the Order Police battalions in occupational policy and mass murder,[24] but we still don't know much about what these men did before they committed mass murder in eastern Europe. How did former experiences change their worldview and prepare them for the "war against the Jews"? We have already learnt that before the police battalions participated in mass murder some carried out forced deportations of non-Jewish and Jewish

Poles from the *Warthegau*, annexed to the Reich, to the rest of occupied Poland, the so-called General Government in 1939–40.[25] Yet, from 1933 onwards one of the daily routines of the Order Police in Germany was to arrest Jews who did not obey anti-Jewish laws. The Order Police worked closely with the Gestapo and handed Jews over for internment in concentration camps.[26] What did those policemen do during the April Boycott of 1933, the summer riots of 1935 and the November pogrom of 1938? How did their daily experience of persecuting Jews prepare them for their murderous work in the east?

In contrast, many of the older family men who were only drafted as reserve policemen during the war and who participated in mass murder had not had the same experience. But did they profit at home and at work from the persecution of Jews from the year 1933 onwards? As the war started, everyone who lived in the Third Reich had been socialized by individual experience or by regular observance of the persecution of others, especially the Jews. The experience of six years of escalating violence and discrimination as a social practise in German society might have had a bigger impact on the minds of many men and women and on their inclination to participate in mass crimes than the short-term propaganda put out by Goebbels.

On the other hand, much of the documented radicalism depended upon individual decisions. One of the most striking results of recent research is that officials at every administrative level and in every region, whether inside or outside Germany, found plenty of leeway for their actions. The traditional notion of the Third Reich as a top-down dictatorship where subaltern officials had no other choice than to follow what Hitler and his entourage mandated is obsolete. This concept dates back to the exculpation strategies of many Nazi defendants after the war. The radicalisation of anti-Jewish policy cannot be understood as solely driven by central orders. Kershaw demonstrated in his biography of Hitler how people tended to work towards the *Führer*. At the same time, it is important to notice that everyone also had plenty of latitude in which to make their own choices and to resist. This leads us to the previously overlooked question of individual responsibility: there was not only a personal responsibility for actively participating in mass crimes but also for not resisting the Nazi mainstream. It is hard to speak of a passive complicity of the majority of the Germans any longer because anti-Jewish policy would have been on the verge of their interests.[27] On the contrary, the research of the last two decades has revealed that millions of employees in a wide range of German public and private institutions, and also a countless number of other individuals, were involved in the persecution in one way or another. Consequently, the application of the "bystander category" to the majority of the Germans seems to be a postwar construct that is far from being based on the reality of the Third Reich.

The mayors and the main city officials alone amounted to approximately half a million people in Germany, and many of them were not members of the Nazi Party. Nonetheless, most cities and many of their departments introduced anti-Jewish policies after 1933, even before national laws were enacted. Jewish employees were dismissed and contracts with Jewish enterprises were cancelled. Garden departments forbade Jews access to public parks and later used them as forced laborers; welfare departments discriminated against the Jewish needy and market departments excluded Jewish merchants from public fairs. Such local initiatives, whether first in Germany or later in the Protectorate and occupied Poland, fuelled the radicalization of anti-Jewish policy and had a hitherto under-estimated impact on the central decision-making process. On the other hand, there was always room to manoeuvre: up until the spring of 1938 only half of the fifty-six German cities with municipal pawn shops had decided to established rules against Jews.[28] Similar developments are seen in local and regional courts, school district departments and in regional and local tax offices.[29]

While the number of people actively involved in persecution greatly increases in this way, so does the potential quantity of people who, confronted with a decision, might have disliked, opposed or resisted discriminatory measures. For a complete account of the Holocaust, such oppositional behaviour needs to be addressed, as Friedländer also demands. There was no uniform response, as he demonstrates with regard to the protests of the Heidelberg medical department against the dismissal of their colleagues in April 1933.[30] Such activities need to be systematically examined as an alternative strand of history, especially when one realizes that inside the apparatus, civil servants and employees were not really punished after failing to obey national laws or local rules, as the following case demonstrates. In 1937, the Munich city employee V. J. Weiss refused to comply with a local order to limit welfare benefits for needy Jews. This measure, issued by the head of the Munich welfare department, was not covered by any existing law. Moreover, Weiss even assigned a weeklong stay in a health resort for a Jewish client who had suffered from "nervous exhaustion." This was a courageous act for which he was later criticized by his supervisor, but not harmed in any way.[31]

The biographies of people employed by public and private institutions who disobeyed anti-Jewish policies need to be further examined, as well as the biographies of those who resigned in protest. Moreover, non-Jewish Germans who spoke out against persecution deserve our attention. In 1935, Dr Elisabeth Schmitz wrote a long critical memorandum about the deteriorating situation of the German Jews under Nazi persecution, in order to inspire her Protestant Church's protest – however to no avail.[32] Heinrich Meißeler, born in 1892, publicly blamed the Nazi government for organising the pogrom of November 1938 and was arrested by the Berlin police as an enemy of the German state.[33] Systematic research on individual resistance against anti-Jewish policy would improve our understanding as to why so few people developed and expressed opposing views. No critical voice should be dismissed because of certain argu-ments, as historians often make with the Germans who only criticized the negative economic consequences of the 1938 pogrom. One can hardly judge today, whether these critiques prove the inhuman perspective of those Germans or whether they were produced as rational, yet powerful arguments to which a regime was receptive. On the other hand, the lack of visible signs of opposition towards persecution did not always mean that everyone believed in antisemitism, as people often shared other goals with the regime and therefore accepted the attacks against the Jews.

Consequently, the question of which interests, goals and motivations led people to oppose or participate in antisemitic acts should be addressed more thoroughly in the future. One important fact is that the Nazi regime provided great social opportunities and career chances beyond class, status, generation and gender. Jakob Sprenger, born in 1884, worked as an employee in a local post office in Frankfurt am Main for decades. After 1933, he ruled the German state Hesse as the *NSDAP Gauleiter* and *Reichsstatthalter*. Dr Kurt Jeserich, an academic, was 29 years old in 1933 when he was appointed manager of the newly founded German Council of Municipalities (*Deutscher Gemeindetag*), of which more than 60,000 German cities and towns were forced members. The Berlin headquarters alone employed 200 officials. In contrast to Sprenger, who joined the Nazi Party around 1922, Jeserich was never a Party member. People such as Jeserich profited with great careers and exchanged their loyalty for hard currency: power, a higher income and a social reputation.[34]

In 1933, when the Nazi government started to partly replace the old republican elite in ministries, universities and municipalities, men and women grabbed the opportunities. Many more prospects opened up when private organizations and businesses followed suit. Later, the war provided even greater possibilities for both Nazis and ordinary people to make profits and to climb up the career ladder. Civil servants as well as white- and blue-collar employees of every strand of the German administration, whether national, regional or local, were recruited or voluntarily went first to the annexed territories and later to the occupied territories. Hans Cramer, who was mayor of the small Bavarian town Dachau from 1933 onwards, became *Stadtkommissar* of the biggest city in occupied Lithuania, Kowno (Kaunas).[35] Emil Zörner, who took office as lord mayor of Dresden in 1933, was during the war appointed *Stadthauptmann* of Cracow, the new capital of the General Government, and later was named governor of the notorious district of Lublin.[36] German mayors in conquered Poland or the Soviet Union not only ruled bigger city administrations, but were often also responsible for the local ghettos and the lives of tens or hundreds of thousands of Jews. Since many of those leading city officials functioned well in such murderous settings, a close analysis of their careers may explain the smooth transition from persecuting people to the establishing of an environment of murder.

While some of the careers of civil servants as perpetrators in the east are well known, though not well researched to date, one wonders what personal experiences of persecuting Jews or other groups the local officials had before they arrived in the Protectorate, in Poland or in the Soviet Union. Common practices introduced by mayors and city officials in pre-war Germany not only encompassed the exclusion of Jews from public facilities and resources, segregation in urban spaces and exploitation as cheap labor forces, but also discrimination against so called gypsies: many city governments excluded gypsies from welfare benefits and interned them in municipal camps. Later, during the war, municipalities discriminated against Polish and Russian forced laborers – most of those segregationist measures were neither demanded nor covered by any national law.[37]

For a long time, the assumption of the powerlessness of German cities in Nazi domestic policy served to obstruct more intensive investigation in this area.[38] Since the late 1980s, this picture has begun to erode due to new books on the evacuations of the Jews from residential quarters,[39] the "Aryanization" of property[40] and the "Jewish experience" in various cities.[41] Comparative research now demonstrates that local persecution driven by municipalities produced original developments that paralleled the general course. From 1933, local governments discriminated against Jewish residents socially, culturally and economically. The majority of those measures either anticipated Nazi legislation or went beyond existing decrees. Hitler had provided an important prerequisite for this development. After postulating the expulsion of the Jews as a general aim for the new state, for years he omitted to formulate concrete instructions as to how to achieve this goal. Consequently, local, regional and even central institutions besides the government gained enormous latitude in which to act. With their anti-Jewish measures, local governments shaped the daily life of the local Jewish population during the 1930s and even during the war. Moreover, municipal initiatives played a decisive role in generating the dynamism of the anti-Jewish policy. The Nazi leadership and the government repeatedly intervened to slow down local radicalization for economic or diplomatic reasons, yet tolerated most of the process. To a certain extent, one can speak of a controlled decentralization of anti-Jewish policy before 1938 and even beyond.[42] This characterization holds true for other institutions – for example, local and regional branches of Reich institutions such as labor and tax offices. Both profited from the leeway given when executing state policies. Not waiting for central orders, they initiated an abundance of measures which later informed Reich policies. Local tax officials, for example, imposed special policies on Jewish emigrants and later invented ways in which to organize the expropriation of the property of the Jewish population.[43]

The participation of such a variety of central, regional and local organizations frequently gave rise to differing, and sometimes conflicting developments that affected the local Jewish population. Hence, persecution at the local level should be systematically examined as having particular value, not simply being understood as mere illustration or effect of the general course.[44] Moreover, research needs to take into account the significance of the interaction between local, regional and central administration and its personnel during the course of persecution. Measures initiated by local and regional administration had a hitherto underestimated impact on the central decision-making process, mainly by providing blueprints for national decrees. For example, the Reich Ministry of the Interior picked up discussions about municipal experiences in segregating Jewish patients in public hospitals and in health resorts and issued analogous national decrees in the summer of 1938.[45]

The anti-Jewish initiatives in the annexed and occupied territories should also not be neglected. After the mayors of Vienna and Linz individually ordered the segregation of Jewish pupils in public schools, in June 1938, the Austrian Ministry of Education legalized those measures for the annexed territory. A corresponding decree for the German Reich was enacted six months later.[46] Even under German control, local governments in the Protectorate of Bohemia and Moravia obtained sufficient leeway to introduce anti-Jewish measures. When, in August 1940, the German Security Police issued a decree to segregate the Czech Jews in public, most of the proposed measures had already been established by local and regional governments.[47] Describing the establishment of the ghettos, Christopher Browning demonstrated the importance of local and regional agencies for the radicalization of the anti-Jewish policy in the General Government.[48] From the 1990s onwards, the importance of regional factors for the unfolding mass extermination surfaced in studies on occupied Poland and the Soviet Union.[49] Hence, the mutual dynamic between local, regional and national policies seems to show a pattern for the newly annexed and occupied territories as well, a fact which needs to be researched more intensively.

Particularly, the persecution policies developed in the annexed territories deserve closer attention in order to understand the specific momentum German policies gained from them. For example, by the end of the summer of 1938, forced labor for unemployed Jews was introduced in Austria; this inspired the Nazi government to establish a similar programme nationwide after the November pogrom.[50] While most books on the Holocaust acknowledge (though rarely analyze) the brutal effects of the annexation of Austria on anti-Jewish policies, they invariably neglect to mention the impact of the seizure of the Czech territories.[51] Anti-Jewish policy in the Protectorate of Bohemia and Moravia fell between the cracks of Austria's annexation and the war with Poland, although it produced certain repercussions for German policies.[52] In 1939, the heads of the civil administration of the German army introduced the first measures controlling Jewish property in Bohemia and Moravia as they also did later during the invasion of Poland. In July 1941, demands to introduce a "yellow star" for Jews in the Protectorate reached Berlin and reignited a two-year-old debate among the Nazi leadership about marking the Jews in Germany. The accordant central decree was issued in September 1941 for the Greater German Reich including the Protectorate and the other annexed territories, because deportations from all those regions were now imminent.[53]

Hence, only a thorough comparison of the political and social approaches in the different territories under Nazi rule promises to illuminate the origins of further radicalization against the Jews and other indigenous populations[54] as well as the impact the annexations had on the general course of the Third Reich and, specifically, on the subsequent occupational policy in Poland. To understand how the various stages of persecution affected the Jewish population and how this process finally transformed into mass murder, the establishment of occupational administrations in Europe needs to be carefully studied; the same applies to the interaction of its various German and indigenous branches.[55]

For the annexed and occupied territories, a focus on the local level may enlighten the previously overlooked responsibilities of civil administrations for shaping the life of the persecuted. For example, for the smooth exploitation of Jewish forced labor in Poland the labor offices collaborated with the municipalities, the police, the local or regional branches of the railway, the German army and the welfare, forest and water construction departments of the General Government, as well as with private enterprises. Many of the former institutions were responsible for the establishment of labor camps and for the dire living conditions of the Jewish forced laborers.[56]

Moreover, differences and inconsistencies in the various territories have to be addressed. Why was there no forced labor program introduced during the first year of occupation, either in the Protectorate of Bohemia and Moravia or in the annexed *Warthegau*, whilst in Germany, Austria and the General Government forced labor for Jews was the daily norm? Why did the second biggest ghetto of Polish Jews still exist in 1944 in the annexed *Warthegau*, a territory predestined to be germanized? If one compares the introduction of anti-Jewish policy in the annexed and occupied territories, there was no uniform application of German legislation. Different timelines are obvious and have to be addressed. Variations may have resulted from the overall goals of occupation, the pragmatic German response to specific political, economic and social conditions of those countries, autonomous local and regional developments, the collaboration of the non-Jewish indigenous population as well as the (re)actions of the persecuted Jews.

Regarding the Jewish population in the various annexed and occupied territories, the Nazi government pursued certain aims, which sometimes collided with regional interests and vice versa. In 1939, the German government pushed to extend the March 1938 decree against the Jewish communities onto Austria. However, Eichmann and the Gestapo successfully blocked the attempt of the Reich Finance Ministry to withdraw their tax exemption status as public corporations because of the financial crises of the Austrian Jewish communities and the immediate need to feed the impoverished local Jews.[57]

As the aims and interests of anti-Jewish policies – and thus the responsible agencies and the relationship between them – changed over the course of time, this resulted in seemingly contradictory policies. In October 1939, after the occupation of Poland which created the General Government, as a new radical step the SS were given the task of organizing Jewish labor battalions whilst in Germany and Austria the labor offices were still responsible for Jewish forced labor. Yet, having produced chaos and having neglected economic needs for months, the SS was forced to hand over authority to the labor department of the General Government in the summer of 1940. For the following two years, the local and regional labor offices successfully arranged forced labor of hundreds of thousands of Jewish men and women according to the demands of the war labor market. Only in the summer of 1942, when the mass extermination orchestrated by the SS was in full swing, did the SS regain power over the mass of forced laborers in the General Government. Nevertheless, the SS still had to take into consideration labor force needs for the war effort, for example those of the army and private industries. As in Poland, the course of the forced labor programme depended elsewhere in Europe on the national, regional and local economic needs of the war labor market and cannot be interpreted as a sole means for racial extermination.[58]

Instead of widespread conflict, as often assumed, cooperation and shared interests between the various occupational forces prevailed.[59] Their interactions and dependencies must be examined. Hence, an integrated history of the Holocaust would also need to be based on interregional and international studies. The latter is an important point which Friedländer touches upon, when he demands here to "include the initiatives and reactions of authorities, institutions, and of the most diverse social groups throughout the occupied and satellite countries of German-controlled Europe."[60] However, following his demands, one should not focus exclusively on the widespread antisemitism in some of those countries. Instead, an examination of territories with a previous positive history of incorporation and assimilation of the Jewish minority, like Czechoslovakia, would raise even more questions. Whilst two of the very rare public protests against the deportations of the Jews in Europe are documented for October 1939 in Czech towns, the question must be addressed why more support for the persecuted Jews did not evolve there later.[61] Recent studies on Aryanization and expropriation of Jewish property, which targeted the problem on a European scale, prove the fruitfulness of this comparative approach and reveal the multiple national and local interests in resources, profit or ideological gain shared by so many involved German and non-German agencies.[62] Only once we analyze the complex historical process including its inconsistencies, driven by multiple agencies and diverse factors, will we develop an understanding of how this affected and shaped the daily life of the victims in the different territories.

One of the widely acclaimed achievements of Friedländer's two-volume account is his rich use of diaries. He provides the reader with insights about the decision-making process in the top echelons of European states (Vichy France and Romania) and, even more importantly, about the perception and experiences of the Jews in different countries. He urges historians to dedicate more emphasis to "the Jewish dimension of the history of the Holocaust" by paying respect to the everyday life of the individuals and their communities.[63] Whilst Friedländer's claim that one can only restore Jewish life during the Third Reich by using contemporary accounts of the victims holds true, a full reconstruction seems only possible when these are complemented with other sources and thus contextualized.

To rely exclusively on one set of sources may restrict our insights in some ways, as can be seen in various studies. For example, Marion Kaplan achieves a great deal in her terrific book, *Between Dignity and Despair*, by unearthing the varying experiences and reactions of Jewish men and women in Germany under the swastika. Yet, all the persecution measures mentioned, which stemmed from cited memoirs, are understood as originating equally in the German government, irrespective of whether they have been national laws or municipal orders.[64] A similar problem surfaces in recent research on ghettos, in which historians rely exclusively on survivor testimonies to describe Jewish life under occupation and fail to complement these personal accounts with administrative data. As a result, anonymous Germans or Nazis seem to have oppressed the life of the Jews, whilst the actual shares of various agencies are obfuscated and the motivations as well as the individual responsibilities of perpetrators are not even addressed.[65]

Only the careful analysis of a rich set of sources might help uncover the different origins of the persecution and explain its disturbing effects on people. Hence, to dedicate time and resources to perpetrator research does not mean to neglect the victims. On the contrary, new insight into the complexity of persecution and its inconsistencies provide us with more detailed knowledge about the differing and changing living conditions of the oppressed. If we fail to analyze and compare Nazi policies at all levels and in all regions, we will never understand what it was the Jews responded to. Ultimately, we would portray the victims, once again, as passive and forlorn people.

To liberate the Jewish role from the existence of a passive and "amorphous mass"[66] we need to do more than just tell individual stories – what is necessary is the meticulous investigation of the Jewish response. Historians must explore the (re)actions of Jewish individuals as well as those of their organizations (as Friedländer also insists) to particular elements of Nazi persecution, in order to understand how they lived even under horrific circumstances. Whilst searching for organized and armed group resistance, historians often overlook how many Jewish men and women, as individuals or as representatives and employees of Jewish communities and associations, actively tried to protest, block, stop, circumvent or at least ease discrimination. Only such an approach may avoid the trap of subscribing to the myth of the victims' passivity, as even Friedländer unconsciously does when he states that it is the hope of the vast majority of the Jews of Europe to gain time and survive hardships they imagined, that partly explains the victims' passivity and the smooth development of the whole process of deportation and extermination.[67]

However, exclusively using diaries and testimonies for this honest purpose also constitutes a methodological problem, since it often connects and compares the micro history of individual Jews with the macro history of the Nazi regime. A comparable macro history would require the analysis of national, regional and local Jewish organizations, and their structures, developments, personnel and communications with the relevant Nazi institutions. At the national level, the umbrella organization for the German Jews, the *Reichsvertretung*, founded in 1933, tried to negotiate with the Nazi government and with the ministries in order to attempt to stop or ease persecution. After 1938 its successor, the *Reichsvereinigung*, also attempted to manipulate Nazi institutions – sometimes with limited success. At a local level, in 1933, the Jewish community in Berlin repeatedly sent complaints about persecution to the municipality and to the government and responded to exclusionary measures by increasing the funds for Jewish schools and by raising the support for small businessmen. Like other Jewish communities, Berlin later dramatically expanded its social, cultural, religious and educational institutions and services in reaction to segregationist municipal policies.[68]

Moreover, on a micro level studies often fail to describe how Jewish individuals interacted with their daily surroundings and how they responded to persecution in private and in public. For example Rosalie Mielzynski publicly criticized the anti-Jewish summer riots of 1935 in Berlin: "Since the Nazi state does not know anymore how to proceed, the government is attacking the Jews." She was interned in a concentration camp.[69] Or the remarkable story of the small shopkeeper Kurt Rosenberg, who was arrested in the late summer of 1938 after a denunciation. His neighbor had filed a complaint that Rosenberg was blocking the sidewalk in front of his small shop with some of his ceramic goods. Once brought to the nearest police station, Rosenberg was interrogated by the highest-ranking police officer. Rosenberg, however, did not hesitate to confront the officer and asked him bluntly if he perceived himself to be a "small Hitler" who had established a dictatorship over his district and mistreated people simply because they were Jews. In addition, Rosenberg openly criticized several central and local anti-Jewish measures and expressed the expectation that Germany would soon assign limited food to Jews on yellow ration cards. There is nothing, he added, that the German state does not invent to oppress the Jews.[70] Both stories prove the importance of the research of perpetrator files, though, since they had been uncovered buried in the archival holdings of the Berlin police. Only the description of more of such courageous acts of opposition and resistance by Jewish individuals across Europe may, in the end, give the victims their full voice back.


## CONCLUSION

After the masterful description of the Holocaust and its impact on the Jewish population in Europe which Saul Friedländer delivers in his two volume account, the question for further research remains unanswered: How did Germany turn into a genocidal society? To address this question we need to focus more on the preliminary stages than on the mass murder period of 1941–5. Moreover, as for the investigation of genocide in general, the periods in which the choice of alternative roads still could have changed the path to mass murder, seem crucial for the analysis. Without a thorough and complex examination of its "twisted road," the genocide against the Jewish people will remain incomprehensible.

The Holocaust should be understood as a highly complex historical process that unfolded through various steps and encompassed people from all strata of the Greater German Reich. In Germany and in its annexed and occupied territories, an oscillating array of perpetrator agencies as well as countless individuals decisively shaped the course of anti-Jewish policies. Whilst a strict division of tasks dominated for most of the time, authorities over certain fields of persecution also changed because of particular historical circumstances, political interests or war needs. This situation led to shifted gears, altered courses and frequent inconsistencies. Hence, a thorough analysis of local, regional and central institutions, and their developments, interactions and dependencies is absolutely necessary. This would most certainly illuminate their mutual dynamics as the overlooked, but essential pattern of the radicalization of anti-Jewish policy in Germany and beyond. No dictatorship can survive only by terror and top-down decisions without support and initiative from the bottom. The broad participation of major parts of the German population besides the Nazi Party members in the persecution seems to be an important impulse for its rapid radicalization and an overlooked factor that would explain the unusual stability of the Nazi regime during the war.

The broad involvement of the German people also points to the imminent question of the responsibility of individuals. Hence, it seems imperative to combine comparative macro studies with comparative micro investigations in order to fully comprehend how the Nazi regime and persecution functioned at all levels. Whilst a macro perspective gives the opportunity to compare anti-Jewish policy and the responses of Jewish organizations in different regions, only a micro perspective can truly provide insight into individual perpetrator actions or resistance. In addition to a more complex and contextualized display of the diverse political and social developments, we have to find out which alternatives to the known route to Auschwitz existed and why those responsible did not choose them. Sophisticated biographical studies of all levels of Third Reich society are required in order to examine what set of motives and interests caused people to participate in or even instigate persecution and mass crimes. On the other hand, the micro perspective would allow us to investigate the individual Jewish experiences of contradictory local, regional and central persecution measures and may also explain the differing responses of the victims of persecution and reveal their acts of courage, opposition and resistance.

A multi-dimensional research approach towards a history of the Holocaust promises to offer fresh insight into the following key aspects: the impulses, dynamics and different layers of the persecution; the reasons for seemingly contradictory historical developments, the different experiences of the Jewish population at different localities as well as the diverse interests and motives of the multiple non-Jewish protagonists participating in persecution and mass crime. The latter is especially significant since "the German" which is often present in literature on the Holocaust never existed; rather countless individuals who bore responsibility and had to make choices.

While, as Friedländer demonstrated, antisemitism as a European phenomenon constituted an important element of the persecution process, the situational context for social interaction, as well as economic factors and individual motives, need to be addressed and examined as well. A future historical account of the Holocaust would require integrating a more in-depth analysis of perpetrator biographies, inter-institutional networks and relationships, interregional ties, the mutual dynamics of national, regional and local administrations, and alternatives and inconsistencies of the historical course. It would need to explore their impact on the Jewish population and their responses, the opposition and resistance of non-Jews and Jews and would ultimately connect the Holocaust to the broader realm of genocides and mass violence in world history. Through examining people, factors and contexts we might come closer to comprehending the multi-faceted historical developments which turned Germany into a genocidal society. In my view, such an approach would provide us with new means to reduce what Heinrich Vierbücher, in 1930, called the "inconceivable" dimension of systematic mass murder and to reach a clearer understanding of the Holocaust.

*Notes*

1    Heinrich Vierbücher, *Was die kaiserliche Regierung den deutschen Untertanen verschwiegen hat: Armenien 1915. Die Abschlachtung eines Kulturvolkes durch die Türken* (Berlin: n.p., 1930), 55.

2    Saul Friedländer, *Nazi Germany and the Jews*, vol. I: *The Years of Persecution, 1933–1939* (New York: HarperCollins, 1996); idem, *The Years of Extermination: Nazi Germany and the Jews, 1939–1945* (New York: HarperCollins, 2007).

3    In the first volume, Friedländer downplayed interpretations like Mommsen's thesis of the cumulative radicalism of competing agencies and rejected Götz Aly's and Susanne Heim's ideas regarding the cruel results produced by cost-benefits calculating technocrats (Friedländer, *Nazi Germany and the Jews*, 3). In the introduction to his second volume, Friedländer states that he would not discuss common explanation models such as the German *Sonderweg*, the dominating role of bureaucracy, totalitarianism, Fascism, and modernity (Friedländer, *The Years of Extermination*, xvi).

4    E.g. Daniel J. Goldhagen, *Hitler's Willing Executioners: Ordinary Germans and the Holocaust* (New York: Vintage, 1997); Jeffrey Herf, *The Jewish Enemy: Nazi Propaganda during World War II and the Holocaust* (Cambridge, MA: Belknap Press, 2006). Even Christopher Browning, after having made such a strong case for the importance of situational dynamics in his seminal study *Ordinary Men*, recently used antisemitism as the leitmotiv in his study on the origins of the "Final Solution" where he scarcely discusses social factors or economical causes; see Christopher R. Browning, *The Origins of the Final Solution: The Evolution of Nazi Jewish Policy, September 1939 – March 1942* (Lincoln: Nebraska University Press, 2004).

5    Stefan Kühl, "The Cooperation of German Racial Hygienists and American Eugenicists before and after 1933," in Michael Berenbaum and Abraham J. Peck (eds), *The Holocaust and History: The Known, the Unknown, the Disputed, and the Reexamined* (Bloomington and Indianapolis: Indiana University Press, 1998), 134–52.

6    Ian Kershaw, *Hitler 1889–1936: Hubris* (London: Allen Lane, The Penguin Press, 1998); Ian Kershaw, *Hitler 1936–1945: Nemesis* (London: Allen Lane, The Penguin Press, 2000).

7    Eleanor Hancock, *Ernst Röhm: Hitler's SA Chief of Staff* (New York: Palgrave Macmillan, 2008).

8    Richard Breitman, *The Architect of Genocide: Himmler and the Final Solution* (New York: Knopf, 1991); Peter Longerich, *Heinrich Himmler. Biographie* (Munich: Siedler, 2008).

9    Günter Neliba, *Wilhelm Frick. Der Legalist des Unrechtsstaates. Eine politische Biographie* (Paderborn: Schöningh, 1992); Albert Fischer, *Hjalmar Schacht und Deutschlands "Judenfrage". Der "Wirtschaftsdiktator" und die Vertreibung der Juden aus der deutschen Wirtschaft* (Cologne: Böhlau Verlag, 1995).

10   Peter Longerich, *The Unwritten Order: Hitler's Role in the Final Solution* (Stroud: Tempus, 2001).

11   Fischer, *Hjalmar Schacht*; on von Krosigk see Martin Friedenberger, Klaus D. Gössel and Eberhard Schönknecht (eds), *Die Reichsfinanzverwaltung im Nationalsozialismus. Darstellung und Dokumente* (Bremen: Ed. Temmen, 2002); Götz Aly, *Hitlers Volksstaat. Raub, Rassenkrieg und nationaler Sozialismus* (Frankfurt am Main: S. Fischer, 2005).

12   Hans Safrian, *Die Eichmann-Männer* (Vienna and Zurich: Europa-Verlag, 1993); Yaakov

Lozowick, *Hitler's Bureaucrats, The Nazi Security Police and the Banality of Evil* (London and New York: Continuum, 2000).

13   Michael Wildt, *Generation des Unbedingten. Das Führungskorps des Reichssicherheitshauptamtes* (Hamburg: Hamburger Edition, 2003).

14   Mario R. Dederichs, *Heydrich. Das Gesicht des Bösen* (Munich and Zurich: Piper, 2005); Andreas Seeger, *"Gestapo-Müller": Die Karriere eins Schreibtischtäters* (Berlin: Metropol, 1996); Joachim Bornschein, *Gestapochef Heinrich Müller. Technokrat des Terrors* (Leipzig: Militzke, 2004); Ulrich Herbert, *Best. Biographische Studien über Radikalismus, Weltanschauung und Vernunft 1903–1989* (Bonn: Verlag J. H. W. Dietz Nachf., 2nd ed. 1996); David Cesarani, *Becoming Eichmann: Rethinking the Life, Crimes and Trial of a "Desk Murderer"* (Cambridge: Da Capo Press, 2004); Siegfried J. Pucher, *". . . in der Bewegung führend tätig". Odilo Globocznik – Kämpfer für den "Anschluß", Vollstrecker des Holocaust* (Klagenfurt: Drava, 1997); Berndt Rieger, *Creator of Nazi Death Camps. The Life of Odilo Globocnik* (London: Vallentine Mitchell, 2007).

15   For examples see Alfons Kenkmann and Bernd A. Rusinek (eds), *Verfolgung und Verwaltung. Die wirtschaftliche Ausplünderung der Juden und die westfälischen Finanzbehörden* (Münster: Villa ten Hompel et.al., 1999); Wolf Gruner, *Öffentliche Wohlfahrt und Judenverfolgung. Wechselwirkungen lokaler und zentraler Politik im NS-Staat (1933–1942)* (Munich: Oldenbourg Verlag, 2002); and see various articles in Gerald D. Feldman and Wolfgang Seibel (eds), *Networks of Nazi Persecution: Bureaucracy, Business and the Organization of the Holocaust* (New York: Berghahn Books, 2005).

16   For examples in Poland see Bogdan Musial, *Deutsche Zivilverwaltung und Judenverfolgung im Generalgouvernement. Eine Fallstudie zum Distrikt Lublin 1939–1944* (Wiesbaden: Harrasowitz, 1999). For the Netherlands see Gerard Aalders, "Organized looting: the Nazi seizure of Jewish property in the Netherlands, 1940–1945," in Feldman and Seibel (eds), *Networks of Persecution*, 168–88.

17   See the impressive recent account by Dieter Pohl, *Die Herrschaft der Wehrmacht. Deutsche Militärbesatzung und einheimische Bevölkerung in der Sowjetunion 1941–1944* (Munich: Oldenbourg Verlag, 2008).

18   Johannes Hürter, *Hitlers Heerführer. Die deutschen Oberbefehlshaber im Krieg gegen die Sowjetunion 1941/42* (Munich: Oldenbourg Wissenschaftsverlag, 2006); Christian Hartmann (ed.), *Von Feldherren und Gefreiten. Zur biographischen Dimension des Zweiten Weltkriegs* (Munich: Oldenbourg Verlag, 2008); Thomas Kühne, *Kameradschaft. Die Soldaten des nationalsozialistischen Krieges und das 20. Jahrhundert* (Göttingen: Vandenhoeck & Ruprecht, 2006).

19   Gerald D. Feldman, *Allianz and the German Insurance Business, 1933 1945* (Cambridge: Cambridge University Press, 2001); Harold James, *The Deutsche Bank and the Nazi Economic War against the Jews* (Cambridge: Cambridge University Press, 2001); Peter Hayes, *From Cooperation to Complicity: Degussa in the Third Reich* (New York: Cambridge University Press, 2004); Dieter Ziegler (ed.), *Banken und "Arisierungen" in Mitteleuropa während des Nationalsozialismus* (Stuttgart: Steiner, 2002); Ludolf Herbst and Thomas Weihe (eds), *Die Commerzbank und die Juden 1933–1945* (Munich, C. H. Beck, 2004); Harald Wixforth, *Die Dresdner Bank im Dritten Reich*, vol. 3: *Die Expansion der Dresdner Bank in Europa* (Munich, Oldenbourg, 2006).

20   Ulrich Herbert, *Best. Biographische Studien über Radikalismus, Weltanschauung und Vernunft 1903–1989, passim*; Michael Wildt, *Generation des Unbedingten. Das Führungskorps des Reichssicherheitshauptamtes* (Hamburg: Hamburger Edition, 2003, English Edition 2010).

21   For this see Wolf Gruner, "Die NS-Judenverfolgung und die Kommunen. Zur wechselseitigen Dynamisierung von zentraler und lokaler Politik 1933–1941," *Vierteljahrshefte für Zeitgeschichte* 48 (2000): 75–126; Gruner, *Öffentliche Wohlfahrt und Judenverfolgung*.

22   Sebastian Weitkamp, *Braune Diplomaten. Horst Wagner und Eberhard von Thadden als Funktionäre der Endlösung* (Bonn: Dietz, 2008); Gerhard Stuby, *Vom "Kronjuristen" zum "Kronzeugen". Friedrich Wilhelm Gaus: Ein Leben im Auswärtigen Amt der Wilhelmstraße* (Hamburg: VSA Verlag, 2008). Currently, a commission of historians is investigating the role of the foreign office in the Third Reich, which will expand our knowledge within a few years.

23   Goldhagen, *Hitler's Willing Executioners*; Christopher R. Browning, *Ordinary Men: Reserve Battalion 101 and the Final Solution in Poland* (New York: HarperCollins, 1992).

24   Wolfgang Curilla, *Die deutsche Ordnungspolizei und der Holocaust im Baltikum und in Weissrussland 1941–1944* (Paderborn: Ferdinand Schöningh, 2006); Stefan Klemp, *"Nicht*

*ermittelt"*. *Polizeibataillone und die Nachkriegsjustiz – Ein Handbuch* (Essen: Klartext Verlag, 2005); Edward B. Westermann, *Hitler's Police Battalions: Enforcing Racial War in the East* (Lawrence, KS: University of Kansas Press, 2005). The first biography of one individual policeman I came across is Karl Schneider, *Zwischen allen Stühlen – Der Bremer Kaufmann Hans Hespe im Reserve-Polizeibattaillon 105* (Bremen: Edition Temmen, 2007).

25  Browning, *The Origins of the Final Solution*, 94.

26  There are examples in the journals of several police stations, e.g.: Landesarchiv Berlin, A Pr.Br. Rep. 030, Tit. 95, Nr. 21618 Bd. 3 and Landesarchiv Berlin, B Rep. 020, Acc. 1201, Nr. 6948. For some cases see Wolf Gruner, *Judenverfolgung in Berlin 1933–1945. Eine Chronologie der Behördenmaßnahmen in der Reichshauptstadt*, 2nd rev. and expanded edn (Berlin: Stiftung Topographie des Terrors, 2009).

27  See Friedländer, *Nazi Germany and the Jews*, 324.

28  Gruner, "Die NS-Judenverfolgung und die Kommunen"; Wolf Gruner, „Local Initiatives, Central Coordination. German Municipal Administration and the Holocaust", in Feldman and Seibel (eds), *Networks of Persecution*, 269–94; Gruner, *Judenverfolgung in Berlin 1933–1945*.

29  Kenkmann and Rusinek, *Verfolgung und Verwaltung*; Friedenberger, Gössel, and Schönknecht (eds), Die Reichsfinanzverwaltung im Nationalsozialismus; Diemut Majer, *"Non-Germans" under the Third Reich* (Baltimore: Johns Hopkins University Press, 2003).

30  Friedländer, *Nazi Germany and the Jews*, 52.

31  Gruner, *Öffentliche Wohlfahrt*, 102-3.

32  The memorandum is printed in Hannelore Erhart, Ilse Meseberg-Haubold, and Dietgard Meyer, *Von der Gestapo verfolgt, von der Kirchenbehörde fallengelassen: Katharina Staritz (1903-1953), Dokumentation Band 1: 1903-1942* (Neukirchen-Vluyn: Neukirchener Verlag 2002), 220–61.

33  Landesarchiv Berlin, A Pr.Br.Rep. 030, Tit. 95., Nr. 21620 Bd. 5, Bl. 83.

34  Stephanie Zibell, *Jakob Sprenger (1884–1945). NS-Gauleiter und Reichsstatthalter in Hessen* (Darmstadt and Marburg: Selbstverlag der Hessischen Historischen Kommission Darmstadt und der Historischen Kommission für Hessen, 1999); Gruner, *Öffentliche Wohlfahrt*, 37–8.

35  Jürgen Matthäus, "Das Ghetto Kaunas und die 'Endlösung' in Litauen," in Wolfgang Benz and Marion Neiss (eds), *Judenmord in Litauen. Studien und Dokumente* (Berlin: Metropol Verlag, 1999), 97–112, here 104.

36  Marcus Gryglewski, "Zur Geschichte der nationalsozialistischen Judenverfolgung in Dresden 1933–1945," in Norbert Haase, Stefi Jersch-Wenzel and Hermann Simon (eds), *Fotografien und Dokumente zur nationalsozialistischen Judenverfolgung in Dresden 1933–1945* (Leipzig: Gustav Kiepenheuer Verlag, 1998), 87–150, here 109.

37  See the chapters on Roma and Sinti in Gruner, *Öffentliche Wohlfahrt*; and Rüdiger Fleiter, *Stadtverwaltung im Dritten Reich. Verfolgungspolitik auf kommunaler Ebene am Beispiel Hannovers* (Hannover: Verlag Hahnsche Buchhandlung, 2006). On Polish and Russian forced laborers see Ulrich Herbert, *Hitler's Foreign Workers: Enforced Foreign Labor in Germany Under the Third Reich* (Cambridge: Cambridge University Press 1997).

38  See Horst Matzerath, *Nationalsozialismus und kommunale Selbstverwaltung* (Stuttgart: Kohlhammer, 1970).

39  Marlis Buchholz, *Die hannoverschen Judenhäuser. Zur Situation der Juden in der Zeit der Ghettoisierung und Verfolgung 1941 bis 1945* (Hildesheim: Lax, 1987); Konrad Kwiet, "Nach dem Pogrom. Stufen der Ausgrenzung," in Wolfgang Benz (ed.), *Die Juden in Deutschland 1933–1945. Leben unter nationalsozialistischer Herrschaft* (Munich: C. H. Beck 1988), 545–659, here 633–59.

40  See Barbara Händler-Lachmann and Thomas Werther, *Vergessene Geschäfte – Verlorene Geschichte. Jüdisches Wirtschaftsleben in Marburg und seine Vernichtung im Nationalsozialismus* (Marburg: Hitzeroth, 1992); Frank Bajohr, *"Arisierung" in Hamburg. Die Verdrängung jüdischer Unternehmer 1933–1945* (Hamburg: Christians, 1997); Alex Bruns-Wüstefeld, *Lohnende Geschäfte. Die "Entjudung" der Wirtschaft am Beispiel Göttingens*, ed. Geschichtswerkstatt Göttingen (Hannover: Fackelträger-Verlag, 1997), 57.

41  Günther von Roden, *Geschichte der Duisburger Juden* (Duisburg: W. Braun, 1986); Josef Werner, *Hakenkreuz und Judenstern. Das Schicksal der Karlsruher Juden im Dritten Reich* (Karlsruhe: Badenia-Verlag, 1990); Wolf Gruner, *Judenverfolgung in Berlin 1933–1945. Eine Chronologie der Behördenmaßnahmen in der Reichshauptstadt*, ed. Reinhard Rürup (Berlin: Hentrich, 1996).

42  More on this subject in Gruner, "Die NS-Judenverfolgung und die Kommunen," 75–126, or

idem, "Local Initiatives, Central Coordination," 269–94; and idem, "Anti-Jewish policy in Nazi Germany 1933–1945: From Exclusion and Expulsion to Segregation and Deportation. New Perspectives on Developments, Actors and Goals," in *The Comprehensive History of the Holocaust: Germany*, ed. Yad Vashem Jerusalem (Lincoln: Nebraska University Press, forthcoming 2010). For more research on municipal policy and the persecution of Jews and other groups see Sabine Mecking and Andreas Wirsching, *Stadtverwaltung im Nationalsozialismus. Systemstabilisierende Dimensionen kommunaler Herrschaft* (Paderborn et.al.: Schöningh, 2005); and Fleiter, *Stadtverwaltung im Dritten Reich.*

43   Kenkmann and Rusinek (eds), *Verfolgung und Verwaltung*; Walter Rummel and Jochen Rath (eds), *"Dem Reich verfallen" – "den Berechtigten zurückzuerstatten". Enteignung und Rückerstattung jüdischen Vermögens im Gebiet des heutigen Rheinland-Pfalz 1938–1953* (Koblenz: Verlag der Landesarchivverwaltung Rheinland-Pfalz, 2001); Susanne Meinl and Jutta Zwilling (eds), *Legalisierter Raub. Die Ausplünderung der Juden im Nationalsozialismus durch die Reichsfinanzverwaltung in Hessen* (Frankfurt am Main: Campus-Verlag, 2004).

44   Although Peter Longerich describes in his study a large number of local violent actions and municipal measures, he doesn't analyze those systematically; see Peter Longerich, *Politik der Vernichtung. Eine Gesamtdarstellung der nationalsozialistischen Judenverfolgung* (Munich: Piper, 1998, new English edition 2010).

45   For more details see Wolf Gruner, "Settings: Greater Germany," in *The Oxford Handbook of Holocaust Studies*, Peter Hayes and John K. Roth (eds), (New York: Oxford University Press, forthcoming 2010).

46   For more details see Wolf Gruner, *Zwangsarbeit und Verfolgung. Österreichische Juden im NS-Staat 1938–1945* (Innsbruck et.al.: Studien-Verlag, 2000).

47   Wolf Gruner, "Das Protektorat Böhmen/Mähren und die antijüdische Politik 1939–1941. Lokale Initiativen, regionale Maßnahmen und zentrale Entscheidungen im 'Großdeutschen Reich,'" in: *Theresienstädter Studien und Dokumente 2005* (Prague: Sefer, 2005), 27–62.

48   Browning, *The Origins of the Final Solution*, 111–68.

49   For Poland see Dieter Pohl, *Von der "Judenpolitik" zum Judenmord. Der Distrikt Lublin des Generalgouvernements 1939–1944* (Frankfurt am Main: Peter Lang, 1993); Dieter Pohl, *Nationalsozialistische Judenverfolgung in Ostgalizien. Organisation und Durchführung eines staatlichen Massenverbrechens* (Munich: Oldenbourg, 1996); Musial, *Deutsche Zivilverwaltung und Judenverfolgung im Generalgouvernement*; Sybille Steinbacher, *"Musterstadt" Auschwitz. Germanisierungspolitik und Judenmord in Ostoberschlesien* (Munich: Saur, 2000). For the occupied Soviet Union: Christian Gerlach on Belorussia and Christoph Dieckmann on Lithuania in Ulrich Herbert (ed.), *National-Socialist Extermination Policies* (New York: Berghahn Books, 2000), 210–75; Wendy Lower on Ukraine in Feldman and Seibel (eds), *Networks of Nazi Persecution*, 236–56. Cf. the recent study by Andrej Angrick and Peter Klein, *Die "Endlösung" in Riga. Ausbeutung und Vernichtung 1941–1944* (Darmstadt: Wissenschaftliche Buchgesellschaft, 2006).

50   Gruner, *Zwangsarbeit und Verfolgung*, 45–92.

51   See for example: Peter Longerich, *Politik der Vernichtung*; Browning, *The Origins of the Final Solution*; Friedländer, *Nazi Germany and the Jews*, Vol. I.

52   Most surveys on the Third Reich do not include accounts of the protectorate. Until now only a few studies on this subject have been available: John G. Lexa, "Anti-Jewish laws and regulations in the Protectorate of Bohemia and Moravia," in Avigdor Dagan (ed.), *The Jews of Czechoslovakia: Historical Studies and Surveys*, Vol. 3 (Philadelphia and New York: Jewish Publication Society of America, 1984), 75–193; Livia Rothkirchen, *The Jews of Bohemia and Moravia: Facing the Holocaust* (Lincoln: University of Nebraska Press, 2005).

53   For a recent survey on anti-Jewish policy in the Protectorate and a preliminary discussion on its impact on the Reich see: Gruner, "Das Protektorat Böhmen/Mähren und die antijüdische Politik 1939–1941," 27–62.

54   For the latter see Chad Carl Bryant, *Prague in Black: Nazi Rule and Czech Nationalism* (Cambridge, MA: Harvard University Press, 2007).

55   See for example P. Verheyde, "The Looting of Jewish Property and Franco-German Rivalry 1940–1944," in Feldman and Seibel (eds), *Networks of Persecution*, 69–87. For other examples, see Aly, *Hitlers Volksstaat.*

56   For details see Christopher R. Browning, *Nazi Policy, Jewish Workers, German Killers* (Cambridge:

Cambridge University Press, 2000); Wolf Gruner, *Jewish Forced Labor under the Nazis. Economic Needs and Racial Aims (1938–1944)* (Cambridge: Cambridge University Press, 2006).

57 Gruner, *Zwangsarbeit und Verfolgung*, 103.

58 Gruner, *Jewish Forced Labor under the Nazis*, 177–275. For the suggestion that forced labor was merely a means for destruction, see Goldhagen, *Hitler's Willing Executioners*.

59 Christian Gerlach, *Kalkulierte Morde: Die deutsche Wirtschafts- und Vernichtungspolitik in Weißrußland 1941 bis 1944* (Hamburg: Hamburger Edition, 1999); Angrick and Klein, *Die "Endlösung" in Riga*; Gruner, *Jewish Forced Labor under the Nazis*.

60 See Saul Friedländer in this volume, p. 212.

61 Bundesarchiv Berlin, R 70 Böhmen und Mähren, No. 9, no folio No.: Note of the Gestapo Mährisch-Ostrau, 23. 10. 1939; cf. ibid.: Daily report, 19. 10. 1939, p. 3; Bundesarchiv Berlin, R 30 Reichsprotektor in Böhmen und Mähren, No. 56, fol. 45: RFSS/SD-central office for Bohemia and Moravia, daily report No. 129 Prague, 28. 10. 1939, p. 5. See Wolf Gruner, *Widerstand in der Rosenstraße. Die Fabrik-Aktion und die Verfolgung der "Mischehen" 1943* (Frankfurt am Main: S. Fischer-Verlag, 2005), 40–1.

62 Aly, *Hitlers Volksstaat*; Martin Dean, *Robbing the Jews: The Confiscation of Jewish Property in the Holocaust, 1933–1945* (Cambridge: Cambridge University Press in association with the US Holocaust Memorial Museum, 2008).

63 Friedländer, *The Years of Extermination*,

64 Marion Kaplan, *Between Dignity and Despair: Jewish Life in Nazi Germany* (New York: Oxford University Press, 1998).

65 See several articles in Christoph Dieckmann, and Babette Quinkert (eds), *Im Ghetto. Neue Forschungen zu Alltag und Umfeld* (Göttingen: Wallstein Verlag, 2009).

66 See Saul Friedländer in this volume, p. 23.

67 ibid., p. 23.

68 Gruner, "Anti-Jewish policy in Nazi Germany 1933–1945"; Gruner, *Judenverfolgung in Berlin*.

69 Otto D. Kulka and Ernst Jäckel (eds), *Die Juden in den geheimen NS-Stimmungsberichten 1933–1945* (Düsseldorf: Droste, 2004), CD-No. 1004: Gestapo (statepolice district) Berlin, July report 1935. For the application of the so called "*Heimtücke*" law in such cases see Bernward Dörner, "*Heimtücke": Das Gesetz als Waffe* (Paderborn: Schöningh, 1998).

70 LA Berlin, A Pr.Br.Rep. 030, Tit. 95, Nr. 21619 Bd. 4, fol. 321+RS: Note of 26.9.1938.

# 18

# Nazi Germany and the Jews *and the Future of Holocaust Historiography*

*Dan Stone*

Saul Friedländer is the "theorist historian" who, more than any other scholar, has made major contributions both to writing the history of the Holocaust and to the theoretical discussions about the metahistorical issues at stake in this history-writing. Here I want to ask whether Friedländer has conformed to his own theoretical guidelines concerning the writing of Holocaust history in *The Years of Persecution* and *The Years of Extermination*, and to consider what the answer to this question tells us about where Holocaust historiography now stands. Steven Aschheim suggests that there is no reason why Friedländer's theoretical writings should mesh exactly with his "concrete history,"[1] but even so it is instructive to note where the gap between the two lies. I argue that where narrative structure, multivocality and the incorporation of memory and testimony are concerned, Friedländer's two-volume history does indeed follow quite closely his theoretical demand to produce an "integrated history of the Holocaust" that does not domesticate the past.[2] But I go on to suggest that, somewhat ironically, by conforming to his own guidelines, Friedländer has brought about precisely that which he appeared to want to resist: the historicization of the Holocaust. I will not argue that this is a bad outcome! Instead, Friedländer's achievement rests in bringing about a practical reconciliation between himself and Broszat by furthering a process of historicization (Broszat's aim), but maintaining the Holocaust as the central point of importance in the consideration of the Nazi regime (the loss of which was Friedländer's fear in the exchange). *The Years of Extermination* shows that the historian is able "to consider the Nazi era *as any other era*, in terms of historical analysis" and reveals how Friedländer was working in the book towards proving his earlier assertion that "historicization can be completed only if the crimes of the Nazi regime are entirely integrated within a complex historical context."[3] One could go so far as to say that with his historicization of the Holocaust, Friedländer finally emerges victorious on a practical level (he had always been victorious on a moral and theoretical level) in his debate with Broszat.

   In revisiting the famous "controversy" with Broszat on the question of historicization, I want first to suggest that Friedländer has made a major contribution to the historicization of the Holocaust despite his earlier warnings about the risks of such an attempt. Although there are many seminal texts on the historical representation of the Holocaust (one thinks of the writings of Dominick LaCapra, Berel Lang, Lawrence Langer and Dan Diner among others[4]), the Friedländer/

Broszat exchange has been described as "perhaps the exemplary document of a tough, entirely candid, post-Shoah German-Jewish dialogue."[5] It speaks to the preoccupations of the generation of historians who had lived through the war (and in Broszat's case, though it was not known at the time, had applied to join the NSDAP in 1944 as a young man[6]) and who wanted to write the history of the war and the Holocaust, but equally feared the consequences of doing so. The exchange thus foreshadowed the thrust of the debates about Holocaust representation that were just beginning to take off in the late 1980s, debates which centered around the question of "postmodernism." The questions raised by historians like Friedländer and Diner, in Nicolas Berg's opinion, "were so important in the case of Germany because they pointed out at an early stage of the historiographical debate the theoretical shortcomings of descriptive and purely empirical research."[7] The implications of these objections were felt much more widely in the historical profession and were not confined to Germany, although the continued stress on a more or less positivist methodology in the history-writing of the Holocaust – especially in perpetrator research – suggests that this debate needs reviving.[8] But, as Berg notes: "No document in the history of historiography has revealed with such clarity the blind spots in German historiographical research" as the Friedländer/Broszat exchange.[9]

I will not provide here a detailed summary of the well-known encounter.[10] The basic disagreement between the two historians rested on their understanding of whether representatives of the perpetrators and victims could present objective scholarship on the subject. Broszat maintained that Jewish historians, by virtue of their subject position, could not do so, but that non-Jewish German historians could. He further argued that the process of doing so would contribute to the desirable outcome of historicizing National Socialism. The "epistemological difference" between them consisted in Broszat's attempt "to ascribe the opposition between "history" and "memory" to the respective situations of the writers concerned."[11] For Broszat "memory," which was legitimate in its own right, was "a matter for Jews" and their experience of mourning, but Jews could not be expected to write "history," which is scientific and objective. Friedländer, by contrast, "regarded the binary visions as fundamental to both sides"[12]; that is, he believed that German historians were every bit as likely as Jewish historians to base their choice of interpretive perspective on their personal experience (whether consciously or unconsciously). Both "memory" and "history", for Friedländer, inhered in the process of writing history, and historicization that aspired only to the latter at the expense of the former would be sterile and morally problematic.

It is important to recall that Friedländer was never opposed to the idea of historicization per se: "for any historian, historicization, understood in its most general sense as the approach to the Nazi era with all the methods at the disposal of the historian, without any forbidden questions, is self-evident."[13] His fear was that a form of historicization, notably that which focused on the "normal" aspects of the Third Reich, would miss the point that our interest in that regime is generated by its extraordinary crimes and our post-Holocaust inability fully to incorporate them into existing frameworks of thought. Thus he wrote to Broszat:

> I agree with you that the historian, as historian, cannot consider the Nazi era from its catastrophic end only. According to the accepted historical method, we have to start at the beginning and follow the manifold paths as they present themselves, including numerous developments within German society which had little to do with Auschwitz, and this throughout the history of the era. But the historian knows the end and he shares this knowledge with his reader. This knowledge should not hamper the exploration of all the possible avenues and interpretations, but it compels the historian to choose the central elements around which his unfolding narrative is implicitly built. In short, we come back to the problem of the dominant focus.[14]

Or, as he wrote elsewhere, "if one admits that the Jewish problem was at the center, was the very essence of the system, many of these studies lose their coherence, and historiography is confronted with an anomaly that defies the normal interpretive categories."[15] No wonder that he could claim, in 1994, that Jewish historians too were:

> at a loss to produce an overall history of the extermination of the Jews of Europe that is not a mere textbook presentation, or an analysis of the internal cogs and wheels of the destruction machinery, or a compendium of separate monographs. The 'Final Solution' in its epoch has not yet found its historian; and the problem cannot be reduced to a mere technical issue.[16]

Still, by the time the first volume of *Nazi Germany and the Jews* appeared just a few years later, as Aschheim notes, Friedländer "considerably modified his opposition to what he took to be a crucial methodological tool of historicization – *Alltagsgeschichte* (the history of everyday life) – and his suspicion that it essentially served "normalizing" tendencies."[17] In fact – and perhaps contrary to the expectations of some historians[18] – the process of writing the history of everyday life under Nazism as it transpired in the post-unification context of the 1990s did not promote apologetic tendencies. Rather, German historiography of the Holocaust has not only grown in size and sophistication, but has retained its position as a barometer of the German public sphere. In fact, focusing on "normality" need not be a zero-sum game with the focus on genocide, as Charles Maier presciently pointed out some years earlier when, in reply to the question "must the effort at 'historicization' end in apology?" he argued that "it must risk apology but need not lead to it."[19] What Friedländer achieves with *The Years of Extermination*, in fact, is a historicization that preserves the Holocaust as the centerpiece of the Third Reich and thus of the historical enterprise. One can still write histories of aspects of Nazi Germany that are not directly about the persecution of the Jews before World War II or the Holocaust, but it is no longer possible to write about the Third Reich without mentioning racial policy, antisemitism, the exclusion of "others" from the *Volksgemeinschaft* or genocide as the culminating point of the regime, just as it is no longer possible for serious historians to write histories of the war – even strictly military histories – without referring to the murder of the Jews.[20] Even if, as some have started to assert, the "racial state" paradigm overstates the extent of the Third Reich's internal coherence and takes the regime's self-image too readily at its own word, the importance of the Holocaust for understanding the Third Reich as such is now very widely accepted amongst historians.

Apart from the fundamental issue of historicization, Friedländer also penned a number of essays in the 1980s and 1990s that dealt with historical methodology. Among his concerns were, as I suggested at the outset, questions of narrative structure, multivocality and the incorporation of memory and testimony into the historian's text. Let us see how the structures and guidelines laid down by Friedländer in those essays corresponds to his practice in the two volumes of *Nazi Germany and the Jews* and, more important, whether they brought about the kind of results that Friedländer anticipated.

In order to combat the problems of mythologization, avoidance and traumatic transference, Friedländer proposed a number of desiderata for future historians. Foremost among them was the "self-awareness of the historian" which necessitates "the sporadic but forceful presence of commentary." The voice of the historian should be clearly heard, Friedländer recommended, in order not to succumb to what we might call the "mythical real" or the "idyllic law" of narrative, that is, the sense that a compelling narrative describes the world fully, transparently and with mimetic accuracy.[21] "The commentary," Friedländer continued, in a much-cited passage, "should disrupt the facile linear progression of the narration, introduce alternative interpretations, question any partial conclusion, withstand the need for closure." Friedländer's belief was that this insertion of the historian's voice into the text, fragmenting its narrative progression, would "allow for an integration of the so-called 'mythic memory' of the victims within the overall representation of the past, without it becoming an 'obstacle' for 'rational historiography.'"[22] Here one sees a methodological statement put forward in order to help the reader understand what Friedländer wanted to achieve in the two volumes of *Nazi Germany and the Jews*.

In volume one, *The Years of Persecution*, readers noted the interspersing of Nazi decrees with diaries and letters of their victims; they noted Friedländer's sensitivity to the responses of the Churches and the world of arts and letters to the persecution of the Jews, his keen eye for the telling details: the moving letter or powerful speech. Over the course of the book, certain individuals recurrently appear, their fates standing for the steadily worsening situation of the German Jews.

Thus on the one hand we see Friedländer fulfilling his requirements for a historical narrative that is fragmented, splintered and fractured by the historian's voice and by the twists and turns of a text that moves ceaselessly between "official" discourse, that is, Nazi documents, the victims and the bystanders. As he wrote: "The *Alltagsgeschichte* of German society has its necessary shadow: the *Alltagsgeschichte* of its victims,"[23] and they do indeed coexist in Friedländer's text. And yet, on the other hand, the text is constructed masterfully, with a sure guiding hand and the control of an apparently all-seeing narrator. As Confino notes, Friedländer presents an "overall interpretative framework" with the result that we are presented with "a sort of a total history (in a historiographical age that repudiates it) that 'penetrates all the nooks and crannies of European space.'"[24] There is indeed a paradox here: in seeking to stay true to (for want of a better term – I suspect that Friedländer, like Hayden White, dislikes it) "postmodern" dictums of resisting closure, offering multiple voices and fracturing the narrative so as to break with what Roland Barthes called the "effect of the real," Friedländer actually produces a text that is impressively coherent, carefully structured and beautifully written. Precisely insofar as it succeeds in achieving its goals, the demand for an alternative history has actually produced the epitome of Holocaust historiography, since it appears to cover almost everything (though this effect disguises the fact that certain major aspects of Holocaust historiography such as perpetrator research are only dealt with fleetingly, at least on an explicit level), and to have contained all this information within a narrative frame that is at once highly readable, controlled and clearly argued. Even the intrusion of the historian's voice does not alienate, but provides a curious comfort, as one senses that one is in the hands of a sure guide.

Friedländer will not be dissatisfied with this outcome. As noted above, in his exchange with Broszat he did not oppose historicization as such. Thus, if he has succeeded in historicizing the Holocaust in such a way that it contains the "mythic memory" of the victims and "rational historiography" in a single structure then this would appear to be a victory of historical methodology over oft-heard mystical demands to maintain the Holocaust as an event "outside of history," for fear that in historicizing it, it would lose this "sacred" aura. Friedländer wants to say that one can treat the Holocaust as history, like any other event, and still retain a sense of the *tremendum*.

This is not to say that objections against the book cannot be raised. In the light of the last two decades' research on the decision-making process for the "Final Solution," Friedländer's strongly intentionalist perspective seems at times a somewhat blunt instrument. Nevertheless, he is explicit about his explanatory framework, noting his belief in "the centrality of ideological-cultural factors as the prime movers of Nazi policies in regard to the Jewish issue."[25] Even so, by making "redemptive antisemitism" function as his overall explanatory and interpretive framework – a stance that he had long held, of course[26] – the "postmodern" textual devices such as fracturing the narrative are well contained. Thus the sense of order and continuity that is the overall impression one takes from reading the book: the narrative may be broken, multiple voices may inhabit its pages, but the analytical tool holding it all together is clear and straightforward. Interestingly, in an age of testimony and autobiographical fiction where we have become accustomed to hearing the author's voice and to chronological acrobatics,

Friedländer's conceptual framework is more controversial – certainly amongst Holocaust historians – than the self-consciously "literary" devices he uses in constructing the text. Whilst there has been a "return of ideology" in the historiography, the many "regional" and institutional studies that have appeared over the last decade or so, and especially the rapid growth of "perpetrator research" (*Täterforschung*) suggest that the interplay between center and periphery, and between ideological and "pragmatic" factors (such as greed) as motors of the killing process is extremely complex.[27] For many historians, "redemptive antisemitism", especially as it was adhered to by only a minority – albeit the most influential – of the Nazi leaders, may be a necessary but not sufficient explanation.

Perhaps more worrying, Friedländer's emphasis on bringing in the "voices" of the victims perpetuates, according to one critic, the divide between the German and European history of the Nazi genocide on the one hand and the Jewish history of the Shoah on the other. Friedländer handles testimonies and diaries far more sensitively than most historians of the Holocaust, and writes at the outset of his book that: "The voices of the victims will be heard in this volume, and yet all of them, as different as they may be, offer but a faint glimpse of the extraordinary diversity that was the world of European Jewry on the edge of destruction."[28] However, as Amos Goldberg explains:

> Jewish sources indeed play a major role in the book but they always appear as "voices." Contrary to the integration of the perpetrators' personal accounts into the narrative, the integration of the victims' diaries and accounts lacks almost any synthetic, analytic or conceptual framework. They are simply there, somehow piercing or punctuating the narrative. They therefore re-present the bare experience of the victim within the historical account. Thus, while the perpetrators have a narrative and a history, the victims have only experiences and voices.[29]

Goldberg's argument is that in the "era of the witness" in which we now live, it is not so daring to bring out these voices as it was, say, when Gideon Hausner made the same decision at the Eichmann trial in 1961, allowing witness after witness to take the stand, even though this was not strictly necessary for the purpose of proving Eichmann guilty.[30] By appearing in a way that is more or less expected in a culture suffused with narratives of victimhood, Friedländer's strategy means that these voices also create a kind of "melancholic pleasure."[31] Instead of a situation where disembodied "raw voices" appear as bearers of the disbelief that Friedländer hopes to sustain, Goldberg proposes to subject these texts to rigorous scrutiny "not only in order to confer a sense of disbelief but also to conceptualize and gain a better understanding of what this disbelief is made of."[32]

All great works of history appear both as the last word on their subject and act as spurs to more research and debate. By bringing about this remarkable synthesis, historicizing the Holocaust in a context that ensures its centrality to the history of the Third Reich and World War II, I agree with Alon Confino that *The Years of Extermination* marks in some ways the end-point of Holocaust historiography as it has thus far been conceived.[33] In the remainder of this chapter I want to consider how the book also opens up new ways of thinking.

***

Friedländer has written that the problem of incomprehension, of the feeling of opaqueness that remains after all explanations have been offered, results from:

> the breaking of a taboo, possibly the most fundamental of all taboos: the Nazi perpetration of systematic, prolonged extermination of categories of human beings considered as non-human. Such behavior causes instinctive repulsion at the level of the species as well as that of the individual. The very disappearance of these psychological (or sociobiological) barriers concerning the "scientific" mass killing of other human beings represents, it seems to me, the first and foremost issue for which our usual categories of interpretation are insufficient.[34]

He is quite right, of course, to note that some aspect of the Holocaust remains, for want of a better expression, "mysterious"; indeed, I would argue that that is a good thing, for to have concluded otherwise is a quite frightening prospect and would go beyond merely historicizing the Holocaust. But I would also argue that these conclusions apply not only to the Holocaust. How will scholars, artists and politicians "explain" the essential truth about the Rwandan genocide? Friedländer's comments about the limits of representation are quite correct, but no less applicable to other genocides or, as Kershaw notes, to writing the history of Soviet society under Stalin.[35] Furthermore, if Friedländer is right that the overcoming of the normal barriers of "civilization" constitutes the main blockage of our comprehension, then perhaps we can expect to go no further than his remarkable poly-vocal and multi-narrative synthesis, since it marks the end-point of the historicization process. Incorporating *Alltagsgeschichte* and the voices of the victims, breaking the linear narrative and taking numerous vantage points, *The Years of Extermination* is not only the culmination of the theoretical guidelines Friedländer has set out over many years, but also proof that, irrespective of the innovativeness of the narrative, there remains "an opaqueness at the core." I assume that Friedländer would be more worried if we were to conclude that such opaqueness were not present. Just as Raul Hilberg once (somewhat unexpectedly) voiced the concern that "some people might read what I have written in the mistaken belief that here, on my printed pages, they will find the true ultimate Holocaust as it really happened,"[36] so Friedländer's magnum opus implies the same fear. Nevertheless, there is a remarkable tension between the all-encompassing nature of his massive narrative and the desire, implicit in it and on the basis of Friedländer's earlier theoretical writings, to "question any partial conclusion, to withstand the need for closure."[37]

Whilst I share Friedländer's sense that Nazism's radical anthropology – the attack on the human species *qua* species – takes us to the heart of its ideology and worldview, and thus to the Holocaust, I would like to develop this point by suggesting that precisely in this claim lies a clue to one of the ways in which Holocaust historiography will develop in the near future. In fact, the breaking of this barrier – which I prefer to call "anthropological" rather than psychological or sociobiological – is the concern of scholars such as Alon Confino, who are starting to look at Nazism and the Holocaust through the lenses of cultural history. Although several of these scholars, notably Amos Goldberg and Manuela Consonni, are using cultural history to think about Nazism's Jewish victims, the future of *Täterforschung* lies, in my opinion, less in social psychology (in the manner of Harald Welzer, Steven K. Baum or James Waller) or prosopography (such as Michael Mann's large-scale study of perpetrator biographies) and more in cultural history, by which I mean (*pace* Lynn Hunt) the study of the past from a symbolic point of view; the search for meaning in the past rather than for causal explanation.[38] To take one example; Goldberg has written that the way in which Nazi ideology worked was to unite the signifier, the signified and the real referent, so that real Jews became inseparable from what was said about them: "[A] Jew as a signifier is a Jew as a concept is a Jew as a real material body." They were reduced (dehumanized, in the usual vocabulary) to their representation, blocking any vital and open identity, and bringing about their "symbolic death." "The subject," writes Goldberg, "receives the imposed signifier in a way that fills all voids and lacks in his or her being; the search for a transformative identity and for new objects of desire comes to a halt and the subject of desire is murdered."[39] This is a suggestive line of argument, and is of a piece with Goebbels' words of November 1941, following the introduction of the yellow star in Germany: "There is no difference between Jews and Jews."[40] I suggest that it can be equally usefully applied to the perpetrators, for they too imposed on themselves "total identification with symbols that represent[ed] them"; that is to say, those that made up the "true believers" reduced themselves in a not dissimilar way to the way in which they reduced their victims. As Arne Johan Vetlesen has argued, in cases of human evil we witness the phenomenon of "double dehumanization," in which perpetrators dehumanize their victims but also themselves: "In making the ends of a master into his own ends, the individual allows himself to turn into a mere means in his persecution and eventual killing of persons who are regarded not as (Kantian) ends in themselves but as mere means."[41] Or, more poetically, in the words of Edmond Jabès: racists are "people who refused their differences, but acted on this position only with regard to others."[42]

In the light of the recent explosion of *Täterforschung* mentioned above, we can see that there is much to be gained by a cultural-historical exploration of the world of the perpetrators.[43] The vast literature on perpetrators encompasses biographies of leading figures in the Third Reich,[44] studies of groups or institutions such as the Order Police or the RSHA[45] and examinations of the interplay of the various motives that underpinned participation in violent and/or criminal acts.[46] In terms of explaining the complexities of human behaviour, this body of research has considerably deepened our understanding of perpetrators, who are no longer viewed as sadists on the one hand, or driven solely by ideology, on the other. We now know that the same person could be both a "desk killer" and a "shooter,"[47] and that even those who most decisively and radically attacked the Jews as the root of all evil could also engage in or excuse looting, that is to say that a "high-minded" belief in the Nazis' "world-historical mission" was compatible with base violence and gangsterism.[48]

These studies, however, all examine perpetrators "from outside," so to speak, that is to say based on their writings, speeches and actions, in the way that historians might write about a group of coalminers or Renaissance scholars. We need instead to focus on perpetrators "from the inside," in other words, to grasp the ways in which they sought to shape and to understand the world. Two examples will serve to show what I mean: Thomas Kühne's study of male bonding in the *Wehrmacht* and Michael Wildt's work on the symbolic use of violence in the creation of the people's community (*Volksgemeinschaft*). In his work on *Kameradschaft* (comradeship) in the *Wehrmacht*, Kühne argues that German soldiers fought so bitterly not only because they were hardened antisemites or because they unquestioningly followed orders, but because of their desire to create a community, which they did through mass violence. Kühne cites Michael Geyer's concept of the "*Vergesellschaftung der Gewalt*" ("socialization of violence"), and argues that *Kameradschaft* is a guiding concept through which to provide an "experience history" (*Erfahrungsgeschichte*) not only of National Socialism but of Germany's transition from Nazism to democracy.[49] In other words, *Kameradschaft* was a symbolic form that provided a way for the war generation to understand itself, although not all soldiers identified with the myth of *Kameradschaft* to the same extent. Even so, Kühne argues that although there was "a plurality of experiences" among soldiers, these led in the direction not of "cultural pluralism" but of "social unity": "the cohesion of the National Socialist '*Volksgemeinschaft*' and its soldiers in the war." *Kameradschaft* is the *Leitbild* and myth that held the *Volksgemeinschaft* and soldiers together, and provided this conjunction with continuity.[50] Thus, Kühne expands his argument out from the military to say that the *Volksgemeinschaft* "presented itself as a total society of comrades."[51] *Kameradschaft* became official state doctrine under Nazism. Whilst the home front was of course not equivalent to a barracks on the eastern front, this is an insightful concept for understanding the self-identity of the Third Reich.

What applied to the *Wehrmacht*, Kühne suggests, was applicable to the Third Reich in general, for the military was held up as the embodiment of German values. Michael Wildt's study of the development of the *Volksgemeinschaft* not only shows (particularly through some striking photographs) how rapidly and wholeheartedly the majority of the "Aryan" population adapted themselves to the new racial paradigm, but also that this development was double-edged. Nazi culture, Wildt explains, meant the entwinement of the cosy and *gemütlich* with extraordinary violence:

From the very start, the inclusive moment of the 'Volksgemeinschaft' was bound together with the violent exclusion of the so-called 'asocial,' of the supposedly hereditarily inferior and, above all, the Jews. What former 'Volksgenossen' eagerly wanted to keep separate in their memories, namely the persecution of the Jews and the experience of community under National Socialism, belonged inseparably together, indeed made up the two sides of a political project: the destruction of civil society and the building of a new, racial order. [. . .] Antisemitic violence not only represented a tool of National Socialist politics; violence against Jews was the core of this politics.[52]

Or, as he writes elsewhere, "The Nazi regime communalised violence [*vergemein-schaftete die Gewalt*], permitting 'Volksgenossen' to participate in it."[53]

Here we can profitably bring in Eelco Runia's provocative claim that: "People start to make history not *despite* the fact that it is at odds with – yes, destroys – the stories they live by, but *because* it destroys the stories they live by."[54] The examples of the *Wehrmacht* and the *Volksgemeinschaft*, as explicated by Kühne and Wildt, show this process in action: even as they ended up destroying themselves, these institutions acquired more and more prestige and devotion to them grew ever more frenzied. Part of the problem in commemorating the destruction they wrought – apart from guilt and resentment – has been the sense that Runia describes of feeling severed from the past because although we cannot deny that terrible actions took place, "we cannot really imagine the position from which we came to commit them."[55] Importantly, for our topic, Runia also notes that the incommensurability between these acts (which he calls "sublime 'acts of people'") and the ability to acknowledge having committed them stems from the fact that the explanations for the acts are under-determined, and that the sense of loss to which this feeling gives rise "expunges the thought that we could ever have jumped upon it – and it miraculously transforms agents into victims."[56] It is true that Runia runs the risk of importing the past into the present, as if it were a living thing, and I do not wish to suggest that I agree with Runia that the past is enduringly present.[57] But for our purposes here, it suffices to suggest that one way of understanding the Third Reich and its agents from within is by asking after their construction and destruction of the stories by which they made sense (and non-sense) of the world around them.[58] The approach that I am proposing here is not a biopolitical one derived from Foucault or Agamben, as one might suspect when confronted with Friedländer's reference to the threat to "the species." It is rather a cultural history that seeks to understand the past through symbolic action, in particular through the stories that actors in the past told themselves.[59]

Such an approach has become possible thanks in part to the synthetic work of Friedländer and other leading historians of the Holocaust. We have, in *The Years of Persecution* and *The Years of Extermination*, the culmination of the great narrative analyses of the Holocaust. It is an extraordinary achievement. But Friedländer's text – precisely because it incorporates so generously many different voices and approaches to the past – seems less of an artifice and more of an all-inclusive narrative than his theoretical writings suggested such a text would be; thus it pushes the historicization process forward maybe even more than he expected or desired. In other words, it is in some ways a victim of its own success, although whether or not Friedländer consciously decided to give up the "productive tension" between his metahistory and his "concrete history" in favour of the latter remains to be determined. Thus, if we want to rest assured that the "opaqueness at the core" remains apparent, the best way to do so now is to probe it directly, not with the hope of rendering it transparent, but perhaps of arriving at a state of translucence. Here then we must push at the issues that leave us uncomprehending, most notably the Nazi break with moral law in favour of redefining "the human."[60] This behaviour does indeed repulse us at the level of the species, as well as the individual. But with "traditional" Holocaust historiography, based on archival documents and a quite restricted methodological repertoire, now reaching its logical end-point in *The Years of Extermination* (precisely because that book is more far-reaching methodologically and stylistically than most synthetic histories, not because it is "restricted") the way is now open for some metahistorical reflection to take place, something which has been off the agenda since the considerable impact of Friedländer's *Probing the Limits of Representation* of 1992. The opportunity now exists for new ways of thinking historically about the Holocaust to be developed, with historians breaking free of what Friedländer himself described many years ago as a "moral imperative" to talk of the Holocaust only within "certain accepted norms of aesthetic collaboration or intellectual discourse."[61] With such research we will still be left with a feeling that, as Friedländer put it, quoting Jean-François Lyotard, "The Shoah carries an *excess*, and this excess cannot be defined except by some sort of general statement about something 'which must be able to be put into phrases [but] cannot yet be.'"[62] Indeed, the new research is aimed not at producing synthetic narrative accounts of the "how" of the Holocaust, its "mechanics"; nor even of producing an all-embracing history of the victims. Rather, it will begin to open up what Dan Diner called the "black box" of history that is Auschwitz.[63] Just as a flight recorder can tell us what happened in a technological or mechanical sense, without providing emotional respite, so historical explanation can probe deeply into the mindset of the Nazis whilst hopefully resisting Friedländer's fear that "whether one wishes it or not, the very momentum of historiography may serve to neutralize the past."[64] Saul Friedländer has not only pointed the way since the 1970s by being a rare example of a historian who is willing to go beyond the normal domains of historical research (think of *L'antisémitisme Nazi*, *History and Psychoanalysis*, and *Reflections of Nazism*), but is also, now, the author of the most ambitious narrative history of the Holocaust, one that combines scholarly rigour with dignity and, if it is not too oxymoronic, an emotional dispassion.

*Notes*

1    Steven E. Aschheim, "On Saul Friedländer," *History & Memory* 9 (1997): 11–46, here 38. My thanks to Amos Goldberg, Wulf Kansteiner and Dirk Moses for their valuable comments on earlier drafts of this chapter.

2    On memory in Friedländer's work see Karolin Machtans, "History and Memory: Saul Friedländer's Historiography of the Shoah," in Martin L. Davies and Claus-Christian Szejnmann (eds), *How the Holocaust Looks Now: International Perspectives* (Basingstoke: Palgrave Macmillan, 2007), 199–207; Robert Eaglestone, *The Holocaust and the Postmodern* (Oxford: Oxford University Press, 2004), chapter 6; Saul Friedländer, *The Years of Extermination: Nazi Germany and the Jews, 1939–1945* (London: HarperCollins, 2007), xiii–xxvi; Saul Friedländer, "Eine integrierte Geschichte des Holocaust," *Aus Politik und Zeitgeschichte* 14–15 (2 April 2007): 7–14. On the relationship between "theory" and "practice" in Friedländer's work, see also Wulf Kansteiner, "Historical Synthesis and Methodological Normalization: Ending the Peculiarities of Holocaust Historiography," in Dan Stone (ed.), *The Holocaust and Historical Methodology* (New York: Berghahn Books, forthcoming).

3    Saul Friedländer, "Some Reflections on the Historicization of National Socialism," in Peter Baldwin (ed.), *Reworking the Past: Hitler, the Holocaust, and the Historians' Debate* (Boston: Beacon Press, 1990), 88–101, here 94 and 99.

4    Dominick LaCapra, *Representing the Holocaust: History, Theory, Trauma* (Ithaca: Cornell University Press, 1994); Dominick LaCapra, *History and Memory after Auschwitz* (Ithaca: Cornell University Press, 1998); Dominick LaCapra, *Writing History, Writing Trauma* (Baltimore: Johns Hopkins University Press, 2001); Berel Lang, *Act and Idea in the Nazi Genocide* (Chicago: University of Chicago Press, 1990); Berel Lang, *The Future of the Holocaust: Between History and Memory* (Ithaca: Cornell University Press, 1999); Berel Lang, *Post-Holocaust: Interpretation, Misinterpretation, and the Claims of History* (Bloomington: Indiana University Press, 2005); Berel Lang (ed.), *Writing and the Holocaust* (New York: Holmes & Meier, 1988); Lawrence L. Langer, *Admitting the Holocaust: Collected Essays* (New York: Oxford University Press, 1995); Lawrence L. Langer, *Preempting the Holocaust* (New Haven: Yale University Press, 1998); Dan Diner, *Beyond the Conceivable: Studies on Germany, Nazism, and the Holocaust* (Berkeley: University of California Press, 2000); Dan Diner, *Gegenläufige Gedächtnisse: Über Geltung und Wirkung des Holocaust* (Göttingen: Vandenhoeck & Ruprecht, 2007); Moishe Postone and Eric Santner (eds), *Catastrophe and Meaning: The Holocaust and the Twentieth Century* (Chicago: University of Chicago Press, 2003); Nicolas Berg, Jess Jochimsen and Bernd Stiegler (eds), *Shoah: Formen der Erinnerung. Geschichte, Philosophie, Literatur, Kunst* (Munich: Wilhelm Fink, 1996).

5    Aschheim, "On Saul Friedländer," 17.

6    Nicolas Berg, *Der Holocaust und die westdeutschen Historiker: Erforschung und Erinnerung* (Göttingen: Wallstein, 2003). See also Helmut Walser Smith, *The Continuities of German History: Nation, Religion, and Race across the Long Nineteenth Century* (Cambridge: Cambridge University Press, 2008), 31.

7    Nicholas Berg, "The Holocaust and the West German Historians: Historical Research and Memory," in Moshe Zimmermann (ed.), *On Germans and Jews under the Nazi Regime: Essays by Three Generations of Historians* (Jerusalem: The Hebrew University Magnes Press, 2006), 85–103, here 87.

8    Which is one of the aims of Stone (ed.), *The Holocaust and Historical Methodology*.

9    Berg, "The Holocaust and the West German Historians," 102.

10   More detail can be found in Eaglestone, *The Holocaust and the Postmodern*, chapter 6; Peter Baldwin, "The *Historikerstreit* in Context," in Baldwin (ed.), *Reworking the Past*, 3–37; Charles E. Maier, *The Unmasterable Past: History, Holocaust, and German National Identity* (Cambridge, MA: Harvard University Press, 1988); Jörn Rüsen, "The Logic of Historicization: Metahistorical Reflections on the Debate between Friedländer and Broszat," *History & Memory* 9 (1997): 113–44.

11   Berg, "The Holocaust and the West German Historians," 103.

12   Ibid.

13   Friedländer, "Some Reflections on the Historicization of National Socialism," 89.

14   Martin Broszat and Saul Friedländer, "A Controversy about the Historicization of National Socialism," *New German Critique* 44 (1988): 85–126, here 106–7.

15 Saul Friedländer, "Introduction," in Gerald Fleming, *Hitler and the Final Solution* (Oxford: Oxford University Press, 1986), xxxii–xxxiii.

16 Saul Friedländer, "Trauma, Memory and Transference," in Geoffrey H. Hartman (ed.), *Holocaust Remembrance: The Shapes of Memory* (Oxford: Blackwell, 1994), 252–63, here 259.

17 Aschheim, "On Saul Friedländer," 44 n59. Cf. Gulie Ne'eman Arad, "'Nazi Germany and the Jews': Reflections on a Beginning, a Middle, and an Open End," *History & Memory* 9 (1997): 409–33, here 420, where she speaks of Friedländer's decision "to return to this history *qua* history . . ."

18 See especially Karl-Heinz Roth, "Revisionist Tendencies in Historical Research into German Fascism," *International Review of Social History* 39 (1994): 429–55; Ian Kershaw, *The Nazi Dictatorship: Problems and Perspectives of Interpretation*, 3rd ed. (London: Edward Arnold, 1993), 205ff.

19 Maier, *The Unmasterable Past*, 93. Or, as Kershaw notes (in *Hitler, the Germans, and the Final Solution* (New Haven: Yale University Press, 2008), 289), "the implications of historicization might be less serious both in theory and in practice than Friedländer fears."

20 Gerhard L. Weinberg, "Two Separate Issues? Historiography of World War II and the Holocaust," in David Bankier and Dan Michman (eds), *Holocaust Historiography in Context: Emergence, Challenges, Polemics and Achievements* (Jerusalem: Yad Vashem, 2008), 379–401.

21 "Idyllic law of narrative" comes from Sarah Kofman, *Paroles suffoquées* (Paris: Galilée, 1987), 43.

22 Friedländer, "Trauma, Memory, and Transference," 261.

23 Ibid., 262.

24 Friedländer, *The Years of Extermination*, xix, cited in Alon Confino, "Narrative Form and Historical Sensation: On Saul Friedländer's *The Years of Extermination*," *History and Theory* 48 (2009): 199–219, here 203.

25 Friedländer, *The Years of Extermination*, xvii.

26 See, for example, Saul Friedländer, "On the Possibility of the Holocaust: An Approach to a Historical Synthesis," in Yehuda Bauer and Nathan Rotenstreich (eds), *The Holocaust as Historical Experience: Essays and a Discussion* (New York: Holmes & Meier, 1981), 1–21; Saul Friedländer, "From Anti-Semitism to Extermination: A Historiographical Study of Nazi Policies Toward the Jews and an Essay in Interpretation," in François Furet (ed.), *Unanswered Questions: Nazi Germany and the Genocide of the Jews* (New York: Schocken Books, 1989), 3–31; Saul Friedländer, "The Extermination of the European Jews in Historiography: Fifty Years Later," in Alvin A. Rosenfeld (ed.), *Thinking about the Holocaust after Fifty Years* (Bloomington: Indiana University Press, 1997), 3–17.

27 On perpetrators, see Dan Stone, *Histories of the Holocaust* (Oxford: Oxford University Press, 2010), ch2; Mark Roseman, "Beyond Conviction? Perpetrators, Ideas and Action in the Holocaust in Historiographical Perspective," in Frank Biess, Mark Roseman and Hanna Schissler (eds), *Conflict, Catastrophe, and Continuity: Essays on Modern German History* (New York: Berghahn Books, 2007), 83–103; Jürgen Matthäus, "Historiography and the Perpetrators of the Holocaust," in Dan Stone (ed.), *The Historiography of the Holocaust* (New York: Palgrave Macmillan, 2004), 197–215; Gerhard Paul, "Von Psychopathen, Technokraten des Terrors und 'ganz gewöhnlichen' Deutschen: Die Täter der Shoah im Spiegel der Forschung," in Paul (ed.), *Die Täter der Shoah: Fanatische Nationalsozialisten oder ganz normale Deutsche?* (Göttingen: Wallstein, 2002), 13–90.

28 Friedländer, *The Years of Extermination*, 4–5; see also p. 64.

29 Amos Goldberg, "The Victim's Voice and Melodramatic Aesthetics in History," *History and Theory* 48 (2009): 220–237, here 222.

30 Shoshana Felman, "Theaters of Justice: Arendt in Jerusalem, the Eichmann Trial, and the Redefinition of Legal Meaning in the Wake of the Holocaust," *Critical Inquiry* 27 (2001), 201–38.

31 Goldberg, "The Victim's Voice," 229.

32 Ibid., 237. See also Amos Goldberg, *Holocaust Diaries as Life Stories* (Jerusalem: Yad Vashem, 2004).

33 Confino, "Narrative Form and Historical Sensation."

34 Saul Friedländer, *Memory, History, and the Extermination of the Jews of Europe* (Bloomington: Indiana University Press, 1993), 49.

35 Kershaw, *Hitler, the Germans, and the Final Solution*, 295.

36   Raul Hilberg, "I Was Not There," in Berel Lang (ed.), *Writing and the Holocaust* (New York: Holmes & Meier, 1988), 17–35, here 25.

37   Friedländer, *Memory, History*, 132.

38   Lynn Hunt, "Introduction: History, Culture, and Text," in Lynn Hunt (ed.), *The New Cultural History* (Berkeley: University of California Press, 1989), 1–22, here 12; Alon Confino, "A World Without Jews: Interpreting the Holocaust," *German History* 27 (2009): 531–559.

39   Amos Goldberg, "Trauma, Narrative, and Two Forms of Death," *Literature and Medicine* 25 (2006): 122–41, here 132 and 124.

40   Joseph Goebbels, "Die Juden sind Schuld!," *Das Reich*, 16 November 1941, cited in Peter Fritzsche, *Life and Death in the Third Reich* (Cambridge, MA: Harvard University Press, 2008), 210.

41   Arne Johan Vetlesen, *Evil and Human Agency* (Cambridge: Cambridge University Press, 2005), 72.

42   Edmond Jabès, *A Foreigner Carrying in the Crook of His Arm a Tiny Book* (Hanover: Wesleyan University Press, 1993), 12.

43   For some of Friedländer's thoughts on this issue, see his "Mosse's Influence on the Historiography of the Holocaust," in Stanley G. Payne, David J. Sorkin and John S. Tortorice (eds), *What History Tells: George L. Mosse and the Culture of Modern Europe* (Madison: University of Wisconsin Press, 2004), 134–47.

44   Most notably Peter Longerich, *Heinrich Himmler: Biographie* (Munich: Siedler, 2008). Also Ulrich Herbert, *Best: Biographische Studien über Radikalismus, Weltanschauung und Vernunft, 1903–1989* (Bonn: Dietz, 1996); Lutz Hachmeister, *Der Gegnerforscher: Die Karriere des SS-Führers Franz Alfred Six* (Munich: C. H. Beck, 1998).

45   Karin Orth, *Die Konzentrationslager-SS: Sozialstrukturelle Analysen und biographische Studien* (Munich: Deutscher Taschenbuch Verlag, 2004); Michael Wildt, *Generation des Unbedingten: Das Führungskorps des Reichssicherheitshauptamtes* (Hamburg: Hamburger Edition, 2002); Isabel Heinemann, *Rasse, Siedlung, deutsches Blut: Das Rasse- und Siedlungshauptamt der SS und die rassenpolitische Neuordnung Europas* (Göttingen: Wallstein, 2003).

46   For example, George C. Browder, "Perpetrator Character and Motivation: An Emerging Consensus?," *Holocaust and Genocide Studies* 17 (2003): 480–97; Edward B. Westermann, "Shaping the Police Soldier as an Instrument for Annihilation," in Alan E. Steinweis and Daniel E. Rogers (eds), *The Impact of Nazism: New Perspectives on the Third Reich and Its Legacy* (Lincoln: University of Nebraska Press, 2003), 129–50; Jürgen Matthäus, "Controlled Escalation: Himmler's Men in the Summer of 1941 and the Holocaust in the Occupied Soviet Territories," *Holocaust and Genocide Studies* 21 (2007): 218–42.

47   See for example, Jürgen Matthäus, "Georg Heuser – Routinier des sicherheitspolizeilichen Osteinsatzes," in Klaus-Michael Mallmann and Gerhard Paul, (eds), *Karrieren der Gewalt: Nationalsozialistische Täterbiographien* (Darmstadt: Wissenschaftliche Buchgesellschaft, 2004), 115–25.

48   Martin Dean, *Robbing the Jews: The Confiscation of Jewish Property in the Holocaust, 1933–1945* (Cambridge: Cambridge University Press, 2008).

49   Thomas Kühne, *Kameradschaft: Die Soldaten des nationalsozialistischen Krieges und das 20. Jahrhundert* (Göttingen: Vandenhoeck & Ruprecht, 2006), 14–5. Michael Geyer, "Der zur Organisation erhobene Burgfrieden. Heeresrüstung und das Problem des Militarismus in der Weimarer Republik," in Klaus-Jürgen Müller and Eckardt Opitz (eds), *Militär und Militarismus in der Weimarer Republik* (Düsseldorf: Droste, 1978), 15–100, here 27. On "Erfahrungsgeschichte" see Frank R. Ankersmit, "Die drei Sinnbildungsebenen der Geschichtsschreibung," in Klaus E. Müller and Jörn Rüsen (eds), *Historische Sinnbildung: Problemstellung, Zeitkonzepte, Wahrnehmungshorizonte, Darstellungsstrategien* (Reinbek: Rowohlt, 1997), 98–117 and the other works by Ankersmit listed on pp. 116–117, fn. 2 in that article.

50   Kühne, *Kameradschaft*, 19.

51   Ibid., 97.

52   Michael Wildt, *Volksgemeinschaft als Selbstermächtigung: Gewalt gegen Juden in der deutschen Provinz 1919 bis 1939* (Hamburg: Hamburger Edition, 2007), 68.

53   Michael Wildt, "Gewalt als Partizipation: Der Nationalsozialismus als Ermächtigungsregime," in Alf Lüdtke and Michael Wildt (eds.), *Staats-Gewalt: Ausnahmezustand und Sicherheitsregimes. Historische Perspektiven* (Göttingen: Wallstein, 2008), 215–40, here 239.

54  Eelco Runia, "Burying the Dead, Creating the Past," *History and Theory* 46 (2007): 313–25, here 319.
55  Ibid., 318.
56  Ibid.
57  Anita Kasabova, "Memory, Memorials, and Commemoration," *History and Theory* 47 (2008): 331–50 is a critique of Runia's work.
58  On sense and non-sense see Reinhart Koselleck, "Vom Sinn und Unsinn der Geschichte," in Müller and Rüsen (eds), *Historische Sinnbildung*, 79–97.
59  For more detail see my "Holocaust Historiography and Cultural History," *Dapim* 23 (2009) and responses to the article in the same issue by Carolyn J. Dean, Federico Finchelstein, Dominick LaCapra, Wendy Lower and Dan Michman.
60  See my "The Holocaust and 'the Human,'" in Richard H. King and Dan Stone (eds), *Hannah Arendt and the Uses of History: Imperialism, Nation, Race, and Genocide* (New York: Berghahn Books, 2007), 232–49.
61  Saul Friedländer, "On the Representation of the Shoah in Present-Day Western Culture," in Yehuda Bauer (ed.), *Remembering for the Future* (Oxford: Pergamon Press, 1989), vol. 3, 3092–97, here 3097.
62  Saul Friedländer, "Introduction," in Friedländer (ed.), *Probing the Limits of Representation: Nazism and the "Final Solution"* (Cambridge, MA: Harvard University Press, 1992), 19–20.
63  Dan Diner, "Zwischen Aporie und Vernunft: Über Grenzen der Historisierbarkeit des Nationalsozialismus," in Diner (ed.), *Ist der Nationalsozialismus Geschichte? Zu Historisierung und Historikerstreit* (Frankfurt am Main: Fischer Taschenbuch Verlag, 1993), 62–73, here 70.
64  Friedländer, *Memory, History*, 5–6.

# Index